MAD's GREATEST ARTISTS

FIVE DECADES OF HIS FINEST WORKS

FOREWORD BY
MICHAEL J. FOX

RUNNING PRESS
PHILADELPHIA · LONDON

I wanted to be Mort Drucker—in my mind, the greatest caricaturist and cartoonist ever to grace the pages of *MAD* Magazine. I would thrill whenever his work would grace the cover of *TV Guide* or a film poster like *Fitzwilly*. His style was kinetic before there was such a word, filled with a sense of action and verve and movement with a trace of naughtiness. No one drew like he did, though many tried.

Alas, there is only one Mort Drucker, and it was fated not to be me. But hallowed be thy name. Hail to thee, Mort Drucker.

—Mick Garris
Filmmaker

TO BARBARA

who has inspired me, supported me
and put up with me for a lifetime,
this book is lovingly dedicated

ACKNOWLEDGEMENTS

The editors would like to thank the following people, whose enthusiasm and generosity of spirit made the production of this book not only a possibility but a true pleasure:

J.J. Abrams, Dave Baronoff, Roger Bonas, Joe Daly, Joe Dante, Frank Darabont, John Fortenberry, Michael J. Fox, Tom Gammill, Mick Garris, Doug Gilford, Bartek Jelonek, George Lucas, Nick Meglin, Sandy Resnick, Irving Schild, Steven Spielberg, Nina Tringali...and, of course, Mort and Barbara Drucker.

Books published by Running Press are available at special discounts for bulk purchases in the United States by corporations, institutions, and other organizations. For more information, please contact the Special Markets Department at the Perseus Books Group, 2300 Chestnut Street, Suite 200, Philadelphia, PA 19103, or call (800) 810-4145, ext. 5000, or e-mail special.markets@perseusbooks.com.

9   8   7   6   5   4   3   2   1
Digit on the right indicates the number of this printing

Library of Congress Control Number: 2012938750

ISBN 978-0-7624-4713-8

Cover Art by Mort Drucker
Cover photo by Irving Schild
Cover and Interior Layouts by Joshua McDonnell
Editor: Greg Jones

For E.C. Publications:
Editor: John Ficarra (MAD)
Art Director: Sam Viviano (MAD)

Running Press Book Publishers
2300 Chestnut St.
Philadelphia, Pennsylvania 19103-4371

Visit us on the web!
www.runningpress.com

Visit Mort Drucker on the web:
www.mortdrucker.com

Visit MAD Magazine on the web:
www.madmagazine.com

CONTENTS

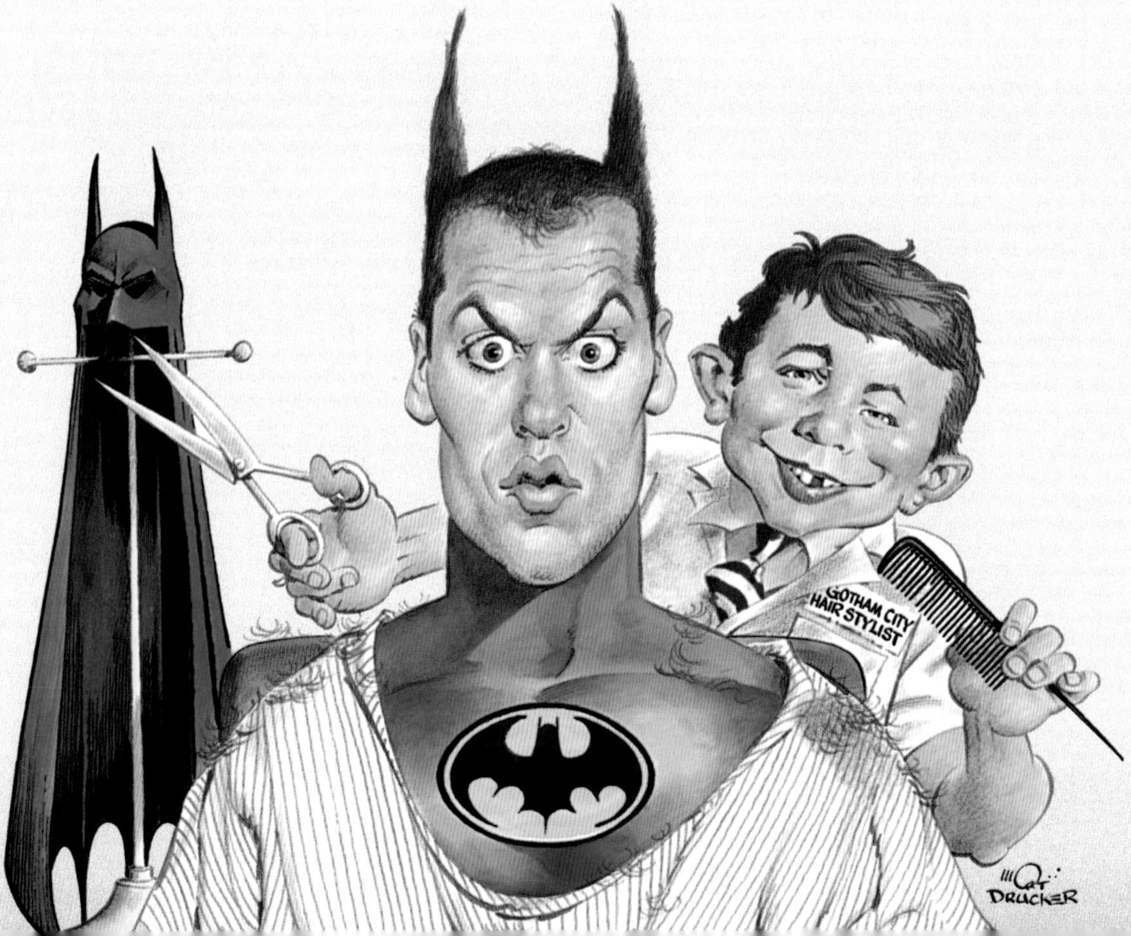
GOTHAM CITY HAIR STYLIST
DRUCKER

FOREWORD

Many years ago, during an appearance on *The Tonight Show*, the late, great Johnny Carson asked me this question: "When did you really know you made it in show business?" That was an easy one. Without a moment's hesitation I replied, "When Mort Drucker drew my head."

I wasn't kidding. An event marked not only in passing or in retrospect, this was actually a fantasy held from the moment I decided to seek fame and fortune in television and film. All through the early years of plain-wrap macaroni and ducking the landlord I knew my success would be realized the instant I opened the pages of *MAD* Magazine and saw my image and idiosyncrasies in Mr. Drucker's riot of ink and line. At the point I appeared on *The Tonight Show*, I believe *Family Tides* (*MAD* #252, January 1985) had already appeared and *Bleak for the Future* (*MAD* #260, January 1986) would be published a year later. It was like having the Beatles write a song about you. Even more important, however, than whatever artistic liberties the genius caricaturist took with the outside of my head, it's the lasting impact he had on the inside of my head which compels me to write this foreword.

I grew up in the '60s and '70s with three sisters and an older brother who, perhaps as amends for all the noogies and purple nurples, allowed me on rare occasion to riff through his impressive stack of *MAD* magazines. Eventually, I directed my paltry allowance toward amassing my own treasured collection. At first suspicious of this reputedly subversive periodical, my parents eventually realized that reading *MAD* kept me occupied and out of their hair. So, in effect, Mort Drucker, Dave Berg, Don Martin, Sergio Aragonés, Al Jaffee, Antonio Prohias, et al, became babysitters during my formative years. Oh, the damage done.

As a Canadian kid, I had an outsider's fascination with all things American, greedily consuming whatever T.V., film and music leaked northward of the border. With the number of U.S. channels limited, and most of the really cool films restricted (18 and older), I needed another way to tap into the U.S. zeitgeist. Enter Mort Drucker.

In panel after panel, Mort's artistry, in concert with the satirical brilliance of *MAD* scribes like Dick DeBartolo, Larry Siegel and Stan Hart, provided a window on American culture, a perspective that, for me at least, transcended parody. In fact, *MAD*'s send-ups of film, television and politics existed as sort of an inverse parody given that I had never personally seen much of the original material that was getting the Mort Drucker treatment. For example, I couldn't compare Mort Drucker's rendering of Dustin Hoffman with the real actor; it might be years later before I could compare the real guy with his depiction in *MAD*. As a 12-year-old, I knew that Richard Nixon was a creep not because Walter Cronkite told me so on the news but because Mort Drucker had drawn him that way in *MAD*. These weren't just likenesses, but stunning masterworks of unadulterated detail.

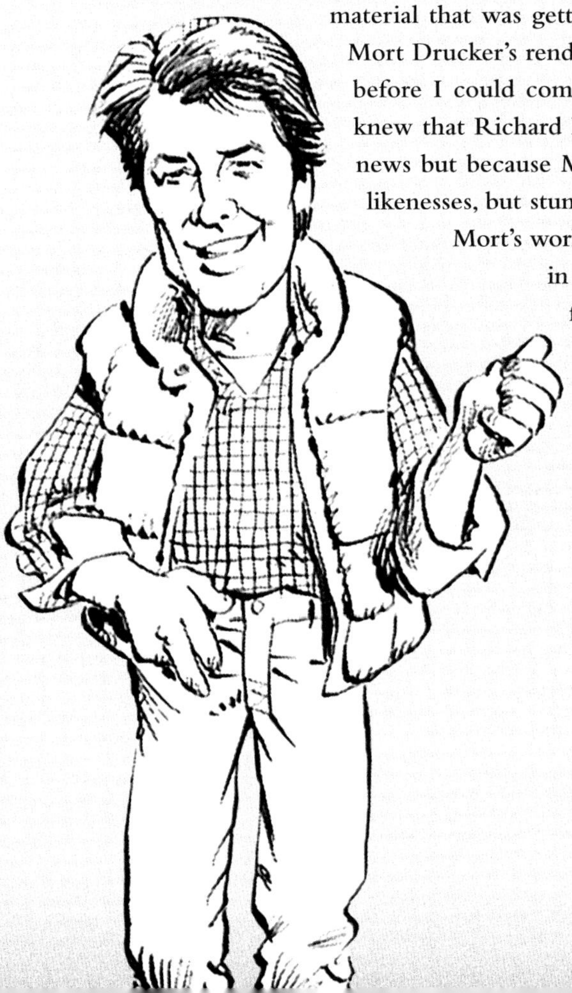

Mort's work is hardly economical but it is exacting. There is so much to discover in each figure, and that's just the foreground. I always scour each panel for the miniature miscreants and insouciant oddballs lurking in the background providing a sideshow to the main event. Oh, and he draws the girls sexy, too.

So thanks, Mort, for drawing (and filling) my head. It is a true honor.

—Michael J. Fox

INTRODUCTION

One of my first responsibilities when I began working at *MAD* as an associate editor was to gather reference material—photos of the stars and scenes from movies we were satirizing—for Mort Drucker and other *MAD* artists. This was well before the age of the internet, where nowadays you can readily find photos of just about anything. And the actual movie studios were no help whatsoever. Most hated *MAD* and refused to cooperate no matter how much I begged.

So I had to get creative. I scrounged. Often I relied on friends who worked at "legitimate" magazines to help me obtain an official press kit and the 6-12 black-and-white still photos it contained. Other times I resorted to the black market. (Yes, there was a black market in movie stills back then.)

Whenever I spoke to Mort about this problem, he would always say the same thing to me: "I just need one good full frontal shot and one profile." More times than I care to admit, that was all I was able to get Mort.

Now that I've pulled back the curtain a bit, I implore you to go back and reread any movie satire Mort Drucker illustrated. Notice how many times he was asked to draw a caricature of the movie's leading actors and actresses over the course of a typical seven-page satire. Twelve? Fifteen? Eighteen? How many different expressions on the stars' faces did the script call for? Serious . . . laughing . . . crying . . . screaming . . . confused . . . bemused . . . and more.

And oh yeah, Mort, in all cases make sure the likeness is dead on, but *funny*.

Now consider that Mort was able to brilliantly accomplish all of this, to twist and exaggerate the stars' facial features *and bodies*, with only one or two measly photographs for reference. You begin to see why the word genius is often found in the same sentence as the name Mort Drucker.

This book is a fitting tribute to the man who created the *MAD* movie satire form, and then brilliantly perfected it over the following decades. It's filled with page after page of masterful pen work, stunning caricatures, wonderfully engaging storytelling and just plain funny artwork. It is my pleasure as *MAD*'s editor to be a part of it and my pleasure as a lifelong fan of Mort Drucker's art to own it.

My congratulations to Mort on a magnificent body of work. My congratulations to you for buying this fabulous book! Enjoy!

John Ficarra
Editor, *MAD*
April 2012

P.S. In case you're wondering, some things never change. To this day most studios refuse to have any association with *MAD*.

A MAD LOOK AT MORT DRUCKER

FORMER *MAD* EDITOR NICK MEGLIN TALKS WITH THE LEGENDARY CARTOONIST

The following interview was conducted for this book by Nick Meglin—longtime MAD magazine editor and close friend of Mort Drucker. It offers background, highlights, and insights into Drucker's approach to drawing throughout his legendary and remarkable career.

NICK MEGLIN: Let's start at the beginning—Brooklyn's famed Erasmus High School. Did Erasmus have any art courses that started you in your artistic direction?

MORT DRUCKER: Not that I recall, and certainly nothing in the cartoon or commercial art area. Erasmus was always an extraordinary school with a high standard of academic learning. But I didn't take any art classes beyond the standard curriculum, like Art Appreciation. I don't think they offered art courses beyond that at the time.

NM: Did you ever have any kind of formal art training?

MD: No.

NM: So you're a graduate from the self-schooled school of art.

MD: Yes. As you and so many of my talented artist friends have said, you learn to draw by drawing. You can go to the best art school in the world, but if you don't do the work you've wasted your time and money.

NM: Another brilliant caricaturist, David Levine, was also an Erasmus graduate. Did you know him?

MD: David attended a few years before me, so I didn't know him back then. He's one of my heroes. I've always marveled at his pen and ink work especially, which was my prime interest.

NM: In many art institutes, student competition can be either a driving force or a pressure that is sometimes very difficult to overcome. How does that work when you're self-educated?

MD: I don't know about others, but for me, I was my own competition and drove myself hard to constantly improve my work. That can be just as pressure-laden, don't you think?

NM: Sometimes more, depending upon the driver. When did you actually start taking your drawing seriously?

MD: Long before high school.

NM: That far back?

MD: Even farther, before newspapers and magazines were around. It was very difficult drawing on those cave walls, believe me.

NM: Sorry I asked. I'll rephrase the question. Okay, when did your desire to draw professionally take root?

MD: There's no specific moment for something like that; it's an evolving process. I was drawing at age six, you know, the regular kid stuff—people, animals, race cars, planes, boats—and as I got older I just kind of knew that's what I wanted to do in life.

NM: Did anyone else in your family have artistic talent?

MD: My mother's father was an artist in Austria. He made his living painting murals and portraits. But when religious discrimination forced him to escape the country with his family, he came to America and the only opportunity available to him as a painter was on walls and house exteriors, so that's what he settled in for as his life's work in this country. He had four children and several grandchildren besides me, but I seemed to be the only one who carried the gene. I always loved to draw and to this day drawing plays a part of my everyday life, whether a commercial assignment or sketching at the local coffee shop for myself.

NM: Early on, did you make a distinction between fine and commercial art?

MD: Not that I was aware of. I always wanted to be as diversified as possible and not be concerned about a particular style or approach. But since I was attracted to the daily and Sunday comic strips and later on comic books, I leaned in that direction.

NM: Early influences seem to stay with all creative people forever and tend to direct us, whether consciously or not. Do you think there's a loss of freedom once you and/or your work becomes categorized, labeled, or defined—like as a cartoonist, comic strip artist, illustrator, fine artist?

MD: Of course. Labels are meaningless—we're all capable of jumping over the fences people seem to want to confine us within. But when the label gets you work, then that's what you do. Making a living is most often the determining factor as to what art direction you travel.

NM: Other than your famed reputation as a world-class caricaturist, your work, whether *MAD*, advertising, *Time* magazine cover, or personal, always showcases your versatility. Do you enjoy any phase of your art more than another?

MD: Not especially. I enjoy illustrating a movie satire in a realistic way as much as I enjoy doing a simple, funny gag drawing.

NM: You've always done both in your *MAD* work.

MD: *MAD* has always allowed me the freedom to fool around, to put my own silly stuff here and there that isn't an integral part of the story. That freedom makes it a lot more fun for me.

NM: I'll bet some of your favorite satires are the ones you had the most fun doing, right?

MD: Of course. It always seems to work out that way.

NM: Would you say the greater percentage of the art you chose to include in this book reflects that sentiment?

MD: Without question. But there's more than one factor about an assignment that contributes to the fun. Sometimes I respond with added enthusiasm because I particularly enjoyed the movie or TV show, or I'm interested in the subject matter...

NM: ...as a genre or as interest in drawing as an artist?

MD: Both. And, of course, certain celebrities are just more fun to draw than others.

NM: Fans always enjoy "when I met one of my heroes" stories, and you have one that concerns an artist who was a hero to many of us—Will Eisner, creator of *The Spirit*. That encounter took place before your professional drawing career began?

Nick Meglin (left) and Mort Drucker at the National Cartoonists Society Reuben Awards Banquet in Chicago, 2006.

MD: Yes, right at the start. Will Eisner was such a great artist, designer, storyteller. It turned out that my grandfather (the housepainter) was a friend of Eisner's father who often talked about his son Will, the comic book artist. So one phone call led to another and sure enough I got an appointment to meet Will at his studio on the East Side of Manhattan. He looked at my work and liked it enough to give me the number of a comic strip artist he knew who happened to be looking for an assistant to draw backgrounds and help him with the strip at the time. I worked on the strip for about three months.

NM: And from that, your first freelance employment, you secured your one and only full-time job as a staff artist for DC Comics. What was that like?

MD: The learning experience more than compensated for the minimal wages that kind of job offered in those days when comic books didn't gain the level of respect that they have now. It was a terrific opportunity to see the work of established professionals in its various stages of production and actually be part of the process.

NM: What were your responsibilities?

MD: At first it was erasing, whiting out, touching up, etc., but soon it became making corrections to fit editorial changes or whatever on work that had to be shipped to the press to meet deadlines. There wasn't time for that artist to be called in to make the changes and I quickly learned how to work in each of their styles in a manner that sometimes even the artist couldn't see the difference in the printed page.

NM: Learning your craft on the job is usually a positive experience for those who don't get complacent and stop looking beyond that point, wouldn't you say?

MD: Moving forward will always depend upon the individual opportunity and what one makes from it. For me, working on art created by comic book giants like Al Toth and Carmine Infantino was a positive one all the way down the line. I learned a lot that I carried with me through the next stages of my career.

NM: Which were?

MD: Making a new set of samples that might get me start-to-finish pages of my own.

NM: Which eventually did happen. Do you remember your first solo flights in comic books?

MD: At the beginning I actually wrote and drew teen stories, love and war comics followed, some stories involved my own characters, but nothing earth-shattering. Then I was offered some Bob Hope Comics work that started me off in a new direction—caricature.

NM: Lucky for *MAD* Magazine!

MD: How about lucky for me!

NM: I guess it's time to repeat the tale of how you got to work for *MAD*. You had answered an ad that we had placed looking for artists and I was screening portfolios. . . .

MD: And you liked my work enough to show it to the art department.

NM: Who also liked it enough to show it to editor Al Feldstein and the legendary publisher, Bill Gaines, who had the radio on very loudly so all of us Brooklyn Dodger fans could hear the World Series game against those damn Yankees!

MD: That was before I knew what nutty characters you all were, so when Bill said that "only if the Dodgers won," *MAD* would hire me, I believed him. They won, and here I am!

NM: We threatened to fire you a year later when the Dodgers moved to Los Angeles, but by then you knew why we were called the Usual Gang of Idiots, being one yourself. As for the real reason you were hired, your caricatures transcend the usual criteria for that art form by being neither obviously humorous portraits nor the typical exaggerated likenesses. They're impressions of the total person with features appearing to be accurately drawn, yet realistically distorted, if you will. You're definitely not from the "lollipop school" of caricature where large heads are arbitrarily placed on top of interchangeable bodies.

MD: I've always considered a caricature to be the complete person, not just a likeness. Hands in particular have always been a prime focus for me as they can be as expressive of character as the exaggerations and distortions a caricaturist searches for. I try to capture the essence of the person, not just facial features.

NM: That's always been your hallmark as a storyteller. You're known for capturing the action, nuance, and gesture of your subjects, yet you never experienced the drawing from live model sessions that most art students do. How did you go about expanding that ability?

MD: I'm fortunate in that I seem to retain a lot of visual imagery and once I get a feel for the person—their outstanding features, their posture, the way they move—a lot of it comes out in the rough sketches when I first start creating the scene the writer has described. I get as much photographic research as I can to help me form a three-dimensional model in my mind of what that person would look like from a different viewpoint and apply it to my work.

NM: I've seen some of the research you've used—in some cases it's so minimal it barely supplies the reference for one or two likenesses of a person, let alone twenty or more in a fully-extended *MAD* movie satire, for instance.

MD: It's no exaggeration to say that you can never have enough research, but there are times when you just have to do the best you can with what you've got.

NM: What's the first step in your drawing process?

MD: To read the script and get an overview of what the satire is about in the way of location, mood and all the other distinguishing qualities. I then read the dialogue which has been set in type and pasted down on the actual drawing pages *MAD* provides to see how the action will move along.

NM: You've already seen the film the satire is based on.

MD: Whenever possible. There were often times when we wanted our take-off to be on the stands at the same time the movie was making the rounds and the satire was written with guesswork, projection, and comic twists and turns to camouflage the fact that none of us involved had seen the actual film.

NM: Thanks for blowing *MAD*'s cover as being a responsible, honest magazine.

MD: We all know *MAD* never had that reputation!

NM: True, but let's go on. What next?

MD: I call it "director time," as that's what the artist is actually doing—creating his own storyboard for the film. I become the "camera" and look for angles, lighting, close-ups, wide angles, long shots—just as a director does to tell the story in the most visually interesting way he can. My first sketches are as much composition and design ideas as they are character and action images.

NM: So at this point the page is filled with only rough pencil sketches and no likenesses or details.

MD: Correct. Very rough—I'm still exploring, not drawing and I don't want to get too involved in the juicy parts since some of what I'm doing will be modified or discarded completely as I get further involved in the storytelling. I then stand back and look at the page as a complete unit to make sure it's designed well.

NM: Give us an idea of something you felt wasn't designed well.

MD: Hmmm, three close-up panels in a row of characters talking. Better change that middle panel to a far shot. Maybe make that panel an open vignette. This one could be dramatically handled in light and dark areas—like that.

NM: Then you go on to the next page in the same way?

MD: Yes, but if the satire is three pages or more, then I place the facing pages together and look at how the spread holds together and sometimes make changes based on that. Then I tighten up the pencils, solve the problems, nail down the likenesses—the fun part. *MAD* always wants to see the complete job in its tight-pencil stage before I can go ahead with the inking.

NM: Yes, more for us to make sure the article is working and that nothing was misinterpreted in the script. Then the final rendering. Your favorite materials for the students among us, please.

MD: I use a mechanical pencil with an F grade lead for the roughs, a fine line fountain pen which I use as a dip-in pen, a number three red sable watercolor brush, and a bottle of the thickest India ink I can find. For color work, I use mostly colored inks. That's it.

NM: Which means that if I use these very same materials I'll be able to produce art on the same level as yours.

MD: Exactly!

NM: Your *MAD* art became so familiar to the American public that it brought you outside work in areas I'm sure you never dreamed possible in the days when all you hoped for was a career in comics.

MD: Absolutely true.

NM: The poster for the movie *American Graffiti*, album covers, major ad campaigns, covers for *Time* and *TV Guide*—it's quite a formidable list.

MD: I owe a lot to *MAD* for presenting my work to such a wide, bright audience.

NM: Can you recall a time, or perhaps a piece of work, that transformed your previous image of yourself and forced you to acknowledge that you were indeed "'THE' Mort Drucker," world-famous artist?

MD: I guess that happened in a way when I was awarded the Reuben, the National Cartoonist Society's highest honor. The voting is by your fellow artists, the most talented group ever assembled, so their acknowledgement meant the world to me.

NM: Speaking of the respect of your peers, I had the honor of introducing you at two significant events a few years apart that spoke volumes about your highly-regarded position in the profession. Both Hanna-Barbera and Walt Disney Productions initiated celebrity artist programs and asked their famed art departments to vote on who they wanted as the first speaker to address their assembly. You headed the list at both of those studios.

MD: I was stunned to learn that at each of those events.

NM: No one else was. Back to drawing. One frequently-asked question concerns your approach to each assignment.

MD: In truth, I don't think about it much and prefer instead to get totally involved with drawing and let the work evolve in directions it wants to go. My focus is on how I'm going to tell the story visually—so composition, setting the scene, action and all I've already described talking about the rough pencil stage.

NM: How about the caricatures themselves?

MD: I've discovered through years of working at capturing a humorous likeness that it's not about the features themselves as much as the space between the features. We all have two eyes, a nose, a mouth, hair and jaw lines, but yet we all look different. What makes that so is the space between them.

NM: What is your starting point?

MD: I take a visual journey around the features of someone I'm portraying as if I was creating a sort of topographical map and then begin to refine the lines that seem to be capturing the likeness best. Believe me, there's a lot of erasing and redrawing completely in the process as it doesn't always come easy.

NM: Which subjects are the hardest to draw?

MD: Those with near-perfect features, like very beautiful women, since with even the slightest exaggeration or distortion you can lose the likeness.

NM: Is there anyone in particular you just can't secure a good likeness of to the page?

MD: Apropos of what I just said, drawing my beautiful wife, Barbara, has always been difficult.

NM: You met Barbara at Erasmus High School, correct?

MD: Yes. We met in high school and we were obviously both young and inexperienced about so many factors of life—but we were married a year after graduation and it worked out well for us.

NM: When people have asked me about the man behind the art, I'm always happy to respond with what you've always considered to be your prime focus—being a devoted, loving husband, father, and friend and believing everything you achieve after that is just icing on the cake.

MD: Isn't that what dedication to your work is for all of us? To be able to provide the best you can for your family through your efforts whether you're an artist, a farmer, or a carpenter? Your work provides you with the necessities, and if you're as fortunate as I've been that the work is more love than labor, it's a win-win situation.

AWARDS DEPT.

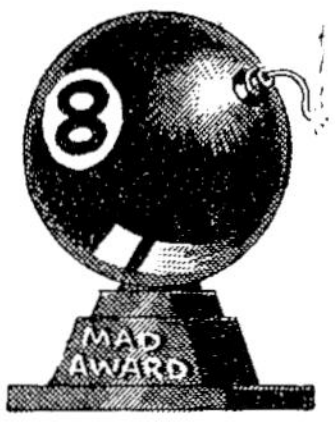
8
MAD AWARD

MAD'S ADVERTISING AWARD
goes to the most nauseating
T.V. COMMERCIAL OF 1956

THE ROLLY CIGARETTE AD

PICTURES BY MORT DRUCKER

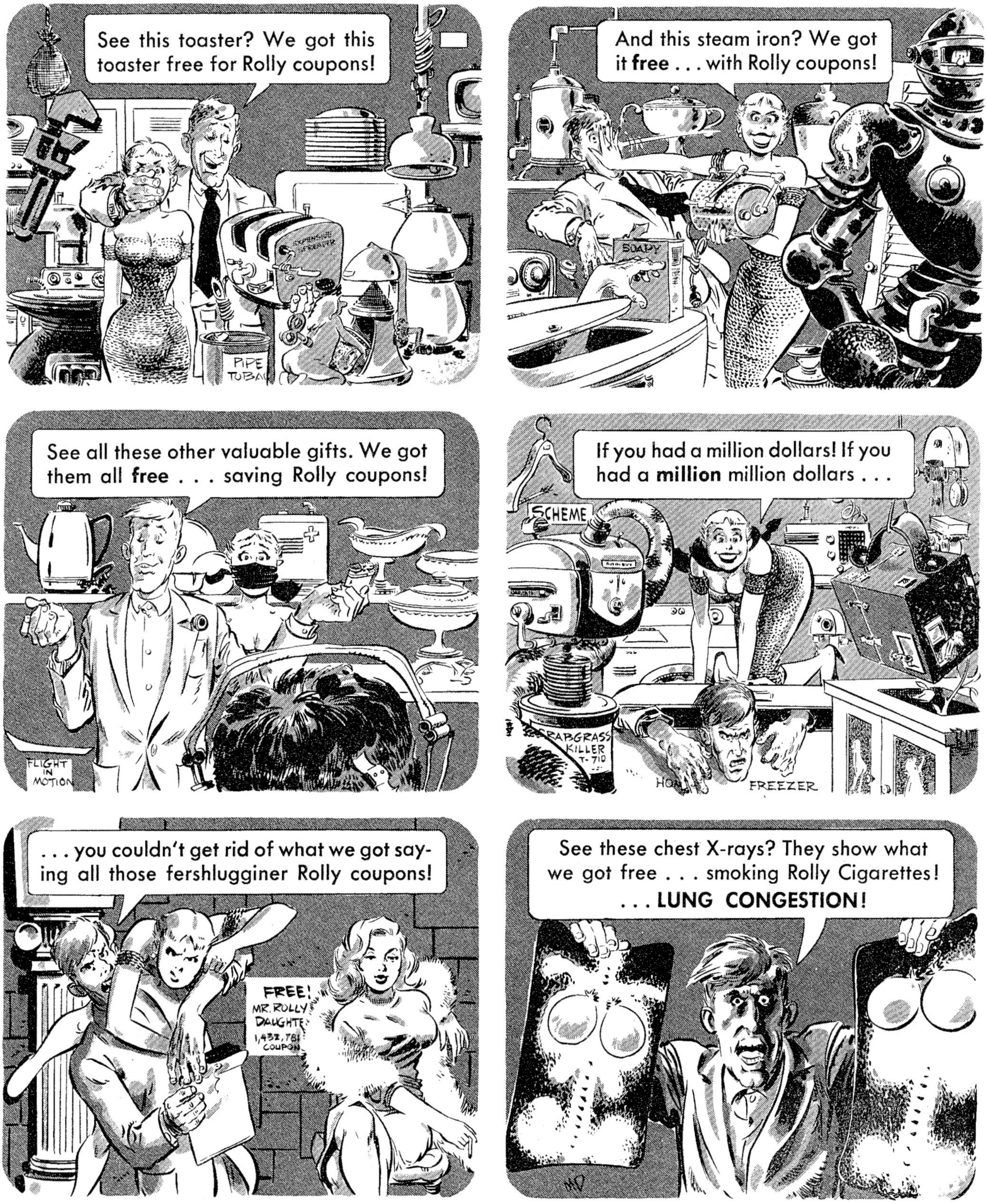
See this toaster? We got this toaster free for Rolly coupons!
And this steam iron? We got it **free** . . . with Rolly coupons!
SOAPY
See all these other valuable gifts. We got them all **free** . . . saving Rolly coupons!
FLIGHT IN MOTION
If you had a million dollars! If you had a **million** million dollars . . .
SCHEME
FREEZER
. . . you couldn't get rid of what we got saying all those fershlugginer Rolly coupons!
FREE!
See these chest X-rays? They show what we got free . . . smoking Rolly Cigarettes!
. . . **LUNG CONGESTION!**

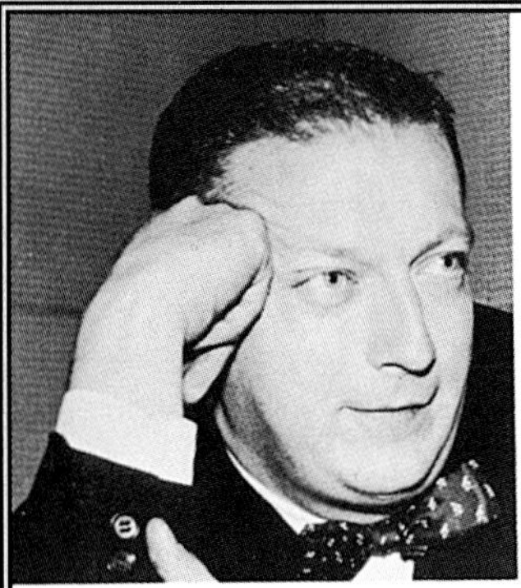

BOB

BOB AND RAY DEPT.

We interrupt this magazine to bring you a special article. Bob and Ray's roving correspondent, Wally Ballew, has just notified us that he's standing by in Newton, Illinois. So if you're ready, come in please, Wally Ballew, with your exciting on-the-spot report of . . .

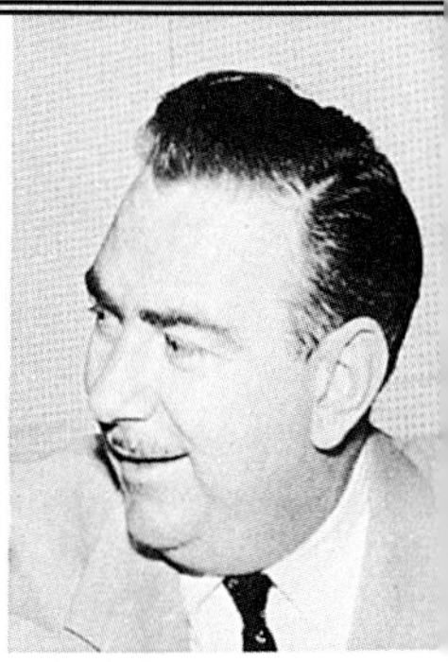

RAY

THE NATIONAL BANNISTER SLIDING CONTESTS

PICTURES BY MORT DRUCKER

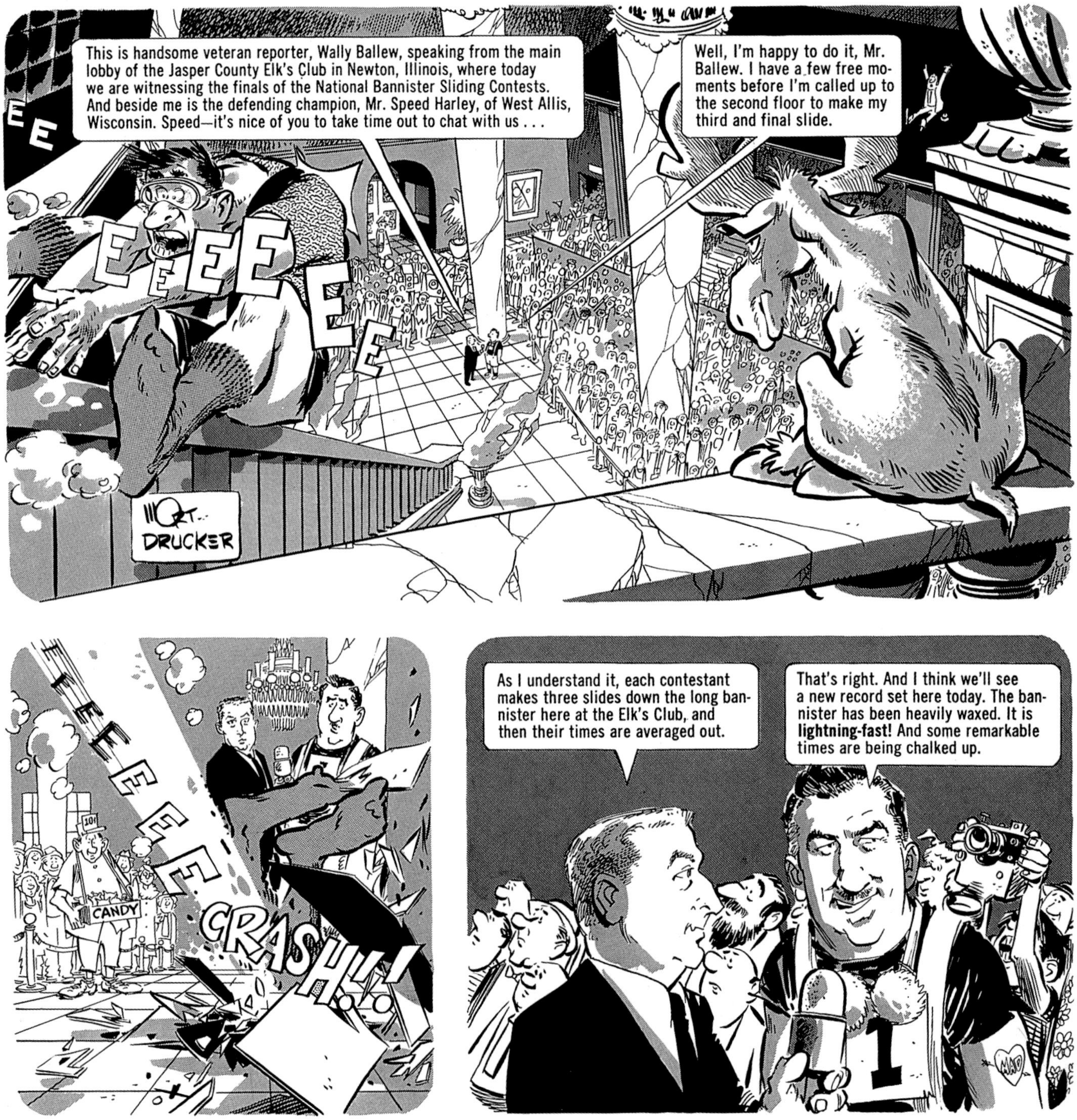
This is handsome veteran reporter, Wally Ballew, speaking from the main lobby of the Jasper County Elk's Club in Newton, Illinois, where today we are witnessing the finals of the National Bannister Sliding Contests. And beside me is the defending champion, Mr. Speed Harley, of West Allis, Wisconsin. Speed—it's nice of you to take time out to chat with us . . .
Well, I'm happy to do it, Mr. Ballew. I have a few free moments before I'm called up to the second floor to make my third and final slide.
MORT DRUCKER
CANDY
CRASH!!!
As I understand it, each contestant makes three slides down the long bannister here at the Elk's Club, and then their times are averaged out.
That's right. And I think we'll see a new record set here today. The bannister has been heavily waxed. It is **lightning-fast!** And some remarkable times are being chalked up.

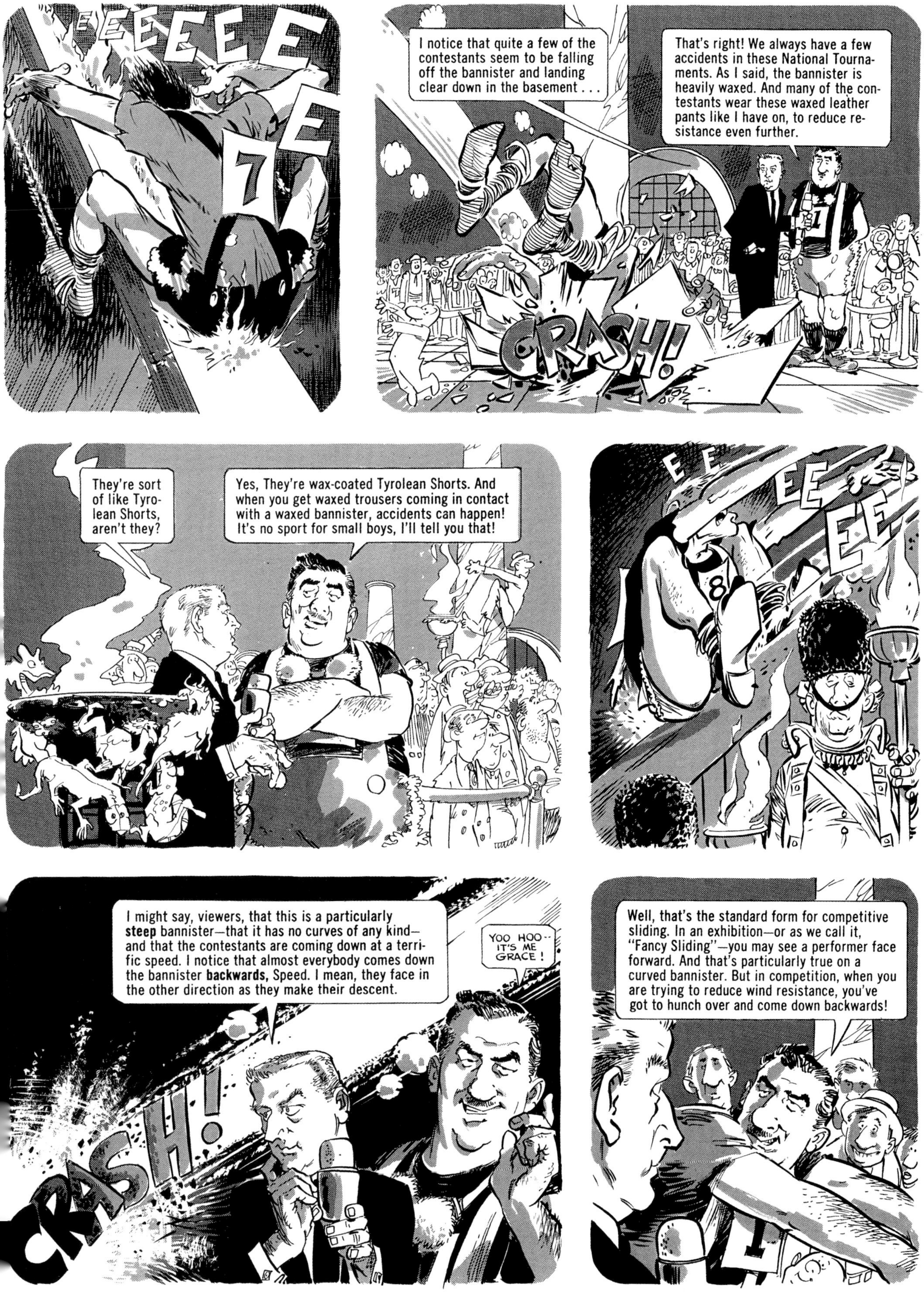
I notice that quite a few of the contestants seem to be falling off the bannister and landing clear down in the basement . . .
That's right! We always have a few accidents in these National Tournaments. As I said, the bannister is heavily waxed. And many of the contestants wear these waxed leather pants like I have on, to reduce resistance even further.
CRASH!
They're sort of like Tyrolean Shorts, aren't they?
Yes, They're wax-coated Tyrolean Shorts. And when you get waxed trousers coming in contact with a waxed bannister, accidents can happen! It's no sport for small boys, I'll tell you that!
I might say, viewers, that this is a particularly **steep** bannister—that it has no curves of any kind—and that the contestants are coming down at a terrific speed. I notice that almost everybody comes down the bannister **backwards,** Speed. I mean, they face in the other direction as they make their descent.
YOO HOO-- IT'S ME GRACE!
CRASH!
Well, that's the standard form for competitive sliding. In an exhibition—or as we call it, "Fancy Sliding"—you may see a performer face forward. And that's particularly true on a curved bannister. But in competition, when you are trying to reduce wind resistance, you've got to hunch over and come down backwards!

CONTINUED ON NEXT PAGE

You certainly seem to be an expert on the subject, Speed. I presume you have been sliding for years.

That's right. I began to slide just for the fun of it when I was a kid. Then a group of businessmen set up a Sunday Morning Sliding Club in West Allis. I won several club championships there. I've been coming down here for the Nationals every year since '51.

And, of course, you won the Men's Title here last year.

Yes, I posted an average speed of 81.327 miles per hour. That, my friend, was good enough to win.

Well, I notice you are pulling your goggles down now. Does that mean you are about ready to go up for your 3rd and final slide of this year's meet?

That's right. I'm on deck now, so I guess I'll have to be going.

Well, thanks very much for talking with us, Speed.

Thank you, Mr. Ballew.

Speed is mounting the stairway now . . .
He climbs on to the bannister at the top . . .
He raises his hand as a signal to the offical timer . . .
And here he comes!

This is Wally Ballew in Newton, Illinios, sending it back to **MAD** Magazine in New York.

THE FOUR HORSEMEN OF THE PREPOSTEROUS DEPT.

Several years ago, a Magazine Editor (who was probably separated from his wife) coined the word, "togetherness." And it took the country by storm. We were bombarded with messages of "togetherness" by magazines, newspapers, skywriting, and even deodorant commercials. Now, thanks to television, the ultimate in "togetherness" has been achieved . . . The Family Western. Gone are the gunfights and the killing and the brutality. Instead, we're getting love and romance and even compatible color—in . . .

BANANZ

The "Family Togetherness" Western

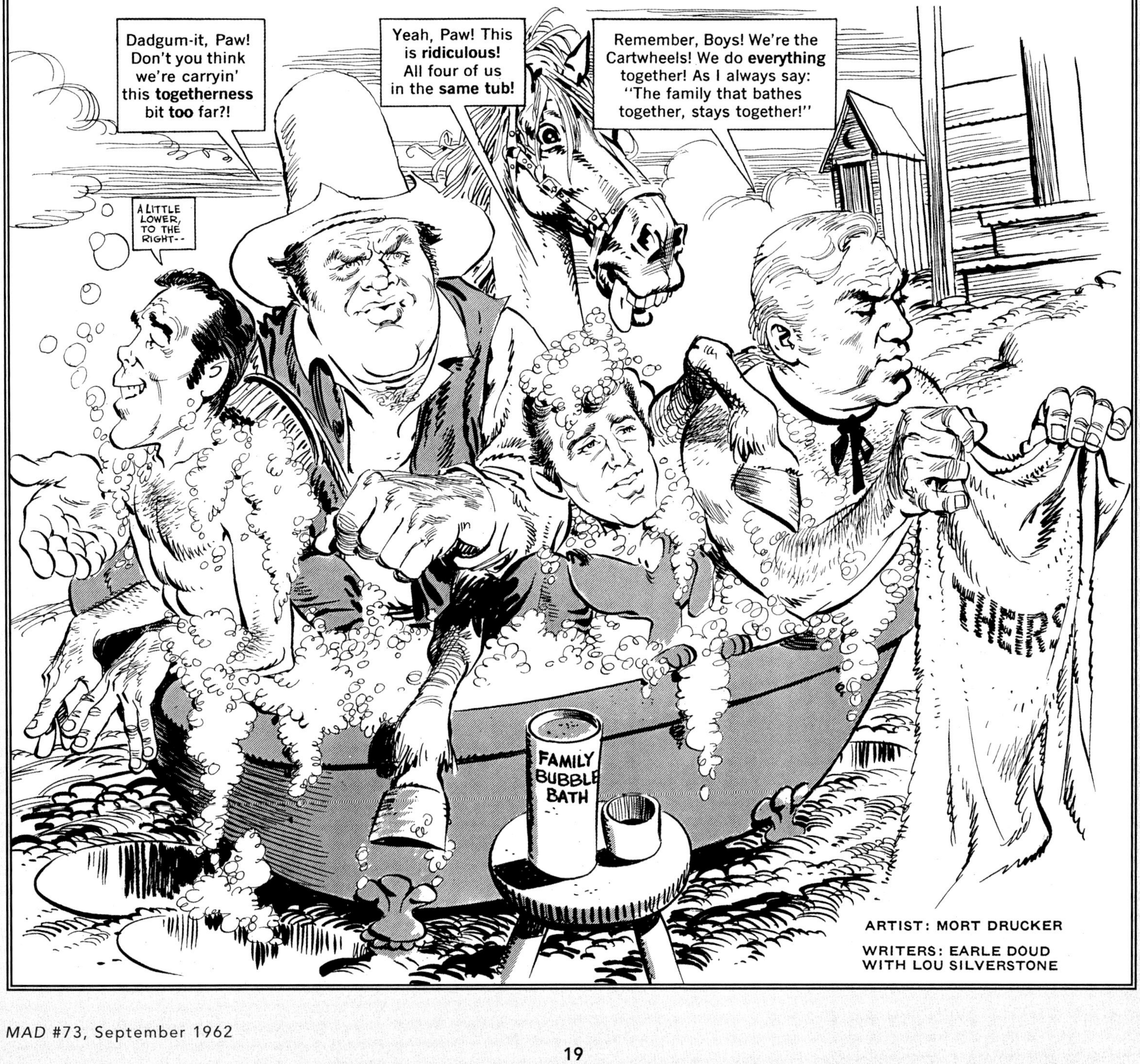
Dadgum-it, Paw! Don't you think we're carryin' this **togetherness** bit **too** far?!
Yeah, Paw! This is **ridiculous!** All four of us in the **same tub!**
Remember, Boys! We're the Cartwheels! We do **everything** together! As I always say: "The family that bathes together, stays together!"
A LITTLE LOWER, TO THE RIGHT--
FAMILY BUBBLE BATH
THEIRS

ARTIST: MORT DRUCKER

WRITERS: EARLE DOUD WITH LOU SILVERSTONE

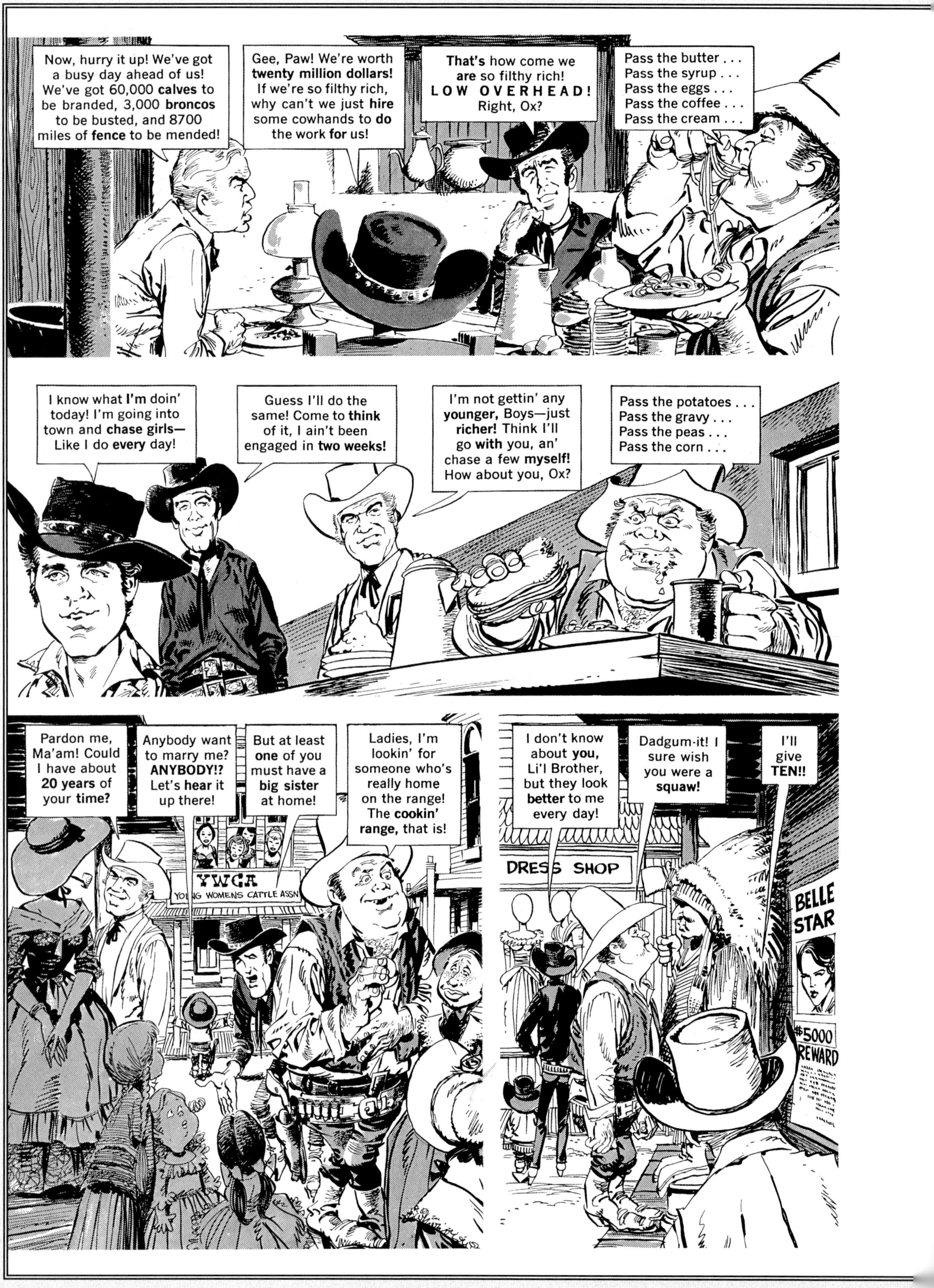
Now, hurry it up! We've got a busy day ahead of us! We've got 60,000 calves to be branded, 3,000 broncos to be busted, and 8700 miles of fence to be mended!
Gee, Paw! We're worth twenty million dollars! If we're so filthy rich, why can't we just hire some cowhands to do the work for us!
That's how come we are so filthy rich! LOW OVERHEAD! Right, Ox?
Pass the butter . . . Pass the syrup . . . Pass the eggs . . . Pass the coffee . . . Pass the cream . . .
I know what I'm doin' today! I'm going into town and chase girls—Like I do every day!
Guess I'll do the same! Come to think of it, I ain't been engaged in two weeks!
I'm not gettin' any younger, Boys—just richer! Think I'll go with you, an' chase a few myself! How about you, Ox?
Pass the potatoes . . . Pass the gravy . . . Pass the peas . . . Pass the corn . . .
Pardon me, Ma'am! Could I have about 20 years of your time?
Anybody want to marry me? ANYBODY!? Let's hear it up there!
But at least one of you must have a big sister at home!
Ladies, I'm lookin' for someone who's really home on the range! The cookin' range, that is!
YWCA
YOUNG WOMENS CATTLE ASSN
I don't know about you, Li'l Brother, but they look better to me every day!
Dadgum-it! I sure wish you were a squaw!
I'll give TEN!!
DRESS SHOP
BELLE STAR
$5000 REWARD

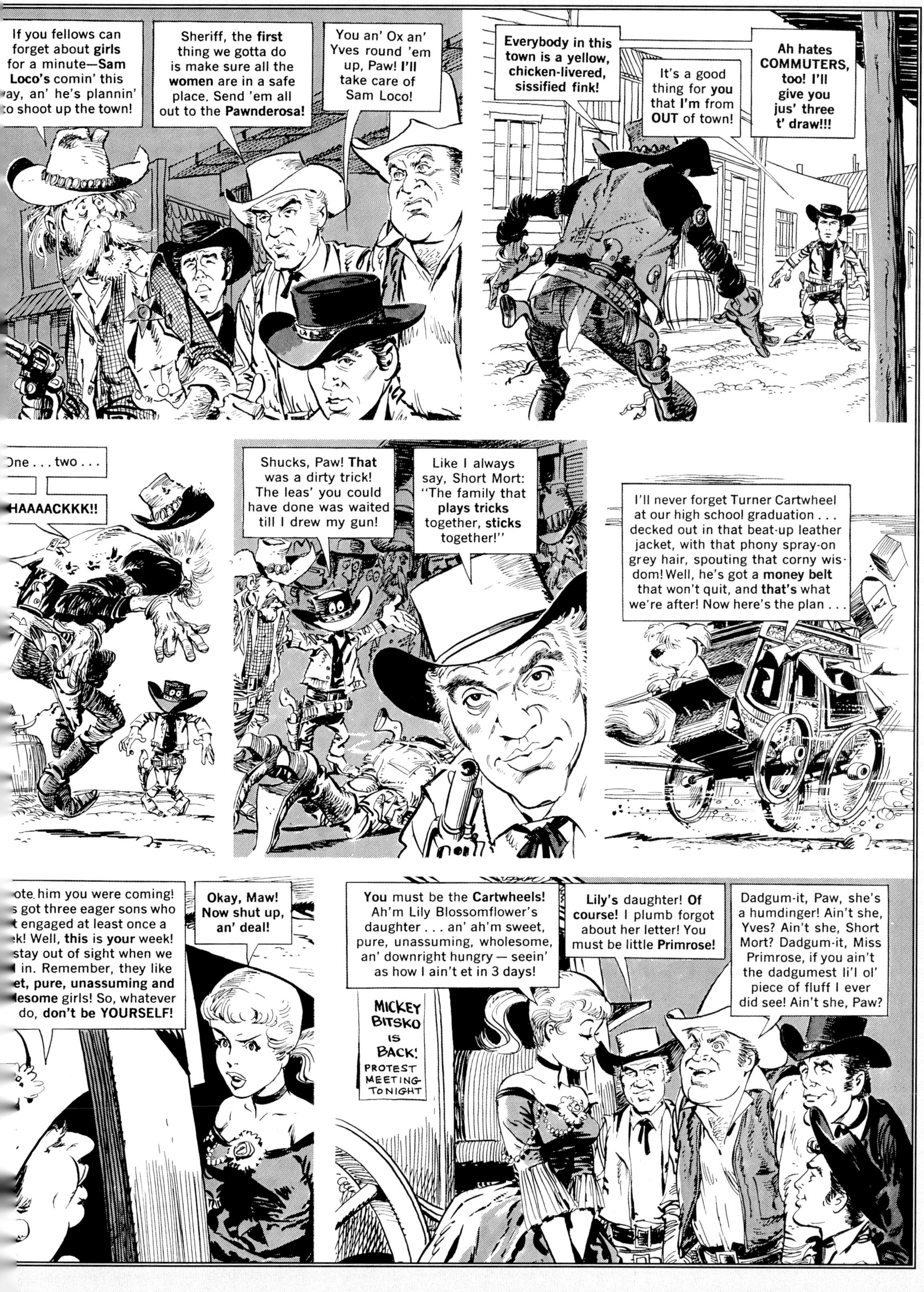
If you fellows can forget about girls for a minute—Sam Loco's comin' this ay, an' he's plannin' o shoot up the town!
Sheriff, the first thing we gotta do is make sure all the women are in a safe place. Send 'em all out to the Pawnderosa!
You an' Ox an' Yves round 'em up, Paw! I'll take care of Sam Loco!
Everybody in this town is a yellow, chicken-livered, sissified fink!
It's a good thing for you that I'm from OUT of town!
Ah hates COMMUTERS, too! I'll give you jus' three t' draw!!!
One . . . two . . .
HAAAACKKK!!
Shucks, Paw! That was a dirty trick! The leas' you could have done was waited till I drew my gun!
Like I always say, Short Mort: "The family that plays tricks together, sticks together!"
I'll never forget Turner Cartwheel at our high school graduation . . . decked out in that beat-up leather jacket, with that phony spray-on grey hair, spouting that corny wisdom! Well, he's got a money belt that won't quit, and that's what we're after! Now here's the plan . . .
ote him you were coming! s got three eager sons who t engaged at least once a k! Well, this is your week! stay out of sight when we in. Remember, they like et, pure, unassuming and lesome girls! So, whatever do, don't be YOURSELF!
Okay, Maw! Now shut up, an' deal!
You must be the Cartwheels! Ah'm Lily Blossomflower's daughter . . . an' ah'm sweet, pure, unassuming, wholesome, an' downright hungry — seein' as how I ain't et in 3 days!
MICKEY BITSKO IS BACK! PROTEST MEETING TONIGHT
Lily's daughter! Of course! I plumb forgot about her letter! You must be little Primrose!
Dadgum-it, Paw, she's a humdinger! Ain't she, Yves? Ain't she, Short Mort? Dadgum-it, Miss Primrose, if you ain't the dadgumest li'l ol' piece of fluff I ever did see! Ain't she, Paw?

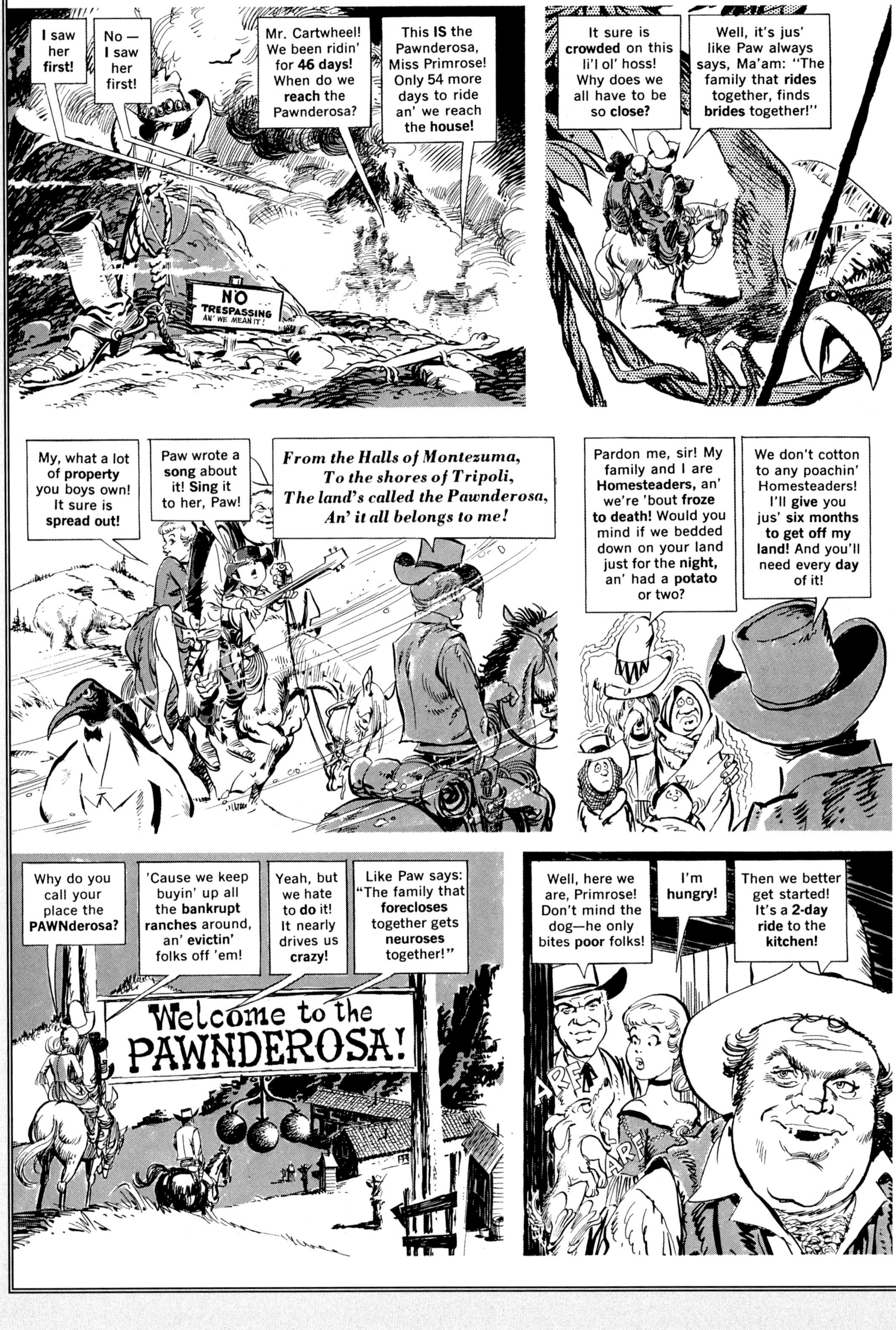
I saw her first!
No — I saw her first!
NO TRESPASSING AN' WE MEAN IT!
Mr. Cartwheel! We been ridin' for 46 days! When do we reach the Pawnderosa?
This IS the Pawnderosa, Miss Primrose! Only 54 more days to ride an' we reach the house!
It sure is crowded on this li'l ol' hoss! Why does we all have to be so close?
Well, it's jus' like Paw always says, Ma'am: "The family that rides together, finds brides together!"
My, what a lot of property you boys own! It sure is spread out!
Paw wrote a song about it! Sing it to her, Paw!
From the Halls of Montezuma, To the shores of Tripoli, The land's called the Pawnderosa, An' it all belongs to me!
Pardon me, sir! My family and I are Homesteaders, an' we're 'bout froze to death! Would you mind if we bedded down on your land just for the night, an' had a potato or two?
We don't cotton to any poachin' Homesteaders! I'll give you jus' six months to get off my land! And you'll need every day of it!
Why do you call your place the PAWNderosa?
'Cause we keep buyin' up all the bankrupt ranches around, an' evictin' folks off 'em!
Yeah, but we hate to do it! It nearly drives us crazy!
Like Paw says: "The family that forecloses together gets neuroses together!"
Welcome to the PAWNDEROSA!
Well, here we are, Primrose! Don't mind the dog—he only bites poor folks!
I'm hungry!
Then we better get started! It's a 2-day ride to the kitchen!
ARF
ARF

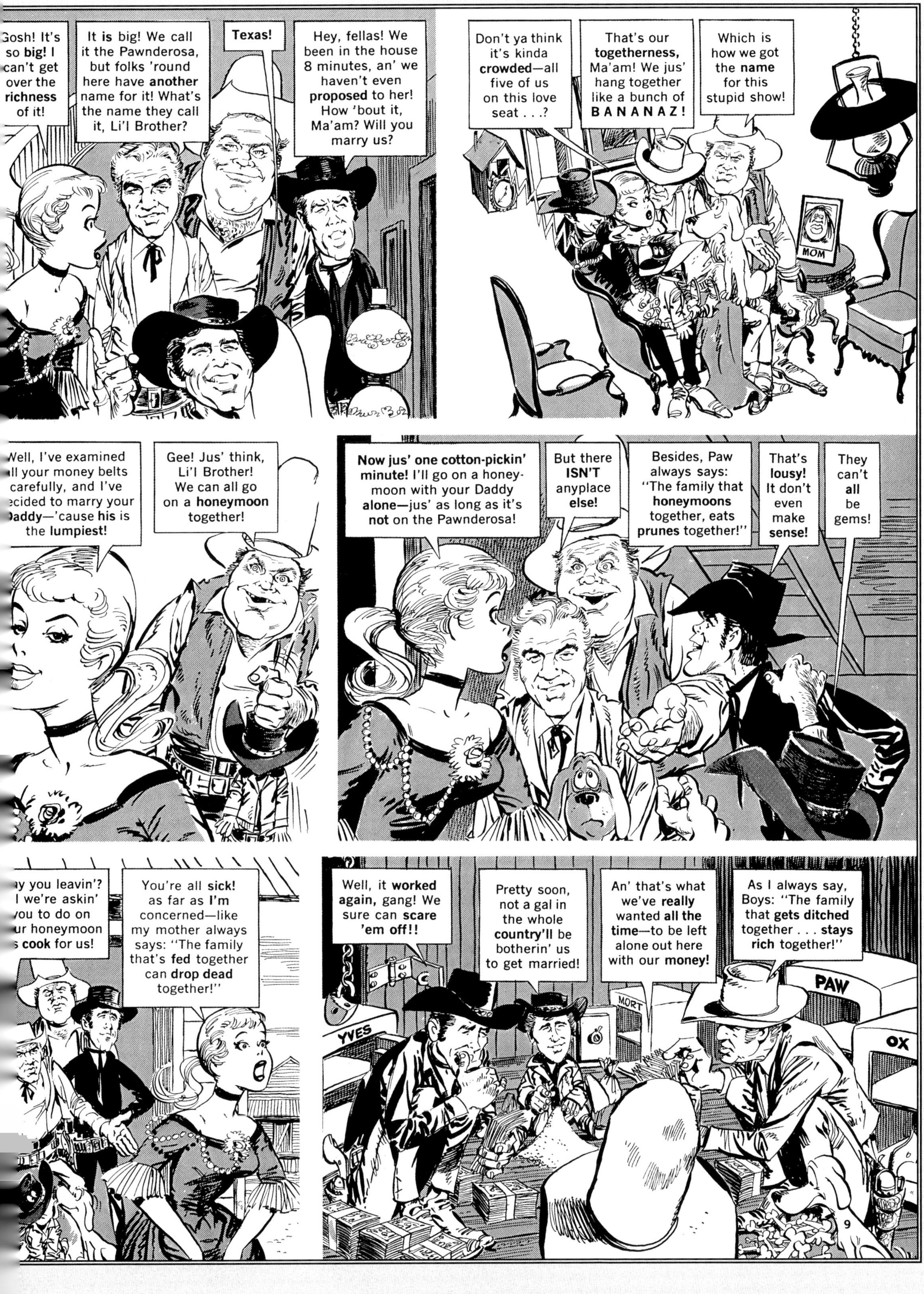
Gosh! It's so big! I can't get over the richness of it!
It is big! We call it the Pawnderosa, but folks 'round here have another name for it! What's the name they call it, Li'l Brother?
Texas!
Hey, fellas! We been in the house 8 minutes, an' we haven't even proposed to her! How 'bout it, Ma'am? Will you marry us?
Don't ya think it's kinda crowded—all five of us on this love seat . . .?
That's our togetherness, Ma'am! We jus' hang together like a bunch of BANANAZ!
Which is how we got the name for this stupid show!
MOM
Well, I've examined all your money belts carefully, and I've decided to marry your Daddy—'cause his is the lumpiest!
Gee! Jus' think, Li'l Brother! We can all go on a honeymoon together!
Now jus' one cotton-pickin' minute! I'll go on a honeymoon with your Daddy alone—jus' as long as it's not on the Pawnderosa!
But there ISN'T anyplace else!
Besides, Paw always says: "The family that honeymoons together, eats prunes together!"
That's lousy! It don't even make sense!
They can't all be gems!
y you leavin'? I we're askin' you to do on ur honeymoon s cook for us!
You're all sick! as far as I'm concerned—like my mother always says: "The family that's fed together can drop dead together!"
Well, it worked again, gang! We sure can scare 'em off!!
Pretty soon, not a gal in the whole country'll be botherin' us to get married!
An' that's what we've really wanted all the time—to be left alone out here with our money!
As I always say, Boys: "The family that gets ditched together . . . stays rich together!"
YVES
MORT
PAW
OX
9

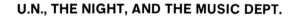

U.N., THE NIGHT, AND THE MUSIC DEPT.

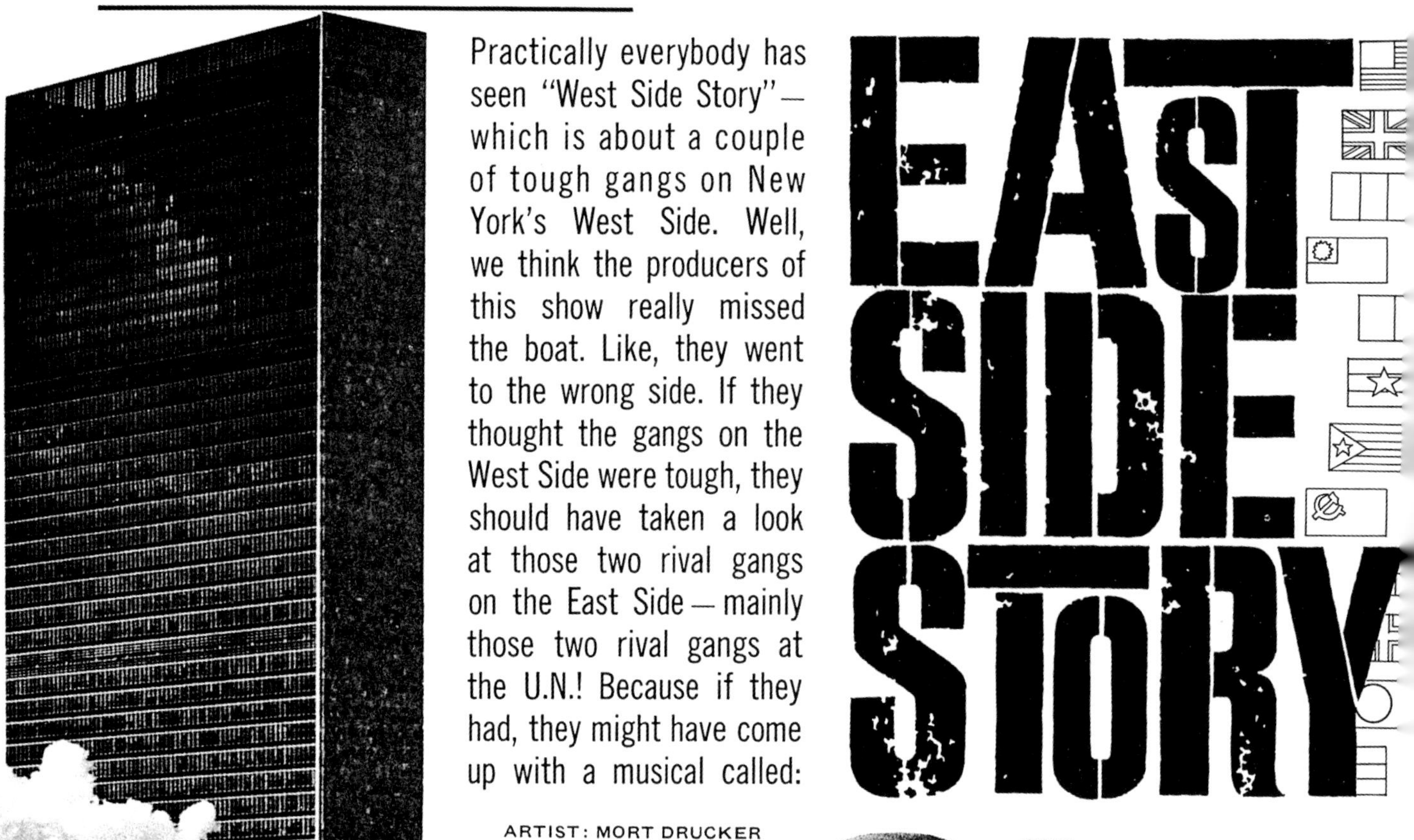

Practically everybody has seen "West Side Story"—which is about a couple of tough gangs on New York's West Side. Well, we think the producers of this show really missed the boat. Like, they went to the wrong side. If they thought the gangs on the West Side were tough, they should have taken a look at those two rival gangs on the East Side—mainly those two rival gangs at the U.N.! Because if they had, they might have come up with a musical called:

EAST SIDE STORY

ARTIST: MORT DRUCKER
WRITER: FRANK JACOBS

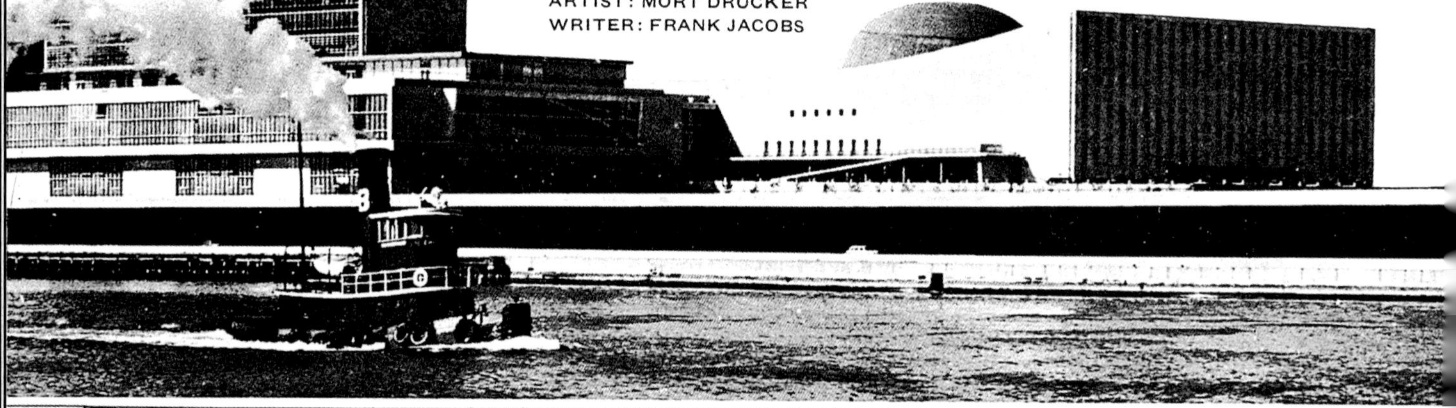

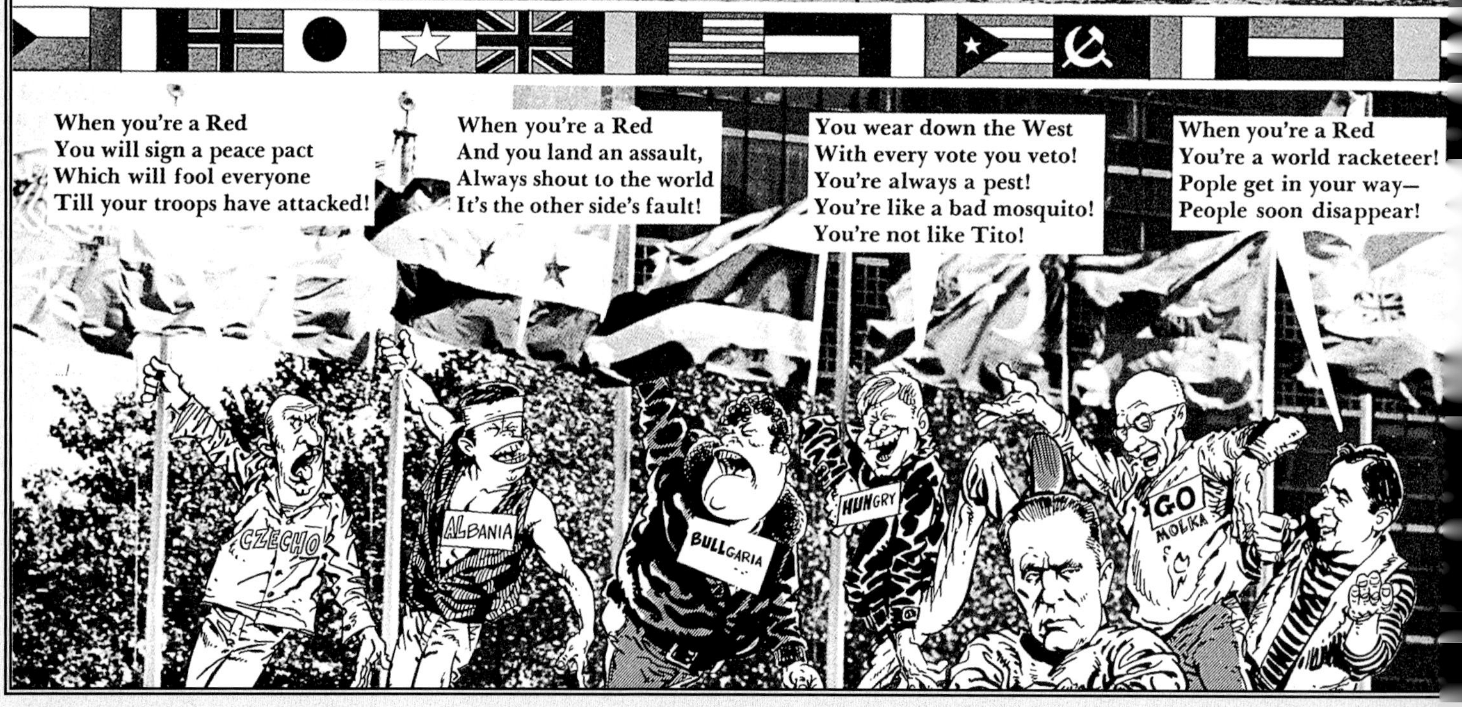
When you're a Red
You will sign a peace pact
Which will fool everyone
Till your troops have attacked!
When you're a Red
And you land an assault,
Always shout to the world
It's the other side's fault!
You wear down the West
With every vote you veto!
You're always a pest!
You're like a bad mosquito!
You're not like Tito!
When you're a Red
You're a world racketeer!
Pople get in your way—
People soon disappear!
CZECHO
ALBANIA
BULLGARIA
HUNGRY
GO
MOLKA

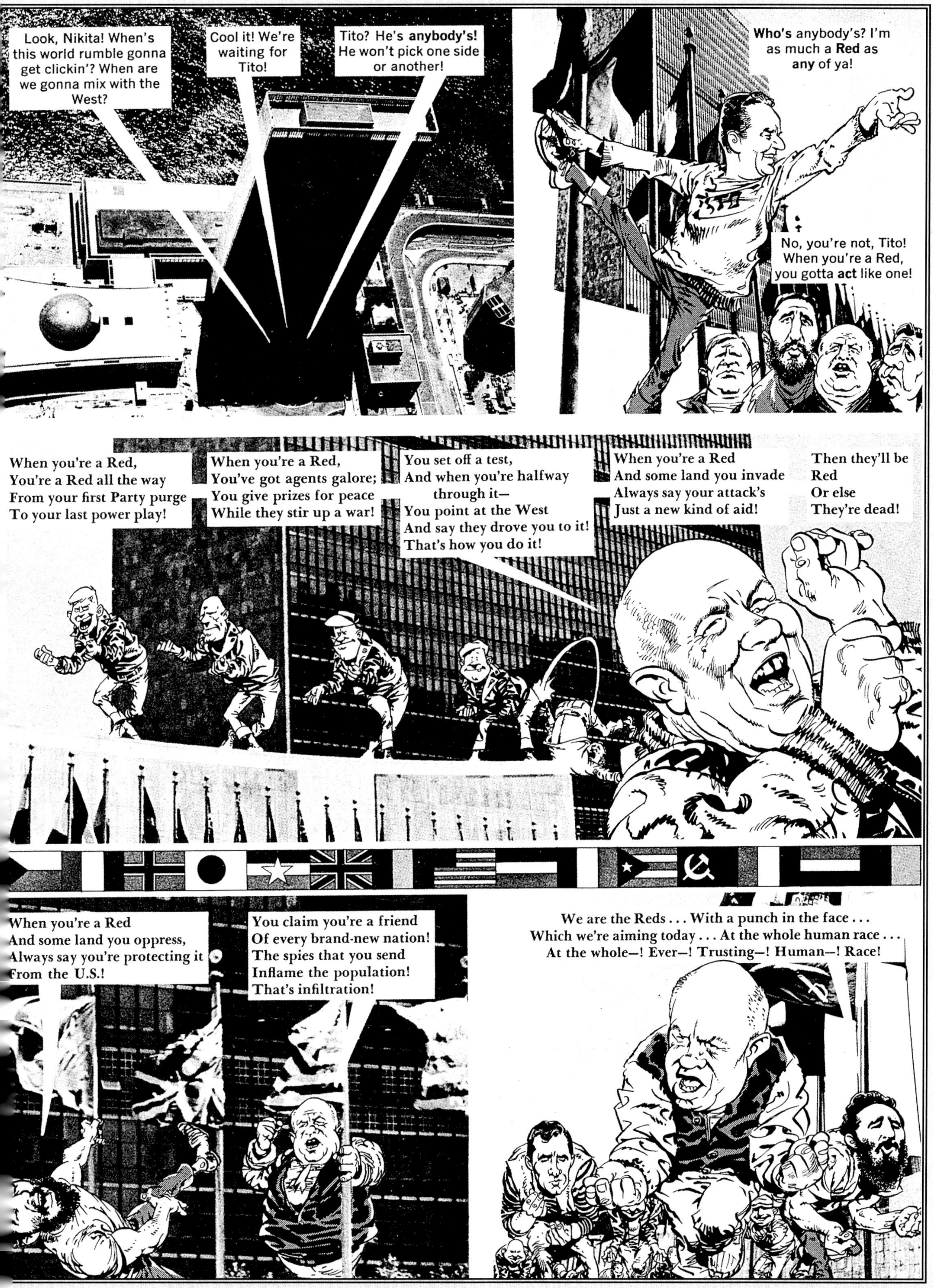
Look, Nikita! When's this world rumble gonna get clickin'? When are we gonna mix with the West?
Cool it! We're waiting for Tito!
Tito? He's **anybody's!** He won't pick one side or another!
Who's anybody's? I'm as much a **Red** as **any** of ya!
No, you're not, Tito! When you're a Red, you gotta **act** like one!
When you're a Red, You're a Red all the way From your first Party purge To your last power play!
When you're a Red, You've got agents galore; You give prizes for peace While they stir up a war!
You set off a test, And when you're halfway through it— You point at the West And say they drove you to it! That's how you do it!
When you're a Red And some land you invade Always say your attack's Just a new kind of aid!
Then they'll be Red Or else They're dead!
When you're a Red And some land you oppress, Always say you're protecting it From the U.S.!
You claim you're a friend Of every brand-new nation! The spies that you send Inflame the population! That's infiltration!
We are the Reds . . . With a punch in the face . . . Which we're aiming today . . . At the whole human race . . . At the whole—! Ever—! Trusting—! Human—! Race!

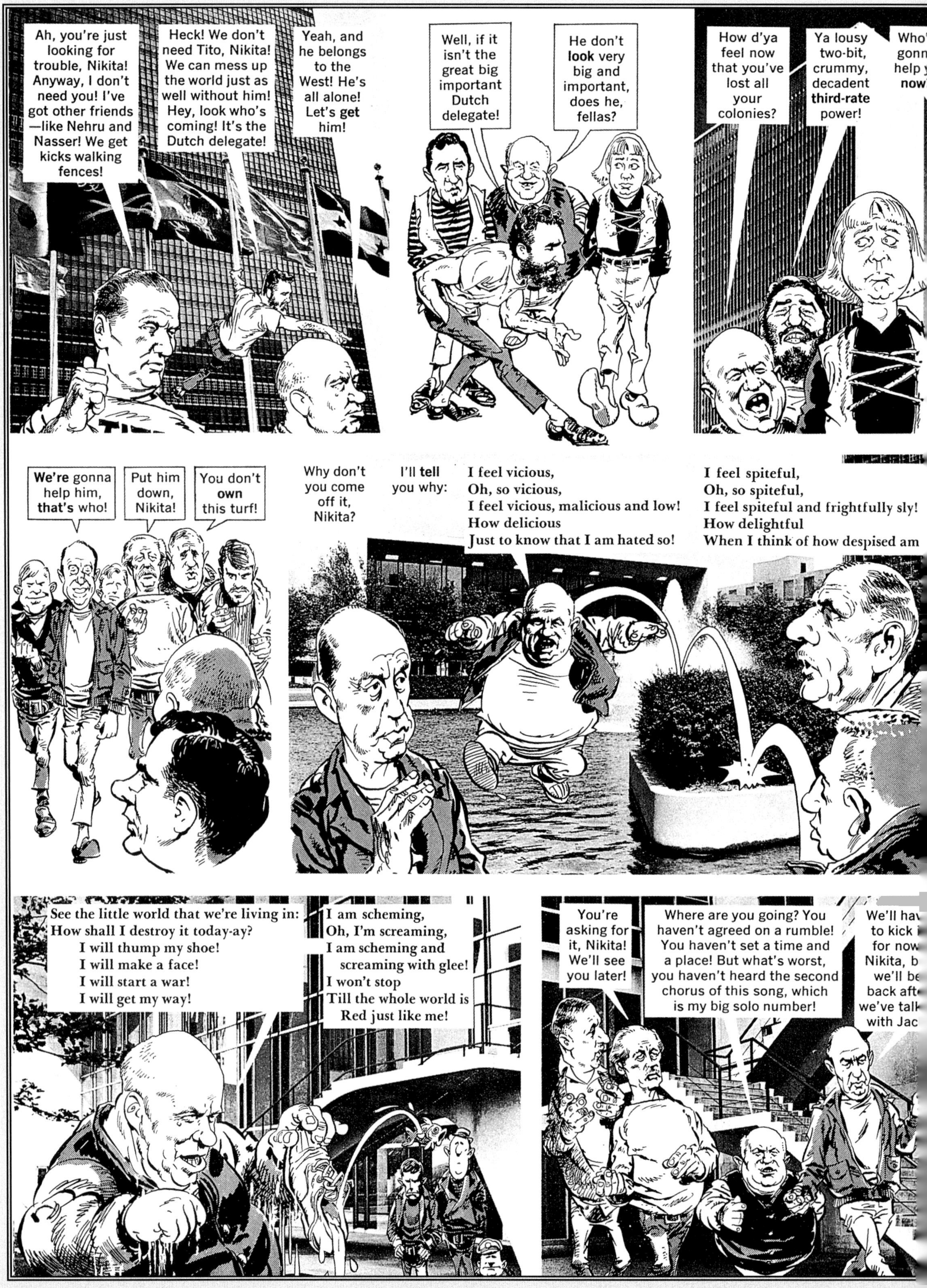
Ah, you're just looking for trouble, Nikita! Anyway, I don't need you! I've got other friends—like Nehru and Nasser! We get kicks walking fences!
Heck! We don't need Tito, Nikita! We can mess up the world just as well without him! Hey, look who's coming! It's the Dutch delegate!
Yeah, and he belongs to the West! He's all alone! Let's **get** him!
Well, if it isn't the great big important Dutch delegate!
He don't **look** very big and important, does he, fellas?
How d'ya feel now that you've lost all your colonies?
Ya lousy two-bit, crummy, decadent **third-rate** power!
We're gonna help him, **that's** who!
Put him down, Nikita!
You don't **own** this turf!
Why don't you come off it, Nikita?
I'll **tell** you why:
I feel vicious,
Oh, so vicious,
I feel vicious, malicious and low!
How delicious
Just to know that I am hated so!
I feel spiteful,
Oh, so spiteful,
I feel spiteful and frightfully sly!
How delightful
When I think of how despised am
See the little world that we're living in:
How shall I destroy it today-ay?
I will thump my shoe!
I will make a face!
I will start a war!
I will get my way!
I am scheming,
Oh, I'm screaming,
I am scheming and screaming with glee!
I won't stop
Till the whole world is Red just like me!
You're asking for it, Nikita! We'll see you later!
Where are you going? You haven't agreed on a rumble! You haven't set a time and a place! But what's worst, you haven't heard the second chorus of this song, which is my big solo number!

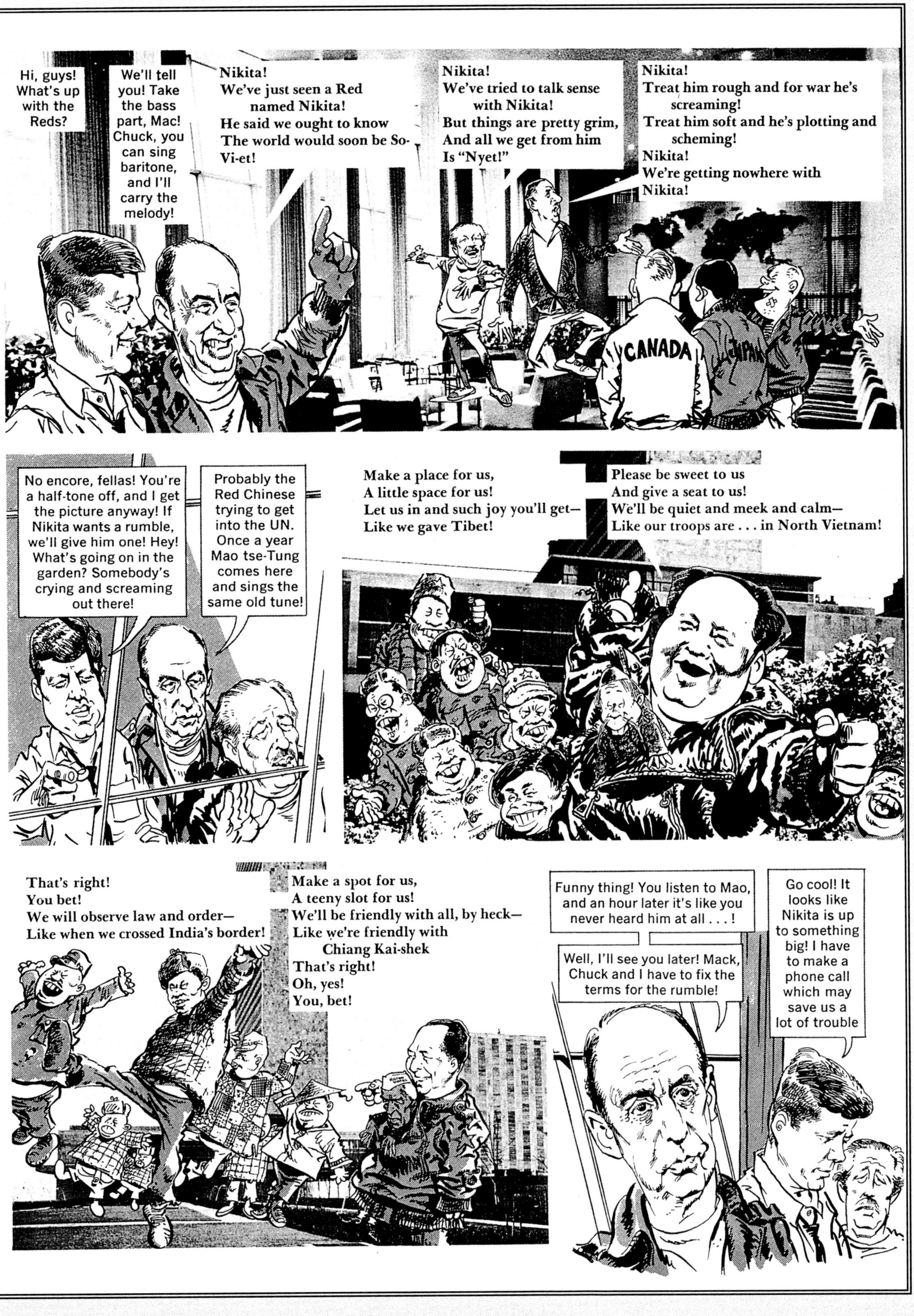
Hi, guys! What's up with the Reds?
We'll tell you! Take the bass part, Mac! Chuck, you can sing baritone, and I'll carry the melody!
Nikita!
We've just seen a Red named Nikita!
He said we ought to know
The world would soon be So-Vi-et!
Nikita!
We've tried to talk sense with Nikita!
But things are pretty grim,
And all we get from him
Is "Nyet!"
Nikita!
Treat him rough and for war he's screaming!
Treat him soft and he's plotting and scheming!
Nikita!
We're getting nowhere with Nikita!
CANADA
JAPAN
No encore, fellas! You're a half-tone off, and I get the picture anyway! If Nikita wants a rumble, we'll give him one! Hey! What's going on in the garden? Somebody's crying and screaming out there!
Probably the Red Chinese trying to get into the UN. Once a year Mao tse-Tung comes here and sings the same old tune!
Make a place for us,
A little space for us!
Let us in and such joy you'll get—
Like we gave Tibet!
Please be sweet to us
And give a seat to us!
We'll be quiet and meek and calm—
Like our troops are . . . in North Vietnam!
That's right!
You bet!
We will observe law and order—
Like when we crossed India's border!
Make a spot for us,
A teeny slot for us!
We'll be friendly with all, by heck—
Like we're friendly with Chiang Kai-shek
That's right!
Oh, yes!
You, bet!
Funny thing! You listen to Mao, and an hour later it's like you never heard him at all . . . !
Well, I'll see you later! Mack, Chuck and I have to fix the terms for the rumble!
Go cool! It looks like Nikita is up to something big! I have to make a phone call which may save us a lot of trouble

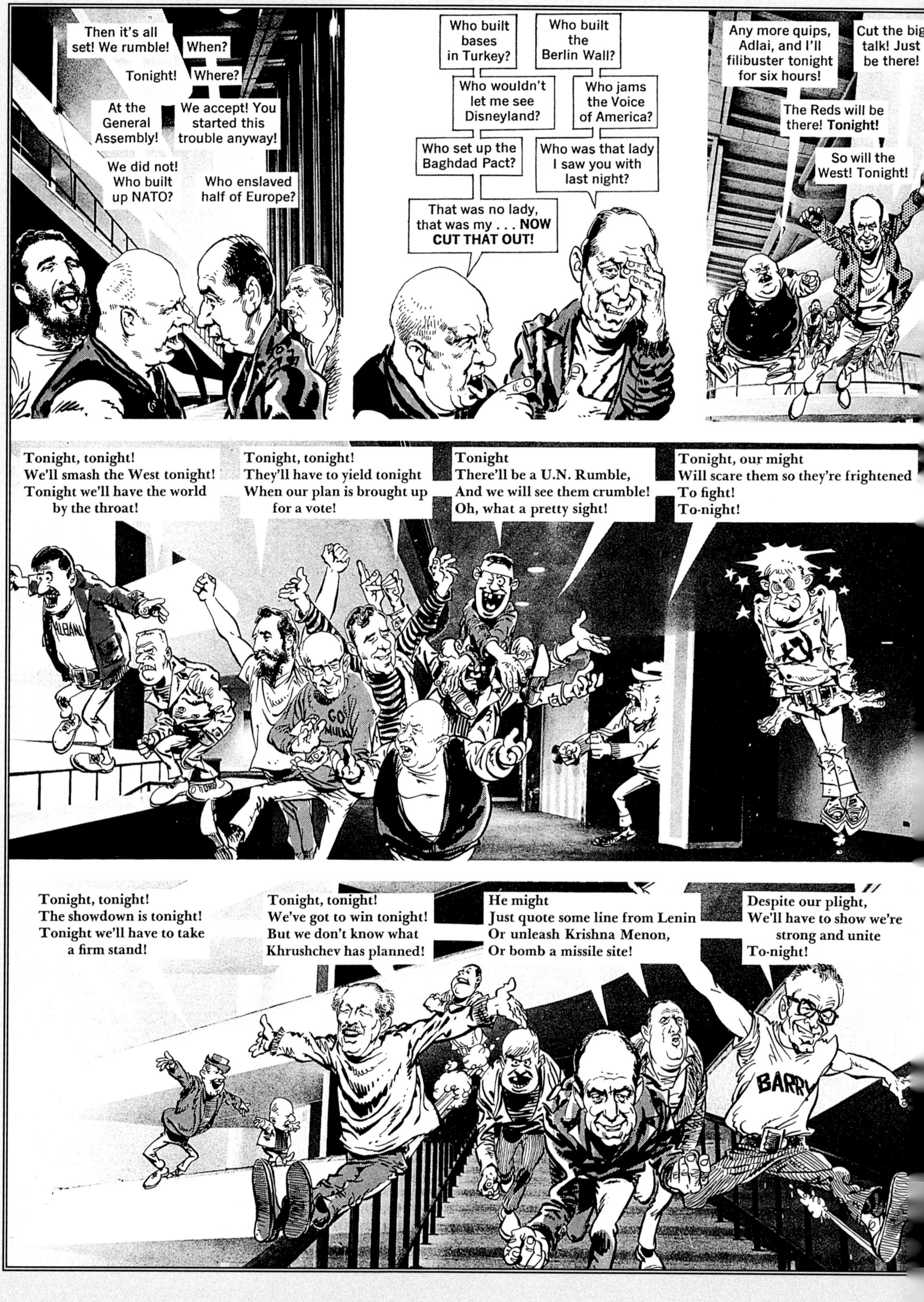
Then it's all set! We rumble!
When?
Tonight!
Where?
At the General Assembly!
We accept! You started this trouble anyway!
We did not! Who built up NATO?
Who enslaved half of Europe?
Who built bases in Turkey?
Who built the Berlin Wall?
Who wouldn't let me see Disneyland?
Who jams the Voice of America?
Who set up the Baghdad Pact?
Who was that lady I saw you with last night?
That was no lady, that was my . . . NOW CUT THAT OUT!
Any more quips, Adlai, and I'll filibuster tonight for six hours!
Cut the big talk! Just be there!
The Reds will be there! Tonight!
So will the West! Tonight!
Tonight, tonight! We'll smash the West tonight! Tonight we'll have the world by the throat!
Tonight, tonight! They'll have to yield tonight When our plan is brought up for a vote!
Tonight There'll be a U.N. Rumble, And we will see them crumble! Oh, what a pretty sight!
Tonight, our might Will scare them so they're frightened To fight! To-night!
Tonight, tonight! The showdown is tonight! Tonight we'll have to take a firm stand!
Tonight, tonight! We've got to win tonight! But we don't know what Khrushchev has planned!
He might Just quote some line from Lenin Or unleash Krishna Menon, Or bomb a missile site!
Despite our plight, We'll have to show we're strong and unite To-night!

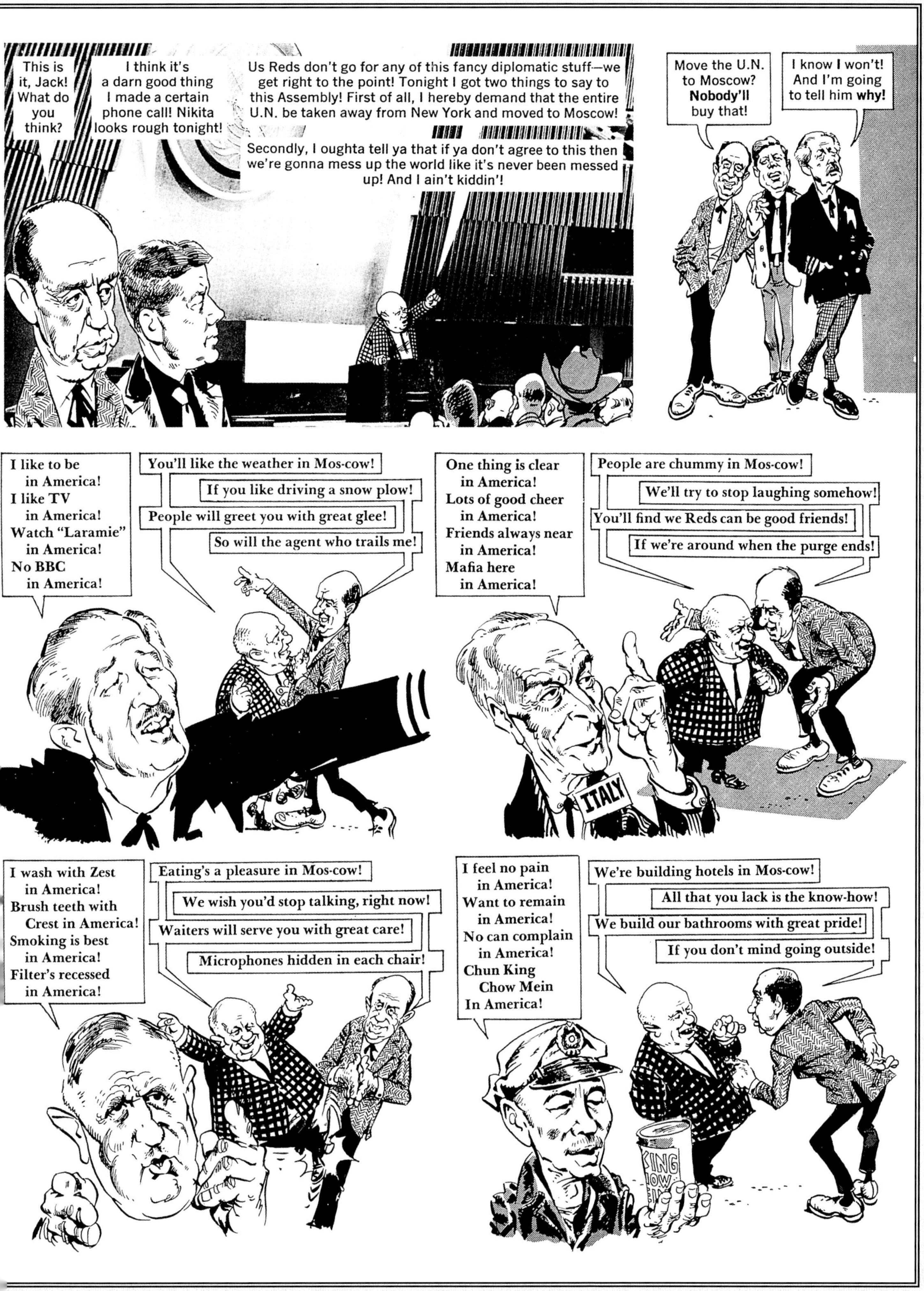
This is it, Jack! What do you think?
I think it's a darn good thing I made a certain phone call! Nikita looks rough tonight!
Us Reds don't go for any of this fancy diplomatic stuff—we get right to the point! Tonight I got two things to say to this Assembly! First of all, I hereby demand that the entire U.N. be taken away from New York and moved to Moscow!
Secondly, I oughta tell ya that if ya don't agree to this then we're gonna mess up the world like it's never been messed up! And I ain't kiddin'!
Move the U.N. to Moscow? **Nobody'll** buy that!
I know **I** won't! And I'm going to tell him **why!**
I like to be in America! I like TV in America! Watch "Laramie" in America! No BBC in America!
You'll like the weather in Mos-cow!
If you like driving a snow plow!
People will greet you with great glee!
So will the agent who trails me!
One thing is clear in America! Lots of good cheer in America! Friends always near in America! Mafia here in America!
People are chummy in Mos-cow!
We'll try to stop laughing somehow!
You'll find we Reds can be good friends!
If we're around when the purge ends!
ITALY
I wash with Zest in America! Brush teeth with Crest in America! Smoking is best in America! Filter's recessed in America!
Eating's a pleasure in Mos-cow!
We wish you'd stop talking, right now!
Waiters will serve you with great care!
Microphones hidden in each chair!
I feel no pain in America! Want to remain in America! No can complain in America! Chun King Chow Mein In America!
We're building hotels in Mos-cow!
All that you lack is the know-how!
We build our bathrooms with great pride!
If you don't mind going outside!

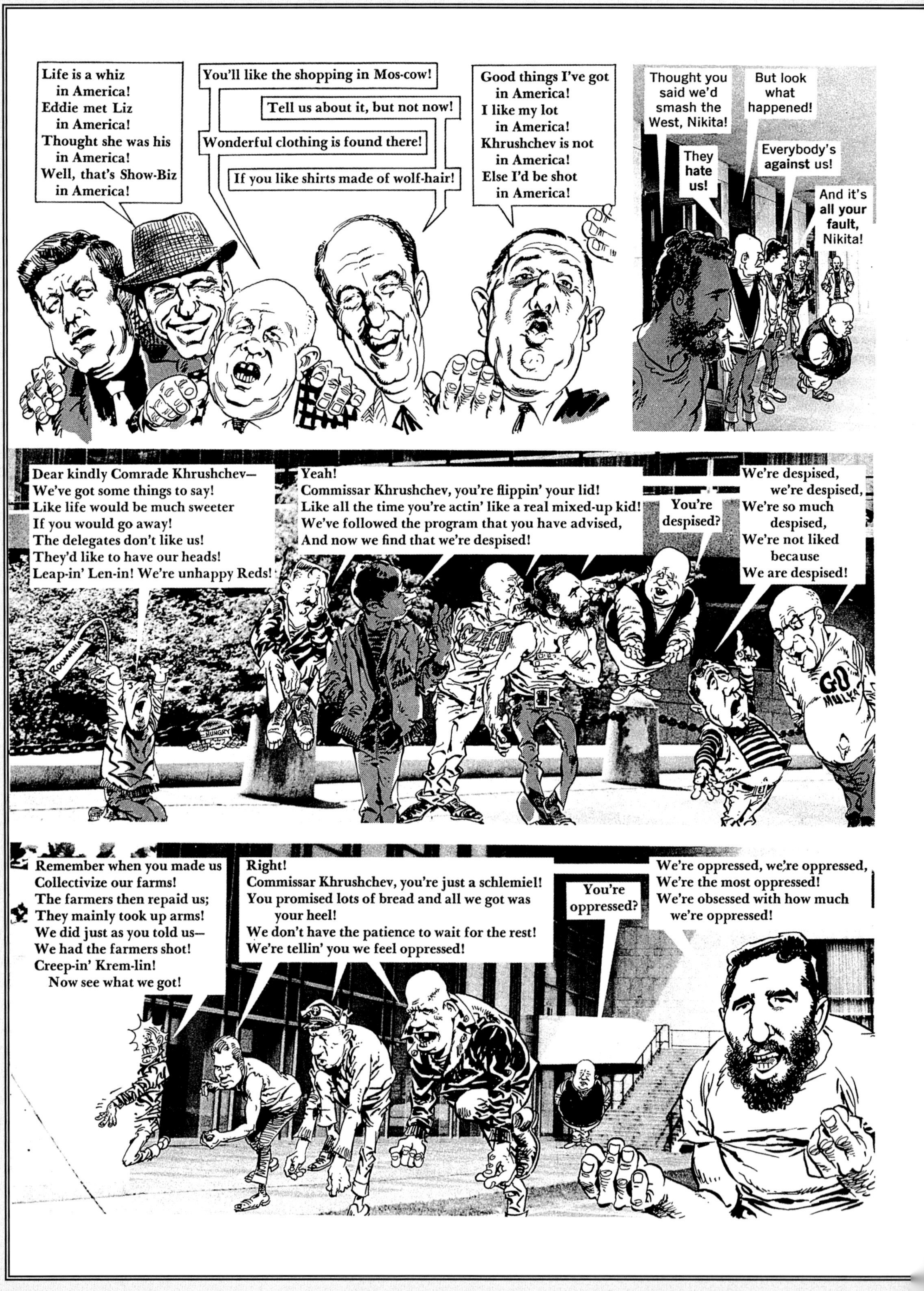
Life is a whiz in America! Eddie met Liz in America! Thought she was his in America! Well, that's Show-Biz in America!
You'll like the shopping in Mos-cow!
Tell us about it, but not now!
Wonderful clothing is found there!
If you like shirts made of wolf-hair!
Good things I've got in America! I like my lot in America! Khrushchev is not in America! Else I'd be shot in America!
Thought you said we'd smash the West, Nikita!
But look what happened!
They hate us!
Everybody's against us!
And it's all your fault, Nikita!
Dear kindly Comrade Khrushchev— We've got some things to say! Like life would be much sweeter If you would go away! The delegates don't like us! They'd like to have our heads! Leap-in' Len-in! We're unhappy Reds!
Yeah! Commissar Khrushchev, you're flippin' your lid! Like all the time you're actin' like a real mixed-up kid! We've followed the program that you have advised, And now we find that we're despised!
You're despised?
We're despised, we're despised, We're so much despised, We're not liked because We are despised!
ROUMANIA
HUNGRY
AL BANIA
CZECH
GO MULKA
Remember when you made us Collectivize our farms! The farmers then repaid us; They mainly took up arms! We did just as you told us— We had the farmers shot! Creep-in' Krem-lin! Now see what we got!
Right! Commissar Khrushchev, you're just a schlemiel! You promised lots of bread and all we got was your heel! We don't have the patience to wait for the rest! We're tellin' you we feel oppressed!
You're oppressed?
We're oppressed, we're oppressed, We're the most oppressed! We're obsessed with how much we're oppressed!

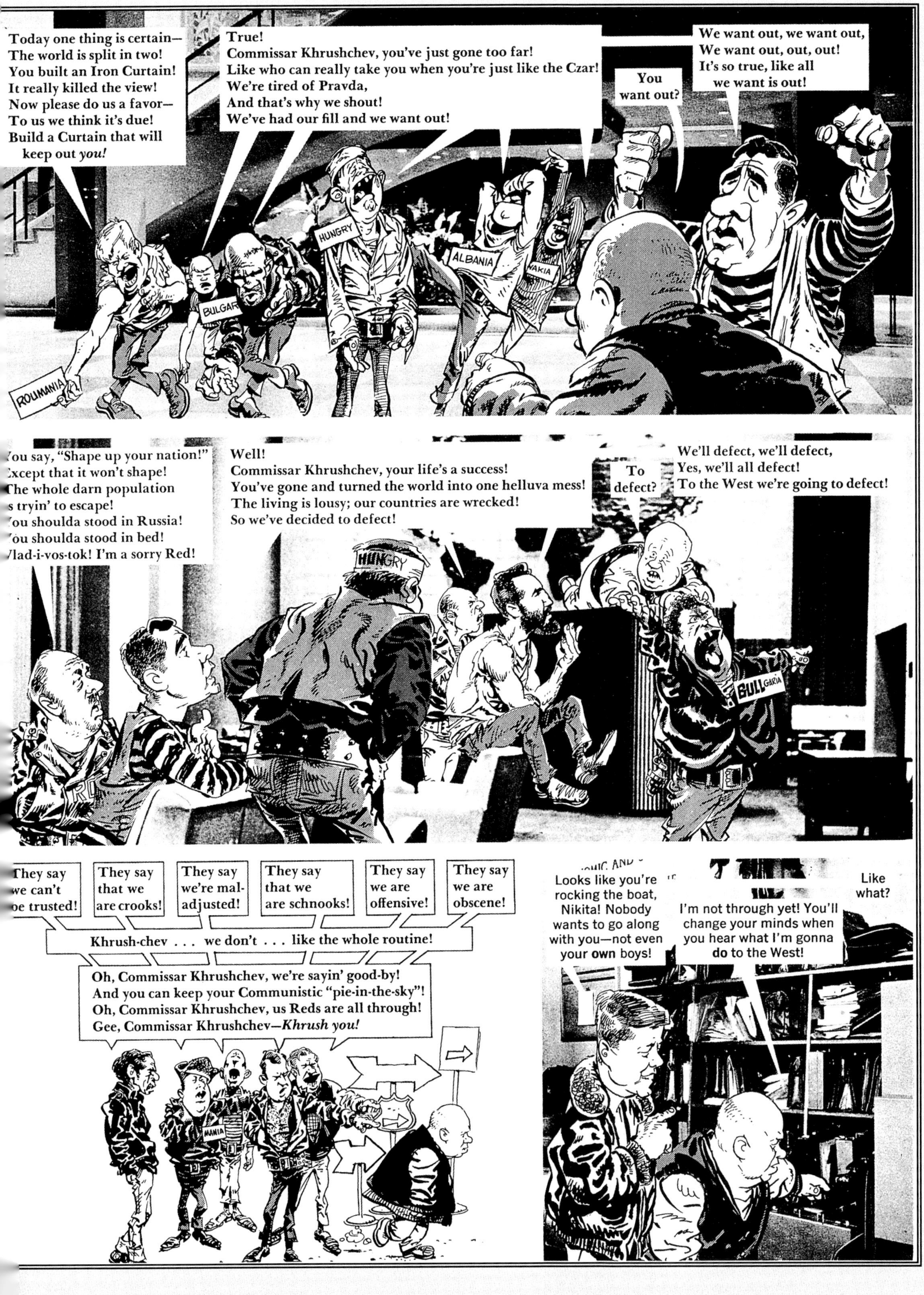
Today one thing is certain—
The world is split in two!
You built an Iron Curtain!
It really killed the view!
Now please do us a favor—
To us we think it's due!
Build a Curtain that will keep out *you!*
True!
Commissar Khrushchev, you've just gone too far!
Like who can really take you when you're just like the Czar!
We're tired of Pravda,
And that's why we shout!
We've had our fill and we want out!
You want out?
We want out, we want out,
We want out, out, out!
It's so true, like all we want is out!
ROUMANIA
BULGAR
HUNGRY
ALBANIA
AKIA
ou say, "Shape up your nation!"
xcept that it won't shape!
The whole darn population
s tryin' to escape!
ou shoulda stood in Russia!
ou shoulda stood in bed!
lad-i-vos-tok! I'm a sorry Red!
Well!
Commissar Khrushchev, your life's a success!
You've gone and turned the world into one helluva mess!
The living is lousy; our countries are wrecked!
So we've decided to defect!
To defect?
We'll defect, we'll defect,
Yes, we'll all defect!
To the West we're going to defect!
HUNGRY
BULLGARIA
hey say we can't e trusted!
They say that we are crooks!
They say we're maladjusted!
They say that we are schnooks!
They say we are offensive!
They say we are obscene!
Khrush-chev . . . we don't . . . like the whole routine!
Oh, Commissar Khrushchev, we're sayin' good-by!
And you can keep your Communistic "pie-in-the-sky"!
Oh, Commissar Khrushchev, us Reds are all through!
Gee, Commissar Khrushchev—*Khrush you!*
MANIA
Looks like you're rocking the boat, Nikita! Nobody wants to go along with you—not even your **own** boys!
Like what?
I'm not through yet! You'll change your minds when you hear what I'm gonna **do** to the West!

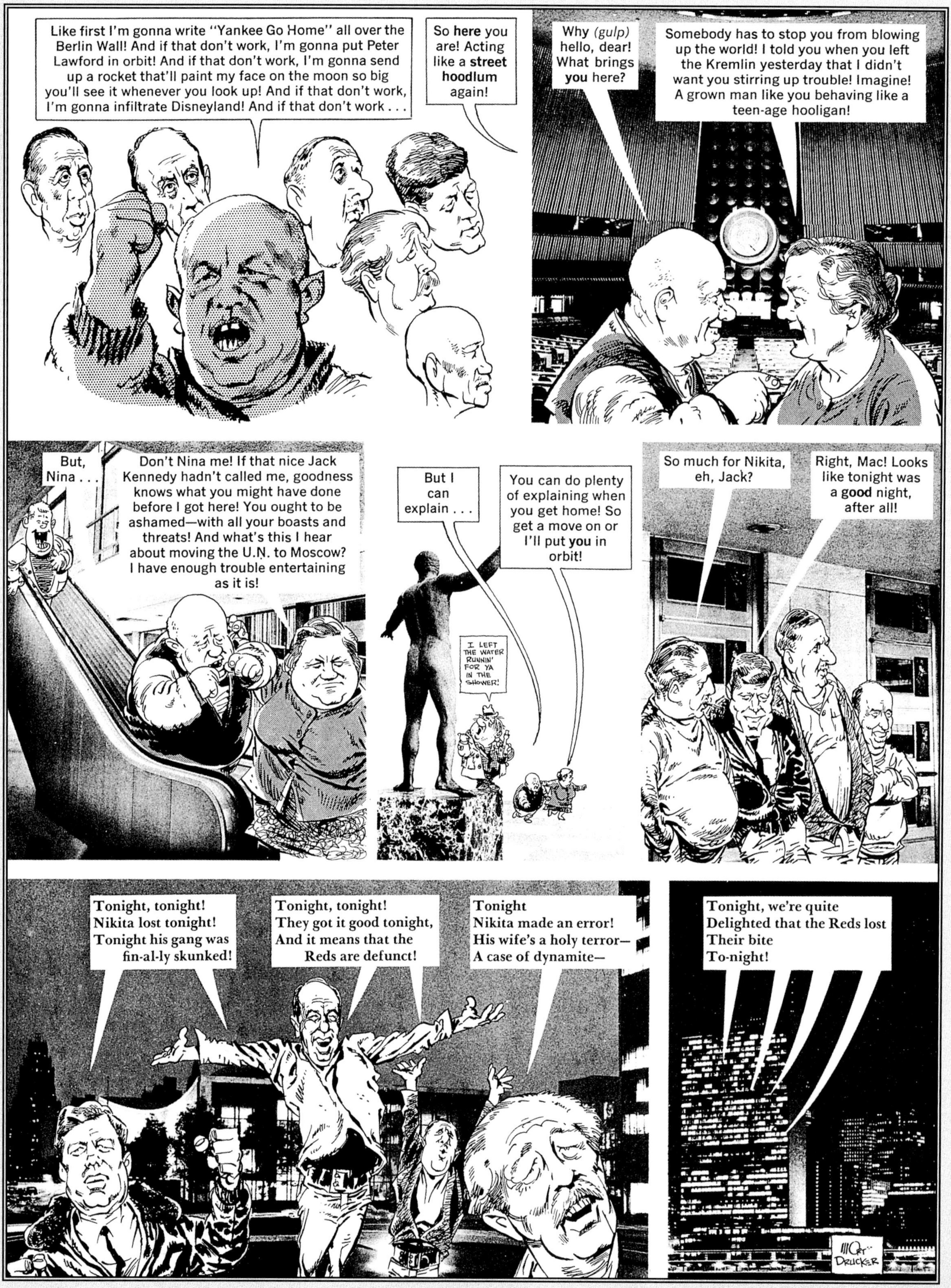

Like first I'm gonna write "Yankee Go Home" all over the Berlin Wall! And if that don't work, I'm gonna put Peter Lawford in orbit! And if that don't work, I'm gonna send up a rocket that'll paint my face on the moon so big you'll see it whenever you look up! And if that don't work, I'm gonna infiltrate Disneyland! And if that don't work . . .
So **here** you are! Acting like a **street hoodlum** again!
Why *(gulp)* hello, dear! What brings **you** here?
Somebody has to stop you from blowing up the world! I told you when you left the Kremlin yesterday that I didn't want you stirring up trouble! Imagine! A grown man like you behaving like a teen-age hooligan!
But, Nina . . .
Don't Nina me! If that nice Jack Kennedy hadn't called me, goodness knows what you might have done before I got here! You ought to be ashamed—with all your boasts and threats! And what's this I hear about moving the U.N. to Moscow? I have enough trouble entertaining as it is!
But I can explain . . .
You can do plenty of explaining when you get home! So get a move on or I'll put **you** in orbit!
I LEFT THE WATER RUNNIN' FOR YA IN THE SHOWER!
So much for Nikita, eh, Jack?
Right, Mac! Looks like tonight was a **good** night, after all!
Tonight, tonight! Nikita lost tonight! Tonight his gang was fin-al-ly skunked!
Tonight, tonight! They got it good tonight, And it means that the Reds are defunct!
Tonight Nikita made an error! His wife's a holy terror— A case of dynamite—
Tonight, we're quite Delighted that the Reds lost Their bite To-night!
MORT DRUCKER

IT'S TRUE! BONDS DO HAVE MORE FUN DEPT.

There's a new trend on Broadway these days—which is to make musicals based on great British literary figures. First there was "Camelot", based on the story of King Arthur...then there was "Oliver", based on Charles Dickens' novel "Oliver Twist"... and this fall, there is "Baker Street", based on the adventures of Sherlock Holmes. That's why we at MAD feel that it's only a matter of time before Broadway does a musical on the most sure-fire British literary hero of all. We mean, of course, James Bond, Special Agent 007, of the British Secret Service, the creation of the late Ian Fleming. Perhaps someday there may be a real James Bond musical. But until then, you'll just have to put up with a MAD James *Bomb* musical, which we've titled:

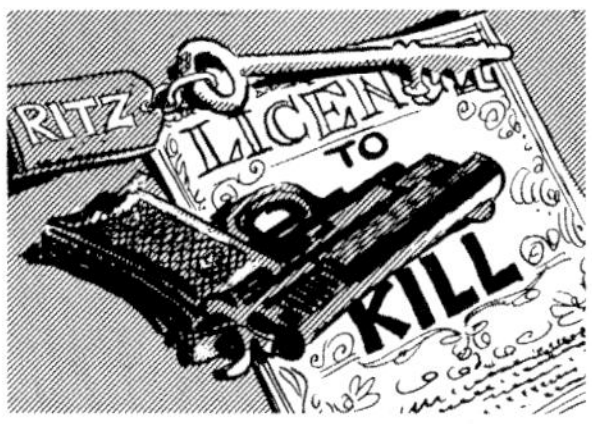
RITZ
LICENSE TO KILL

007

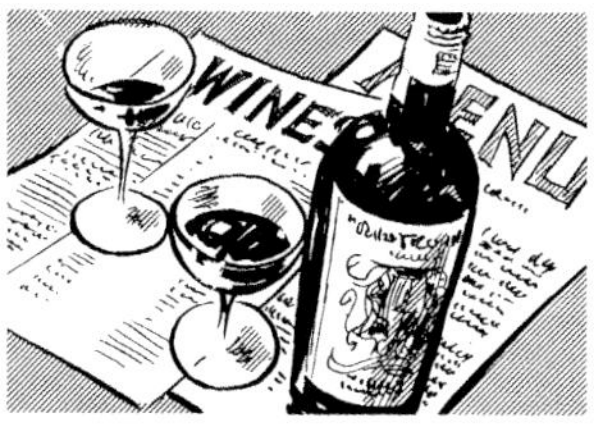
WINE

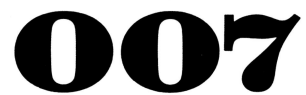

ACT I, SCENE 1: THE LONDON HEADQUARTERS OF THE BRITISH SECRET SERVICE

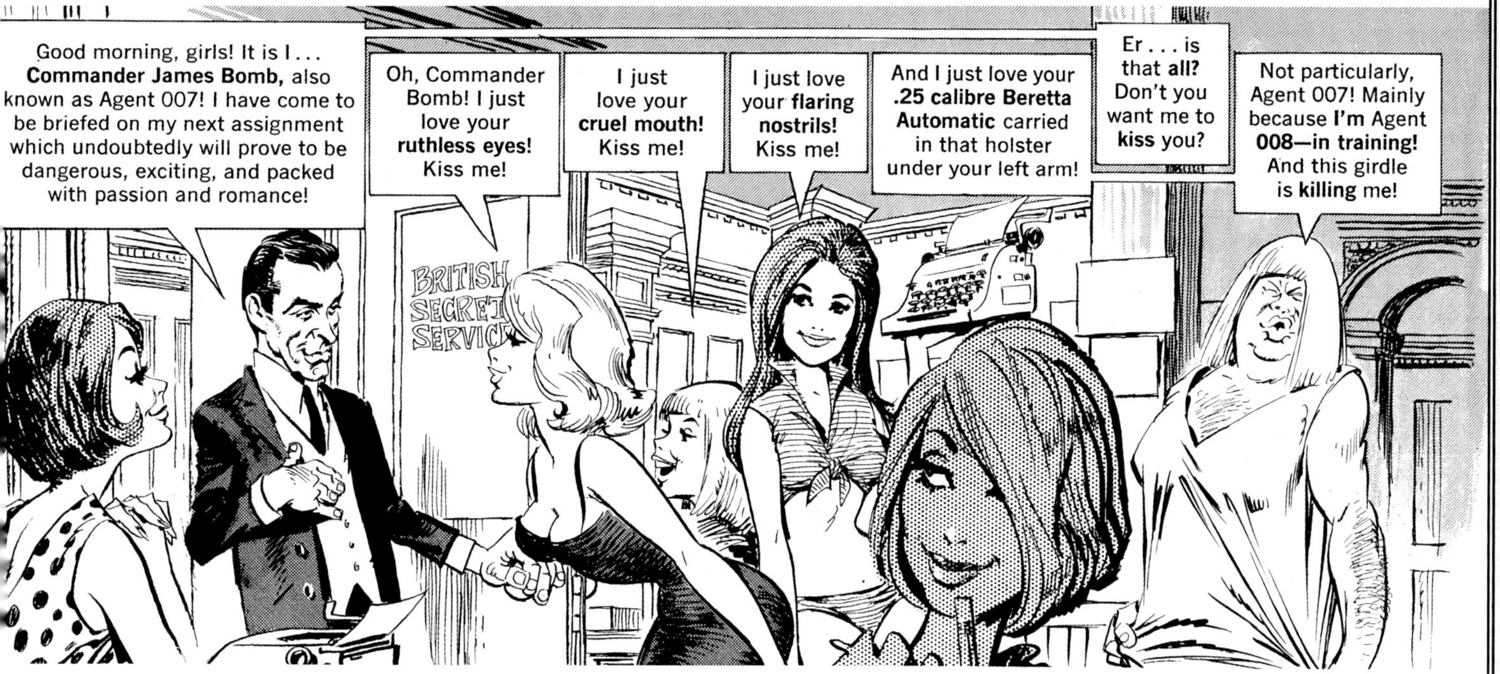
Good morning, girls! It is I... **Commander James Bomb,** also known as Agent 007! I have come to be briefed on my next assignment which undoubtedly will prove to be dangerous, exciting, and packed with passion and romance!
Oh, Commander Bomb! I just love your **ruthless eyes!** Kiss me!
I just love your **cruel mouth!** Kiss me!
I just love your **flaring nostrils!** Kiss me!
And I just love your **.25 calibre Beretta Automatic** carried in that holster under your left arm!
Er... is that **all?** Don't you want me to **kiss** you?
Not particularly, Agent 007! Mainly because **I'm Agent 008—in training!** And this girdle is **killing** me!
BRITISH SECRET SERVICE

ARTIST: MORT DRUCKER WRITER: FRANK JACOBS

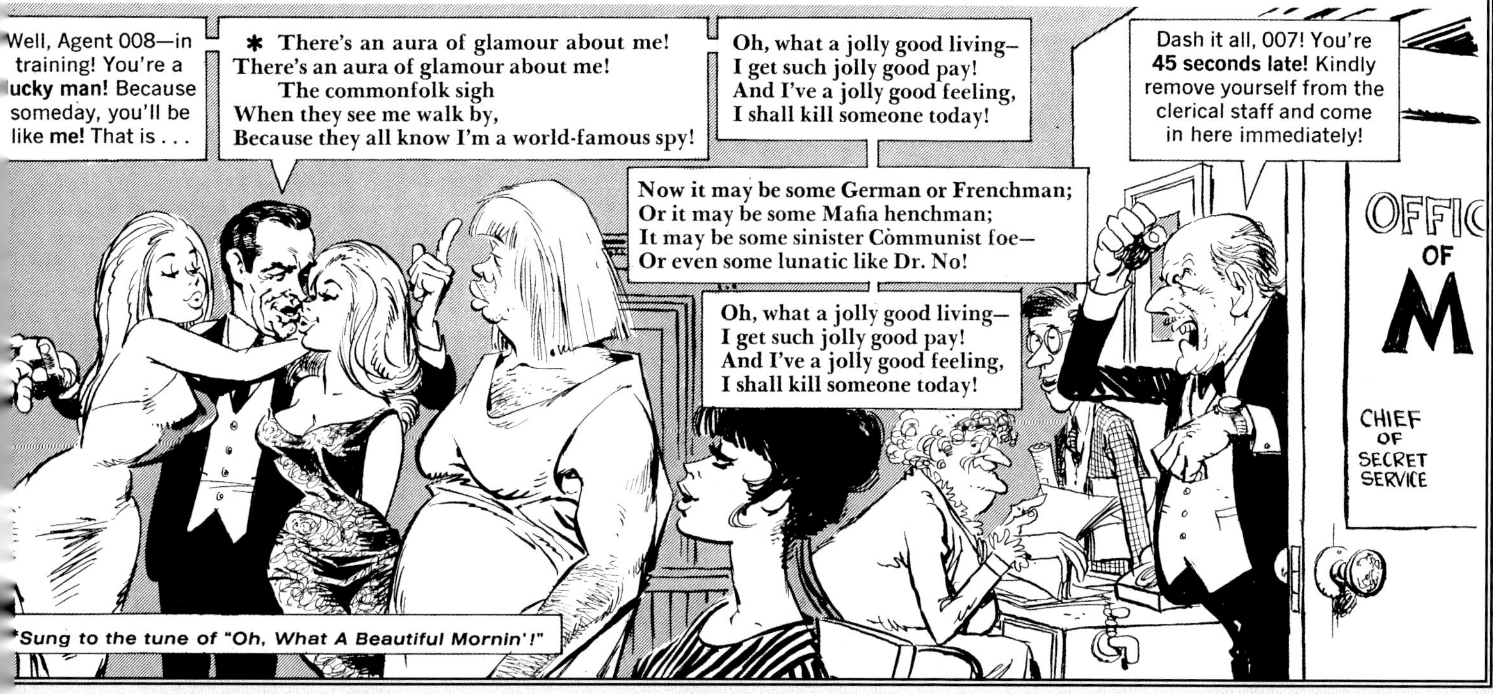
Well, Agent 008—in training! You're a **lucky man!** Because someday, you'll be like **me!** That is...
* There's an aura of glamour about me!
There's an aura of glamour about me!
The commonfolk sigh
When they see me walk by,
Because they all know I'm a world-famous spy!
Oh, what a jolly good living—
I get such jolly good pay!
And I've a jolly good feeling,
I shall kill someone today!
Dash it all, 007! You're **45 seconds late!** Kindly remove yourself from the clerical staff and come in here immediately!
Now it may be some German or Frenchman;
Or it may be some Mafia henchman;
It may be some sinister Communist foe—
Or even some lunatic like Dr. No!
Oh, what a jolly good living—
I get such jolly good pay!
And I've a jolly good feeling,
I shall kill someone today!
OFFIC OF M
CHIEF OF SECRET SERVICE
*Sung to the tune of "Oh, What A Beautiful Mornin'!"

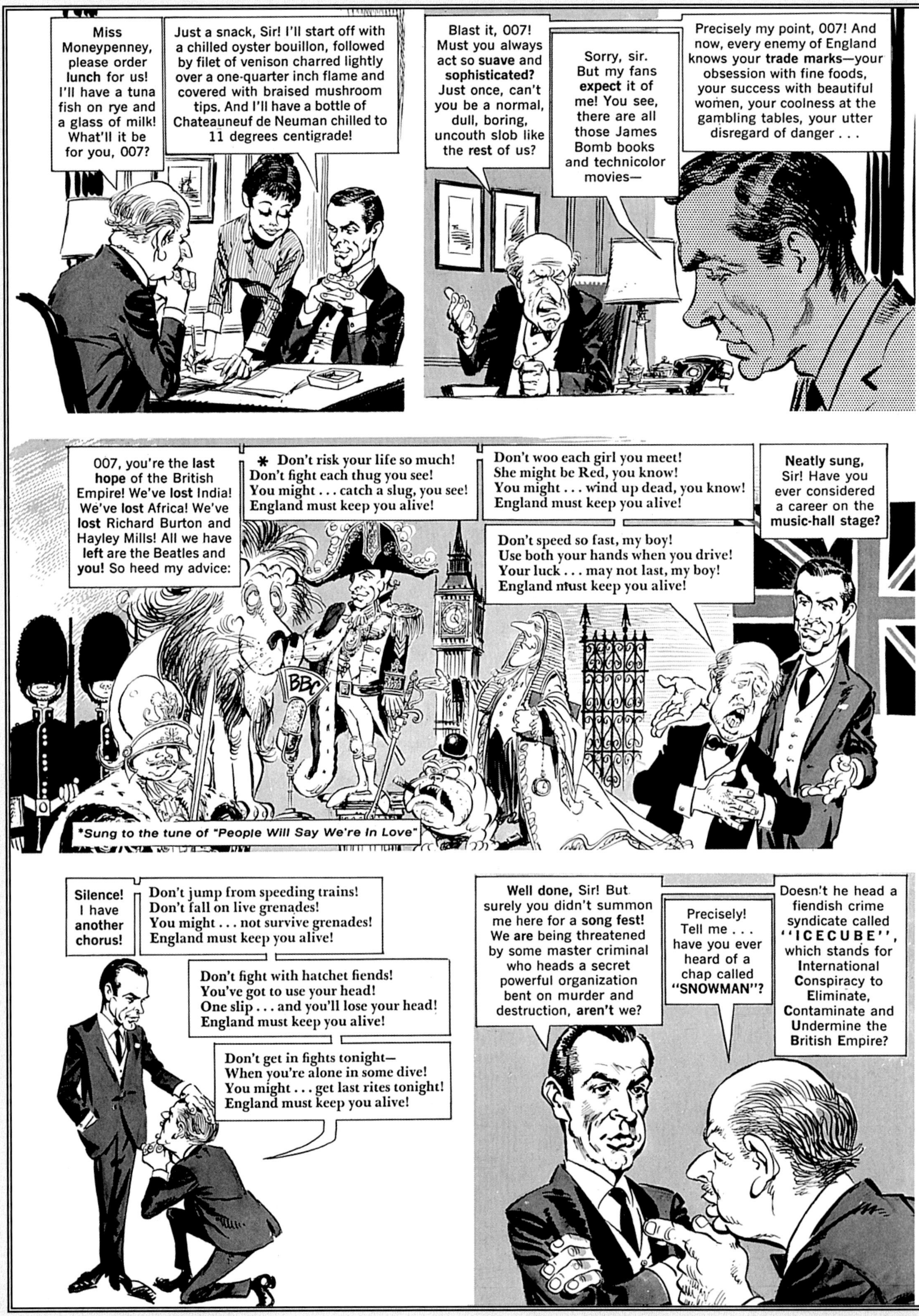
Miss Moneypenney, please order lunch for us! I'll have a tuna fish on rye and a glass of milk! What'll it be for you, 007?
Just a snack, Sir! I'll start off with a chilled oyster bouillon, followed by filet of venison charred lightly over a one-quarter inch flame and covered with braised mushroom tips. And I'll have a bottle of Chateauneuf de Neuman chilled to 11 degrees centigrade!
Blast it, 007! Must you always act so suave and sophisticated? Just once, can't you be a normal, dull, boring, uncouth slob like the rest of us?
Sorry, sir. But my fans expect it of me! You see, there are all those James Bomb books and technicolor movies—
Precisely my point, 007! And now, every enemy of England knows your trade marks—your obsession with fine foods, your success with beautiful women, your coolness at the gambling tables, your utter disregard of danger . . .
007, you're the last hope of the British Empire! We've lost India! We've lost Africa! We've lost Richard Burton and Hayley Mills! All we have left are the Beatles and you! So heed my advice:
* Don't risk your life so much! Don't fight each thug you see! You might . . . catch a slug, you see! England must keep you alive!
Don't woo each girl you meet! She might be Red, you know! You might . . . wind up dead, you know! England must keep you alive!
Don't speed so fast, my boy! Use both your hands when you drive! Your luck . . . may not last, my boy! England must keep you alive!
Neatly sung, Sir! Have you ever considered a career on the music-hall stage?
BBC
*Sung to the tune of "People Will Say We're In Love"
Silence! I have another chorus!
Don't jump from speeding trains! Don't fall on live grenades! You might . . . not survive grenades! England must keep you alive!
Don't fight with hatchet fiends! You've got to use your head! One slip . . . and you'll lose your head! England must keep you alive!
Don't get in fights tonight— When you're alone in some dive! You might . . . get last rites tonight! England must keep you alive!
Well done, Sir! But surely you didn't summon me here for a song fest! We are being threatened by some master criminal who heads a secret powerful organization bent on murder and destruction, aren't we?
Precisely! Tell me . . . have you ever heard of a chap called "SNOWMAN"?
Doesn't he head a fiendish crime syndicate called "ICECUBE", which stands for International Conspiracy to Eliminate, Contaminate and Undermine the British Empire?

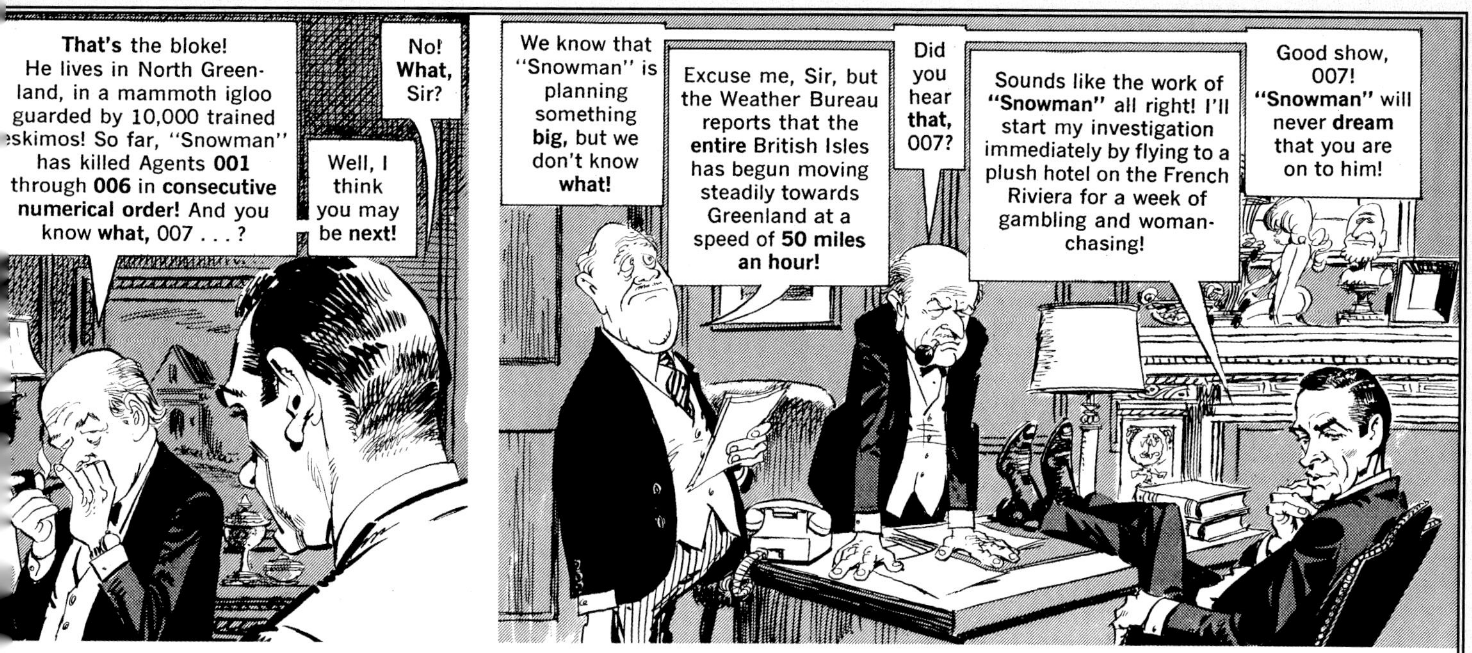
That's the bloke! He lives in North Green-land, in a mammoth igloo guarded by 10,000 trained skimos! So far, "Snowman" has killed Agents 001 through 006 in consecutive numerical order! And you know what, 007 . . . ?
No! What, Sir?
Well, I think you may be next!
We know that "Snowman" is planning something big, but we don't know what!
Excuse me, Sir, but the Weather Bureau reports that the entire British Isles has begun moving steadily towards Greenland at a speed of 50 miles an hour!
Did you hear that, 007?
Sounds like the work of "Snowman" all right! I'll start my investigation immediately by flying to a plush hotel on the French Riviera for a week of gambling and woman-chasing!
Good show, 007! "Snowman" will never dream that you are on to him!

ACT I, SCENE 2: A LONDON STREET

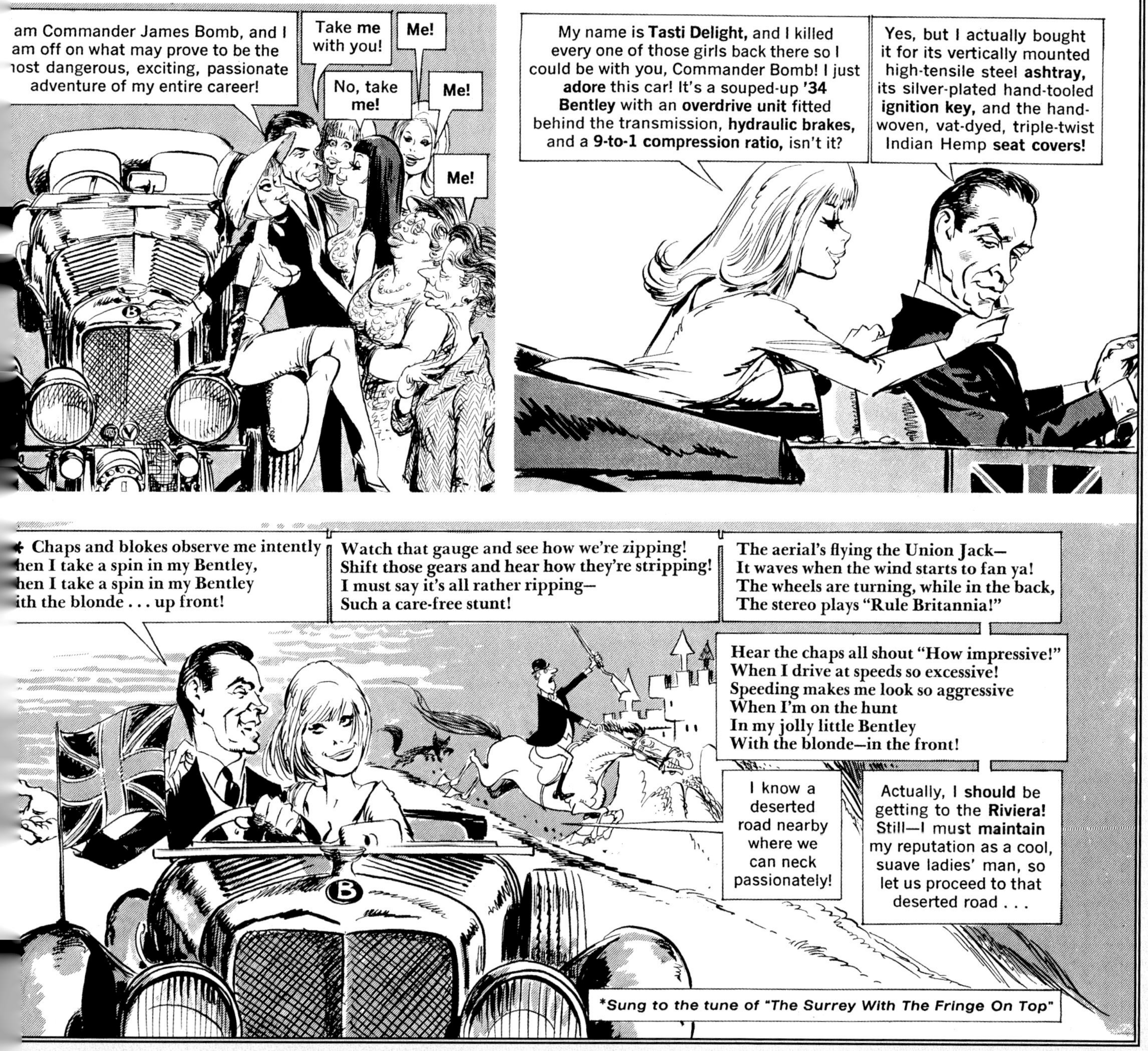
am Commander James Bomb, and I am off on what may prove to be the ost dangerous, exciting, passionate adventure of my entire career!
Take me with you!
Me!
No, take me!
Me!
Me!
My name is Tasti Delight, and I killed every one of those girls back there so I could be with you, Commander Bomb! I just adore this car! It's a souped-up '34 Bentley with an overdrive unit fitted behind the transmission, hydraulic brakes, and a 9-to-1 compression ratio, isn't it?
Yes, but I actually bought it for its vertically mounted high-tensile steel ashtray, its silver-plated hand-tooled ignition key, and the hand-woven, vat-dyed, triple-twist Indian Hemp seat covers!
* Chaps and blokes observe me intently
hen I take a spin in my Bentley,
hen I take a spin in my Bentley
ith the blonde . . . up front!
Watch that gauge and see how we're zipping!
Shift those gears and hear how they're stripping!
I must say it's all rather ripping—
Such a care-free stunt!
The aerial's flying the Union Jack—
It waves when the wind starts to fan ya!
The wheels are turning, while in the back,
The stereo plays "Rule Britannia!"
Hear the chaps all shout "How impressive!"
When I drive at speeds so excessive!
Speeding makes me look so aggressive
When I'm on the hunt
In my jolly little Bentley
With the blonde—in the front!
I know a deserted road nearby where we can neck passionately!
Actually, I should be getting to the Riviera! Still—I must maintain my reputation as a cool, suave ladies' man, so let us proceed to that deserted road . . .
*Sung to the tune of "The Surrey With The Fringe On Top"

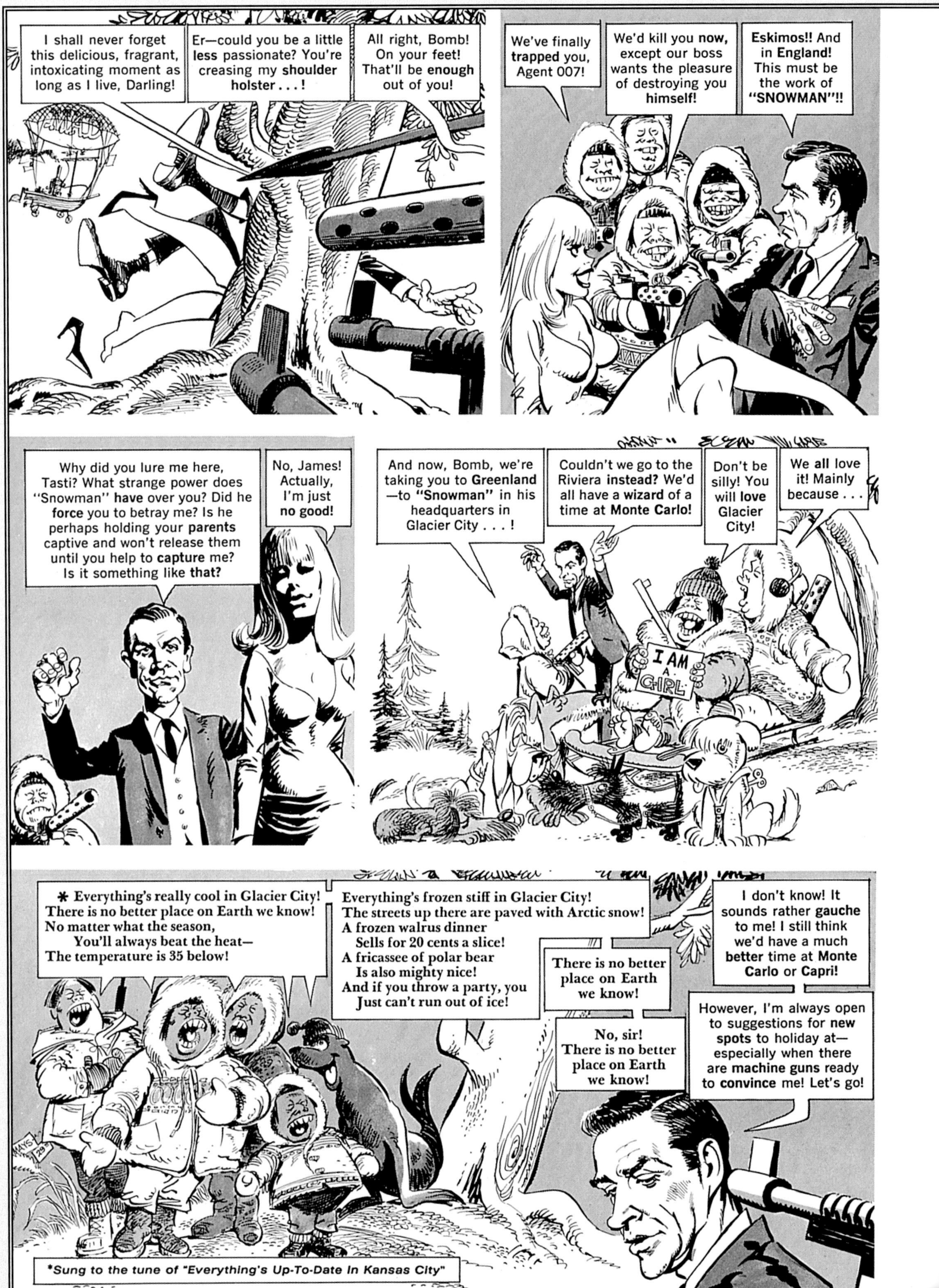
I shall never forget this delicious, fragrant, intoxicating moment as long as I live, Darling!
Er—could you be a little less passionate? You're creasing my shoulder holster . . . !
All right, Bomb! On your feet! That'll be enough out of you!
We've finally trapped you, Agent 007!
We'd kill you now, except our boss wants the pleasure of destroying you himself!
Eskimos!! And in England! This must be the work of "SNOWMAN"!!
Why did you lure me here, Tasti? What strange power does "Snowman" have over you? Did he force you to betray me? Is he perhaps holding your parents captive and won't release them until you help to capture me? Is it something like that?
No, James! Actually, I'm just no good!
And now, Bomb, we're taking you to Greenland—to "Snowman" in his headquarters in Glacier City . . . !
Couldn't we go to the Riviera instead? We'd all have a wizard of a time at Monte Carlo!
Don't be silly! You will love Glacier City!
We all love it! Mainly because . . .
I AM A GIRL
* Everything's really cool in Glacier City! There is no better place on Earth we know! No matter what the season, You'll always beat the heat— The temperature is 35 below!
Everything's frozen stiff in Glacier City! The streets up there are paved with Arctic snow! A frozen walrus dinner Sells for 20 cents a slice! A fricassee of polar bear Is also mighty nice! And if you throw a party, you Just can't run out of ice!
There is no better place on Earth we know!
No, sir! There is no better place on Earth we know!
I don't know! It sounds rather gauche to me! I still think we'd have a much better time at Monte Carlo or Capri!
However, I'm always open to suggestions for new spots to holiday at—especially when there are machine guns ready to convince me! Let's go!
*Sung to the tune of "Everything's Up-To-Date In Kansas City"

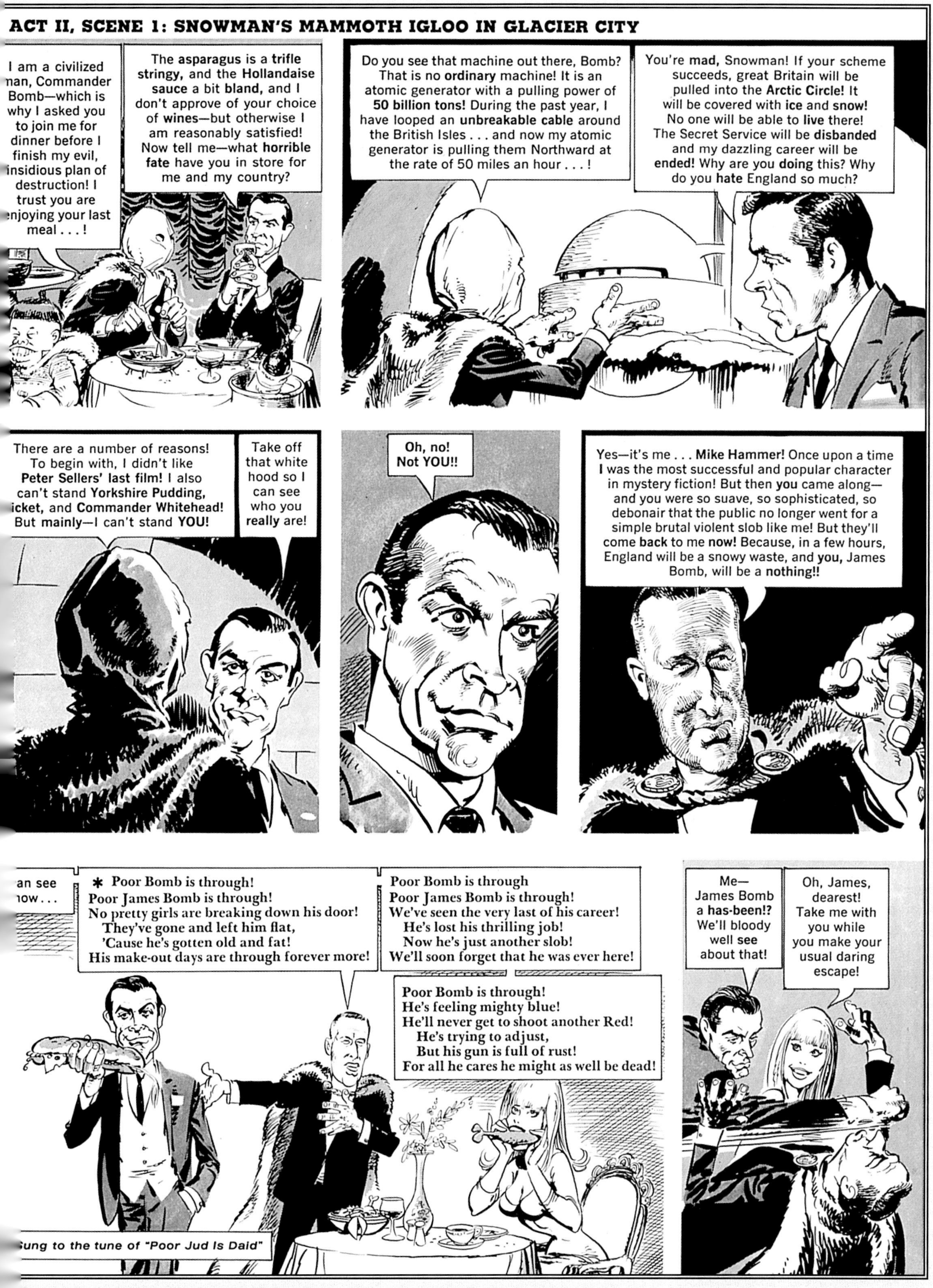
ACT II, SCENE 1: SNOWMAN'S MAMMOTH IGLOO IN GLACIER CITY
I am a civilized man, Commander Bomb—which is why I asked you to join me for dinner before I finish my evil, insidious plan of destruction! I trust you are enjoying your last meal . . . !
The asparagus is a trifle stringy, and the Hollandaise sauce a bit bland, and I don't approve of your choice of wines—but otherwise I am reasonably satisfied! Now tell me—what horrible fate have you in store for me and my country?
Do you see that machine out there, Bomb? That is no ordinary machine! It is an atomic generator with a pulling power of 50 billion tons! During the past year, I have looped an unbreakable cable around the British Isles . . . and now my atomic generator is pulling them Northward at the rate of 50 miles an hour . . . !
You're mad, Snowman! If your scheme succeeds, great Britain will be pulled into the Arctic Circle! It will be covered with ice and snow! No one will be able to live there! The Secret Service will be disbanded and my dazzling career will be ended! Why are you doing this? Why do you hate England so much?
There are a number of reasons! To begin with, I didn't like Peter Sellers' last film! I also can't stand Yorkshire Pudding, icket, and Commander Whitehead! But mainly—I can't stand YOU!
Take off that white hood so I can see who you really are!
Oh, no! Not YOU!!
Yes—it's me . . . Mike Hammer! Once upon a time I was the most successful and popular character in mystery fiction! But then you came along—and you were so suave, so sophisticated, so debonair that the public no longer went for a simple brutal violent slob like me! But they'll come back to me now! Because, in a few hours, England will be a snowy waste, and you, James Bomb, will be a nothing!!
an see now . . .
* Poor Bomb is through!
Poor James Bomb is through!
No pretty girls are breaking down his door!
They've gone and left him flat,
'Cause he's gotten old and fat!
His make-out days are through forever more!
Poor Bomb is through
Poor James Bomb is through!
We've seen the very last of his career!
He's lost his thrilling job!
Now he's just another slob!
We'll soon forget that he was ever here!
Poor Bomb is through!
He's feeling mighty blue!
He'll never get to shoot another Red!
He's trying to adjust,
But his gun is full of rust!
For all he cares he might as well be dead!
Me—James Bomb a has-been!? We'll bloody well see about that!
Oh, James, dearest! Take me with you while you make your usual daring escape!
Sung to the tune of "Poor Jud Is Daid"

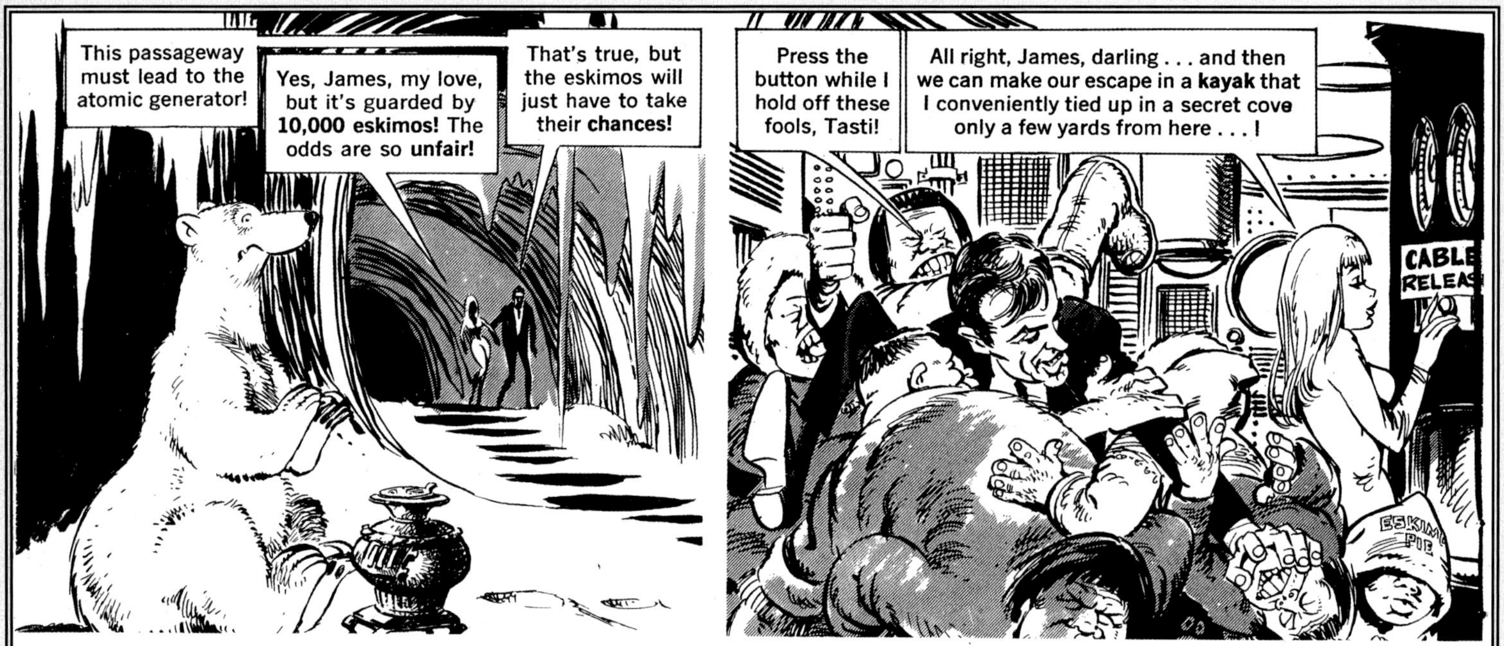
This passageway must lead to the atomic generator!
Yes, James, my love, but it's guarded by **10,000 eskimos!** The odds are so **unfair!**
That's true, but the eskimos will just have to take their **chances!**
Press the button while I hold off these fools, Tasti!
All right, James, darling . . . and then we can make our escape in a **kayak** that I conveniently tied up in a secret cove only a few yards from here . . . !
CABLE RELEAS
ESKIMO PIE

ACT II, SCENE 2: THE LONDON HEADQUARTERS OF THE BRITISH SECRET SERVICE

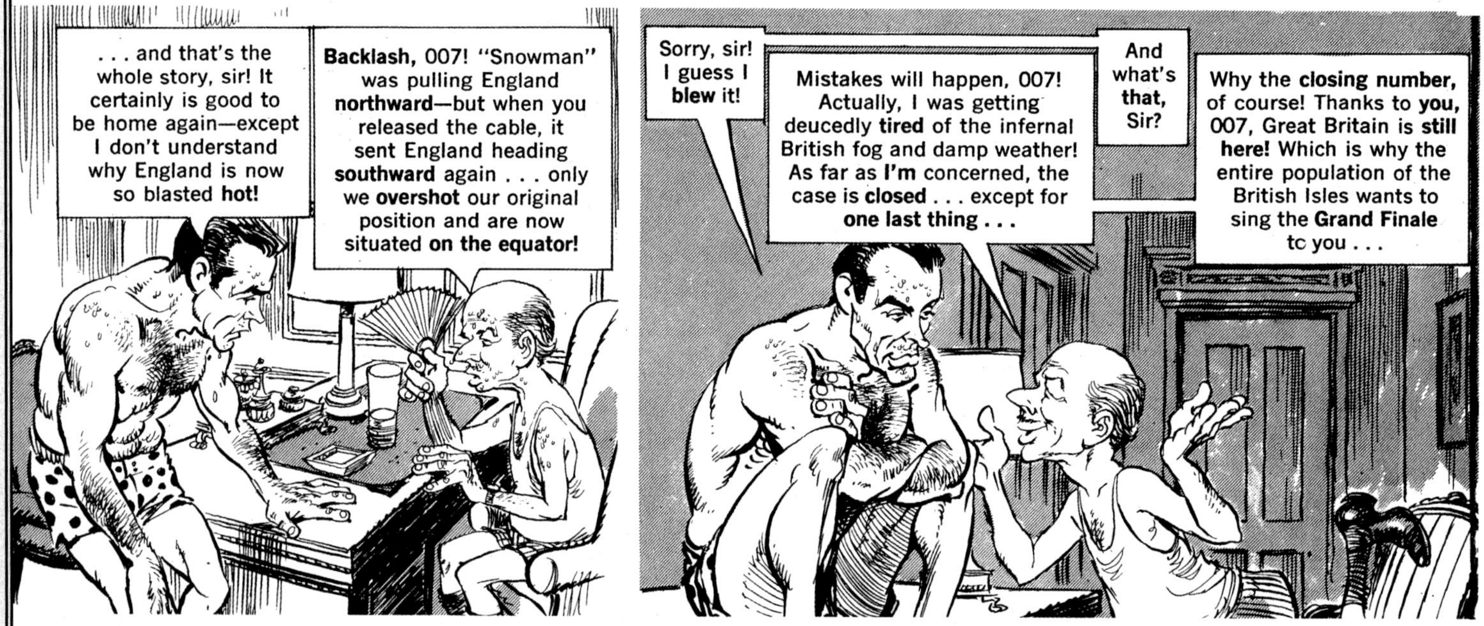
. . . and that's the whole story, sir! It certainly is good to be home again—except I don't understand why England is now so blasted **hot!**
Backlash, 007! "Snowman" was pulling England **northward**—but when you released the cable, it sent England heading **southward** again . . . only we **overshot** our original position and are now situated **on the equator!**
Sorry, sir! I guess I **blew** it!
Mistakes will happen, 007! Actually, I was getting deucedly **tired** of the infernal British fog and damp weather! As far as **I'm** concerned, the case is **closed** . . . except for **one last thing . . .**
And what's **that,** Sir?
Why the **closing number,** of course! Thanks to **you,** 007, Great Britain is **still here!** Which is why the entire population of the British Isles wants to sing the **Grand Finale** to you . . .

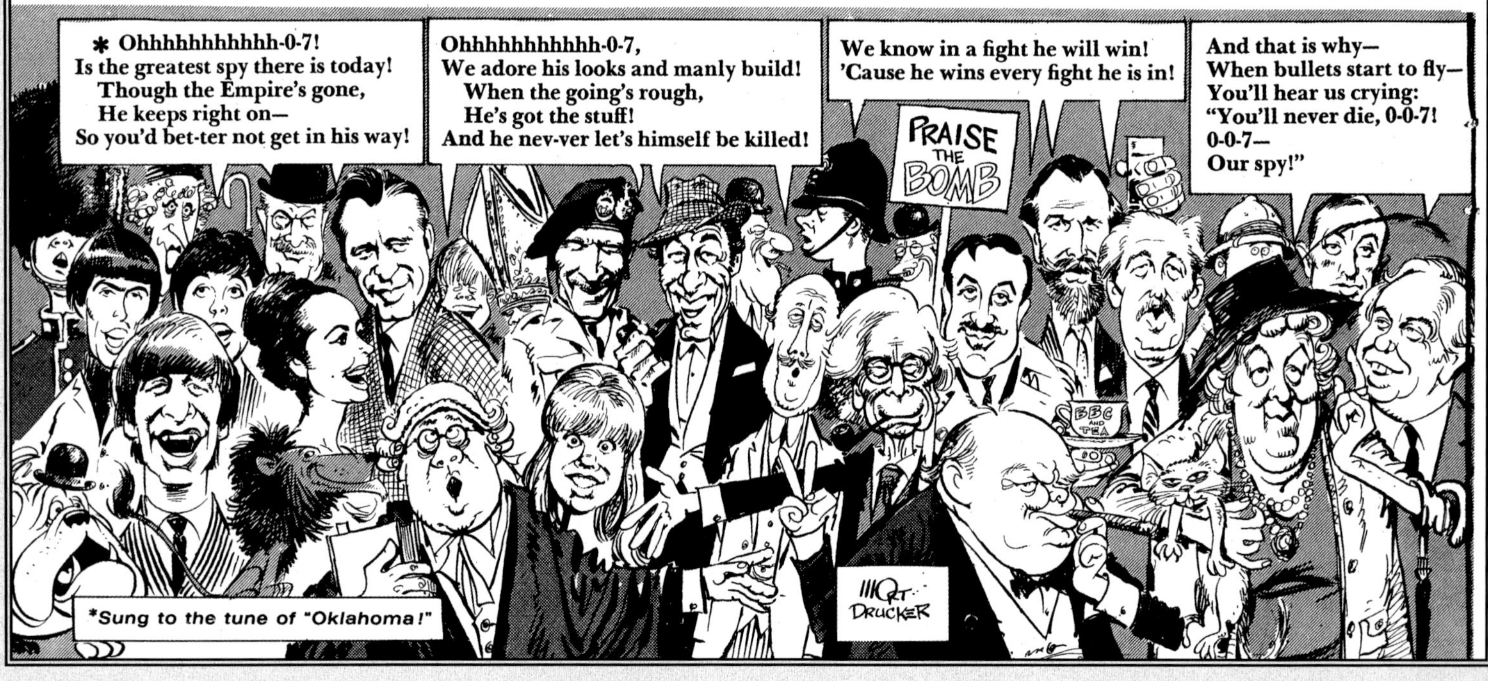
* Ohhhhhhhhhhh-0-7!
Is the greatest spy there is today!
Though the Empire's gone,
He keeps right on—
So you'd bet-ter not get in his way!
Ohhhhhhhhhhh-0-7,
We adore his looks and manly build!
When the going's rough,
He's got the stuff!
And he nev-ver let's himself be killed!
We know in a fight he will win!
'Cause he wins every fight he is in!
And that is why—
When bullets start to fly—
You'll hear us crying:
"You'll never die, 0-0-7!
0-0-7—
Our spy!"
PRAISE THE BOMB
*Sung to the tune of "Oklahoma!"
MORT DRUCKER

AIDE-DE-"CAMP" DEPT.

Everybody's going wild over that new TV show featuring "The Caped Crusader" and his teenage side-kick. But has anyone ever wondered what it would really be like as the side-kick of a "Caped Crusader"? Would a typical red-blooded teenage boy really be happy dressing in some far-out costume and spending all of his free time chasing crooks? Or would he much prefer dressing in chinos and go-go boots and spending all of his free time chasing chicks? We at MAD think the latter! In fact, we're ready to prove it! Let's take a MAD look at "Boy Wonderful" as he is slowly being driven

BATS-MAN

ARTIST: MORT DRUCKER WRITER: LOU SILVERSTONE

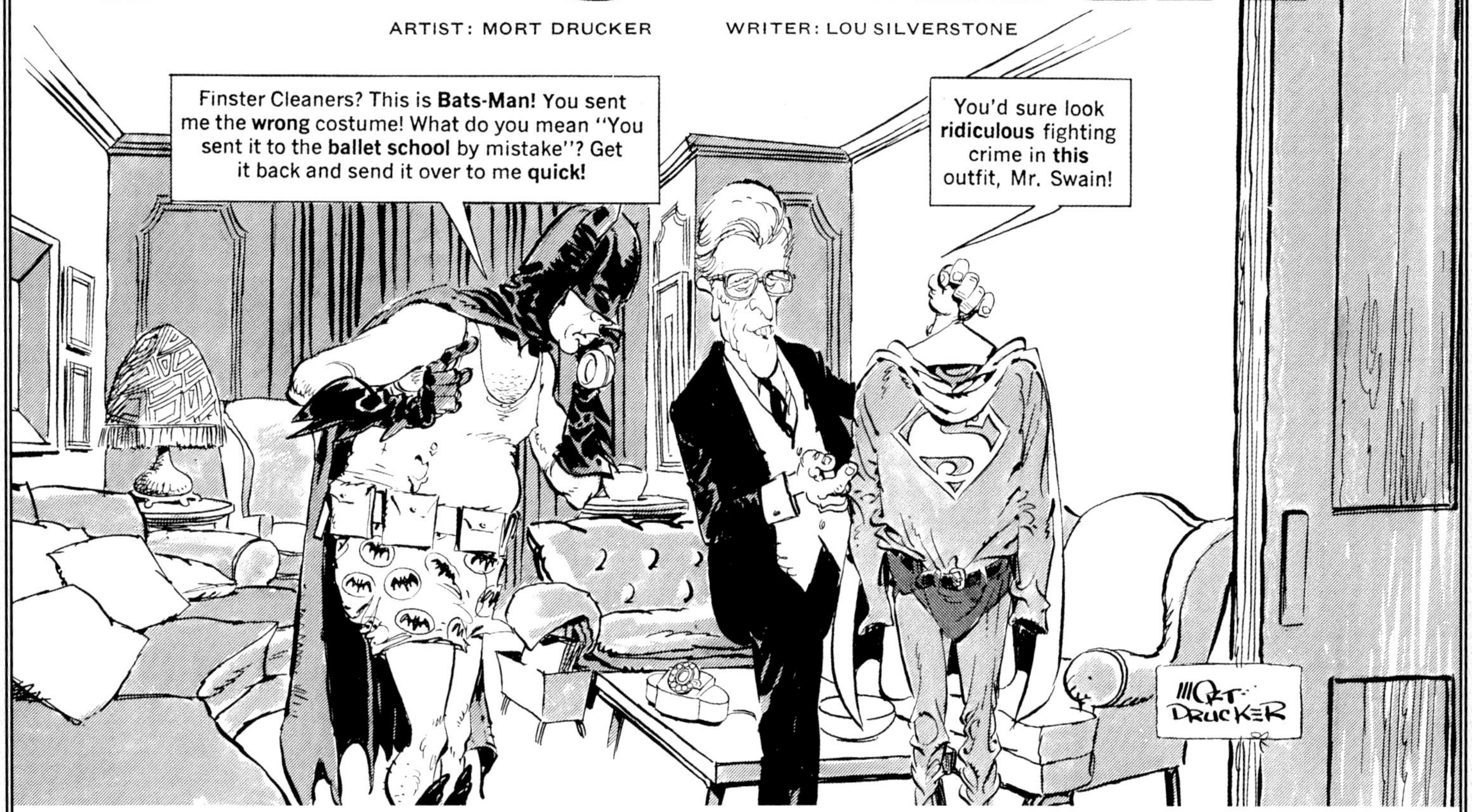
Finster Cleaners? This is Bats-Man! You sent me the wrong costume! What do you mean "You sent it to the ballet school by mistake"? Get it back and send it over to me quick!
You'd sure look ridiculous fighting crime in this outfit, Mr. Swain!
MORT DRUCKER

Meanwhile, at Franklin D. Wilson High School . . .

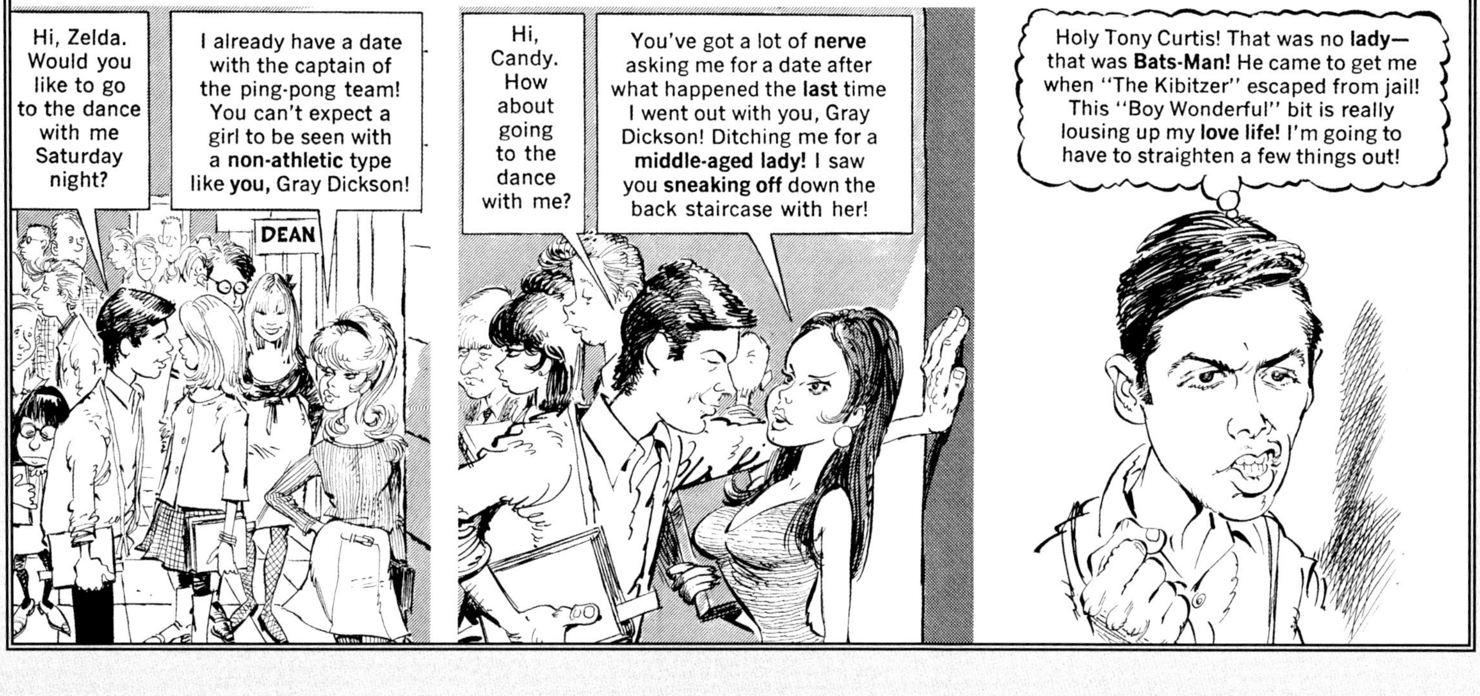
Hi, Zelda. Would you like to go to the dance with me Saturday night?
I already have a date with the captain of the ping-pong team! You can't expect a girl to be seen with a non-athletic type like you, Gray Dickson!
DEAN
Hi, Candy. How about going to the dance with me?
You've got a lot of nerve asking me for a date after what happened the last time I went out with you, Gray Dickson! Ditching me for a middle-aged lady! I saw you sneaking off down the back staircase with her!
Holy Tony Curtis! That was no lady—that was Bats-Man! He came to get me when "The Kibitzer" escaped from jail! This "Boy Wonderful" bit is really lousing up my love life! I'm going to have to straighten a few things out!

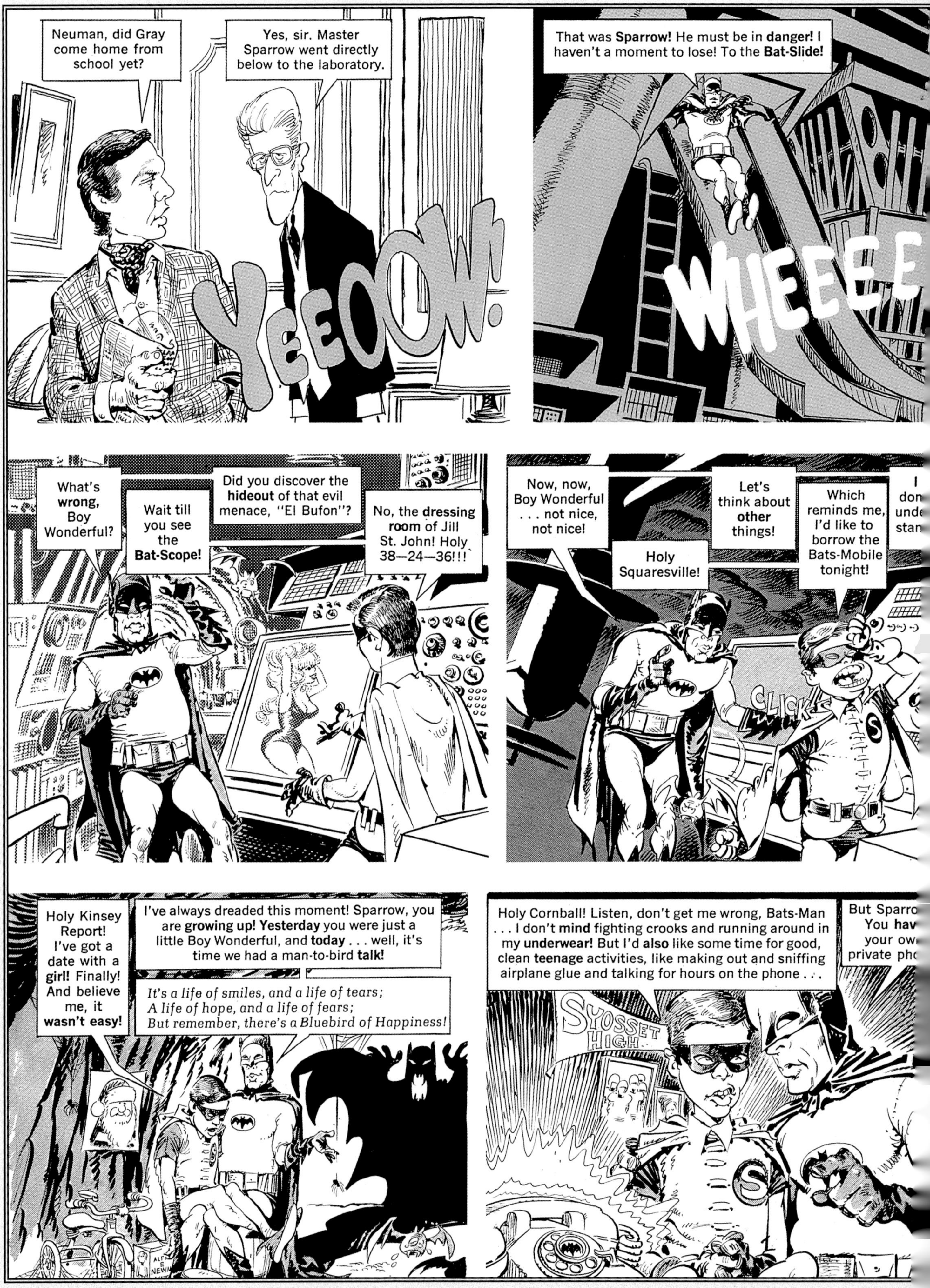
Neuman, did Gray come home from school yet?
Yes, sir. Master Sparrow went directly below to the laboratory.
YEEOOW!
That was **Sparrow!** He must be in **danger!** I haven't a moment to lose! To the **Bat-Slide!**
WHEEEE
What's **wrong,** Boy Wonderful?
Wait till you see the **Bat-Scope!**
Did you discover the **hideout** of that evil menace, "El Bufon"?
No, the **dressing room** of Jill St. John! Holy 38—24—36!!!
Now, now, Boy Wonderful . . . not nice, not nice!
Holy Squaresville!
Let's think about **other** things!
Which reminds me, I'd like to borrow the Bats-Mobile tonight!
CLICK
Holy Kinsey Report! I've got a date with a **girl!** Finally! And believe me, it **wasn't easy!**
I've always dreaded this moment! Sparrow, you are **growing up! Yesterday** you were just a little Boy Wonderful, and **today** . . . well, it's time we had a man-to-bird **talk!**
It's a life of smiles, and a life of tears; A life of hope, and a life of fears; But remember, there's a Bluebird of Happiness!
Holy Cornball! Listen, don't get me wrong, Bats-Man . . . I don't **mind** fighting crooks and running around in my **underwear!** But I'd **also** like some time for good, clean **teenage** activities, like making out and sniffing airplane glue and talking for hours on the phone . . .
SYOSSET HIGH

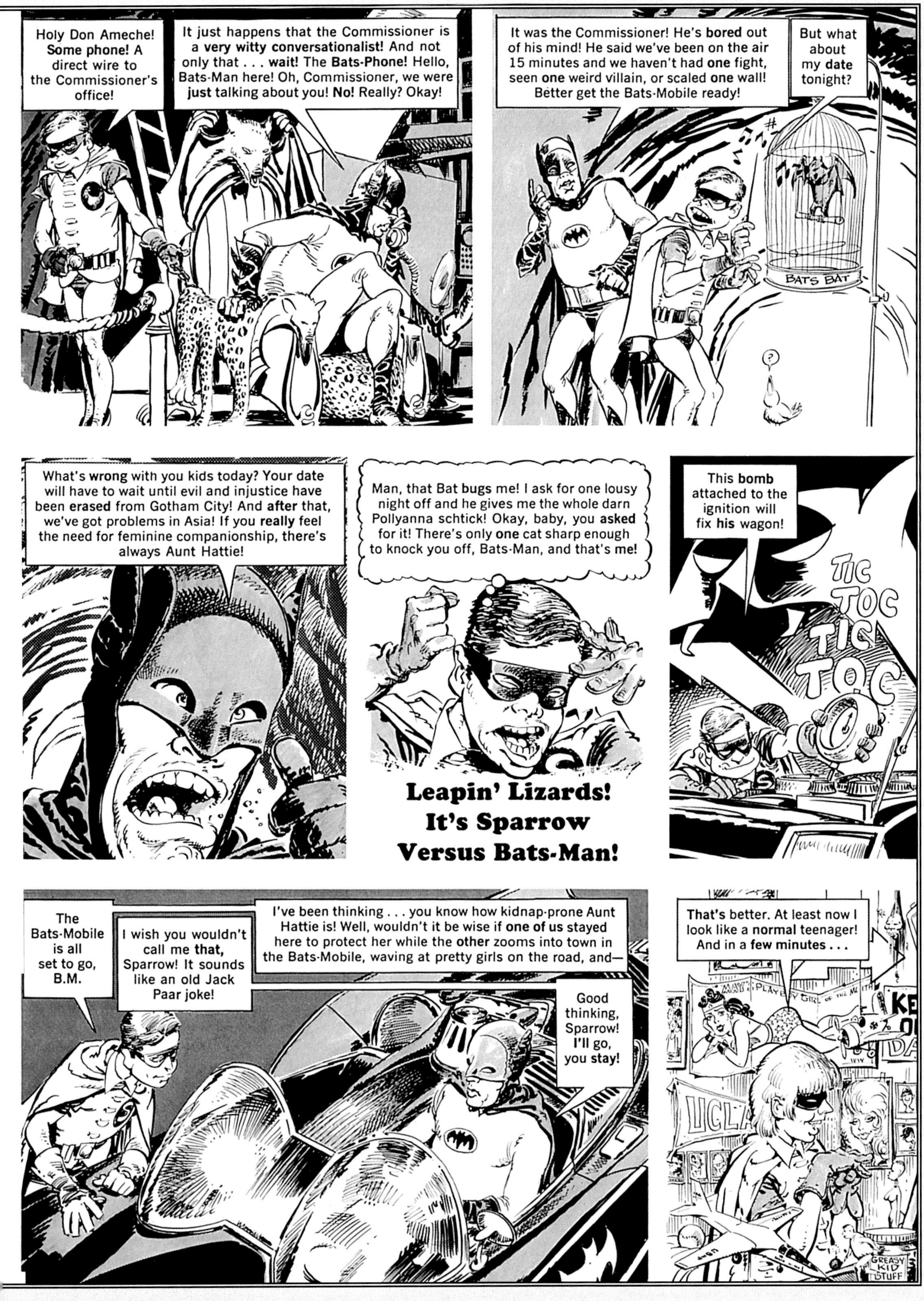
Holy Don Ameche! Some phone! A direct wire to the Commissioner's office!
It just happens that the Commissioner is a very witty conversationalist! And not only that . . . wait! The Bats-Phone! Hello, Bats-Man here! Oh, Commissioner, we were just talking about you! No! Really? Okay!
It was the Commissioner! He's bored out of his mind! He said we've been on the air 15 minutes and we haven't had one fight, seen one weird villain, or scaled one wall! Better get the Bats-Mobile ready!
But what about my date tonight?
BATS BAT
?
What's wrong with you kids today? Your date will have to wait until evil and injustice have been erased from Gotham City! And after that, we've got problems in Asia! If you really feel the need for feminine companionship, there's always Aunt Hattie!
Man, that Bat bugs me! I ask for one lousy night off and he gives me the whole darn Pollyanna schtick! Okay, baby, you asked for it! There's only one cat sharp enough to knock you off, Bats-Man, and that's me!
Leapin' Lizards! It's Sparrow Versus Bats-Man!
This bomb attached to the ignition will fix his wagon!
TIC TOC TIC TOC
The Bats-Mobile is all set to go, B.M.
I wish you wouldn't call me that, Sparrow! It sounds like an old Jack Paar joke!
I've been thinking . . . you know how kidnap-prone Aunt Hattie is! Well, wouldn't it be wise if one of us stayed here to protect her while the other zooms into town in the Bats-Mobile, waving at pretty girls on the road, and—
Good thinking, Sparrow! I'll go, you stay!
That's better. At least now I look like a normal teenager! And in a few minutes . . .
UCLA
GREASY KID STUFF

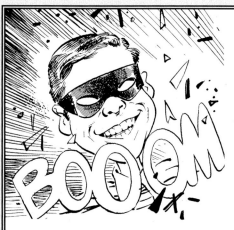

BOOOM
Holy Mushroom Cloud! Can That Be The End Of Bats-Man?!
Bats-Man! Are you all right?
That was a close call, Boy Wonderful! If I hadn't fallen out of the Bats-Mobile on that sharp turn outside the Bats-Cave, I'd be Bats-Burger by now! The car is a total loss, though . . . better call the Insurance Adjuster and uncrate the alternate Bats-Mobile!
Hmmm . . . getting this Bat off my back is going to be tougher than I figured. But my next idea won't fail!
Holy Socks! What Bird-Brained Scheme Is Sparrow Hatching Now
Mr. Bats-Man, sir, this package just arrived. I took the liberty of opening it for you—It's a new electric razor!
Probably a gift from one of my many admirers. Come to think of it, I can use a shave right now!
Just wait until he uses that razor! It's really a Laser beam! So long, you old Bat!
Suffering Sunbeam! Is This The End For Bats-Man, Or Just Another Close Shave?
It's the Commissioner, sir. Some diabolical fiend has just robbed the Wessel Foundation Museum . . .
Tell him not to worry—the paintings are all insured for more than they're worth!
Not just the paintings, sir—they stole the whole museum!
What? Give me that phone!
BZZZZ
TO THE MOST POPULAR BAT ON TV GOOD LUCK DRACULA
They put the whole museum on wheels and stole it in broad daylight? Astounding! Sounds like a new menace has come to Gotham City—or maybe it's just the Seven Santini Brothers!?
Yeeaahhhh!!!
Holy Ichabod Crane!
Oh dear, and good domestics are so hard to find, nowadays!
That death ray was meant for me! I'm up against the archest arch criminal in my career! Warm up the alternate Bats-Mobile!

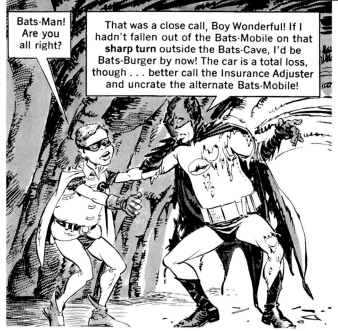

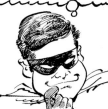

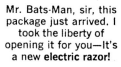

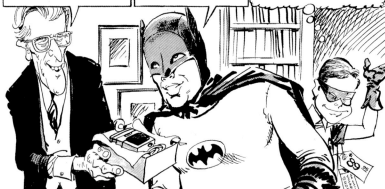

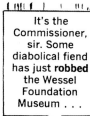

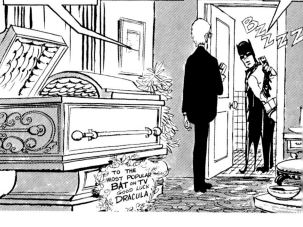

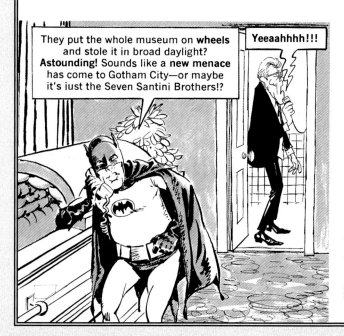

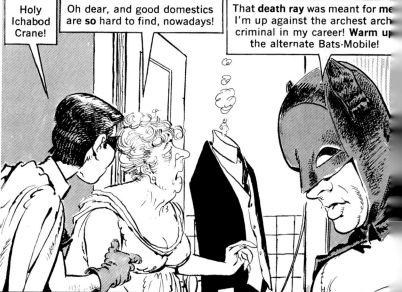

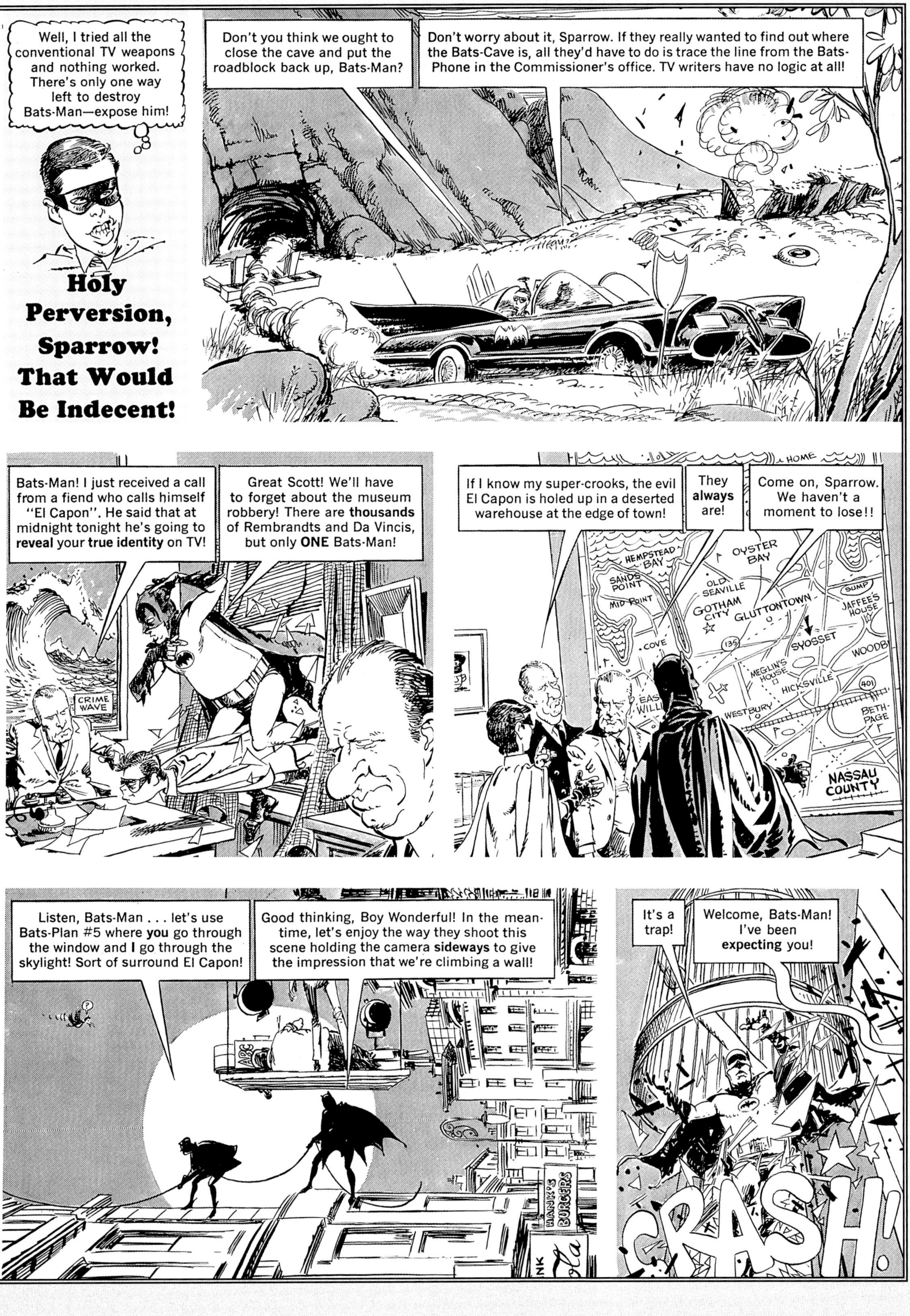

Well, I tried all the conventional TV weapons and nothing worked. There's only one way left to destroy Bats-Man—expose him!
Holy Perversion, Sparrow! That Would Be Indecent!
Don't you think we ought to close the cave and put the roadblock back up, Bats-Man?
Don't worry about it, Sparrow. If they really wanted to find out where the Bats-Cave is, all they'd have to do is trace the line from the Bats-Phone in the Commissioner's office. TV writers have no logic at all!
Bats-Man! I just received a call from a fiend who calls himself "El Capon". He said that at midnight tonight he's going to **reveal** your **true identity** on TV!
Great Scott! We'll have to forget about the museum robbery! There are **thousands** of Rembrandts and Da Vincis, but only **ONE** Bats-Man!
CRIME WAVE
If I know my super-crooks, the evil El Capon is holed up in a deserted warehouse at the edge of town!
They **always** are!
Come on, Sparrow. We haven't a moment to lose!!
HOME
HEMPSTEAD BAY
OYSTER BAY
SANDS POINT
MID POINT
OLD SEAVILLE
GOTHAM CITY
GLUTTONTOWN
SUMP
JAFFEE'S HOUSE
COVE
SYOSSET
MEGLIN'S HOUSE
HICKSVILLE
WESTBURY
BETH-PAGE
NASSAU COUNTY
Listen, Bats-Man . . . let's use Bats-Plan #5 where **you** go through the window and **I** go through the skylight! Sort of surround El Capon!
Good thinking, Boy Wonderful! In the mean-time, let's enjoy the way they shoot this scene holding the camera **sideways** to give the impression that we're climbing a wall!
HANK'S BURGERS
It's a trap!
Welcome, Bats-Man! I've been **expecting** you!
CRASH!

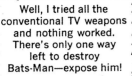

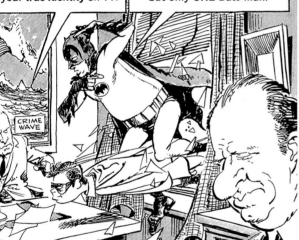

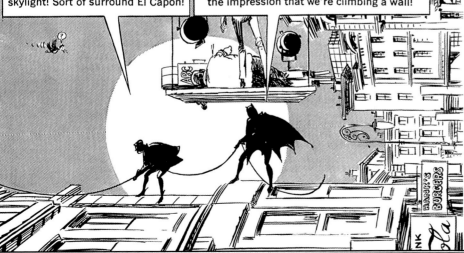

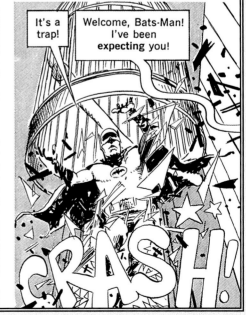

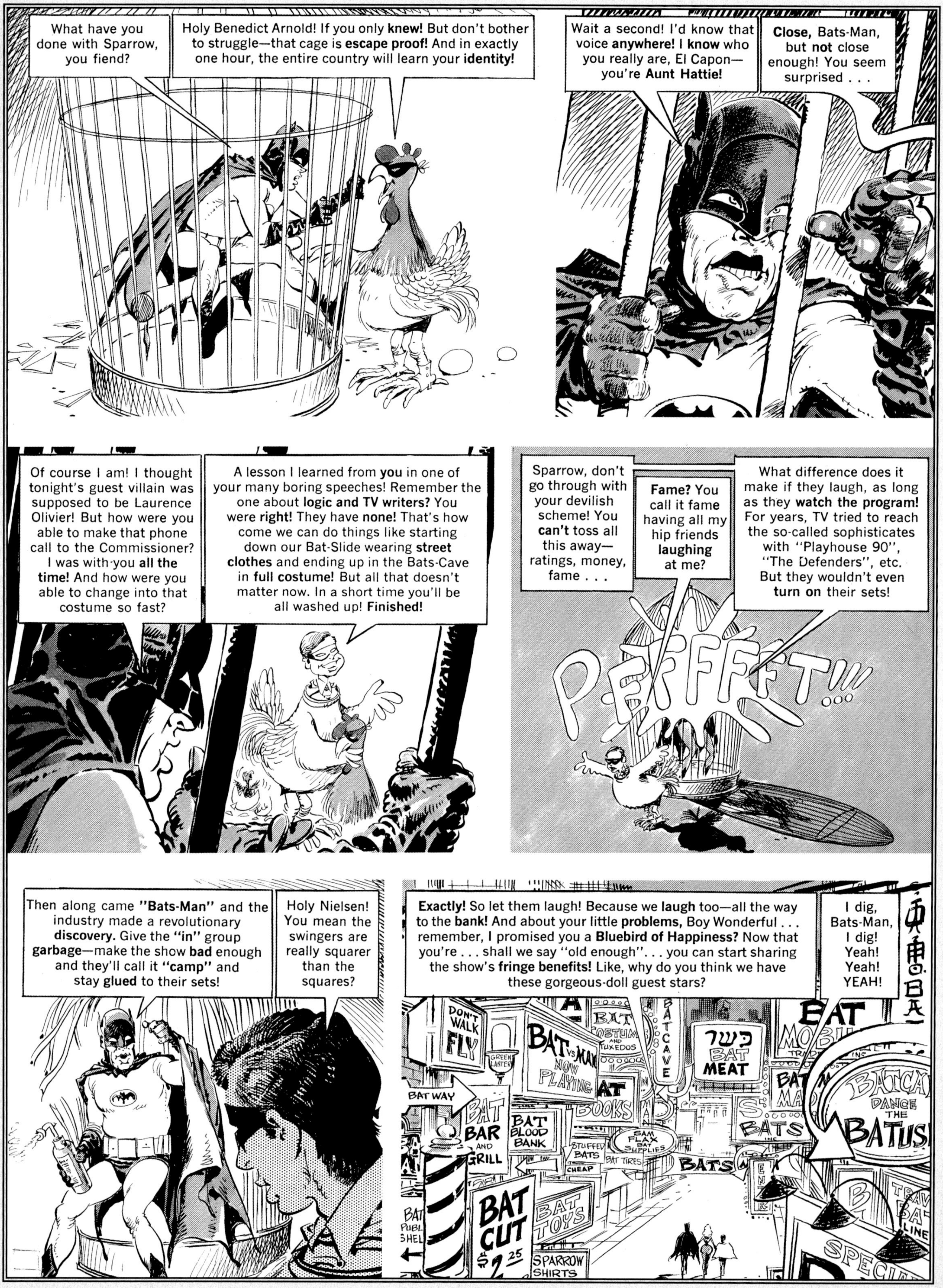
What have you done with Sparrow, you fiend?
Holy Benedict Arnold! If you only **knew!** But don't bother to struggle—that cage is **escape proof!** And in exactly one hour, the entire country will learn your **identity!**
Wait a second! I'd know that voice **anywhere! I know** who you really are, El Capon—you're **Aunt Hattie!**
Close, Bats-Man, but **not** close enough! You seem surprised . . .
Of course I am! I thought tonight's guest villain was supposed to be Laurence Olivier! But how were you able to make that phone call to the Commissioner? I was with you **all the time!** And how were you able to change into that costume so fast?
A lesson I learned from **you** in one of your many boring speeches! Remember the one about **logic and TV writers?** You were **right!** They have **none!** That's how come we can do things like starting down our Bat-Slide wearing **street clothes** and ending up in the Bats-Cave in **full costume!** But all that doesn't matter now. In a short time you'll be all washed up! **Finished!**
Sparrow, don't go through with your devilish scheme! You **can't** toss all this away—ratings, money, fame . . .
Fame? You call it fame having all my hip friends **laughing** at me?
What difference does it make if they laugh, as long as they **watch the program!** For years, TV tried to reach the so-called sophisticates with "Playhouse 90", "The Defenders", etc. But they wouldn't even **turn on** their sets!
PFFFFT!!!
Then along came **"Bats-Man"** and the industry made a revolutionary **discovery.** Give the **"in"** group **garbage**—make the show **bad** enough and they'll call it **"camp"** and stay **glued** to their sets!
Holy Nielsen! You mean the swingers are really squarer than the squares?
Exactly! So let them laugh! Because we **laugh** too—all the way to the **bank!** And about your little **problems,** Boy Wonderful . . . remember, I promised you a **Bluebird of Happiness?** Now that you're . . . shall we say "old enough" . . . you can start sharing the show's **fringe benefits!** Like, why do you think we have these gorgeous-doll guest stars?
I dig, Bats-Man, I dig! Yeah! Yeah! YEAH!
DON'T WALK FLY
BAT vs MAN NOW PLAYING
BATCAVE
כשר BAT MEAT
BAT WAY
BAT BAR AND GRILL
BAT BLOOD BANK
STUFFED BATS CHEAP
SAM FLAX BAT SUPPLIES
BAT TIRES
BAT CUT $2.25
BAT TOYS
SPARROW SHIRTS

KEY TO THE REMOVABLE POSTER:

Mort Drucker's 1965 Calendar from *MAD Follies* #2

This poster originally appeared on the gatefold back cover of *MAD Follies* #2, part of a 1965 calendar included as an added bonus to the magazine, which otherwise consisted of reprint material from past issues of *MAD*. As Mort Drucker had not yet begun working regularly in color, he asked a neighbor to assist him by adding color to his ink drawing. The neighbor was Frank Frazetta, now a legend in his own right for his work in comics, movie posters and book covers. This work may represent the only collaboration of these two giants of the profession.

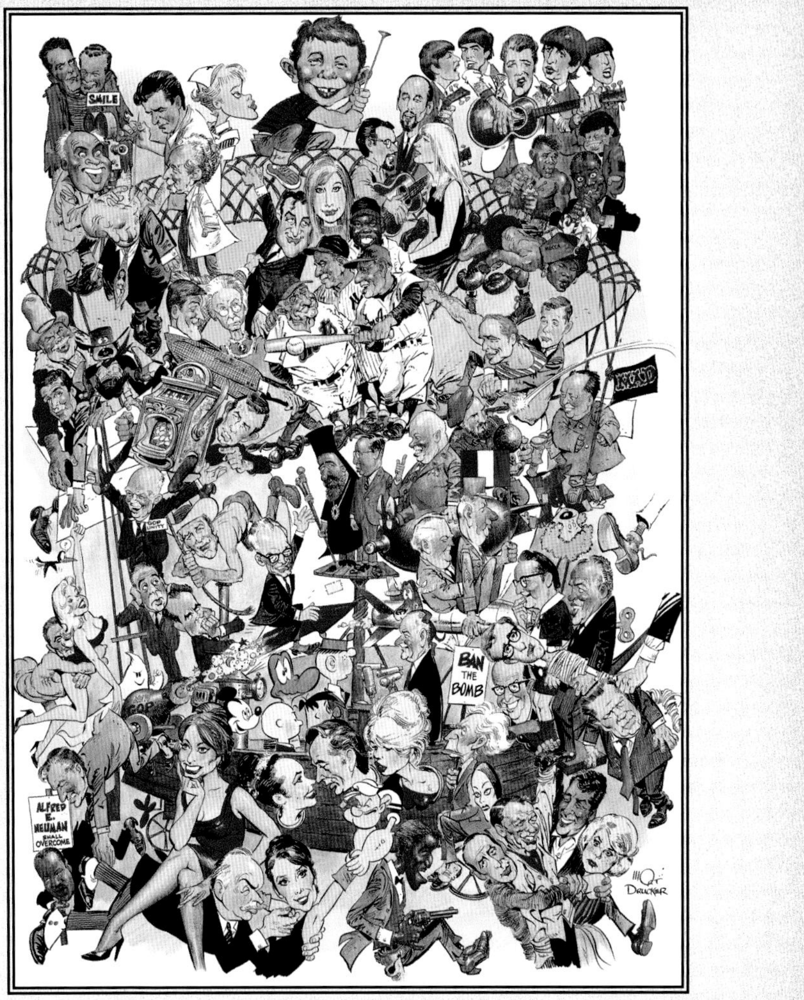
SMILE
BAN THE BOMB
ALFRED E. NEUMAN SHALL OVERCOME
DRUCKER

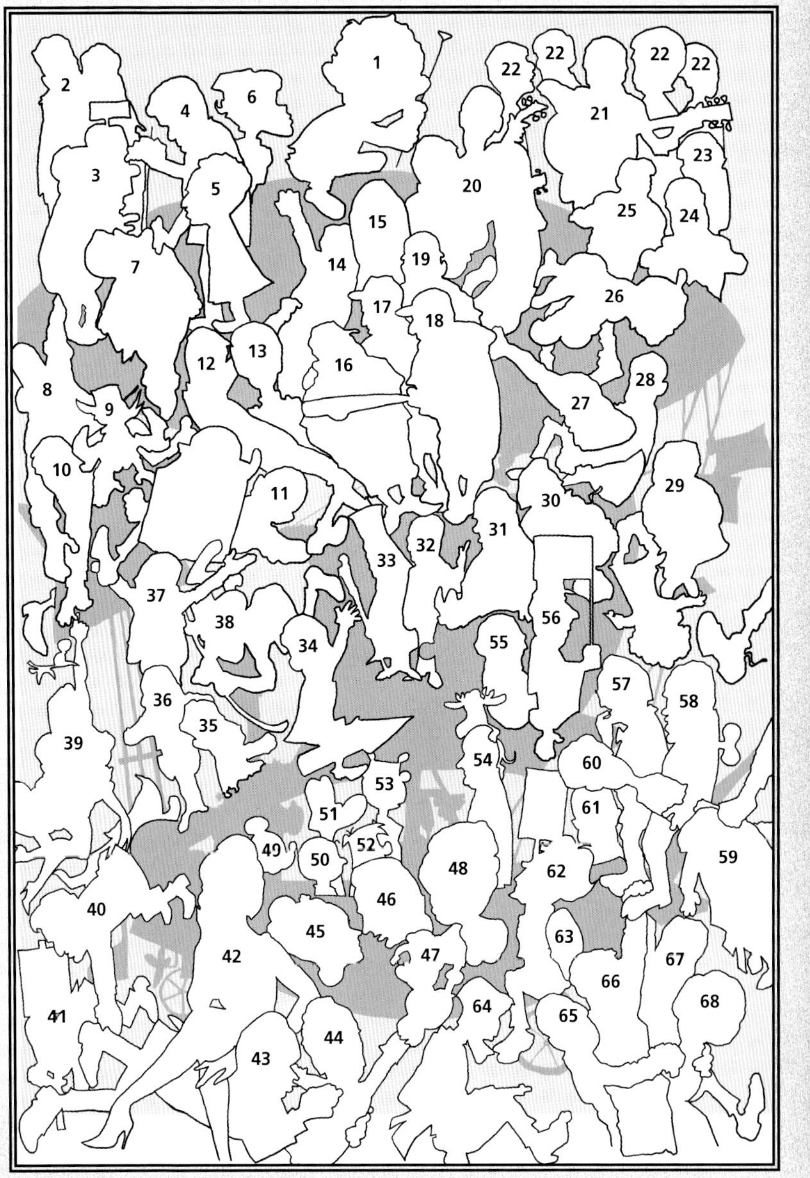

1. Alfred E. Neuman, *MAD Magazine* cover boy
2. Chet Huntley and David Brinkley, NBC news anchors
3. Allen Funt, creator and host, *Candid Camera*
4. Vince Edwards, title star, *Ben Casey*
5. Sam Jaffee, "Dr. Zorba" on *Ben Casey*
6. Zina Bethune, "Gail Lucas" on *The Doctors and the Nurses*
7. Alfred Hitchock, film director
8. Dan Blocker, "Hoss Cartwright" on *Bonanza*
9. Michael Landon, "Little Joe" on *Bonanza*
10. Gene Barry, "Amos Burke" on *Burke's Law*
11. David Janssen, "Dr. Richard Kimble" on *The Fugitive*
12. Dick Van Dyke, "Rob Petrie" on *The Dick Van Dyke Show*
13. Irene Ryan, "Granny" on *The Beverly Hillbillies*
14. Peter Sellers, actor
15. Barbra Streisand, Broadway actress and singer
16. Casey Stengel, New York Mets manager
17. Ralph Houk, New York Yankees manager
18. Leo Durocher, Los Angeles Dodgers coach
19. Willie Mays, New York/San Francisco Giants center fielder
20. Peter, Paul and Mary, folk music trio
21. Elvis Presley, rock and roll performer
22. Paul McCartney, George Harrison, Ringo Starr, John Lennon: The Beatles
23. Happy Beatles Fan
24. Louis Armstrong, jazz musician
25. Floyd Patterson, former heavyweight boxing champion
26. Muhammad Ali, heavyweight boxing champion
27. Marlon Brando, actor
28. Johnny Carson, *The Tonight Show* host
29. Mao Tse-tung, Chairman of the Communist Party of China
30. Fidel Castro, Prime Minister of Cuba
31. Nikita Khrushev, Premier of the Soviet Union
32. U Thant, Secretary-General of the United Nations
33. Archbishop Makarios III, Present of Cyprus
34. Barry Goldwater, 1964 Republican presidential nominee
35. Richard M. Nixon, former Vice-President of the U.S.
36. William Scranton, Governor of Pennsylvania
37. Dwight D. Eisenhower, former President of the U.S.
38. Paul Newman, actor
39. Jayne Mansfield, actress, with husband Mickey Hargitay, Mr. Universe 1955
40. Nelson Rockefeller, Governor of New York
41. Martin Luther King Jr., civil rights activist
42. Sophia Loren, Italian film star
43. Charles Boyer, actor
44. Audrey Hepburn, actress
45. Elizabeth Taylor, actress
46. Richard Burton, actor
47. Popeye the Sailor, cartoon character
48. Bridgitte Bardot, French film star
49. Mickey Mouse, cartoon character
50. Charlie Brown, comic strip character (Charles Schulz's *Peanuts)*
51. Albert Alligator, comic strip character (Walt Kelly's *Pogo*)
52. Fred Flintstone, cartoon character
53. Beetle Bailey, comic strip character
54. Lyndon Baines Johnson, President of the United States
55. Harold MacMillan, Prime Minister of England
56. Charles deGaulle, President of France
57. Steve Allen, television personality
58. Ed Sullivan, host of *The Ed Sullivan Show*
59. Jimmy Hoffa, President of the Teamsters Union
60. Woody Allen, comedian
61. Phil Silvers, comedian
62. Bertrand Russell, philosopher
63. Morticia Addams, *New Yorker* cartoon character
64. Sammy Davis Jr., performer
65. Joey Bishop, television personality
66. Frank Sinatra, performer
67. Dean Martin, performer
68. Doris Day, actress

THE BAINES OF OUR EXISTENCE DEPT.

And now, the Editors of MAD would like to sing our praises of "The Great Society"! We'd like to, but we can

"HELLO

OR "MY FAIR

ARTIST: MORT DRUCKER

Hello, Lyndon! How did things go today?

Well, naturally I got everything I **wanted**! I always **do**! But let me tell you something —it **wasn't easy**! You have to know how to **handle** people! You see—it's like this:

✱ The people in this land elect a Congress, Which is both bold and independent, too. They've got much courage, All those men in Congress . . . But! With a little twist of arm, With a little twist of arm, They will do just what I want them to!

With a little twist . . . With a little twist . . . With a little twist of arm I own that crew!

62% OF THE PEOPLE BACK LBJ

VIET NAM POLICY
LOAN TO INDIA
MEDICARE BILL

*Sung to the tune of "With A Little Bit Of Luck"

JLBJLBJLBJLBJLBJLBJLBJLBJLBJHEILBJLBJLBJLBJLBJLBJLBJLBJLBJLBJLBJLBJLBJLBJLBJLBJLBJLBJLBJLB

It's been a wonderful three years so far, Lyndon!

I couldn't have done it without **your help**, Lady Bird!

Did you **hear** that, girls? He **admitted** it! I always **told** you he was nothing but a **hick High School Teacher** until he met me! **I** taught him everything he **knows**! So how about a little **credit** where credit is **due**? Repeat after me:

Oh—Lyndon Baines reigns mainly with my brains!

Oh, Lyndon Baines reigns mainly with your brains!

Again!

Oh—Lyndon Baines reigns mainly with your brains!

By George, you've got it! I think you've got it!

Drucker

64% OF THE PEOPLE BACK LBJ

SURVEY POLL

*Sung to the tune of "The Rain In Spain"

very much to sing our praises about! So instead, we'd like YOU to sing, mainly this new MAD Musical…

YNDON!"

ADY BIRD"

ITER: LARRY SIEGEL

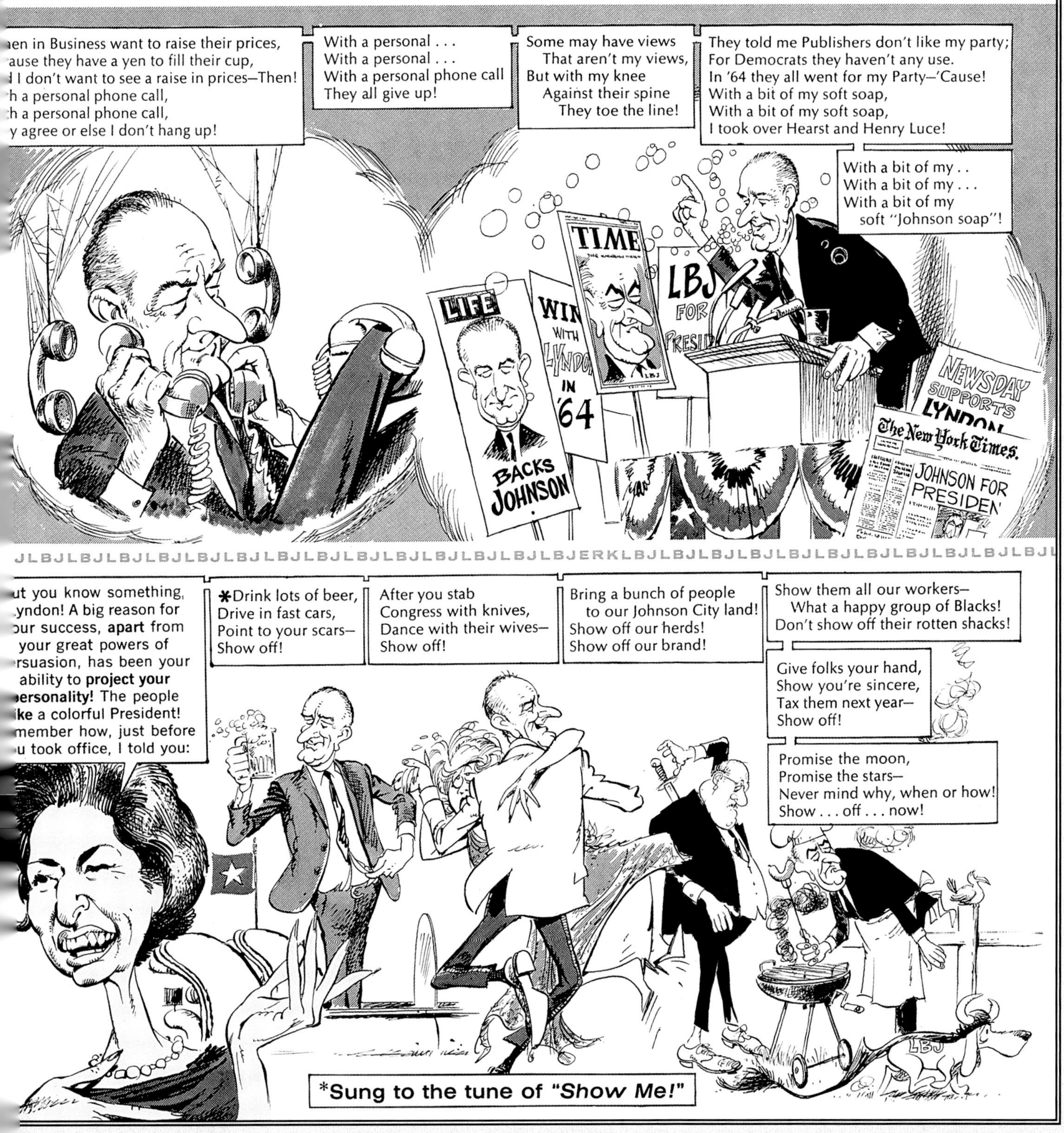

en in Business want to raise their prices,
ause they have a yen to fill their cup,
I don't want to see a raise in prices—Then!
h a personal phone call,
h a personal phone call,
y agree or else I don't hang up!
With a personal . . .
With a personal . . .
With a personal phone call
They all give up!
Some may have views
That aren't my views,
But with my knee
Against their spine
They toe the line!
They told me Publishers don't like my party;
For Democrats they haven't any use.
In '64 they all went for my Party—'Cause!
With a bit of my soft soap,
With a bit of my soft soap,
I took over Hearst and Henry Luce!
With a bit of my . .
With a bit of my . . .
With a bit of my
soft "Johnson soap"!
TIME
LIFE
BACKS JOHNSON
WIN WITH LYNDON IN '64
LBJ FOR PRESID
NEWSDAY SUPPORTS LYNDON
The New York Times
JOHNSON FOR PRESIDEN
JLBJLBJLBJLBJLBJLBJLBJLBJLBJLBJLBJLBJERKLBJLBJLBJLBJLBJLBJLBJLBJLBJLBJLBJ
ut you know something, yndon! A big reason for our success, apart from your great powers of rsuasion, has been your ability to project your personality! The people ike a colorful President! member how, just before u took office, I told you:
*Drink lots of beer,
Drive in fast cars,
Point to your scars—
Show off!
After you stab
Congress with knives,
Dance with their wives—
Show off!
Bring a bunch of people
to our Johnson City land!
Show off our herds!
Show off our brand!
Show them all our workers—
What a happy group of Blacks!
Don't show off their rotten shacks!
Give folks your hand,
Show you're sincere,
Tax them next year—
Show off!
Promise the moon,
Promise the stars—
Never mind why, when or how!
Show . . . off . . . now!
LBJ
*Sung to the tune of "Show Me!"

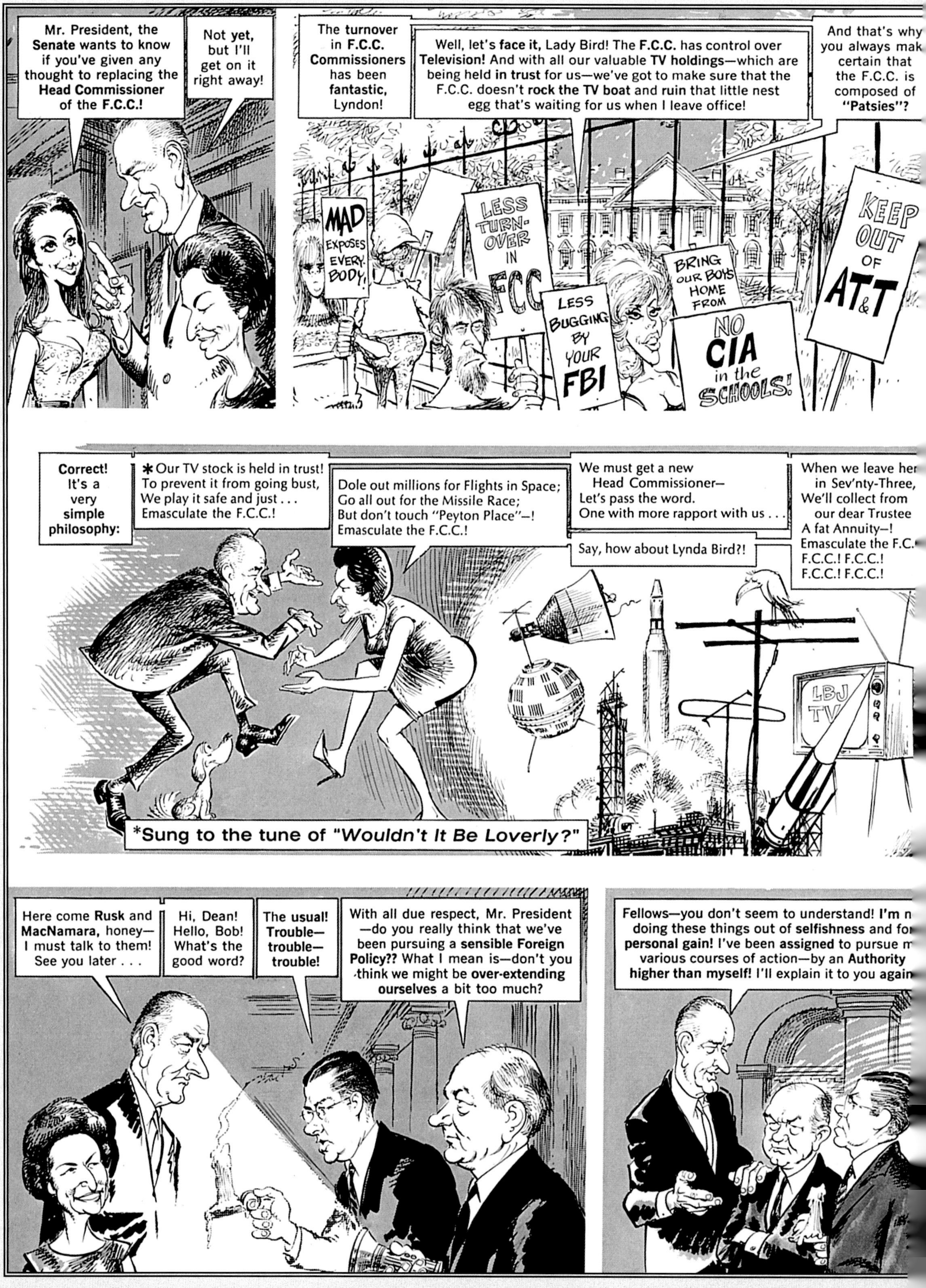
Mr. President, the Senate wants to know if you've given any thought to replacing the Head Commissioner of the F.C.C.!
Not yet, but I'll get on it right away!
The turnover in F.C.C. Commissioners has been fantastic, Lyndon!
Well, let's face it, Lady Bird! The F.C.C. has control over Television! And with all our valuable TV holdings—which are being held in trust for us—we've got to make sure that the F.C.C. doesn't rock the TV boat and ruin that little nest egg that's waiting for us when I leave office!
And that's why you always mak certain that the F.C.C. is composed of "Patsies"?
MAD EXPOSES EVERY-BODY
LESS TURN-OVER IN FCC
LESS BUGGING BY YOUR FBI
BRING OUR BOYS HOME FROM
NO CIA in the SCHOOLS!
KEEP OUT OF AT&T
Correct! It's a very simple philosophy:
*Our TV stock is held in trust!
To prevent it from going bust,
We play it safe and just . . .
Emasculate the F.C.C.!
Dole out millions for Flights in Space;
Go all out for the Missile Race;
But don't touch "Peyton Place"—!
Emasculate the F.C.C.!
We must get a new
Head Commissioner—
Let's pass the word.
One with more rapport with us . . .
Say, how about Lynda Bird?!
When we leave her
in Sev'nty-Three,
We'll collect from
our dear Trustee
A fat Annuity—!
Emasculate the F.C.
F.C.C.! F.C.C.!
F.C.C.! F.C.C.!
LBJ TV
*Sung to the tune of "Wouldn't It Be Loverly?"
Here come Rusk and MacNamara, honey—I must talk to them! See you later . . .
Hi, Dean! Hello, Bob! What's the good word?
The usual! Trouble—trouble—trouble!
With all due respect, Mr. President—do you really think that we've been pursuing a sensible Foreign Policy?? What I mean is—don't you think we might be over-extending ourselves a bit too much?
Fellows—you don't seem to understand! I'm n doing these things out of selfishness and fo personal gain! I've been assigned to pursue m various courses of action—by an Authority higher than myself! I'll explain it to you again

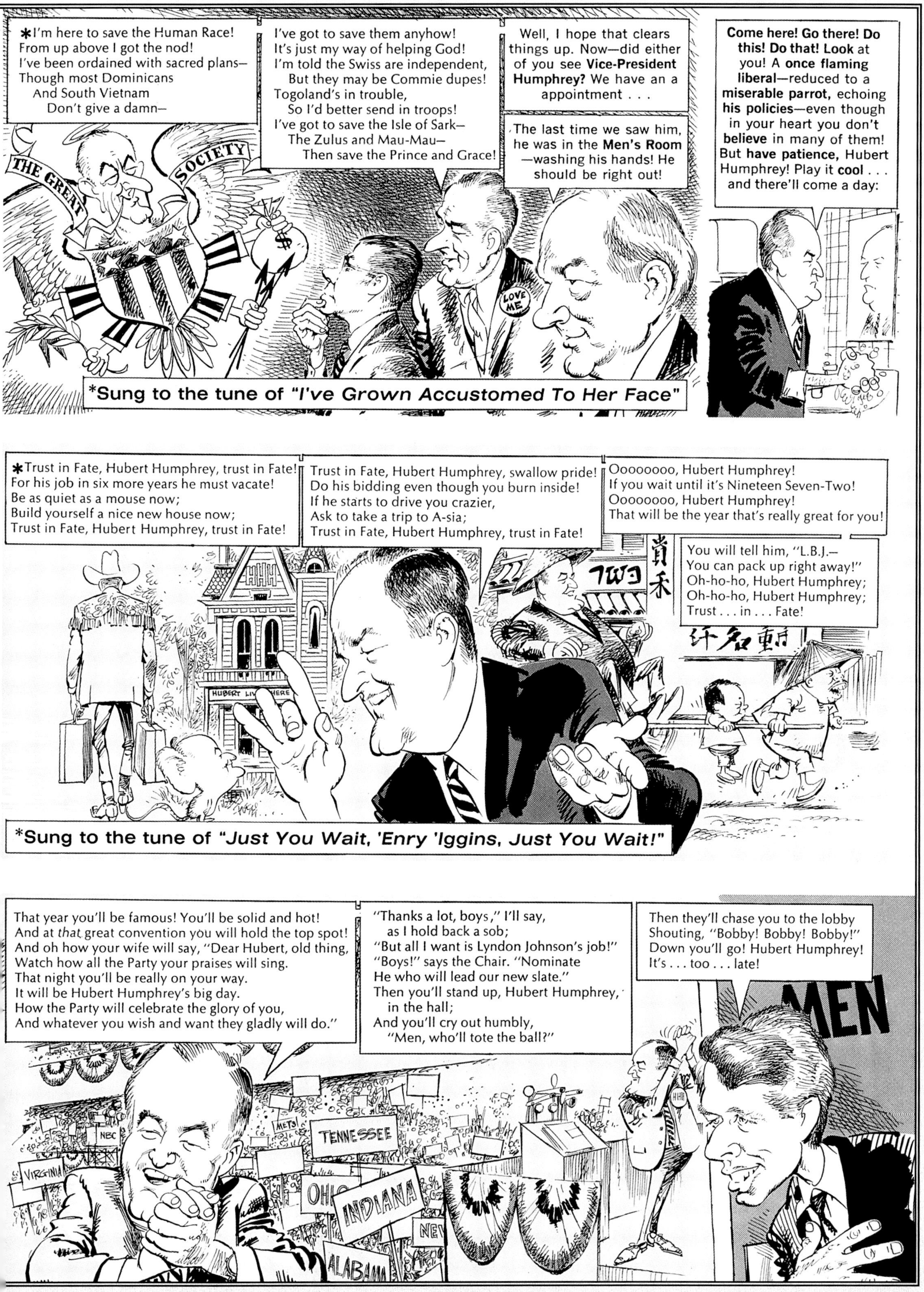
*I'm here to save the Human Race!
From up above I got the nod!
I've been ordained with sacred plans—
Though most Dominicans
And South Vietnam
Don't give a damn—
THE GREAT SOCIETY
I've got to save them anyhow!
It's just my way of helping God!
I'm told the Swiss are independent,
But they may be Commie dupes!
Togoland's in trouble,
So I'd better send in troops!
I've got to save the Isle of Sark—
The Zulus and Mau-Mau—
Then save the Prince and Grace!
Well, I hope that clears things up. Now—did either of you see **Vice-President Humphrey?** We have an a appointment . . .
The last time we saw him, he was in the **Men's Room** —washing his hands! He should be right out!
LOVE ME
Come here! Go there! Do this! Do that! Look at you! A **once flaming liberal**—reduced to a **miserable parrot,** echoing **his policies**—even though in your heart you don't **believe** in many of them! But **have patience,** Hubert Humphrey! Play it **cool** . . . and there'll come a day:
*Sung to the tune of "I've Grown Accustomed To Her Face"
*Trust in Fate, Hubert Humphrey, trust in Fate!
For his job in six more years he must vacate!
Be as quiet as a mouse now;
Build yourself a nice new house now;
Trust in Fate, Hubert Humphrey, trust in Fate!
Trust in Fate, Hubert Humphrey, swallow pride!
Do his bidding even though you burn inside!
If he starts to drive you crazier,
Ask to take a trip to A-sia;
Trust in Fate, Hubert Humphrey, trust in Fate!
Oooooooo, Hubert Humphrey!
If you wait until it's Nineteen Seven-Two!
Oooooooo, Hubert Humphrey!
That will be the year that's really great for you!
You will tell him, "L.B.J.—
You can pack up right away!"
Oh-ho-ho, Hubert Humphrey;
Oh-ho-ho, Hubert Humphrey;
Trust . . . in . . . Fate!
*Sung to the tune of "Just You Wait, 'Enry 'Iggins, Just You Wait!"
That year you'll be famous! You'll be solid and hot!
And at *that* great convention you will hold the top spot!
And oh how your wife will say, "Dear Hubert, old thing,
Watch how all the Party your praises will sing.
That night you'll be really on your way.
It will be Hubert Humphrey's big day.
How the Party will celebrate the glory of you,
And whatever you wish and want they gladly will do."
"Thanks a lot, boys," I'll say,
as I hold back a sob;
"But all I want is Lyndon Johnson's job!"
"Boys!" says the Chair. "Nominate
He who will lead our new slate."
Then you'll stand up, Hubert Humphrey,
in the hall;
And you'll cry out humbly,
"Men, who'll tote the ball?"
Then they'll chase you to the lobby
Shouting, "Bobby! Bobby! Bobby!"
Down you'll go! Hubert Humphrey!
It's . . . too . . . late!
NBC
VIRGINIA
METS
TENNESSEE
OHIO
INDIANA
ALABAMA
MEN

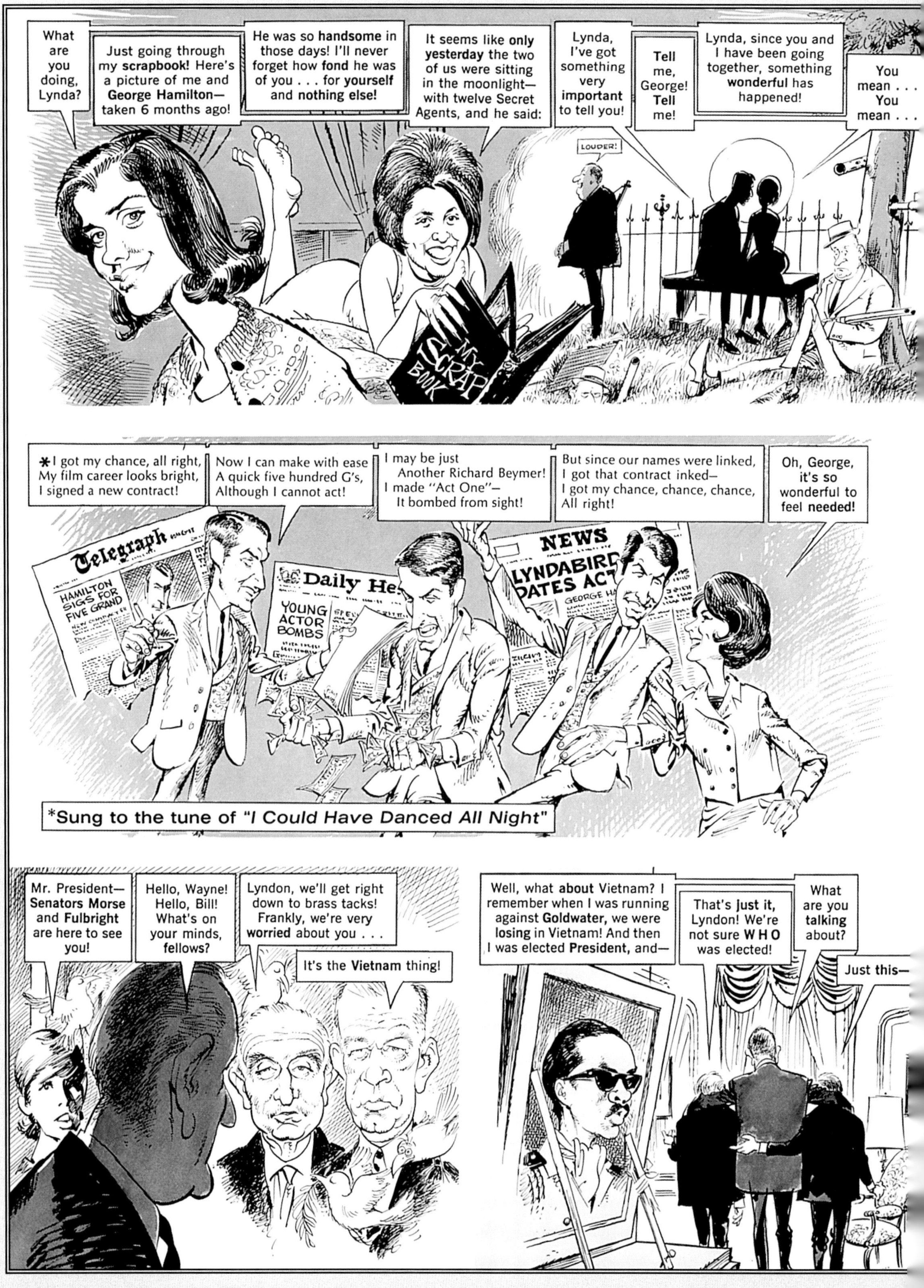
What are you doing, Lynda?
Just going through my scrapbook! Here's a picture of me and George Hamilton—taken 6 months ago!
He was so handsome in those days! I'll never forget how fond he was of you . . . for yourself and nothing else!
It seems like only yesterday the two of us were sitting in the moonlight—with twelve Secret Agents, and he said:
Lynda, I've got something very important to tell you!
Tell me, George! Tell me!
Lynda, since you and I have been going together, something wonderful has happened!
You mean . . . You mean . . .
LOUDER!
MY SCRAP BOOK
*I got my chance, all right, My film career looks bright, I signed a new contract!
Now I can make with ease A quick five hundred G's, Although I cannot act!
I may be just Another Richard Beymer! I made "Act One"— It bombed from sight!
But since our names were linked, I got that contract inked— I got my chance, chance, chance, All right!
Oh, George, it's so wonderful to feel needed!
Telegraph
HAMILTON SIGS FOR FIVE GRAND
Daily He
YOUNG ACTOR BOMBS
NEWS
LYNDABIRD DATES ACT
*Sung to the tune of "I Could Have Danced All Night"
Mr. President—Senators Morse and Fulbright are here to see you!
Hello, Wayne! Hello, Bill! What's on your minds, fellows?
Lyndon, we'll get right down to brass tacks! Frankly, we're very worried about you . . .
It's the Vietnam thing!
Well, what about Vietnam? I remember when I was running against Goldwater, we were losing in Vietnam! And then I was elected President, and—
That's just it, Lyndon! We're not sure WHO was elected!
What are you talking about?
Just this—

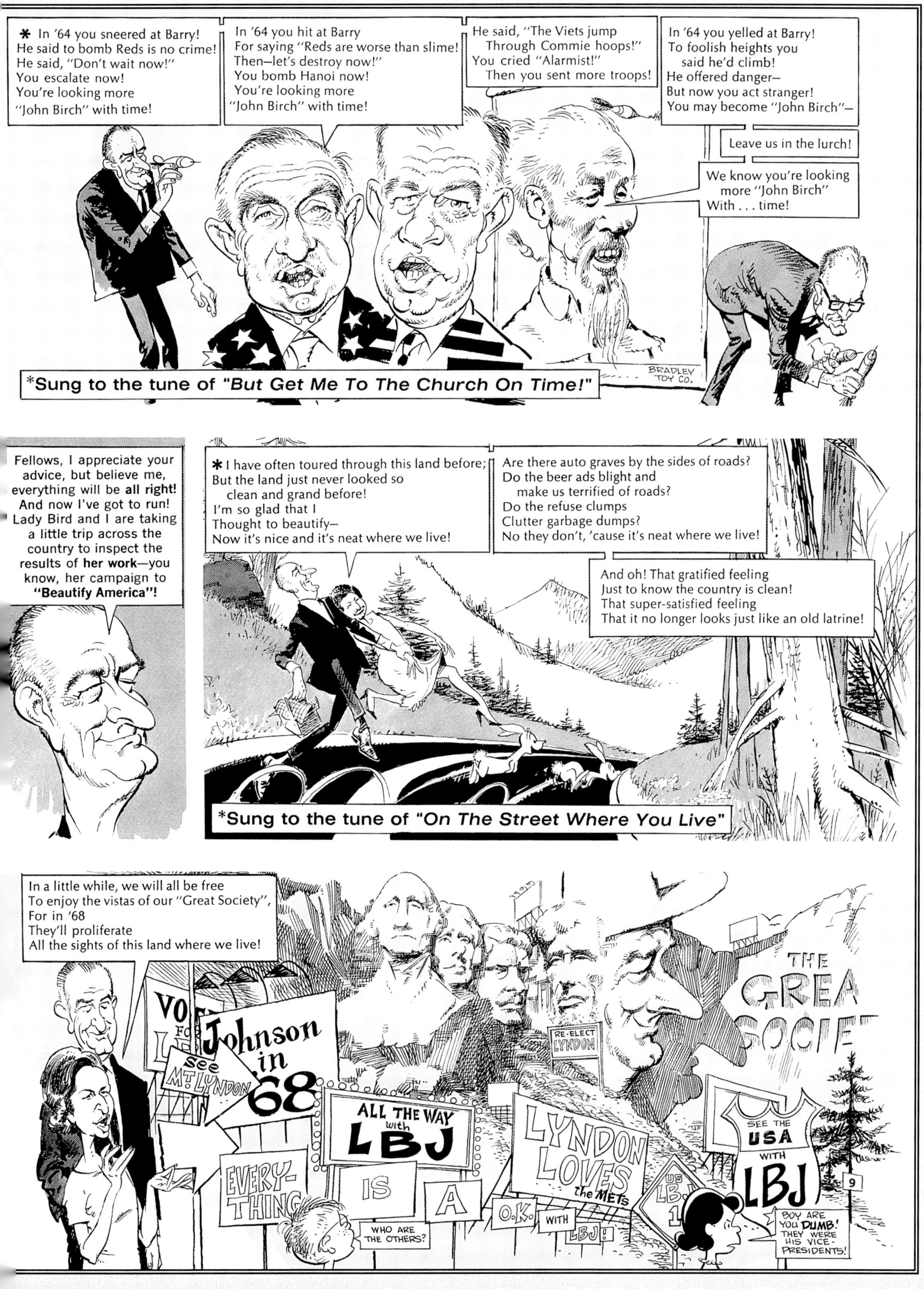
* In '64 you sneered at Barry! He said to bomb Reds is no crime! He said, "Don't wait now!" You escalate now! You're looking more "John Birch" with time!
In '64 you hit at Barry For saying "Reds are worse than slime! Then—let's destroy now!" You bomb Hanoi now! You're looking more "John Birch" with time!
He said, "The Viets jump Through Commie hoops!" You cried "Alarmist!" Then you sent more troops!
In '64 you yelled at Barry! To foolish heights you said he'd climb! He offered danger— But now you act stranger! You may become "John Birch"—
Leave us in the lurch!
We know you're looking more "John Birch" With . . . time!
BRADLEY TOY CO.
*Sung to the tune of "But Get Me To The Church On Time!"
Fellows, I appreciate your advice, but believe me, everything will be all right! And now I've got to run! Lady Bird and I are taking a little trip across the country to inspect the results of her work—you know, her campaign to "Beautify America"!
* I have often toured through this land before; But the land just never looked so clean and grand before! I'm so glad that I Thought to beautify— Now it's nice and it's neat where we live!
Are there auto graves by the sides of roads? Do the beer ads blight and make us terrified of roads? Do the refuse clumps Clutter garbage dumps? No they don't, 'cause it's neat where we live!
And oh! That gratified feeling Just to know the country is clean! That super-satisfied feeling That it no longer looks just like an old latrine!
*Sung to the tune of "On The Street Where You Live"
In a little while, we will all be free To enjoy the vistas of our "Great Society", For in '68 They'll proliferate All the sights of this land where we live!
Johnson in 68
SEE MT. LYNDON
RE-ELECT LYNDON
THE GREA SOCIET
ALL THE WAY with LBJ
EVERY-THING
IS
A
O.K.
WITH
LBJ!
LYNDON LOVES the METS
US LBJ 1
SEE THE USA WITH LBJ
9
WHO ARE THE OTHERS?
BOY ARE YOU DUMB! THEY WERE HIS VICE-PRESIDENTS!

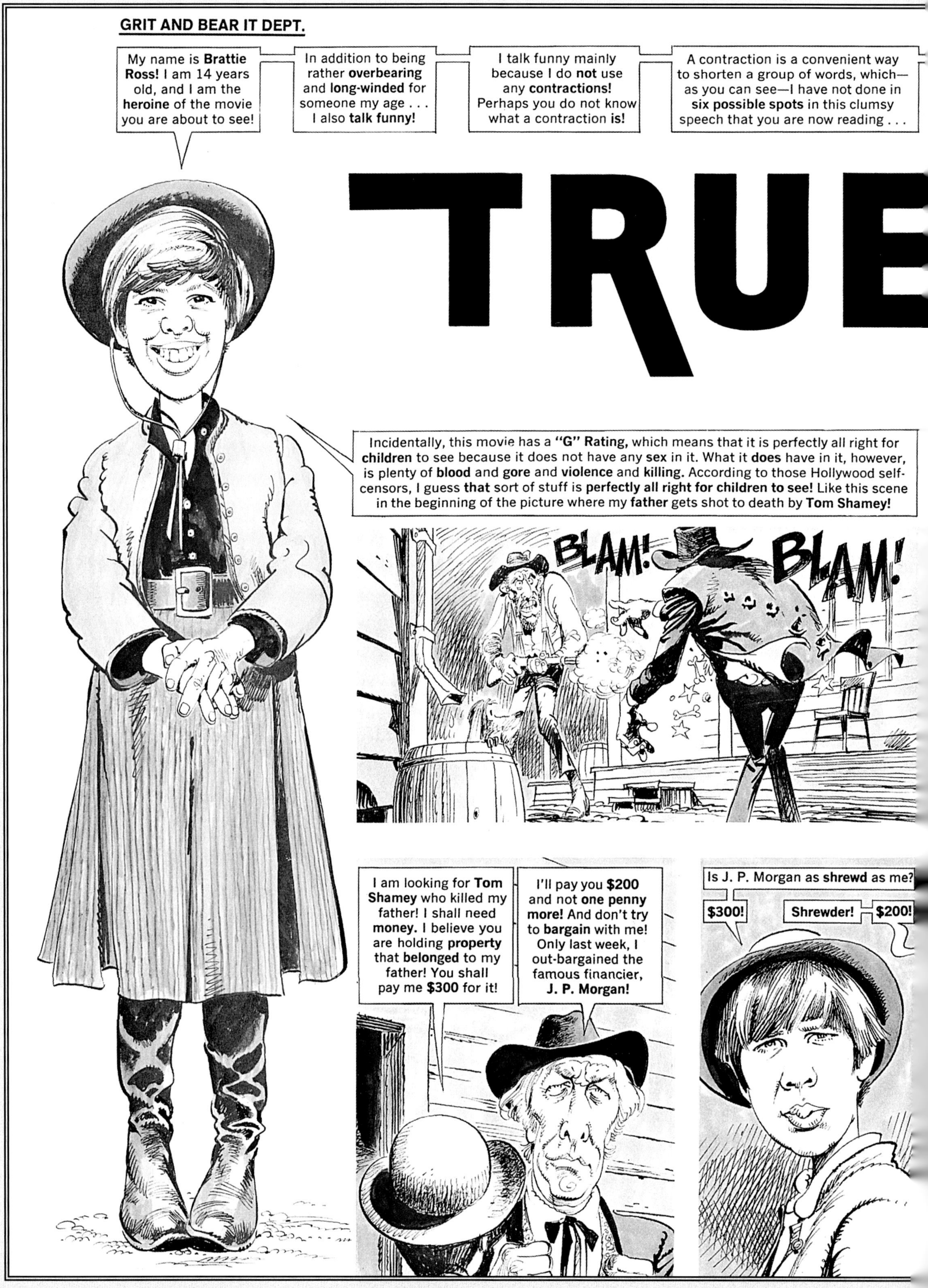
GRIT AND BEAR IT DEPT.
My name is Brattie Ross! I am 14 years old, and I am the heroine of the movie you are about to see!
In addition to being rather overbearing and long-winded for someone my age . . . I also talk funny!
I talk funny mainly because I do not use any contractions! Perhaps you do not know what a contraction is!
A contraction is a convenient way to shorten a group of words, which—as you can see—I have not done in six possible spots in this clumsy speech that you are now reading . . .
TRUE
Incidentally, this movie has a "G" Rating, which means that it is perfectly all right for children to see because it does not have any sex in it. What it does have in it, however, is plenty of blood and gore and violence and killing. According to those Hollywood self-censors, I guess that sort of stuff is perfectly all right for children to see! Like this scene in the beginning of the picture where my father gets shot to death by Tom Shamey!
BLAM!
BLAM!
I am looking for Tom Shamey who killed my father! I shall need money. I believe you are holding property that belonged to my father! You shall pay me $300 for it!
I'll pay you $200 and not one penny more! And don't try to bargain with me! Only last week, I out-bargained the famous financier, J. P. Morgan!
Is J. P. Morgan as shrewd as me?
$300!
Shrewder!
$200!

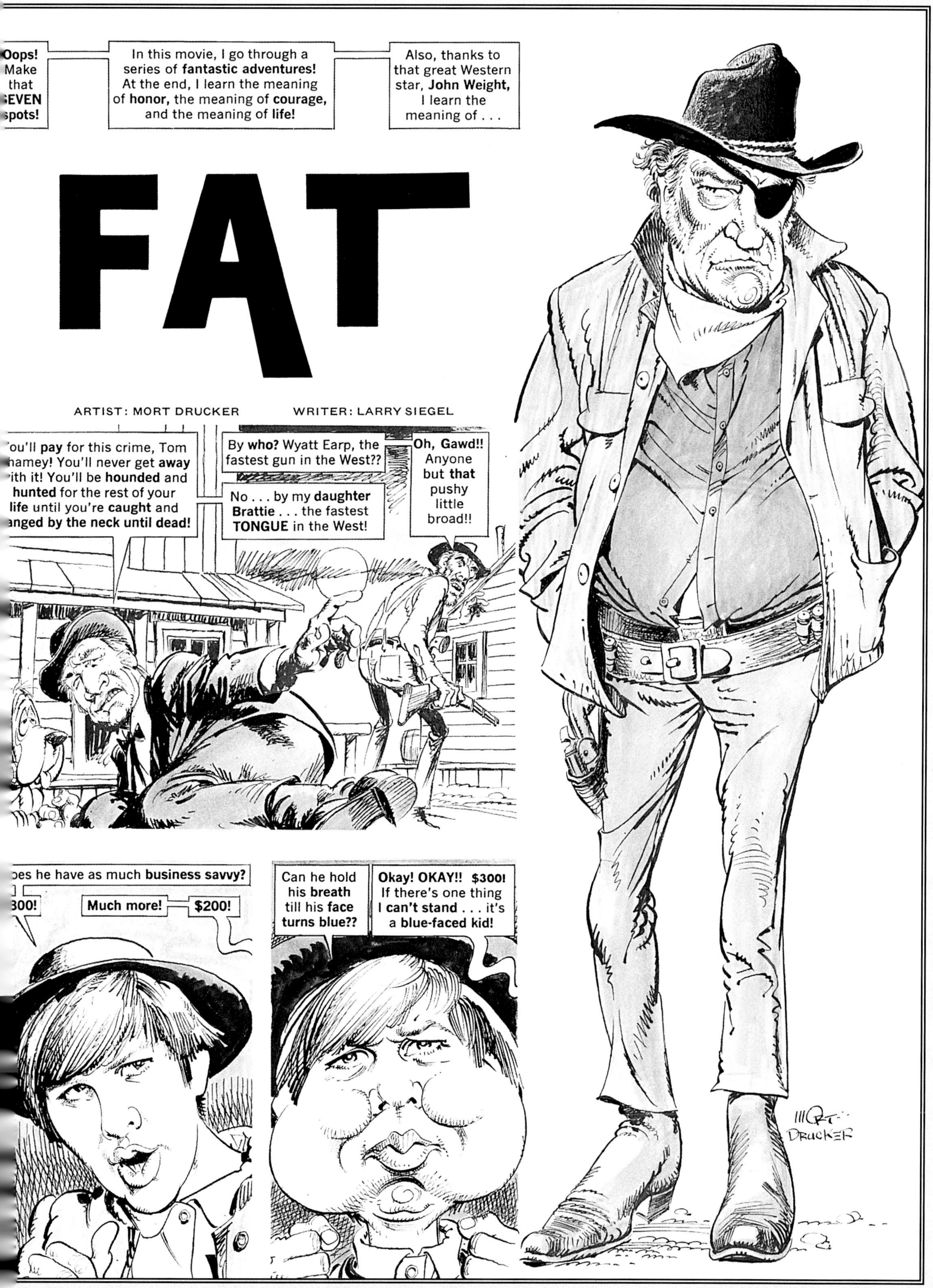
Oops! Make that SEVEN spots!
In this movie, I go through a series of fantastic adventures! At the end, I learn the meaning of honor, the meaning of courage, and the meaning of life!
Also, thanks to that great Western star, John Weight, I learn the meaning of . . .
FAT
ARTIST: MORT DRUCKER
WRITER: LARRY SIEGEL
ou'll pay for this crime, Tom hamey! You'll never get away ith it! You'll be hounded and hunted for the rest of your life until you're caught and anged by the neck until dead!
By who? Wyatt Earp, the fastest gun in the West??
No . . . by my daughter Brattie . . . the fastest TONGUE in the West!
Oh, Gawd!! Anyone but that pushy little broad!!
oes he have as much business savvy?
300!
Much more!
$200!
Can he hold his breath till his face turns blue??
Okay! OKAY!! $300! If there's one thing I can't stand . . . it's a blue-faced kid!
MORT DRUCKER

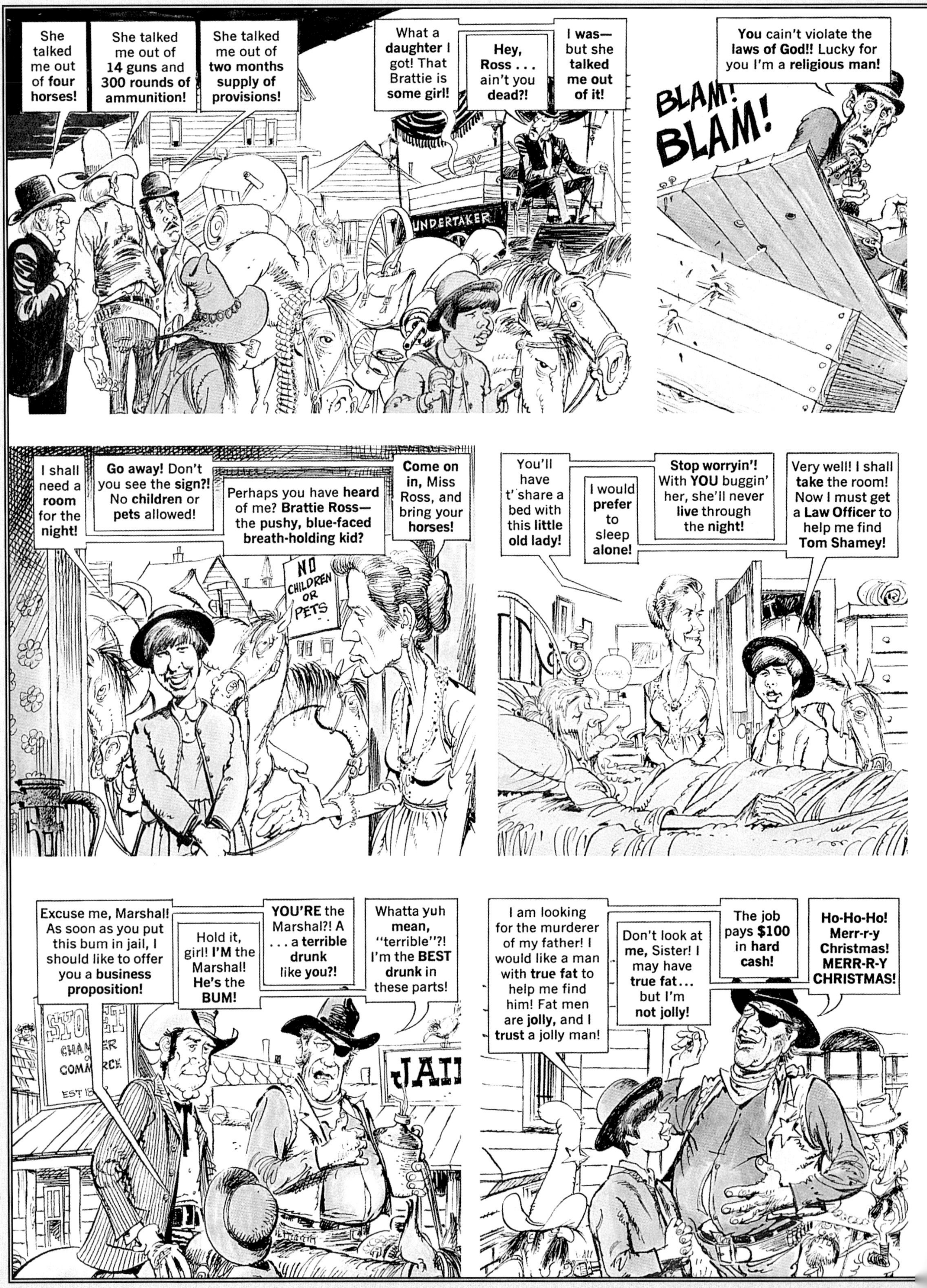
She talked me out of four horses!
She talked me out of 14 guns and 300 rounds of ammunition!
She talked me out of two months supply of provisions!
What a daughter I got! That Brattie is some girl!
Hey, Ross . . . ain't you dead?!
I was—but she talked me out of it!
UNDERTAKER
You cain't violate the laws of God!! Lucky for you I'm a religious man!
BLAM! BLAM!
I shall need a room for the night!
Go away! Don't you see the sign?! No children or pets allowed!
Perhaps you have heard of me? Brattie Ross—the pushy, blue-faced breath-holding kid?
Come on in, Miss Ross, and bring your horses!
NO CHILDREN OR PETS
You'll have t' share a bed with this little old lady!
I would prefer to sleep alone!
Stop worryin'! With YOU buggin' her, she'll never live through the night!
Very well! I shall take the room! Now I must get a Law Officer to help me find Tom Shamey!
Excuse me, Marshal! As soon as you put this bum in jail, I should like to offer you a business proposition!
Hold it, girl! I'M the Marshal! He's the BUM!
YOU'RE the Marshal?! A . . . a terrible drunk like you?!
Whatta yuh mean, "terrible"?! I'm the BEST drunk in these parts!
I am looking for the murderer of my father! I would like a man with true fat to help me find him! Fat men are jolly, and I trust a jolly man!
Don't look at me, Sister! I may have true fat . . . but I'm not jolly!
The job pays $100 in hard cash!
Ho-Ho-Ho! Merr-r-y Christmas! MERR-R-Y CHRISTMAS!

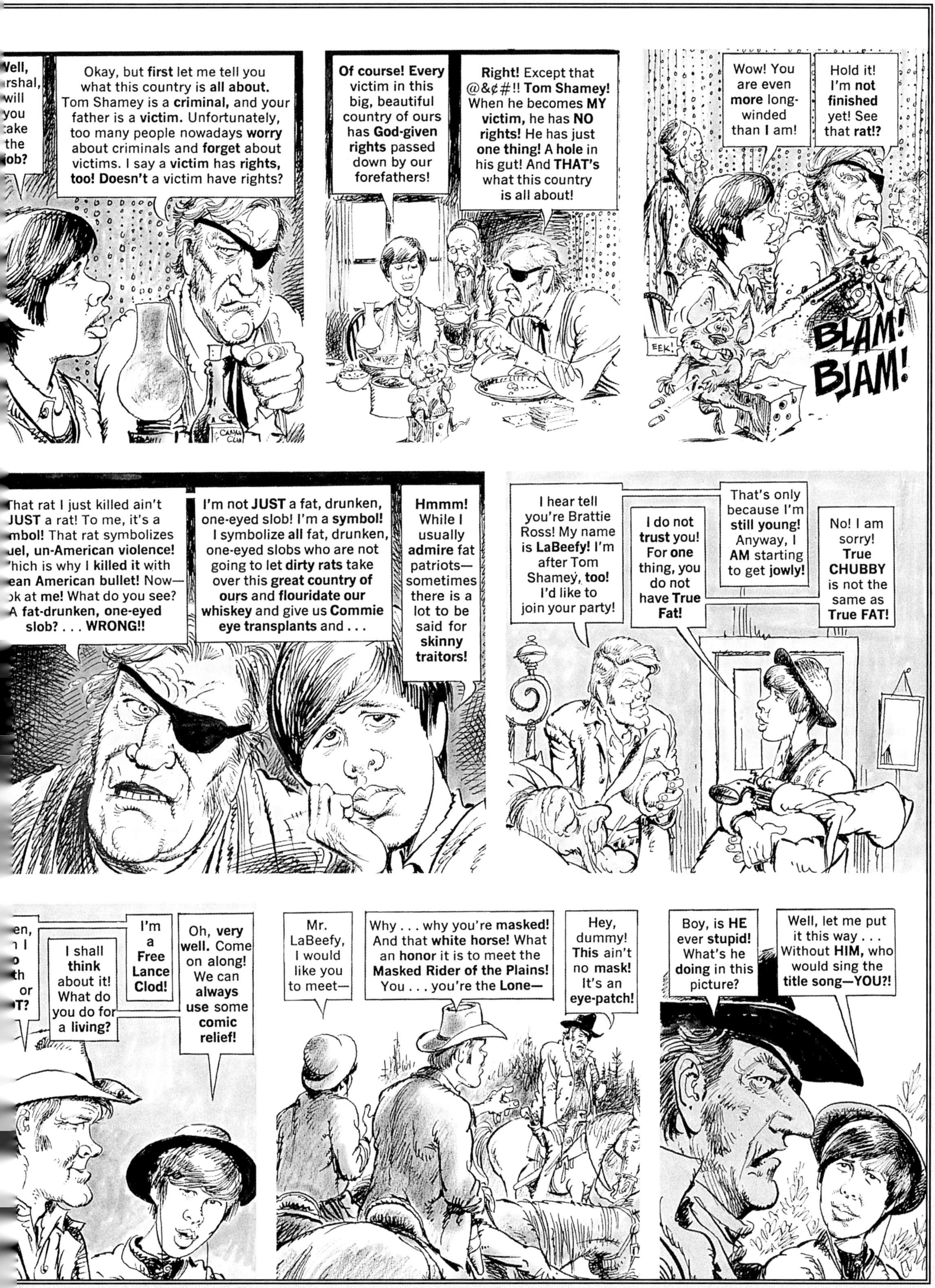
ell, rshal, will you ake the ob?
Okay, but first let me tell you what this country is all about. Tom Shamey is a criminal, and your father is a victim. Unfortunately, too many people nowadays worry about criminals and forget about victims. I say a victim has rights, too! Doesn't a victim have rights?
Of course! Every victim in this big, beautiful country of ours has God-given rights passed down by our forefathers!
Right! Except that @&¢#!! Tom Shamey! When he becomes MY victim, he has NO rights! He has just one thing! A hole in his gut! And THAT's what this country is all about!
Wow! You are even more long-winded than I am!
Hold it! I'm not finished yet! See that rat!?
EEK!
BLAM! BJAM!
hat rat I just killed ain't JUST a rat! To me, it's a mbol! That rat symbolizes uel, un-American violence! hich is why I killed it with ean American bullet! Now— ok at me! What do you see? A fat-drunken, one-eyed slob? . . . WRONG!!
I'm not JUST a fat, drunken, one-eyed slob! I'm a symbol! I symbolize all fat, drunken, one-eyed slobs who are not going to let dirty rats take over this great country of ours and flouridate our whiskey and give us Commie eye transplants and . . .
Hmmm! While I usually admire fat patriots—sometimes there is a lot to be said for skinny traitors!
I hear tell you're Brattie Ross! My name is LaBeefy! I'm after Tom Shamey, too! I'd like to join your party!
I do not trust you! For one thing, you do not have True Fat!
That's only because I'm still young! Anyway, I AM starting to get jowly!
No! I am sorry! True CHUBBY is not the same as True FAT!
I shall think about it! What do you do for a living?
I'm a Free Lance Clod!
Oh, very well. Come on along! We can always use some comic relief!
Mr. LaBeefy, I would like you to meet—
Why . . . why you're masked! And that white horse! What an honor it is to meet the Masked Rider of the Plains! You . . . you're the Lone—
Hey, dummy! This ain't no mask! It's an eye-patch!
Boy, is HE ever stupid! What's he doing in this picture?
Well, let me put it this way . . . Without HIM, who would sing the title song—YOU?!

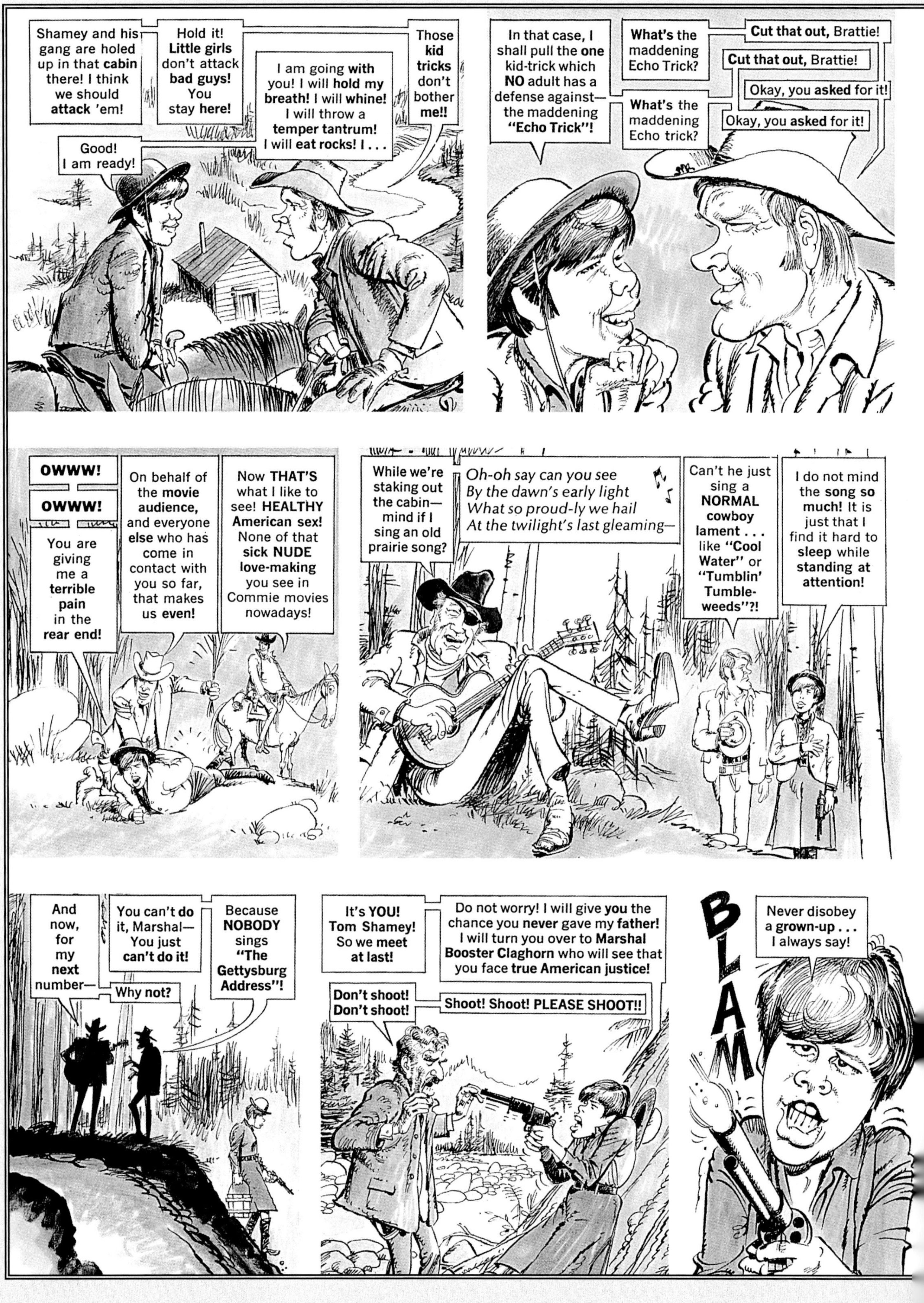
Shamey and his gang are holed up in that cabin there! I think we should attack 'em!
Hold it! Little girls don't attack bad guys! You stay here!
Good! I am ready!
I am going with you! I will hold my breath! I will whine! I will throw a temper tantrum! I will eat rocks! I . . .
Those kid tricks don't bother me!!
In that case, I shall pull the one kid-trick which NO adult has a defense against—the maddening "Echo Trick"!
What's the maddening Echo Trick?
What's the maddening Echo trick?
Cut that out, Brattie!
Cut that out, Brattie!
Okay, you asked for it!
Okay, you asked for it!
OWWW!
OWWW!
You are giving me a terrible pain in the rear end!
On behalf of the movie audience, and everyone else who has come in contact with you so far, that makes us even!
Now THAT'S what I like to see! HEALTHY American sex! None of that sick NUDE love-making you see in Commie movies nowadays!
While we're staking out the cabin—mind if I sing an old prairie song?
Oh-oh say can you see By the dawn's early light What so proud-ly we hail At the twilight's last gleaming—
Can't he just sing a NORMAL cowboy lament . . . like "Cool Water" or "Tumblin' Tumble-weeds"?!
I do not mind the song so much! It is just that I find it hard to sleep while standing at attention!
And now, for my next number—
You can't do it, Marshal—You just can't do it!
Why not?
Because NOBODY sings "The Gettysburg Address"!
It's YOU! Tom Shamey! So we meet at last!
Do not worry! I will give you the chance you never gave my father! I will turn you over to Marshal Booster Claghorn who will see that you face true American justice!
Don't shoot! Don't shoot!
Shoot! Shoot! PLEASE SHOOT!!
BLAM
Never disobey a grown-up . . . I always say!

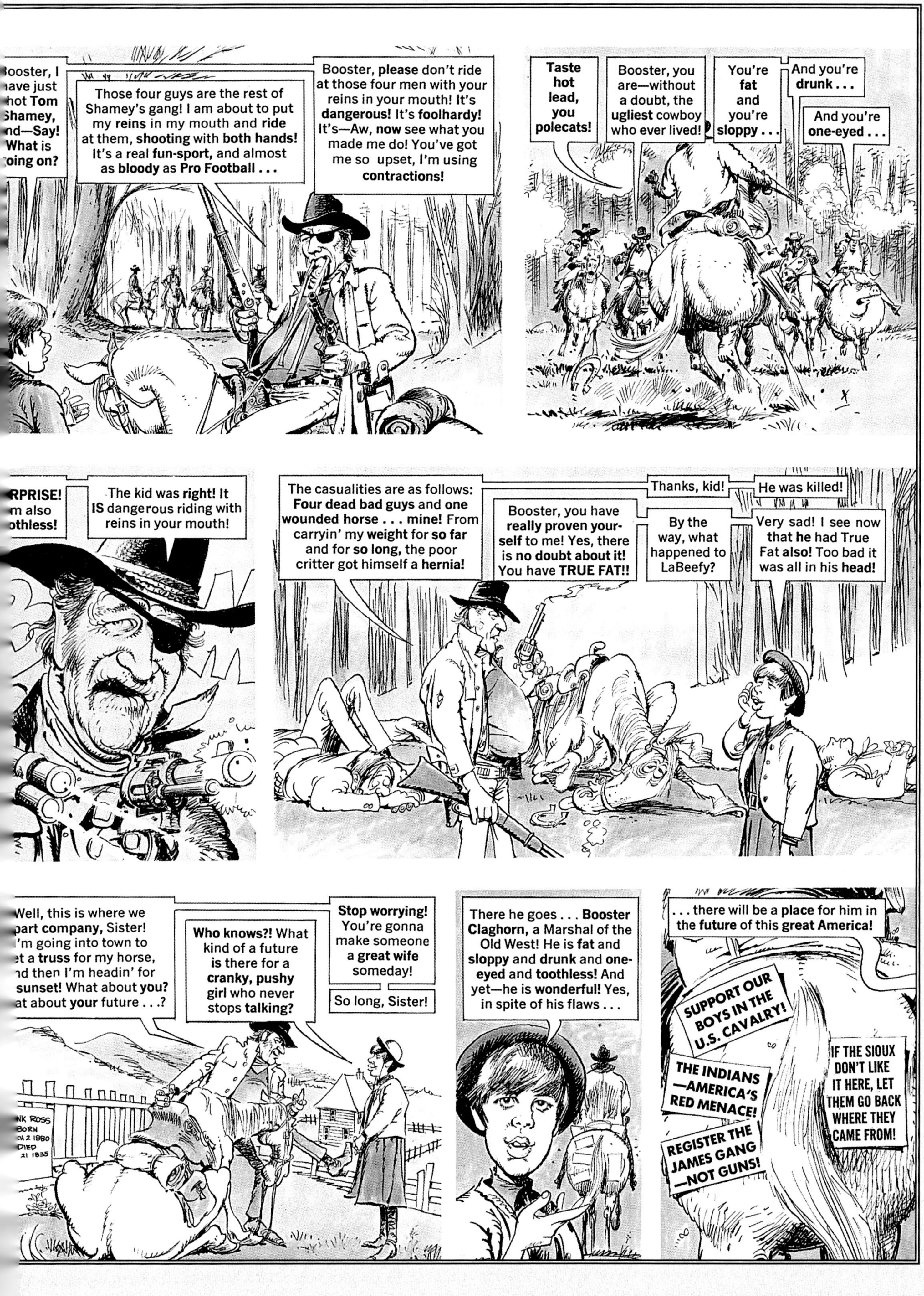
ooster, I ave just hot Tom Shamey, nd—Say! What is oing on?
Those four guys are the rest of Shamey's gang! I am about to put my reins in my mouth and ride at them, shooting with both hands! It's a real fun-sport, and almost as bloody as Pro Football . . .
Booster, please don't ride at those four men with your reins in your mouth! It's dangerous! It's foolhardy! It's—Aw, now see what you made me do! You've got me so upset, I'm using contractions!
Taste hot lead, you polecats!
Booster, you are—without a doubt, the ugliest cowboy who ever lived!
You're fat and you're sloppy . . .
And you're drunk . . .
And you're one-eyed . . .
RPRISE! m also othless!
The kid was right! It IS dangerous riding with reins in your mouth!
The casualities are as follows: Four dead bad guys and one wounded horse . . . mine! From carryin' my weight for so far and for so long, the poor critter got himself a hernia!
Booster, you have really proven yourself to me! Yes, there is no doubt about it! You have TRUE FAT!!
Thanks, kid!
By the way, what happened to LaBeefy?
He was killed!
Very sad! I see now that he had True Fat also! Too bad it was all in his head!
Well, this is where we part company, Sister! 'm going into town to et a truss for my horse, nd then I'm headin' for sunset! What about you? at about your future . . .?
Who knows?! What kind of a future is there for a cranky, pushy girl who never stops talking?
Stop worrying! You're gonna make someone a great wife someday!
So long, Sister!
There he goes . . . Booster Claghorn, a Marshal of the Old West! He is fat and sloppy and drunk and one-eyed and toothless! And yet—he is wonderful! Yes, in spite of his flaws . . .
. . . there will be a place for him in the future of this great America!
SUPPORT OUR BOYS IN THE U.S. CAVALRY!
THE INDIANS —AMERICA'S RED MENACE!
REGISTER THE JAMES GANG —NOT GUNS!
IF THE SIOUX DON'T LIKE IT HERE, LET THEM GO BACK WHERE THEY CAME FROM!

BIG TIME OPERETTA DEPT.

In recent years, MAD has published musicals featuring such way-out characters as mobsters, hippies, student rioters and Barbra Streisand. Now we'd like to present a musical featuring the most far-out characters of all, namely Dick, Pat, Spiro, Henry, Martha and all the other zany cut-ups who wander around that crazy executive mansion down in Washington, D.C. Which is as good a way as any of introducing . . .

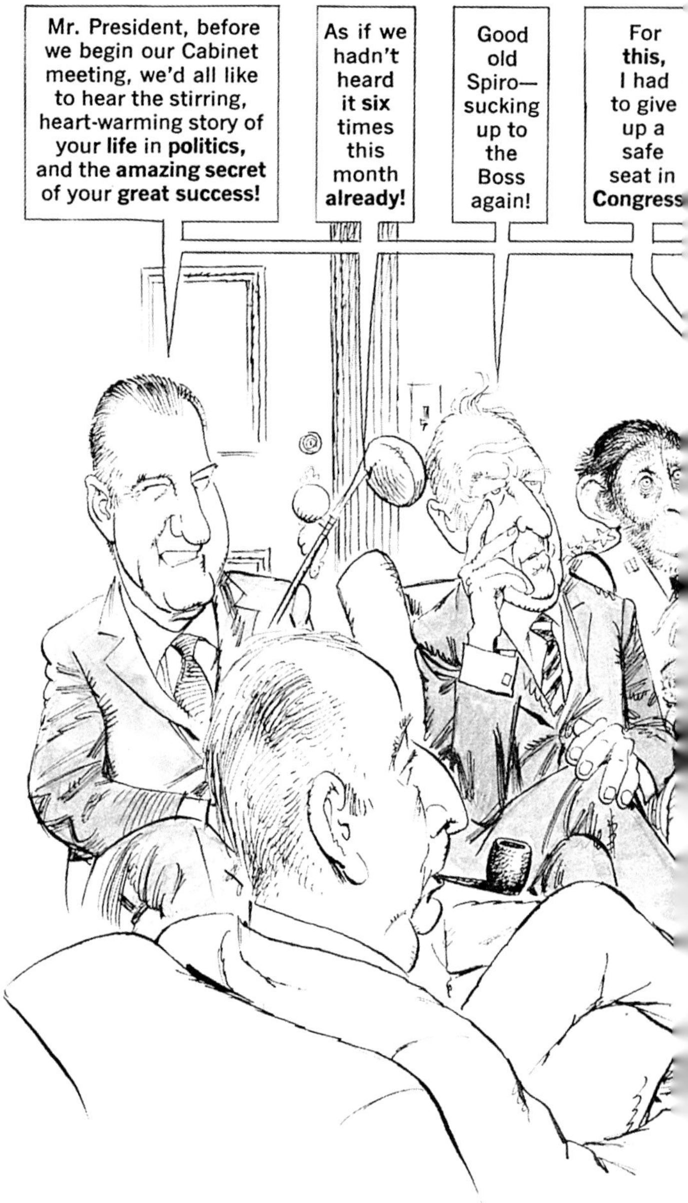
Mr. President, before we begin our Cabinet meeting, we'd all like to hear the stirring, heart-warming story of your life in politics, and the amazing secret of your great success!
As if we hadn't heard it six times this month already!
Good old Spiro—sucking up to the Boss again!
For this, I had to give up a safe seat in Congress

THE WHITE HOUSE FOLLIES OF 1972

(With Apologies To Gilbert & Sullivan)

ARTIST: MORT DRUCKER WRITER: FRANK JACOBS

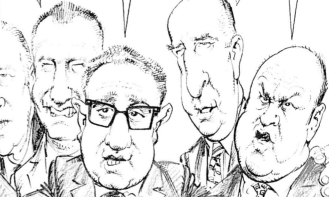

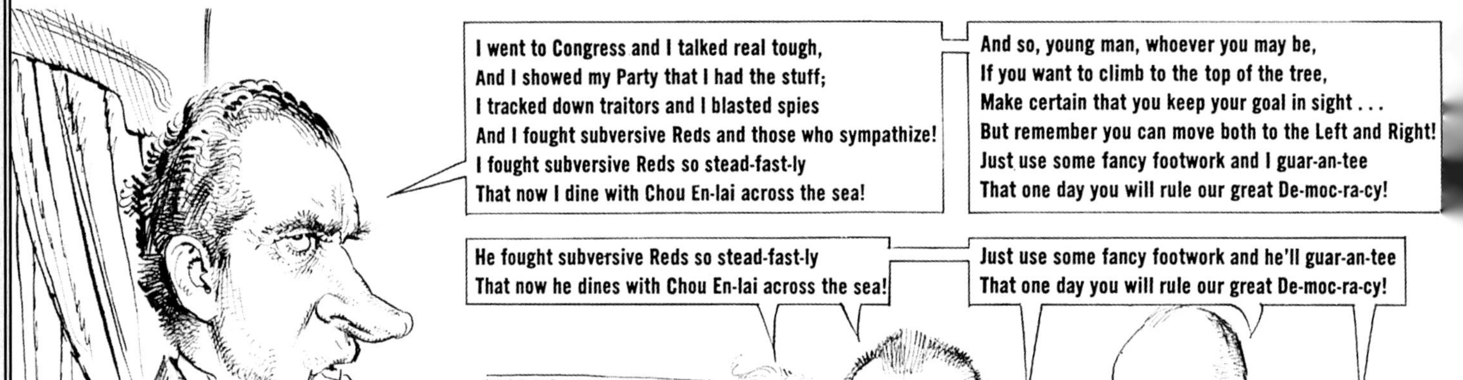
I went to Congress and I talked real tough,
And I showed my Party that I had the stuff;
I tracked down traitors and I blasted spies
And I fought subversive Reds and those who sympathize!
I fought subversive Reds so stead-fast-ly
That now I dine with Chou En-lai across the sea!
And so, young man, whoever you may be,
If you want to climb to the top of the tree,
Make certain that you keep your goal in sight . . .
But remember you can move both to the Left and Right!
Just use some fancy footwork and I guar-an-tee
That one day you will rule our great De-moc-ra-cy!
He fought subversive Reds so stead-fast-ly
That now he dines with Chou En-lai across the sea!
Just use some fancy footwork and he'll guar-an-tee
That one day you will rule our great De-moc-ra-cy!

MAD #150, April 1972

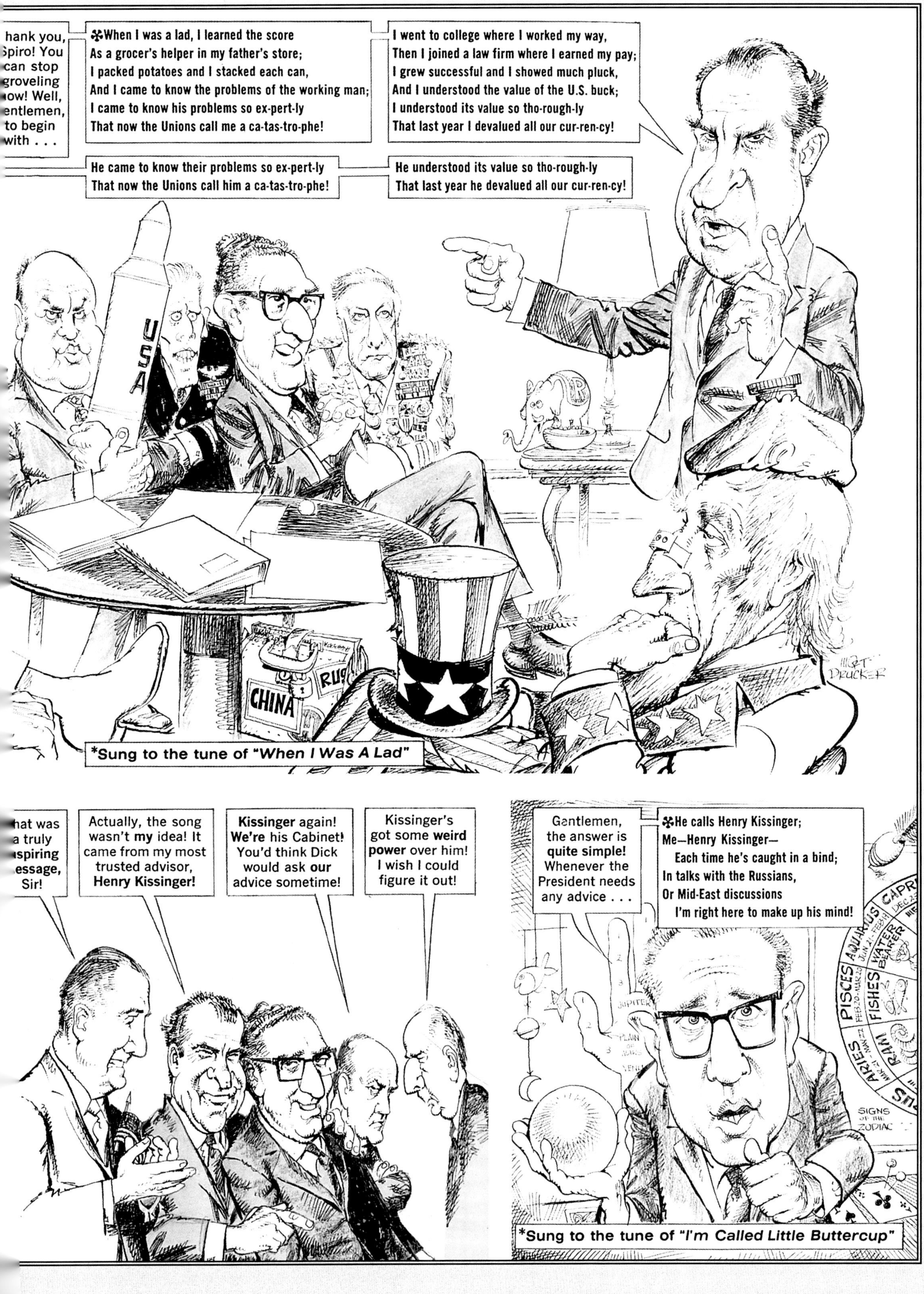
hank you, Spiro! You can stop groveling now! Well, entlemen, to begin with . . .
*When I was a lad, I learned the score
As a grocer's helper in my father's store;
I packed potatoes and I stacked each can,
And I came to know the problems of the working man;
I came to know his problems so ex-pert-ly
That now the Unions call me a ca-tas-tro-phe!
I went to college where I worked my way,
Then I joined a law firm where I earned my pay;
I grew successful and I showed much pluck,
And I understood the value of the U.S. buck;
I understood its value so tho-rough-ly
That last year I devalued all our cur-ren-cy!
He came to know their problems so ex-pert-ly
That now the Unions call him a ca-tas-tro-phe!
He understood its value so tho-rough-ly
That last year he devalued all our cur-ren-cy!
USA
CHINA
RUS
MORT DRUCKER
*Sung to the tune of "When I Was A Lad"
hat was a truly spiring essage, Sir!
Actually, the song wasn't **my** idea! It came from my most trusted advisor, **Henry Kissinger!**
Kissinger again! **We're** his Cabinet! You'd think Dick would ask **our** advice sometime!
Kissinger's got some **weird power** over him! I wish I could figure it out!
Gentlemen, the answer is **quite simple!** Whenever the President needs any advice . . .
*He calls Henry Kissinger;
Me—Henry Kissinger—
Each time he's caught in a bind;
In talks with the Russians,
Or Mid-East discussions
I'm right here to make up his mind!
JUPITER
AQUARIUS
WATER BEARER
CAPRI
PISCES
FISHES
ARIES
RAM
SIGNS OF THE ZODIAC
*Sung to the tune of "I'm Called Little Buttercup"

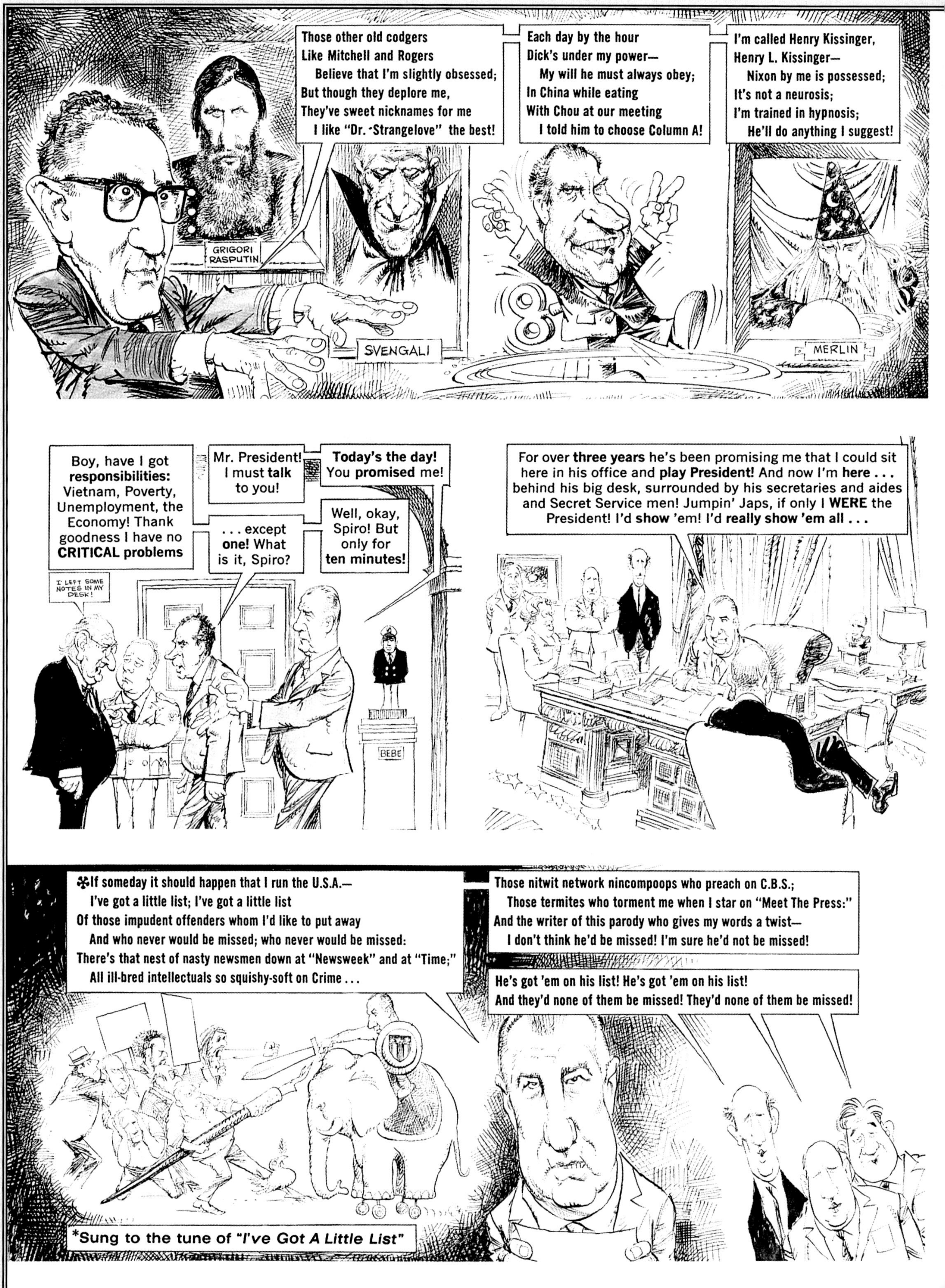
Those other old codgers
Like Mitchell and Rogers
Believe that I'm slightly obsessed;
But though they deplore me,
They've sweet nicknames for me
I like "Dr. Strangelove" the best!
GRIGORI RASPUTIN
SVENGALI
Each day by the hour
Dick's under my power—
My will he must always obey;
In China while eating
With Chou at our meeting
I told him to choose Column A!
I'm called Henry Kissinger,
Henry L. Kissinger—
Nixon by me is possessed;
It's not a neurosis;
I'm trained in hypnosis;
He'll do anything I suggest!
MERLIN
Boy, have I got **responsibilities:** Vietnam, Poverty, Unemployment, the Economy! Thank goodness I have no **CRITICAL problems**
Mr. President! I must **talk** to you!
. . . except **one!** What is it, Spiro?
Today's the day! You **promised** me!
Well, okay, Spiro! But only for **ten minutes!**
I LEFT SOME NOTES IN MY DESK!
BEBE
For over **three years** he's been promising me that I could sit here in his office and **play President!** And now I'm **here . . .** behind his big desk, surrounded by his secretaries and aides and Secret Service men! Jumpin' Japs, if only I **WERE** the President! I'd **show 'em!** I'd **really show 'em all . . .**
*If someday it should happen that I run the U.S.A.—
I've got a little list; I've got a little list
Of those impudent offenders whom I'd like to put away
And who never would be missed; who never would be missed:
There's that nest of nasty newsmen down at "Newsweek" and at "Time;"
All ill-bred intellectuals so squishy-soft on Crime . . .
Those nitwit network nincompoops who preach on C.B.S.;
Those termites who torment me when I star on "Meet The Press:"
And the writer of this parody who gives my words a twist—
I don't think he'd be missed! I'm sure he'd not be missed!
He's got 'em on his list! He's got 'em on his list!
And they'd none of them be missed! They'd none of them be missed!
*Sung to the tune of *"I've Got A Little List"*

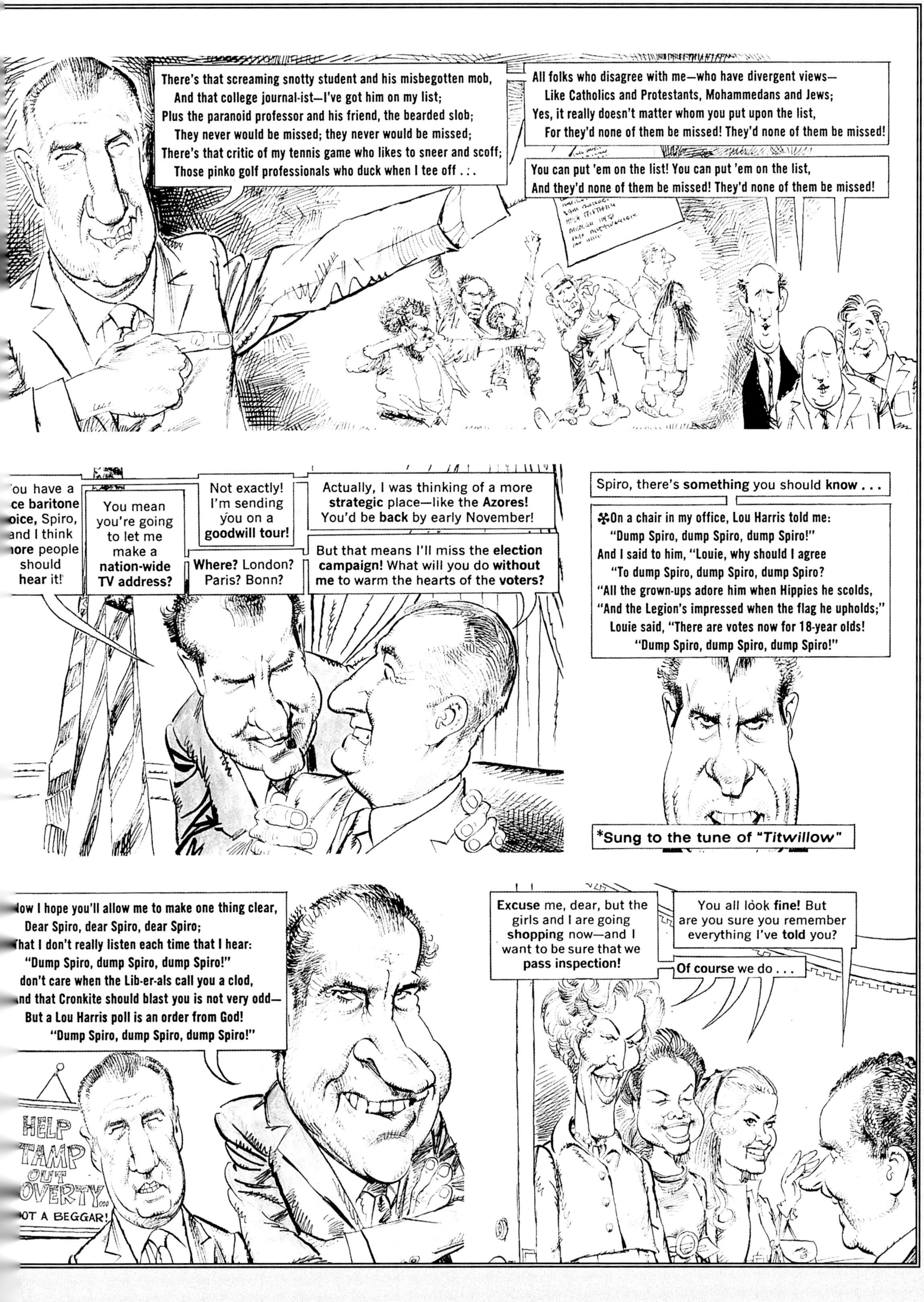
There's that screaming snotty student and his misbegotten mob, And that college journal-ist—I've got him on my list; Plus the paranoid professor and his friend, the bearded slob; They never would be missed; they never would be missed; There's that critic of my tennis game who likes to sneer and scoff; Those pinko golf professionals who duck when I tee off . . .
All folks who disagree with me—who have divergent views— Like Catholics and Protestants, Mohammedans and Jews; Yes, it really doesn't matter whom you put upon the list, For they'd none of them be missed! They'd none of them be missed!
You can put 'em on the list! You can put 'em on the list, And they'd none of them be missed! They'd none of them be missed!
ou have a ce baritone oice, Spiro, and I think nore people should hear it!
You mean you're going to let me make a nation-wide TV address?
Not exactly! I'm sending you on a goodwill tour!
Where? London? Paris? Bonn?
Actually, I was thinking of a more strategic place—like the Azores! You'd be back by early November!
But that means I'll miss the election campaign! What will you do without me to warm the hearts of the voters?
Spiro, there's something you should know . . .
*On a chair in my office, Lou Harris told me: "Dump Spiro, dump Spiro, dump Spiro!" And I said to him, "Louie, why should I agree "To dump Spiro, dump Spiro, dump Spiro? "All the grown-ups adore him when Hippies he scolds, "And the Legion's impressed when the flag he upholds;" Louie said, "There are votes now for 18-year olds! "Dump Spiro, dump Spiro, dump Spiro!"
*Sung to the tune of "Titwillow"
ow I hope you'll allow me to make one thing clear, Dear Spiro, dear Spiro, dear Spiro; hat I don't really listen each time that I hear: "Dump Spiro, dump Spiro, dump Spiro!" don't care when the Lib-er-als call you a clod, nd that Cronkite should blast you is not very odd— But a Lou Harris poll is an order from God! "Dump Spiro, dump Spiro, dump Spiro!"
HELP TAMP OUT OVERTY
OT A BEGGAR!
Excuse me, dear, but the girls and I are going shopping now—and I want to be sure that we pass inspection!
You all look fine! But are you sure you remember everything I've told you?
Of course we do . . .

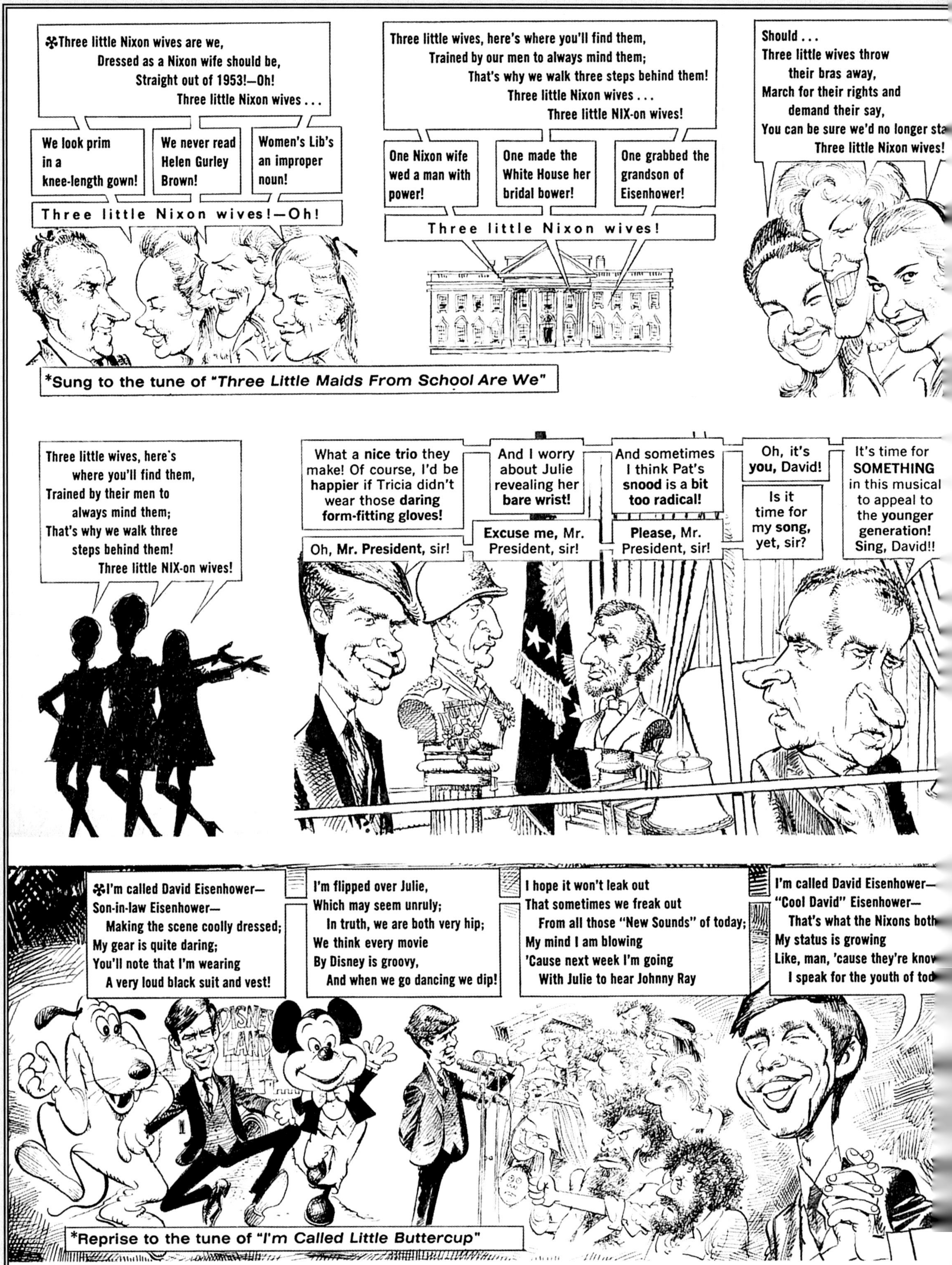
✽Three little Nixon wives are we,
Dressed as a Nixon wife should be,
Straight out of 1953!—Oh!
Three little Nixon wives . . .
We look prim in a knee-length gown!
We never read Helen Gurley Brown!
Women's Lib's an improper noun!
Three little Nixon wives!—Oh!
*Sung to the tune of "Three Little Maids From School Are We"
Three little wives, here's where you'll find them,
Trained by our men to always mind them;
That's why we walk three steps behind them!
Three little Nixon wives . . .
Three little NIX-on wives!
One Nixon wife wed a man with power!
One made the White House her bridal bower!
One grabbed the grandson of Eisenhower!
Three little Nixon wives!
Should . . .
Three little wives throw their bras away,
March for their rights and demand their say,
You can be sure we'd no longer sta
Three little Nixon wives!
Three little wives, here's where you'll find them,
Trained by their men to always mind them;
That's why we walk three steps behind them!
Three little NIX-on wives!
Oh, Mr. President, sir!
What a nice trio they make! Of course, I'd be happier if Tricia didn't wear those daring form-fitting gloves!
Excuse me, Mr. President, sir!
And I worry about Julie revealing her bare wrist!
Please, Mr. President, sir!
And sometimes I think Pat's snood is a bit too radical!
Oh, it's you, David!
Is it time for my song, yet, sir?
It's time for SOMETHING in this musical to appeal to the younger generation! Sing, David!!
✽I'm called David Eisenhower—
Son-in-law Eisenhower—
Making the scene coolly dressed;
My gear is quite daring;
You'll note that I'm wearing
A very loud black suit and vest!
I'm flipped over Julie,
Which may seem unruly;
In truth, we are both very hip;
We think every movie
By Disney is groovy,
And when we go dancing we dip!
I hope it won't leak out
That sometimes we freak out
From all those "New Sounds" of today;
My mind I am blowing
'Cause next week I'm going
With Julie to hear Johnny Ray
I'm called David Eisenhower—
"Cool David" Eisenhower—
That's what the Nixons both
My status is growing
Like, man, 'cause they're kno
I speak for the youth of to
DISNEY LAND
*Reprise to the tune of "I'm Called Little Buttercup"

David's such a **vibrant personality!** Hmm! I **AM** looking for a **new Vice-President!** It sure would make a **keen ticket: NIXON and EISENHOWER!**

But, no! People would say I was **playing politics!** Anyway, I need someone who **tunes in** on the people!

Sir! **J. Edgar Hoover** is waiting for you in the rose garden!

Hoover! Now **THERE'S** someone who **REALLY tunes in** on the people!

Hello, Edgar! I've **called** you here because **Pat** is complaining that you're bugging her **jewel case!**

Well, **that's** Security, Dick! You can't trust **ANYONE** these days!

But she's the wife of the **President!** How would it look if you bugged **MY** possessions?

Better take a look at your **cufflinks!**

As head of the F.B.I., I must use the **latest techniques** so that the **Press** won't think I'm **too old** for my **job!** You see . . .

✱I am the very model of a modern criminologist;
My instinct for survival would intrigue an anthropologist;
For more than forty year's I've clung to my official residence,
Outlasting Walter Lippman, not to mention seven Presidents;

Yet rather than remove me from my post proprietorial,
They'd rather put the hammer to the Jefferson Memorial;
It's known, you see, I have the goods on Congressmen and Senators,
Including information on their children and progenitors;
And should I be tormented by some critic of the media,
The file I've got on him would fill a small encyclopedia.
Of course, in my position one must think like a psychologist;
I am the very model of a modern criminologist.

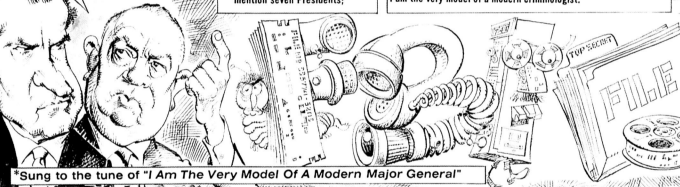

*Sung to the tune of "I Am The Very Model Of A Modern Major General"

I am the very model of a modern criminologist,
As thorough in his findings as a Harvard archaeologist;
I do not care for idle talk; I weigh the facts judicially;
The Mob did not exist until I broke the news officially;

Each agent that surrounds me must possess the right ingredients
Of reverence, fidelity, devotion and obedience,
And should one doubt my wisdom it could lead to the extremity
Of putting him on duty on a mountain in Yosemite;
My men I much prefer to take their exercise unraveling
The evil web of Communists and others fellow-traveling,
Or, failing that, to trail some bearded student idealogist;
I am the very model of a modern criminologist.

Golly! Here comes my **economic advisor, Arthur Burns!** I haven't seen him so upset since **David Rockefeller** forgot to send him a **Christmas card!**

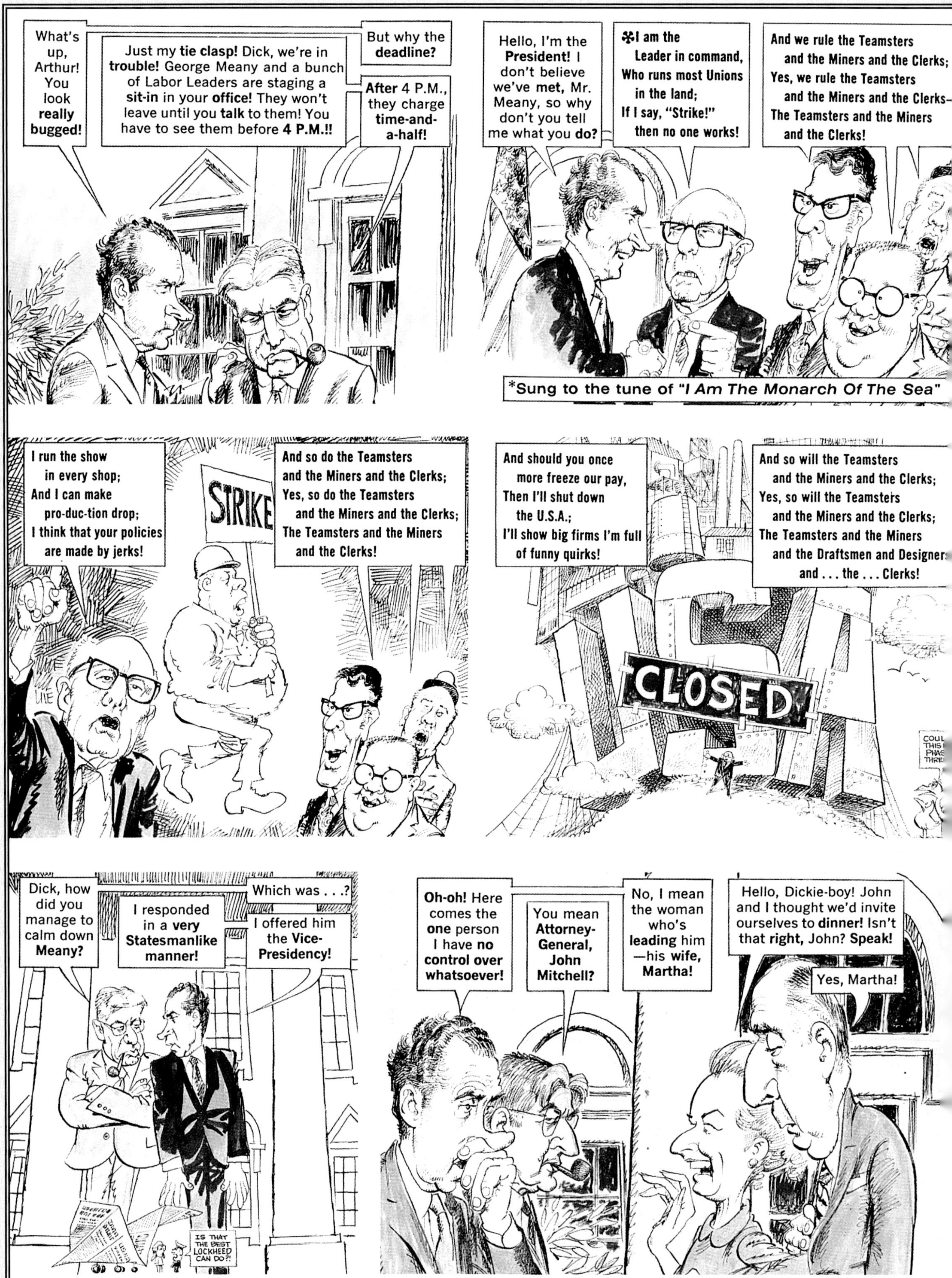
What's up, Arthur! You look really bugged!
Just my tie clasp! Dick, we're in trouble! George Meany and a bunch of Labor Leaders are staging a sit-in in your office! They won't leave until you talk to them! You have to see them before 4 P.M.!!
But why the deadline?
After 4 P.M., they charge time-and-a-half!
Hello, I'm the President! I don't believe we've met, Mr. Meany, so why don't you tell me what you do?
*I am the Leader in command, Who runs most Unions in the land; If I say, "Strike!" then no one works!
And we rule the Teamsters and the Miners and the Clerks; Yes, we rule the Teamsters and the Miners and the Clerks— The Teamsters and the Miners and the Clerks!
*Sung to the tune of "I Am The Monarch Of The Sea"
I run the show in every shop; And I can make pro-duc-tion drop; I think that your policies are made by jerks!
STRIKE
And so do the Teamsters and the Miners and the Clerks; Yes, so do the Teamsters and the Miners and the Clerks; The Teamsters and the Miners and the Clerks!
And should you once more freeze our pay, Then I'll shut down the U.S.A.; I'll show big firms I'm full of funny quirks!
And so will the Teamsters and the Miners and the Clerks; Yes, so will the Teamsters and the Miners and the Clerks; The Teamsters and the Miners and the Draftsmen and Designers and . . . the . . . Clerks!
CLOSED
Dick, how did you manage to calm down Meany?
I responded in a very Statesmanlike manner!
Which was . . .?
I offered him the Vice-Presidency!
IS THAT THE BEST LOCKHEED CAN DO?!
Oh-oh! Here comes the one person I have no control over whatsoever!
You mean Attorney-General, John Mitchell?
No, I mean the woman who's leading him —his wife, Martha!
Hello, Dickie-boy! John and I thought we'd invite ourselves to dinner! Isn't that right, John? Speak!
Yes, Martha!

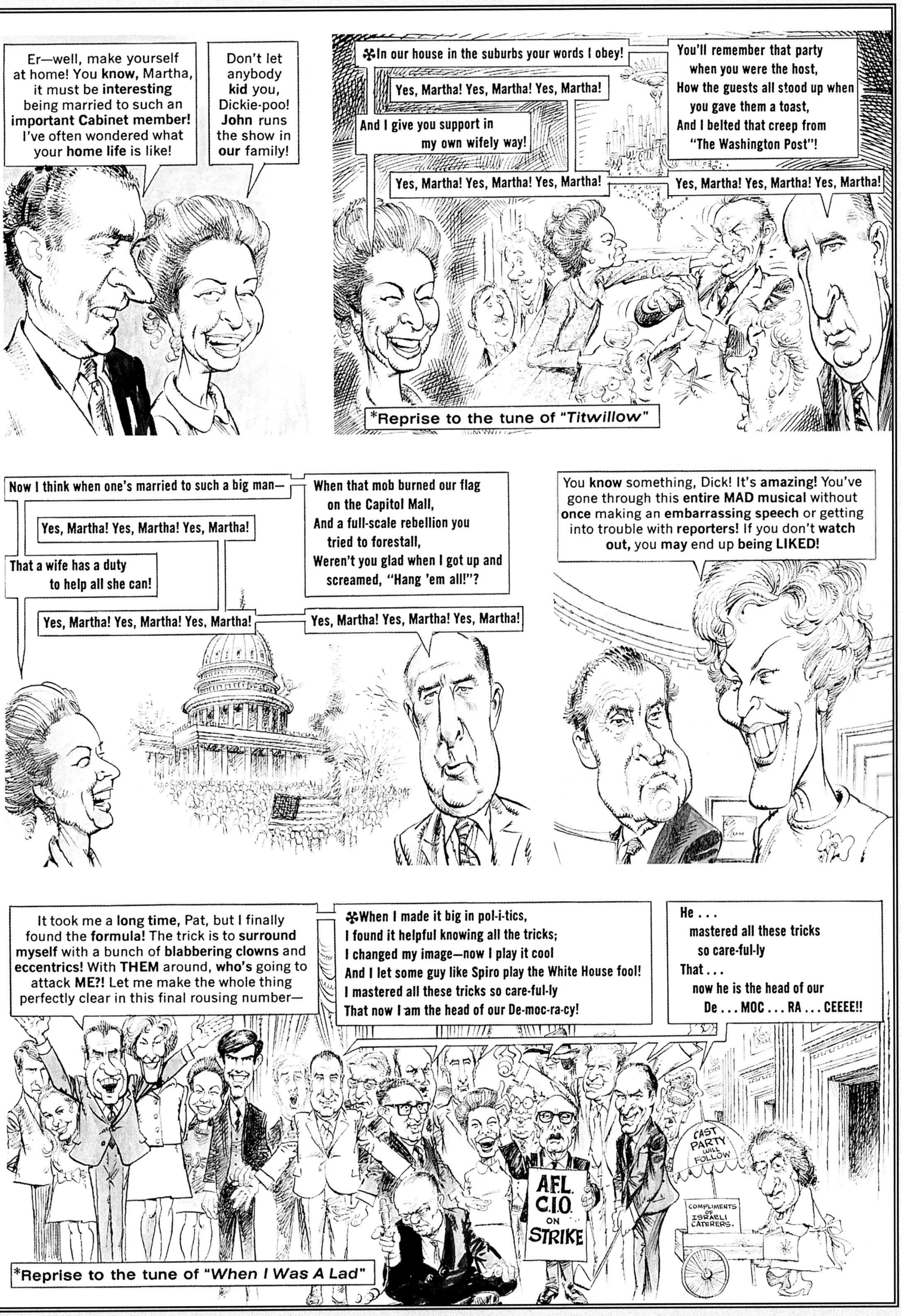
Er—well, make yourself at home! You know, Martha, it must be interesting being married to such an important Cabinet member! I've often wondered what your home life is like!
Don't let anybody kid you, Dickie-poo! John runs the show in our family!
*In our house in the suburbs your words I obey!
Yes, Martha! Yes, Martha! Yes, Martha!
And I give you support in my own wifely way!
Yes, Martha! Yes, Martha! Yes, Martha!
You'll remember that party when you were the host, How the guests all stood up when you gave them a toast, And I belted that creep from "The Washington Post"!
Yes, Martha! Yes, Martha! Yes, Martha!
*Reprise to the tune of "Titwillow"
Now I think when one's married to such a big man—
Yes, Martha! Yes, Martha! Yes, Martha!
That a wife has a duty to help all she can!
Yes, Martha! Yes, Martha! Yes, Martha!
When that mob burned our flag on the Capitol Mall, And a full-scale rebellion you tried to forestall, Weren't you glad when I got up and screamed, "Hang 'em all!"?
Yes, Martha! Yes, Martha! Yes, Martha!
You know something, Dick! It's amazing! You've gone through this entire MAD musical without once making an embarrassing speech or getting into trouble with reporters! If you don't watch out, you may end up being LIKED!
It took me a long time, Pat, but I finally found the formula! The trick is to surround myself with a bunch of blabbering clowns and eccentrics! With THEM around, who's going to attack ME?! Let me make the whole thing perfectly clear in this final rousing number—
*When I made it big in pol-i-tics,
I found it helpful knowing all the tricks;
I changed my image—now I play it cool
And I let some guy like Spiro play the White House fool!
I mastered all these tricks so care-ful-ly
That now I am the head of our De-moc-ra-cy!
He . . . mastered all these tricks so care-ful-ly
That . . . now he is the head of our De . . . MOC . . . RA . . . CEEEE!!
CAST PARTY WILL FOLLOW
AFL. C.I.O. ON STRIKE
COMPLIMENTS OF ISRAELI CATERERS.
*Reprise to the tune of "When I Was A Lad"

THE FAMILY THAT PREYS TOGETHER SLAYS TOGETHER DEPT.

Hey, Gang! Tired of all the garbage they're showing on motion picture screens lately? Well, here's a "Family" film for a change! And now, meet the "Family":

This is Don Vino Minestrone. Not too long ago, he was just a poor immigrant from Sicily. Now he's a leading racketeer, extortionist and killer. How did Don Vino get where he is today? By putting his faith in The American Way of Life.

Here's Mama Minestrone, a typical lovable Sicilian housewife. It seems like only yesterday at another wedding that Mama herself said, "I do!" Come to think of it, that was the last time she opened her mouth.

This is Don Vino's daught Canny, and her bridegroo Carly. Such a nice coup Everyone is saying that D Vino is not really losing daughter. No, actually, this kind of Family, h probably lose a Son-in-l

And so, with such a strange family and such weird childr

THE ODD

This is some swell wedding!

It's THE Social event of 1945!

Everybody who is anybody in organized crime is here!

Look! Here comes the Odd Father!

They say he's the biggest Mafia leader in the country!

Hey, you! I'm with the Italian Anti-Defamation League! Don't you know you're not supposed to use the word "MAFIA" in this picture!?!

Sorry! Er—they say he's th biggest Italian racketeer a murderer in the country

That's much better!

MAD #155, December 1972

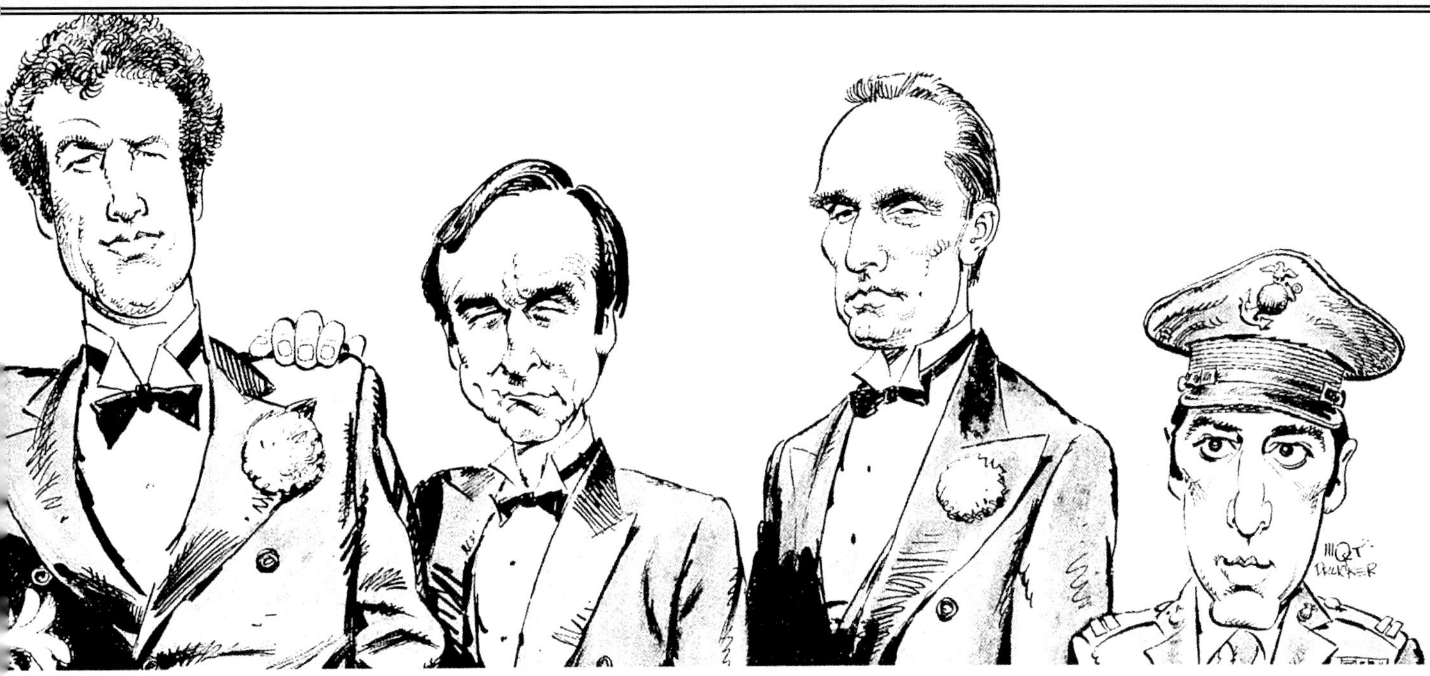

his is Sinny Minestrone, ıe Don's eldest son. He's ext in line, and it's only matter of time before he ets the Family business. hat is, of course, unless rival Family decides to ve him the business first.

This is the Don's second son, Freako. He's a sad, gentle soul. He cries at weddings and all kinds of Family crises. But he can also be a barrel of laughs. Just catch him at a funeral some time.

This is Tim Haven, the Don's adopted son. He's shrewd and smart. All his life, he dreamed of being a criminal lawyer. But he only finished half of his education —the "criminal" part.

And this is Micrin, the Don's youngest son. He's a college graduate, a veteran war hero, an honest law-abiding citizen —and a disgrace to the entire Family.

easy to see why Don Vino Minestrone is known as...

FATHER

ARTIST: MORT DRUCKER

WRITER: LARRY SIEGEL

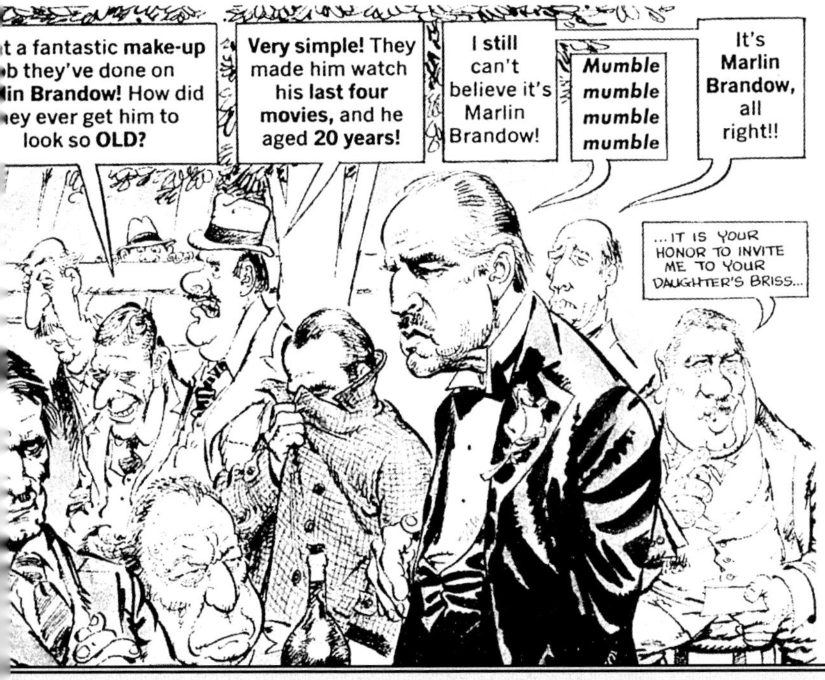
t a fantastic make-up b they've done on lin Brandow! How did ey ever get him to look so OLD?
Very simple! They made him watch his last four movies, and he aged 20 years!
I still can't believe it's Marlin Brandow!
Mumble mumble mumble mumble
It's Marlin Brandow, all right!!
...IT IS YOUR HONOR TO INVITE ME TO YOUR DAUGHTER'S BRISS...

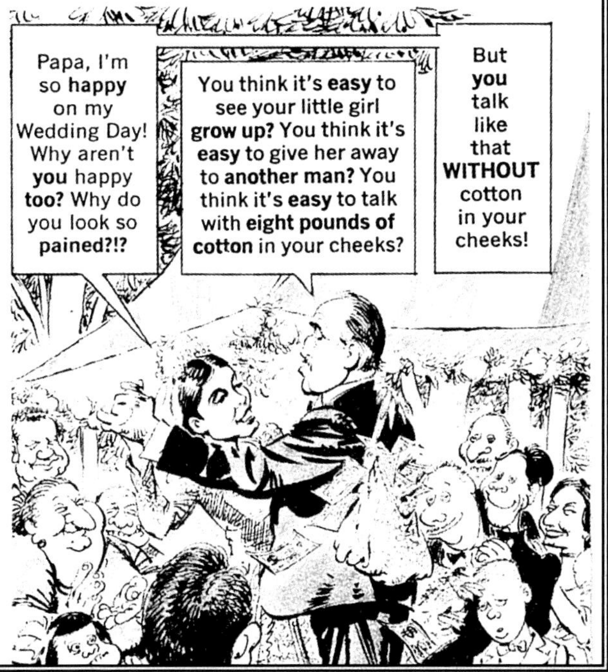
Papa, I'm so happy on my Wedding Day! Why aren't you happy too? Why do you look so pained?!?
You think it's easy to see your little girl grow up? You think it's easy to give her away to another man? You think it's easy to talk with eight pounds of cotton in your cheeks?
But you talk like that WITHOUT cotton in your cheeks!

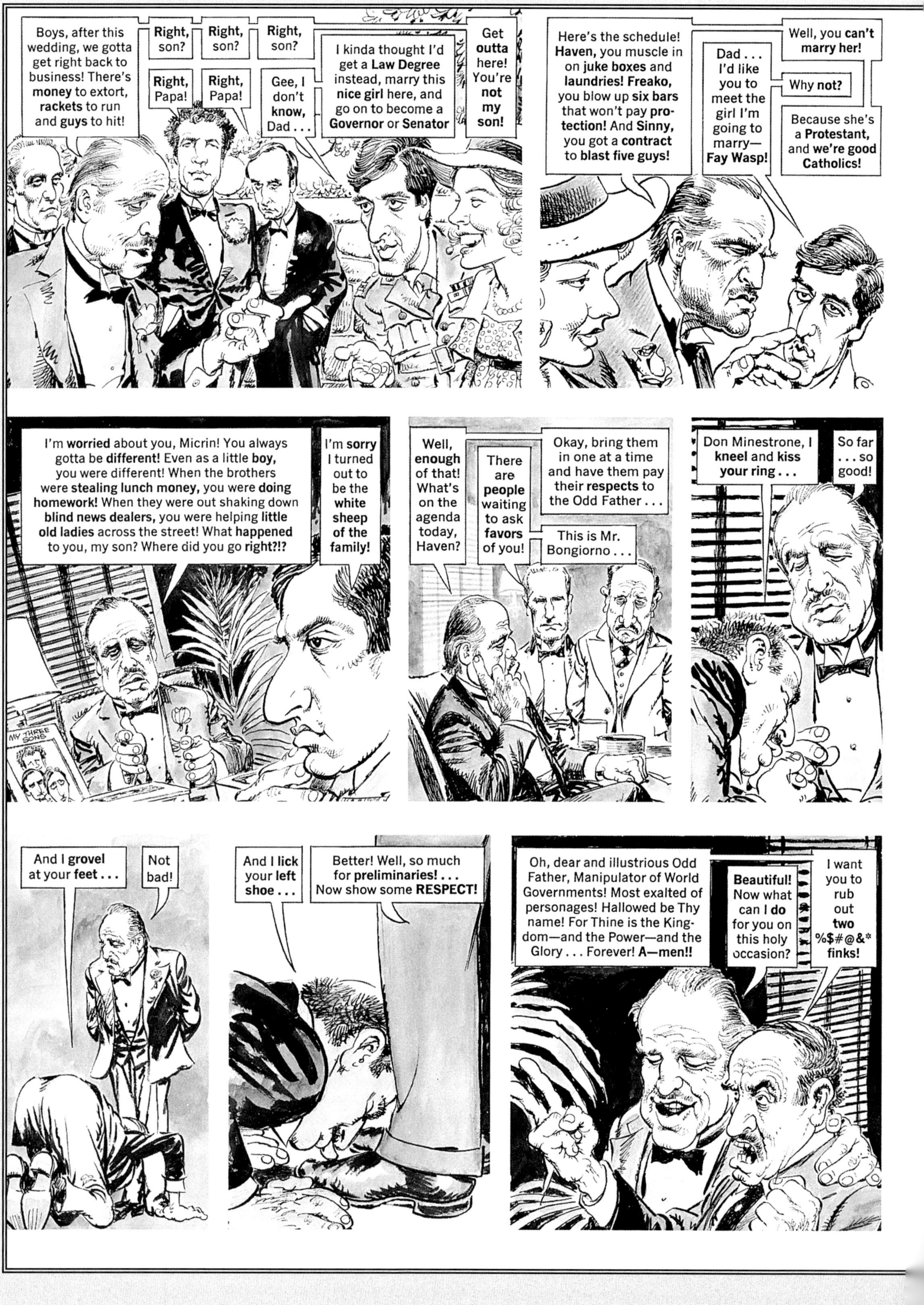
Boys, after this wedding, we gotta get right back to business! There's money to extort, rackets to run and guys to hit!
Right, son?
Right, Papa!
Right, son?
Right, Papa!
Right, son?
Gee, I don't know, Dad . . .
I kinda thought I'd get a Law Degree instead, marry this nice girl here, and go on to become a Governor or Senator
Get outta here! You're not my son!
Here's the schedule! Haven, you muscle in on juke boxes and laundries! Freako, you blow up six bars that won't pay protection! And Sinny, you got a contract to blast five guys!
Dad . . . I'd like you to meet the girl I'm going to marry—Fay Wasp!
Well, you can't marry her!
Why not?
Because she's a Protestant, and we're good Catholics!
I'm worried about you, Micrin! You always gotta be different! Even as a little boy, you were different! When the brothers were stealing lunch money, you were doing homework! When they were out shaking down blind news dealers, you were helping little old ladies across the street! What happened to you, my son? Where did you go right?!?
I'm sorry I turned out to be the white sheep of the family!
MY THREE SONS
Well, enough of that! What's on the agenda today, Haven?
There are people waiting to ask favors of you!
Okay, bring them in one at a time and have them pay their respects to the Odd Father . . .
This is Mr. Bongiorno . . .
Don Minestrone, I kneel and kiss your ring . . .
So far . . . so good!
And I grovel at your feet . . .
Not bad!
And I lick your left shoe . . .
Better! Well, so much for preliminaries! . . . Now show some RESPECT!
Oh, dear and illustrious Odd Father, Manipulator of World Governments! Most exalted of personages! Hallowed be Thy name! For Thine is the Kingdom—and the Power—and the Glory . . . Forever! A—men!!
Beautiful! Now what can I do for you on this holy occasion?
I want you to rub out two %$#@&* finks!

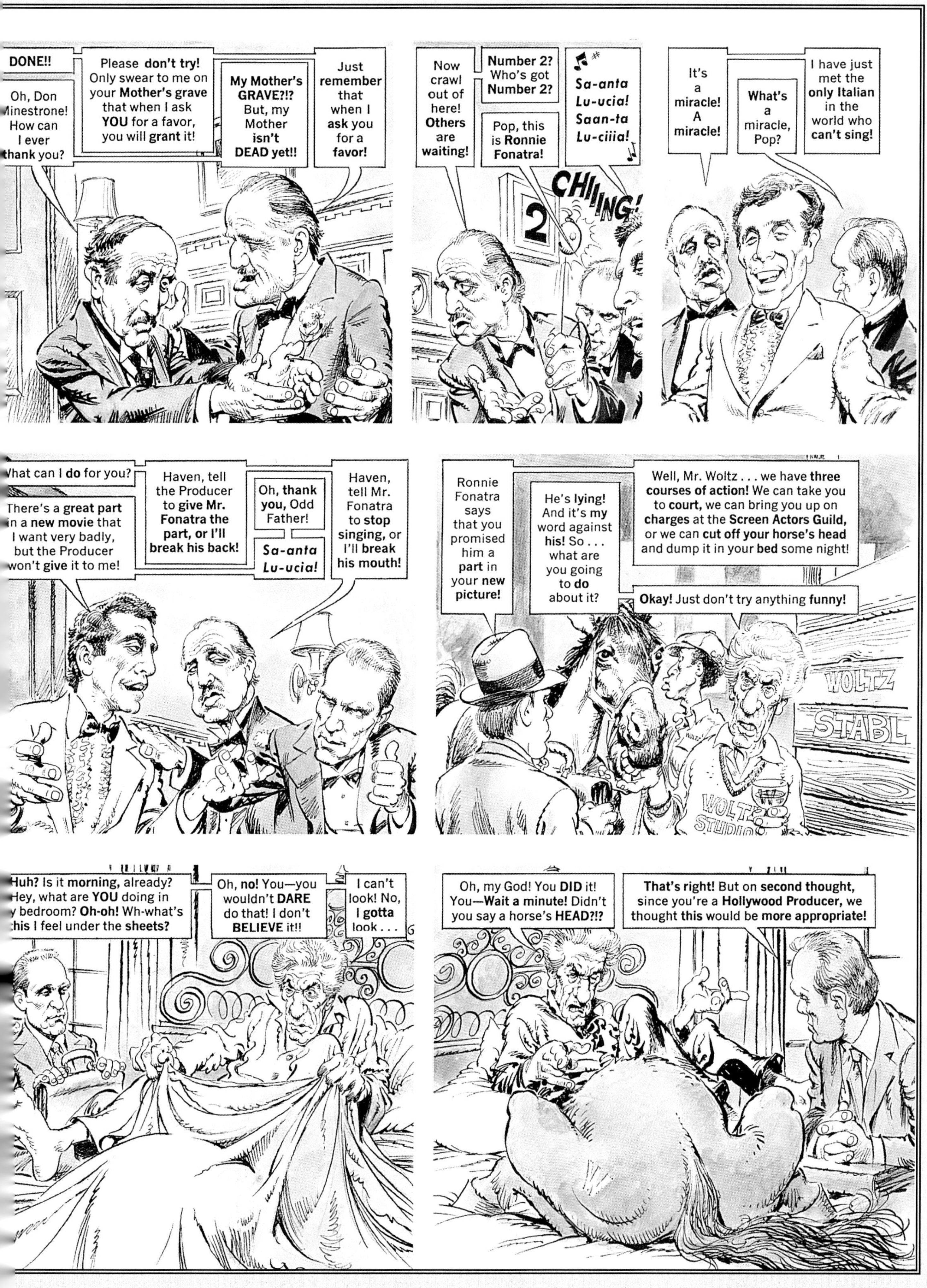
DONE!!
Oh, Don Minestrone! How can I ever thank you?
Please don't try! Only swear to me on your Mother's grave that when I ask YOU for a favor, you will grant it!
My Mother's GRAVE?!? But, my Mother isn't DEAD yet!!
Just remember that when I ask you for a favor!
Now crawl out of here! Others are waiting!
Number 2? Who's got Number 2?
Pop, this is Ronnie Fonatra!
Sa-anta Lu-ucia! Saan-ta Lu-ciiia!
CHIIING!
2
It's a miracle! A miracle!
What's a miracle, Pop?
I have just met the only Italian in the world who can't sing!
What can I do for you?
There's a great part in a new movie that I want very badly, but the Producer won't give it to me!
Haven, tell the Producer to give Mr. Fonatra the part, or I'll break his back!
Oh, thank you, Odd Father!
Sa-anta Lu-ucia!
Haven, tell Mr. Fonatra to stop singing, or I'll break his mouth!
Ronnie Fonatra says that you promised him a part in your new picture!
He's lying! And it's my word against his! So . . . what are you going to do about it?
Well, Mr. Woltz . . . we have three courses of action! We can take you to court, we can bring you up on charges at the Screen Actors Guild, or we can cut off your horse's head and dump it in your bed some night!
Okay! Just don't try anything funny!
WOLTZ
STABL
WOLTZ STUDIOS
Huh? Is it morning, already? Hey, what are YOU doing in y bedroom? Oh-oh! Wh-what's this I feel under the sheets?
Oh, no! You—you wouldn't DARE do that! I don't BELIEVE it!!
I can't look! No, I gotta look . . .
Oh, my God! You DID it! You—Wait a minute! Didn't you say a horse's HEAD?!?
That's right! But on second thought, since you're a Hollywood Producer, we thought this would be more appropriate!

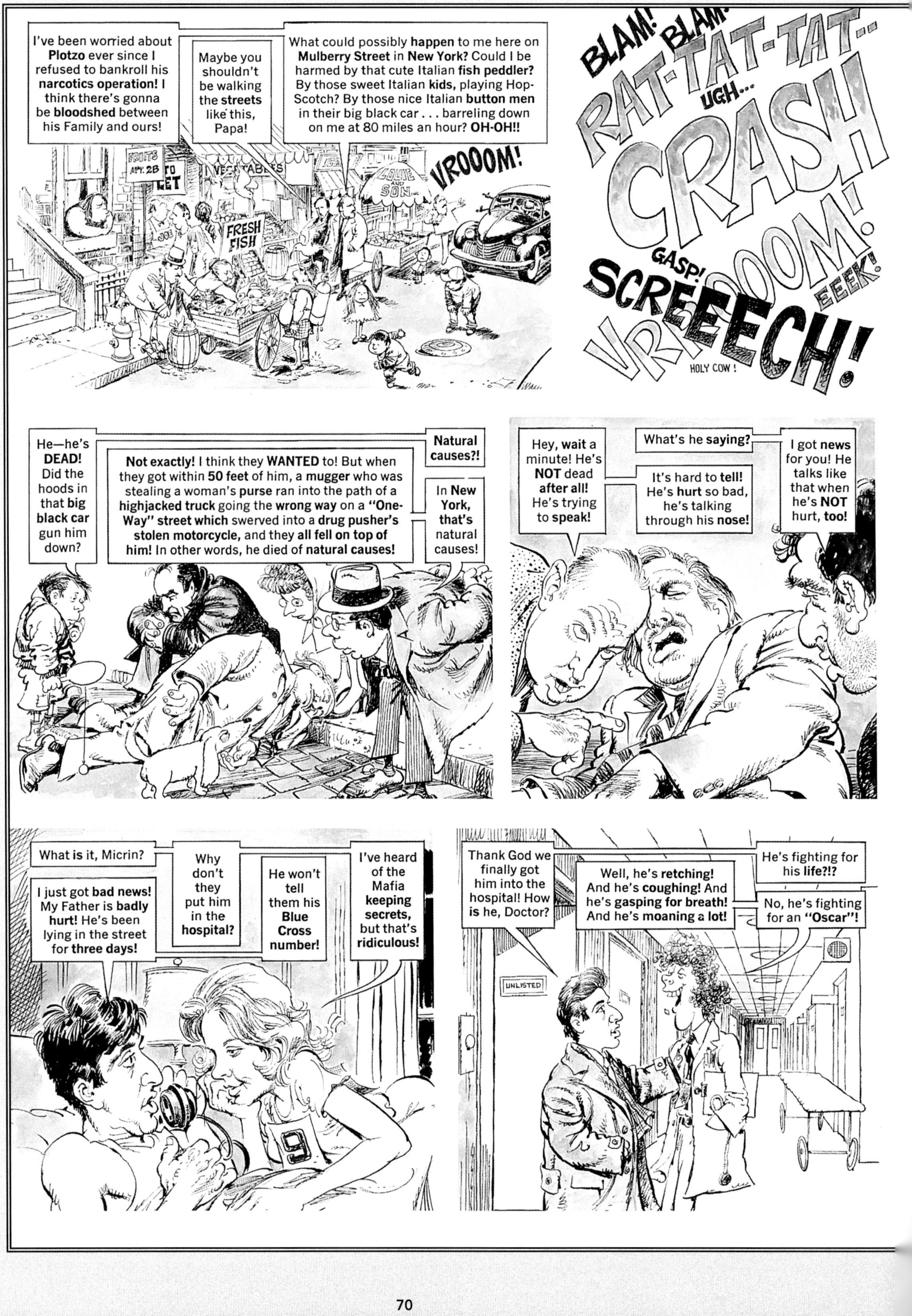
I've been worried about Plotzo ever since I refused to bankroll his narcotics operation! I think there's gonna be bloodshed between his Family and ours!
Maybe you shouldn't be walking the streets like this, Papa!
What could possibly happen to me here on Mulberry Street in New York? Could I be harmed by that cute Italian fish peddler? By those sweet Italian kids, playing Hop-Scotch? By those nice Italian button men in their big black car . . . barreling down on me at 80 miles an hour? OH-OH!!
FRUITS
APT. 2B
TO LET
FRESH FISH
VROOOM!
BLAM! BLAM!
RAT-TAT-TAT...
UGH...
CRASH
VROOOM!
GASP!
SCREEECH!
EEEK!
HOLY COW!
He—he's DEAD! Did the hoods in that big black car gun him down?
Not exactly! I think they WANTED to! But when they got within 50 feet of him, a mugger who was stealing a woman's purse ran into the path of a highjacked truck going the wrong way on a "One-Way" street which swerved into a drug pusher's stolen motorcycle, and they all fell on top of him! In other words, he died of natural causes!
Natural causes?!
In New York, that's natural causes!
Hey, wait a minute! He's NOT dead after all! He's trying to speak!
What's he saying?
It's hard to tell! He's hurt so bad, he's talking through his nose!
I got news for you! He talks like that when he's NOT hurt, too!
What is it, Micrin?
I just got bad news! My Father is badly hurt! He's been lying in the street for three days!
Why don't they put him in the hospital?
He won't tell them his Blue Cross number!
I've heard of the Mafia keeping secrets, but that's ridiculous!
Thank God we finally got him into the hospital! How is he, Doctor?
Well, he's retching! And he's coughing! And he's gasping for breath! And he's moaning a lot!
He's fighting for his life?!?
No, he's fighting for an "Oscar"!
UNLISTED

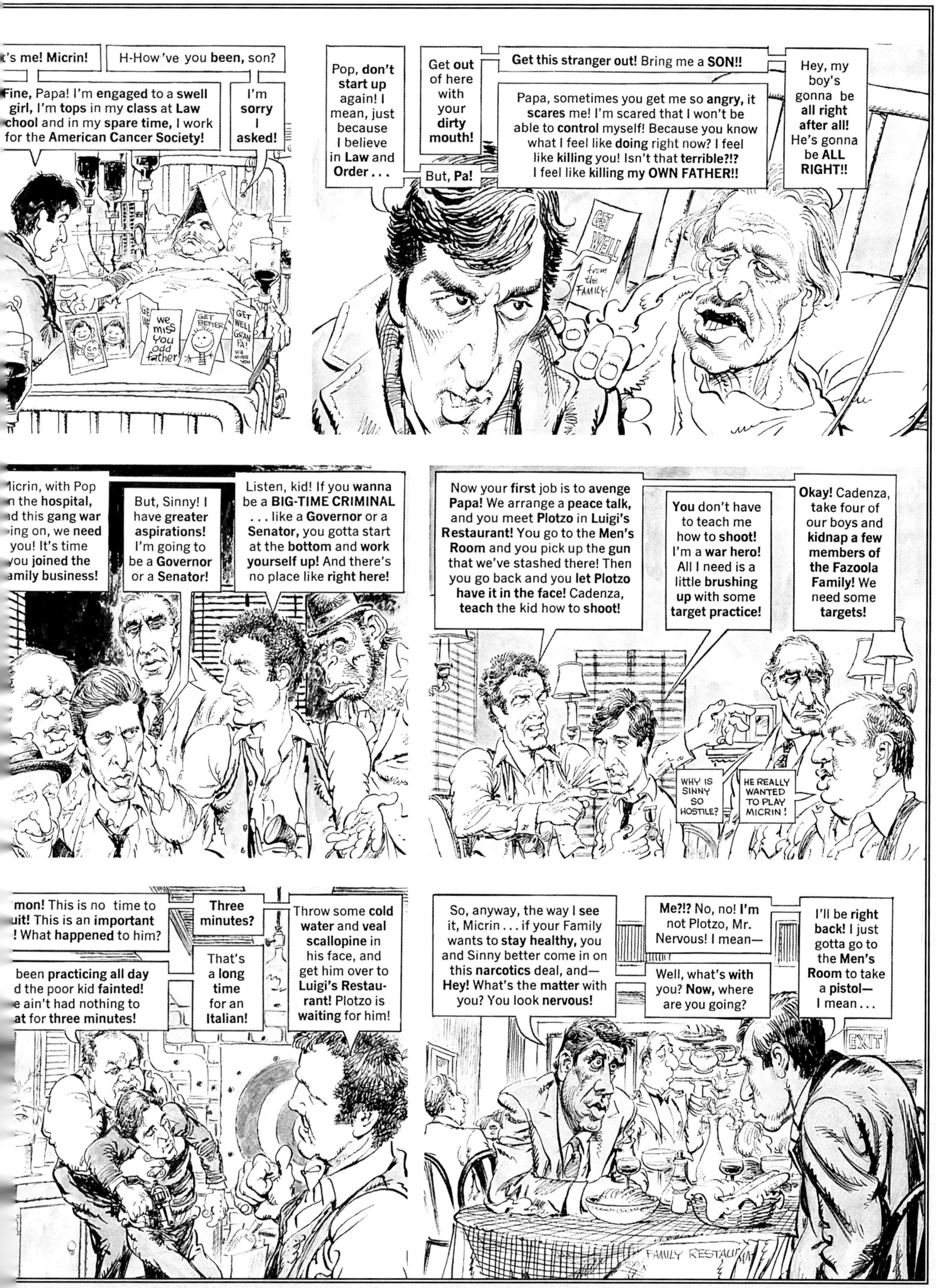

's me! Micrin!
H-How've you been, son?
Fine, Papa! I'm engaged to a swell girl, I'm tops in my class at Law chool and in my spare time, I work for the American Cancer Society!
I'm sorry I asked!
GET WELL GRAN PA!
we miss you odd father
GET BETTER
Pop, don't start up again! I mean, just because I believe in Law and Order . . .
Get out of here with your dirty mouth!
But, Pa!
Get this stranger out! Bring me a SON!!
Papa, sometimes you get me so angry, it scares me! I'm scared that I won't be able to control myself! Because you know what I feel like doing right now? I feel like killing you! Isn't that terrible?!? I feel like killing my OWN FATHER!!
Hey, my boy's gonna be all right after all! He's gonna be ALL RIGHT!!
GET WELL from the FAMILY
icrin, with Pop n the hospital, d this gang war ing on, we need you! It's time you joined the amily business!
But, Sinny! I have greater aspirations! I'm going to be a Governor or a Senator!
Listen, kid! If you wanna be a BIG-TIME CRIMINAL . . . like a Governor or a Senator, you gotta start at the bottom and work yourself up! And there's no place like right here!
Now your first job is to avenge Papa! We arrange a peace talk, and you meet Plotzo in Luigi's Restaurant! You go to the Men's Room and you pick up the gun that we've stashed there! Then you go back and you let Plotzo have it in the face! Cadenza, teach the kid how to shoot!
You don't have to teach me how to shoot! I'm a war hero! All I need is a little brushing up with some target practice!
Okay! Cadenza, take four of our boys and kidnap a few members of the Fazoola Family! We need some targets!
WHY IS SINNY SO HOSTILE?
HE REALLY WANTED TO PLAY MICRIN!
mon! This is no time to uit! This is an important ! What happened to him?
Three minutes?
been practicing all day d the poor kid fainted! e ain't had nothing to at for three minutes!
That's a long time for an Italian!
Throw some cold water and veal scallopine in his face, and get him over to Luigi's Restau- rant! Plotzo is waiting for him!
So, anyway, the way I see it, Micrin . . . if your Family wants to stay healthy, you and Sinny better come in on this narcotics deal, and— Hey! What's the matter with you? You look nervous!
Me?!? No, no! I'm not Plotzo, Mr. Nervous! I mean—
Well, what's with you? Now, where are you going?
I'll be right back! I just gotta go to the Men's Room to take a pistol— I mean . . .
EXIT
FAMILY RESTAURANT

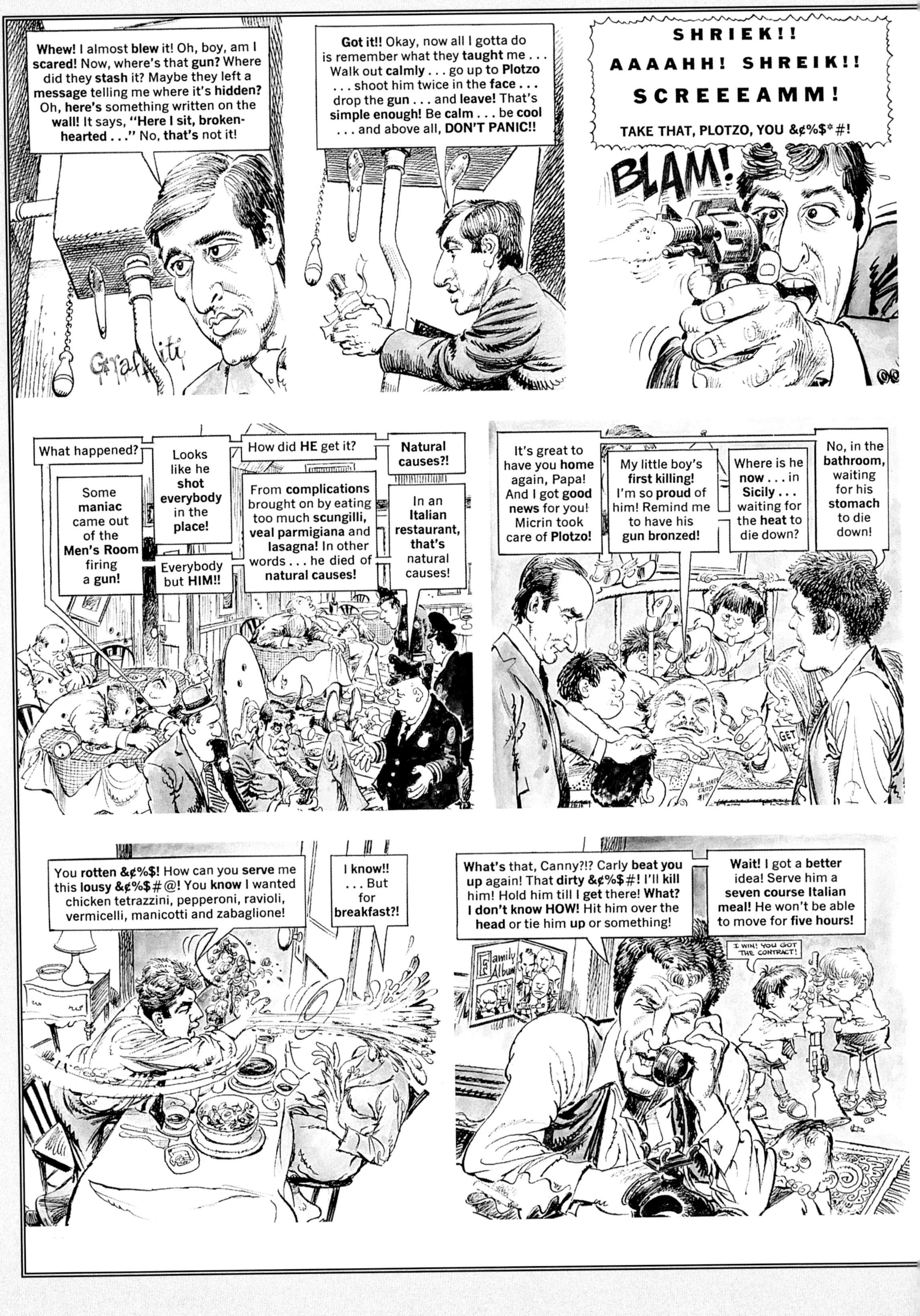
Whew! I almost blew it! Oh, boy, am I scared! Now, where's that gun? Where did they stash it? Maybe they left a message telling me where it's hidden? Oh, here's something written on the wall! It says, "Here I sit, broken-hearted . . ." No, that's not it!
Graffiti
Got it!! Okay, now all I gotta do is remember what they taught me . . . Walk out calmly . . . go up to Plotzo . . . shoot him twice in the face . . . drop the gun . . . and leave! That's simple enough! Be calm . . . be cool . . . and above all, DON'T PANIC!!
SHRIEK!! AAAAHH! SHREIK!! SCREEEAMM!
TAKE THAT, PLOTZO, YOU &¢%$*#!
BLAM!
What happened?
Some maniac came out of the Men's Room firing a gun!
Looks like he shot everybody in the place!
Everybody but HIM!!
How did HE get it?
From complications brought on by eating too much scungilli, veal parmigiana and lasagna! In other words . . . he died of natural causes!
Natural causes?!
In an Italian restaurant, that's natural causes!
It's great to have you home again, Papa! And I got good news for you! Micrin took care of Plotzo!
My little boy's first killing! I'm so proud of him! Remind me to have his gun bronzed!
Where is he now . . . in Sicily . . . waiting for the heat to die down?
No, in the bathroom, waiting for his stomach to die down!
You rotten &¢%$! How can you serve me this lousy &¢%$#@! You know I wanted chicken tetrazzini, pepperoni, ravioli, vermicelli, manicotti and zabaglione!
I know!! . . . But for breakfast?!
What's that, Canny?!? Carly beat you up again! That dirty &¢%$#! I'll kill him! Hold him till I get there! What? I don't know HOW! Hit him over the head or tie him up or something!
Wait! I got a better idea! Serve him a seven course Italian meal! He won't be able to move for five hours!
Family Album
I WIN! YOU GOT THE CONTRACT!

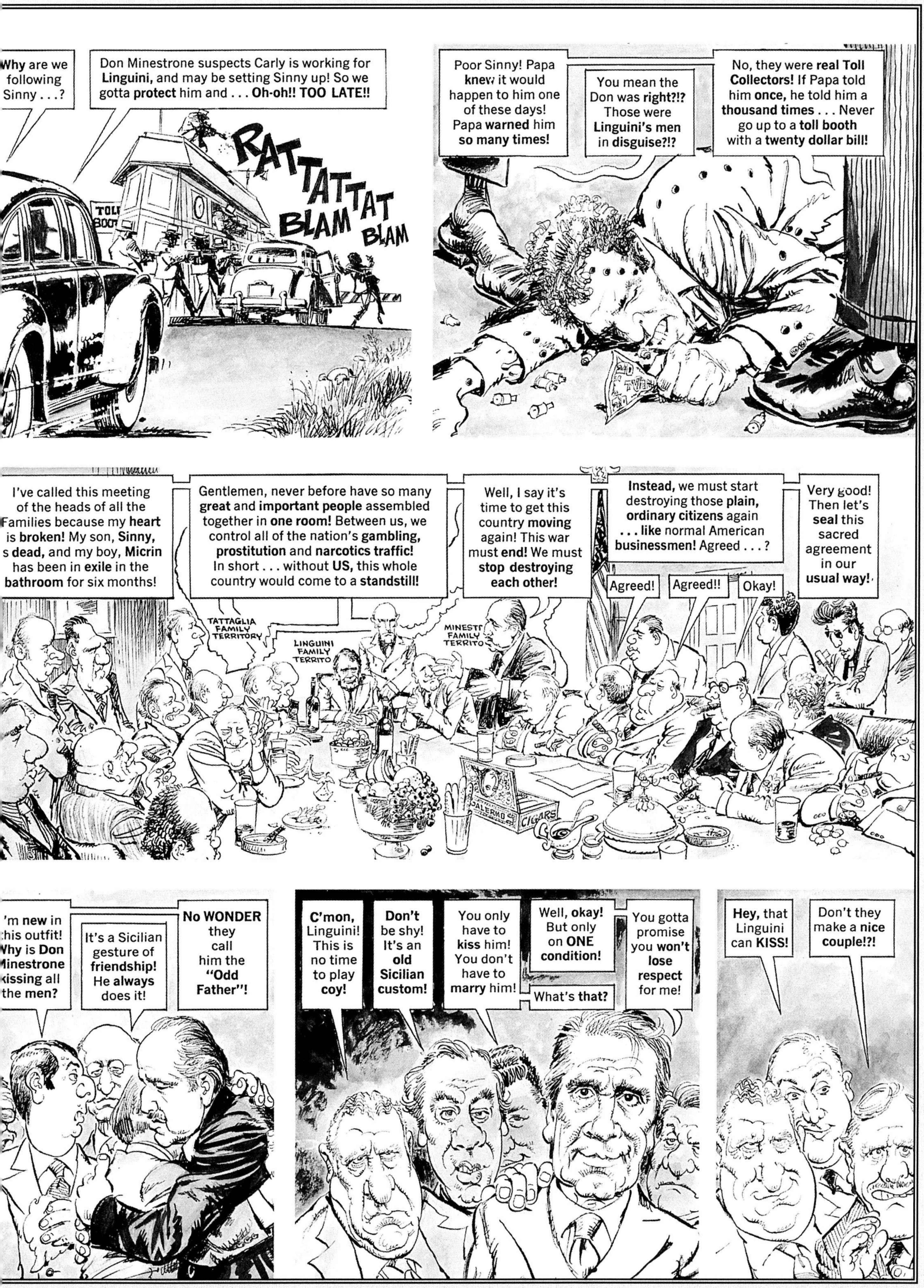
Why are we following Sinny . . . ?
Don Minestrone suspects Carly is working for **Linguini,** and may be setting Sinny up! So we gotta **protect** him and . . . **Oh-oh!! TOO LATE!!**
TOL BOOT
RATTATTAT
BLAM
BLAM
Poor Sinny! Papa **knew** it would happen to him one of these days! Papa **warned** him **so many times!**
You mean the Don was **right?!?** Those were **Linguini's men** in **disguise?!?**
No, they were **real Toll Collectors!** If Papa told him **once,** he told him a **thousand times . . .** Never go up to a **toll booth** with a **twenty dollar bill!**
I've called this meeting of the heads of all the Families because my **heart** is **broken!** My son, **Sinny,** s **dead,** and my boy, **Micrin** has been in **exile** in the **bathroom** for six months!
Gentlemen, never before have so many **great** and **important people** assembled together in **one room!** Between us, we control all of the nation's **gambling, prostitution** and **narcotics traffic!** In short . . . without **US,** this whole country would come to a **standstill!**
Well, I say it's time to get this country **moving** again! This war must **end!** We must **stop destroying each other!**
Instead, we must start destroying those **plain, ordinary citizens** again **. . . like** normal American **businessmen! Agreed . . . ?**
Agreed!
Agreed!!
Okay!
Very good! Then let's **seal** this sacred agreement in our **usual way!**
TATTAGLIA FAMILY TERRITORY
LINGUINI FAMILY TERRITO
MINESTI FAMILY TERRITO
PALERMO CIGARS
'm **new** in his outfit! Why is **Don** Minestrone kissing all the **men?**
It's a Sicilian gesture of **friendship!** He always does it!
No WONDER they call him the **"Odd Father"!**
C'mon, Linguini! This is no time to play **coy!**
Don't be shy! It's an **old Sicilian custom!**
You only have to **kiss** him! You don't have to **marry** him!
Well, **okay!** But only on **ONE condition!**
What's **that?**
You gotta promise you **won't lose respect** for me!
Hey, that Linguini can **KISS!**
Don't they make a **nice couple!?!**

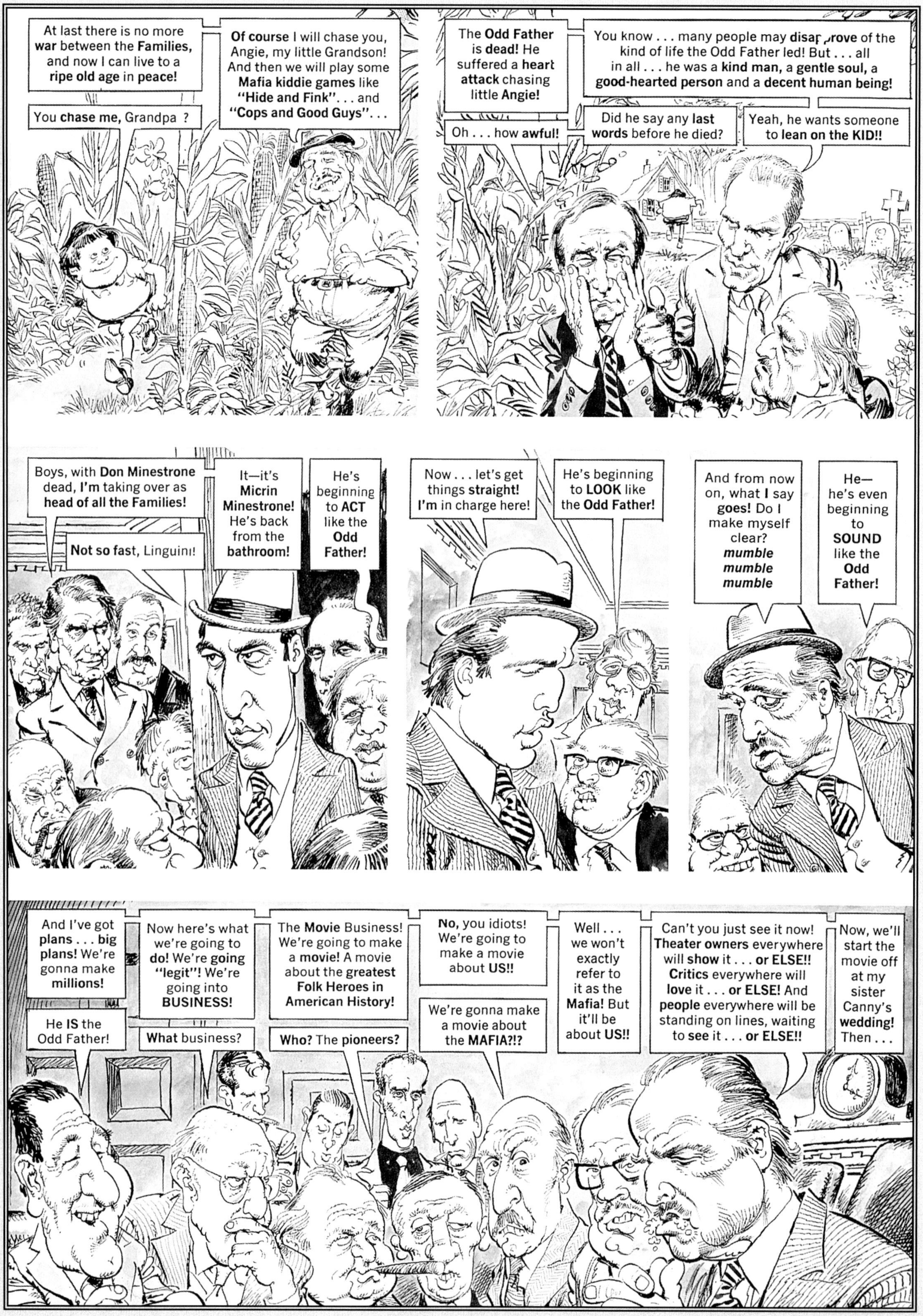
At last there is no more war between the Families, and now I can live to a ripe old age in peace!
You chase me, Grandpa ?
Of course I will chase you, Angie, my little Grandson! And then we will play some Mafia kiddie games like "Hide and Fink". . . and "Cops and Good Guys". . .
The Odd Father is dead! He suffered a heart attack chasing little Angie!
Oh . . . how awful!
You know . . . many people may disapprove of the kind of life the Odd Father led! But . . . all in all . . . he was a kind man, a gentle soul, a good-hearted person and a decent human being!
Did he say any last words before he died?
Yeah, he wants someone to lean on the KID!!
Boys, with Don Minestrone dead, I'm taking over as head of all the Families!
Not so fast, Linguini!
It—it's Micrin Minestrone! He's back from the bathroom!
He's beginning to ACT like the Odd Father!
Now . . . let's get things straight! I'm in charge here!
He's beginning to LOOK like the Odd Father!
And from now on, what I say goes! Do I make myself clear? mumble mumble mumble
He— he's even beginning to SOUND like the Odd Father!
And I've got plans . . . big plans! We're gonna make millions!
He IS the Odd Father!
Now here's what we're going to do! We're going "legit"! We're going into BUSINESS!
What business?
The Movie Business! We're going to make a movie! A movie about the greatest Folk Heroes in American History!
Who? The pioneers?
No, you idiots! We're going to make a movie about US!!
We're gonna make a movie about the MAFIA?!?
Well . . . we won't exactly refer to it as the Mafia! But it'll be about US!!
Can't you just see it now! Theater owners everywhere will show it . . . or ELSE!! Critics everywhere will love it . . . or ELSE! And people everywhere will be standing on lines, waiting to see it . . . or ELSE!!
Now, we'll start the movie off at my sister Canny's wedding! Then . . .

TO A LYING SWEETHEART

The sweet talk oozes from your lips
  Like barrels of molasses;
If all your lies were dollars, you
  Could buy and sell Onassis!

"*MAD* Nasty Cards" were a bonus feature in 1969's *MAD Follies* #7.
Written by Frank Jacobs, *MAD*'s "poet laureate," they were illustrated by
an assortment of the magazine's regular artists. This one—an early example
of his full-color work—was Mort Drucker's contribution to the feature.

THERE'S GOLD IN OLDIES DEPT.

What's been just about the biggest thing going in the movies for the pa couple of years? Nostalgia, right? The film-makers took us back to the 1920 in "The Boy Friend", to the '30's in "Paper Moon", to the '40's in "Summer '42", and to the '50's in "The Last Picture Show". So that just about uses u all the important nostalgia decades, and now on to other things, right? Wron

AMERICAN

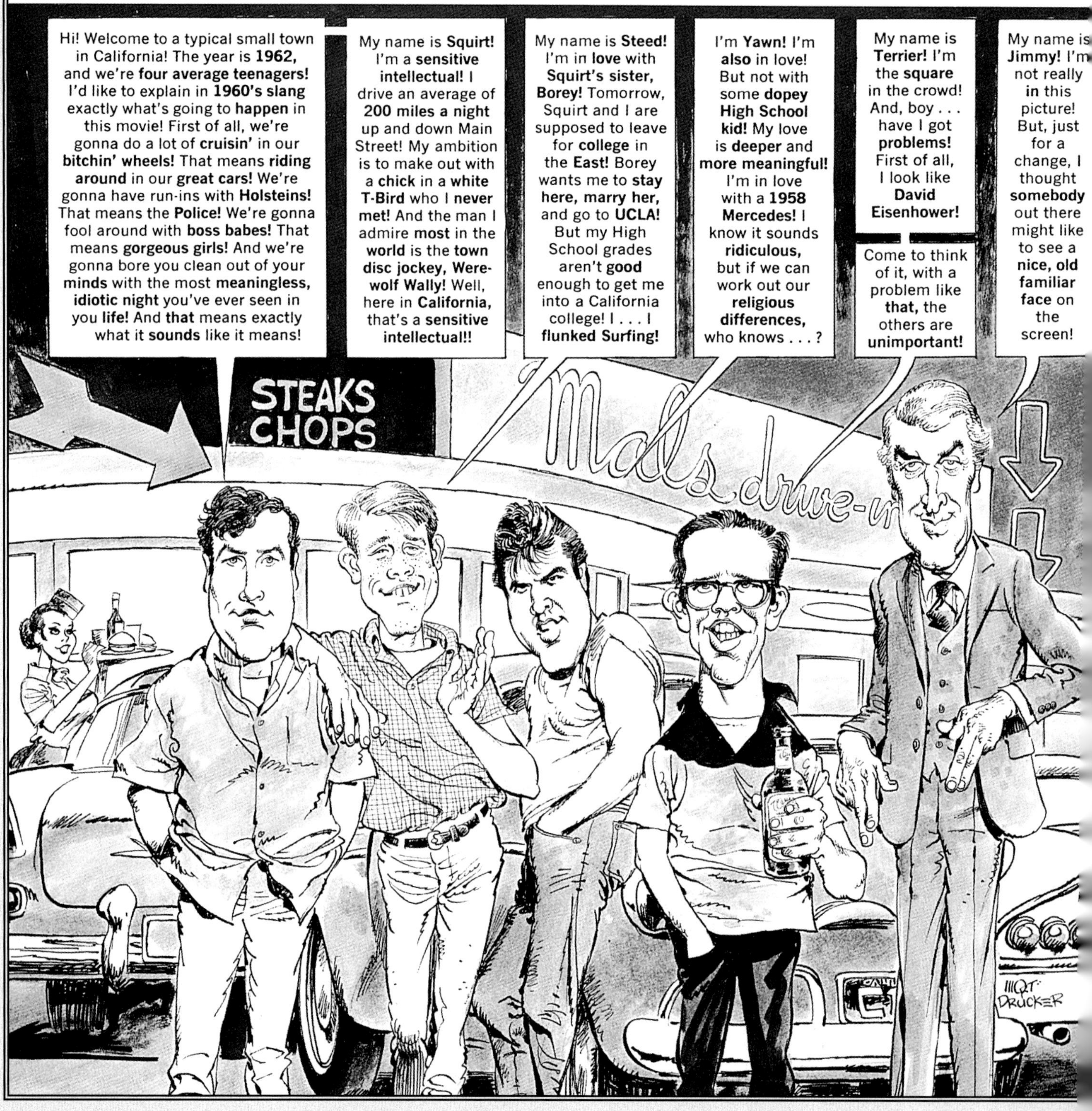
Hi! Welcome to a typical small town in California! The year is **1962**, and we're **four average teenagers!** I'd like to explain in **1960's slang** exactly what's going to **happen** in this movie! First of all, we're gonna do a lot of **cruisin'** in our **bitchin' wheels!** That means **riding around** in our **great cars!** We're gonna have run-ins with **Holsteins!** That means the **Police!** We're gonna fool around with **boss babes!** That means **gorgeous girls!** And we're gonna bore you clean out of your **minds** with the most **meaningless, idiotic night** you've ever seen in you **life!** And **that** means exactly what it **sounds** like it means!
My name is **Squirt!** I'm a **sensitive intellectual!** I drive an average of **200 miles a night** up and down Main Street! My ambition is to make out with a **chick** in a **white T-Bird** who I **never met!** And the man I admire **most** in the **world** is the **town disc jockey, Werewolf Wally!** Well, here in **California,** that's a **sensitive intellectual!!**
My name is **Steed!** I'm in **love** with **Squirt's sister, Borey!** Tomorrow, Squirt and I are supposed to leave for **college** in the **East!** Borey wants me to **stay here, marry her,** and go to **UCLA!** But my High School grades aren't **good** enough to get me into a California college! I . . . I **flunked Surfing!**
I'm **Yawn!** I'm **also** in love! But not with some **dopey High School kid!** My love is **deeper** and **more meaningful!** I'm in love with a **1958 Mercedes!** I know it sounds **ridiculous,** but if we can work out our **religious differences,** who knows . . . ?
My name is **Terrier!** I'm the **square** in the crowd! And, boy . . . have I got **problems!** First of all, I look like **David Eisenhower!**
Come to think of it, with a problem like **that,** the others are **unimportant!**
My name is **Jimmy!** I'm not really **in** this picture! But, just for a change, I thought **somebody** out there might like to see a **nice, old familiar face** on the screen!
STEAKS CHOPS
Mel's drive-in
DRUCKER

Some producer has just discovered another decade! What else? The 1960's! Okay, all you nostalgic 12-year-olds out there, it's time now to go back to the "Soaring Sixties" and reminisce over your glorious past—just a few minutes ago. So bring out the banners, fall into line, and get ready to march in one more parade down "Memory Lane, U.S.A."...while we here at MAD start tossing

CONFETTI

ARTIST:
MORT DRUCKER

WRITER:
LARRY SIEGEL

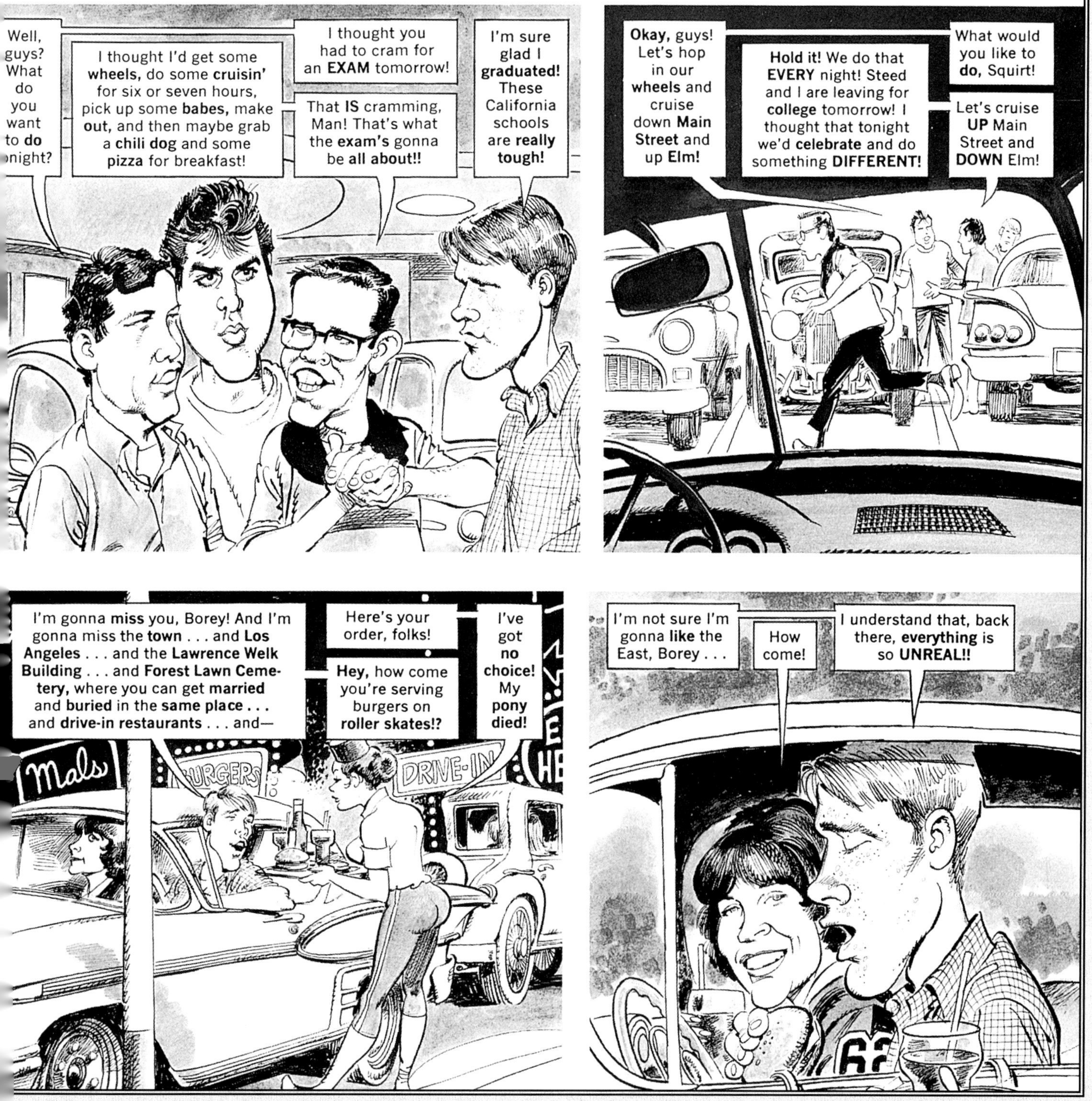
Well, guys? What do you want to do tonight?
I thought I'd get some wheels, do some cruisin' for six or seven hours, pick up some babes, make out, and then maybe grab a chili dog and some pizza for breakfast!
I thought you had to cram for an EXAM tomorrow!
That IS cramming, Man! That's what the exam's gonna be all about!!
I'm sure glad I graduated! These California schools are really tough!
Okay, guys! Let's hop in our wheels and cruise down Main Street and up Elm!
Hold it! We do that EVERY night! Steed and I are leaving for college tomorrow! I thought that tonight we'd celebrate and do something DIFFERENT!
What would you like to do, Squirt!
Let's cruise UP Main Street and DOWN Elm!
I'm gonna miss you, Borey! And I'm gonna miss the town . . . and Los Angeles . . . and the Lawrence Welk Building . . . and Forest Lawn Cemetery, where you can get married and buried in the same place . . . and drive-in restaurants . . . and—
Here's your order, folks!
Hey, how come you're serving burgers on roller skates!?
I've got no choice! My pony died!
Mals
BURGERS
DRIVE-IN
I'm not sure I'm gonna like the East, Borey . . .
How come!
I understand that, back there, everything is so UNREAL!!

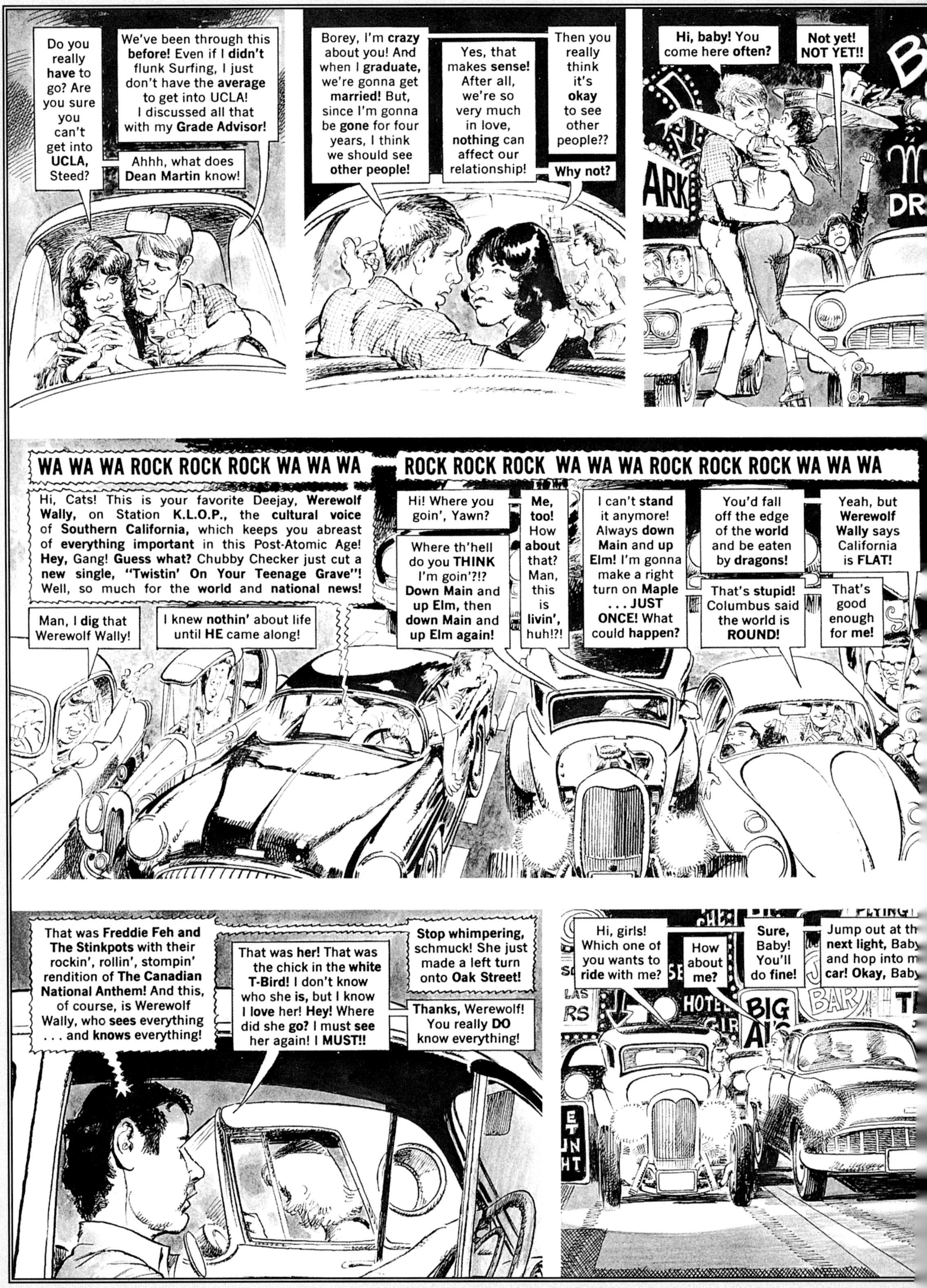
Do you really have to go? Are you sure you can't get into UCLA, Steed?
We've been through this before! Even if I didn't flunk Surfing, I just don't have the average to get into UCLA! I discussed all that with my Grade Advisor!
Ahhh, what does Dean Martin know!
Borey, I'm crazy about you! And when I graduate, we're gonna get married! But, since I'm gonna be gone for four years, I think we should see other people!
Yes, that makes sense! After all, we're so very much in love, nothing can affect our relationship!
Then you really think it's okay to see other people??
Why not?
Hi, baby! You come here often?
Not yet! NOT YET!!
WA WA WA ROCK ROCK ROCK WA WA WA
ROCK ROCK ROCK WA WA WA ROCK ROCK ROCK WA WA WA
Hi, Cats! This is your favorite Deejay, Werewolf Wally, on Station K.L.O.P., the cultural voice of Southern California, which keeps you abreast of everything important in this Post-Atomic Age! Hey, Gang! Guess what? Chubby Checker just cut a new single, "Twistin' On Your Teenage Grave"! Well, so much for the world and national news!
Man, I dig that Werewolf Wally!
I knew nothin' about life until HE came along!
Hi! Where you goin', Yawn?
Where th'hell do you THINK I'm goin'?!? Down Main and up Elm, then down Main and up Elm again!
Me, too! How about that? Man, this is livin', huh!?!
I can't stand it anymore! Always down Main and up Elm! I'm gonna make a right turn on Maple . . . JUST ONCE! What could happen?
You'd fall off the edge of the world and be eaten by dragons!
Yeah, but Werewolf Wally says California is FLAT!
That's stupid! Columbus said the world is ROUND!
That's good enough for me!
That was Freddie Feh and The Stinkpots with their rockin', rollin', stompin' rendition of The Canadian National Anthem! And this, of course, is Werewolf Wally, who sees everything . . . and knows everything!
That was her! That was the chick in the white T-Bird! I don't know who she is, but I know I love her! Hey! Where did she go? I must see her again! I MUST!!
Stop whimpering, schmuck! She just made a left turn onto Oak Street!
Thanks, Werewolf! You really DO know everything!
Hi, girls! Which one of you wants to ride with me?
How about me?
Sure, Baby! You'll do fine!
Jump out at th next light, Baby and hop into m car! Okay, Baby

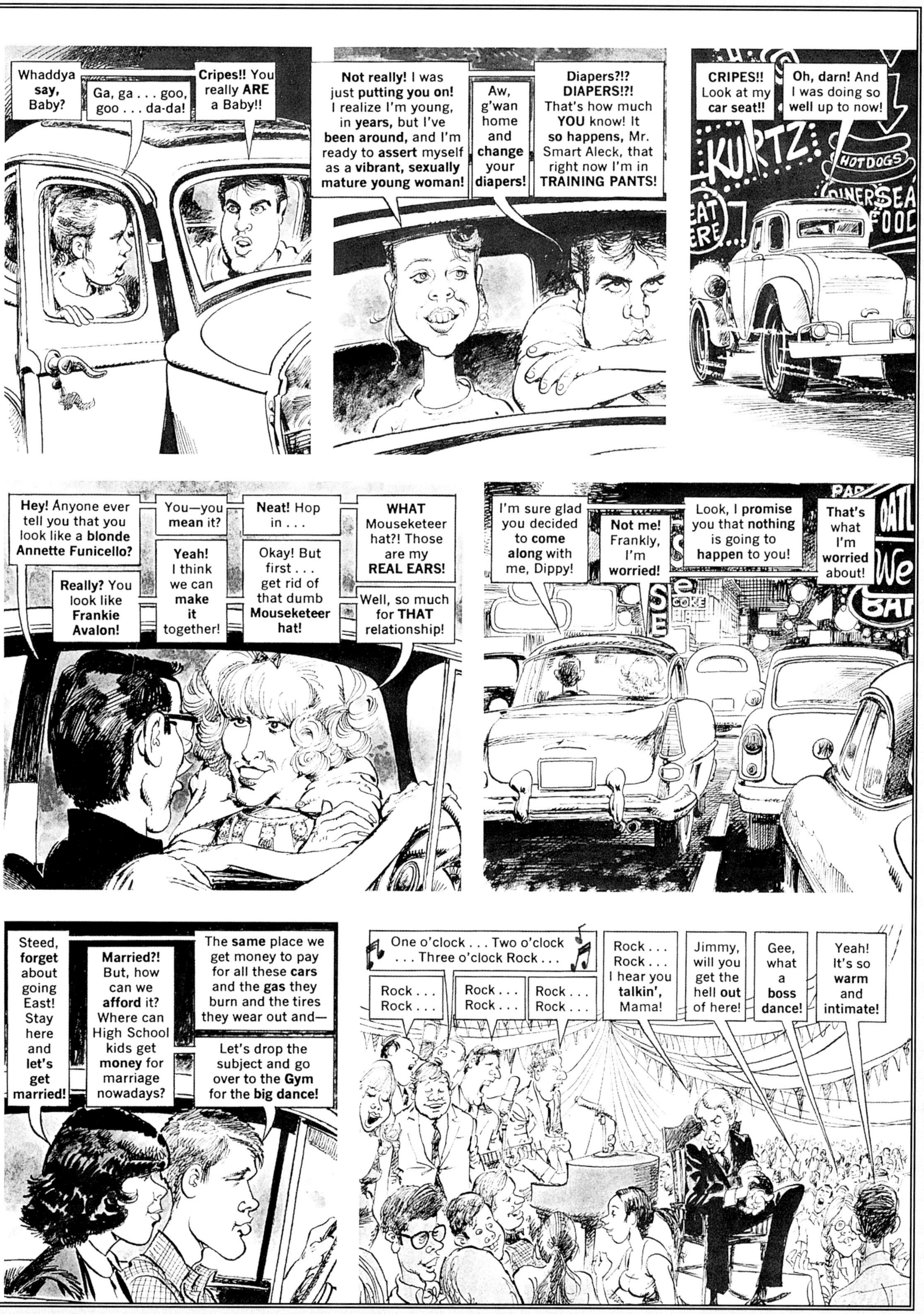
Whaddya say, Baby?
Ga, ga . . . goo, goo . . . da-da!
Cripes!! You really ARE a Baby!!
Not really! I was just putting you on! I realize I'm young, in years, but I've been around, and I'm ready to assert myself as a vibrant, sexually mature young woman!
Aw, g'wan home and change your diapers!
Diapers?!? DIAPERS!?! That's how much YOU know! It so happens, Mr. Smart Aleck, that right now I'm in TRAINING PANTS!
CRIPES!! Look at my car seat!!
Oh, darn! And I was doing so well up to now!
KURTZ
HOT DOGS
DINER SEA FOOD
EAT HERE
Hey! Anyone ever tell you that you look like a blonde Annette Funicello?
Really? You look like Frankie Avalon!
You—you mean it?
Yeah! I think we can make it together!
Neat! Hop in . . .
Okay! But first . . . get rid of that dumb Mouseketeer hat!
WHAT Mouseketeer hat?! Those are my REAL EARS!
Well, so much for THAT relationship!
I'm sure glad you decided to come along with me, Dippy!
Not me! Frankly, I'm worried!
Look, I promise you that nothing is going to happen to you!
That's what I'm worried about!
Steed, forget about going East! Stay here and let's get married!
Married?! But, how can we afford it? Where can High School kids get money for marriage nowadays?
The same place we get money to pay for all these cars and the gas they burn and the tires they wear out and—
Let's drop the subject and go over to the Gym for the big dance!
One o'clock . . . Two o'clock . . . Three o'clock Rock . . .
Rock . . . Rock . . .
Rock . . . Rock . . .
Rock . . . Rock . . .
Rock . . . Rock . . . I hear you talkin', Mama!
Jimmy, will you get the hell out of here!
Gee, what a boss dance!
Yeah! It's so warm and intimate!

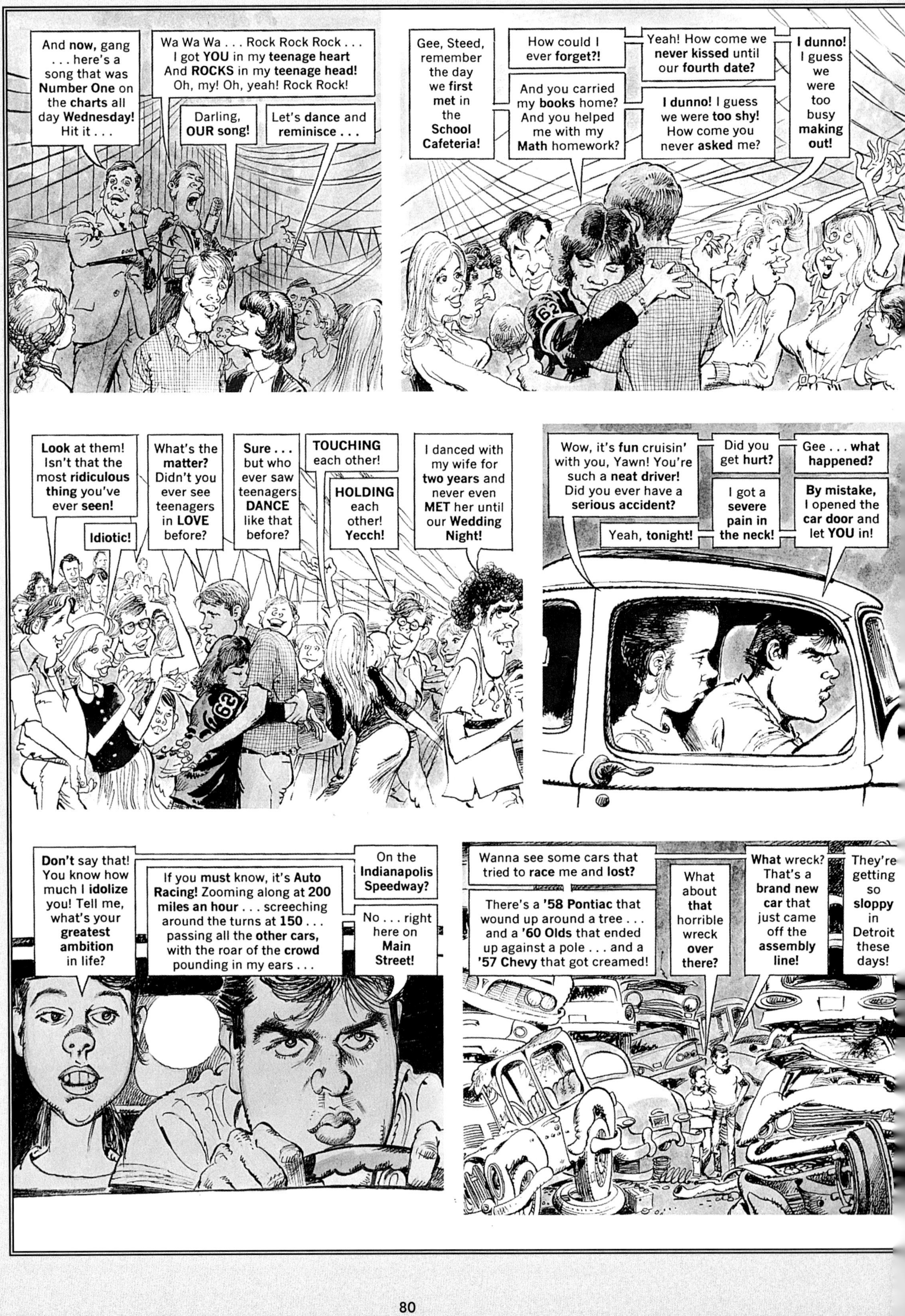
And now, gang . . . here's a song that was Number One on the charts all day Wednesday! Hit it . . .
Wa Wa Wa . . . Rock Rock Rock . . . I got YOU in my teenage heart And ROCKS in my teenage head! Oh, my! Oh, yeah! Rock Rock!
Darling, OUR song!
Let's dance and reminisce . . .
Gee, Steed, remember the day we first met in the School Cafeteria!
How could I ever forget?!
And you carried my books home? And you helped me with my Math homework?
Yeah! How come we never kissed until our fourth date?
I dunno! I guess we were too shy! How come you never asked me?
I dunno! I guess we were too busy making out!
Look at them! Isn't that the most ridiculous thing you've ever seen!
Idiotic!
What's the matter? Didn't you ever see teenagers in LOVE before?
Sure . . . but who ever saw teenagers DANCE like that before?
TOUCHING each other!
HOLDING each other! Yecch!
I danced with my wife for two years and never even MET her until our Wedding Night!
Wow, it's fun cruisin' with you, Yawn! You're such a neat driver! Did you ever have a serious accident?
Yeah, tonight!
Did you get hurt?
I got a severe pain in the neck!
Gee . . . what happened?
By mistake, I opened the car door and let YOU in!
Don't say that! You know how much I idolize you! Tell me, what's your greatest ambition in life?
If you must know, it's Auto Racing! Zooming along at 200 miles an hour . . . screeching around the turns at 150 . . . passing all the other cars, with the roar of the crowd pounding in my ears . . .
On the Indianapolis Speedway?
No . . . right here on Main Street!
Wanna see some cars that tried to race me and lost?
There's a '58 Pontiac that wound up around a tree . . . and a '60 Olds that ended up against a pole . . . and a '57 Chevy that got creamed!
What about that horrible wreck over there?
What wreck? That's a brand new car that just came off the assembly line!
They're getting so sloppy in Detroit these days!

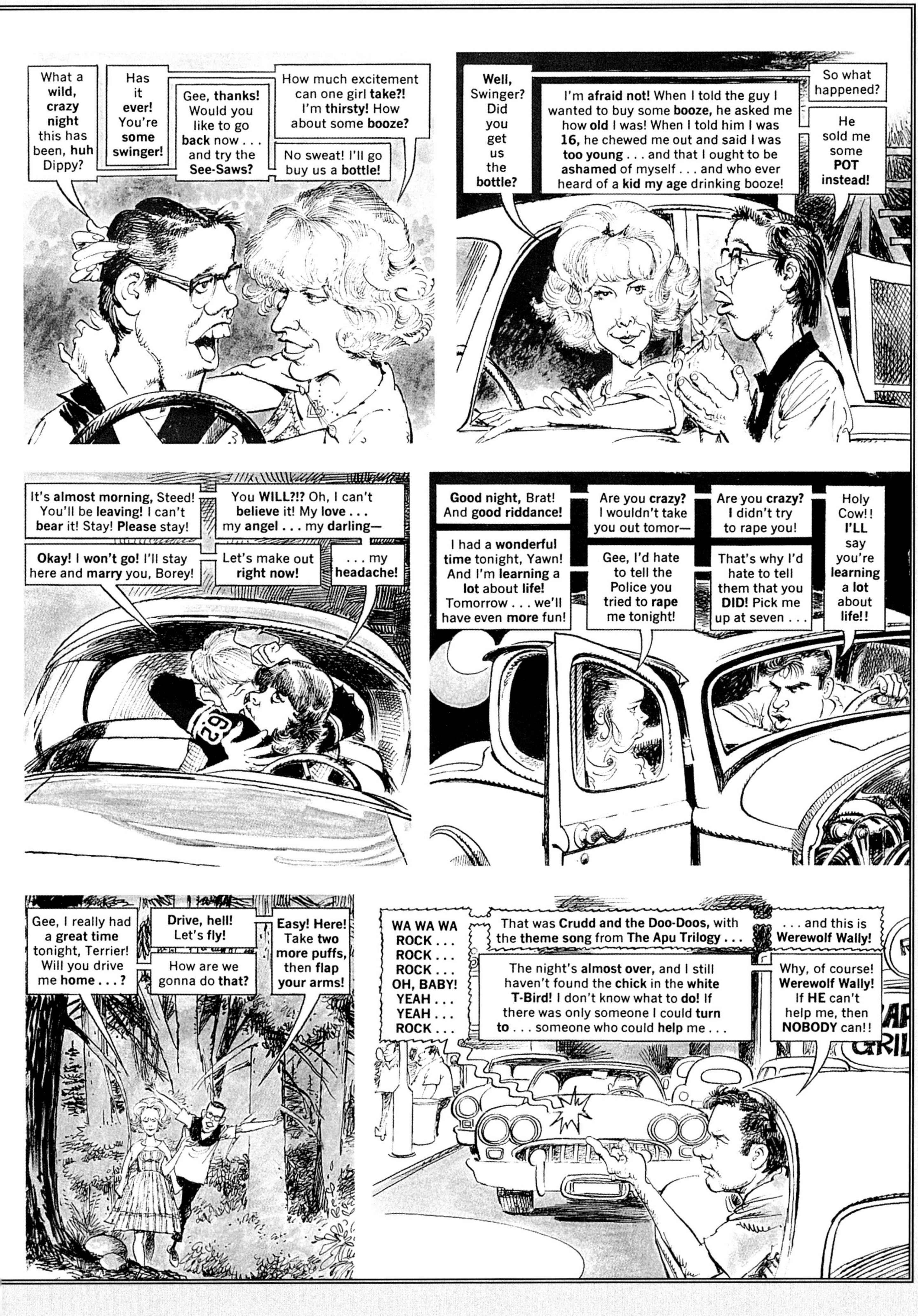
What a wild, crazy night this has been, huh Dippy?
Has it ever! You're some swinger!
Gee, thanks! Would you like to go back now . . . and try the See-Saws?
How much excitement can one girl take?! I'm thirsty! How about some booze?
No sweat! I'll go buy us a bottle!
Well, Swinger? Did you get us the bottle?
I'm afraid not! When I told the guy I wanted to buy some booze, he asked me how old I was! When I told him I was 16, he chewed me out and said I was too young . . . and that I ought to be ashamed of myself . . . and who ever heard of a kid my age drinking booze!
So what happened?
He sold me some POT instead!
It's almost morning, Steed! You'll be leaving! I can't bear it! Stay! Please stay!
Okay! I won't go! I'll stay here and marry you, Borey!
You WILL?!? Oh, I can't believe it! My love . . . my angel . . . my darling—
Let's make out right now!
. . . my headache!
Good night, Brat! And good riddance!
I had a wonderful time tonight, Yawn! And I'm learning a lot about life! Tomorrow . . . we'll have even more fun!
Are you crazy? I wouldn't take you out tomor—
Gee, I'd hate to tell the Police you tried to rape me tonight!
Are you crazy? I didn't try to rape you!
That's why I'd hate to tell them that you DID! Pick me up at seven . . .
Holy Cow!! I'LL say you're learning a lot about life!!
Gee, I really had a great time tonight, Terrier! Will you drive me home . . . ?
Drive, hell! Let's fly!
How are we gonna do that?
Easy! Here! Take two more puffs, then flap your arms!
WA WA WA ROCK . . . ROCK . . . ROCK . . . OH, BABY! YEAH . . . YEAH . . . ROCK . . .
That was Crudd and the Doo-Doos, with the theme song from The Apu Trilogy . . .
. . . and this is Werewolf Wally!
The night's almost over, and I still haven't found the chick in the white T-Bird! I don't know what to do! If there was only someone I could turn to . . . someone who could help me . . .
Why, of course! Werewolf Wally! If HE can't help me, then NOBODY can!!

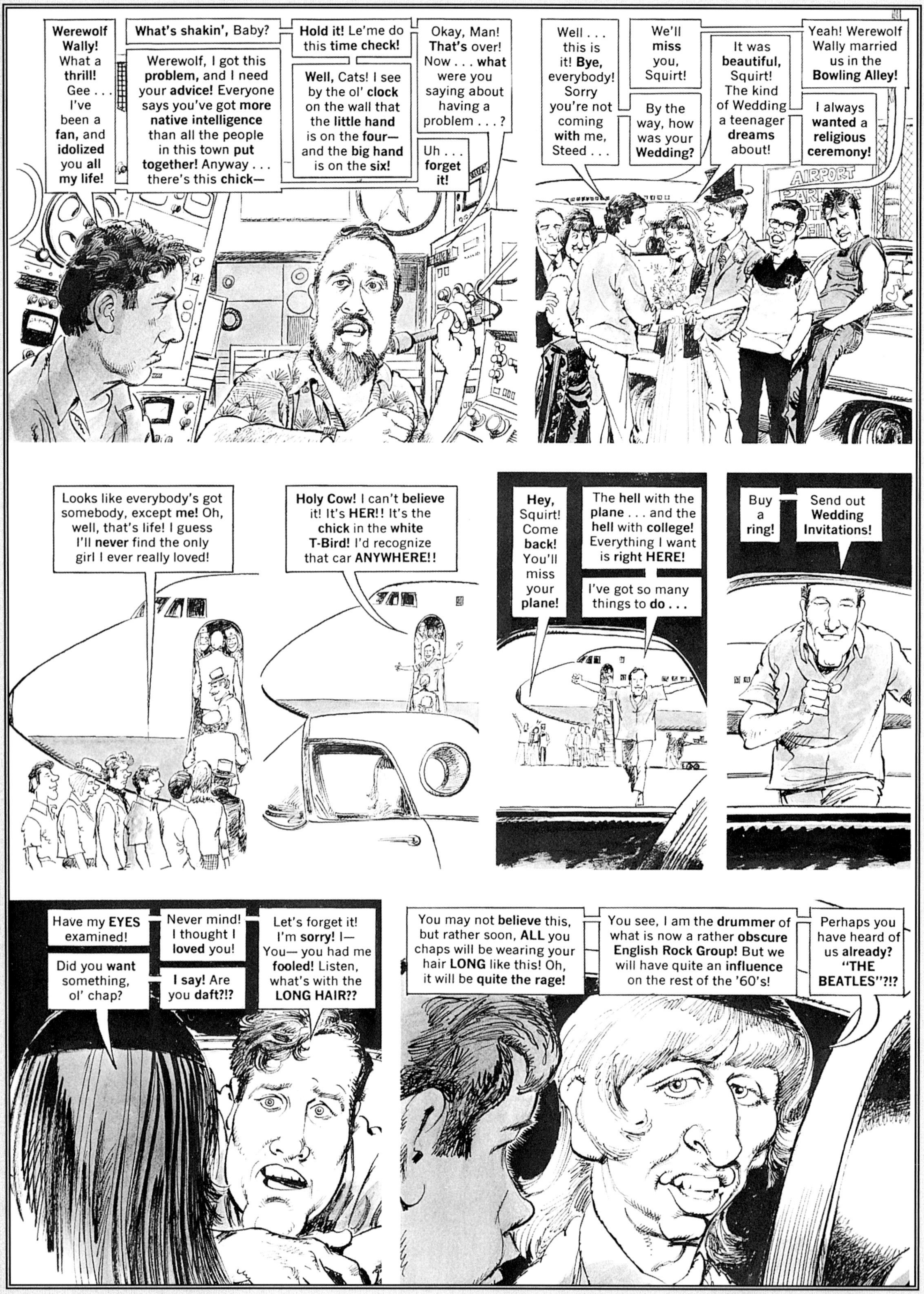
Werewolf Wally! What a thrill! Gee . . . I've been a fan, and idolized you all my life!
What's shakin', Baby?
Werewolf, I got this problem, and I need your advice! Everyone says you've got more native intelligence than all the people in this town put together! Anyway . . . there's this chick—
Hold it! Le'me do this time check!
Well, Cats! I see by the ol' clock on the wall that the little hand is on the four— and the big hand is on the six!
Okay, Man! That's over! Now . . . what were you saying about having a problem . . . ?
Uh . . . forget it!
Well . . . this is it! Bye, everybody! Sorry you're not coming with me, Steed . . .
We'll miss you, Squirt!
By the way, how was your Wedding?
It was beautiful, Squirt! The kind of Wedding a teenager dreams about!
Yeah! Werewolf Wally married us in the Bowling Alley!
I always wanted a religious ceremony!
AIRPORT
Looks like everybody's got somebody, except me! Oh, well, that's life! I guess I'll never find the only girl I ever really loved!
Holy Cow! I can't believe it! It's HER!! It's the chick in the white T-Bird! I'd recognize that car ANYWHERE!!
Hey, Squirt! Come back! You'll miss your plane!
The hell with the plane . . . and the hell with college! Everything I want is right HERE!
I've got so many things to do . . .
Buy a ring!
Send out Wedding Invitations!
Have my EYES examined!
Did you want something, ol' chap?
Never mind! I thought I loved you!
I say! Are you daft?!?
Let's forget it! I'm sorry! I— You— you had me fooled! Listen, what's with the LONG HAIR??
You may not believe this, but rather soon, ALL you chaps will be wearing your hair LONG like this! Oh, it will be quite the rage!
You see, I am the drummer of what is now a rather obscure English Rock Group! But we will have quite an influence on the rest of the '60's!
Perhaps you have heard of us already? "THE BEATLES"?!?

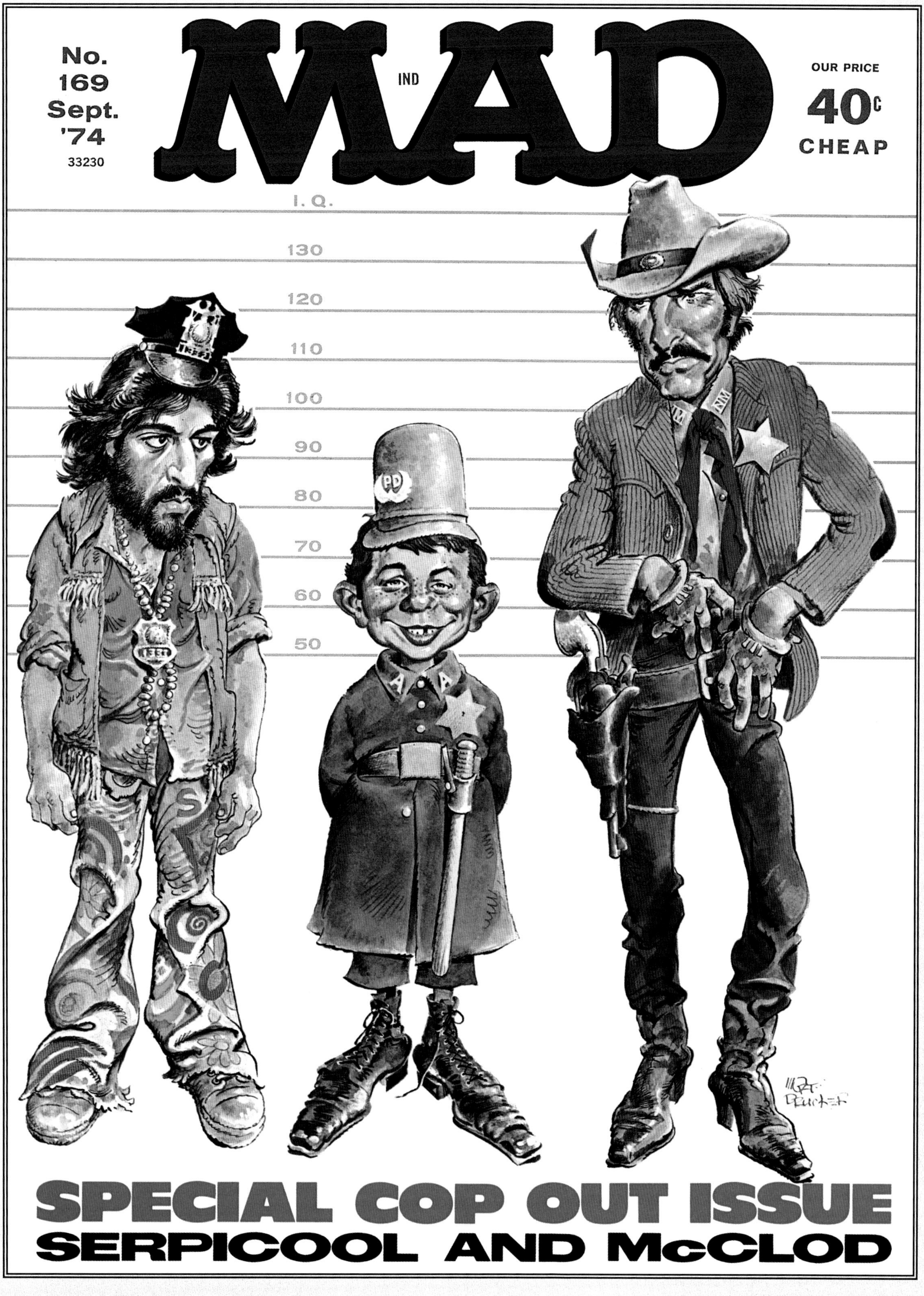
No. 169 Sept. '74
33230
MAD
IND
OUR PRICE 40¢ CHEAP
I. Q.
130
120
110
100
90
80
70
60
50
MORT DRUCKER
SPECIAL COP OUT ISSUE
SERPICOOL AND McCLOD

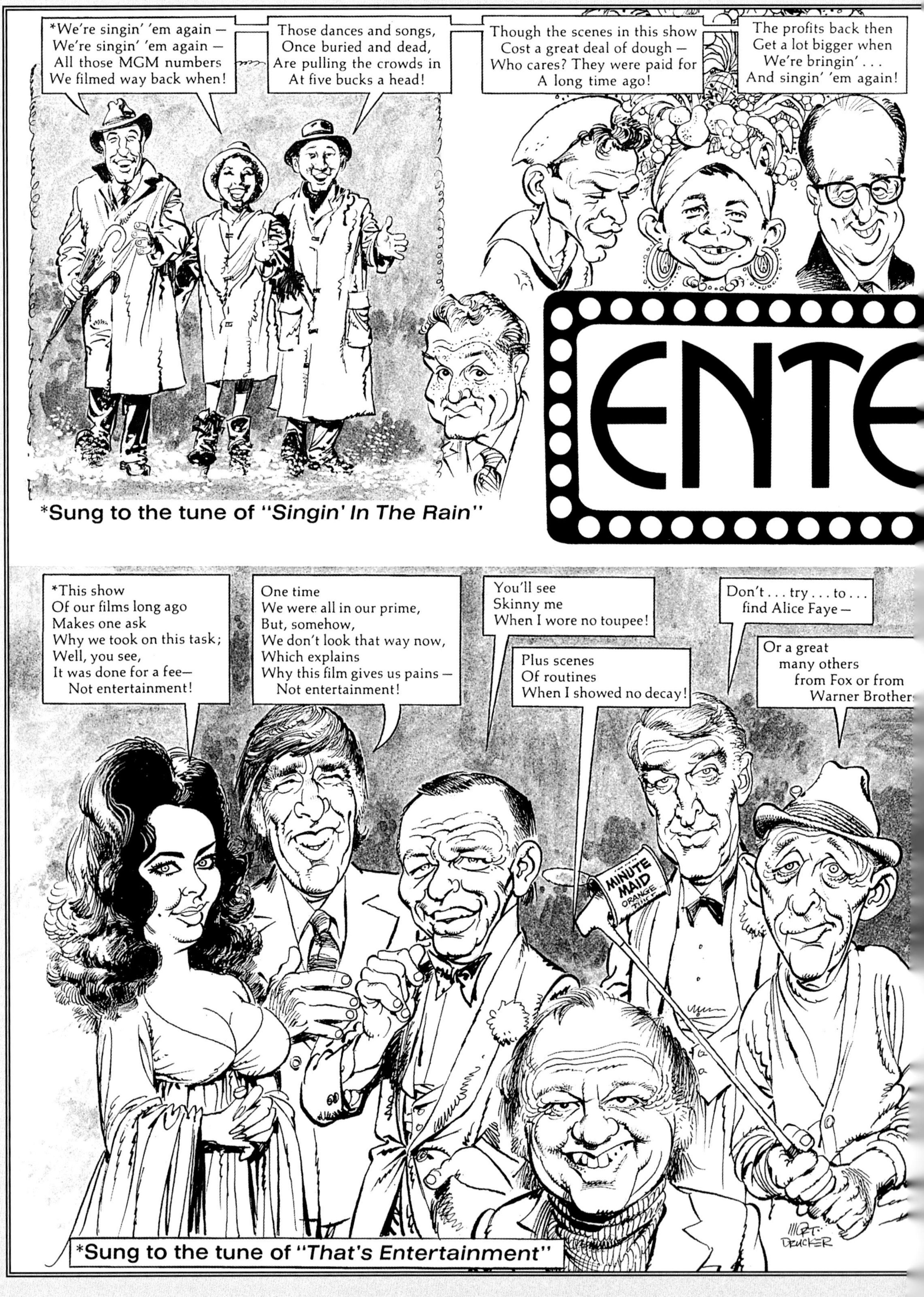
*We're singin' 'em again —
We're singin' 'em again —
All those MGM numbers
We filmed way back when!
Those dances and songs,
Once buried and dead,
Are pulling the crowds in
At five bucks a head!
Though the scenes in this show
Cost a great deal of dough —
Who cares? They were paid for
A long time ago!
The profits back then
Get a lot bigger when
We're bringin' . . .
And singin' 'em again!
ENTE
*Sung to the tune of "Singin' In The Rain"
*This show
Of our films long ago
Makes one ask
Why we took on this task;
Well, you see,
It was done for a fee—
Not entertainment!
One time
We were all in our prime,
But, somehow,
We don't look that way now,
Which explains
Why this film gives us pains —
Not entertainment!
You'll see
Skinny me
When I wore no toupee!
Plus scenes
Of routines
When I showed no decay!
Don't . . . try . . . to . . .
find Alice Faye —
Or a great
many others
from Fox or from
Warner Brothers
MINUTE MAID ORANGE JUICE
MORT DRUCKER
*Sung to the tune of "That's Entertainment"

BEST FOOTAGE FORWARD DEPT.

That's right! They're singin' 'em again . . . in a successful new film . . . all them outdated songs from all them corny old MGM Musicals! And what's even *more* amazing is: People are standing in line and paying good money to see this movie! And it hasn't even got a plot! Which makes us kinda wonder . . .

WHAT'S RTAINMENT?

ARTIST: MORT DRUCKER WRITER: FRANK JACOBS

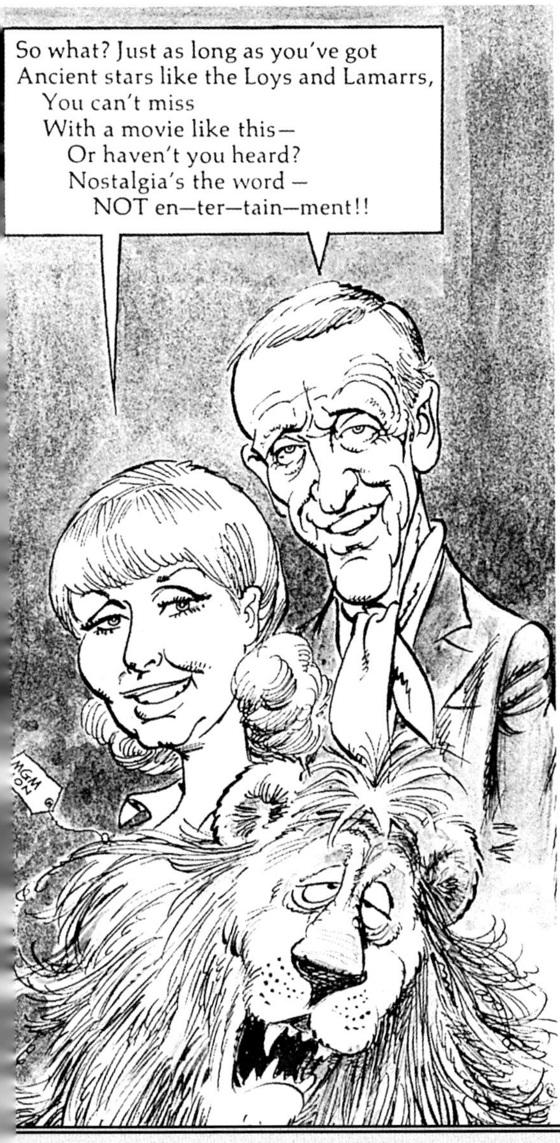

So what? Just as long as you've got Ancient stars like the Loys and Lamarrs, You can't miss With a movie like this— Or haven't you heard? Nostalgia's the word — NOT en—ter—tain—ment!!
MGM LION

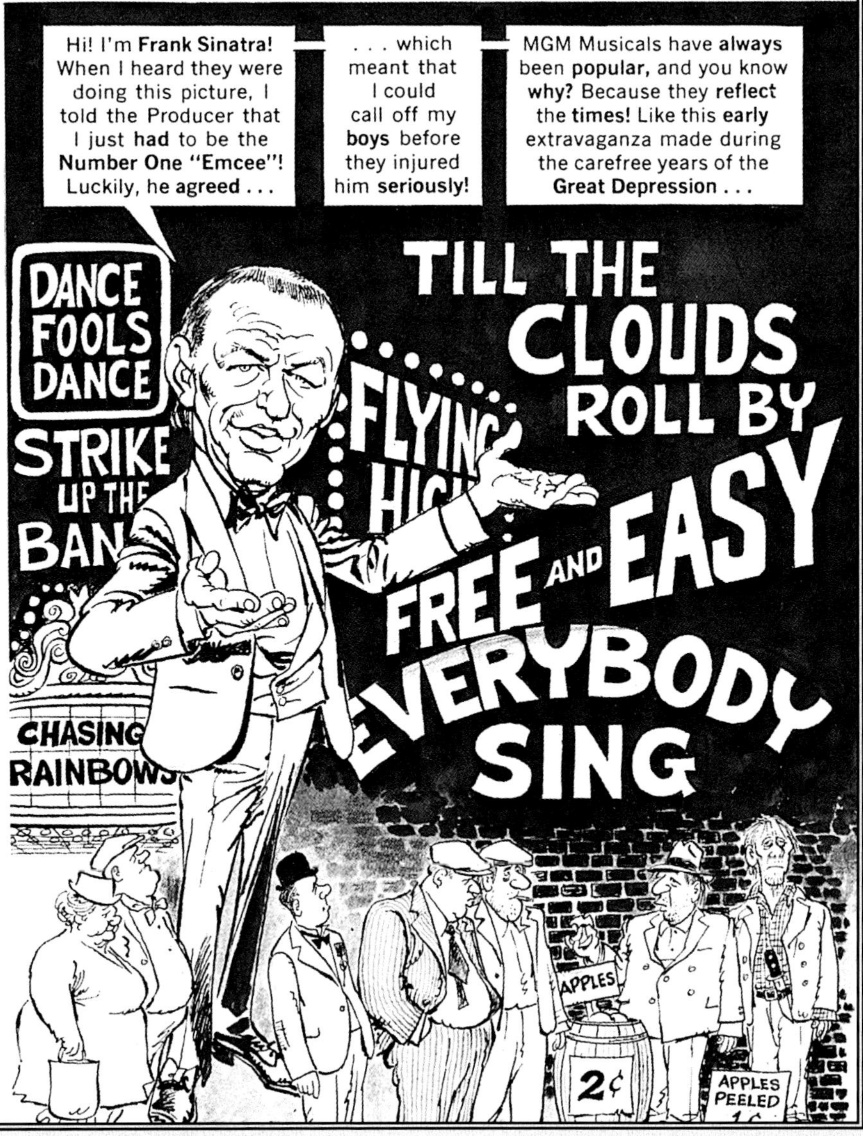

Hi! I'm Frank Sinatra! When I heard they were doing this picture, I told the Producer that I just had to be the Number One "Emcee"! Luckily, he agreed . . .
. . . which meant that I could call off my boys before they injured him seriously!
MGM Musicals have always been popular, and you know why? Because they reflect the times! Like this early extravaganza made during the carefree years of the Great Depression . . .
DANCE FOOLS DANCE
STRIKE UP THE BAN
FLYIN
CHASING RAINBOW
TILL THE CLOUDS ROLL BY
FREE AND EASY
EVERYBODY SING
APPLES
2¢
APPLES PEELED

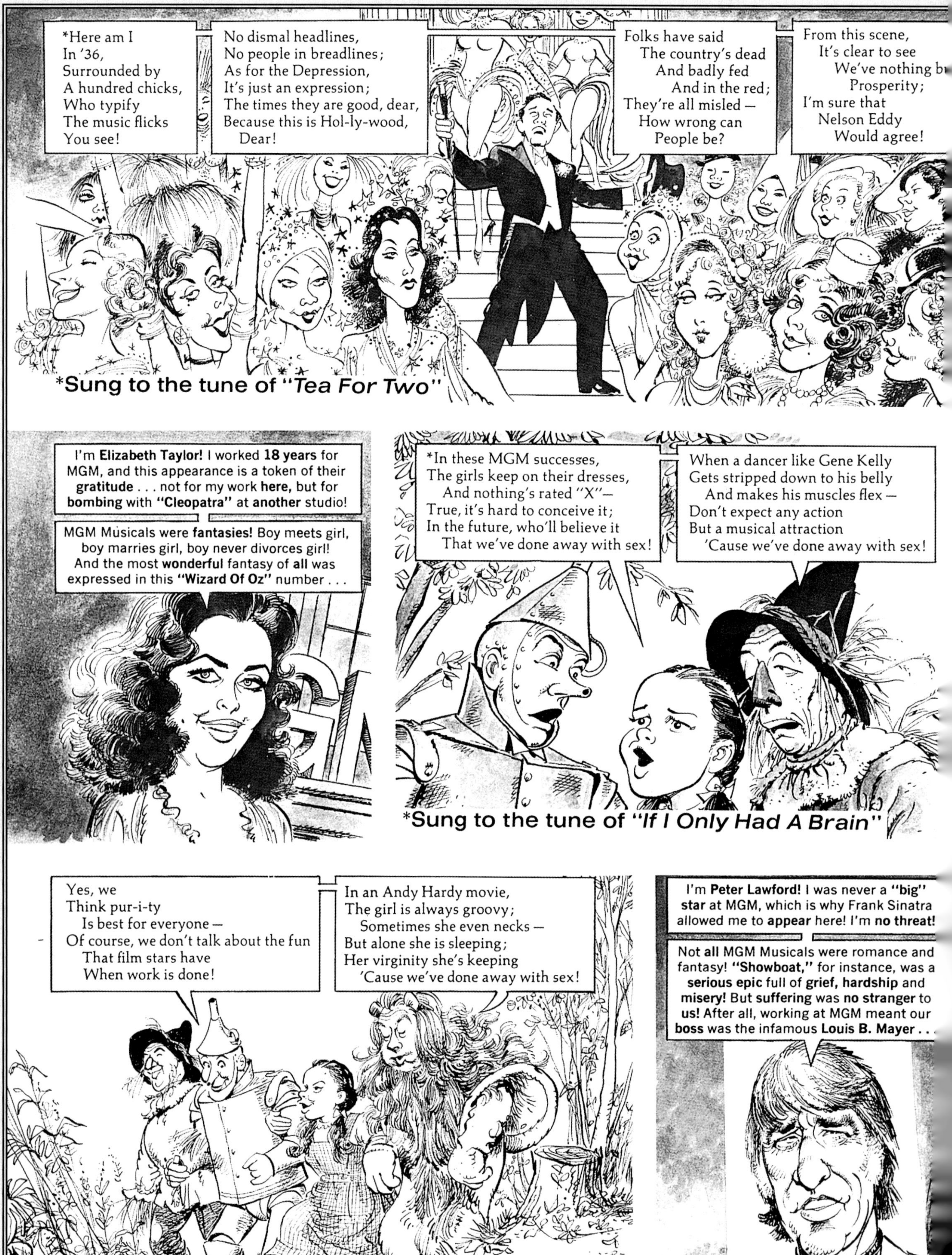
*Here am I In '36, Surrounded by A hundred chicks, Who typify The music flicks You see!
No dismal headlines, No people in breadlines; As for the Depression, It's just an expression; The times they are good, dear, Because this is Hol-ly-wood, Dear!
Folks have said The country's dead And badly fed And in the red; They're all misled — How wrong can People be?
From this scene, It's clear to see We've nothing b Prosperity; I'm sure that Nelson Eddy Would agree!
*Sung to the tune of "Tea For Two"
I'm Elizabeth Taylor! I worked 18 years for MGM, and this appearance is a token of their gratitude . . . not for my work here, but for bombing with "Cleopatra" at another studio!
MGM Musicals were fantasies! Boy meets girl, boy marries girl, boy never divorces girl! And the most wonderful fantasy of all was expressed in this "Wizard Of Oz" number . . .
*In these MGM successes, The girls keep on their dresses, And nothing's rated "X"— True, it's hard to conceive it; In the future, who'll believe it That we've done away with sex!
When a dancer like Gene Kelly Gets stripped down to his belly And makes his muscles flex — Don't expect any action But a musical attraction 'Cause we've done away with sex!
*Sung to the tune of "If I Only Had A Brain"
Yes, we Think pur-i-ty Is best for everyone — Of course, we don't talk about the fun That film stars have When work is done!
In an Andy Hardy movie, The girl is always groovy; Sometimes she even necks — But alone she is sleeping; Her virginity she's keeping 'Cause we've done away with sex!
I'm Peter Lawford! I was never a "big" star at MGM, which is why Frank Sinatra allowed me to appear here! I'm no threat!
Not all MGM Musicals were romance and fantasy! "Showboat," for instance, was a serious epic full of grief, hardship and misery! But suffering was no stranger to us! After all, working at MGM meant our boss was the infamous Louis B. Mayer . . .

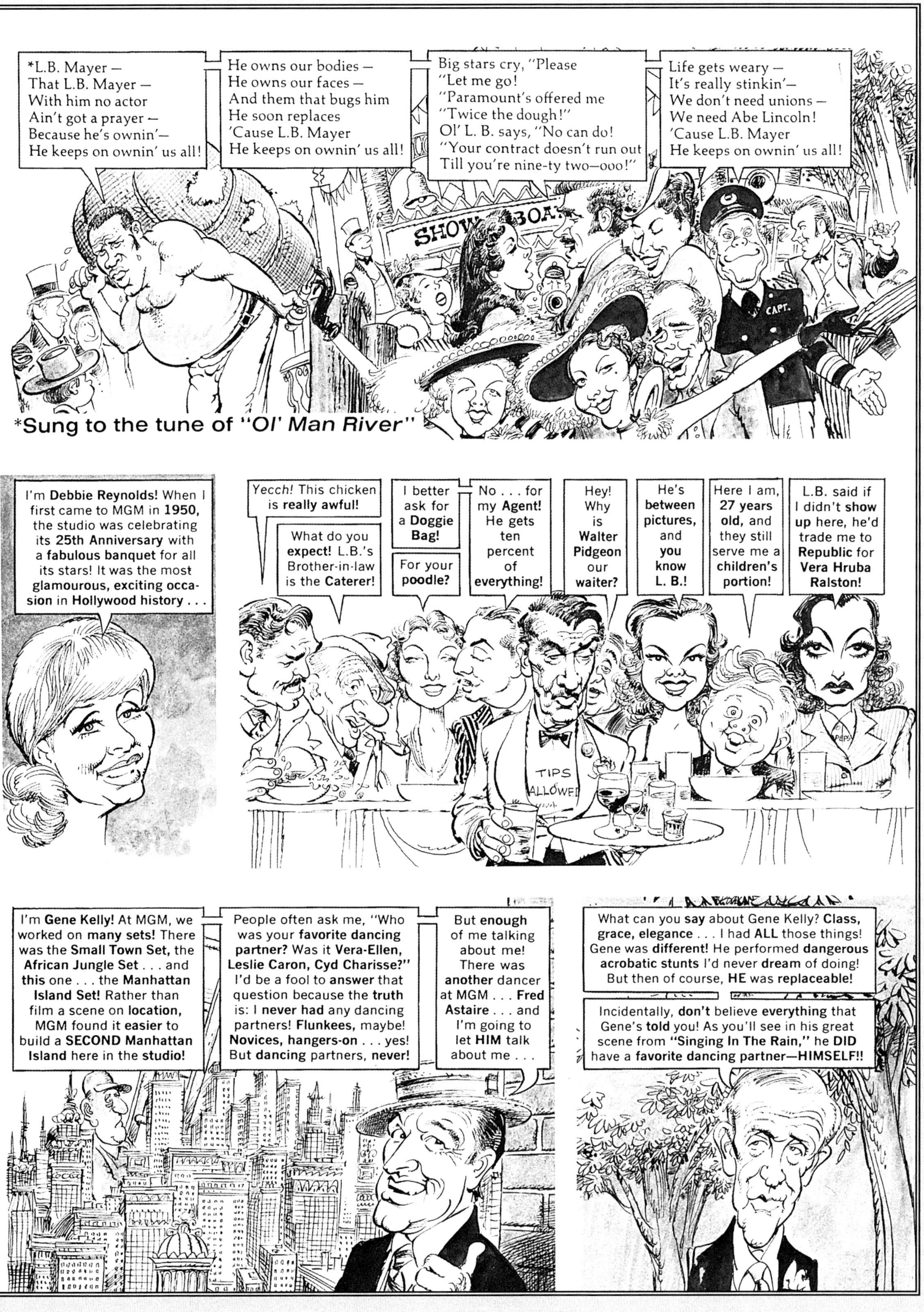
*L.B. Mayer —
That L.B. Mayer —
With him no actor
Ain't got a prayer —
Because he's ownin'—
He keeps on ownin' us all!
He owns our bodies —
He owns our faces —
And them that bugs him
He soon replaces
'Cause L.B. Mayer
He keeps on ownin' us all!
Big stars cry, "Please
"Let me go!
"Paramount's offered me
"Twice the dough!"
Ol' L. B. says, "No can do!
"Your contract doesn't run out
Till you're nine-ty two—ooo!"
Life gets weary —
It's really stinkin'—
We don't need unions —
We need Abe Lincoln!
'Cause L.B. Mayer
He keeps on ownin' us all!
SHOW BOAT
CAPT.
*Sung to the tune of "Ol' Man River"
I'm Debbie Reynolds! When I first came to MGM in 1950, the studio was celebrating its 25th Anniversary with a fabulous banquet for all its stars! It was the most glamourous, exciting occasion in Hollywood history . . .
Yecch! This chicken is really awful!
What do you expect! L.B.'s Brother-in-law is the Caterer!
I better ask for a Doggie Bag!
For your poodle?
No . . . for my Agent! He gets ten percent of everything!
Hey! Why is Walter Pidgeon our waiter?
He's between pictures, and you know L. B.!
Here I am, 27 years old, and they still serve me a children's portion!
L.B. said if I didn't show up here, he'd trade me to Republic for Vera Hruba Ralston!
TIPS ALLOWED
I'm Gene Kelly! At MGM, we worked on many sets! There was the Small Town Set, the African Jungle Set . . . and this one . . . the Manhattan Island Set! Rather than film a scene on location, MGM found it easier to build a SECOND Manhattan Island here in the studio!
People often ask me, "Who was your favorite dancing partner? Was it Vera-Ellen, Leslie Caron, Cyd Charisse?" I'd be a fool to answer that question because the truth is: I never had any dancing partners! Flunkees, maybe! Novices, hangers-on . . . yes! But dancing partners, never!
But enough of me talking about me! There was another dancer at MGM . . . Fred Astaire . . . and I'm going to let HIM talk about me . . .
What can you say about Gene Kelly? Class, grace, elegance . . . I had ALL those things! Gene was different! He performed dangerous acrobatic stunts I'd never dream of doing! But then of course, HE was replaceable!
Incidentally, don't believe everything that Gene's told you! As you'll see in his great scene from "Singing In The Rain," he DID have a favorite dancing partner—HIMSELF!!

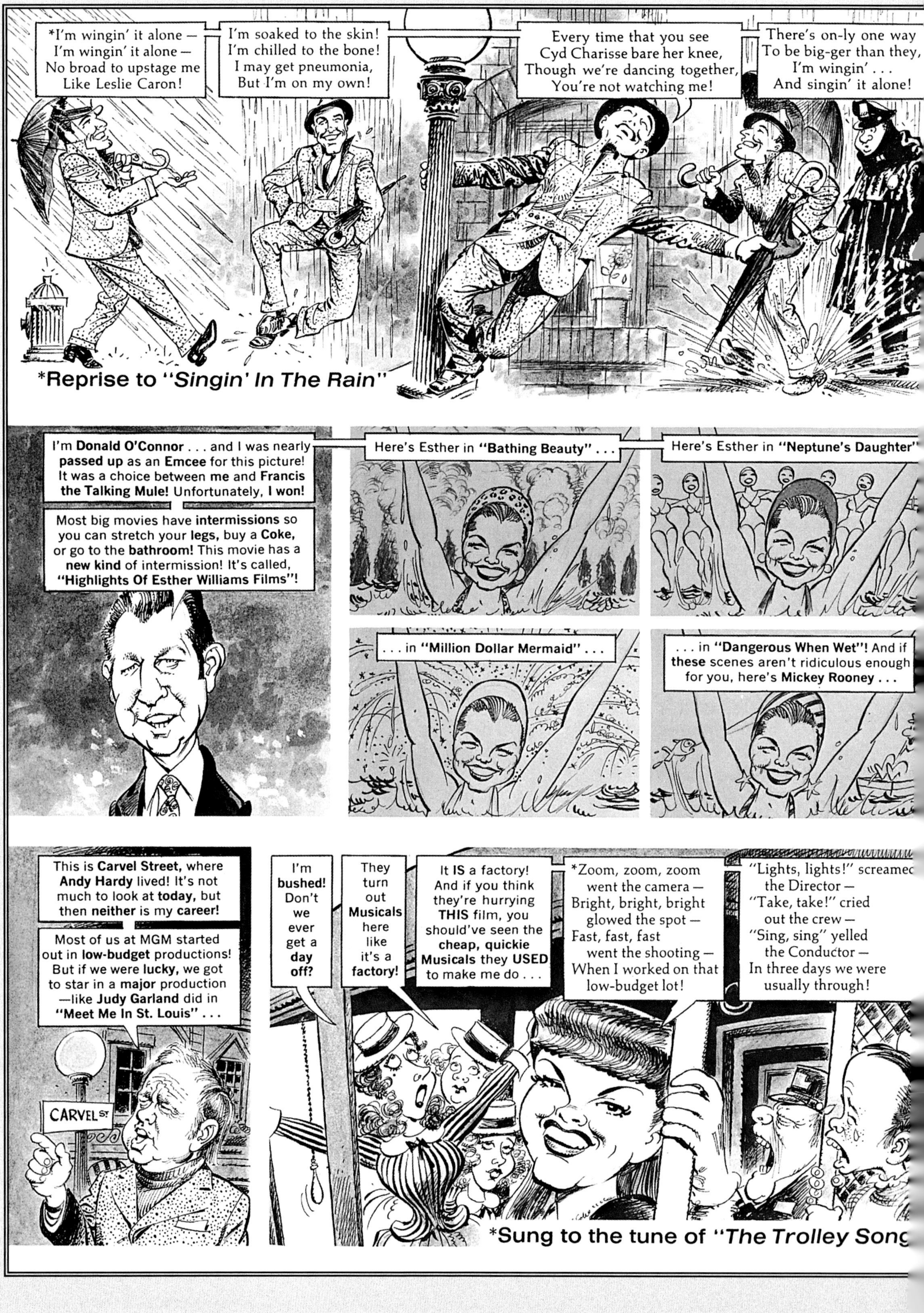
*I'm wingin' it alone — I'm wingin' it alone — No broad to upstage me Like Leslie Caron!
I'm soaked to the skin! I'm chilled to the bone! I may get pneumonia, But I'm on my own!
Every time that you see Cyd Charisse bare her knee, Though we're dancing together, You're not watching me!
There's on-ly one way To be big-ger than they, I'm wingin' . . . And singin' it alone!
*Reprise to "Singin' In The Rain"
I'm Donald O'Connor . . . and I was nearly passed up as an Emcee for this picture! It was a choice between me and Francis the Talking Mule! Unfortunately, I won!
Most big movies have intermissions so you can stretch your legs, buy a Coke, or go to the bathroom! This movie has a new kind of intermission! It's called, "Highlights Of Esther Williams Films"!
Here's Esther in "Bathing Beauty" . . .
Here's Esther in "Neptune's Daughter"
. . . in "Million Dollar Mermaid" . . .
. . . in "Dangerous When Wet"! And if these scenes aren't ridiculous enough for you, here's Mickey Rooney . . .
This is Carvel Street, where Andy Hardy lived! It's not much to look at today, but then neither is my career!
Most of us at MGM started out in low-budget productions! But if we were lucky, we got to star in a major production —like Judy Garland did in "Meet Me In St. Louis" . . .
CARVEL ST
I'm bushed! Don't we ever get a day off?
They turn out Musicals here like it's a factory!
It IS a factory! And if you think they're hurrying THIS film, you should've seen the cheap, quickie Musicals they USED to make me do . . .
*Zoom, zoom, zoom went the camera — Bright, bright, bright glowed the spot — Fast, fast, fast went the shooting — When I worked on that low-budget lot!
"Lights, lights!" screamed the Director — "Take, take!" cried out the crew — "Sing, sing" yelled the Conductor — In three days we were usually through!
*Sung to the tune of "The Trolley Song

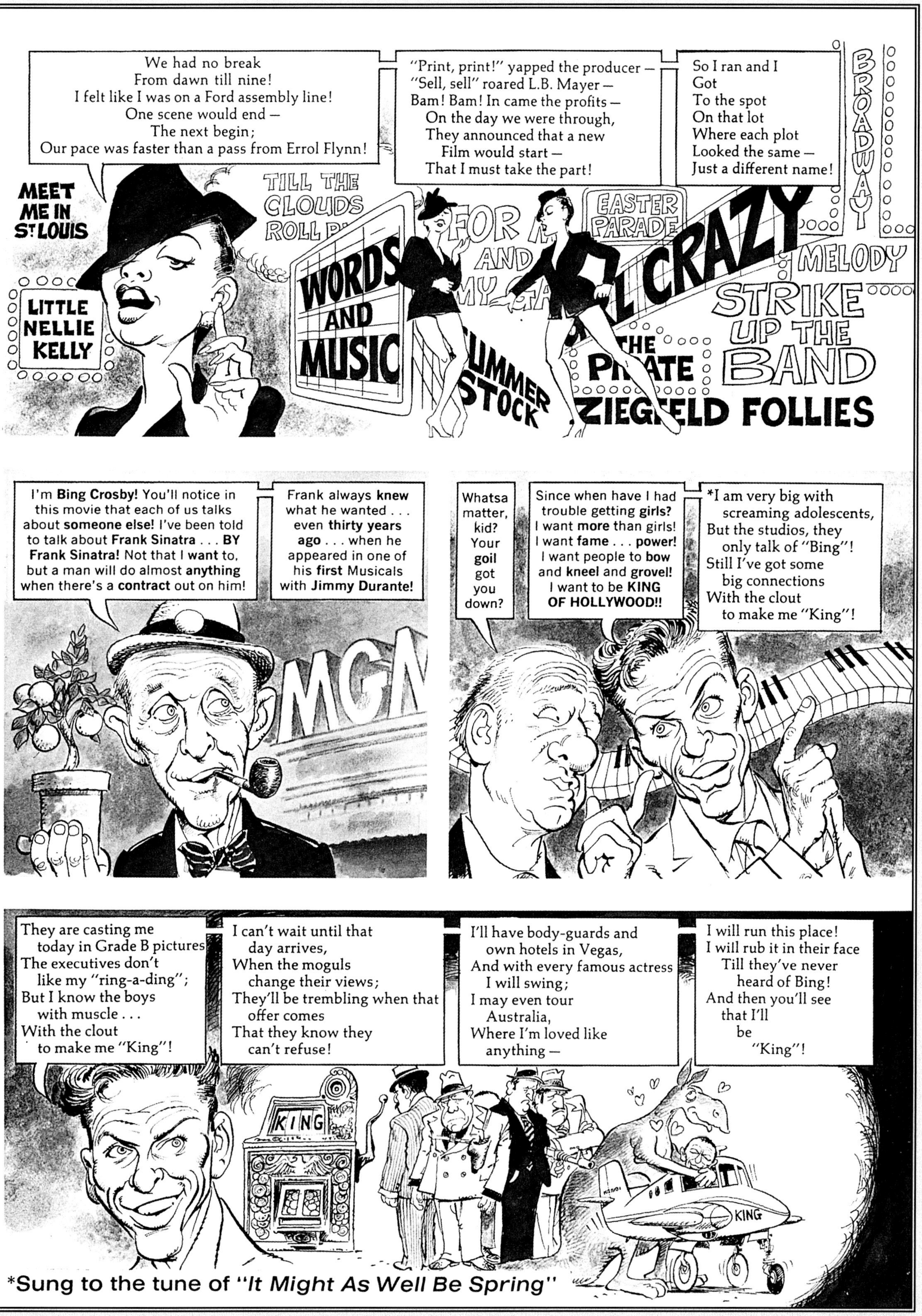
We had no break
From dawn till nine!
I felt like I was on a Ford assembly line!
One scene would end –
The next begin;
Our pace was faster than a pass from Errol Flynn!
"Print, print!" yapped the producer –
"Sell, sell" roared L.B. Mayer –
Bam! Bam! In came the profits –
On the day we were through,
They announced that a new
Film would start –
That I must take the part!
So I ran and I
Got
To the spot
On that lot
Where each plot
Looked the same –
Just a different name!
BROADWAY
MEET ME IN ST. LOUIS
LITTLE NELLIE KELLY
WORDS AND MUSIC
EASTER PARADE
MELODY
STRIKE UP THE BAND
SUMMER STOCK
ZIEGFELD FOLLIES
I'm **Bing Crosby!** You'll notice in this movie that each of us talks about **someone else!** I've been told to talk about **Frank Sinatra** . . . **BY Frank Sinatra!** Not that I **want** to, but a man will do almost **anything** when there's a **contract** out on him!
Frank always **knew** what he wanted . . . even **thirty years ago** . . . when he appeared in one of his **first** Musicals with **Jimmy Durante!**
MGM
Whatsa matter, kid? Your **goil** got you down?
Since when have I had trouble getting **girls?** I want **more** than girls! I want **fame** . . . **power!** I want people to **bow** and **kneel** and **grovel!** I want to be **KING OF HOLLYWOOD!!**
*I am very big with
screaming adolescents,
But the studios, they
only talk of "Bing"!
Still I've got some
big connections
With the clout
to make me "King"!
They are casting me
today in Grade B pictures
The executives don't
like my "ring-a-ding";
But I know the boys
with muscle . . .
With the clout
to make me "King"!
I can't wait until that
day arrives,
When the moguls
change their views;
They'll be trembling when that
offer comes
That they know they
can't refuse!
I'll have body-guards and
own hotels in Vegas,
And with every famous actress
I will swing;
I may even tour
Australia,
Where I'm loved like
anything –
I will run this place!
I will rub it in their face
Till they've never
heard of Bing!
And then you'll see
that I'll
be
"King"!
KING
KING
*Sung to the tune of "*It Might As Well Be Spring*"

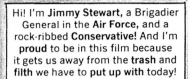

Hi! I'm **Jimmy Stewart**, a Brigadier General in the **Air Force**, and a rock-ribbed **Conservative!** And I'm **proud** to be in this film because it gets us away from the **trash** and **filth** we have to **put up with** today!

Just look at the **clean, fresh-faced kids** in these old Musical scenes, and you'll see **why** America used to be such a **great** place to **live in!**

*We can't make a film that's true to life, baby!

We can't show a man divorce his wife, baby!

Filthy slums, Drunken bums — They don't exist!

Cops and Feds Busting heads Aren't the stuff that dreams are made of!

*To the tune of "*I Can't Give You Anything But Love*"

When boy meets girl we like to keep it light, baby!
Bubbly, pro-Establishment and trite, baby!

Just make sure the boy and girl are white, baby!
We can't make a film that's true to life!

Over the years, MGM has made more than **200 Musicals!** If you had to pick **one** as "**best**," I think **everyone** would vote for "**West Side Story**"! Unfortunately, **that one** was made by **United Artists!**

But that's YOUR tough luck, because **this** show is **over!** And if you ask **us**—

*There's no movies
Like old movies
Like no movies
Today!

Pardon us if we sound egotistic,
When we tell you that they filled the house!
Even though they seemed a bit simplistic,
And realistic . . . as Mickey Mouse!

There's no pictures,
Like our pictures!
What's more, they're
Rated "G"!

But we must confess
    though each one was a gem,
THIS one's a rip-off from MGM!
If you stay at home,
    you could be seeing them
For free . . . on your TV!

ZIEG
BROADWAY MELODY
GOOD NEWS
RIO RITA
HIGH SOCIETY
KISMET
GIGI
LILI
LES GIRLS

*Sung to the tune of "*There's No Business Like Show Business*"

Mort Drucker's timely sense of parody mixed with commentary first made me aware of the culture of our generation. Mort's irreverent and historical caricatures have never been nor will they ever be equaled. He poked fun at all my favorite movies when I was a teenager and when I was a filmmaker, he started going to town on the ones I was making and I loved every frame of his.

—Steven Spielberg
Director, *Jaws*

PLAYING IT FOR SHARK VALUE DEPT.

There's a sick new trend in movies! It started with "Airport", continued with "Towering Inferno", sunk to a low with "Earthquake" and has now reached the depths with the movie that's REALLY packing 'em in, the one about a giant shark that terrorizes a summer community! Yep, it's obvious that people get their kicks out of seeing other people die . . . in every horrible way possible, which includes being . . .

JA

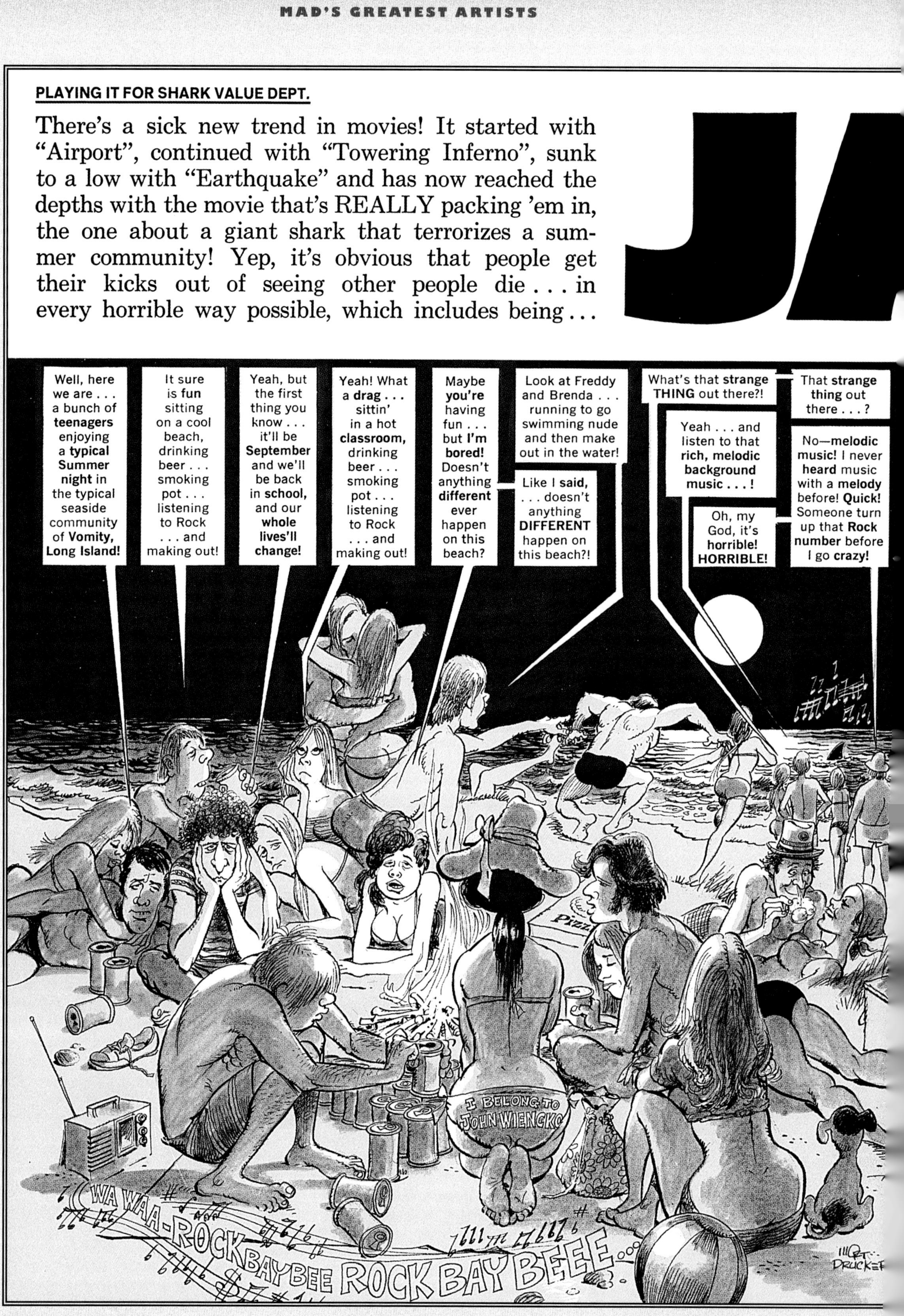
Well, here we are . . . a bunch of teenagers enjoying a typical Summer night in the typical seaside community of Vomity, Long Island!
It sure is fun sitting on a cool beach, drinking beer . . . smoking pot . . . listening to Rock . . . and making out!
Yeah, but the first thing you know . . . it'll be September and we'll be back in school, and our whole lives'll change!
Yeah! What a drag . . . sittin' in a hot classroom, drinking beer . . . smoking pot . . . listening to Rock . . . and making out!
Maybe you're having fun . . . but I'm bored! Doesn't anything different ever happen on this beach?
Look at Freddy and Brenda . . . running to go swimming nude and then make out in the water!
Like I said, . . . doesn't anything DIFFERENT happen on this beach?!
What's that strange THING out there?!
Yeah . . . and listen to that rich, melodic background music . . . !
Oh, my God, it's horrible! HORRIBLE!
That strange thing out there . . . ?
No—melodic music! I never heard music with a melody before! Quick! Someone turn up that Rock number before I go crazy!
I BELONG TO JOHN WIENCKO
WA WAA-ROCK BAYBEE ROCK BAY BEEE
MORT DRUCKER

W'D

ARTIST: MORT DRUCKER WRITER: LARRY SIEGEL

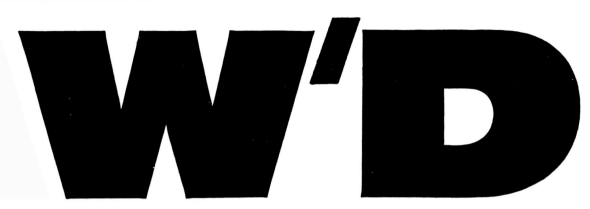

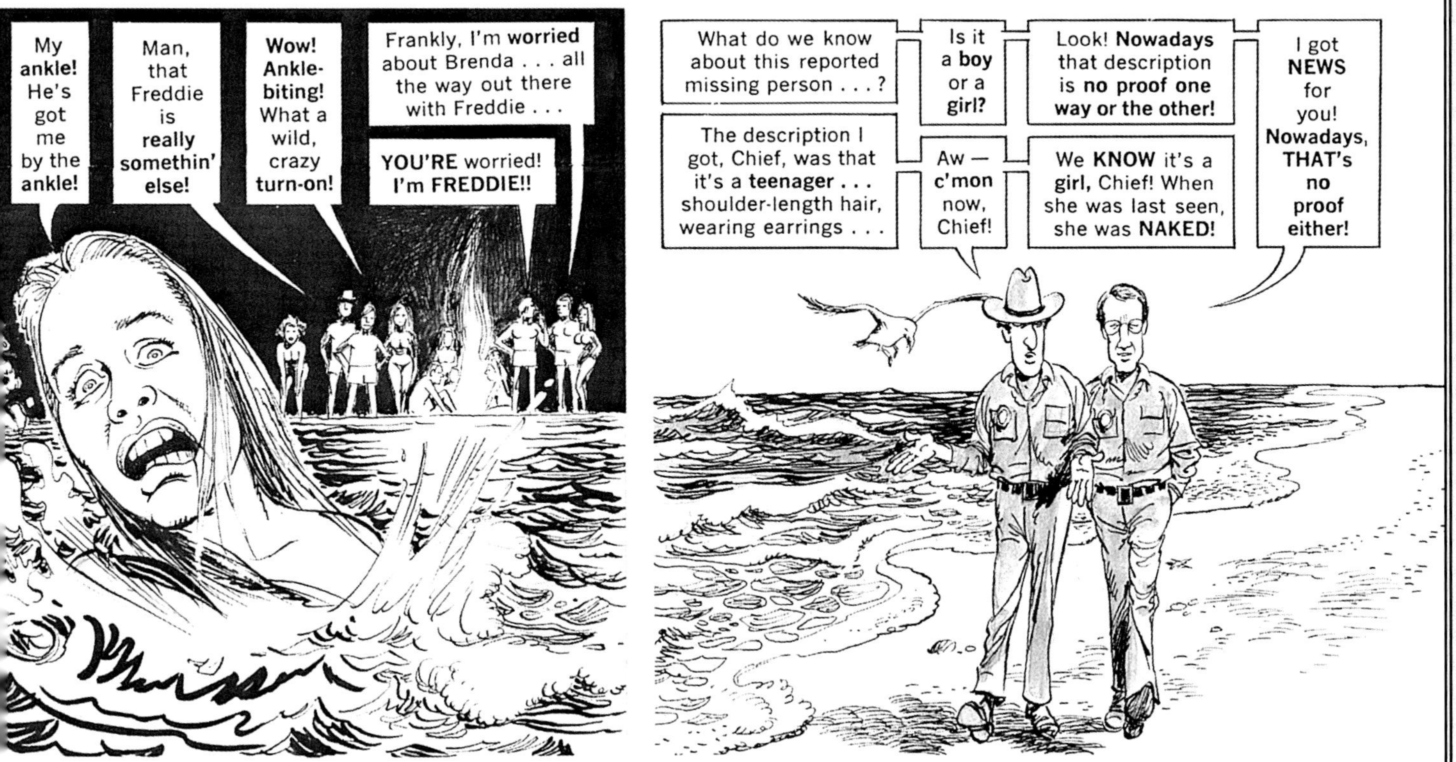
My ankle! He's got me by the ankle!
Man, that Freddie is really somethin' else!
Wow! Ankle-biting! What a wild, crazy turn-on!
Frankly, I'm worried about Brenda . . . all the way out there with Freddie . . .
YOU'RE worried! I'm FREDDIE!!
What do we know about this reported missing person . . . ?
Is it a boy or a girl?
Look! Nowadays that description is no proof one way or the other!
I got NEWS for you! Nowadays, THAT's no proof either!
The description I got, Chief, was that it's a teenager . . . shoulder-length hair, wearing earrings . . .
Aw — c'mon now, Chief!
We KNOW it's a girl, Chief! When she was last seen, she was NAKED!

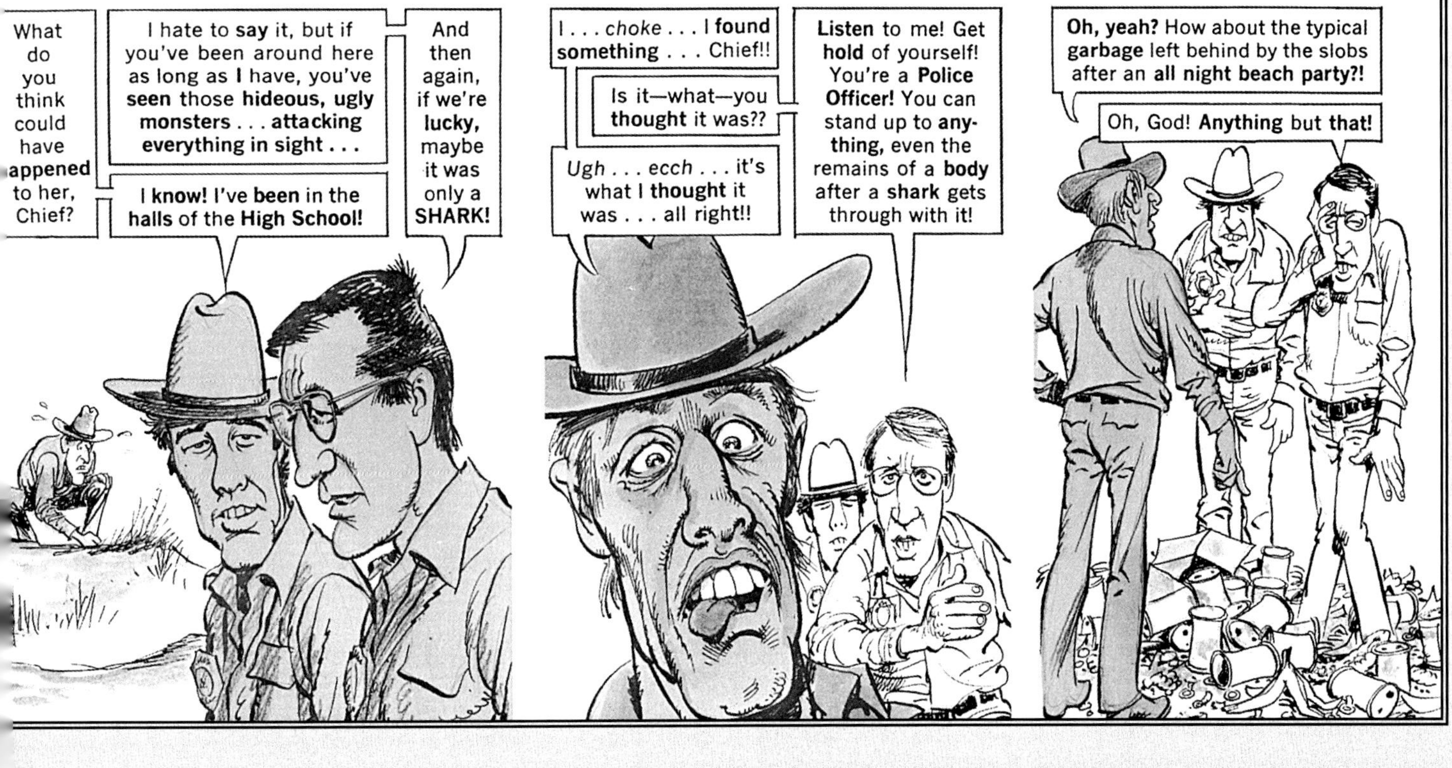
What do you think could have appened to her, Chief?
I hate to say it, but if you've been around here as long as I have, you've seen those hideous, ugly monsters . . . attacking everything in sight . . .
I know! I've been in the halls of the High School!
And then again, if we're lucky, maybe it was only a SHARK!
I . . . choke . . . I found something . . . Chief!!
Is it—what—you thought it was??
Ugh . . . ecch . . . it's what I thought it was . . . all right!!
Listen to me! Get hold of yourself! You're a Police Officer! You can stand up to anything, even the remains of a body after a shark gets through with it!
Oh, yeah? How about the typical garbage left behind by the slobs after an all night beach party?!
Oh, God! Anything but that!

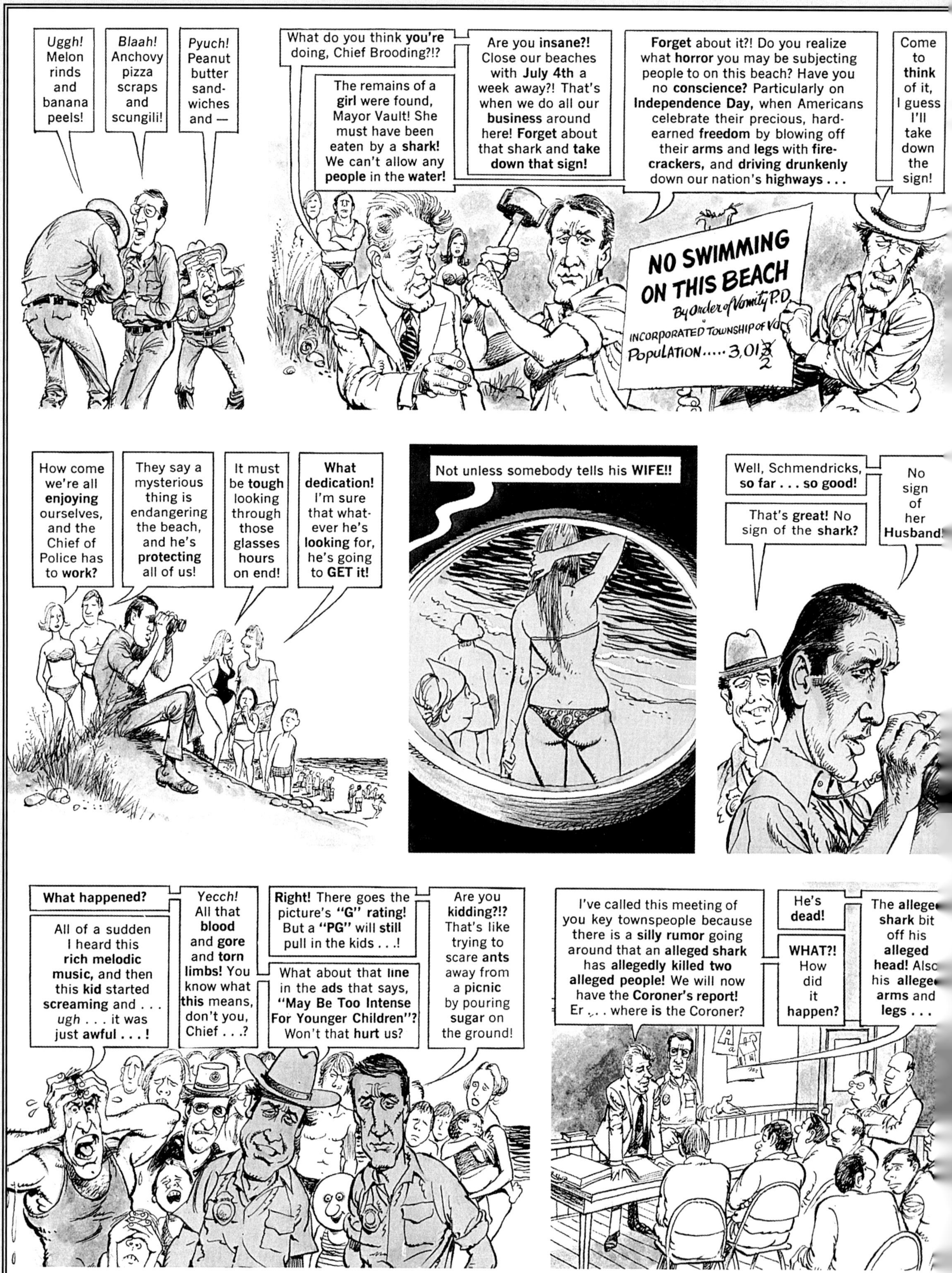

Uggh! Melon rinds and banana peels!
Blaah! Anchovy pizza scraps and scungili!
Pyuch! Peanut butter sand-wiches and —
What do you think **you're** doing, Chief Brooding?!?
The remains of a **girl** were found, Mayor Vault! She must have been eaten by a **shark!** We can't allow any **people** in the **water!**
Are you **insane?!** Close our beaches with **July 4th** a week away?! That's when we do all our **business** around here! **Forget** about that shark and **take down that sign!**
Forget about it?! Do you realize what **horror** you may be subjecting people to on this beach? Have you no **conscience?** Particularly on **Independence Day,** when Americans celebrate their precious, hard-earned **freedom** by blowing off their **arms** and **legs** with **fire-crackers,** and **driving drunkenly** down our nation's **highways . . .**
Come to **think** of it, I guess I'll take down the sign!
NO SWIMMING
ON THIS BEACH
INCORPORATED TOWNSHIP OF
POPULATION
How come we're all **enjoying** ourselves, and the Chief of Police has to **work?**
They say a mysterious thing is endangering the beach, and he's **protecting** all of us!
It must be **tough** looking through those glasses hours on end!
What dedication! I'm sure that what-ever he's **looking** for, he's going to **GET it!**
Not unless somebody tells his **WIFE!!**
Well, Schmendricks, **so far . . . so good!**
That's **great!** No sign of the **shark?**
No sign of her **Husband!**
What happened?
All of a sudden I heard this **rich melodic music,** and then this **kid** started **screaming** and . . . *ugh* . . . it was just **awful . . . !**
Yecch! All that **blood** and **gore** and **torn limbs!** You know what **this** means, don't you, Chief . . .?
Right! There goes the picture's **"G" rating!** But a **"PG"** will **still** pull in the kids . . .!
What about that **line** in the **ads** that says, **"May Be Too Intense For Younger Children"?** Won't that **hurt** us?
Are you **kidding?!?** That's like trying to scare **ants** away from a **picnic** by pouring **sugar** on the ground!
I've called this meeting of you key townspeople because there is a **silly rumor** going around that an **alleged shark** has **allegedly killed two alleged people!** We will now have the **Coroner's report!** Er . . . where **is** the Coroner?
He's **dead!**
WHAT?! How did it **happen?**
The **allege** **shark** bit off his **alleged head!** Als his **allege** **arms** and **legs . . .**

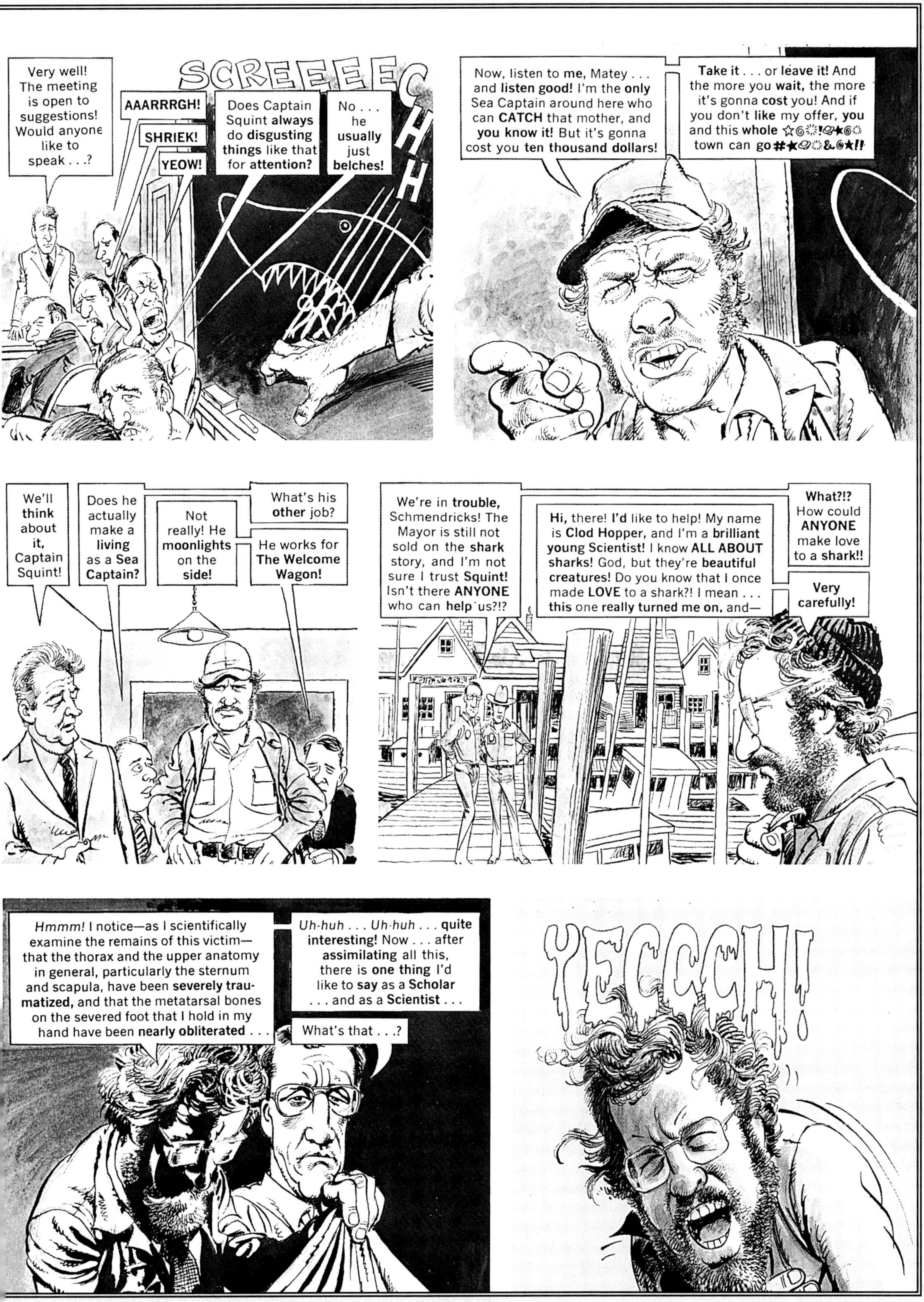

Very well! The meeting is open to suggestions! Would anyone like to speak . . .?
SCREEEECHHH
AAARRRGH!
SHRIEK!
YEOW!
Does Captain Squint always do disgusting things like that for attention?
No . . . he usually just belches!
Now, listen to me, Matey . . . and listen good! I'm the only Sea Captain around here who can CATCH that mother, and you know it! But it's gonna cost you ten thousand dollars!
Take it . . . or leave it! And the more you wait, the more it's gonna cost you! And if you don't like my offer, you and this whole ☆@☼!@★@☼ town can go #★@☼&@★!!
We'll think about it, Captain Squint!
Does he actually make a living as a Sea Captain?
Not really! He moonlights on the side!
What's his other job?
He works for The Welcome Wagon!
We're in trouble, Schmendricks! The Mayor is still not sold on the shark story, and I'm not sure I trust Squint! Isn't there ANYONE who can help us?!?
Hi, there! I'd like to help! My name is Clod Hopper, and I'm a brilliant young Scientist! I know ALL ABOUT sharks! God, but they're beautiful creatures! Do you know that I once made LOVE to a shark?! I mean . . . this one really turned me on, and—
What?!? How could ANYONE make love to a shark!!
Very carefully!
Hmmm! I notice—as I scientifically examine the remains of this victim—that the thorax and the upper anatomy in general, particularly the sternum and scapula, have been severely traumatized, and that the metatarsal bones on the severed foot that I hold in my hand have been nearly obliterated . . .
Uh-huh . . . Uh-huh . . . quite interesting! Now . . . after assimilating all this, there is one thing I'd like to say as a Scholar . . . and as a Scientist . . .
What's that . . .?
YECCCH!

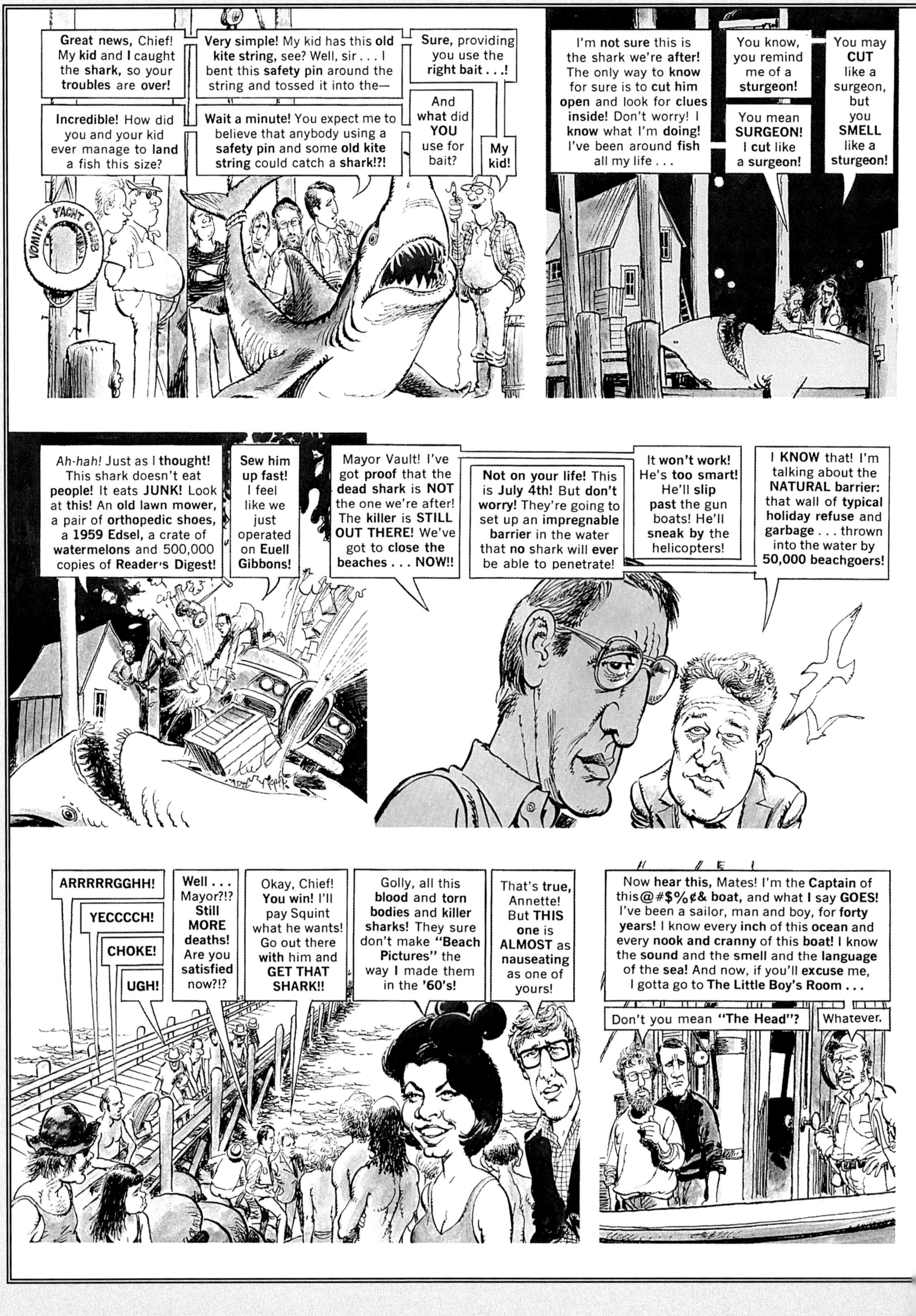
Great news, Chief! My kid and I caught the shark, so your troubles are over!
Incredible! How did you and your kid ever manage to land a fish this size?
Very simple! My kid has this old kite string, see? Well, sir . . . I bent this safety pin around the string and tossed it into the—
Wait a minute! You expect me to believe that anybody using a safety pin and some old kite string could catch a shark!?!
Sure, providing you use the right bait . . .!
And what did YOU use for bait?
My kid!
VOMITY YACHT CLUB
I'm not sure this is the shark we're after! The only way to know for sure is to cut him open and look for clues inside! Don't worry! I know what I'm doing! I've been around fish all my life . . .
You know, you remind me of a sturgeon!
You mean SURGEON! I cut like a surgeon!
You may CUT like a surgeon, but you SMELL like a sturgeon!
Ah-hah! Just as I thought! This shark doesn't eat people! It eats JUNK! Look at this! An old lawn mower, a pair of orthopedic shoes, a 1959 Edsel, a crate of watermelons and 500,000 copies of Reader's Digest!
Sew him up fast! I feel like we just operated on Euell Gibbons!
Mayor Vault! I've got proof that the dead shark is NOT the one we're after! The killer is STILL OUT THERE! We've got to close the beaches . . . NOW!!
Not on your life! This is July 4th! But don't worry! They're going to set up an impregnable barrier in the water that no shark will ever be able to penetrate!
It won't work! He's too smart! He'll slip past the gun boats! He'll sneak by the helicopters!
I KNOW that! I'm talking about the NATURAL barrier: that wall of typical holiday refuse and garbage . . . thrown into the water by 50,000 beachgoers!
ARRRRRGGHH!
YECCCCH!
CHOKE!
UGH!
Well . . . Mayor?!? Still MORE deaths! Are you satisfied now?!?
Okay, Chief! You win! I'll pay Squint what he wants! Go out there with him and GET THAT SHARK!!
Golly, all this blood and torn bodies and killer sharks! They sure don't make "Beach Pictures" the way I made them in the '60's!
That's true, Annette! But THIS one is ALMOST as nauseating as one of yours!
Now hear this, Mates! I'm the Captain of this@#$%¢& boat, and what I say GOES! I've been a sailor, man and boy, for forty years! I know every inch of this ocean and every nook and cranny of this boat! I know the sound and the smell and the language of the sea! And now, if you'll excuse me, I gotta go to The Little Boy's Room . . .
Don't you mean "The Head"?
Whatever.

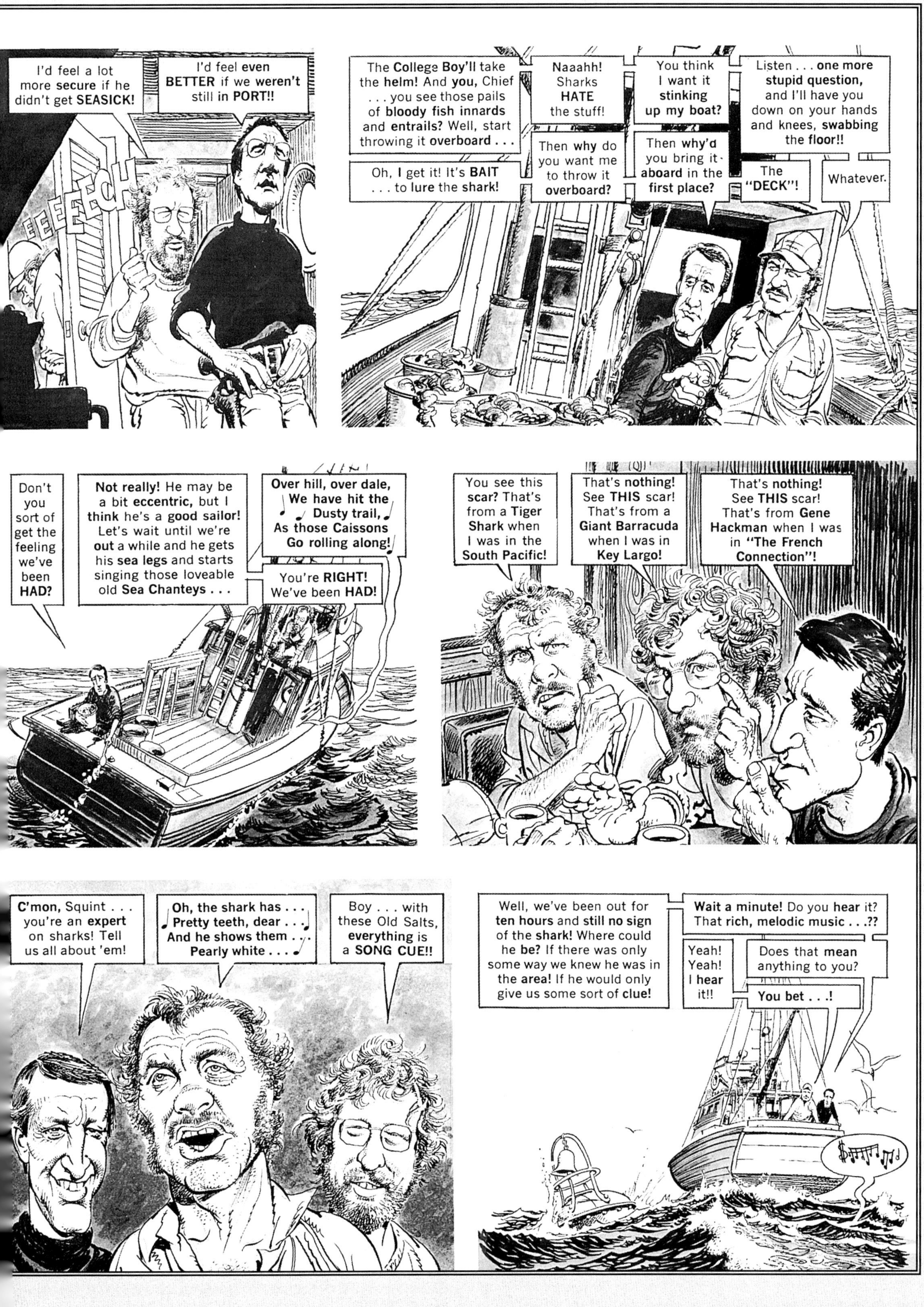
I'd feel a lot more secure if he didn't get SEASICK!
I'd feel even BETTER if we weren't still in PORT!!
EEEEEECH
The College Boy'll take the helm! And you, Chief . . . you see those pails of bloody fish innards and entrails? Well, start throwing it overboard . . .
Oh, I get it! It's BAIT . . . to lure the shark!
Naaahh! Sharks HATE the stuff!
Then why do you want me to throw it overboard?
You think I want it stinking up my boat?
Then why'd you bring it aboard in the first place?
Listen . . . one more stupid question, and I'll have you down on your hands and knees, swabbing the floor!!
The "DECK"!
Whatever.
Don't you sort of get the feeling we've been HAD?
Not really! He may be a bit eccentric, but I think he's a good sailor! Let's wait until we're out a while and he gets his sea legs and starts singing those loveable old Sea Chanteys . . .
Over hill, over dale, We have hit the Dusty trail, As those Caissons Go rolling along!
You're RIGHT! We've been HAD!
You see this scar? That's from a Tiger Shark when I was in the South Pacific!
That's nothing! See THIS scar! That's from a Giant Barracuda when I was in Key Largo!
That's nothing! See THIS scar! That's from Gene Hackman when I was in "The French Connection"!
C'mon, Squint . . . you're an expert on sharks! Tell us all about 'em!
Oh, the shark has . . . Pretty teeth, dear . . . And he shows them . . . Pearly white . . .
Boy . . . with these Old Salts, everything is a SONG CUE!!
Well, we've been out for ten hours and still no sign of the shark! Where could he be? If there was only some way we knew he was in the area! If he would only give us some sort of clue!
Wait a minute! Do you hear it? That rich, melodic music . . .??
Yeah! Yeah! I hear it!!
Does that mean anything to you?
You bet . . .!

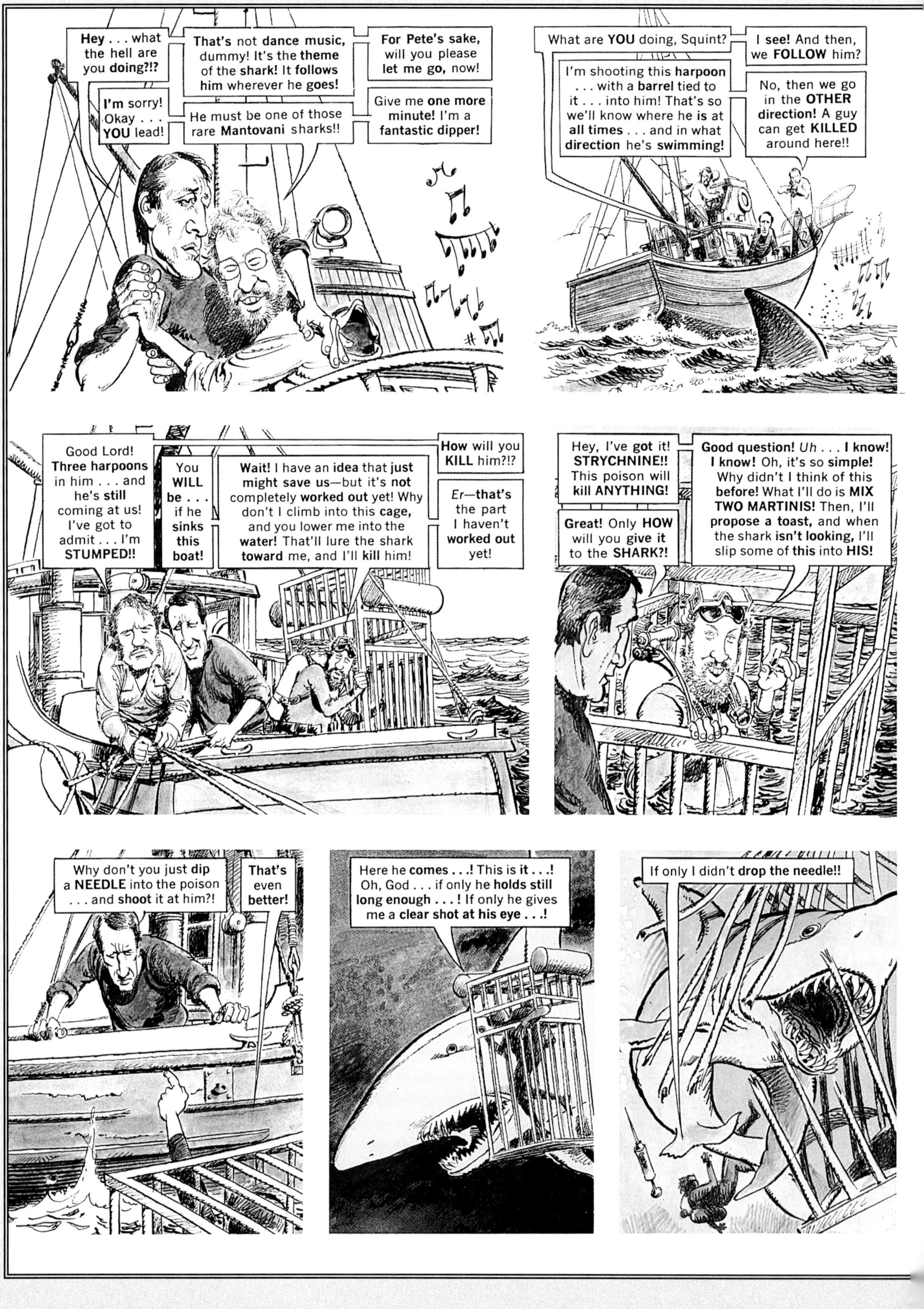
Hey . . . what the hell are you doing?!?
That's not dance music, dummy! It's the theme of the shark! It follows him wherever he goes!
For Pete's sake, will you please let me go, now!
I'm sorry! Okay . . . YOU lead!
He must be one of those rare Mantovani sharks!!
Give me one more minute! I'm a fantastic dipper!
What are YOU doing, Squint?
I'm shooting this harpoon . . . with a barrel tied to it . . . into him! That's so we'll know where he is at all times . . . and in what direction he's swimming!
I see! And then, we FOLLOW him?
No, then we go in the OTHER direction! A guy can get KILLED around here!!
Good Lord! Three harpoons in him . . . and he's still coming at us! I've got to admit . . . I'm STUMPED!!
You WILL be . . . if he sinks this boat!
Wait! I have an idea that just might save us—but it's not completely worked out yet! Why don't I climb into this cage, and you lower me into the water! That'll lure the shark toward me, and I'll kill him!
How will you KILL him?!?
Er—that's the part I haven't worked out yet!
Hey, I've got it! STRYCHNINE!! This poison will kill ANYTHING!
Great! Only HOW will you give it to the SHARK?!
Good question! Uh . . . I know! I know! Oh, it's so simple! Why didn't I think of this before! What I'll do is MIX TWO MARTINIS! Then, I'll propose a toast, and when the shark isn't looking, I'll slip some of this into HIS!
Why don't you just dip a NEEDLE into the poison . . . and shoot it at him?!
That's even better!
Here he comes . . .! This is it . . .! Oh, God . . . if only he holds still long enough . . .! If only he gives me a clear shot at his eye . . .!
If only I didn't drop the needle!!

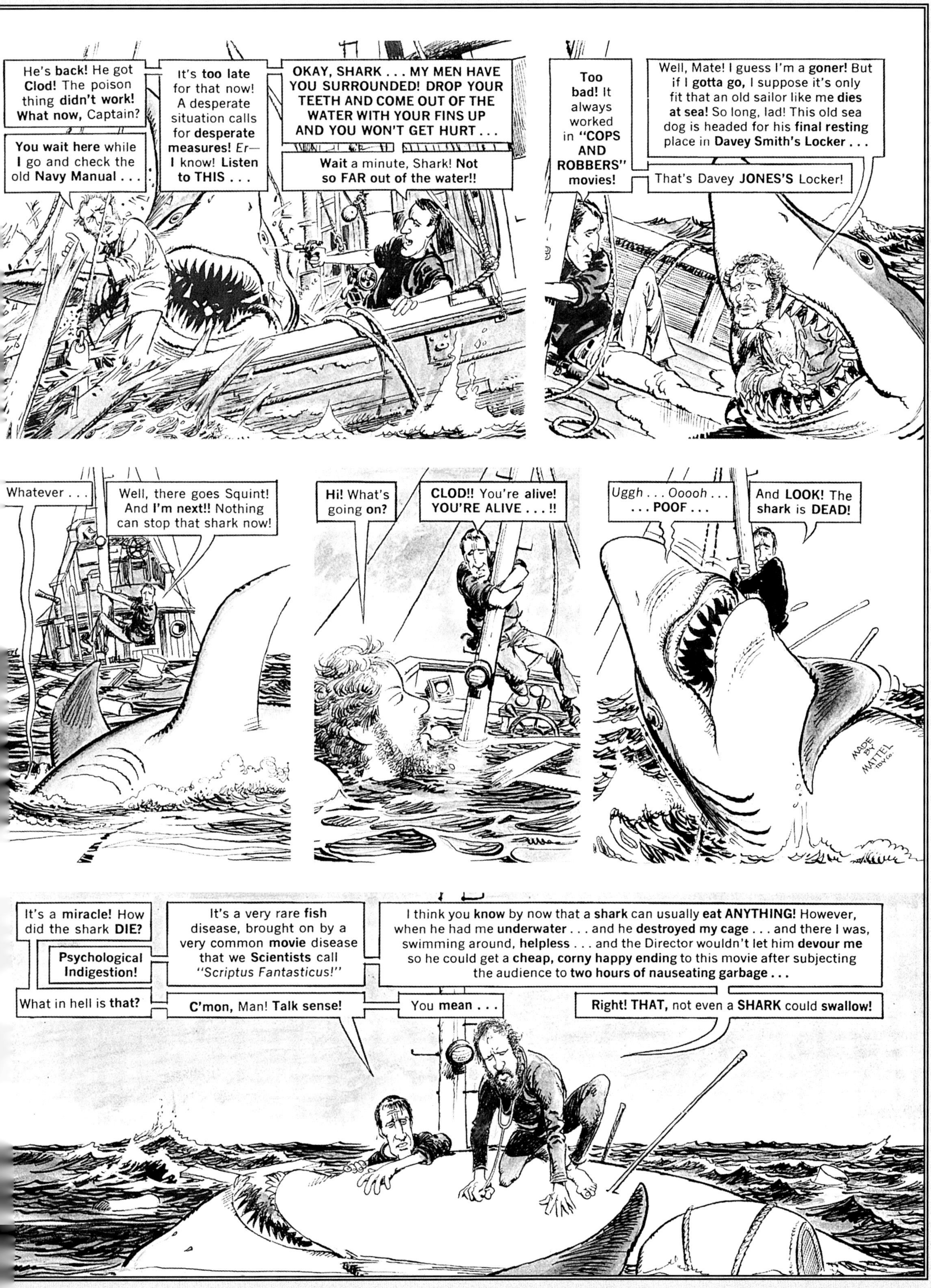
He's back! He got Clod! The poison thing didn't work! What now, Captain?
You wait here while I go and check the old Navy Manual . . .
It's too late for that now! A desperate situation calls for desperate measures! Er— I know! Listen to THIS . . .
OKAY, SHARK . . . MY MEN HAVE YOU SURROUNDED! DROP YOUR TEETH AND COME OUT OF THE WATER WITH YOUR FINS UP AND YOU WON'T GET HURT . . .
Wait a minute, Shark! Not so FAR out of the water!!
Too bad! It always worked in "COPS AND ROBBERS" movies!
Well, Mate! I guess I'm a goner! But if I gotta go, I suppose it's only fit that an old sailor like me dies at sea! So long, lad! This old sea dog is headed for his final resting place in Davey Smith's Locker . . .
That's Davey JONES'S Locker!
Whatever . . .
Well, there goes Squint! And I'm next!! Nothing can stop that shark now!
Hi! What's going on?
CLOD!! You're alive! YOU'RE ALIVE . . . !!
Uggh . . . Ooooh . . . . . . POOF . . .
And LOOK! The shark is DEAD!
MADE BY MATTEL
It's a miracle! How did the shark DIE?
Psychological Indigestion!
What in hell is that?
It's a very rare fish disease, brought on by a very common movie disease that we Scientists call "Scriptus Fantasticus!"
C'mon, Man! Talk sense!
I think you know by now that a shark can usually eat ANYTHING! However, when he had me underwater . . . and he destroyed my cage . . . and there I was, swimming around, helpless . . . and the Director wouldn't let him devour me so he could get a cheap, corny happy ending to this movie after subjecting the audience to two hours of nauseating garbage . . .
You mean . . .
Right! THAT, not even a SHARK could swallow!

LOONEY BINGE DEPT.

HERE WE GO WITH OUR VERSION OF THE RECENT SMASH-HIT-MOVIE ABOUT

ONE CUCKOO FL

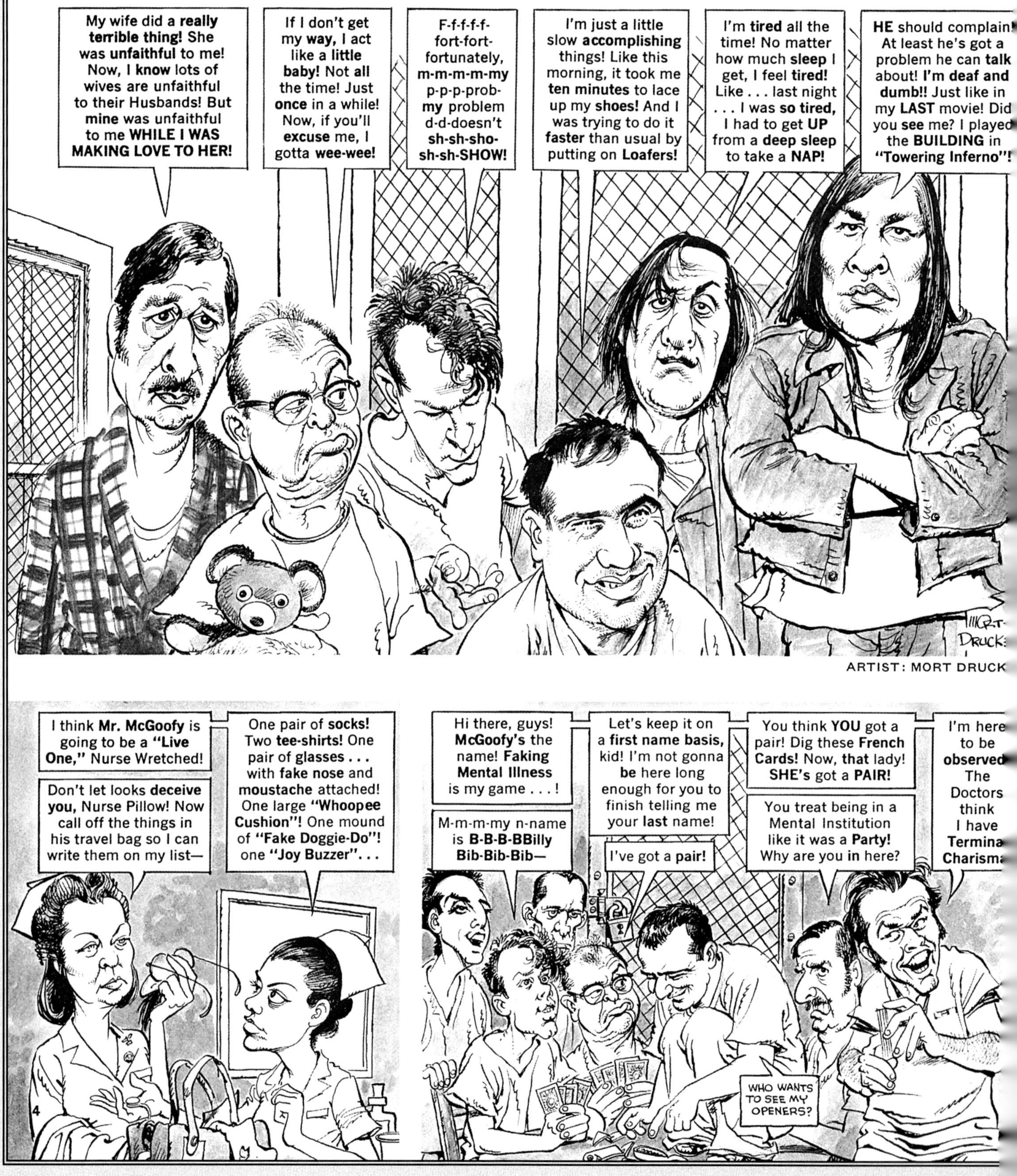
My wife did a really terrible thing! She was unfaithful to me! Now, I know lots of wives are unfaithful to their Husbands! But mine was unfaithful to me WHILE I WAS MAKING LOVE TO HER!
If I don't get my way, I act like a little baby! Not all the time! Just once in a while! Now, if you'll excuse me, I gotta wee-wee!
F-f-f-f-f-fort-fort-fortunately, m-m-m-m-my p-p-p-prob-my problem d-d-doesn't sh-sh-sho-sh-sh-SHOW!
I'm just a little slow accomplishing things! Like this morning, it took me ten minutes to lace up my shoes! And I was trying to do it faster than usual by putting on Loafers!
I'm tired all the time! No matter how much sleep I get, I feel tired! Like . . . last night . . . I was so tired, I had to get UP from a deep sleep to take a NAP!
HE should complain! At least he's got a problem he can talk about! I'm deaf and dumb!! Just like in my LAST movie! Did you see me? I played the BUILDING in "Towering Inferno"!
ARTIST: MORT DRUCK
I think Mr. McGoofy is going to be a "Live One," Nurse Wretched!
Don't let looks deceive you, Nurse Pillow! Now call off the things in his travel bag so I can write them on my list—
One pair of socks! Two tee-shirts! One pair of glasses . . . with fake nose and moustache attached! One large "Whoopee Cushion"! One mound of "Fake Doggie-Do"! one "Joy Buzzer". . .
Hi there, guys! McGoofy's the name! Faking Mental Illness is my game . . . !
M-m-m-my n-name is B-B-B-BBilly Bib-Bib-Bib—
Let's keep it on a first name basis, kid! I'm not gonna be here long enough for you to finish telling me your last name!
I've got a pair!
You think YOU got a pair! Dig these French Cards! Now, that lady! SHE's got a PAIR!
You treat being in a Mental Institution like it was a Party! Why are you in here?
I'm here to be observed The Doctors think I have Termina Charisma
WHO WANTS TO SEE MY OPENERS?

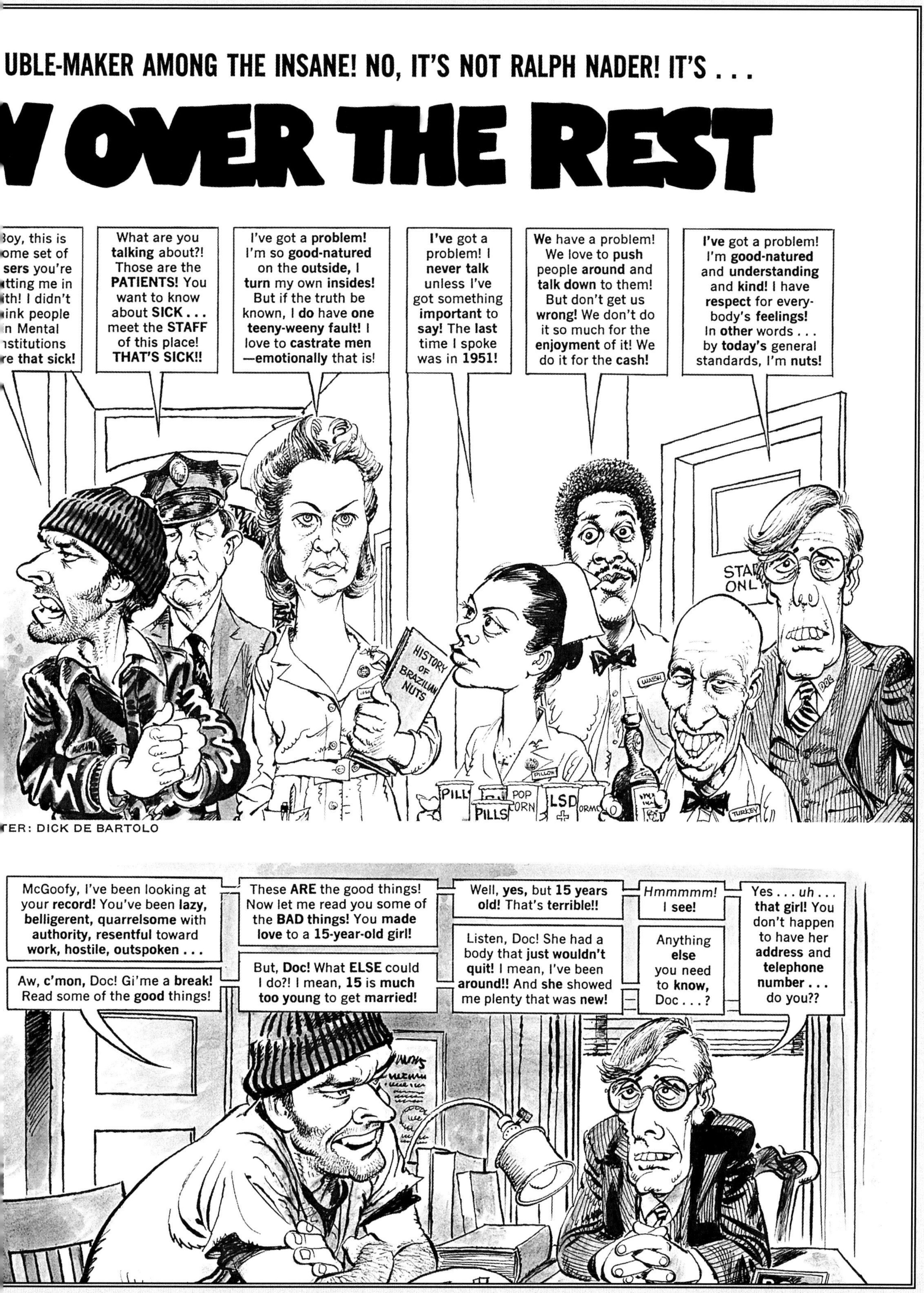
UBLE-MAKER AMONG THE INSANE! NO, IT'S NOT RALPH NADER! IT'S . . .
V OVER THE REST
oy, this is ome set of sers you're tting me in ith! I didn't ink people n Mental nstitutions e that sick!
What are you talking about?! Those are the PATIENTS! You want to know about SICK . . . meet the STAFF of this place! THAT'S SICK!!
I've got a problem! I'm so good-natured on the outside, I turn my own insides! But if the truth be known, I do have one teeny-weeny fault! I love to castrate men —emotionally that is!
I've got a problem! I never talk unless I've got something important to say! The last time I spoke was in 1951!
We have a problem! We love to push people around and talk down to them! But don't get us wrong! We don't do it so much for the enjoyment of it! We do it for the cash!
I've got a problem! I'm good-natured and understanding and kind! I have respect for every-body's feelings! In other words . . . by today's general standards, I'm nuts!
HISTORY OF BRAZILIAN NUTS
STA ONL
PILLS
POP CORN
LSD
TER: DICK DE BARTOLO
McGoofy, I've been looking at your record! You've been lazy, belligerent, quarrelsome with authority, resentful toward work, hostile, outspoken . . .
Aw, c'mon, Doc! Gi'me a break! Read some of the good things!
These ARE the good things! Now let me read you some of the BAD things! You made love to a 15-year-old girl!
But, Doc! What ELSE could I do?! I mean, 15 is much too young to get married!
Well, yes, but 15 years old! That's terrible!!
Listen, Doc! She had a body that just wouldn't quit! I mean, I've been around!! And she showed me plenty that was new!
Hmmmmm! I see!
Anything else you need to know, Doc . . . ?
Yes . . . uh . . . that girl! You don't happen to have her address and telephone number . . . do you??

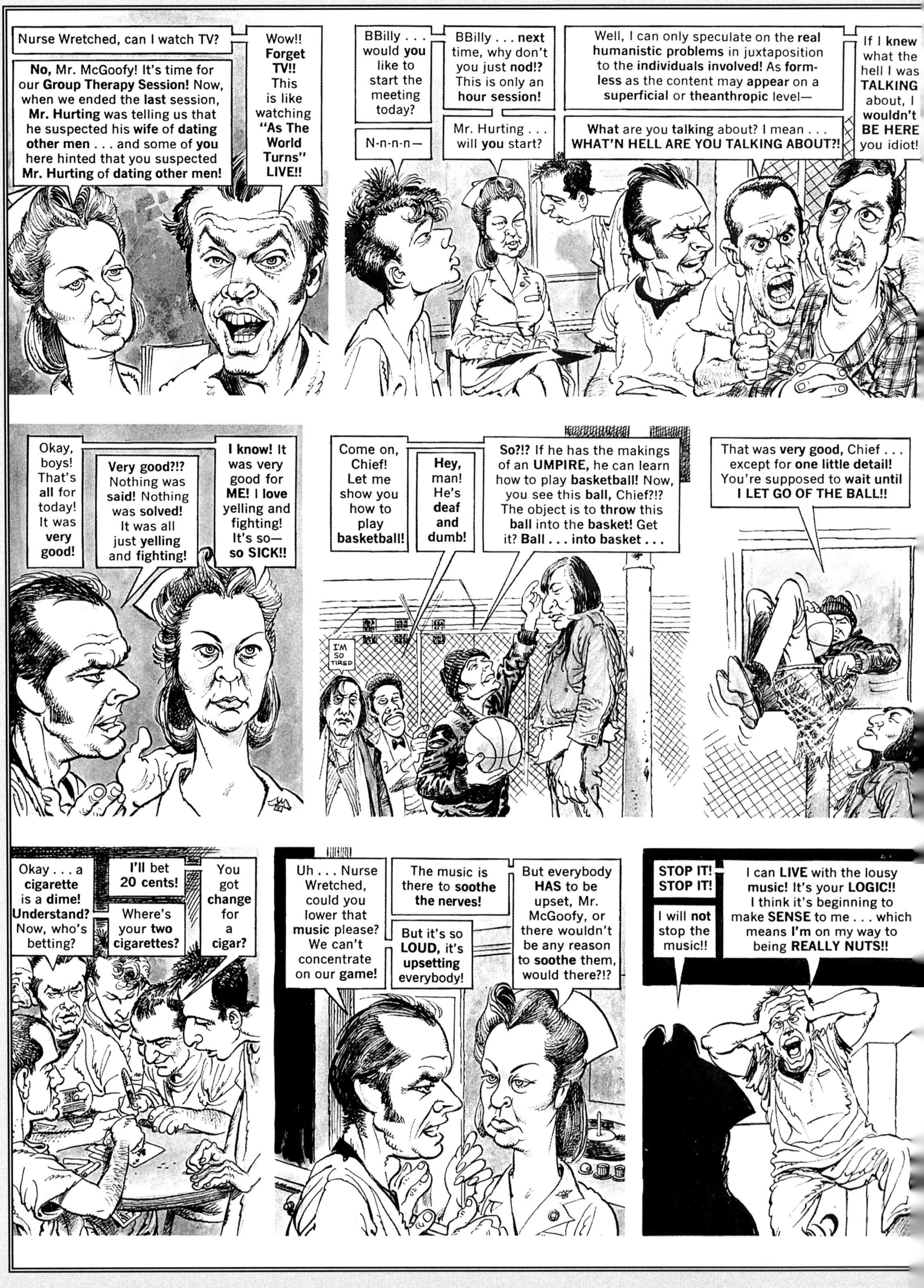
Nurse Wretched, can I watch TV?
No, Mr. McGoofy! It's time for our Group Therapy Session! Now, when we ended the last session, Mr. Hurting was telling us that he suspected his wife of dating other men . . . and some of you here hinted that you suspected Mr. Hurting of dating other men!
Wow!! Forget TV!! This is like watching "As The World Turns" LIVE!!
BBilly . . . would you like to start the meeting today?
N-n-n-n—
BBilly . . . next time, why don't you just nod!? This is only an hour session!
Mr. Hurting . . . will you start?
Well, I can only speculate on the real humanistic problems in juxtaposition to the individuals involved! As formless as the content may appear on a superficial or theanthropic level—
What are you talking about? I mean . . . WHAT'N HELL ARE YOU TALKING ABOUT?!
If I knew what the hell I was TALKING about, I wouldn't BE HERE you idiot!
Okay, boys! That's all for today! It was very good!
Very good?!? Nothing was said! Nothing was solved! It was all just yelling and fighting!
I know! It was very good for ME! I love yelling and fighting! It's so— so SICK!!
Come on, Chief! Let me show you how to play basketball!
Hey, man! He's deaf and dumb!
So?!? If he has the makings of an UMPIRE, he can learn how to play basketball! Now, you see this ball, Chief?!? The object is to throw this ball into the basket! Get it? Ball . . . into basket . . .
I'M SO TIRED
That was very good, Chief . . . except for one little detail! You're supposed to wait until I LET GO OF THE BALL!!
Okay . . . a cigarette is a dime! Understand? Now, who's betting?
I'll bet 20 cents!
Where's your two cigarettes?
You got change for a cigar?
Uh . . . Nurse Wretched, could you lower that music please? We can't concentrate on our game!
The music is there to soothe the nerves!
But it's so LOUD, it's upsetting everybody!
But everybody HAS to be upset, Mr. McGoofy, or there wouldn't be any reason to soothe them, would there?!?
STOP IT! STOP IT!
I will not stop the music!!
I can LIVE with the lousy music! It's your LOGIC!! I think it's beginning to make SENSE to me . . . which means I'm on my way to being REALLY NUTS!!

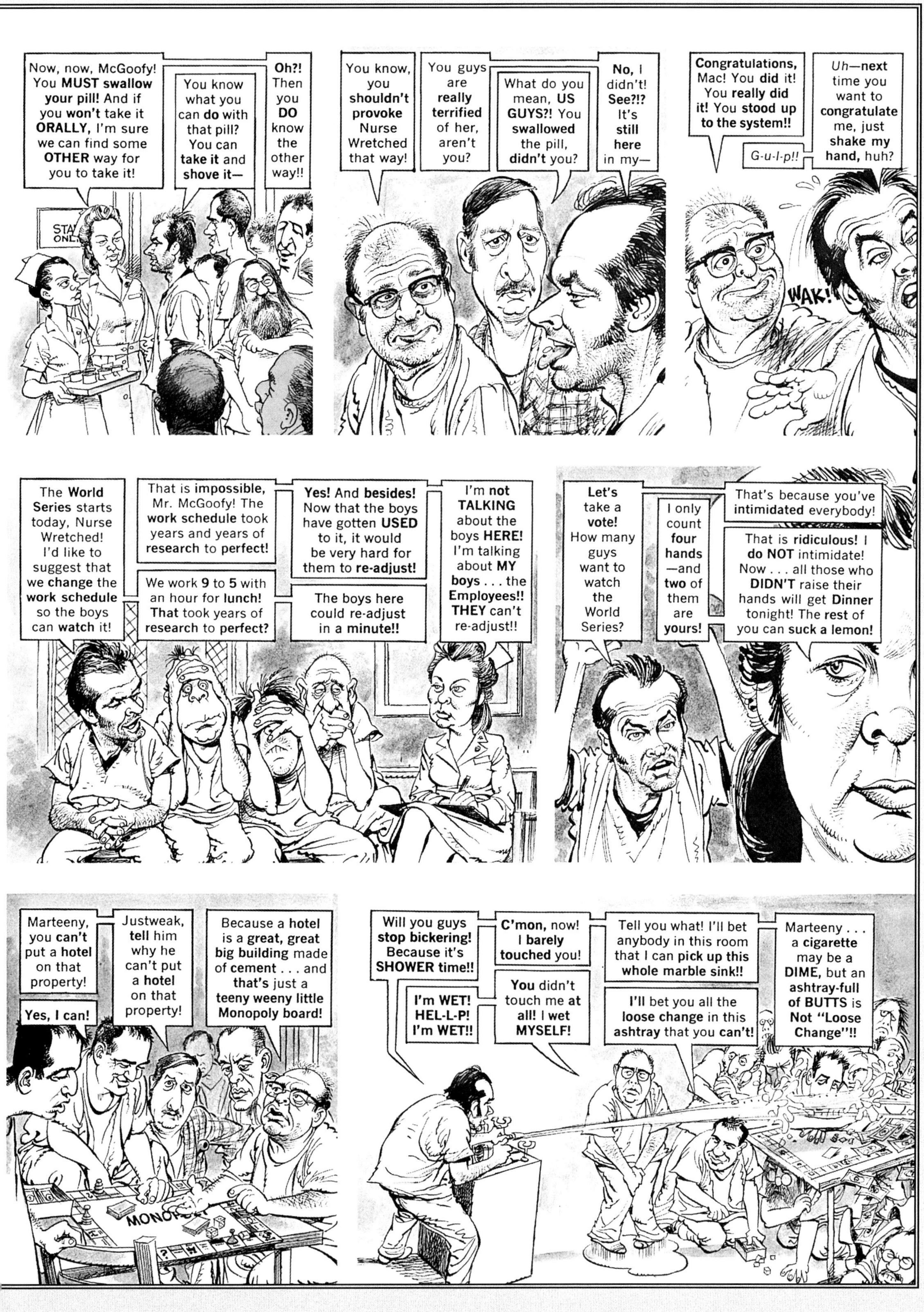
Now, now, McGoofy! You MUST swallow your pill! And if you won't take it ORALLY, I'm sure we can find some OTHER way for you to take it!
You know what you can do with that pill? You can take it and shove it—
Oh?! Then you DO know the other way!!
You know, you shouldn't provoke Nurse Wretched that way!
You guys are really terrified of her, aren't you?
What do you mean, US GUYS?! You swallowed the pill, didn't you?
No, I didn't! See?!? It's still here in my—
Congratulations, Mac! You did it! You really did it! You stood up to the system!!
G-u-l-p!!
WAK!
Uh—next time you want to congratulate me, just shake my hand, huh?
The World Series starts today, Nurse Wretched! I'd like to suggest that we change the work schedule so the boys can watch it!
That is impossible, Mr. McGoofy! The work schedule took years and years of research to perfect!
We work 9 to 5 with an hour for lunch! That took years of research to perfect?
Yes! And besides! Now that the boys have gotten USED to it, it would be very hard for them to re-adjust!
The boys here could re-adjust in a minute!!
I'm not TALKING about the boys HERE! I'm talking about MY boys . . . the Employees!! THEY can't re-adjust!!
Let's take a vote! How many guys want to watch the World Series?
I only count four hands—and two of them are yours!
That's because you've intimidated everybody!
That is ridiculous! I do NOT intimidate! Now . . . all those who DIDN'T raise their hands will get Dinner tonight! The rest of you can suck a lemon!
Marteeny, you can't put a hotel on that property!
Yes, I can!
Justweak, tell him why he can't put a hotel on that property!
Because a hotel is a great, great big building made of cement . . . and that's just a teeny weeny little Monopoly board!
Will you guys stop bickering! Because it's SHOWER time!!
I'm WET! HEL-L-P! I'm WET!!
C'mon, now! I barely touched you!
You didn't touch me at all! I wet MYSELF!
Tell you what! I'll bet anybody in this room that I can pick up this whole marble sink!!
I'll bet you all the loose change in this ashtray that you can't!
Marteeny . . . a cigarette may be a DIME, but an ashtray-full of BUTTS is Not "Loose Change"!!

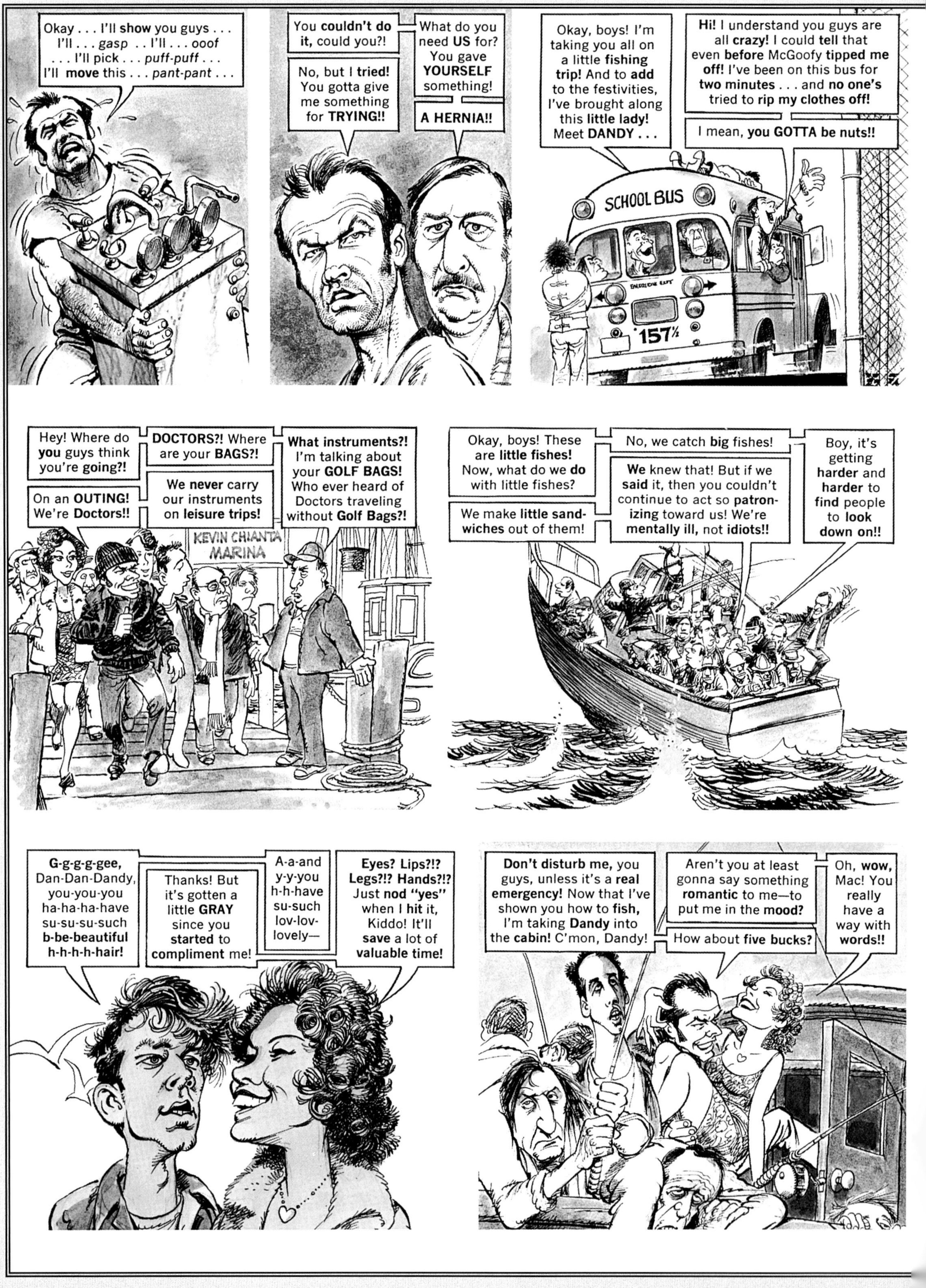
Okay . . . I'll show you guys . . . I'll . . . gasp . . I'll . . . ooof . . . I'll pick . . . puff-puff . . . I'll move this . . . pant-pant . . .
You couldn't do it, could you?!
No, but I tried! You gotta give me something for TRYING!!
What do you need US for? You gave YOURSELF something!
A HERNIA!!
Okay, boys! I'm taking you all on a little fishing trip! And to add to the festivities, I've brought along this little lady! Meet DANDY . . .
Hi! I understand you guys are all crazy! I could tell that even before McGoofy tipped me off! I've been on this bus for two minutes . . . and no one's tried to rip my clothes off!
I mean, you GOTTA be nuts!!
SCHOOL BUS
157½
Hey! Where do you guys think you're going?!
On an OUTING! We're Doctors!!
DOCTORS?! Where are your BAGS?!
We never carry our instruments on leisure trips!
What instruments?! I'm talking about your GOLF BAGS! Who ever heard of Doctors traveling without Golf Bags?!
KEVIN CHIANTA MARINA
Okay, boys! These are little fishes! Now, what do we do with little fishes?
We make little sandwiches out of them!
No, we catch big fishes!
We knew that! But if we said it, then you couldn't continue to act so patronizing toward us! We're mentally ill, not idiots!!
Boy, it's getting harder and harder to find people to look down on!!
G-g-g-g-gee, Dan-Dan-Dandy, you-you-you ha-ha-ha-have su-su-su-such b-be-beautiful h-h-h-h-hair!
Thanks! But it's gotten a little GRAY since you started to compliment me!
A-a-and y-y-you h-h-have su-such lov-lov-lovely—
Eyes? Lips?!? Legs?!? Hands?!? Just nod "yes" when I hit it, Kiddo! It'll save a lot of valuable time!
Don't disturb me, you guys, unless it's a real emergency! Now that I've shown you how to fish, I'm taking Dandy into the cabin! C'mon, Dandy!
Aren't you at least gonna say something romantic to me—to put me in the mood?
How about five bucks?
Oh, wow, Mac! You really have a way with words!!

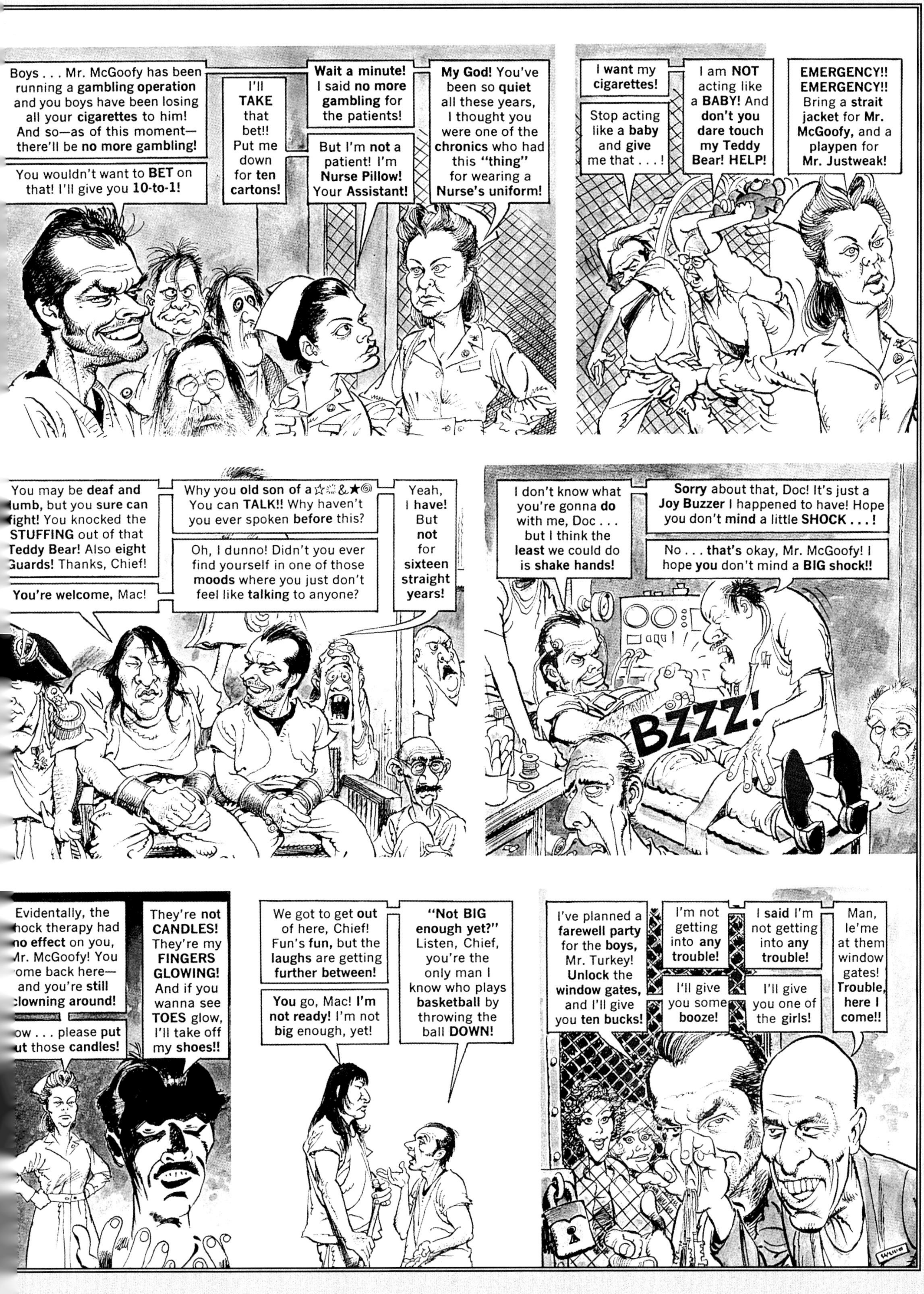
Boys . . . Mr. McGoofy has been running a gambling operation and you boys have been losing all your cigarettes to him! And so—as of this moment—there'll be no more gambling!
You wouldn't want to BET on that! I'll give you 10-to-1!
I'll TAKE that bet!! Put me down for ten cartons!
Wait a minute! I said no more gambling for the patients!
But I'm not a patient! I'm Nurse Pillow! Your Assistant!
My God! You've been so quiet all these years, I thought you were one of the chronics who had this "thing" for wearing a Nurse's uniform!
I want my cigarettes!
Stop acting like a baby and give me that . . . !
I am NOT acting like a BABY! And don't you dare touch my Teddy Bear! HELP!
EMERGENCY!! EMERGENCY!! Bring a strait jacket for Mr. McGoofy, and a playpen for Mr. Justweak!
You may be deaf and umb, but you sure can fight! You knocked the STUFFING out of that Teddy Bear! Also eight Guards! Thanks, Chief!
You're welcome, Mac!
Why you old son of a ☆⁂&★◎ You can TALK!! Why haven't you ever spoken before this?
Oh, I dunno! Didn't you ever find yourself in one of those moods where you just don't feel like talking to anyone?
Yeah, I have! But not for sixteen straight years!
I don't know what you're gonna do with me, Doc . . . but I think the least we could do is shake hands!
Sorry about that, Doc! It's just a Joy Buzzer I happened to have! Hope you don't mind a little SHOCK . . . !
No . . . that's okay, Mr. McGoofy! I hope you don't mind a BIG shock!!
BZZZ!
Evidentally, the hock therapy had no effect on you, Ar. McGoofy! You ome back here—and you're still clowning around!
ow . . . please put ut those candles!
They're not CANDLES! They're my FINGERS GLOWING! And if you wanna see TOES glow, I'll take off my shoes!!
We got to get out of here, Chief! Fun's fun, but the laughs are getting further between!
You go, Mac! I'm not ready! I'm not big enough, yet!
"Not BIG enough yet?" Listen, Chief, you're the only man I know who plays basketball by throwing the ball DOWN!
I've planned a farewell party for the boys, Mr. Turkey! Unlock the window gates, and I'll give you ten bucks!
I'm not getting into any trouble!
I'll give you some booze!
I said I'm not getting into any trouble!
I'll give you one of the girls!
Man, le'me at them window gates! Trouble, here I come!!

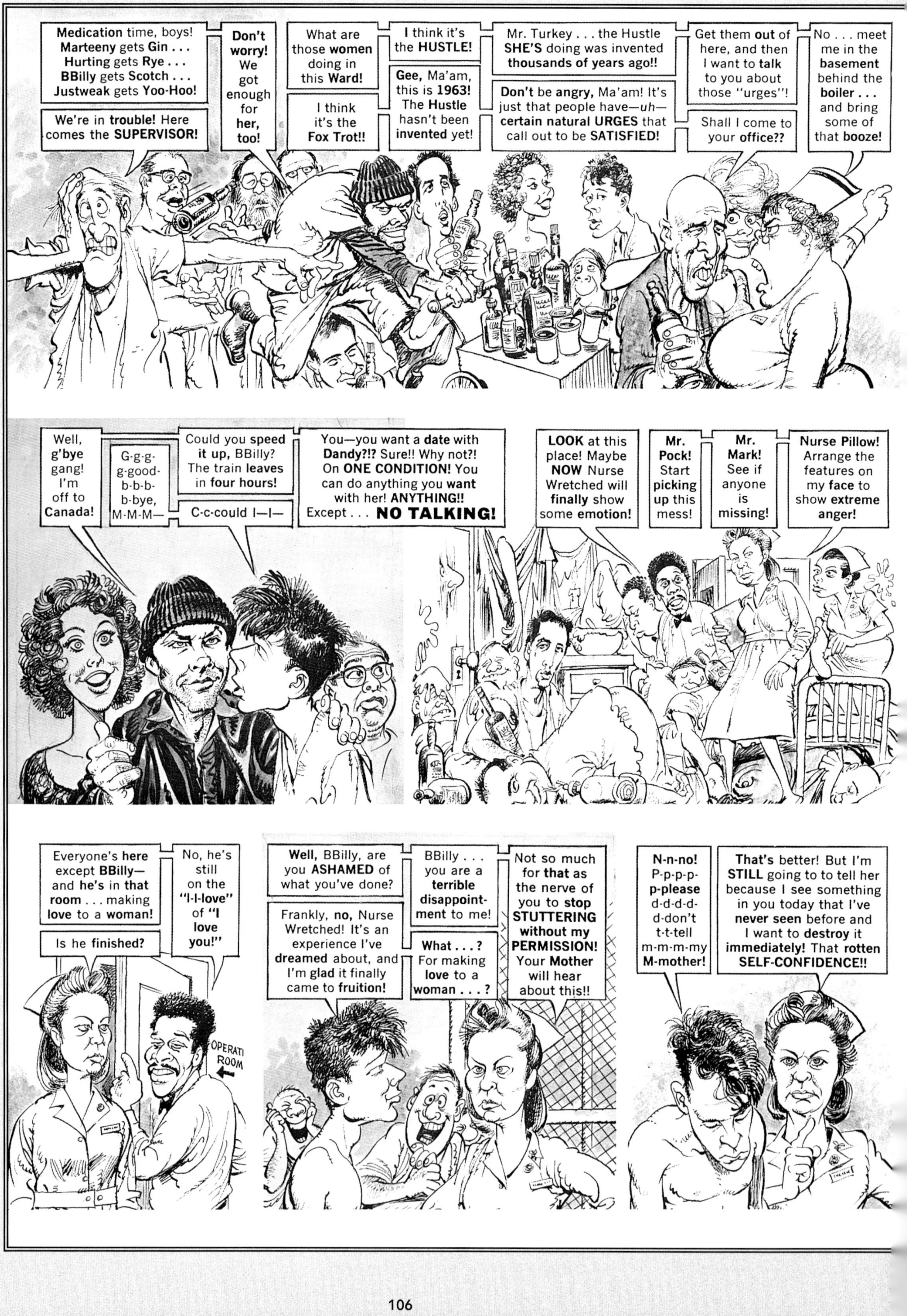
Medication time, boys! Marteeny gets Gin . . . Hurting gets Rye . . . BBilly gets Scotch . . . Justweak gets Yoo-Hoo!
We're in trouble! Here comes the SUPERVISOR!
Don't worry! We got enough for her, too!
What are those women doing in this Ward!
I think it's the Fox Trot!!
I think it's the HUSTLE!
Gee, Ma'am, this is 1963! The Hustle hasn't been invented yet!
Mr. Turkey . . . the Hustle SHE'S doing was invented thousands of years ago!!
Don't be angry, Ma'am! It's just that people have—uh—certain natural URGES that call out to be SATISFIED!
Get them out of here, and then I want to talk to you about those "urges"!
Shall I come to your office??
No . . . meet me in the basement behind the boiler . . . and bring some of that booze!
Well, g'bye gang! I'm off to Canada!
G-g-g-g-good-b-b-b-b-bye, M-M-M—
Could you speed it up, BBilly? The train leaves in four hours!
C-c-could I—I—
You—you want a date with Dandy?!? Sure!! Why not?! On ONE CONDITION! You can do anything you want with her! ANYTHING!! Except . . . NO TALKING!
LOOK at this place! Maybe NOW Nurse Wretched will finally show some emotion!
Mr. Pock! Start picking up this mess!
Mr. Mark! See if anyone is missing!
Nurse Pillow! Arrange the features on my face to show extreme anger!
Everyone's here except BBilly—and he's in that room . . . making love to a woman!
Is he finished?
No, he's still on the "I-I-love" of "I love you!"
OPERATI ROOM
Well, BBilly, are you ASHAMED of what you've done?
Frankly, no, Nurse Wretched! It's an experience I've dreamed about, and I'm glad it finally came to fruition!
BBilly . . . you are a terrible disappointment to me!
What . . . ? For making love to a woman . . . ?
Not so much for that as the nerve of you to stop STUTTERING without my PERMISSION! Your Mother will hear about this!!
N-n-no! P-p-p-p-please d-d-d-d-don't t-t-tell m-m-m-my M-mother!
That's better! But I'm STILL going to to tell her because I see something in you today that I've never seen before and I want to destroy it immediately! That rotten SELF-CONFIDENCE!!

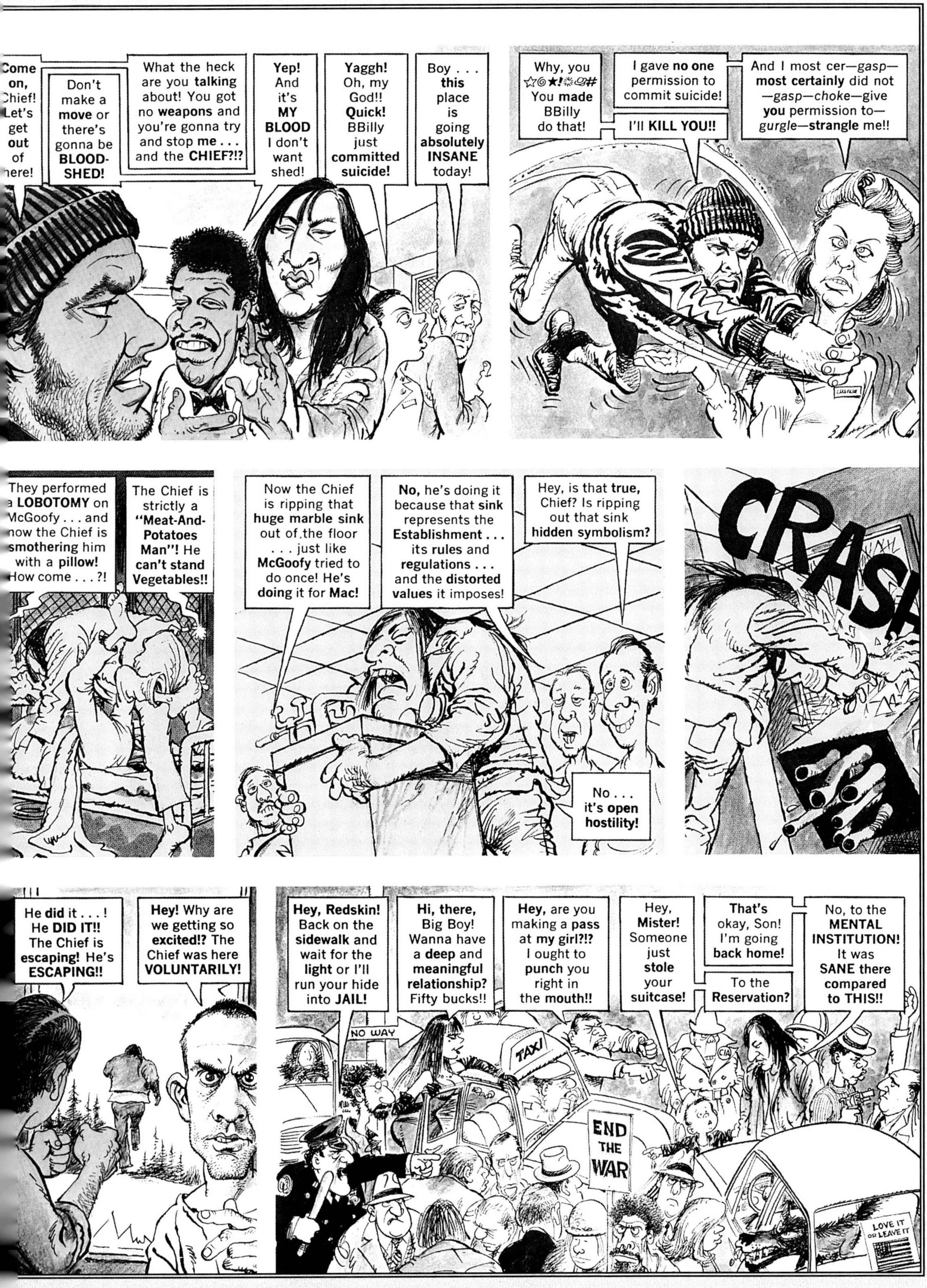
Come on, hief! Let's get out of ere!
Don't make a move or there's gonna be BLOOD-SHED!
What the heck are you talking about! You got no weapons and you're gonna try and stop me . . . and the CHIEF?!?
Yep! And it's MY BLOOD I don't want shed!
Yaggh! Oh, my God!! Quick! BBilly just committed suicide!
Boy . . . this place is going absolutely INSANE today!
Why, you ☆⊚★!※@# You made BBilly do that!
I'll KILL YOU!!
I gave no one permission to commit suicide!
And I most cer—gasp—most certainly did not —gasp—choke—give you permission to—gurgle—strangle me!!
They performed a LOBOTOMY on McGoofy . . . and now the Chief is smothering him with a pillow! How come . . . ?!
The Chief is strictly a "Meat-And-Potatoes Man"! He can't stand Vegetables!!
Now the Chief is ripping that huge marble sink out of the floor . . . just like McGoofy tried to do once! He's doing it for Mac!
No, he's doing it because that sink represents the Establishment . . . its rules and regulations . . . and the distorted values it imposes!
Hey, is that true, Chief? Is ripping out that sink hidden symbolism?
No . . . it's open hostility!
CRASH
He did it . . . ! He DID IT!! The Chief is escaping! He's ESCAPING!!
Hey! Why are we getting so excited!? The Chief was here VOLUNTARILY!
Hey, Redskin! Back on the sidewalk and wait for the light or I'll run your hide into JAIL!
Hi, there, Big Boy! Wanna have a deep and meaningful relationship? Fifty bucks!!
Hey, are you making a pass at my girl?!? I ought to punch you right in the mouth!!
Hey, Mister! Someone just stole your suitcase!
That's okay, Son! I'm going back home!
To the Reservation?
No, to the MENTAL INSTITUTION! It was SANE there compared to THIS!!
NO WAY
TAXI
CIA
END THE WAR
LOVE IT OR LEAVE IT

HIGH TRAVOLTAGE DEPT.

Combine a dynamic young TV star with the soundtrack of a hot, exploitable singin group and some "R"-rated dialogue, insure it with some sub-plots from other hi films like "Rocky," "American Graffiti," "West Side Story," "Mean Streets," an "Beach Blanket Bingo"... and you've got the formula for one of the biggest block buster movies of the year, right? Wrong! Because the best "hustle" may not be th one they're dancing up on the screen, but the one foisted on us by the producers- for making millions on a film that does have spectacular choreography... but no much else! Yep, as far as we at MAD are concerned, you wasted your money on . .

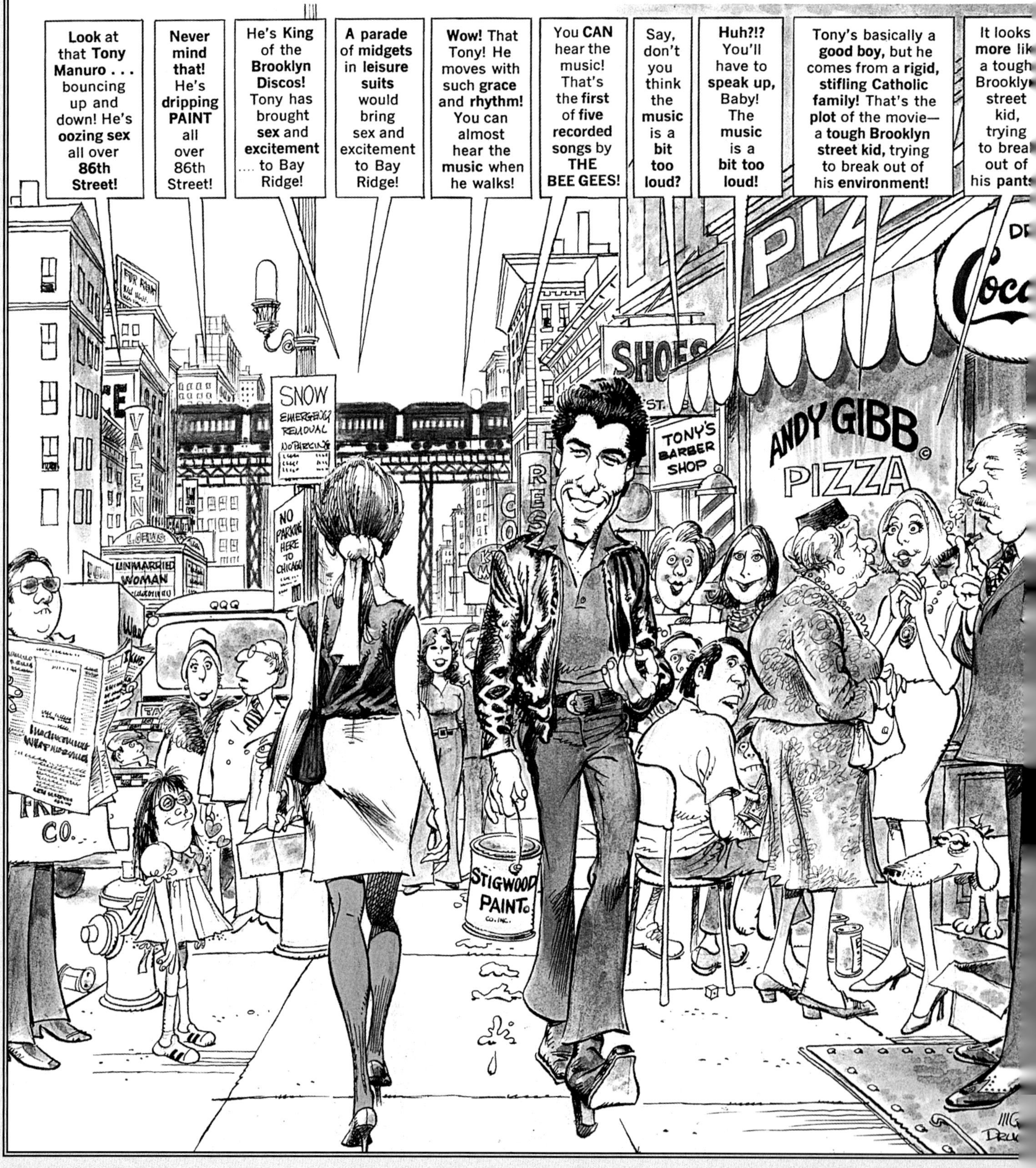
Look at that Tony Manuro . . . bouncing up and down! He's oozing sex all over 86th Street!
Never mind that! He's dripping PAINT all over 86th Street!
He's King of the Brooklyn Discos! Tony has brought sex and excitement .... to Bay Ridge!
A parade of midgets in leisure suits would bring sex and excitement to Bay Ridge!
Wow! That Tony! He moves with such grace and rhythm! You can almost hear the music when he walks!
You CAN hear the music! That's the first of five recorded songs by THE BEE GEES!
Say, don't you think the music is a bit too loud?
Huh?!? You'll have to speak up, Baby! The music is a bit too loud!
Tony's basically a good boy, but he comes from a rigid, stifling Catholic family! That's the plot of the movie— a tough Brooklyn street kid, trying to break out of his environment!
It looks more lik a tough Brookly street kid, trying to brea out of his pant
SNOW
NO PARKING HERE TO CHICAGO
UNMARRIED WOMAN
SHOES
TONY'S BARBER SHOP
ANDY GIBB© PIZZA
STIGWOOD PAINT CO. INC.

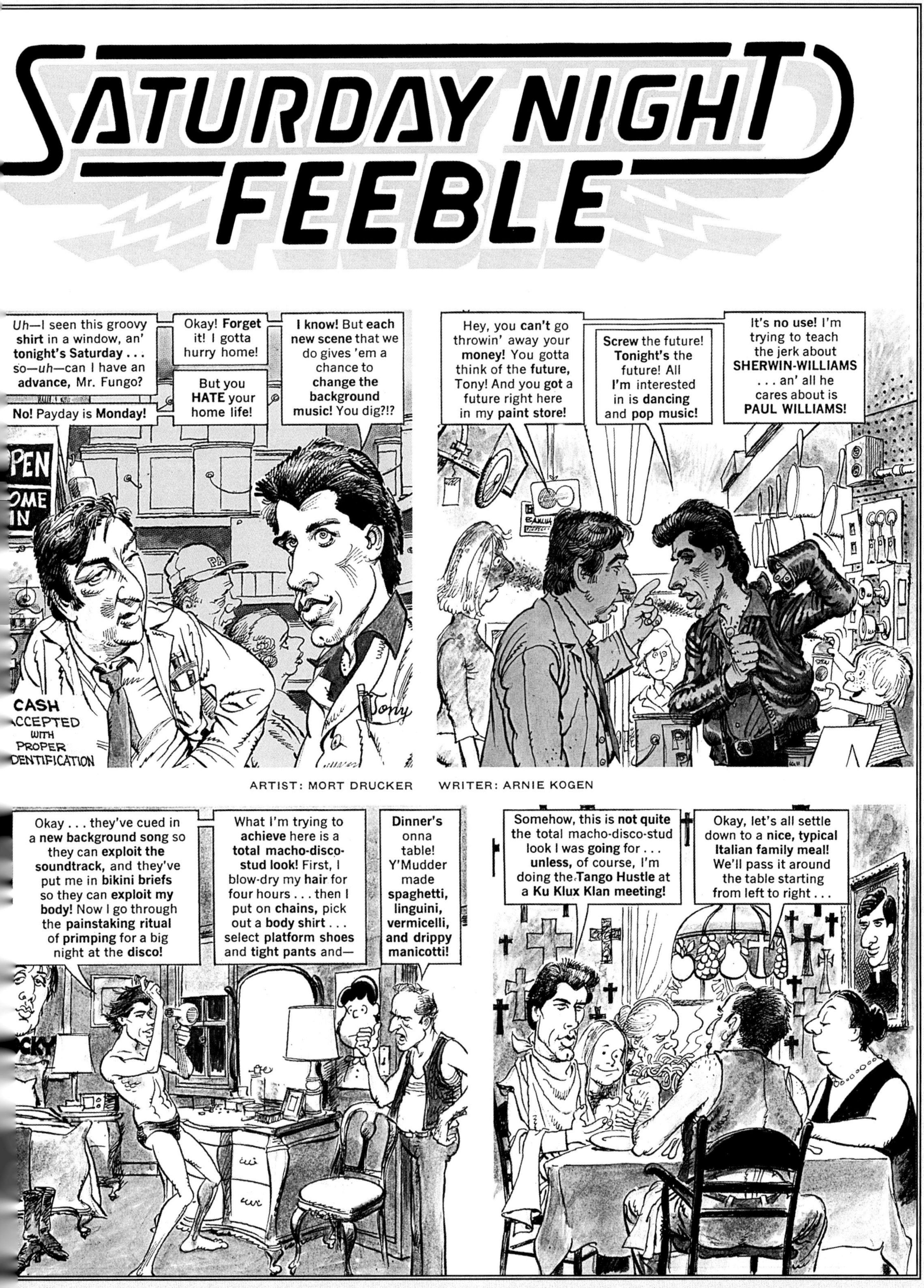
SATURDAY NIGHT FEEBLE
Uh—I seen this groovy shirt in a window, an' tonight's Saturday . . . so—uh—can I have an advance, Mr. Fungo?
No! Payday is Monday!
Okay! Forget it! I gotta hurry home!
But you HATE your home life!
I know! But each new scene that we do gives 'em a chance to change the background music! You dig?!?
CASH
Tony
Hey, you can't go throwin' away your money! You gotta think of the future, Tony! And you got a future right here in my paint store!
Screw the future! Tonight's the future! All I'm interested in is dancing and pop music!
It's no use! I'm trying to teach the jerk about SHERWIN-WILLIAMS . . . an' all he cares about is PAUL WILLIAMS!
ARTIST: MORT DRUCKER WRITER: ARNIE KOGEN
Okay . . . they've cued in a new background song so they can exploit the soundtrack, and they've put me in bikini briefs so they can exploit my body! Now I go through the painstaking ritual of primping for a big night at the disco!
What I'm trying to achieve here is a total macho-disco-stud look! First, I blow-dry my hair for four hours . . . then I put on chains, pick out a body shirt . . . select platform shoes and tight pants and—
Dinner's onna table! Y'Mudder made spaghetti, linguini, vermicelli, and drippy manicotti!
Somehow, this is not quite the total macho-disco-stud look I was going for . . . unless, of course, I'm doing the Tango Hustle at a Ku Klux Klan meeting!
Okay, let's all settle down to a nice, typical Italian family meal! We'll pass it around the table starting from left to right . . .

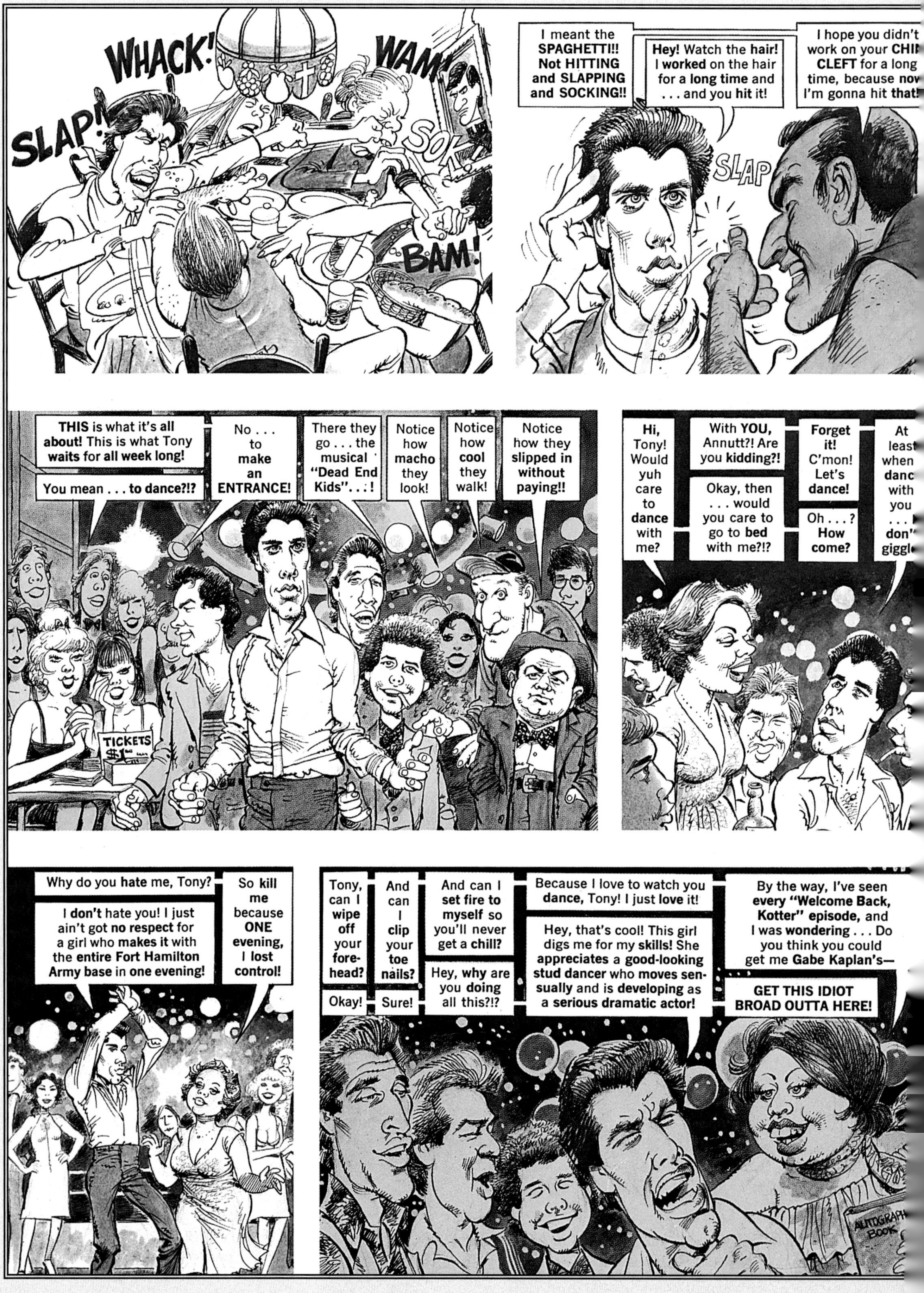
WHACK!
WAM
SLAP!
SOK
BAM!
I meant the SPAGHETTI!! Not HITTING and SLAPPING and SOCKING!!
Hey! Watch the hair! I worked on the hair for a long time and . . . and you hit it!
I hope you didn't work on your CHI CLEFT for a long time, because no I'm gonna hit that!
SLAP
THIS is what it's all about! This is what Tony waits for all week long!
You mean . . . to dance?!?
No . . . to make an ENTRANCE!
There they go . . . the musical "Dead End Kids" . . . !
Notice how macho they look!
Notice how cool they walk!
Notice how they slipped in without paying!!
TICKETS $1
Hi, Tony! Would yuh care to dance with me?
With YOU, Annutt?! Are you kidding?!
Okay, then . . . would you care to go to bed with me?!?
Forget it! C'mon! Let's dance!
Oh . . . ? How come?
At least when danc with you . . . don' giggl
Why do you hate me, Tony?
I don't hate you! I just ain't got no respect for a girl who makes it with the entire Fort Hamilton Army base in one evening!
So kill me because ONE evening, I lost control!
Tony, can I wipe off your fore-head?
Okay!
And can I clip your toe nails?
Sure!
And can I set fire to myself so you'll never get a chill?
Hey, why are you doing all this?!?
Because I love to watch you dance, Tony! I just love it!
Hey, that's cool! This girl digs me for my skills! She appreciates a good-looking stud dancer who moves sen-sually and is developing as a serious dramatic actor!
By the way, I've seen every "Welcome Back, Kotter" episode, and I was wondering . . . Do you think you could get me Gabe Kaplan's—
GET THIS IDIOT BROAD OUTTA HERE!
AUTOGRAPH BOOK

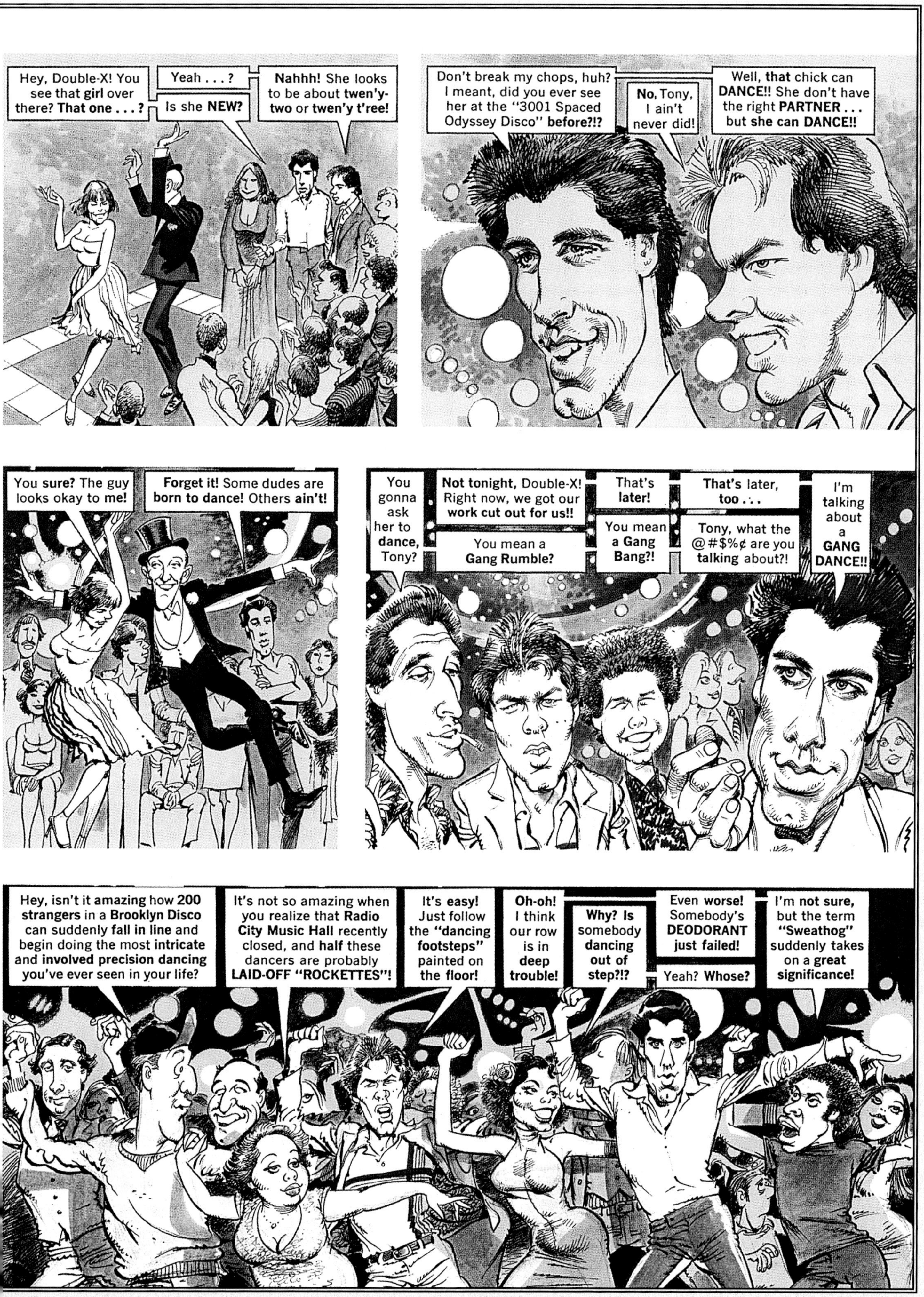
Hey, Double-X! You see that girl over there? That one . . . ?
Yeah . . . ?
Is she NEW?
Nahhh! She looks to be about twen'y-two or twen'y t'ree!
Don't break my chops, huh? I meant, did you ever see her at the "3001 Spaced Odyssey Disco" before?!?
No, Tony, I ain't never did!
Well, that chick can DANCE!! She don't have the right PARTNER . . . but she can DANCE!!
You sure? The guy looks okay to me!
Forget it! Some dudes are born to dance! Others ain't!
You gonna ask her to dance, Tony?
Not tonight, Double-X! Right now, we got our work cut out for us!!
You mean a Gang Rumble?
That's later!
You mean a Gang Bang?!
That's later, too . . .
Tony, what the @#$%¢ are you talking about?!
I'm talking about a GANG DANCE!!
Hey, isn't it amazing how 200 strangers in a Brooklyn Disco can suddenly fall in line and begin doing the most intricate and involved precision dancing you've ever seen in your life?
It's not so amazing when you realize that Radio City Music Hall recently closed, and half these dancers are probably LAID-OFF "ROCKETTES"!
It's easy! Just follow the "dancing footsteps" painted on the floor!
Oh-oh! I think our row is in deep trouble!
Why? Is somebody dancing out of step?!?
Even worse! Somebody's DEODORANT just failed!
Yeah? Whose?
I'm not sure, but the term "Sweathog" suddenly takes on a great significance!

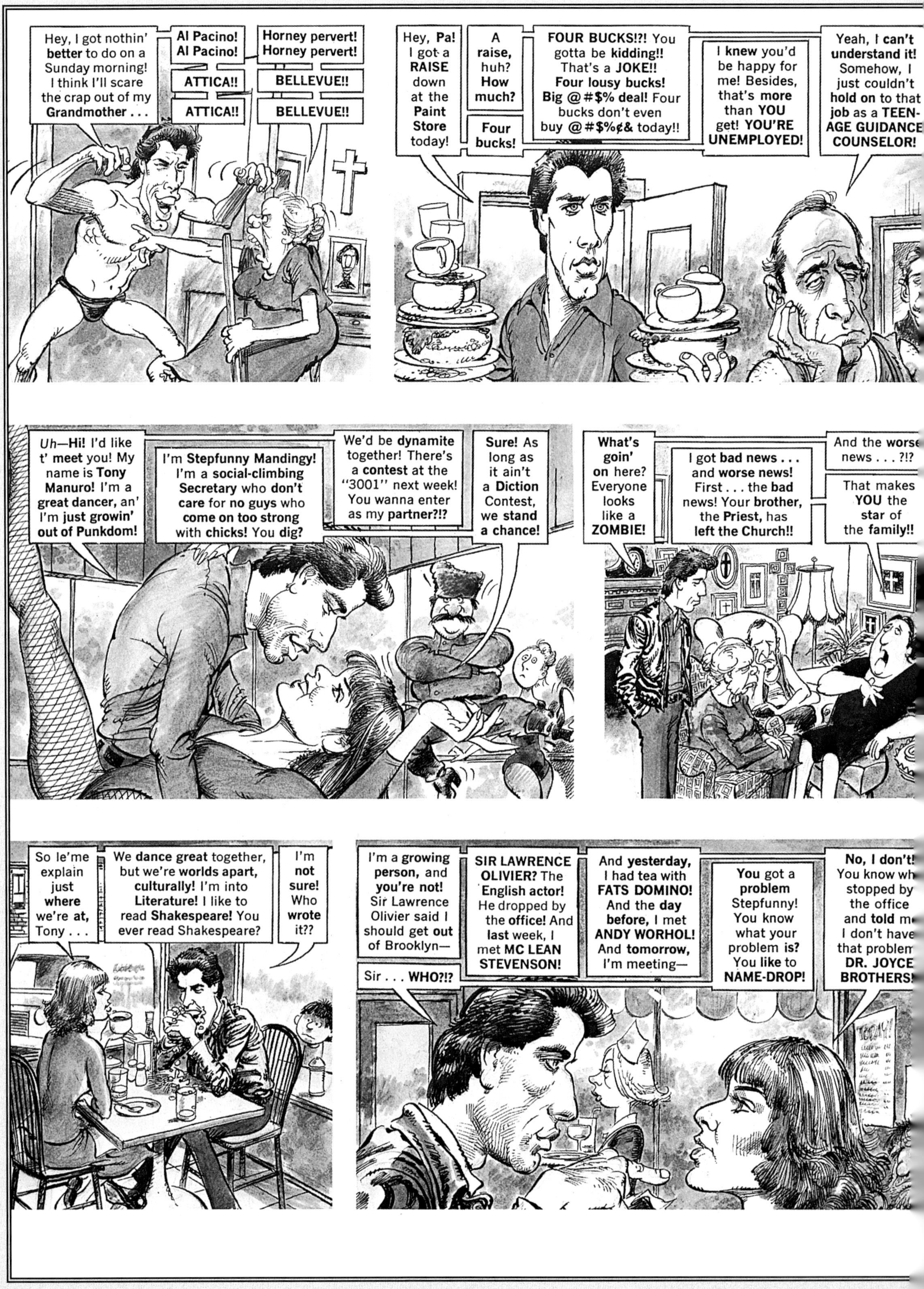

Hey, I got nothin' better to do on a Sunday morning! I think I'll scare the crap out of my Grandmother . . .
Al Pacino! Al Pacino!
Horney pervert! Horney pervert!
ATTICA!!
BELLEVUE!!
ATTICA!!
BELLEVUE!!
Hey, Pa! I got a RAISE down at the Paint Store today!
A raise, huh? How much?
Four bucks!
FOUR BUCKS!?! You gotta be kidding!! That's a JOKE!! Four lousy bucks! Big @#$% deal! Four bucks don't even buy @#$%¢& today!!
I knew you'd be happy for me! Besides, that's more than YOU get! YOU'RE UNEMPLOYED!
Yeah, I can't understand it! Somehow, I just couldn't hold on to that job as a TEEN-AGE GUIDANCE COUNSELOR!
Uh—Hi! I'd like t' meet you! My name is Tony Manuro! I'm a great dancer, an' I'm just growin' out of Punkdom!
I'm Stepfunny Mandingy! I'm a social-climbing Secretary who don't care for no guys who come on too strong with chicks! You dig?
We'd be dynamite together! There's a contest at the "3001" next week! You wanna enter as my partner?!?
Sure! As long as it ain't a Diction Contest, we stand a chance!
What's goin' on here? Everyone looks like a ZOMBIE!
I got bad news . . . and worse news! First . . . the bad news! Your brother, the Priest, has left the Church!!
And the worse news . . . ?!?
That makes YOU the star of the family!!
So le'me explain just where we're at, Tony . . .
We dance great together, but we're worlds apart, culturally! I'm into Literature! I like to read Shakespeare! You ever read Shakespeare?
I'm not sure! Who wrote it??
I'm a growing person, and you're not! Sir Lawrence Olivier said I should get out of Brooklyn—
Sir . . . WHO?!?
SIR LAWRENCE OLIVIER? The English actor! He dropped by the office! And last week, I met MC LEAN STEVENSON!
And yesterday, I had tea with FATS DOMINO! And the day before, I met ANDY WORHOL! And tomorrow, I'm meeting—
You got a problem Stepfunny! You know what your problem is? You like to NAME-DROP!
No, I don't! You know wh stopped by the office and told m I don't have that problem DR. JOYCE BROTHERS!

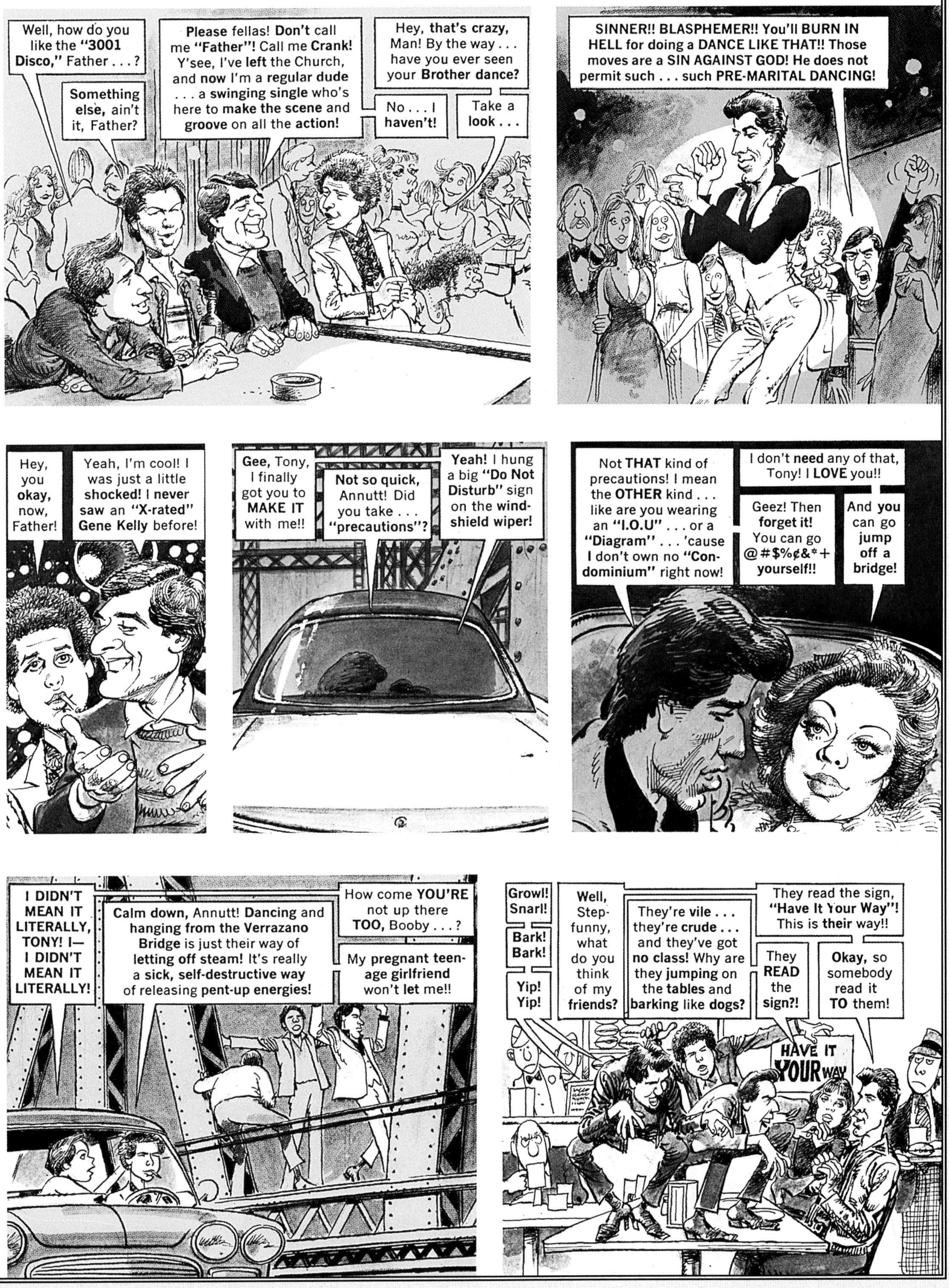
Well, how do you like the "3001 Disco," Father . . . ?
Something else, ain't it, Father?
Please fellas! Don't call me "Father"! Call me Crank! Y'see, I've left the Church, and now I'm a regular dude . . . a swinging single who's here to make the scene and groove on all the action!
Hey, that's crazy, Man! By the way . . . have you ever seen your Brother dance?
No . . . I haven't!
Take a look . . .
SINNER!! BLASPHEMER!! You'll BURN IN HELL for doing a DANCE LIKE THAT!! Those moves are a SIN AGAINST GOD! He does not permit such . . . such PRE-MARITAL DANCING!
Hey, you okay, now, Father!
Yeah, I'm cool! I was just a little shocked! I never saw an "X-rated" Gene Kelly before!
Gee, Tony, I finally got you to MAKE IT with me!!
Not so quick, Annutt! Did you take . . . "precautions"?
Yeah! I hung a big "Do Not Disturb" sign on the wind-shield wiper!
Not THAT kind of precautions! I mean the OTHER kind . . . like are you wearing an "I.O.U" . . . or a "Diagram" . . . 'cause I don't own no "Con-dominium" right now!
I don't need any of that, Tony! I LOVE you!!
Geez! Then forget it! You can go @#$%¢&*+ yourself!!
And you can go jump off a bridge!
I DIDN'T MEAN IT LITERALLY, TONY! I— I DIDN'T MEAN IT LITERALLY!
Calm down, Annutt! Dancing and hanging from the Verrazano Bridge is just their way of letting off steam! It's really a sick, self-destructive way of releasing pent-up energies!
How come YOU'RE not up there TOO, Booby . . . ?
My pregnant teen-age girlfriend won't let me!!
Growl! Snarl!
Bark! Bark!
Yip! Yip!
Well, Step-funny, what do you think of my friends?
They're vile . . . they're crude . . . and they've got no class! Why are they jumping on the tables and barking like dogs?
They read the sign, "Have It Your Way"! This is their way!!
They READ the sign?!
Okay, so somebody read it TO them!
HAVE IT YOUR WAY

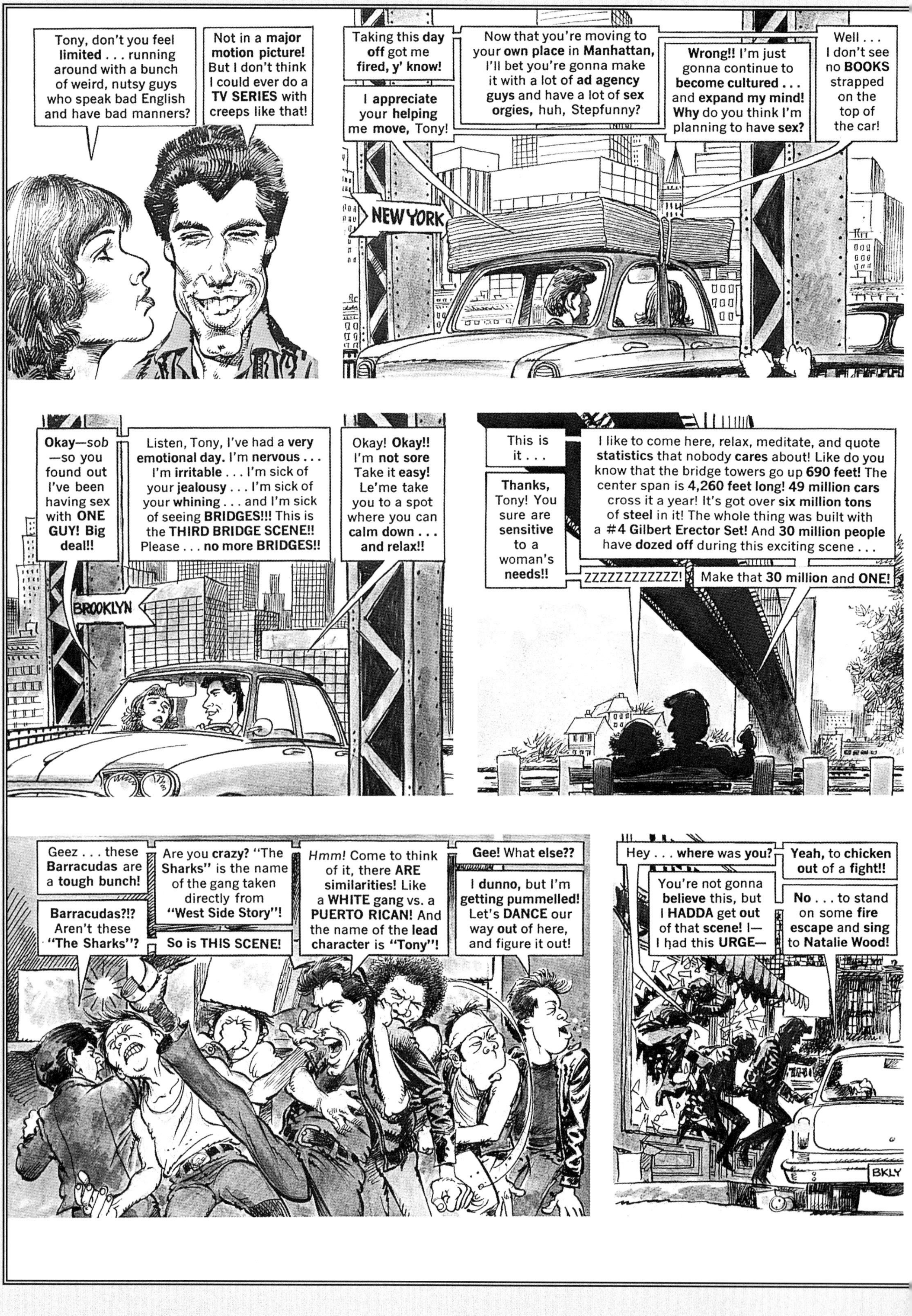
Tony, don't you feel limited . . . running around with a bunch of weird, nutsy guys who speak bad English and have bad manners?
Not in a major motion picture! But I don't think I could ever do a TV SERIES with creeps like that!
Taking this day off got me fired, y' know!
I appreciate your helping me move, Tony!
Now that you're moving to your own place in Manhattan, I'll bet you're gonna make it with a lot of ad agency guys and have a lot of sex orgies, huh, Stepfunny?
Wrong!! I'm just gonna continue to become cultured . . . and expand my mind! Why do you think I'm planning to have sex?
Well . . . I don't see no BOOKS strapped on the top of the car!
NEW YORK
Okay—sob—so you found out I've been having sex with ONE GUY! Big deal!!
Listen, Tony, I've had a very emotional day. I'm nervous . . . I'm irritable . . . I'm sick of your jealousy . . . I'm sick of your whining . . . and I'm sick of seeing BRIDGES!!! This is the THIRD BRIDGE SCENE!! Please . . . no more BRIDGES!!
Okay! Okay!! I'm not sore Take it easy! Le'me take you to a spot where you can calm down . . . and relax!!
BROOKLYN
This is it . . .
Thanks, Tony! You sure are sensitive to a woman's needs!!
I like to come here, relax, meditate, and quote statistics that nobody cares about! Like do you know that the bridge towers go up 690 feet! The center span is 4,260 feet long! 49 million cars cross it a year! It's got over six million tons of steel in it! The whole thing was built with a #4 Gilbert Erector Set! And 30 million people have dozed off during this exciting scene . . .
ZZZZZZZZZZZZ!
Make that 30 million and ONE!
Geez . . . these Barracudas are a tough bunch!
Barracudas?!? Aren't these "The Sharks"?
Are you crazy? "The Sharks" is the name of the gang taken directly from "West Side Story"!
So is THIS SCENE!
Hmm! Come to think of it, there ARE similarities! Like a WHITE gang vs. a PUERTO RICAN! And the name of the lead character is "Tony"!
Gee! What else??
I dunno, but I'm getting pummelled! Let's DANCE our way out of here, and figure it out!
Hey . . . where was you?
You're not gonna believe this, but I HADDA get out of that scene! I— I had this URGE—
Yeah, to chicken out of a fight!!
No . . . to stand on some fire escape and sing to Natalie Wood!
BKLY

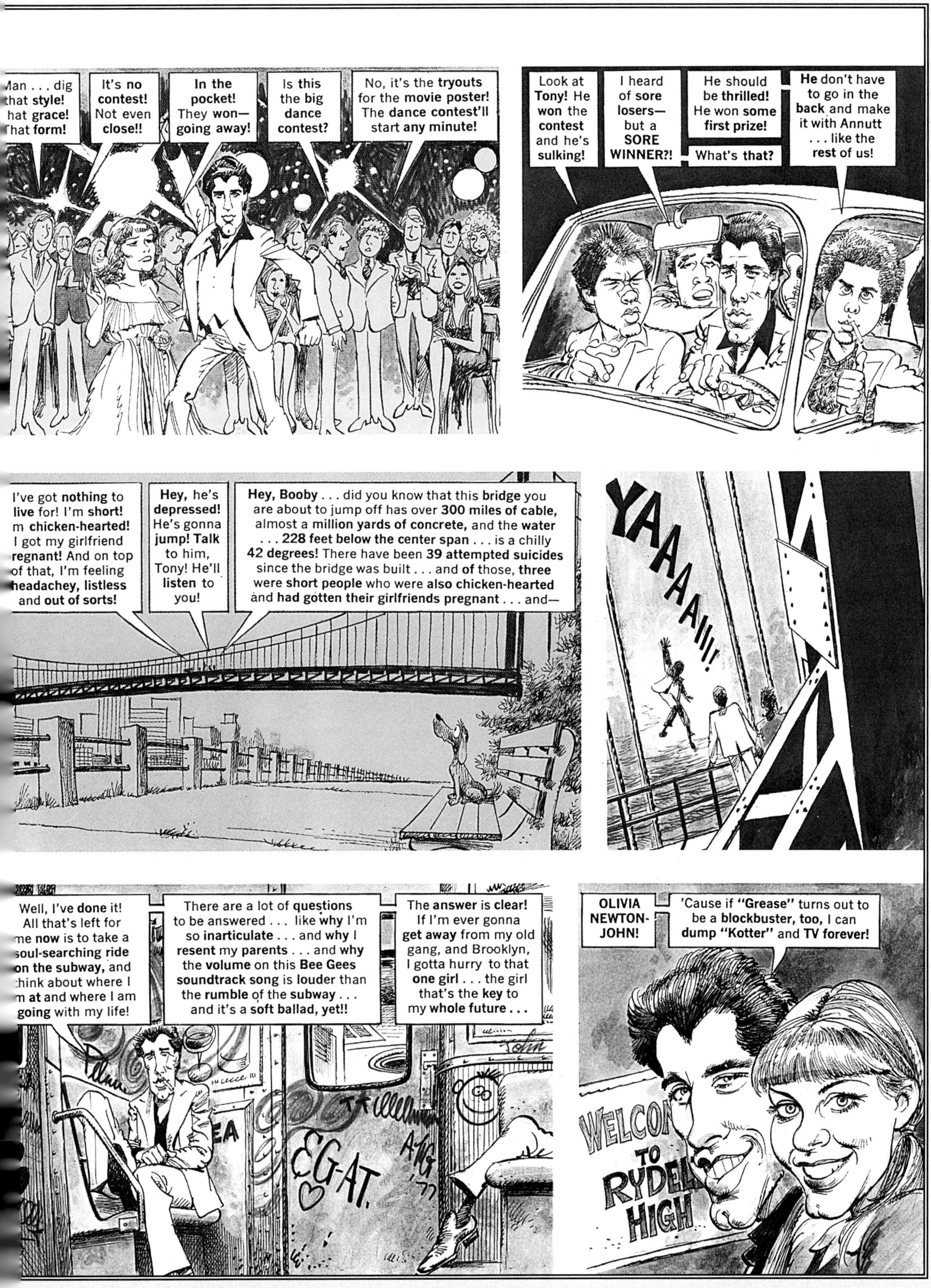
an . . . dig hat style! hat grace! That form!
It's no contest! Not even close!!
In the pocket! They won— going away!
Is this the big dance contest?
No, it's the tryouts for the movie poster! The dance contest'll start any minute!
Look at Tony! He won the contest and he's sulking!
I heard of sore losers— but a SORE WINNER?!
He should be thrilled! He won some first prize!
What's that?
He don't have to go in the back and make it with Annutt . . . like the rest of us!
I've got nothing to live for! I'm short! m chicken-hearted! I got my girlfriend regnant! And on top of that, I'm feeling headachey, listless and out of sorts!
Hey, he's depressed! He's gonna jump! Talk to him, Tony! He'll listen to you!
Hey, Booby . . . did you know that this bridge you are about to jump off has over 300 miles of cable, almost a million yards of concrete, and the water . . . 228 feet below the center span . . . is a chilly 42 degrees! There have been 39 attempted suicides since the bridge was built . . . and of those, three were short people who were also chicken-hearted and had gotten their girlfriends pregnant . . . and—
YAAAAAIII!
Well, I've done it! All that's left for me now is to take a soul-searching ride on the subway, and think about where I m at and where I am going with my life!
There are a lot of questions to be answered . . . like why I'm so inarticulate . . . and why I resent my parents . . . and why the volume on this Bee Gees soundtrack song is louder than the rumble of the subway . . . and it's a soft ballad, yet!!
The answer is clear! If I'm ever gonna get away from my old gang, and Brooklyn, I gotta hurry to that one girl . . . the girl that's the key to my whole future . . .
OLIVIA NEWTON-JOHN!
'Cause if "Grease" turns out to be a blockbuster, too, I can dump "Kotter" and TV forever!
WELCO TO RYDEL HIGH

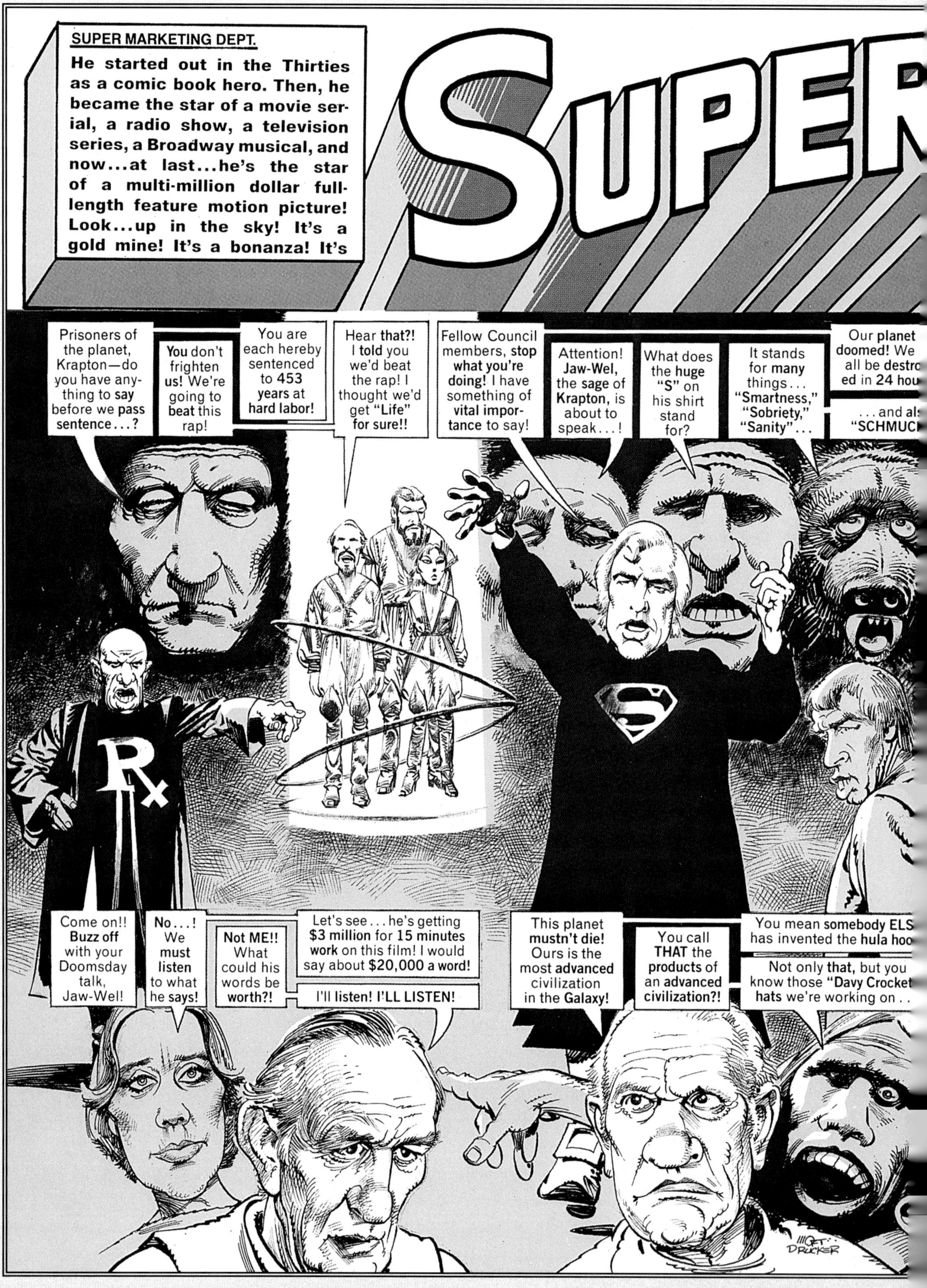
SUPER MARKETING DEPT.
He started out in the Thirties as a comic book hero. Then, he became the star of a movie serial, a radio show, a television series, a Broadway musical, and now...at last...he's the star of a multi-million dollar full-length feature motion picture! Look...up in the sky! It's a gold mine! It's a bonanza! It's
SUPER
Prisoners of the planet, Krapton—do you have anything to say before we pass sentence...?
You don't frighten us! We're going to beat this rap!
You are each hereby sentenced to 453 years at hard labor!
Hear that?! I told you we'd beat the rap! I thought we'd get "Life" for sure!!
Fellow Council members, stop what you're doing! I have something of vital importance to say!
Attention! Jaw-Wel, the sage of Krapton, is about to speak...!
What does the huge "S" on his shirt stand for?
It stands for many things... "Smartness," "Sobriety," "Sanity"...
...and al "SCHMUC
Come on!! Buzz off with your Doomsday talk, Jaw-Wel!
No...! We must listen to what he says!
Not ME!! What could his words be worth?!
Let's see...he's getting $3 million for 15 minutes work on this film! I would say about $20,000 a word!
I'll listen! I'LL LISTEN!
This planet mustn't die! Ours is the most advanced civilization in the Galaxy!
You call THAT the products of an advanced civilization?!
You mean somebody ELS has invented the hula hoo
Not only that, but you know those "Davy Crocket hats we're working on . .
MORT DRUCKER

MAD #208, July 1979

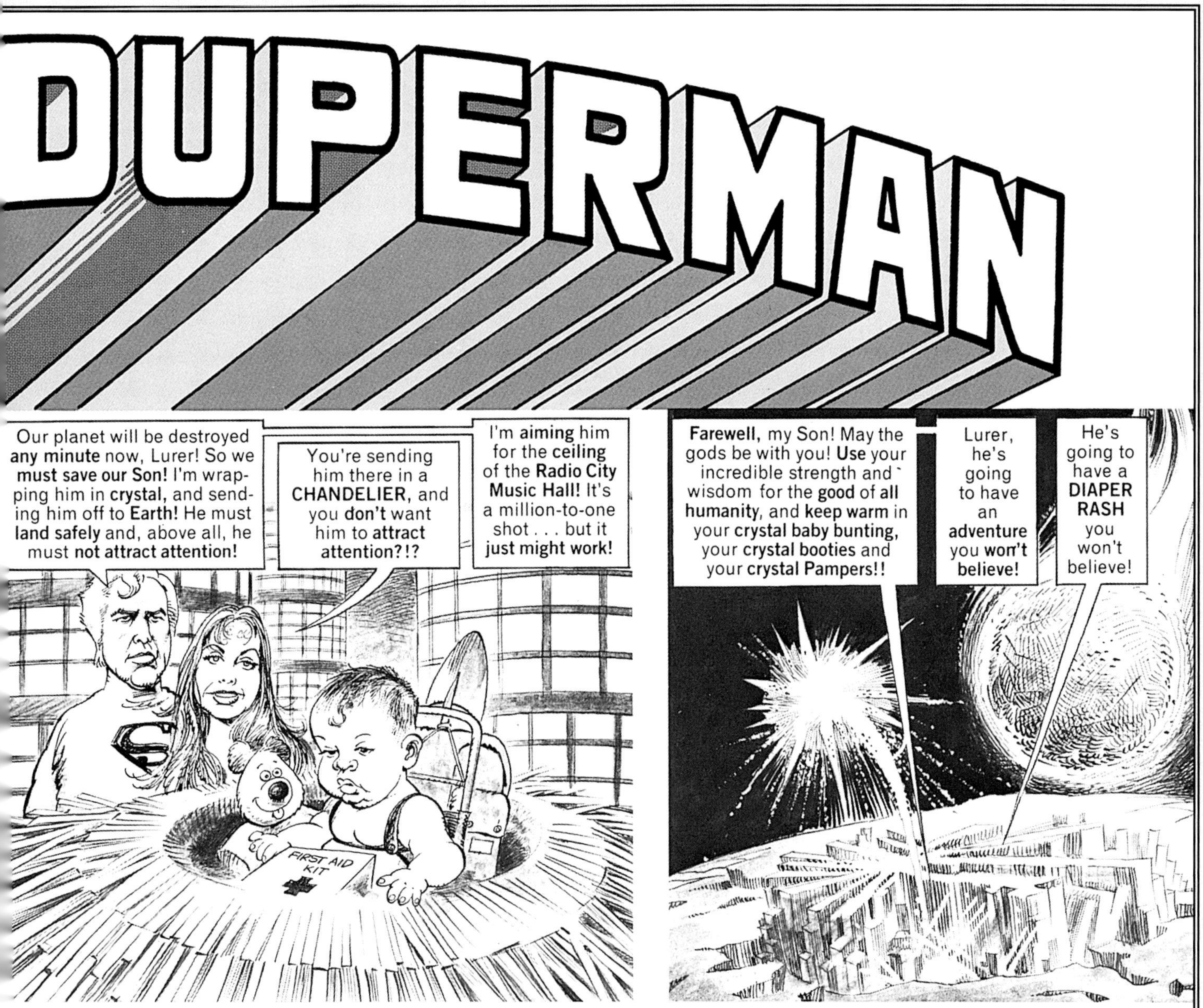
DUPERMAN
Our planet will be destroyed any minute now, Lurer! So we must save our Son! I'm wrapping him in crystal, and sending him off to Earth! He must land safely and, above all, he must not attract attention!
You're sending him there in a CHANDELIER, and you don't want him to attract attention?!?
I'm aiming him for the ceiling of the Radio City Music Hall! It's a million-to-one shot . . . but it just might work!
FIRST AID KIT
Farewell, my Son! May the gods be with you! Use your incredible strength and wisdom for the good of all humanity, and keep warm in your crystal baby bunting, your crystal booties and your crystal Pampers!!
Lurer, he's going to have an adventure you won't believe!
He's going to have a DIAPER RASH you won't believe!

ARTIST: MORT DRUCKER WRITER: LARRY SIEGEL

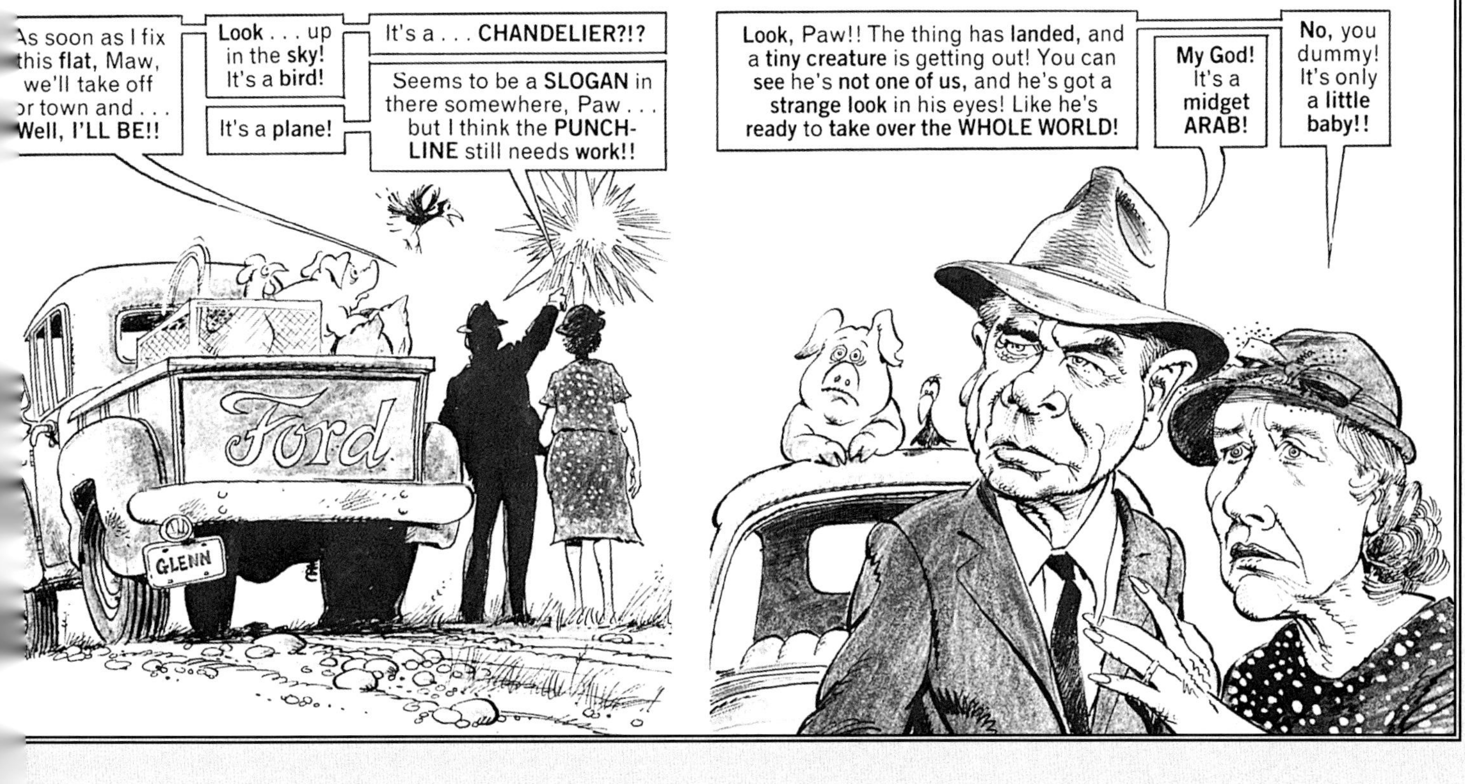
s soon as I fix this flat, Maw, we'll take off r town and . . . Well, I'LL BE!!
Look . . . up in the sky! It's a bird!
It's a plane!
It's a . . . CHANDELIER?!?
Seems to be a SLOGAN in there somewhere, Paw . . . but I think the PUNCH-LINE still needs work!!
Ford
GLENN
Look, Paw!! The thing has landed, and a tiny creature is getting out! You can see he's not one of us, and he's got a strange look in his eyes! Like he's ready to take over the WHOLE WORLD!
My God! It's a midget ARAB!
No, you dummy! It's only a little baby!!

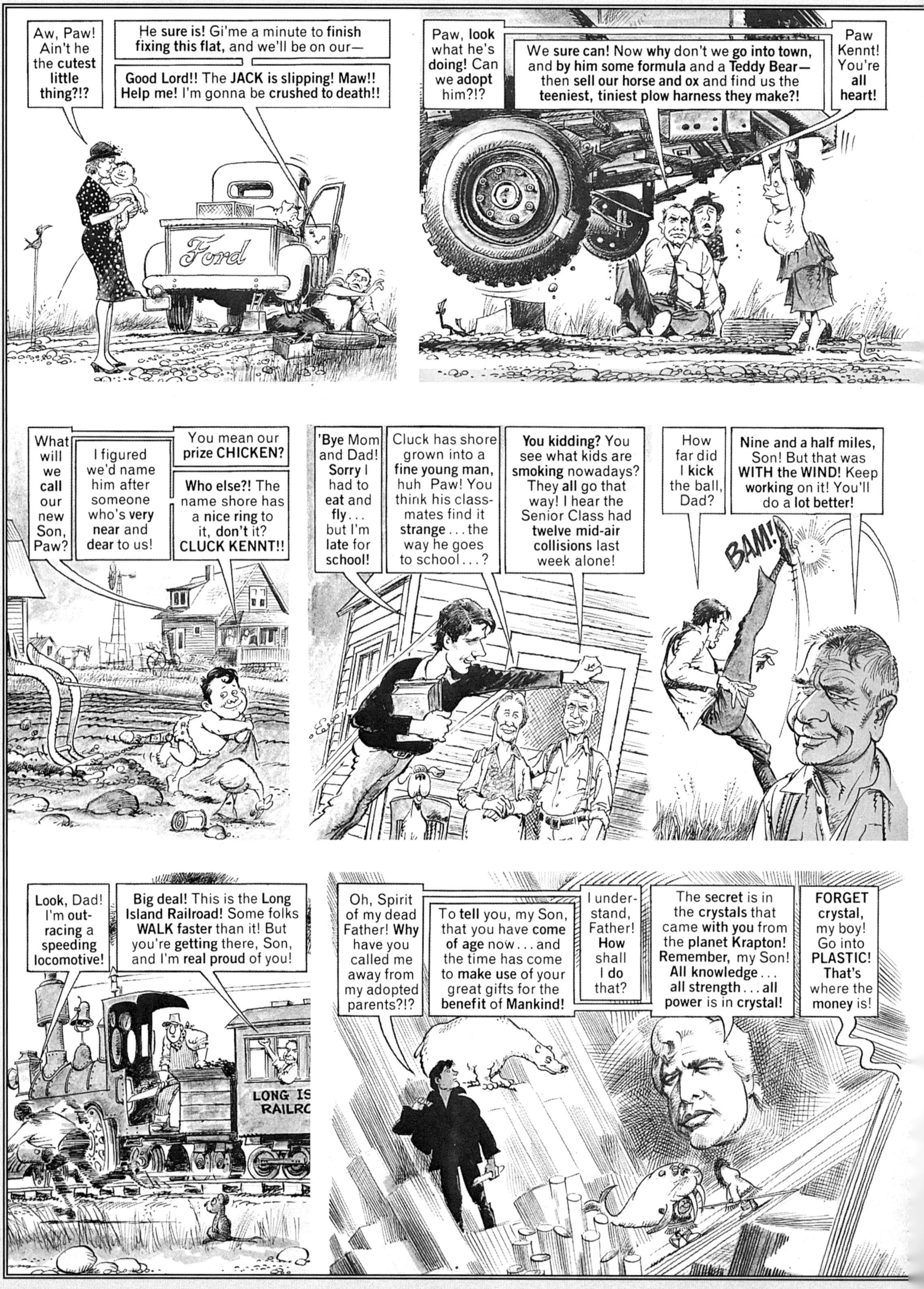
Aw, Paw! Ain't he the cutest little thing?!?
He sure is! Gi'me a minute to finish fixing this flat, and we'll be on our—
Good Lord!! The JACK is slipping! Maw!! Help me! I'm gonna be crushed to death!!
Ford
Paw, look what he's doing! Can we adopt him?!?
We sure can! Now why don't we go into town, and by him some formula and a Teddy Bear— then sell our horse and ox and find us the teeniest, tiniest plow harness they make?!
Paw Kennt! You're all heart!
What will we call our new Son, Paw?
I figured we'd name him after someone who's very near and dear to us!
You mean our prize CHICKEN?
Who else?! The name shore has a nice ring to it, don't it? CLUCK KENNT!!
'Bye Mom and Dad! Sorry I had to eat and fly... but I'm late for school!
Cluck has shore grown into a fine young man, huh Paw! You think his classmates find it strange... the way he goes to school...?
You kidding? You see what kids are smoking nowadays? They all go that way! I hear the Senior Class had twelve mid-air collisions last week alone!
How far did I kick the ball, Dad?
Nine and a half miles, Son! But that was WITH the WIND! Keep working on it! You'll do a lot better!
BAM!
Look, Dad! I'm out-racing a speeding locomotive!
Big deal! This is the Long Island Railroad! Some folks WALK faster than it! But you're getting there, Son, and I'm real proud of you!
LONG IS
RAILRO
Oh, Spirit of my dead Father! Why have you called me away from my adopted parents?!?
To tell you, my Son, that you have come of age now... and the time has come to make use of your great gifts for the benefit of Mankind!
I understand, Father! How shall I do that?
The secret is in the crystals that came with you from the planet Krapton! Remember, my Son! All knowledge... all strength... all power is in crystal!
FORGET crystal, my boy! Go into PLASTIC! That's where the money is!

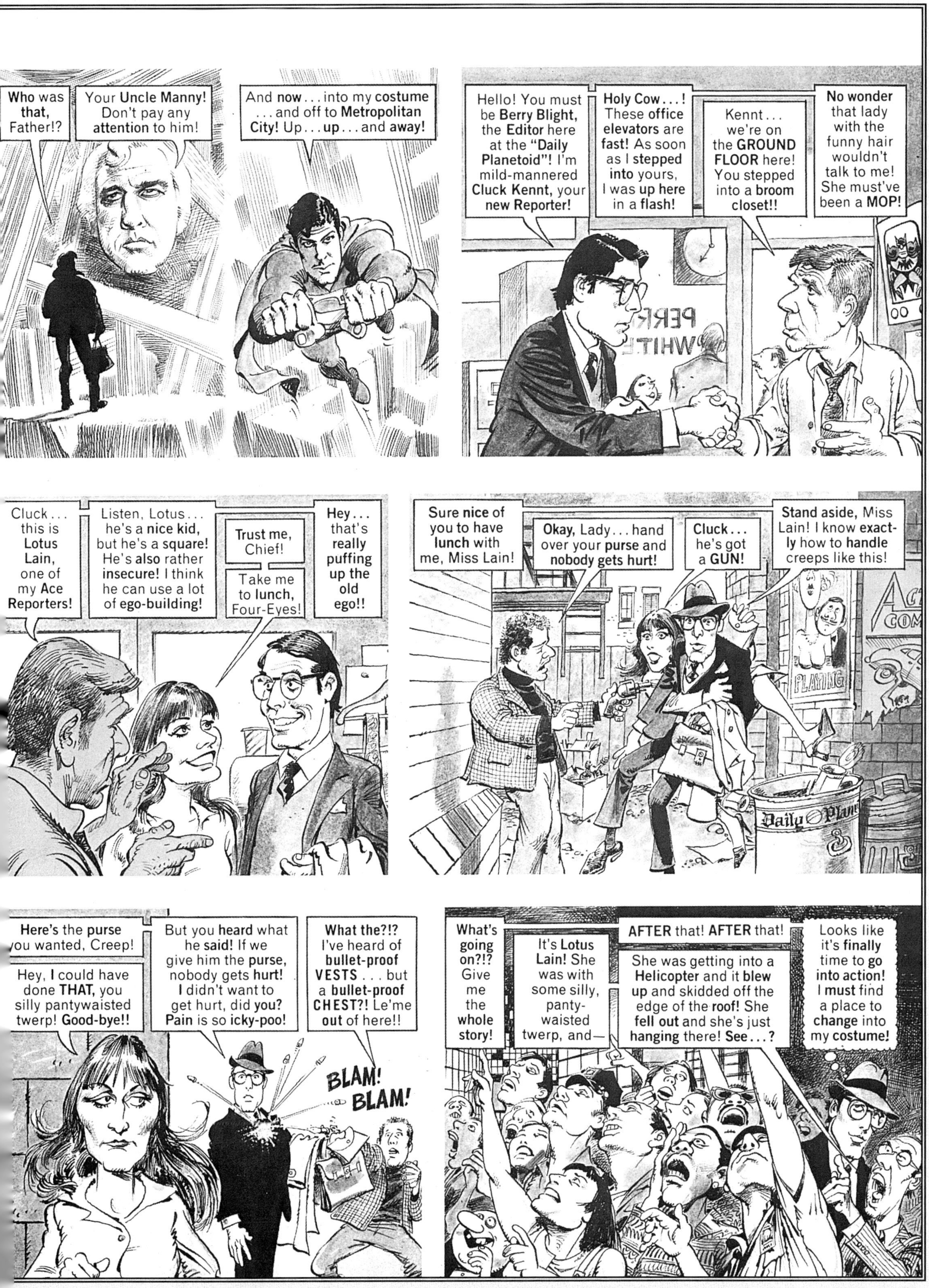
Who was that, Father!?
Your Uncle Manny! Don't pay any attention to him!
And now . . . into my costume . . . and off to Metropolitan City! Up . . . up . . . and away!
Hello! You must be Berry Blight, the Editor here at the "Daily Planetoid"! I'm mild-mannered Cluck Kennt, your new Reporter!
Holy Cow . . . ! These office elevators are fast! As soon as I stepped into yours, I was up here in a flash!
Kennt . . . we're on the GROUND FLOOR here! You stepped into a broom closet!!
No wonder that lady with the funny hair wouldn't talk to me! She must've been a MOP!
Cluck . . . this is Lotus Lain, one of my Ace Reporters!
Listen, Lotus . . . he's a nice kid, but he's a square! He's also rather insecure! I think he can use a lot of ego-building!
Trust me, Chief!
Take me to lunch, Four-Eyes!
Hey . . . that's really puffing up the old ego!!
Sure nice of you to have lunch with me, Miss Lain!
Okay, Lady . . . hand over your purse and nobody gets hurt!
Cluck . . . he's got a GUN!
Stand aside, Miss Lain! I know exactly how to handle creeps like this!
Here's the purse you wanted, Creep!
Hey, I could have done THAT, you silly pantywaisted twerp! Good-bye!!
But you heard what he said! If we give him the purse, nobody gets hurt! I didn't want to get hurt, did you? Pain is so icky-poo!
What the?!? I've heard of bullet-proof VESTS . . . but a bullet-proof CHEST?! Le'me out of here!!
BLAM! BLAM!
What's going on?!? Give me the whole story!
It's Lotus Lain! She was with some silly, panty-waisted twerp, and—
AFTER that! AFTER that!
She was getting into a Helicopter and it blew up and skidded off the edge of the roof! She fell out and she's just hanging there! See . . . ?
Looks like it's finally time to go into action! I must find a place to change into my costume!

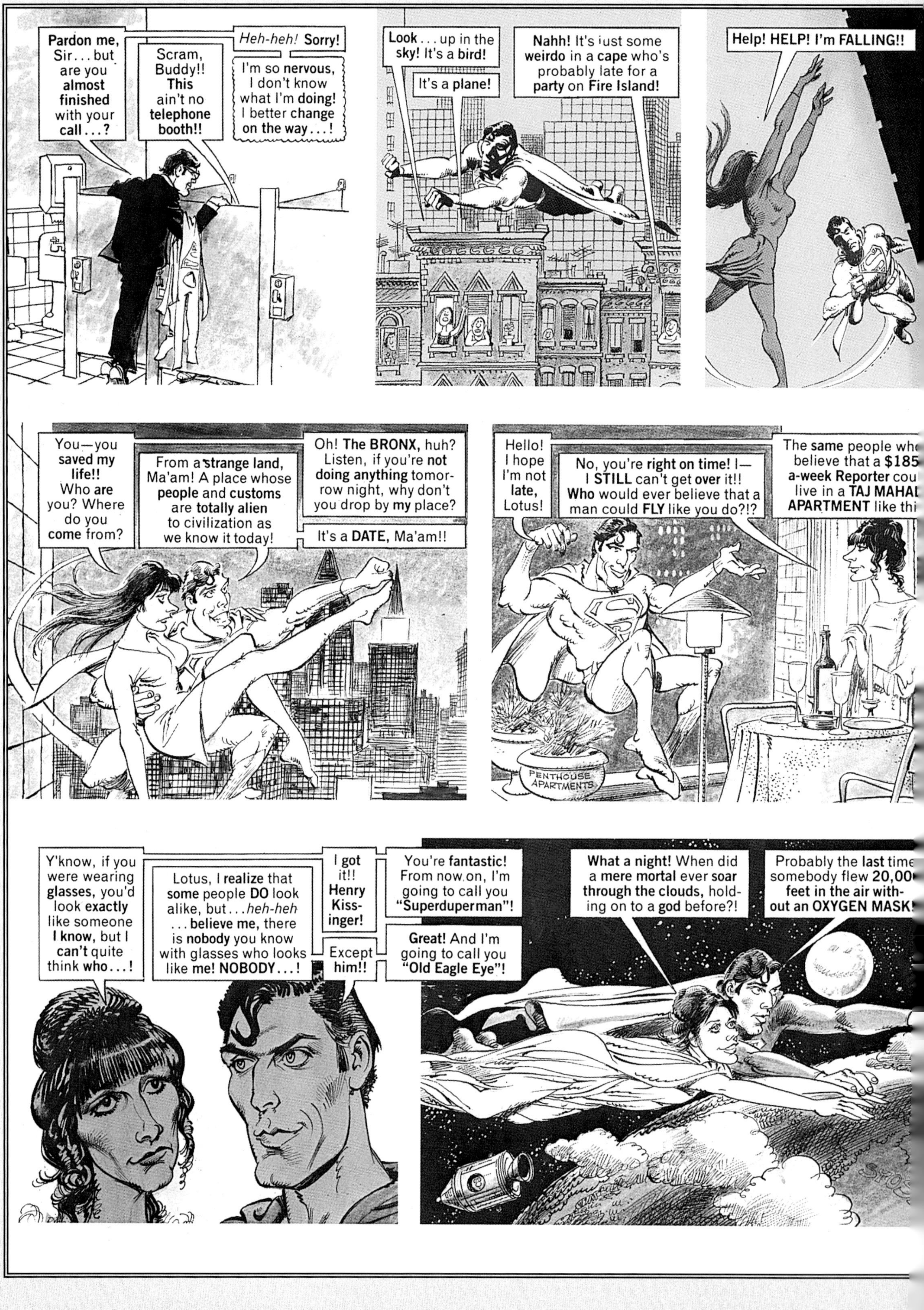

Pardon me, Sir... but are you almost finished with your call...?
Scram, Buddy!! This ain't no telephone booth!!
Heh-heh! Sorry!
I'm so nervous, I don't know what I'm doing! I better change on the way...!
Look... up in the sky! It's a bird!
It's a plane!
Nahh! It's just some weirdo in a cape who's probably late for a party on Fire Island!
Help! HELP! I'm FALLING!!
You—you saved my life!! Who are you? Where do you come from?
From a strange land, Ma'am! A place whose people and customs are totally alien to civilization as we know it today!
Oh! The BRONX, huh? Listen, if you're not doing anything tomorrow night, why don't you drop by my place?
It's a DATE, Ma'am!!
Hello! I hope I'm not late, Lotus!
No, you're right on time! I— I STILL can't get over it!! Who would ever believe that a man could FLY like you do?!?
The same people wh believe that a $185 a-week Reporter cou live in a TAJ MAHA APARTMENT like thi
PENTHOUSE APARTMENTS
Y'know, if you were wearing glasses, you'd look exactly like someone I know, but I can't quite think who...!
Lotus, I realize that some people DO look alike, but...heh-heh ...believe me, there is nobody you know with glasses who looks like me! NOBODY...!
I got it!! Henry Kissinger!
Except him!!
You're fantastic! From now on, I'm going to call you "Superduperman"!
Great! And I'm going to call you "Old Eagle Eye"!
What a night! When did a mere mortal ever soar through the clouds, holding on to a god before?!
Probably the last time somebody flew 20,00 feet in the air without an OXYGEN MASK

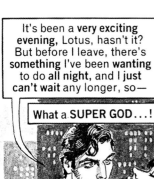

It's been a very exciting evening, Lotus, hasn't it? But before I leave, there's something I've been wanting to do all night, and I just can't wait any longer, so—
What a SUPER GOD...!
Lotus... I want to shake your hand and sincerely thank you from the bottom of my heart for being such a swell date!
What a SUPER DUD!!
Cluck... I just got a tip that Lox Looter, the arch-criminal, is about to pull off a caper that will destroy the entire West Coast!
Didn't you just send Lotus to the Coast on a special assignment?
Yes, and if anything happens to that wonderful girl because of me, I'll throw myself out the window, and...
Mr. Blight, we''re on the Ground Floor!
...I'll sprain my ankle so badly, you won't believe it!
Coca-Cola
MOBIL
I.T.T.
SONY
Listen to me, Onus, my stupid henchman, and Evil, my sexy girlfriend! I, Lox Looter, am about to pull off the most fiendish act in the history of crime... heh-heh...chortle!!
Tell me, Boss, why are you always wreaking vengeance on the world??
It all began 13 years ago when I was turned down for one of the arch-villains on the "Batman" TV Series—for being too boring! But, I'll show 'em!! I'LL show 'em, NOW! NOBODY CAN STOP ME!
"Nobody" is a mighty big word, Lox!
It's Superduperman! But you're too late, my friend! In a few minutes, a 500-megaton bomb will zoom across the country, strike the San Andreas fault, cause a mighty earthquake, and send California into the sea!!
Lox, I plan to stop you ...and have you thrown into jail!
On WHAT CHARGE?!?
Well... for starters, there's always "Pre-Meditated Mischief"!
Don't fight me, Lox! You know there's nothing on this planet that's a match for my super-duper strength!
Oh? How about something from ANOTHER planet, like this piece of Kraptonite, f'rinstance...
No! No! Anything but that!
Starting to get all mushy inside? Starting to get weak in the knees? This Kraptonite is taking its toll, right, "Stupidman"?!
Right! And the broad in the Bikini isn't exactly HELPING THINGS!!
SPRING ST.
Hang in there, Superduperman! I'll save you! Hang in there!
Evil, why are you doing this? You're LOX's girl! He's been sleeping with you for years!!
I know! And just ONCE, I'd like to find me a guy who'll STAY AWAKE!

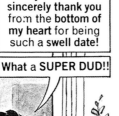

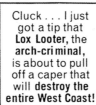

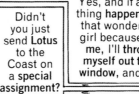

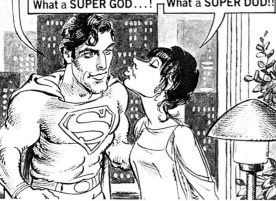

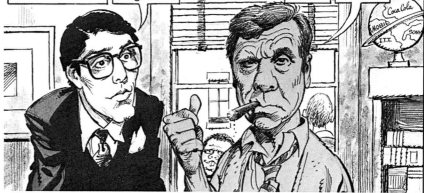

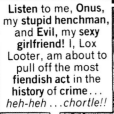

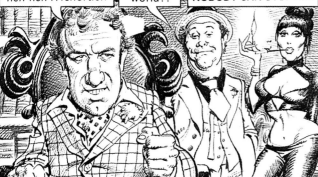

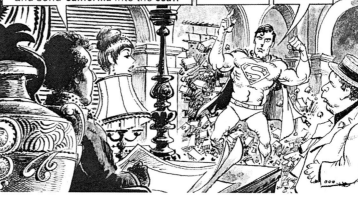

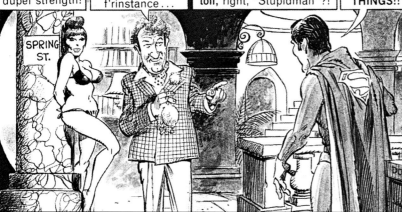

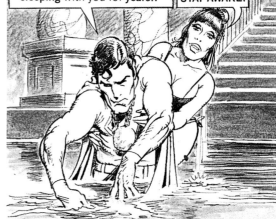

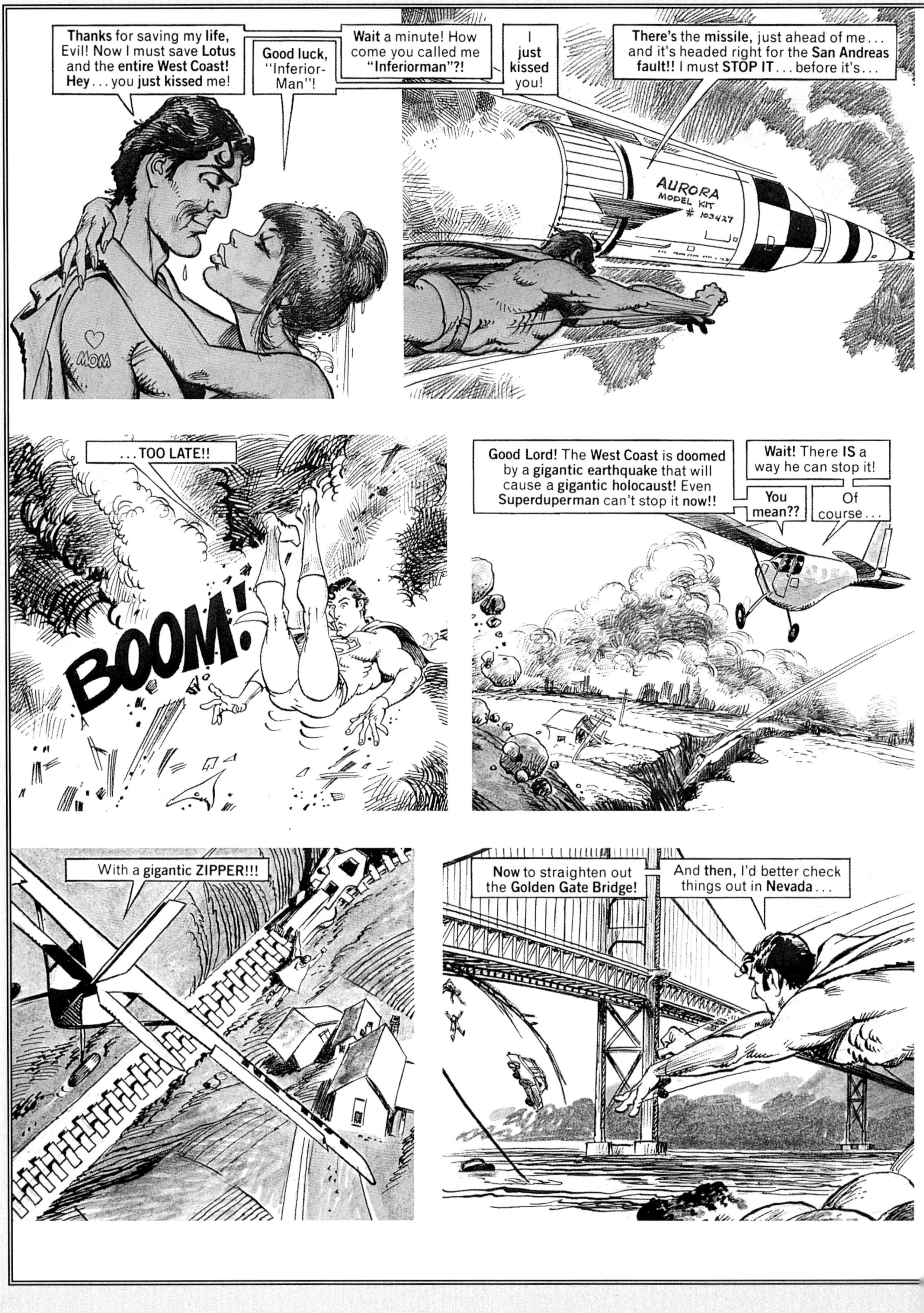
Thanks for saving my life, Evil! Now I must save Lotus and the entire West Coast! Hey . . . you just kissed me!
Good luck, "Inferior-Man"!
Wait a minute! How come you called me "Inferiorman"?!
I just kissed you!
There's the missile, just ahead of me . . . and it's headed right for the San Andreas fault!! I must STOP IT . . . before it's . . .
AURORA MODEL KIT # 103427
MOM
. . . TOO LATE!!
BOOM!
Good Lord! The West Coast is doomed by a gigantic earthquake that will cause a gigantic holocaust! Even Superduperman can't stop it now!!
Wait! There IS a way he can stop it!
You mean??
Of course . . .
With a gigantic ZIPPER!!!
Now to straighten out the Golden Gate Bridge!
And then, I'd better check things out in Nevada . . .

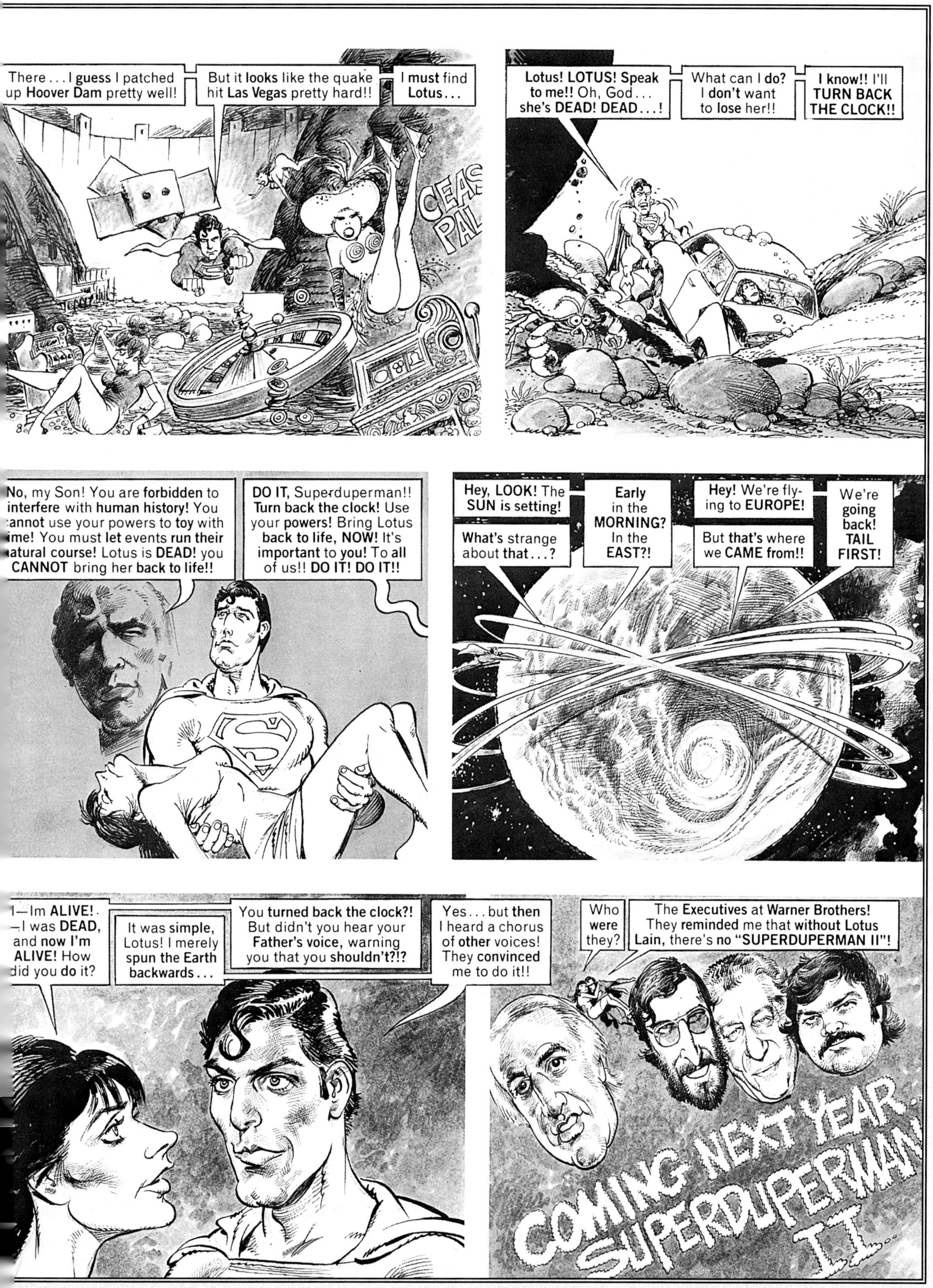

There . . . I guess I patched up Hoover Dam pretty well!
But it looks like the quake hit Las Vegas pretty hard!!
I must find Lotus . . .
CEAS PAL
Lotus! LOTUS! Speak to me!! Oh, God . . . she's DEAD! DEAD . . . !
What can I do? I don't want to lose her!!
I know!! I'll TURN BACK THE CLOCK!!
No, my Son! You are forbidden to interfere with human history! You annot use your powers to toy with ime! You must let events run their atural course! Lotus is DEAD! you CANNOT bring her back to life!!
DO IT, Superduperman!! Turn back the clock! Use your powers! Bring Lotus back to life, NOW! It's important to you! To all of us!! DO IT! DO IT!!
Hey, LOOK! The SUN is setting!
What's strange about that . . . ?
Early in the MORNING? In the EAST?!
Hey! We're flying to EUROPE!
But that's where we CAME from!!
We're going back! TAIL FIRST!
I—Im ALIVE! —I was DEAD, and now I'm ALIVE! How did you do it?
It was simple, Lotus! I merely spun the Earth backwards . . .
You turned back the clock?! But didn't you hear your Father's voice, warning you that you shouldn't?!?
Yes . . . but then I heard a chorus of other voices! They convinced me to do it!!
Who were they?
The Executives at Warner Brothers! They reminded me that without Lotus Lain, there's no "SUPERDUPERMAN II"!
COMING NEXT YEAR. SUPERDUPERMAN II

MUCHO DE NIRO DEPT.

For as long as we can remember, the plot of a "Fight Picture" was usually very simple. An underprivileged kid starts in the gutter, and blasts his way to the top. Then, along comes the first major Fight Picture of the '80's, and what do we get: an underprivileged kid starts in the gutter, and blasts his way to the sewer! Boy, Hollywood has given us our fair share of "anti-heroes" in the past, but now make way for the "anti-anti-anti hero" affectionately known as the . . .

RAV

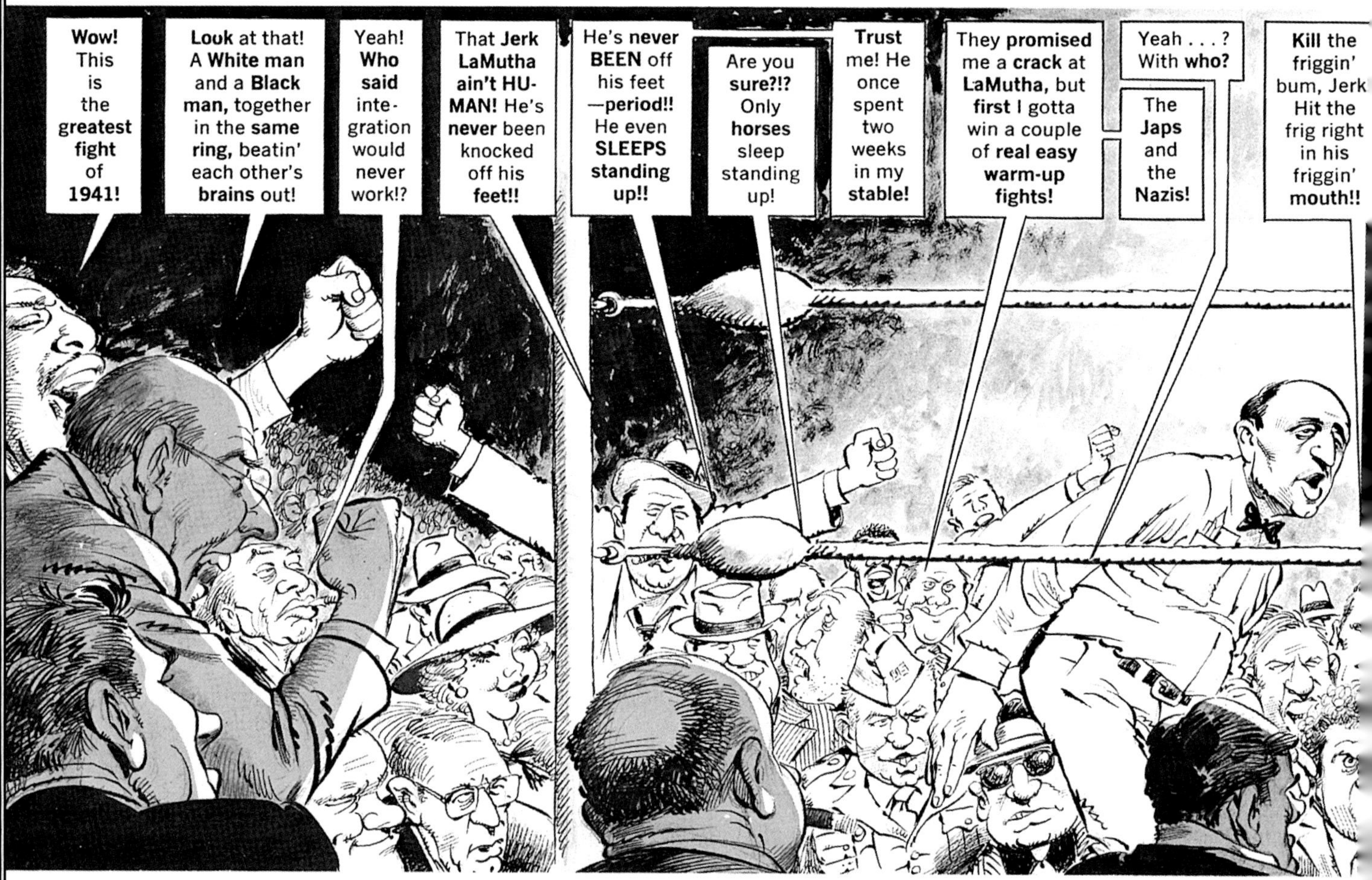
Wow! This is the greatest fight of 1941!
Look at that! A White man and a Black man, together in the same ring, beatin' each other's brains out!
Yeah! Who said integration would never work!?
That Jerk LaMutha ain't HU-MAN! He's never been knocked off his feet!!
He's never BEEN off his feet —period!! He even SLEEPS standing up!!
Are you sure?!? Only horses sleep standing up!
Trust me! He once spent two weeks in my stable!
They promised me a crack at LaMutha, but first I gotta win a couple of real easy warm-up fights!
Yeah . . . ? With who?
The Japs and the Nazis!
Kill the friggin' bum, Jerk Hit the frig right in his friggin' mouth!!

ARTIST: MORT DRUCK

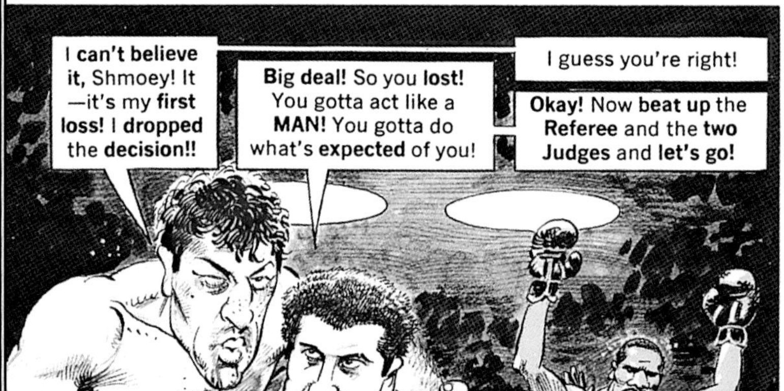
I can't believe it, Shmoey! It —it's my first loss! I dropped the decision!!
Big deal! So you lost! You gotta act like a MAN! You gotta do what's expected of you!
I guess you're right!
Okay! Now beat up the Referee and the two Judges and let's go!
4

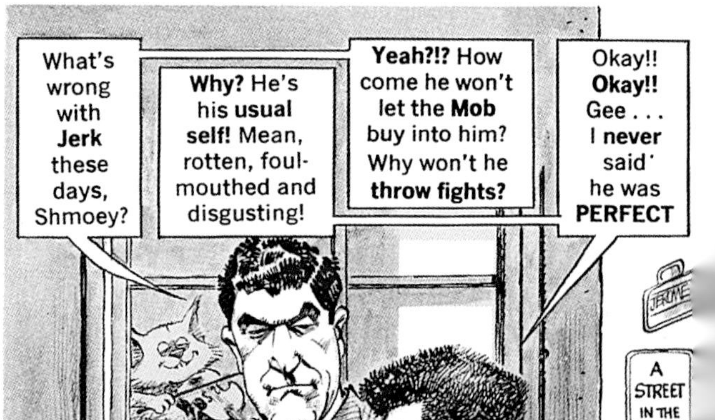
What's wrong with Jerk these days, Shmoey?
Why? He's his usual self! Mean, rotten, foul-mouthed and disgusting!
Yeah?!? How come he won't let the Mob buy into him? Why won't he throw fights?
Okay!! Okay!! Gee . . . I never said' he was PERFECT
A STREET IN THE BRONX N.Y.

NG BULLY

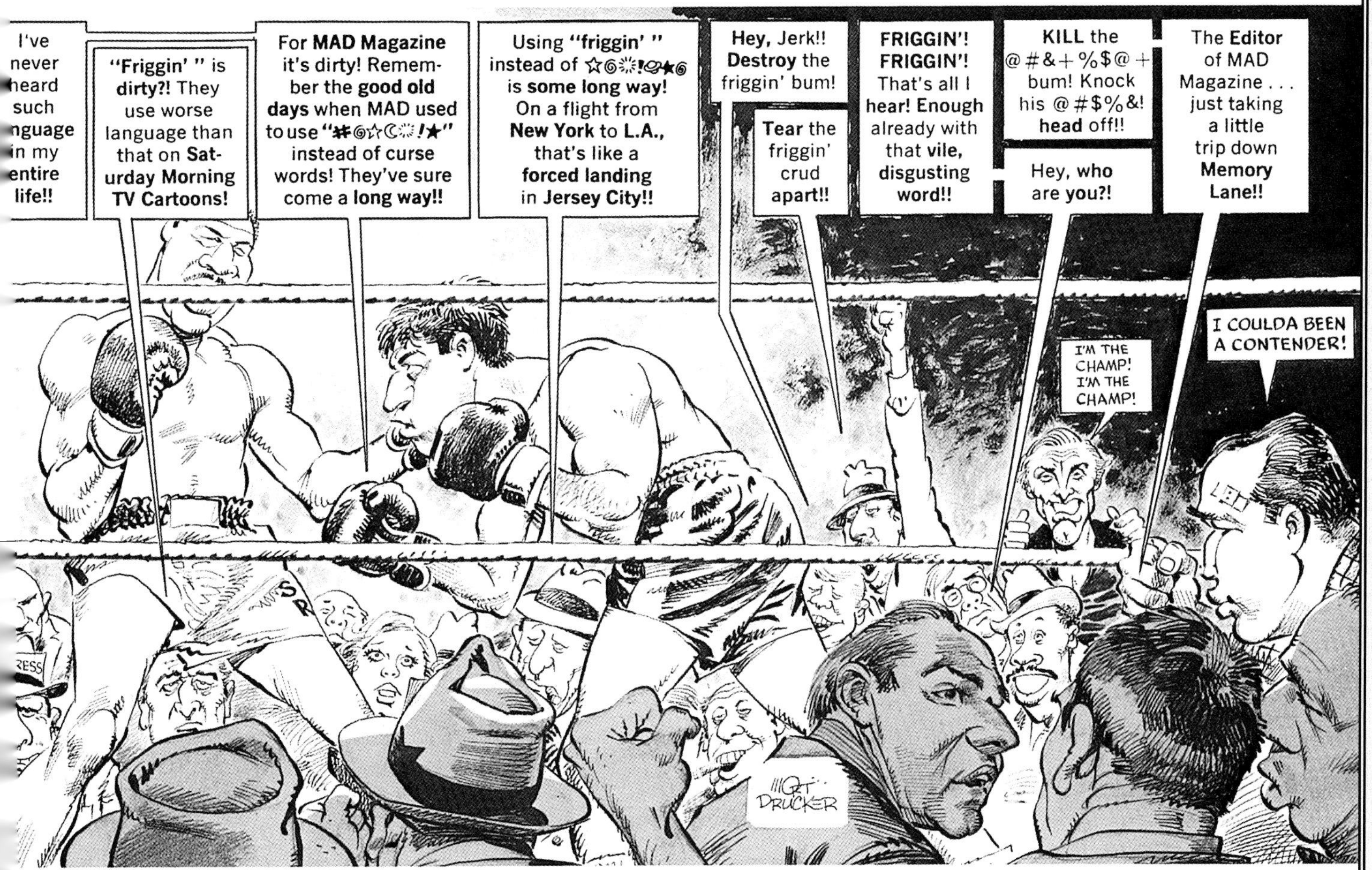

I've never heard such nguage in my entire life!!
"Friggin' " is dirty?! They use worse language than that on Saturday Morning TV Cartoons!
For MAD Magazine it's dirty! Remember the good old days when MAD used to use "✱◎☆☾⁂!★" instead of curse words! They've sure come a long way!!
Using "friggin' " instead of ☆◎⁂!◎★◎ is some long way! On a flight from New York to L.A., that's like a forced landing in Jersey City!!
Hey, Jerk!! Destroy the friggin' bum!
Tear the friggin' crud apart!!
FRIGGIN'! FRIGGIN'! That's all I hear! Enough already with that vile, disgusting word!!
KILL the @#&+%$@+ bum! Knock his @#$%&! head off!!
Hey, who are you?!
The Editor of MAD Magazine . . . just taking a little trip down Memory Lane!!
I'M THE CHAMP! I'M THE CHAMP!
I COULDA BEEN A CONTENDER!
RESS
MORT DRUCKER

TER: LARRY SIEGEL

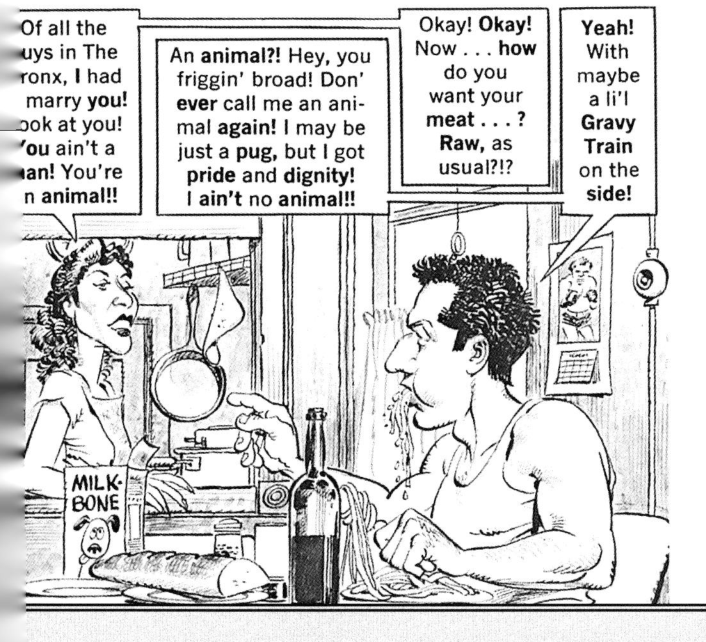

Of all the uys in The ronx, I had marry you! ook at you! 'ou ain't a ian! You're n animal!!
An animal?! Hey, you friggin' broad! Don' ever call me an animal again! I may be just a pug, but I got pride and dignity! I ain't no animal!!
Okay! Okay! Now . . . how do you want your meat . . . ? Raw, as usual?!?
Yeah! With maybe a li'l Gravy Train on the side!
MILK-BONE

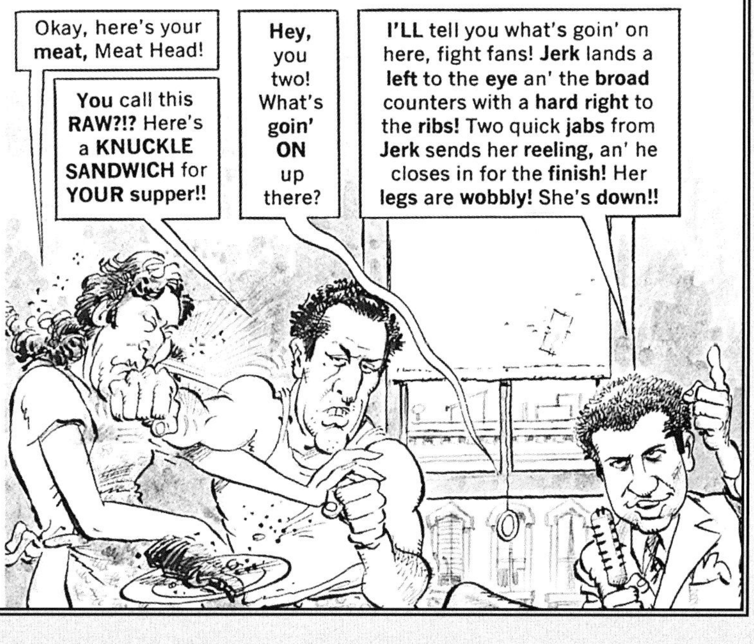

Okay, here's your meat, Meat Head!
You call this RAW?!? Here's a KNUCKLE SANDWICH for YOUR supper!!
Hey, you two! What's goin' ON up there?
I'LL tell you what's goin' on here, fight fans! Jerk lands a left to the eye an' the broad counters with a hard right to the ribs! Two quick jabs from Jerk sends her reeling, an' he closes in for the finish! Her legs are wobbly! She's down!!

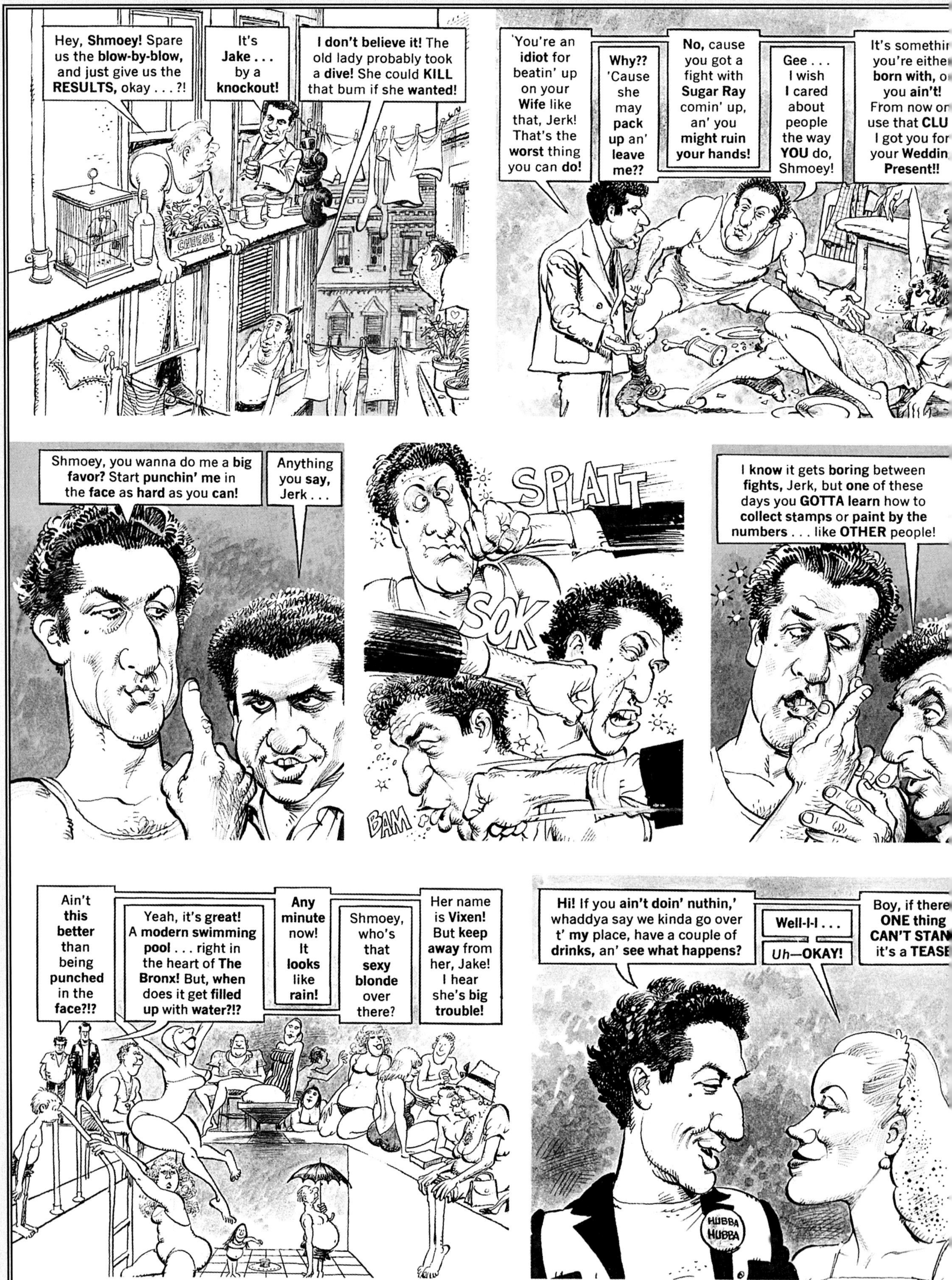
Hey, Shmoey! Spare us the blow-by-blow, and just give us the RESULTS, okay . . . ?!
It's Jake . . . by a knockout!
I don't believe it! The old lady probably took a dive! She could KILL that bum if she wanted!
CHEESE
'You're an idiot for beatin' up on your Wife like that, Jerk! That's the worst thing you can do!
Why?? 'Cause she may pack up an' leave me??
No, cause you got a fight with Sugar Ray comin' up, an' you might ruin your hands!
Gee . . . I wish I cared about people the way YOU do, Shmoey!
It's somethin you're eithe born with, o you ain't! From now on use that CLU I got you for your Weddin Present!!
Shmoey, you wanna do me a big favor? Start punchin' me in the face as hard as you can!
Anything you say, Jerk . . .
SPLATT
SOK
BAM
I know it gets boring between fights, Jerk, but one of these days you GOTTA learn how to collect stamps or paint by the numbers . . . like OTHER people!
Ain't this better than being punched in the face?!?
Yeah, it's great! A modern swimming pool . . . right in the heart of The Bronx! But, when does it get filled up with water?!?
Any minute now! It looks like rain!
Shmoey, who's that sexy blonde over there?
Her name is Vixen! But keep away from her, Jake! I hear she's big trouble!
Hi! If you ain't doin' nuthin,' whaddya say we kinda go over t' my place, have a couple of drinks, an' see what happens?
Well-l-l . . .
Uh—OKAY!
Boy, if there ONE thing CAN'T STAN it's a TEASE
HUBBA HUBBA

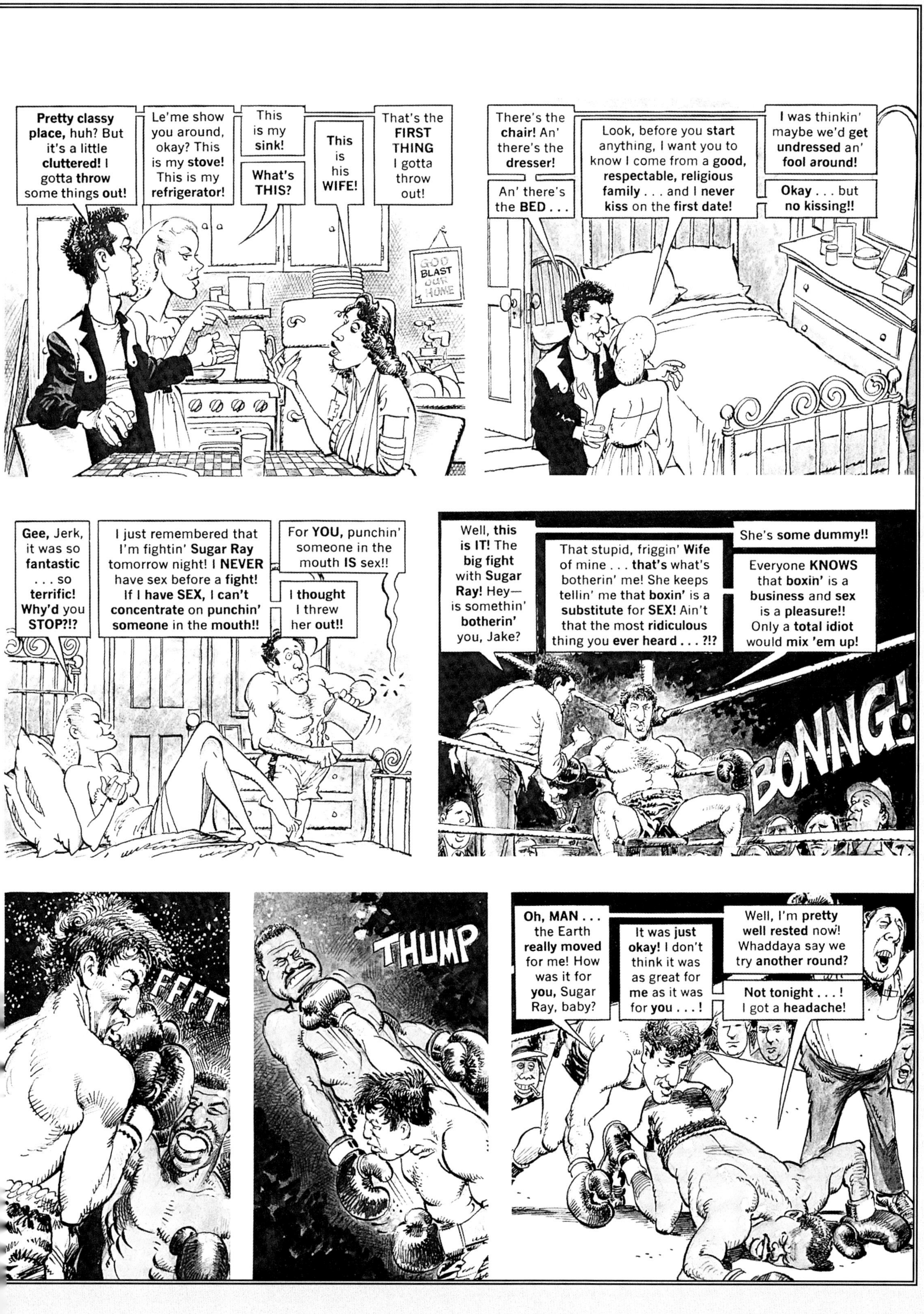
Pretty classy place, huh? But it's a little cluttered! I gotta throw some things out!
Le'me show you around, okay? This is my stove! This is my refrigerator!
This is my sink!
What's THIS?
This is his WIFE!
That's the FIRST THING I gotta throw out!
GOD BLAST OUR HOME
There's the chair! An' there's the dresser!
An' there's the BED . . .
Look, before you start anything, I want you to know I come from a good, respectable, religious family . . . and I never kiss on the first date!
I was thinkin' maybe we'd get undressed an' fool around!
Okay . . . but no kissing!!
Gee, Jerk, it was so fantastic . . . so terrific! Why'd you STOP?!?
I just remembered that I'm fightin' Sugar Ray tomorrow night! I NEVER have sex before a fight! If I have SEX, I can't concentrate on punchin' someone in the mouth!!
For YOU, punchin' someone in the mouth IS sex!!
I thought I threw her out!!
Well, this is IT! The big fight with Sugar Ray! Hey—is somethin' botherin' you, Jake?
That stupid, friggin' Wife of mine . . . that's what's botherin' me! She keeps tellin' me that boxin' is a substitute for SEX! Ain't that the most ridiculous thing you ever heard . . . ?!?
She's some dummy!!
Everyone KNOWS that boxin' is a business and sex is a pleasure!! Only a total idiot would mix 'em up!
BONNG!
FFFT
THUMP
Oh, MAN . . . the Earth really moved for me! How was it for you, Sugar Ray, baby?
It was just okay! I don't think it was as great for me as it was for you . . . !
Well, I'm pretty well rested now! Whaddaya say we try another round?
Not tonight . . . ! I got a headache!

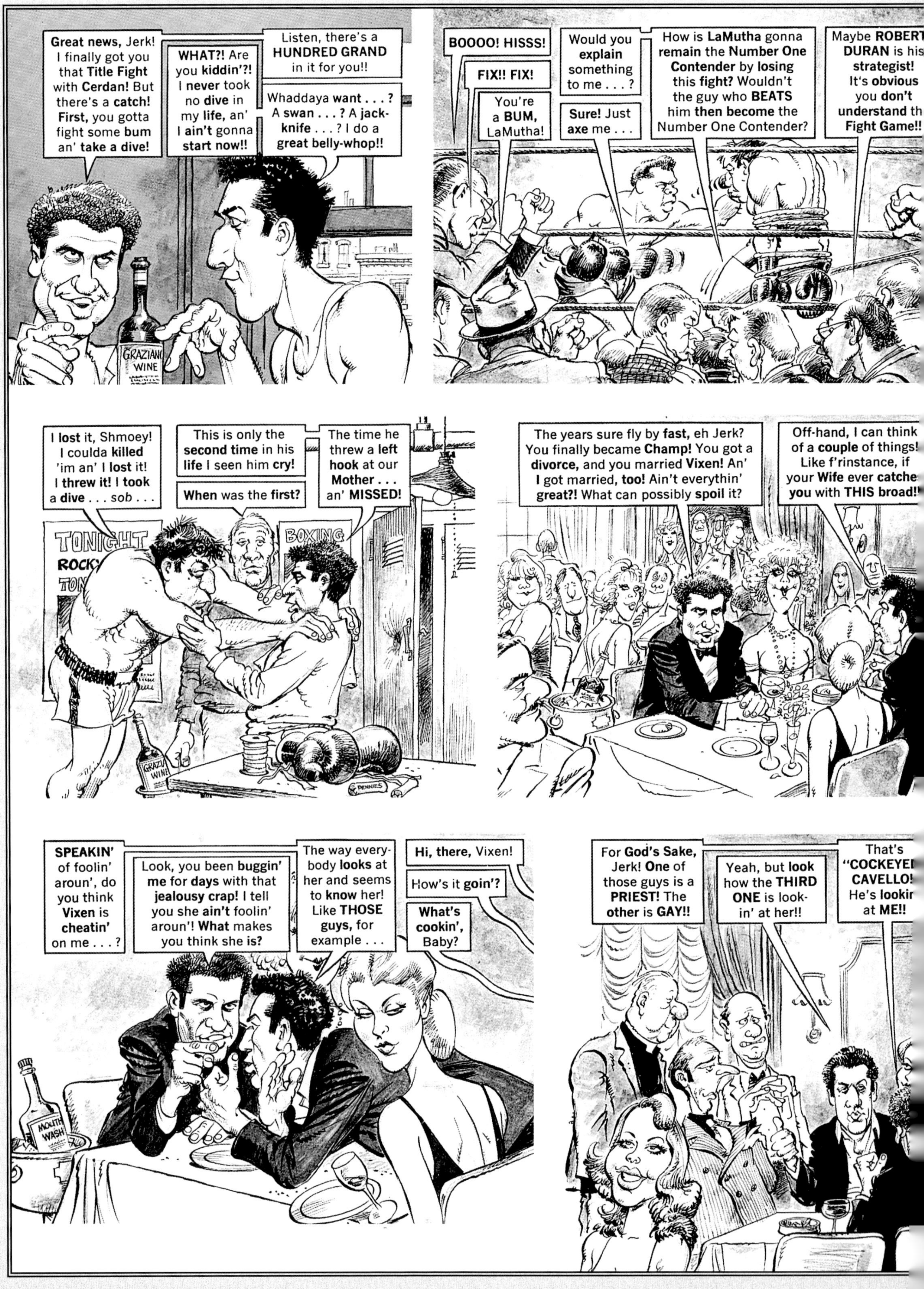
Great news, Jerk! I finally got you that Title Fight with Cerdan! But there's a catch! First, you gotta fight some bum an' take a dive!
WHAT?! Are you kiddin'?! I never took no dive in my life, an' I ain't gonna start now!!
Listen, there's a HUNDRED GRAND in it for you!!
Whaddaya want . . . ? A swan . . . ? A jack-knife . . . ? I do a great belly-whop!!
GRAZIANO WINE
BOOOO! HISSS!
FIX!! FIX!
You're a BUM, LaMutha!
Would you explain something to me . . . ?
Sure! Just axe me . . .
How is LaMutha gonna remain the Number One Contender by losing this fight? Wouldn't the guy who BEATS him then become the Number One Contender?
Maybe ROBERTO DURAN is his strategist! It's obvious you don't understand the Fight Game!!
I lost it, Shmoey! I coulda killed 'im an' I lost it! I threw it! I took a dive . . . sob . . .
This is only the second time in his life I seen him cry!
When was the first?
The time he threw a left hook at our Mother . . . an' MISSED!
TONIGHT ROCKY
BOXING
GRAZIANO WINE
PENNIES
The years sure fly by fast, eh Jerk? You finally became Champ! You got a divorce, and you married Vixen! An' I got married, too! Ain't everythin' great?! What can possibly spoil it?
Off-hand, I can think of a couple of things! Like f'rinstance, if your Wife ever catches you with THIS broad!!
SPEAKIN' of foolin' aroun', do you think Vixen is cheatin' on me . . . ?
Look, you been buggin' me for days with that jealousy crap! I tell you she ain't foolin' aroun'! What makes you think she is?
The way every-body looks at her and seems to know her! Like THOSE guys, for example . . .
Hi, there, Vixen!
How's it goin'?
What's cookin', Baby?
MOUTH WASH
For God's Sake, Jerk! One of those guys is a PRIEST! The other is GAY!!
Yeah, but look how the THIRD ONE is look-in' at her!!
That's "COCKEYED CAVELLO!" He's lookin' at ME!!

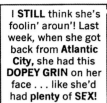

I **STILL** think she's foolin' aroun'! Last week, when she got back from **Atlantic City,** she had this **DOPEY GRIN** on her face . . . like she'd had **plenty** of **SEX!**

You **friggin' idiot! YOU** were with her in Atlantic City!! You were on your **HONEYMOON!**

And I **NEVER TOUCHED** her!! I **TOLD** you she was foolin' aroun'!!

Okay, you dirty two-timing broad!! Where **WERE** you?! Who were you **MESSIN' AROUN'** with?!? **"HOT LIPS"** HOROWITZ? **"LOVER BOY"** LUNDIGAN?!? **"ROMEO"** RICOTTA?!

F'r cryin' out loud!! I **jus'** took out the **GARBAGE!!** I was gone a minute and a half!

You **gotta stop** wearin' yourself **out** like this, Jerk! Listen . . . you got a big **return match** with Sugar Ray comin' up! You gotta **concentrate** on that! You **promise** me you're gonna **concentrate** on **nothin'** but the Sugar Ray fight?

Okay . . . I promise . . .

Way to go, Jerk!!

He's in **terrific form!**

I never **SEEN** him so sharp!!

Now, **you** do that to **SUGAR RAY,** and you're a shoo-in!!

You **friggin' tramp!** Take **that** n' **that! THIS** will teach you to cheat on **ME!**

I **AIN'T** cheatin' on you, you **damn fool!!**

Yes you are! **C'mon!** Tell me **WHO** you been cheatin' **with,** or I'll **KILL** ya . . . !

Okay, you **really wanna know?!** I'll **tell** you! I been cheatin' with **Clark Gable, John Wayne,** Haile Selassie, Pres. Truman, and your **own brother,** Shmoey!

My God! A friggin' ORGY!!

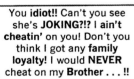

You **idiot!!** Can't you see she's **JOKING?!?** I ain't cheatin' on you! Don't you think I got any **family loyalty!** I would **NEVER** cheat on my **Brother . . . !!**

That's **RIGHT!** I'm **married** to him, and **I know** Shmoey better than **ANYBODY!** He would **NEVER** cheat on his **Brother!** On his **WIFE,** maybe, but **never** his **Brother!**

Boy, that LaMutha sure made a **MESS** out of his life!

Yeah! His own Brother **walked out** on him, his Wife **hardly talks** to him, and now, Sugar Ray is poundin' the **crap** out of him!

And look at the **SHAPE** he's in! You **can't tell ME** he's a Middleweight!

No?!? Take another look at his **middle!**

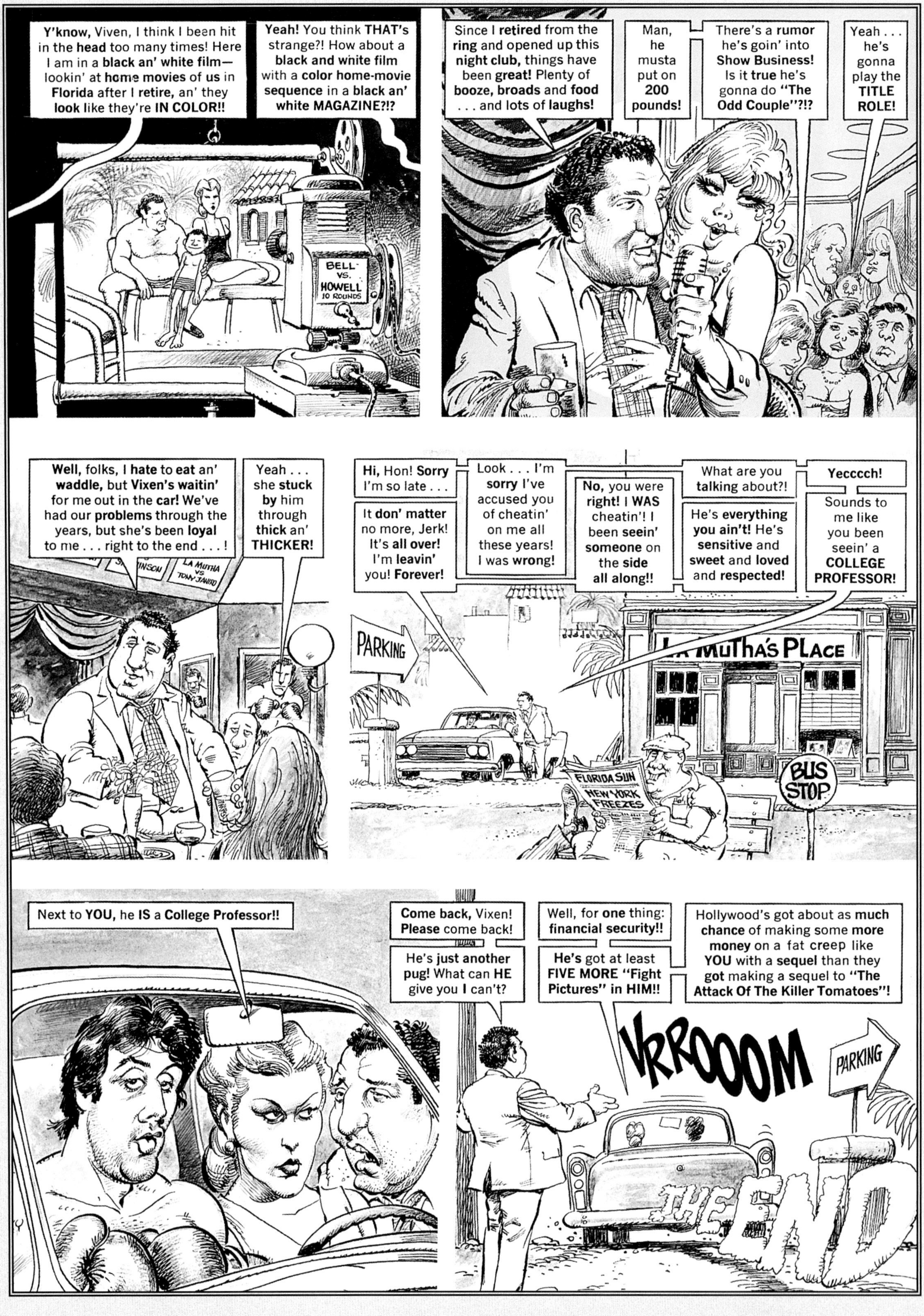
Y'know, Viven, I think I been hit in the head too many times! Here I am in a black an' white film—lookin' at home movies of us in Florida after I retire, an' they look like they're IN COLOR!!
Yeah! You think THAT's strange?! How about a black and white film with a color home-movie sequence in a black an' white MAGAZINE?!?
BELL VS. HOWELL 10 ROUNDS
Since I retired from the ring and opened up this night club, things have been great! Plenty of booze, broads and food . . . and lots of laughs!
Man, he musta put on 200 pounds!
There's a rumor he's goin' into Show Business! Is it true he's gonna do "The Odd Couple"?!?
Yeah . . . he's gonna play the TITLE ROLE!
Well, folks, I hate to eat an' waddle, but Vixen's waitin' for me out in the car! We've had our problems through the years, but she's been loyal to me . . . right to the end . . . !
Yeah . . . she stuck by him through thick an' THICKER!
LA MUTHA VS TONY JANIRO
Hi, Hon! Sorry I'm so late . . .
It don' matter no more, Jerk! It's all over! I'm leavin' you! Forever!
Look . . . I'm sorry I've accused you of cheatin' on me all these years! I was wrong!
No, you were right! I WAS cheatin'! I been seein' someone on the side all along!!
What are you talking about?!
He's everything you ain't! He's sensitive and sweet and loved and respected!
Yeccch!
Sounds to me like you been seein' a COLLEGE PROFESSOR!
PARKING
LA MUTHA'S PLACE
FLORIDA SUN
NEW YORK FREEZES
BUS STOP
Next to YOU, he IS a College Professor!!
Come back, Vixen! Please come back!
He's just another pug! What can HE give you I can't?
Well, for one thing: financial security!!
He's got at least FIVE MORE "Fight Pictures" in HIM!!
Hollywood's got about as much chance of making some more money on a fat creep like YOU with a sequel than they got making a sequel to "The Attack Of The Killer Tomatoes"!
VRROOOM
PARKING
THE END

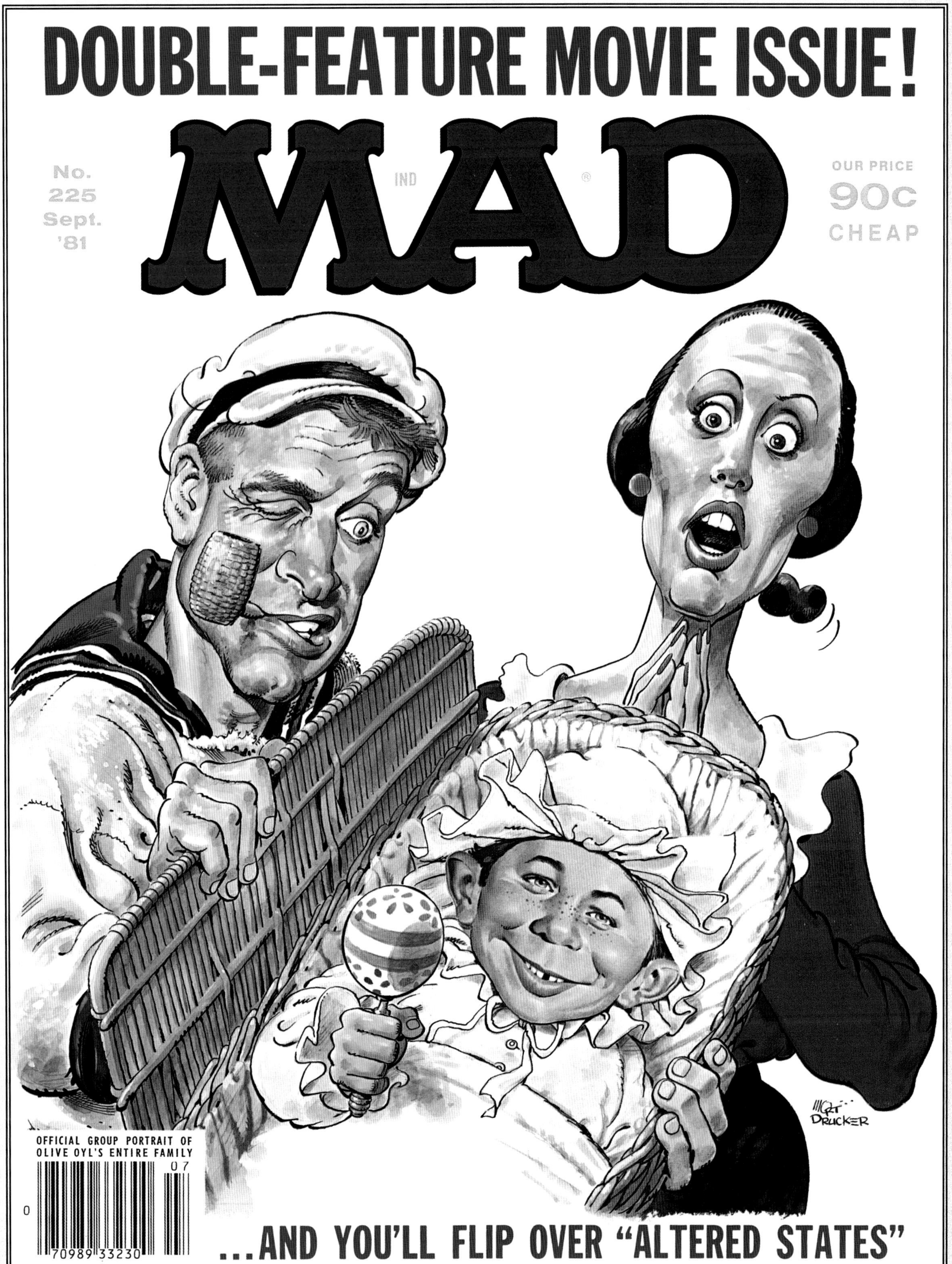
DOUBLE-FEATURE MOVIE ISSUE!
MAD
IND
No. 225 Sept. '81
OUR PRICE 90¢ CHEAP
OFFICIAL GROUP PORTRAIT OF OLIVE OYL'S ENTIRE FAMILY
MORT DRUCKER
...AND YOU'LL FLIP OVER "ALTERED STATES"

CAUGHT IN THE ACTS DEPT.

So you really think that just because Ronald Reagan became President, he gave u acting?! Well, shows how much you know!! Because once an actor, always an acto It's kinda like herpes! And now that he IS President, instead of waiting aroun

RONALD REAGAN NOW STARRIN

...as "Hamlet"...

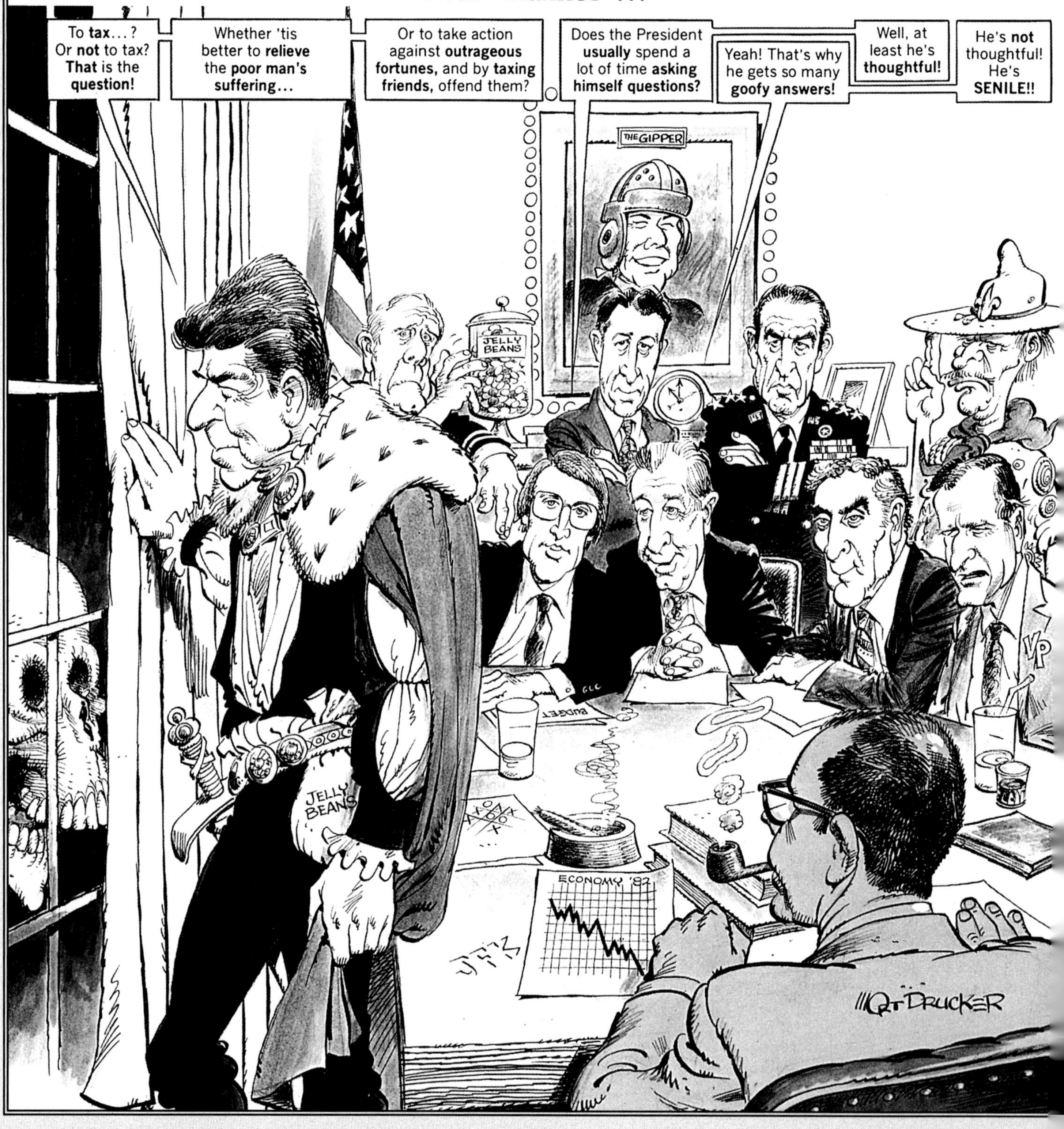
To **tax**...? Or **not** to tax? **That** is the **question!**
Whether 'tis better to **relieve** the **poor man's suffering...**
Or to take action against **outrageous fortunes,** and by **taxing friends,** offend them?
Does the President **usually** spend a lot of time **asking himself questions?**
Yeah! That's why he gets so many **goofy answers!**
Well, at least he's **thoughtful!**
He's **not** thoughtful! He's **SENILE!!**
THE GIPPER
JELLY BEANS
JELLY BEANS
BUDGET
ECONOMY '82
VP

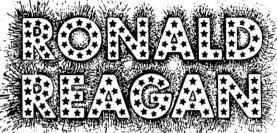

r a great role like "Bonzo's Pal" to come along, Ronnie can play any role that e wants. In fact, we here at MAD have detected him playing many famous, sought-fter parts since he took office. Here are just few we've observed...with...

AT THE WHITE HOUSE

ARTIST: MORT DRUCKER WRITER: STAN HART

..as Ron Corlione... in "The Godfather"...

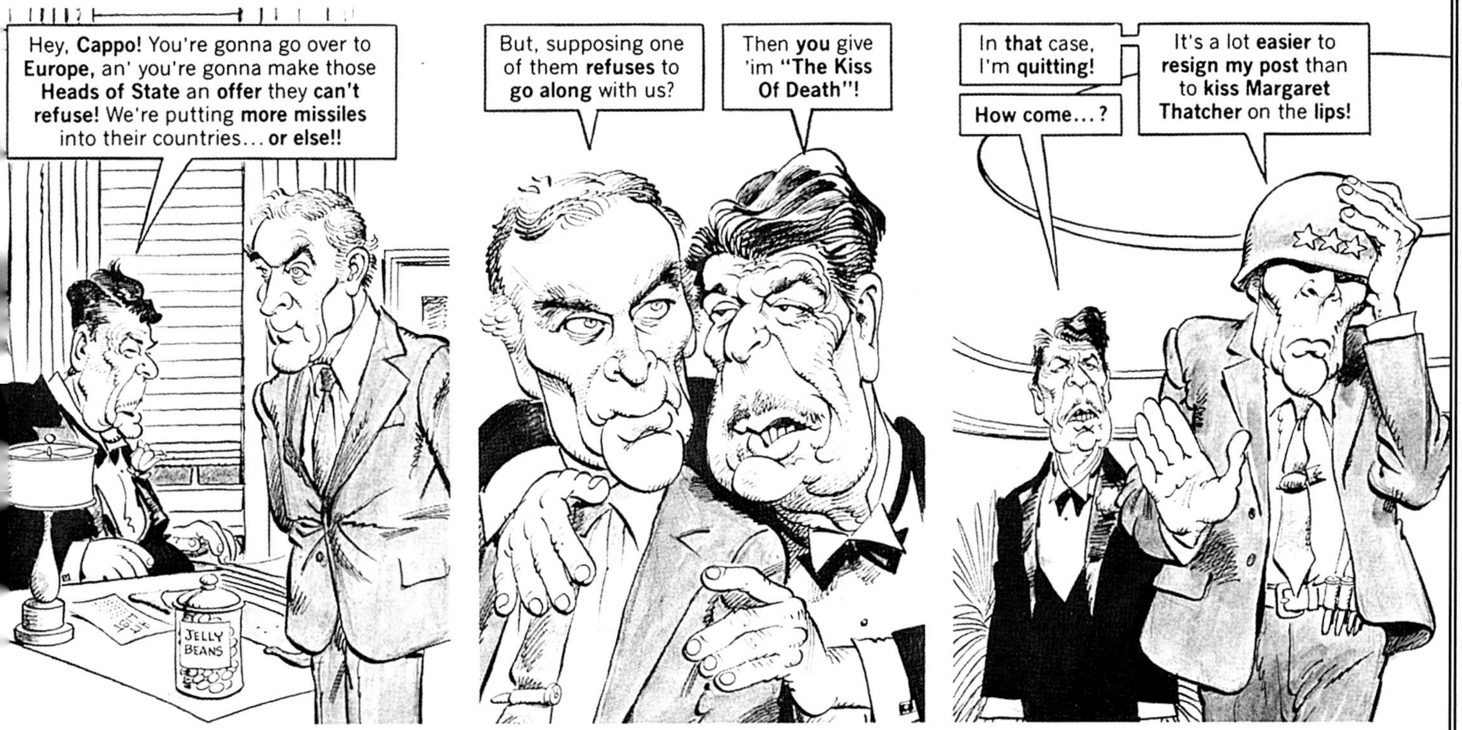
Hey, Cappo! You're gonna go over to Europe, an' you're gonna make those Heads of State an offer they can't refuse! We're putting more missiles into their countries... or else!!
JELLY BEANS
But, supposing one of them refuses to go along with us?
Then you give 'im "The Kiss Of Death"!
In that case, I'm quitting!
How come...?
It's a lot easier to resign my post than to kiss Margaret Thatcher on the lips!

.as Ron Quixote... in "Man Of La Mancha"...

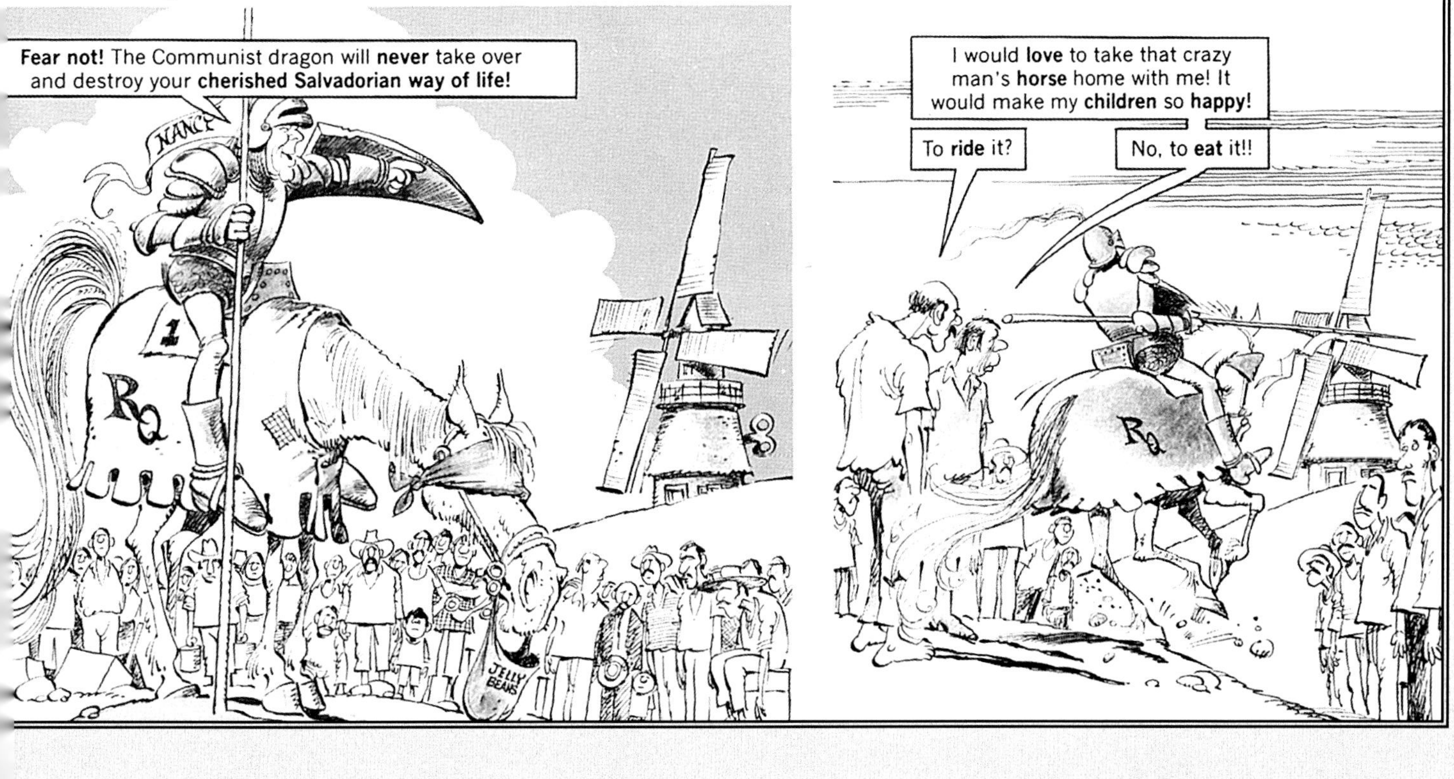
Fear not! The Communist dragon will never take over and destroy your cherished Salvadorian way of life!
NANCY
RQ
JELLY BEANS
I would love to take that crazy man's horse home with me! It would make my children so happy!
To ride it?
No, to eat it!!
RQ

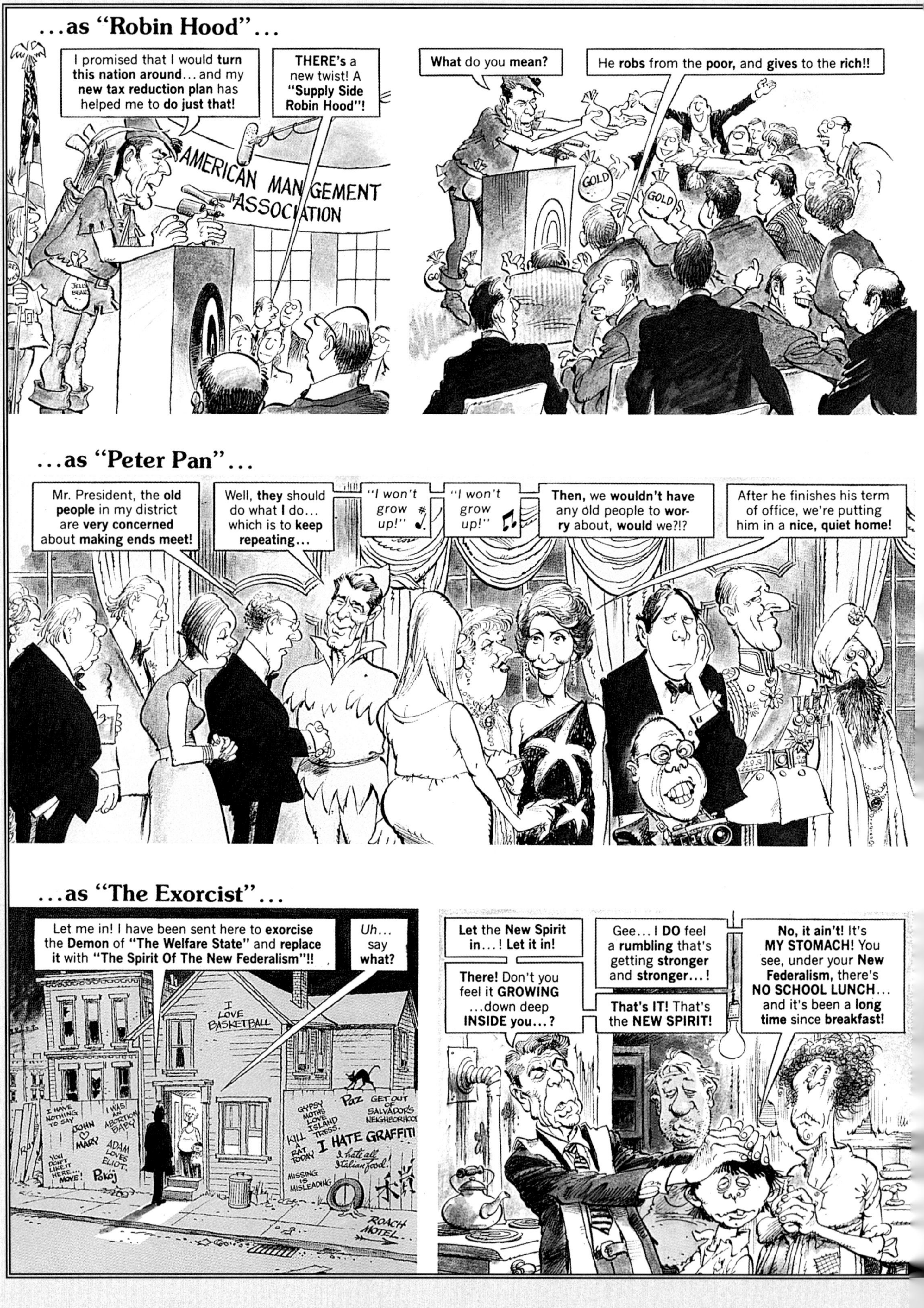
...as "Robin Hood"...
I promised that I would turn this nation around... and my new tax reduction plan has helped me to do just that!
THERE's a new twist! A "Supply Side Robin Hood"!
AMERICAN MANAGEMENT ASSOCIATION
What do you mean?
He robs from the poor, and gives to the rich!!
GOLD
GOLD
...as "Peter Pan"...
Mr. President, the old people in my district are very concerned about making ends meet!
Well, they should do what I do... which is to keep repeating...
"I won't grow up!"
"I won't grow up!"
Then, we wouldn't have any old people to worry about, would we?!?
After he finishes his term of office, we're putting him in a nice, quiet home!
...as "The Exorcist"...
Let me in! I have been sent here to exorcise the Demon of "The Welfare State" and replace it with "The Spirit Of The New Federalism"!!
Uh... say what?
I LOVE BASKETBALL
I HAVE NOTHING TO SAY
I WAS AN ABORTION BABY
JOHN MARY
ADAM LOVES ELIOT.
YOU DON'T LIKE IT HERE... MOVE!
GYPSY MOTHS LOVE ISLAND TREES.
GET OUT OF SALVADOR'S NEIGHBORHOOD
KILL A RAT TODAY
I HATE GRAFFITI
I hate all Italian food.
MISSING IS MISLEADING
ROACH MOTEL
Let the New Spirit in...! Let it in!
There! Don't you feel it GROWING ...down deep INSIDE you...?
Gee... I DO feel a rumbling that's getting stronger and stronger...!
That's IT! That's the NEW SPIRIT!
No, it ain't! It's MY STOMACH! You see, under your New Federalism, there's NO SCHOOL LUNCH... and it's been a long time since breakfast!

...as Moses... in "The Ten Commandments"...

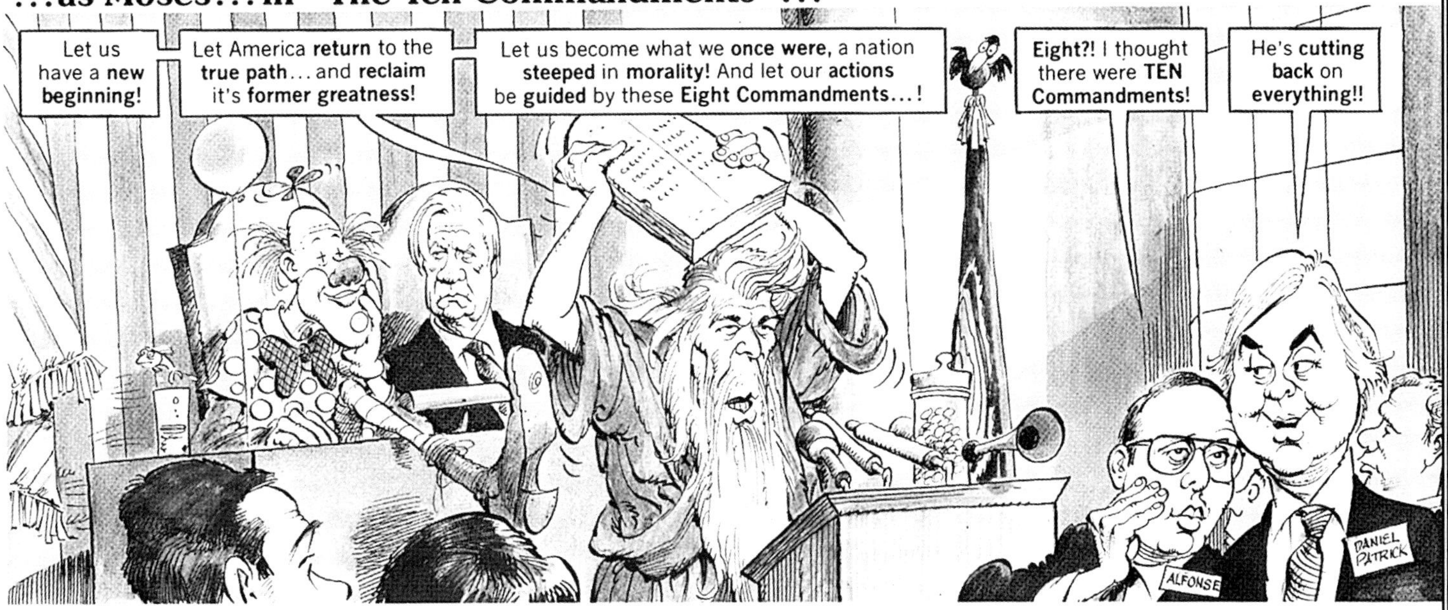
Let us have a new beginning!
Let America return to the true path... and reclaim it's former greatness!
Let us become what we once were, a nation steeped in morality! And let our actions be guided by these Eight Commandments...!
Eight?! I thought there were TEN Commandments!
He's cutting back on everything!!
ALFONSE
DANIEL PATRICK

...as Merlin... in "Camelot"...

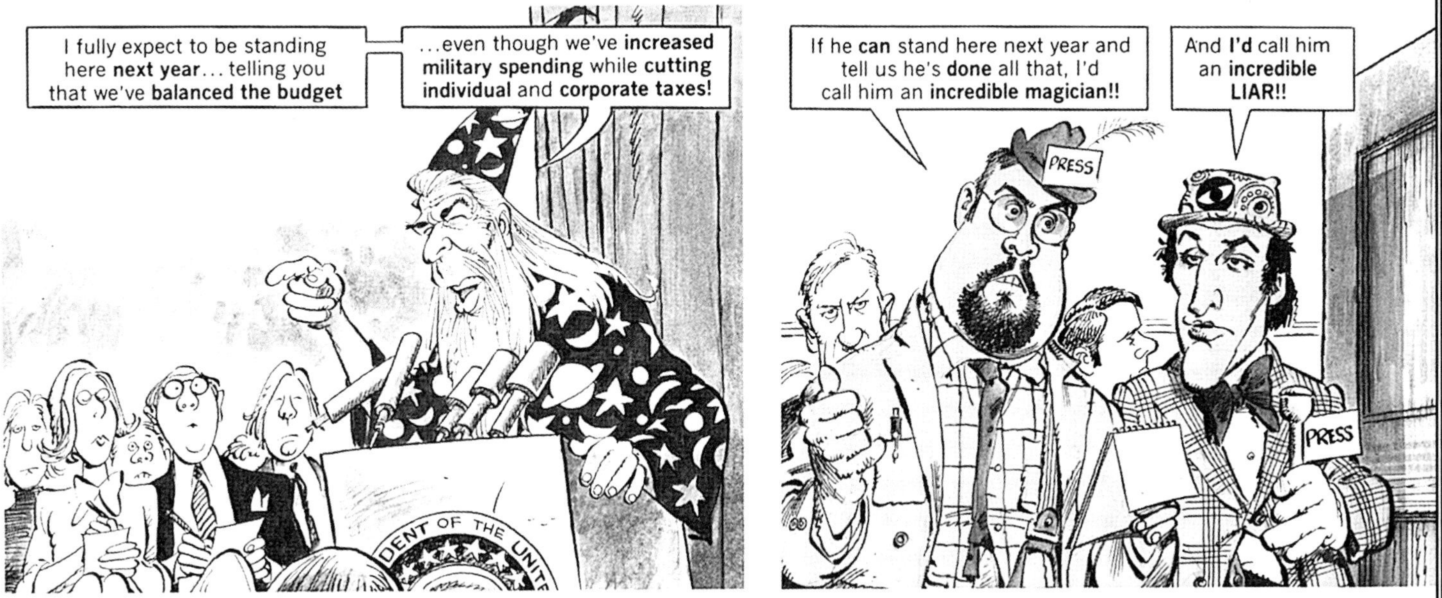
I fully expect to be standing here next year... telling you that we've balanced the budget
...even though we've increased military spending while cutting individual and corporate taxes!
If he can stand here next year and tell us he's done all that, I'd call him an incredible magician!!
And I'd call him an incredible LIAR!!
PRESS
PRESS

...as Scrooge... in "A Christmas Carol"...

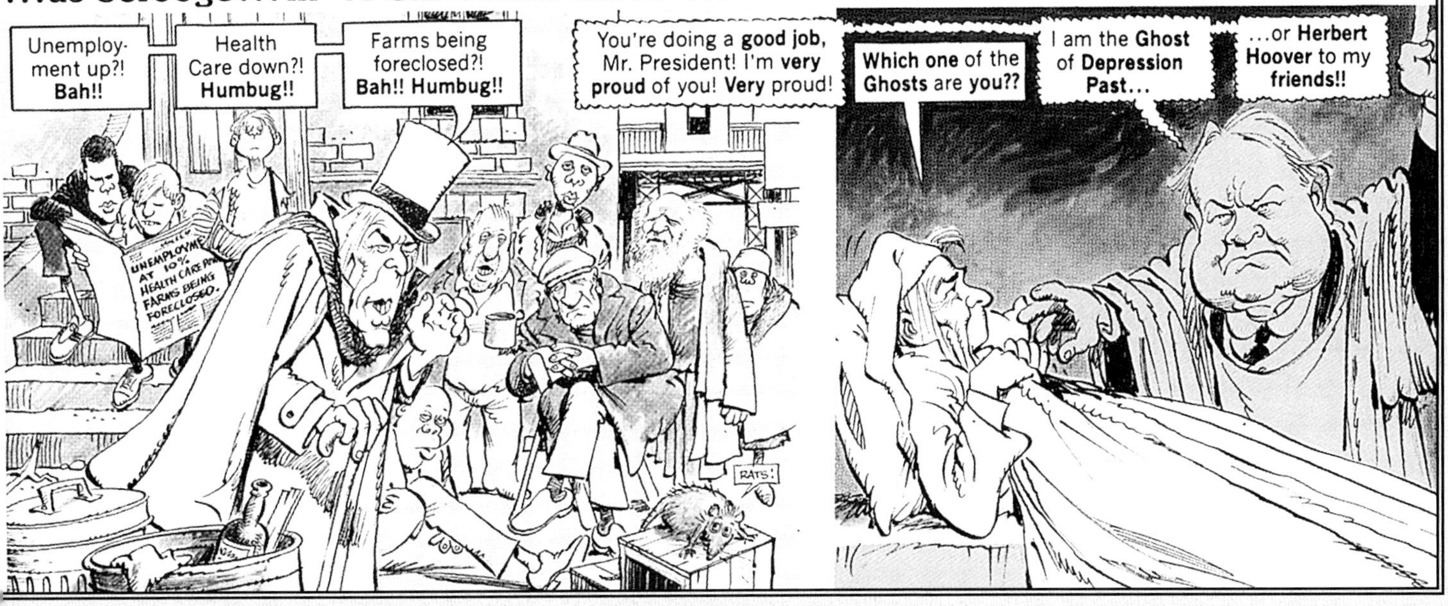
Unemploy-ment up?! Bah!!
Health Care down?! Humbug!!
Farms being foreclosed?! Bah!! Humbug!!
You're doing a good job, Mr. President! I'm very proud of you! Very proud!
Which one of the Ghosts are you??
I am the Ghost of Depression Past...
...or Herbert Hoover to my friends!!
RATS!

...as Simon Legree...in "Uncle Tom's Cabin"...

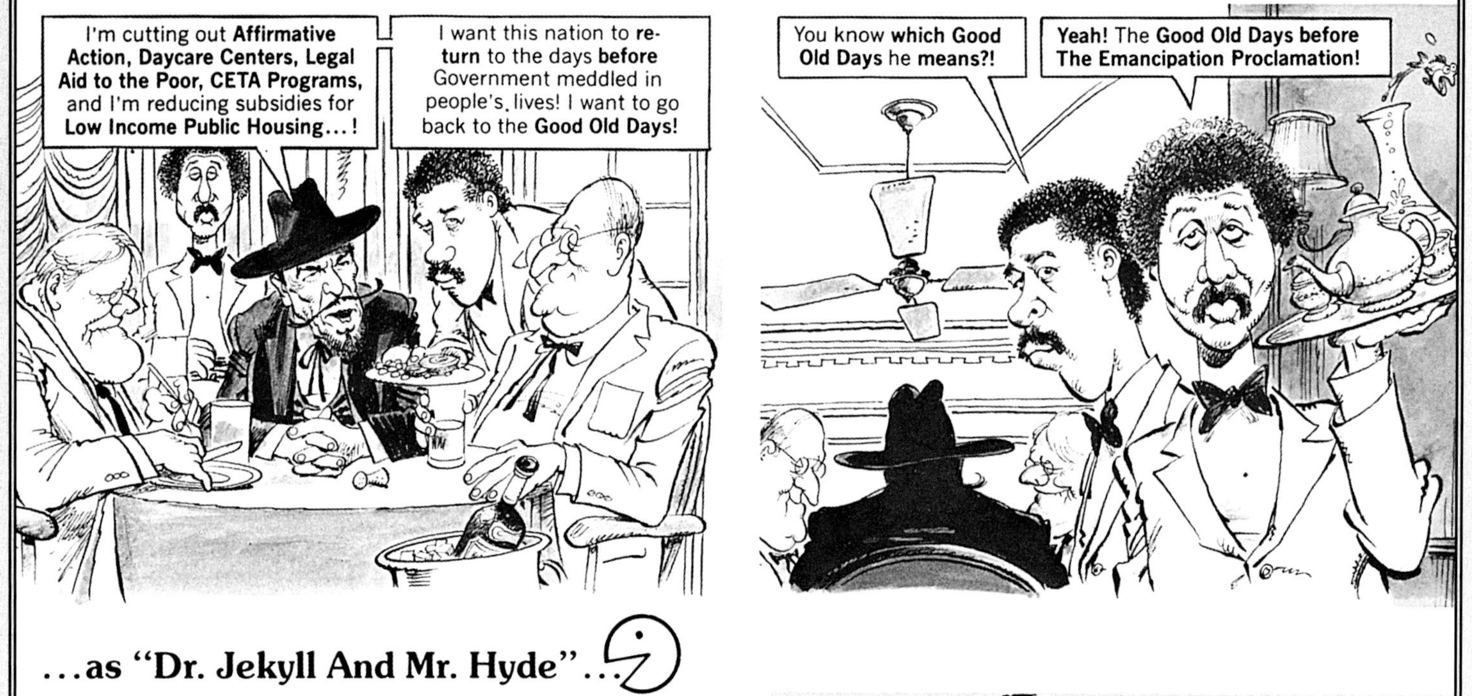
I'm cutting out Affirmative Action, Daycare Centers, Legal Aid to the Poor, CETA Programs, and I'm reducing subsidies for Low Income Public Housing...!
I want this nation to return to the days before Government meddled in people's lives! I want to go back to the Good Old Days!
You know which Good Old Days he means?!
Yeah! The Good Old Days before The Emancipation Proclamation!

...as "Dr. Jekyll And Mr. Hyde"...

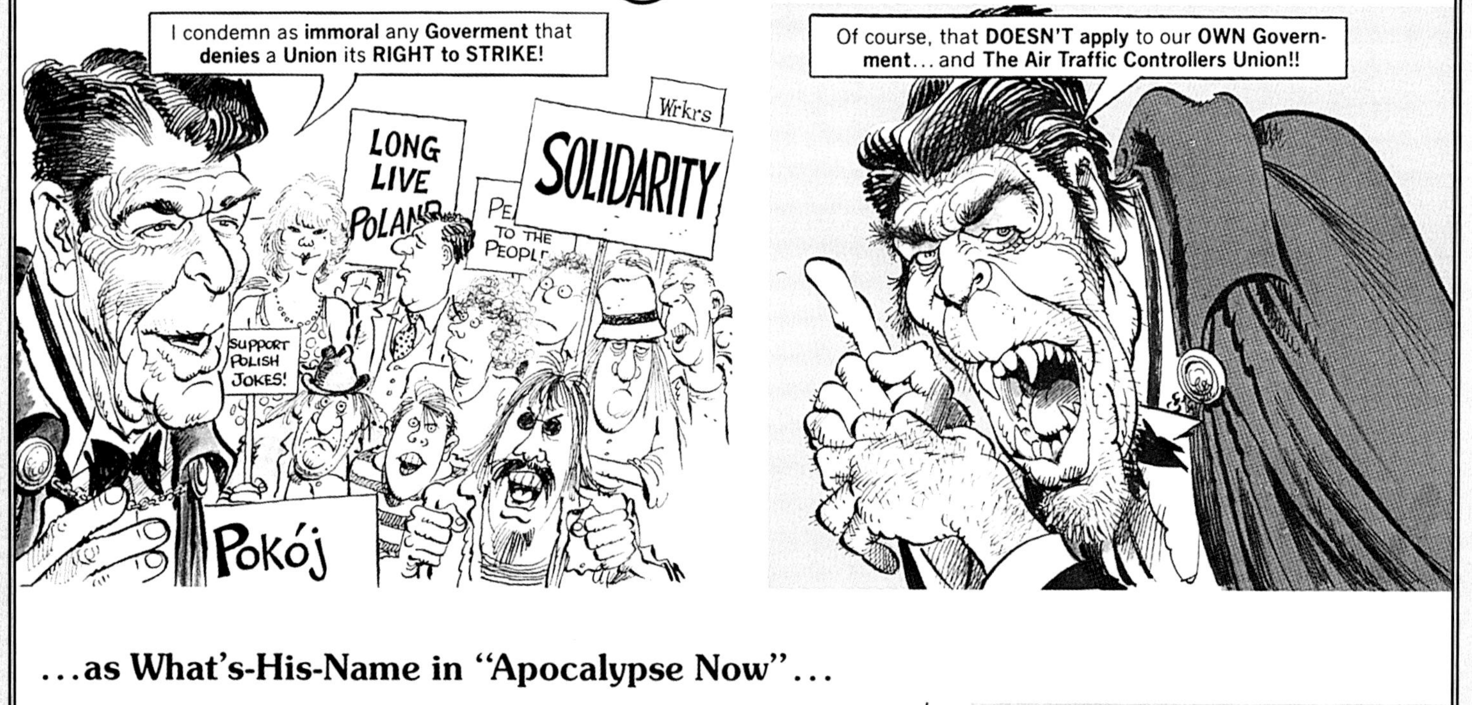
I condemn as immoral any Goverment that denies a Union its RIGHT to STRIKE!
LONG LIVE
SOLIDARITY
Wrkrs
SUPPORT POLISH JOKES!
Pokój
Of course, that DOESN'T apply to our OWN Government... and The Air Traffic Controllers Union!!

...as What's-His-Name in "Apocalypse Now"...

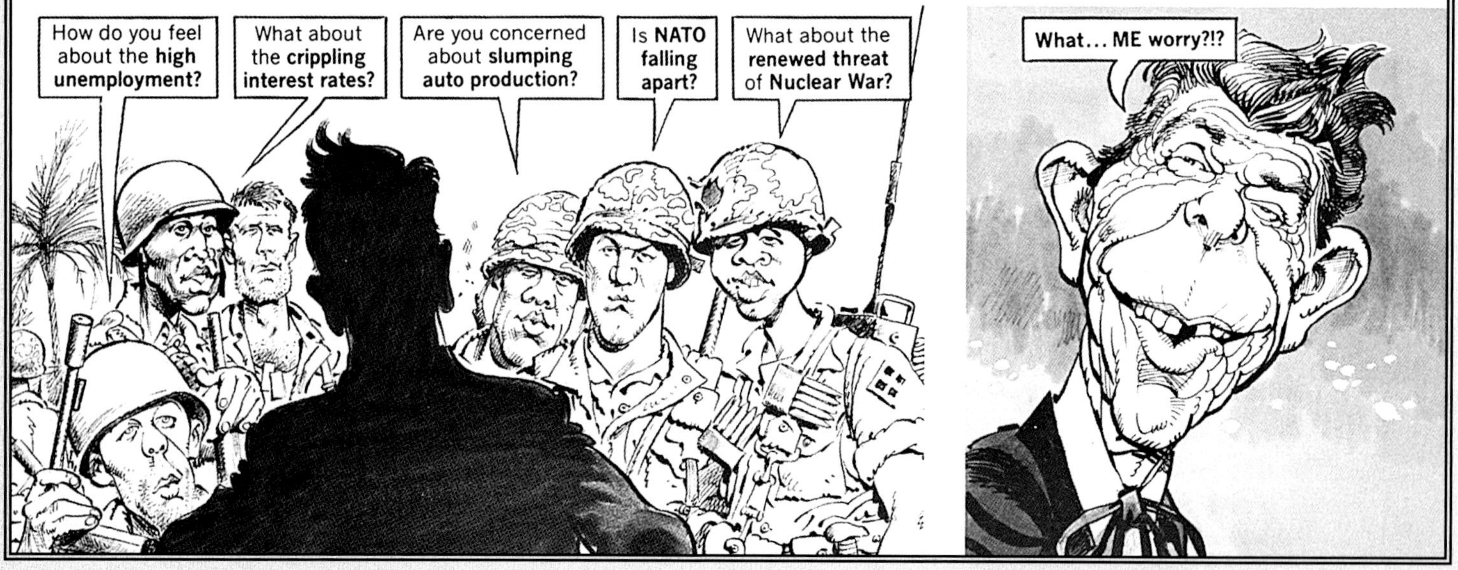
How do you feel about the high unemployment?
What about the crippling interest rates?
Are you concerned about slumping auto production?
Is NATO falling apart?
What about the renewed threat of Nuclear War?
What... ME worry?!?

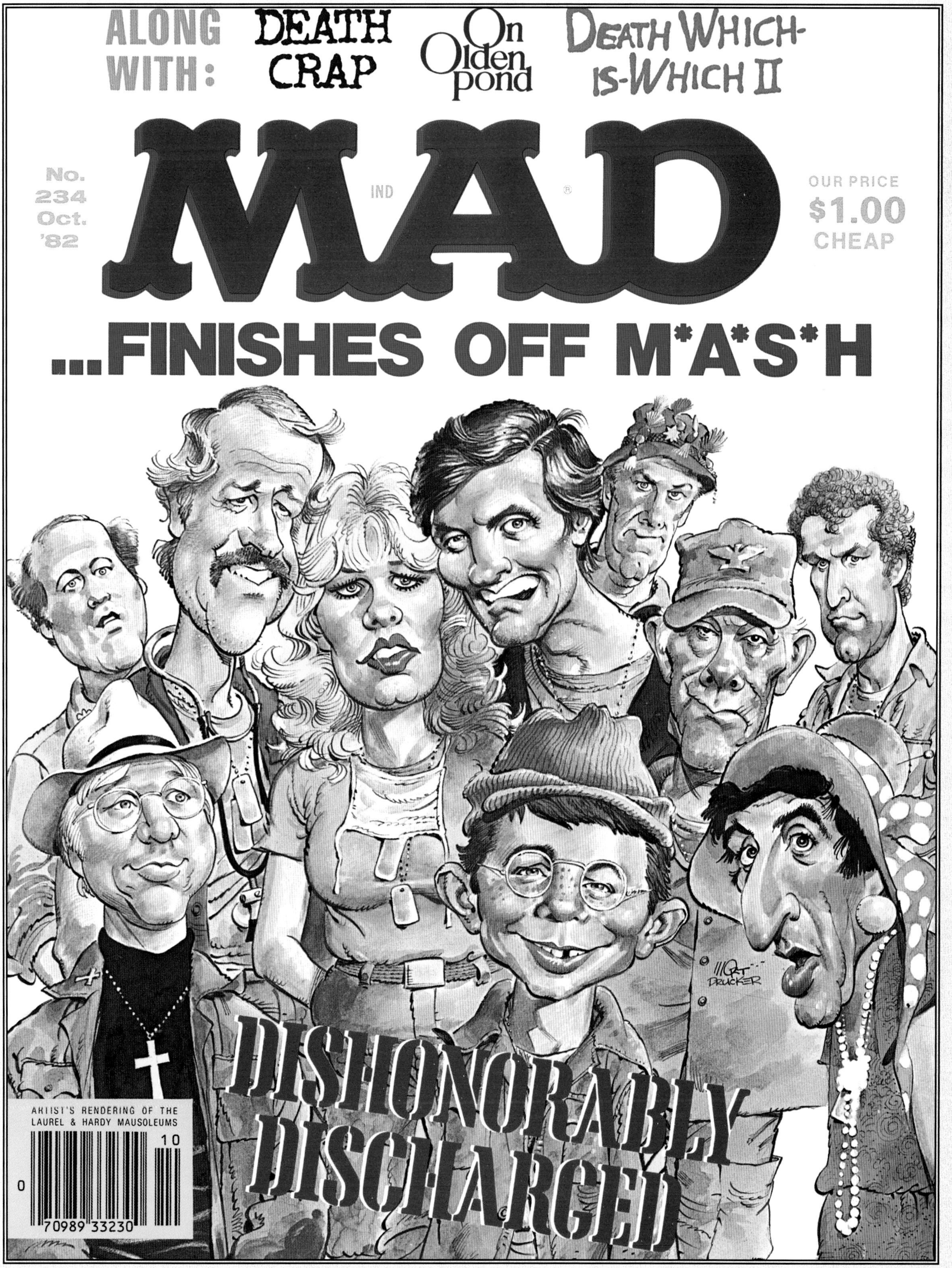
ALONG WITH:
DEATH CRAP
On Olden pond
DEATH WHICH-IS-WHICH II
MAD
No. 234 Oct. '82
IND
OUR PRICE $1.00 CHEAP
...FINISHES OFF M*A*S*H
MORT DRUCKER
DISHONORABLY DISCHARGED
ARTIST'S RENDERING OF THE LAUREL & HARDY MAUSOLEUMS
10
0
70989 33230

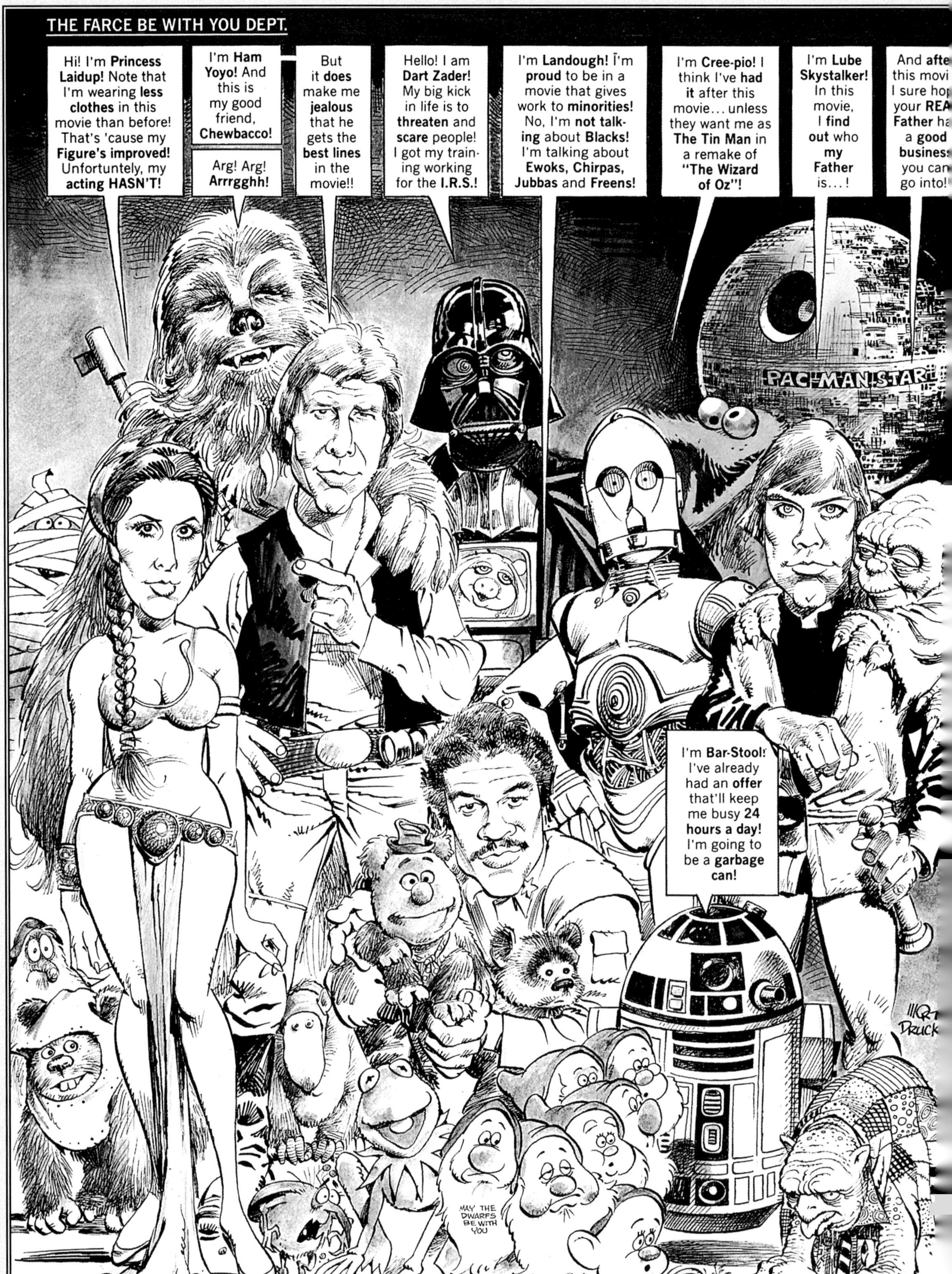
THE FARCE BE WITH YOU DEPT.
Hi! I'm Princess Laidup! Note that I'm wearing less clothes in this movie than before! That's 'cause my Figure's improved! Unfortuntely, my acting HASN'T!
I'm Ham Yoyo! And this is my good friend, Chewbacco!
Arg! Arg! Arrrgghh!
But it does make me jealous that he gets the best lines in the movie!!
Hello! I am Dart Zader! My big kick in life is to threaten and scare people! I got my training working for the I.R.S.!
I'm Landough! I'm proud to be in a movie that gives work to minorities! No, I'm not talking about Blacks! I'm talking about Ewoks, Chirpas, Jubbas and Freens!
I'm Cree-pio! I think I've had it after this movie... unless they want me as The Tin Man in a remake of "The Wizard of Oz"!
I'm Lube Skystalker! In this movie, I find out who my Father is...!
And afte this movi I sure hop your REA Father ha a good busines you can go into!
PAC-MAN STAR
I'm Bar-Stool! I've already had an offer that'll keep me busy 24 hours a day! I'm going to be a garbage can!
MAY THE DWARFS BE WITH YOU

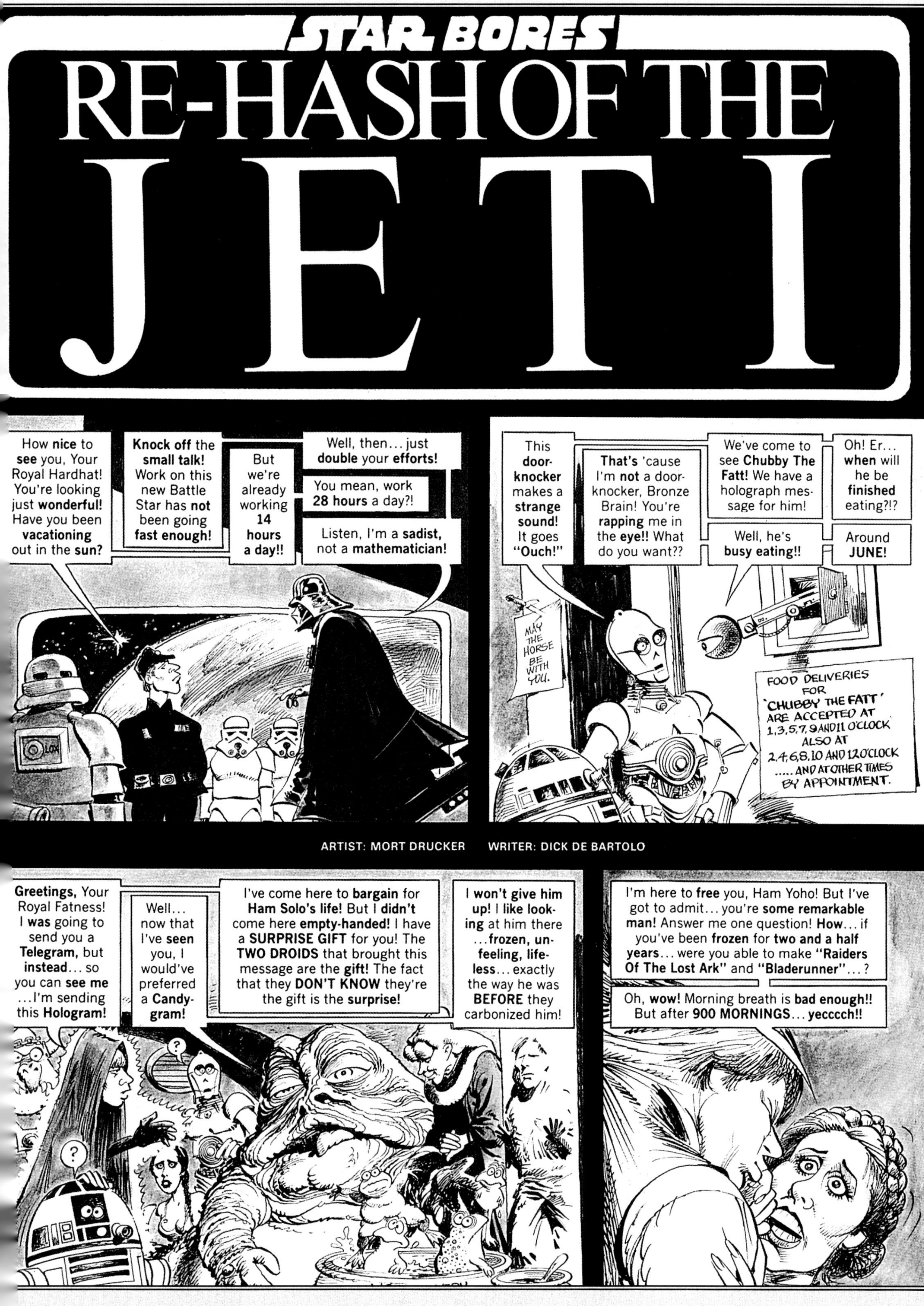
STAR BORES
RE-HASH OF THE JETI
How nice to see you, Your Royal Hardhat! You're looking just wonderful! Have you been vacationing out in the sun?
Knock off the small talk! Work on this new Battle Star has not been going fast enough!
But we're already working 14 hours a day!!
Well, then... just double your efforts!
You mean, work 28 hours a day?!
Listen, I'm a sadist, not a mathematician!
This door-knocker makes a strange sound! It goes "Ouch!"
That's 'cause I'm not a door-knocker, Bronze Brain! You're rapping me in the eye!! What do you want??
We've come to see Chubby The Fatt! We have a holograph message for him!
Well, he's busy eating!!
Oh! Er... when will he be finished eating?!?
Around JUNE!
MAY THE HORSE BE WITH YOU.
FOOD DELIVERIES FOR 'CHUBBY THE FATT' ARE ACCEPTED AT 1,3,5,7,9 AND 11 O'CLOCK ALSO AT 2,4,6,8,10 AND 12 O'CLOCK ..... AND AT OTHER TIMES BY APPOINTMENT.
ARTIST: MORT DRUCKER WRITER: DICK DE BARTOLO
Greetings, Your Royal Fatness! I was going to send you a Telegram, but instead... so you can see me ...I'm sending this Hologram!
Well... now that I've seen you, I would've preferred a Candy-gram!
I've come here to bargain for Ham Solo's life! But I didn't come here empty-handed! I have a SURPRISE GIFT for you! The TWO DROIDS that brought this message are the gift! The fact that they DON'T KNOW they're the gift is the surprise!
I won't give him up! I like looking at him there ...frozen, unfeeling, lifeless... exactly the way he was BEFORE they carbonized him!
?
?
I'm here to free you, Ham Yoho! But I've got to admit... you're some remarkable man! Answer me one question! How... if you've been frozen for two and a half years... were you able to make "Raiders Of The Lost Ark" and "Bladerunner"...?
Oh, wow! Morning breath is bad enough!! But after 900 MORNINGS... yeccch!!

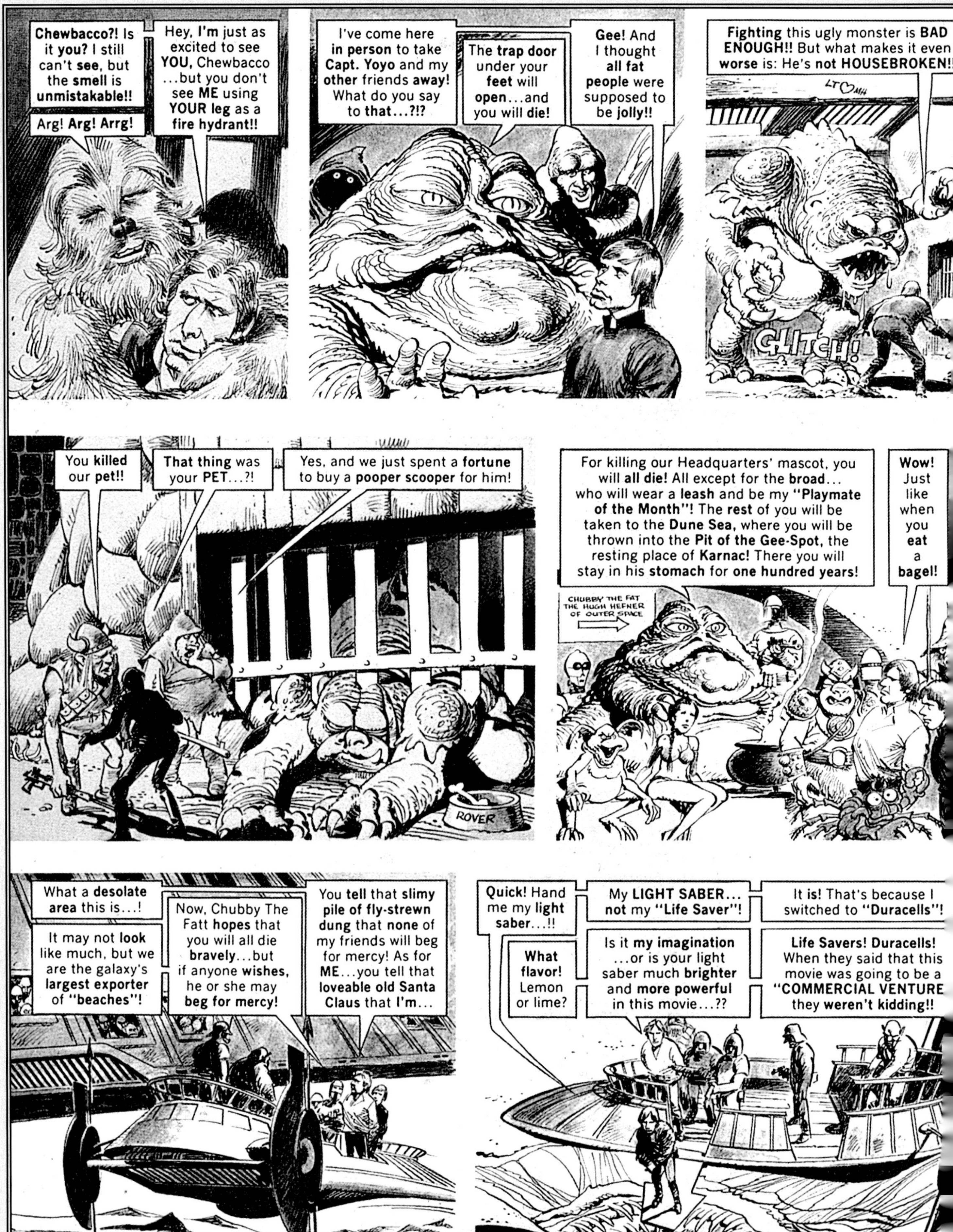
Chewbacco?! Is it you? I still can't see, but the smell is unmistakable!!
Arg! Arg! Arrg!
Hey, I'm just as excited to see YOU, Chewbacco ...but you don't see ME using YOUR leg as a fire hydrant!!
I've come here in person to take Capt. Yoyo and my other friends away! What do you say to that...?!?
The trap door under your feet will open...and you will die!
Gee! And I thought all fat people were supposed to be jolly!!
Fighting this ugly monster is BAD ENOUGH!! But what makes it even worse is: He's not HOUSEBROKEN!!
GLITCH!
You killed our pet!!
That thing was your PET...?!
Yes, and we just spent a fortune to buy a pooper scooper for him!
ROVER
For killing our Headquarters' mascot, you will all die! All except for the broad... who will wear a leash and be my "Playmate of the Month"! The rest of you will be taken to the Dune Sea, where you will be thrown into the Pit of the Gee-Spot, the resting place of Karnac! There you will stay in his stomach for one hundred years!
Wow! Just like when you eat a bagel!
CHUBBY THE FAT THE HUGH HEFNER OF OUTER SPACE
What a desolate area this is...!
It may not look like much, but we are the galaxy's largest exporter of "beaches"!
Now, Chubby The Fatt hopes that you will all die bravely...but if anyone wishes, he or she may beg for mercy!
You tell that slimy pile of fly-strewn dung that none of my friends will beg for mercy! As for ME...you tell that loveable old Santa Claus that I'm...
Quick! Hand me my light saber...!!
What flavor! Lemon or lime?
My LIGHT SABER... not my "Life Saver"!
Is it my imagination ...or is your light saber much brighter and more powerful in this movie...??
It is! That's because I switched to "Duracells"!
Life Savers! Duracells! When they said that this movie was going to be a "COMMERCIAL VENTURE" they weren't kidding!!

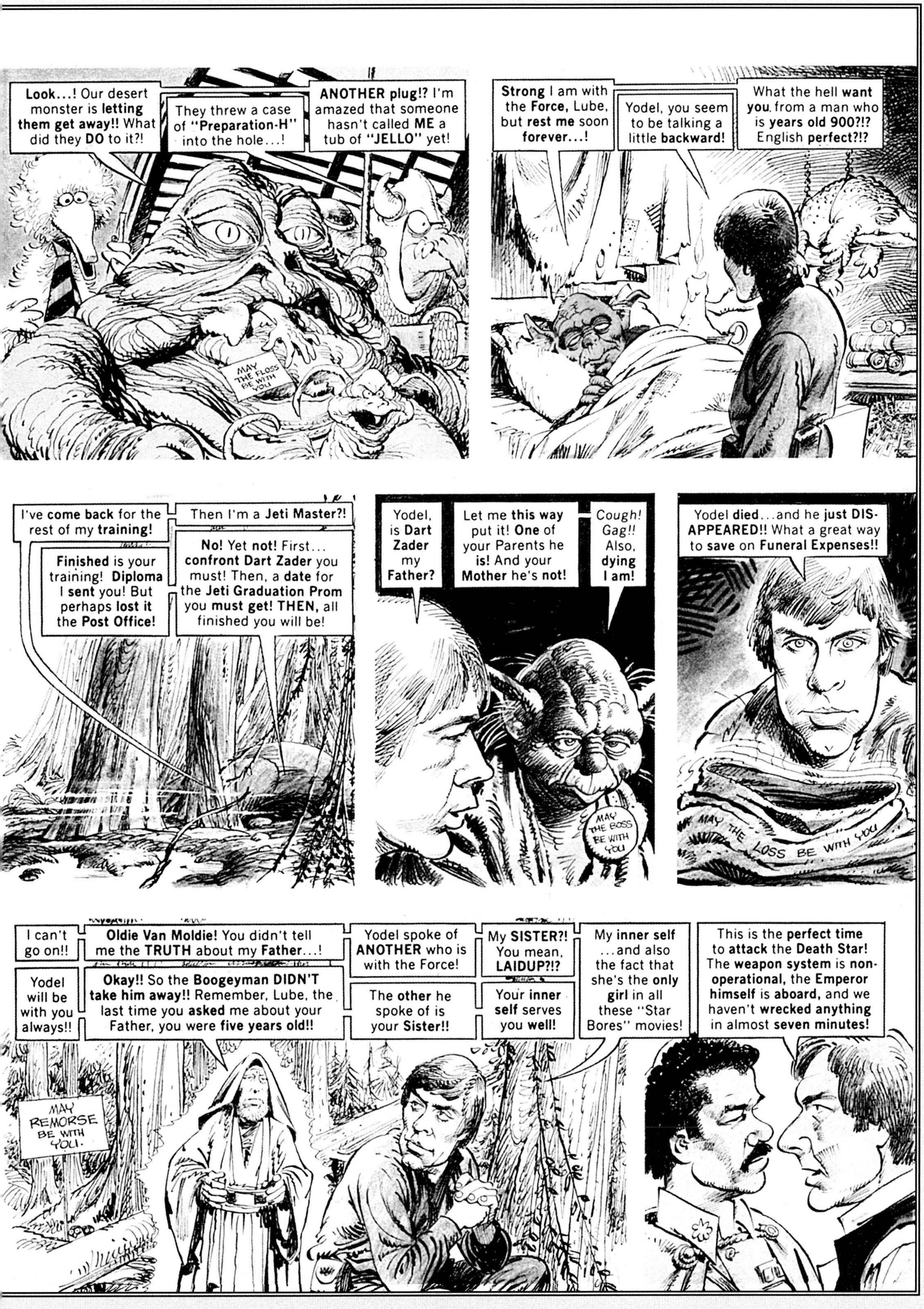
Look...! Our desert monster is letting them get away!! What did they DO to it?!
They threw a case of "Preparation-H" into the hole...!
ANOTHER plug!? I'm amazed that someone hasn't called ME a tub of "JELLO" yet!
MAY THE FLOSS BE WITH YOU
Strong I am with the Force, Lube, but rest me soon forever...!
Yodel, you seem to be talking a little backward!
What the hell want you from a man who is years old 900?!? English perfect?!?
I've come back for the rest of my training!
Finished is your training! Diploma I sent you! But perhaps lost it the Post Office!
Then I'm a Jeti Master?!
No! Yet not! First... confront Dart Zader you must! Then, a date for the Jeti Graduation Prom you must get! THEN, all finished you will be!
Yodel, is Dart Zader my Father?
Let me this way put it! One of your Parents he is! And your Mother he's not!
Cough! Gag!! Also, dying I am!
MAY THE BOSS BE WITH YOU
Yodel died...and he just DISAPPEARED!! What a great way to save on Funeral Expenses!!
MAY THE LOSS BE WITH YOU
I can't go on!!
Yodel will be with you always!!
Oldie Van Moldie! You didn't tell me the TRUTH about my Father...!
Okay!! So the Boogeyman DIDN'T take him away!! Remember, Lube, the last time you asked me about your Father, you were five years old!!
MAY REMORSE BE WITH YOU.
Yodel spoke of ANOTHER who is with the Force!
The other he spoke of is your Sister!!
My SISTER?! You mean, LAIDUP?!?
Your inner self serves you well!
My inner self ...and also the fact that she's the only girl in all these "Star Bores" movies!
This is the perfect time to attack the Death Star! The weapon system is non-operational, the Emperor himself is aboard, and we haven't wrecked anything in almost seven minutes!

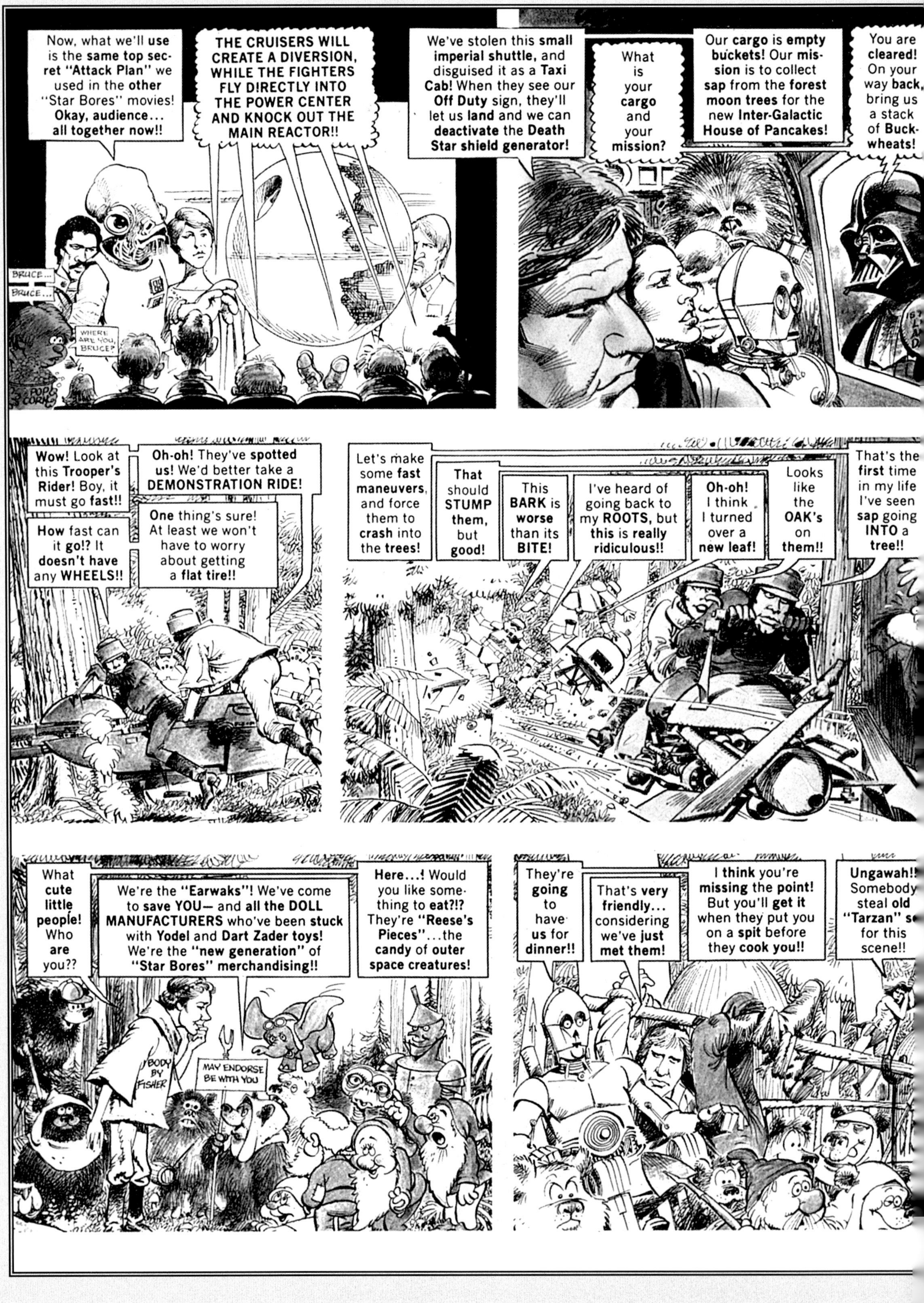
Now, what we'll use is the same top secret "Attack Plan" we used in the other "Star Bores" movies! Okay, audience... all together now!!
THE CRUISERS WILL CREATE A DIVERSION, WHILE THE FIGHTERS FLY DIRECTLY INTO THE POWER CENTER AND KNOCK OUT THE MAIN REACTOR!!
BRUCE...
BRUCE...
WHERE ARE YOU, BRUCE?
We've stolen this small imperial shuttle, and disguised it as a Taxi Cab! When they see our Off Duty sign, they'll let us land and we can deactivate the Death Star shield generator!
What is your cargo and your mission?
Our cargo is empty buckets! Our mission is to collect sap from the forest moon trees for the new Inter-Galactic House of Pancakes!
You are cleared! On your way back, bring us a stack of Buckwheats!
Wow! Look at this Trooper's Rider! Boy, it must go fast!!
Oh-oh! They've spotted us! We'd better take a DEMONSTRATION RIDE!
How fast can it go!? It doesn't have any WHEELS!!
One thing's sure! At least we won't have to worry about getting a flat tire!!
Let's make some fast maneuvers, and force them to crash into the trees!
That should STUMP them, but good!
This BARK is worse than its BITE!
I've heard of going back to my ROOTS, but this is really ridiculous!!
Oh-oh! I think I turned over a new leaf!
Looks like the OAK's on them!!
That's the first time in my life I've seen sap going INTO a tree!!
What cute little people! Who are you??
We're the "Earwaks"! We've come to save YOU— and all the DOLL MANUFACTURERS who've been stuck with Yodel and Dart Zader toys! We're the "new generation" of "Star Bores" merchandising!!
Here...! Would you like something to eat?!? They're "Reese's Pieces"...the candy of outer space creatures!
BODY BY FISHER
MAY ENDORSE BE WITH YOU
They're going to have us for dinner!!
That's very friendly... considering we've just met them!
I think you're missing the point! But you'll get it when they put you on a spit before they cook you!!
Ungawah!! Somebody steal old "Tarzan" s for this scene!!

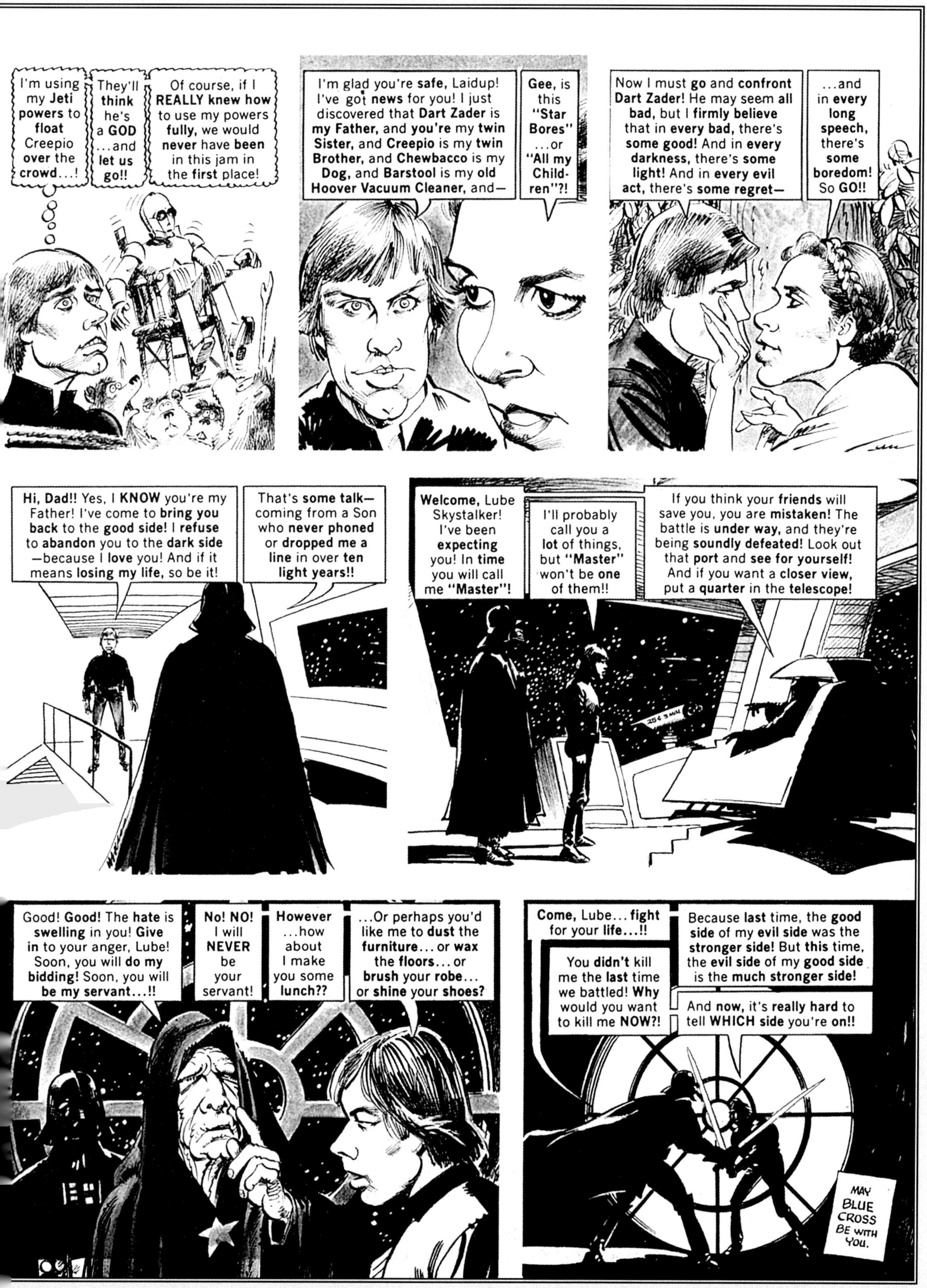
I'm using my Jeti powers to float Creepio over the crowd...!
They'll think he's a GOD ...and let us go!!
Of course, if I REALLY knew how to use my powers fully, we would never have been in this jam in the first place!
I'm glad you're safe, Laidup! I've got news for you! I just discovered that Dart Zader is my Father, and you're my twin Sister, and Creepio is my twin Brother, and Chewbacco is my Dog, and Barstool is my old Hoover Vacuum Cleaner, and—
Gee, is this "Star Bores" ...or "All my Children"?!
Now I must go and confront Dart Zader! He may seem all bad, but I firmly believe that in every bad, there's some good! And in every darkness, there's some light! And in every evil act, there's some regret—
...and in every long speech, there's some boredom! So GO!!
Hi, Dad!! Yes, I KNOW you're my Father! I've come to bring you back to the good side! I refuse to abandon you to the dark side —because I love you! And if it means losing my life, so be it!
That's some talk— coming from a Son who never phoned or dropped me a line in over ten light years!!
Welcome, Lube Skystalker! I've been expecting you! In time you will call me "Master"!
I'll probably call you a lot of things, but "Master" won't be one of them!!
If you think your friends will save you, you are mistaken! The battle is under way, and they're being soundly defeated! Look out that port and see for yourself! And if you want a closer view, put a quarter in the telescope!
25¢ 3 MIN
Good! Good! The hate is swelling in you! Give in to your anger, Lube! Soon, you will do my bidding! Soon, you will be my servant...!!
No! NO! I will NEVER be your servant!
However ...how about I make you some lunch??
...Or perhaps you'd like me to dust the furniture... or wax the floors... or brush your robe... or shine your shoes?
Come, Lube... fight for your life...!!
You didn't kill me the last time we battled! Why would you want to kill me NOW?!
Because last time, the good side of my evil side was the stronger side! But this time, the evil side of my good side is the much stronger side!
And now, it's really hard to tell WHICH side you're on!!
MAY BLUE CROSS BE WITH YOU.

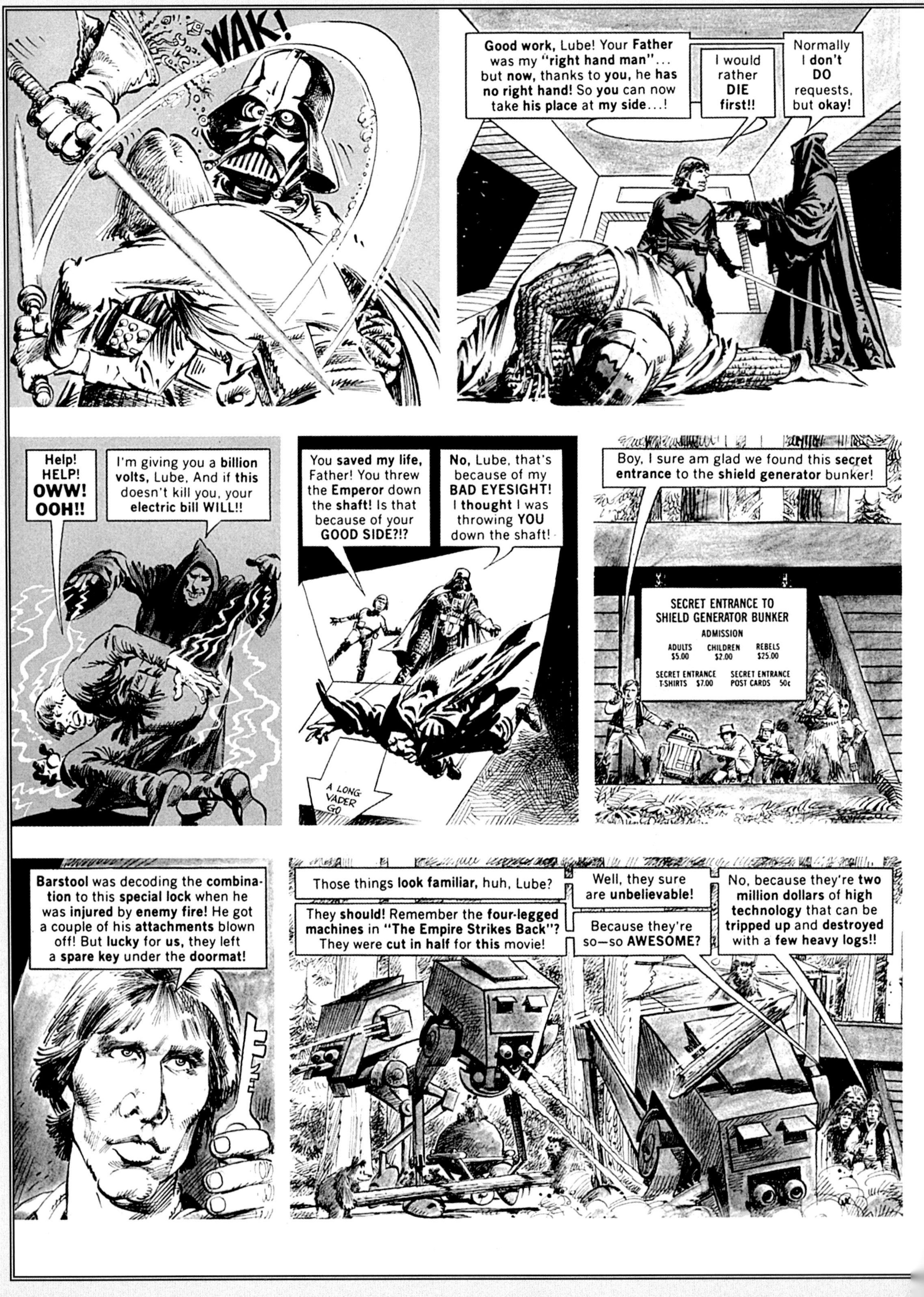
WAK!
Good work, Lube! Your Father was my "right hand man"... but now, thanks to you, he has no right hand! So you can now take his place at my side...!
I would rather DIE first!!
Normally I don't DO requests, but okay!
Help! HELP! OWW! OOH!!
I'm giving you a billion volts, Lube. And if this doesn't kill you, your electric bill WILL!!
You saved my life, Father! You threw the Emperor down the shaft! Is that because of your GOOD SIDE?!?
No, Lube, that's because of my BAD EYESIGHT! I thought I was throwing YOU down the shaft!
A LONG VADER GO
Boy, I sure am glad we found this secret entrance to the shield generator bunker!
SECRET ENTRANCE TO SHIELD GENERATOR BUNKER
ADMISSION
ADULTS $5.00
CHILDREN $2.00
REBELS $25.00
SECRET ENTRANCE T-SHIRTS $7.00
SECRET ENTRANCE POST CARDS 50¢
Barstool was decoding the combination to this special lock when he was injured by enemy fire! He got a couple of his attachments blown off! But lucky for us, they left a spare key under the doormat!
Those things look familiar, huh, Lube?
They should! Remember the four-legged machines in "The Empire Strikes Back"? They were cut in half for this movie!
Well, they sure are unbelievable!
Because they're so—so AWESOME?
No, because they're two million dollars of high technology that can be tripped up and destroyed with a few heavy logs!!

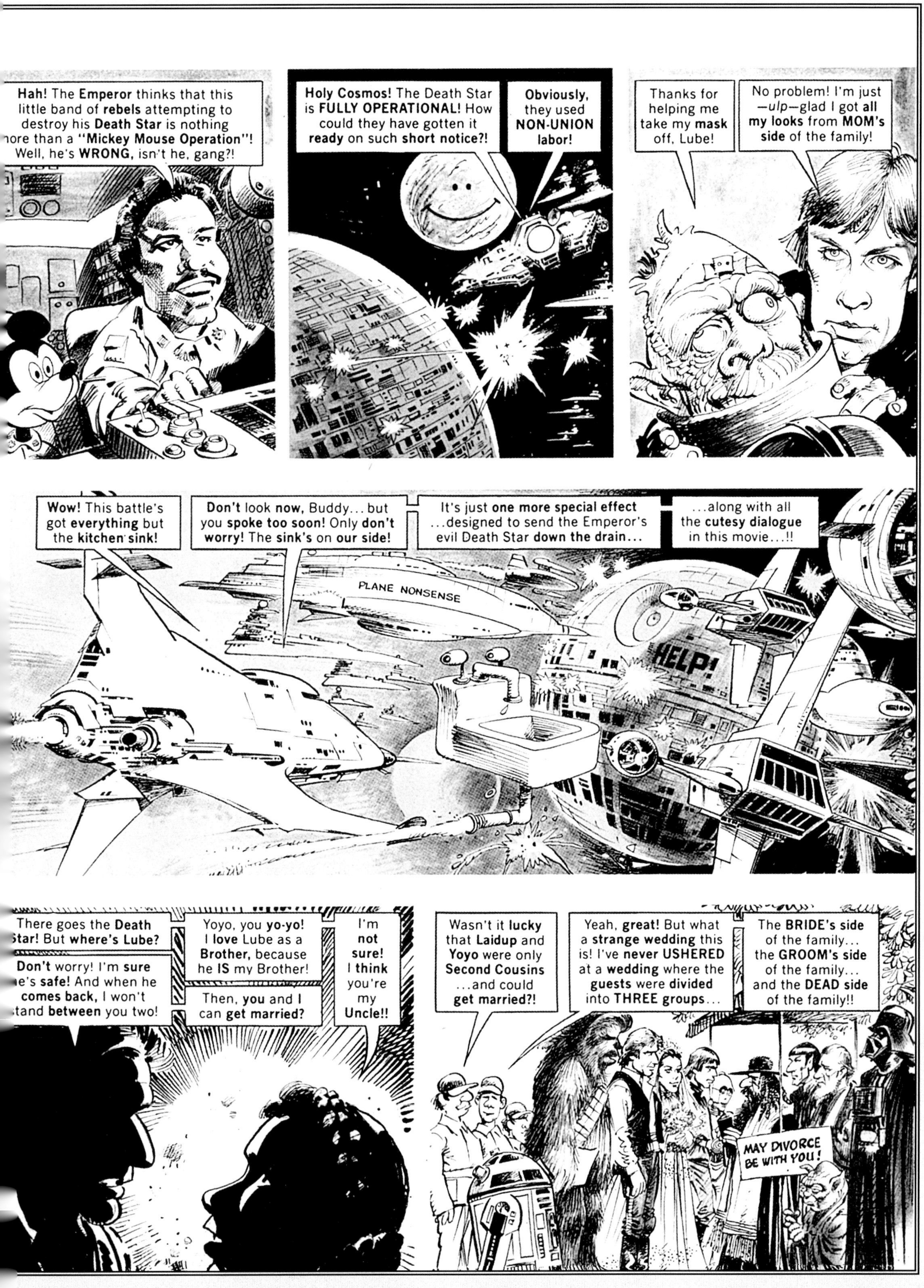
Hah! The Emperor thinks that this little band of rebels attempting to destroy his Death Star is nothing nore than a "Mickey Mouse Operation"! Well, he's WRONG, isn't he, gang?!
Holy Cosmos! The Death Star is FULLY OPERATIONAL! How could they have gotten it ready on such short notice?!
Obviously, they used NON-UNION labor!
Thanks for helping me take my mask off, Lube!
No problem! I'm just —ulp—glad I got all my looks from MOM's side of the family!
Wow! This battle's got everything but the kitchen sink!
Don't look now, Buddy... but you spoke too soon! Only don't worry! The sink's on our side!
It's just one more special effect ...designed to send the Emperor's evil Death Star down the drain...
...along with all the cutesy dialogue in this movie...!!
PLANE NONSENSE
HELP!
There goes the Death tar! But where's Lube?
Don't worry! I'm sure e's safe! And when he comes back, I won't tand between you two!
Yoyo, you yo-yo! I love Lube as a Brother, because he IS my Brother!
Then, you and I can get married?
I'm not sure! I think you're my Uncle!!
Wasn't it lucky that Laidup and Yoyo were only Second Cousins ...and could get married?!
Yeah, great! But what a strange wedding this is! I've never USHERED at a wedding where the guests were divided into THREE groups...
The BRIDE's side of the family... the GROOM's side of the family... and the DEAD side of the family!!
MAY DIVORCE BE WITH YOU!

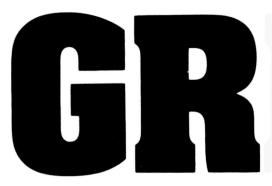

OUR CREATURES PRESENTATION DEPT.

Two summers ago, Steven Spielberg gave us "E.T.", a smash-hit film about a cuddly alien who has to withstand the villainies of us humans to get back home. This summer, Steven's come up with another smash-hit film—with an extra-added wrinkle. Oh, sure, there's a cuddly creature in it again! Why give up a good thing? But now, there are also a lot of evil creatures, too. And they're attacking us humans! But enough of this prose. Look at the pictures... and try reading MAD's version of...

GR

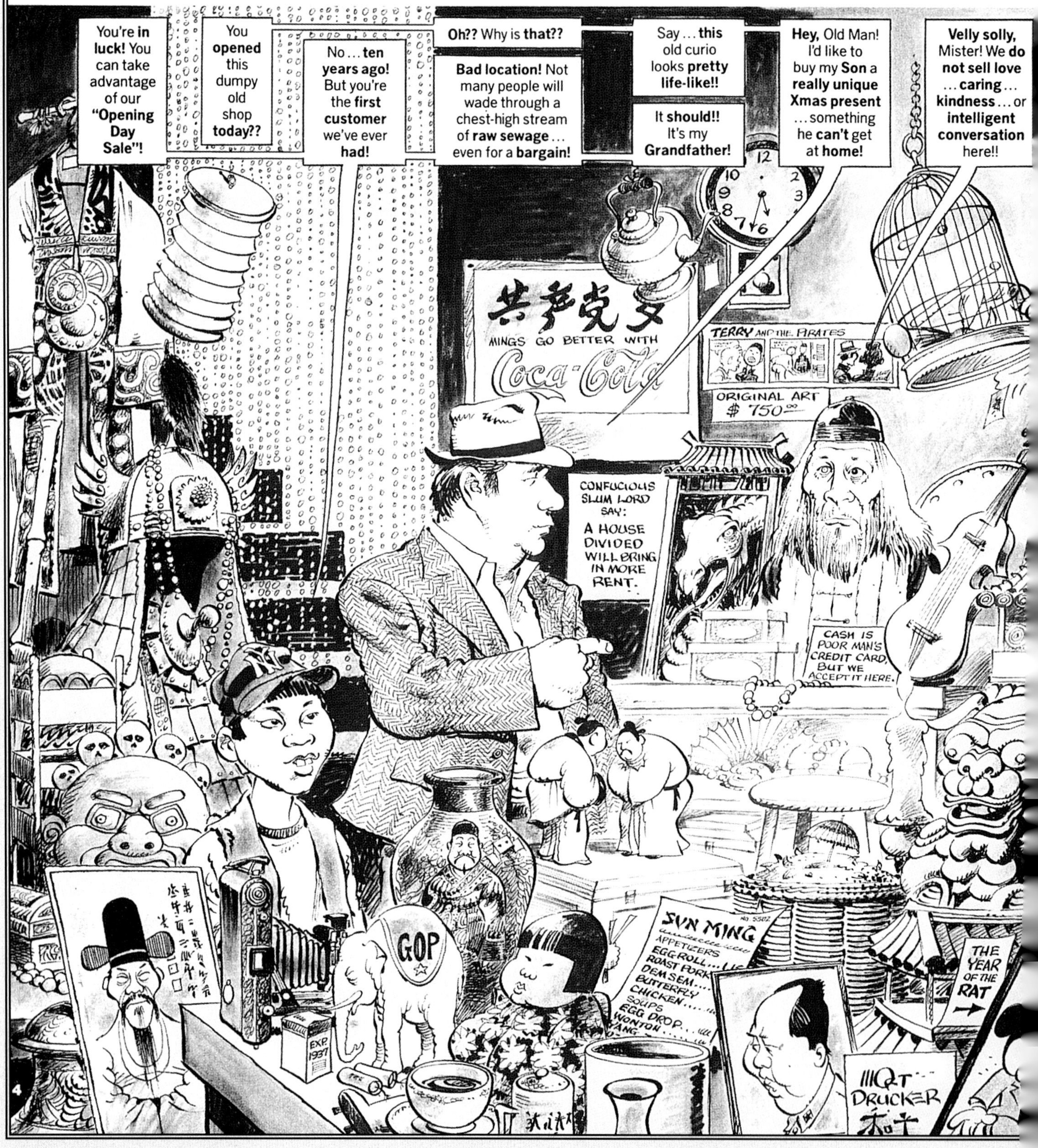
You're in luck! You can take advantage of our "Opening Day Sale"!
You opened this dumpy old shop today??
No... ten years ago! But you're the first customer we've ever had!
Oh?? Why is that??
Bad location! Not many people will wade through a chest-high stream of raw sewage... even for a bargain!
Say... this old curio looks pretty life-like!!
It should!! It's my Grandfather!
Hey, Old Man! I'd like to buy my Son a really unique Xmas present ...something he can't get at home!
Velly solly, Mister! We do not sell love ...caring... kindness... or intelligent conversation here!!
MINGS GO BETTER WITH
Coca-Cola
TERRY AND THE PIRATES
ORIGINAL ART $ 750.00
CONFUCIOUS SLUM LORD SAY: A HOUSE DIVIDED WILL BRING IN MORE RENT.
CASH IS POOR MAN'S CREDIT CARD, BUT WE ACCEPT IT HERE.
GOP
EXP 1937
SUN MING
APPETIZERS
EGG ROLL...
ROAST PORK
DEM SEM...
BUTTERFLY CHICKEN...
SOUPS
EGG DROP...
WONTON
THE YEAR OF THE RAT
DRUCKER

MLINS

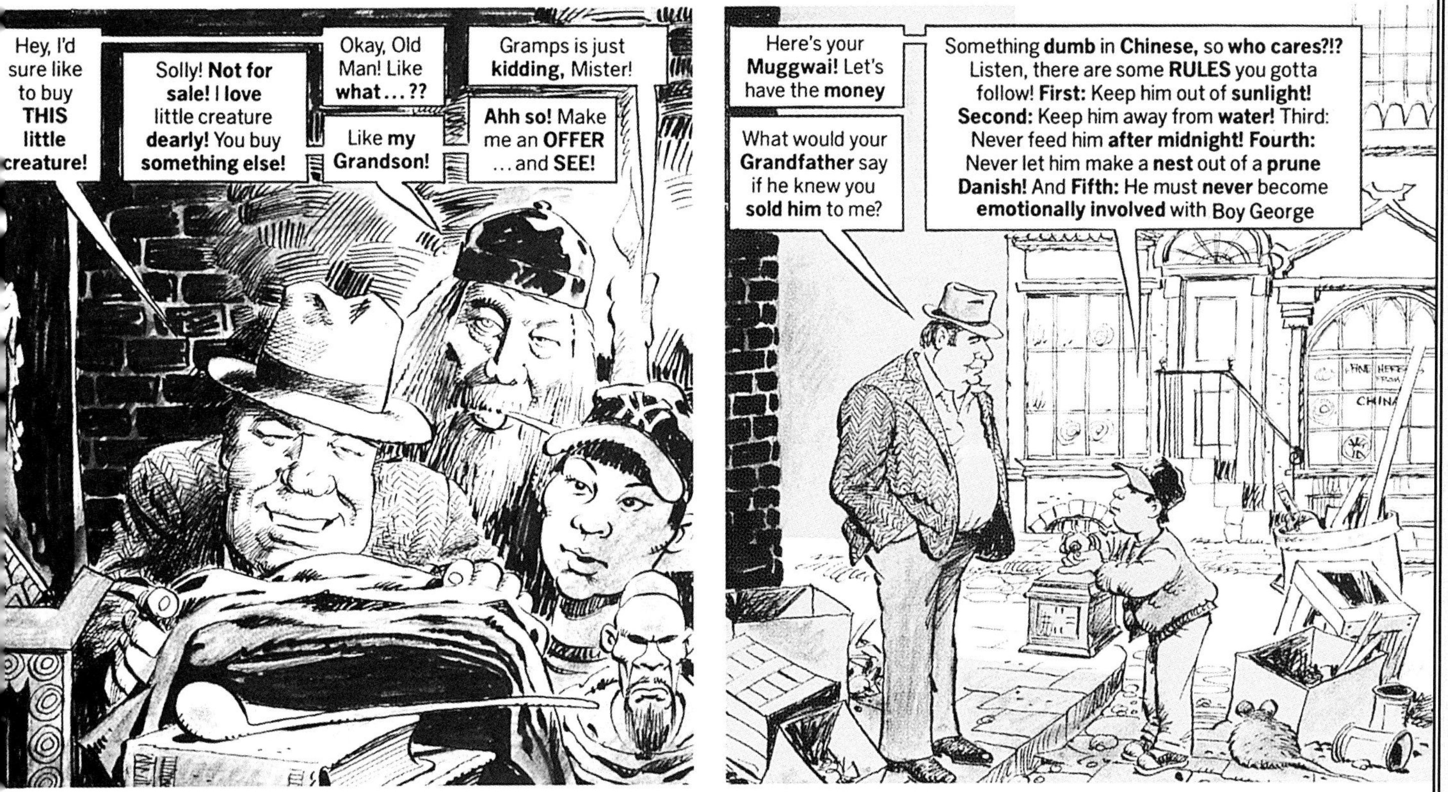

Hey, I'd sure like to buy THIS little creature!
Solly! Not for sale! I love little creature dearly! You buy something else!
Okay, Old Man! Like what...??
Like my Grandson!
Gramps is just kidding, Mister!
Ahh so! Make me an OFFER ...and SEE!
Here's your Muggwai! Let's have the money
What would your Grandfather say if he knew you sold him to me?
Something dumb in Chinese, so who cares?!? Listen, there are some RULES you gotta follow! First: Keep him out of sunlight! Second: Keep him away from water! Third: Never feed him after midnight! Fourth: Never let him make a nest out of a prune Danish! And Fifth: He must never become emotionally involved with Boy George

ARTIST: MORT DRUCKER WRITER: STAN HART

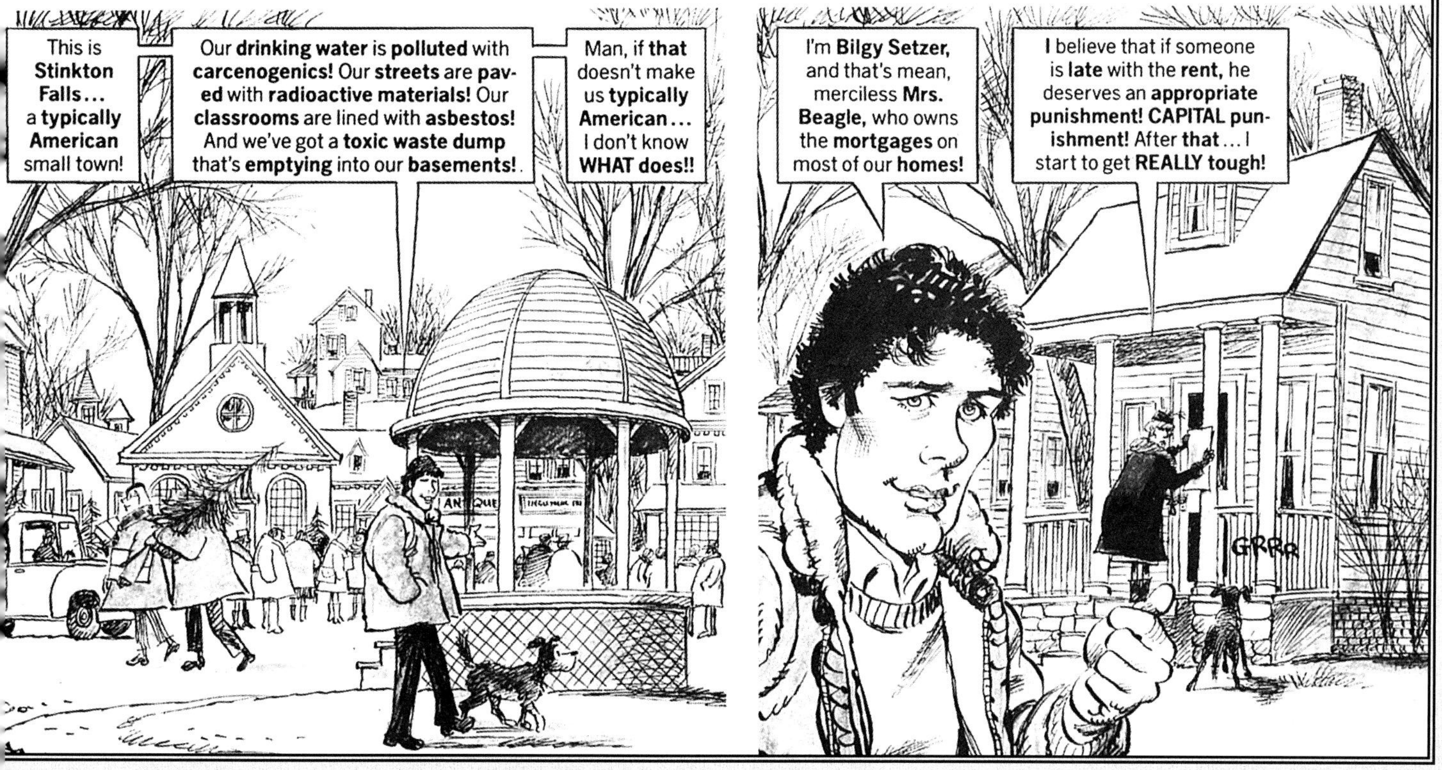

This is Stinkton Falls... a typically American small town!
Our drinking water is polluted with carcenogenics! Our streets are paved with radioactive materials! Our classrooms are lined with asbestos! And we've got a toxic waste dump that's emptying into our basements!
Man, if that doesn't make us typically American... I don't know WHAT does!!
I'm Bilgy Setzer, and that's mean, merciless Mrs. Beagle, who owns the mortgages on most of our homes!
I believe that if someone is late with the rent, he deserves an appropriate punishment! CAPITAL punishment! After that... I start to get REALLY tough!
GRRR

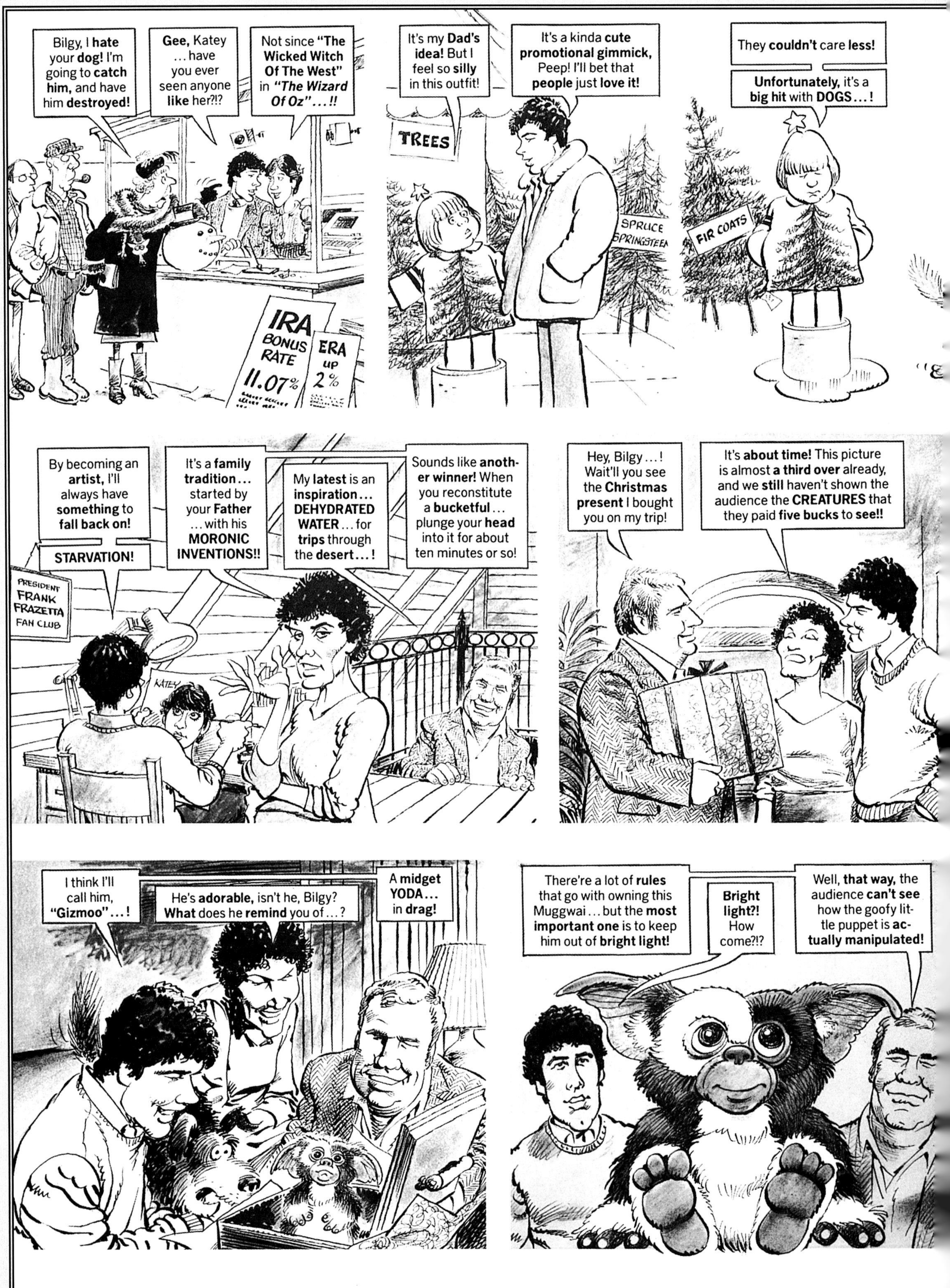
Bilgy, I **hate** your **dog!** I'm going to **catch him,** and have him **destroyed!**
Gee, Katey ... have you ever seen anyone **like** her?!?
Not since **"The Wicked Witch Of The West"** in ***"The Wizard Of Oz"...!!***
IRA BONUS RATE 11.07%
ERA up 2%
It's my **Dad's idea!** But I feel so **silly** in this outfit!
It's a kinda **cute promotional gimmick,** Peep! I'll bet that **people** just **love it!**
TREES
SPRUCE SPRINGSTEEN
They **couldn't** care **less!**
Unfortunately, it's a **big hit** with **DOGS...!**
FIR COATS
By becoming an **artist,** I'll always have **something** to **fall back on!**
STARVATION!
PRESIDENT FRANK FRAZETTA FAN CLUB
It's a **family tradition...** started by your **Father** ... with his **MORONIC INVENTIONS!!**
My **latest** is an **inspiration... DEHYDRATED WATER**... for **trips** through the **desert...!**
Sounds like **another winner!** When you reconstitute a **bucketful...** plunge your **head** into it for about ten minutes or so!
KATEY
Hey, Bilgy...! Wait'll you see the **Christmas present** I bought you on my trip!
It's **about time!** This picture is almost **a third over** already, and we **still** haven't shown the audience the **CREATURES** that they paid **five bucks** to **see!!**
I think I'll call him, **"Gizmoo"...!**
He's **adorable,** isn't he, Bilgy? **What** does he **remind** you of...?
A **midget YODA...** in **drag!**
There're a lot of **rules** that go with owning this Muggwai... but the **most important one** is to keep him out of **bright light!**
Bright light?! How come?!?
Well, **that way,** the audience **can't see** how the goofy little puppet is **actually manipulated!**

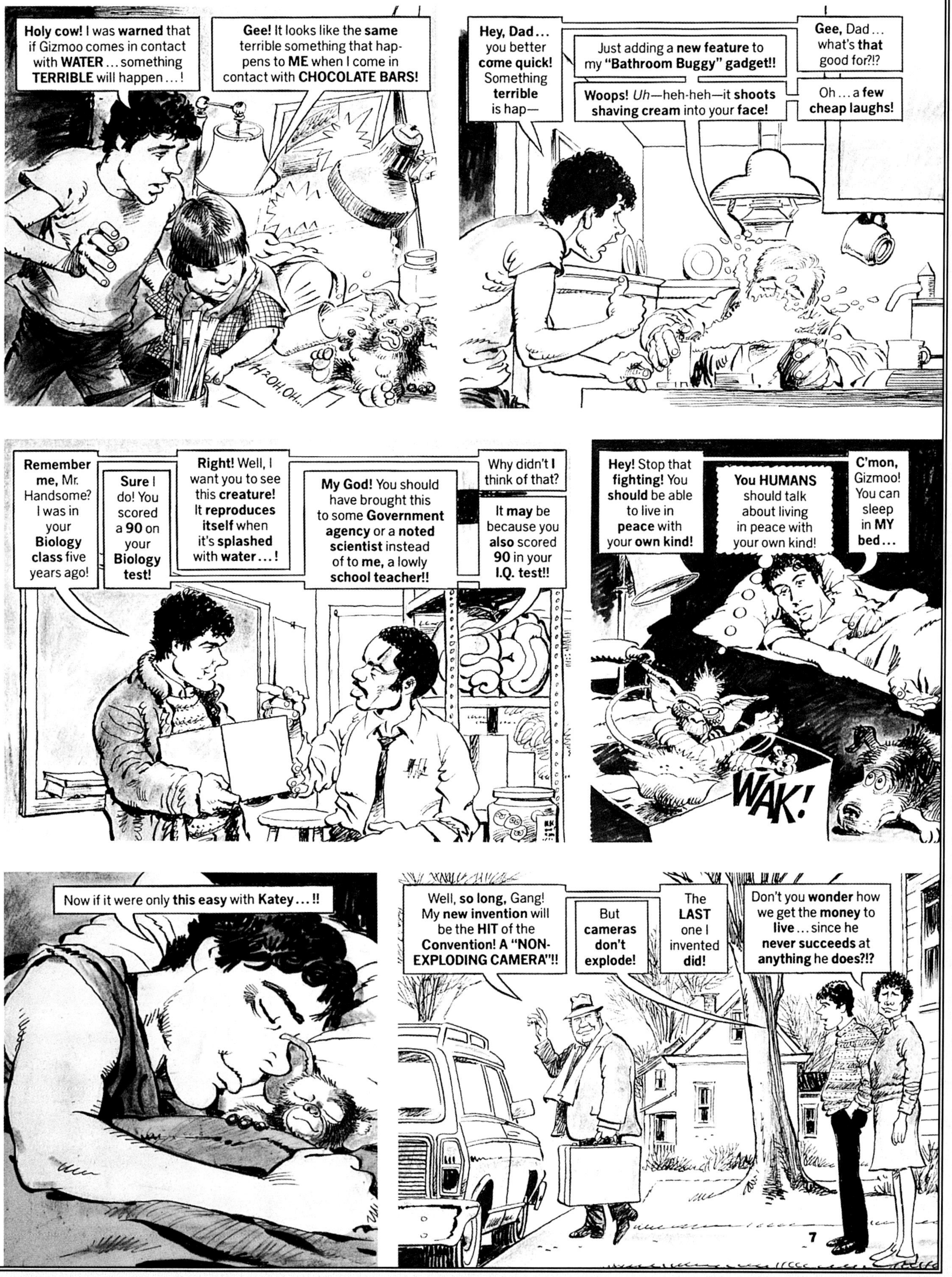
Holy cow! I was warned that if Gizmoo comes in contact with WATER . . . something TERRIBLE will happen . . . !
Gee! It looks like the same terrible something that happens to ME when I come in contact with CHOCOLATE BARS!
Hey, Dad . . . you better come quick! Something terrible is hap—
Just adding a new feature to my "Bathroom Buggy" gadget!!
Woops! Uh—heh-heh—it shoots shaving cream into your face!
Gee, Dad . . . what's that good for?!?
Oh . . . a few cheap laughs!
Remember me, Mr. Handsome? I was in your Biology class five years ago!
Sure I do! You scored a 90 on your Biology test!
Right! Well, I want you to see this creature! It reproduces itself when it's splashed with water . . . !
My God! You should have brought this to some Government agency or a noted scientist instead of to me, a lowly school teacher!!
Why didn't I think of that?
It may be because you also scored 90 in your I.Q. test!!
Hey! Stop that fighting! You should be able to live in peace with your own kind!
You HUMANS should talk about living in peace with your own kind!
C'mon, Gizmoo! You can sleep in MY bed . . .
WAK!
Now if it were only this easy with Katey . . . !!
Well, so long, Gang! My new invention will be the HIT of the Convention! A "NON-EXPLODING CAMERA"!!
But cameras don't explode!
The LAST one I invented did!
Don't you wonder how we get the money to live . . . since he never succeeds at anything he does?!?
7

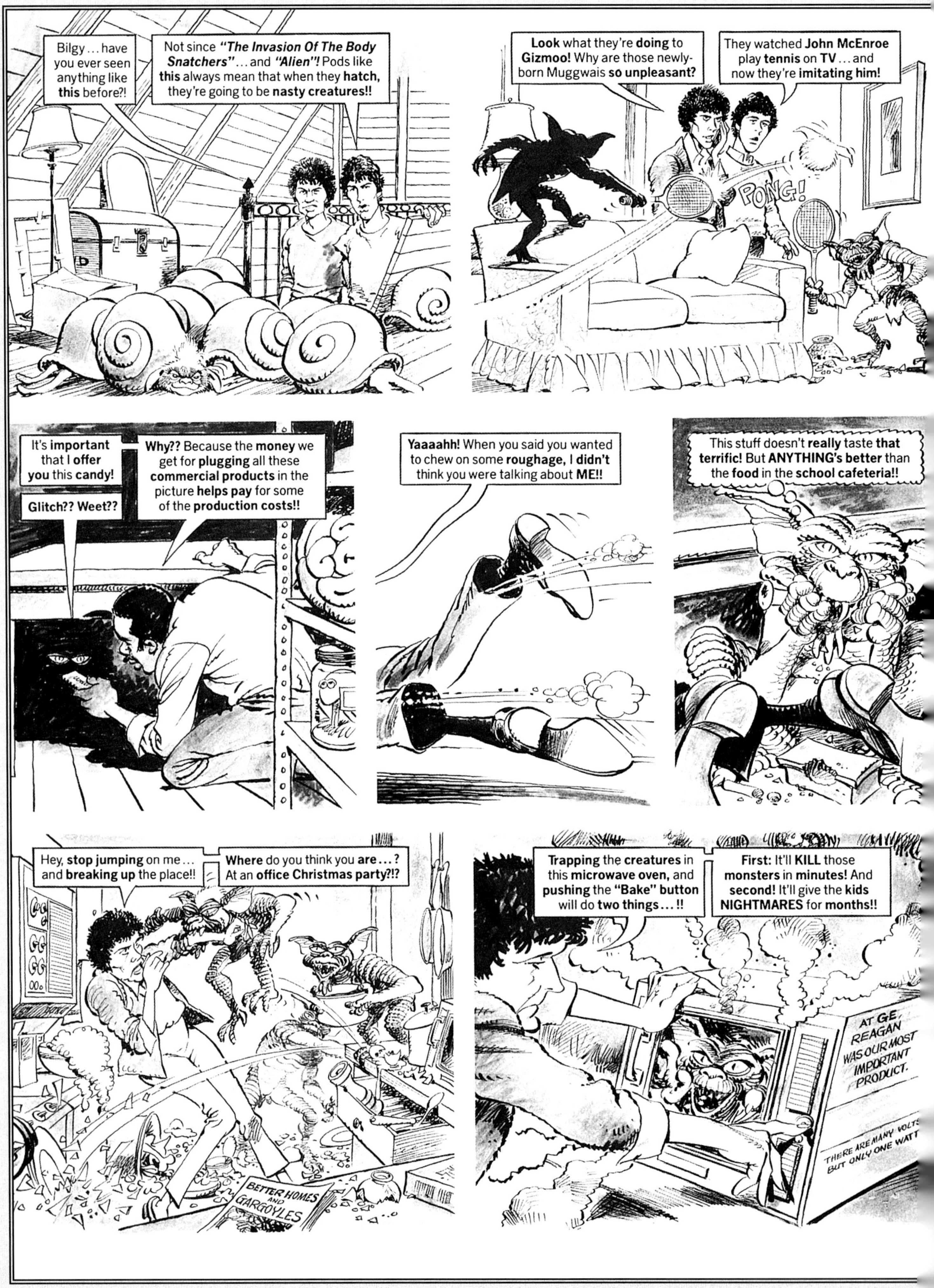
Bilgy... have you ever seen anything like this before?!
Not since "The Invasion Of The Body Snatchers"... and "Alien"! Pods like this always mean that when they hatch, they're going to be nasty creatures!!
Look what they're doing to Gizmoo! Why are those newly-born Muggwais so unpleasant?
They watched John McEnroe play tennis on TV... and now they're imitating him!
PONG!
It's important that I offer you this candy!
Glitch?? Weet??
Why?? Because the money we get for plugging all these commercial products in the picture helps pay for some of the production costs!!
Yaaaahh! When you said you wanted to chew on some roughage, I didn't think you were talking about ME!!
This stuff doesn't really taste that terrific! But ANYTHING's better than the food in the school cafeteria!!
Hey, stop jumping on me... and breaking up the place!!
Where do you think you are...? At an office Christmas party?!?
BETTER HOMES AND GARGOYLES
Trapping the creatures in this microwave oven, and pushing the "Bake" button will do two things...!!
First: It'll KILL those monsters in minutes! And second! It'll give the kids NIGHTMARES for months!!
AT G.E. REAGAN WAS OUR MOST IMPORTANT PRODUCT.
THERE ARE MANY VOLTS BUT ONLY ONE WATT

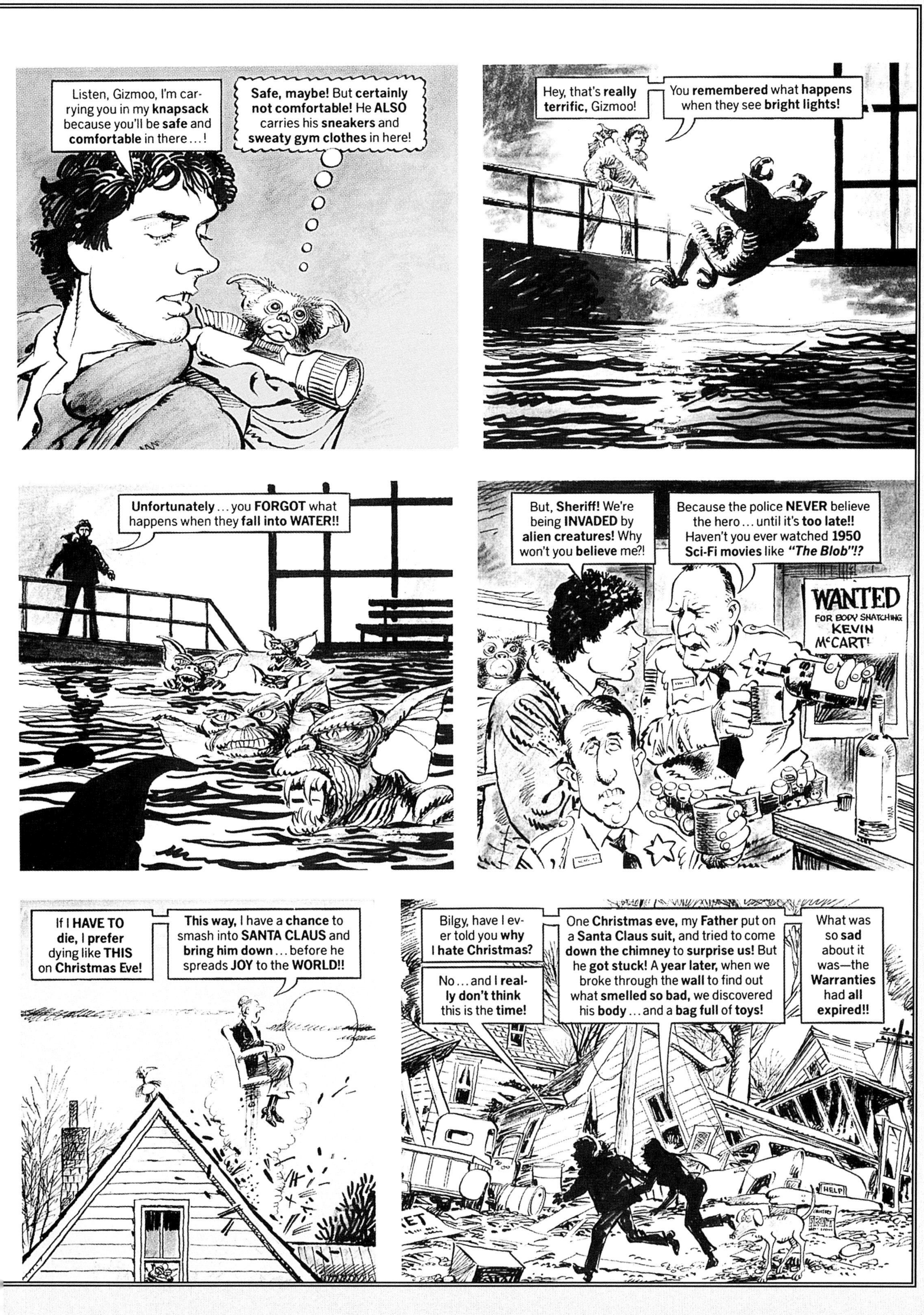
Listen, Gizmoo, I'm carrying you in my **knapsack** because you'll be **safe** and **comfortable** in there…!
Safe, maybe! But **certainly not comfortable!** He **ALSO** carries his **sneakers** and **sweaty gym clothes** in here!
Hey, that's **really terrific,** Gizmoo!
You **remembered** what **happens** when they see **bright lights!**
Unfortunately… you **FORGOT** what happens when they **fall into WATER!!**
But, **Sheriff!** We're being **INVADED** by **alien creatures!** Why won't you **believe** me?!
Because the police **NEVER** believe the hero… until it's **too late!!** Haven't you ever watched **1950 Sci-Fi movies** like ***"The Blob"!?***
WANTED
FOR BODY SNATCHING
KEVIN
McCART!
If I **HAVE TO die, I prefer** dying like **THIS** on **Christmas Eve!**
This way, I have a **chance** to smash into **SANTA CLAUS** and **bring him down**… before he spreads **JOY** to the **WORLD!!**
Bilgy, have I ever told you **why** I **hate Christmas?**
No… and I **really don't think** this is the **time!**
One **Christmas eve,** my **Father** put on a **Santa Claus suit,** and tried to come **down the chimney to surprise us!** But he **got stuck!** A **year later,** when we broke through the **wall** to find out what **smelled so bad,** we discovered his **body**… and a **bag full of toys!**
What was so **sad** about it was—the **Warranties** had **all expired!!**
HELP

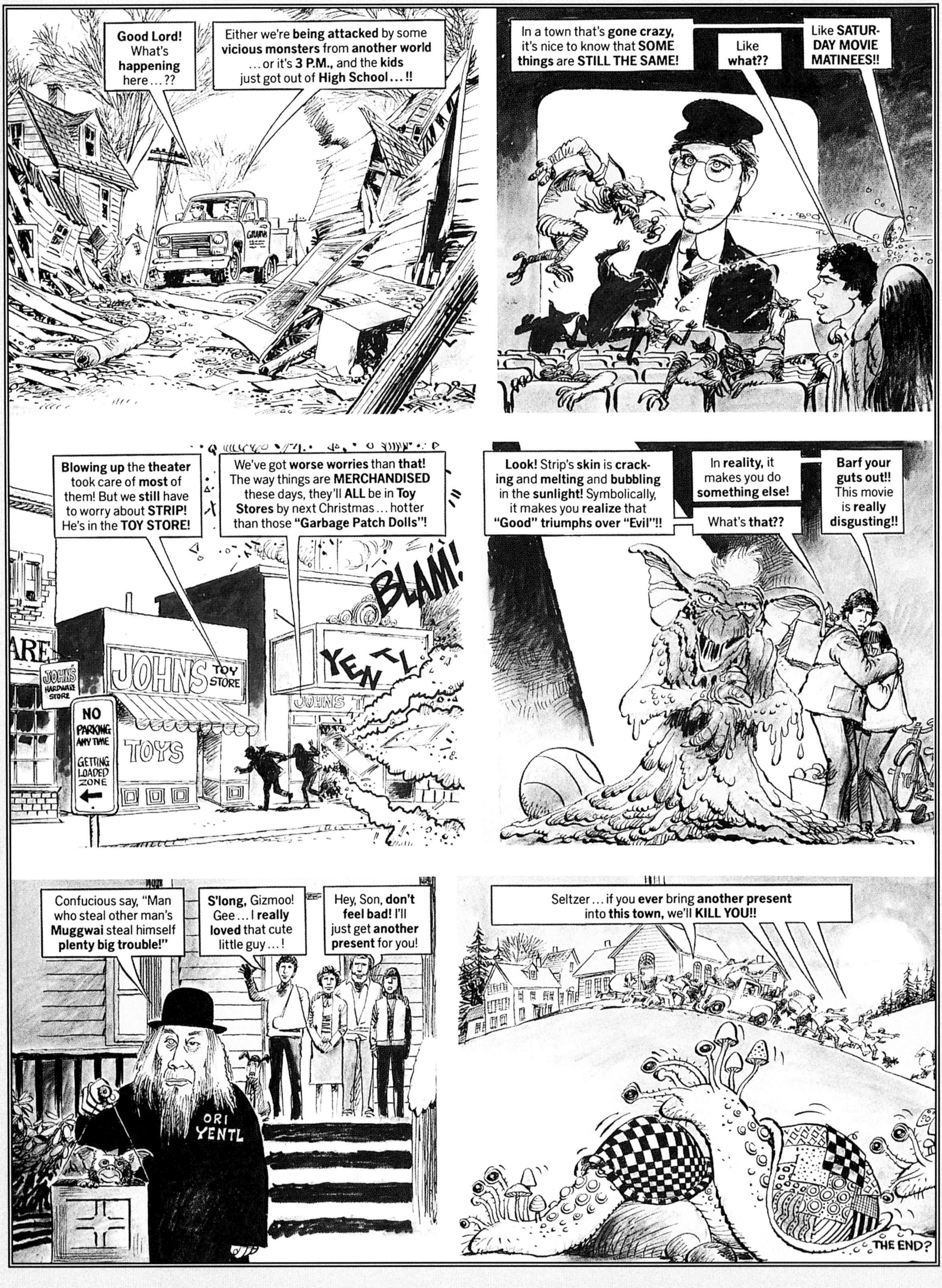
Good Lord! What's happening here...??
Either we're being attacked by some vicious monsters from another world ...or it's 3 P.M., and the kids just got out of High School...!!
In a town that's gone crazy, it's nice to know that SOME things are STILL THE SAME!
Like what??
Like SATURDAY MOVIE MATINEES!!
Blowing up the theater took care of most of them! But we still have to worry about STRIP! He's in the TOY STORE!
We've got worse worries than that! The way things are MERCHANDISED these days, they'll ALL be in Toy Stores by next Christmas... hotter than those "Garbage Patch Dolls"!
BLAM!
YENTL
JOHNS TOY STORE
TOYS
JOHN'S HARDWARE STORE
NO PARKING ANY TIME GETTING LOADED ZONE
Look! Strip's skin is cracking and melting and bubbling in the sunlight! Symbolically, it makes you realize that "Good" triumphs over "Evil"!!
In reality, it makes you do something else!
What's that??
Barf your guts out!! This movie is really disgusting!!
Confucious say, "Man who steal other man's Muggwai steal himself plenty big trouble!"
S'long, Gizmoo! Gee...I really loved that cute little guy...!
Hey, Son, don't feel bad! I'll just get another present for you!
ORI YENTL
Seltzer... if you ever bring another present into this town, we'll KILL YOU!!
THE END?

As a lifelong *MAD* devotee from the time it was a four-color comic, I can tell you that there are few thrills in life quite like seeing your own movie parodied in the pages of *MAD*! So you can imagine my shock and glee when I glommed onto the cover of the September 1984 "*Grimlins*" issue with Alfred E. Neuman as Gizmo, surrounded by horrified Gremlins holding their noses behind him. And even better, what was inside was almost too good to be true: several hilarious pages of clever spoofery by Stan Hart, illustrated with the usual brilliant Mort Drucker comic art!

What an honor.

Let's be clear—Mort Drucker is simply right up there with Hirschfeld as the master American caricaturist.

His pure, unmistakable graphic style has captured an astonishing array of 20th century celebrities and public figures. Even if you didn't know a performer's name you could always place the face. His movie-like staging and composition were unmatched, and the result was artwork that could be revisited time and time again and still yield something new. That particular facet of *MAD* influenced many nascent filmmakers, including myself.

I never actually met the absurdly prolific Mr. Drucker, but I feel I know him through his years of work.

Now there's a legacy few of us can even aspire to!

—Joe Dante
Director, *Gremlins*

GENERATION PAP DEPT.

Throughout TV History, one of the most popular words in series' titles has bee
"Family." We've laughed, cried and cheered at shows like "All In The Family" an
"Family Affair" and "Family Tree" and just plain "Family." Now, let's throw u
over this latest one... as we get a little seasick, bobbing and weaving throug

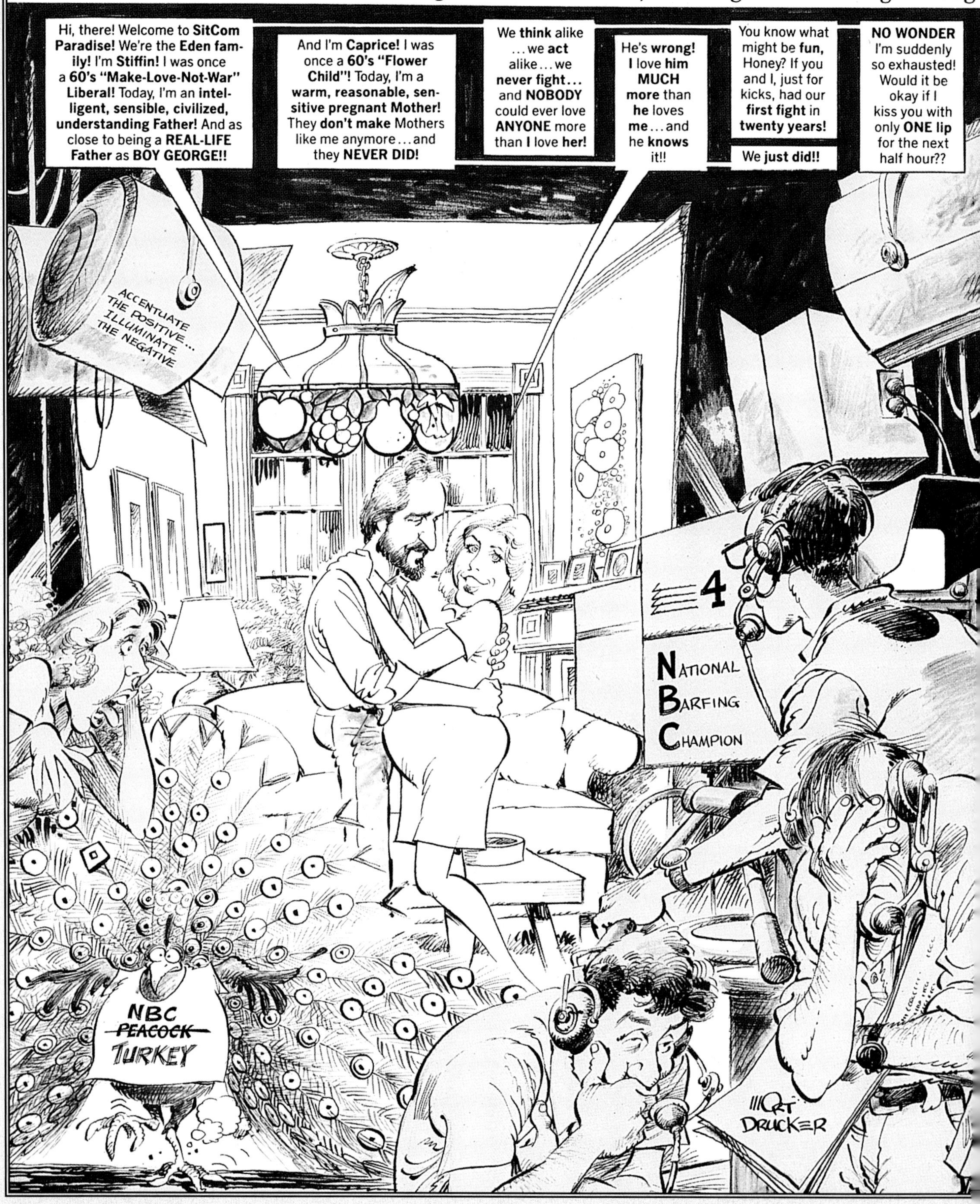
Hi, there! Welcome to SitCom Paradise! We're the Eden family! I'm Stiffin! I was once a 60's "Make-Love-Not-War" Liberal! Today, I'm an intelligent, sensible, civilized, understanding Father! And as close to being a REAL-LIFE Father as BOY GEORGE!!
And I'm Caprice! I was once a 60's "Flower Child"! Today, I'm a warm, reasonable, sensitive pregnant Mother! They don't make Mothers like me anymore... and they NEVER DID!
We think alike ... we act alike ... we never fight ... and NOBODY could ever love ANYONE more than I love her!
He's wrong! I love him MUCH more than he loves me... and he knows it!!
You know what might be fun, Honey? If you and I, just for kicks, had our first fight in twenty years!
We just did!!
NO WONDER I'm suddenly so exhausted! Would it be okay if I kiss you with only ONE lip for the next half hour??
ACCENTUATE THE POSITIVE... ILLUMINATE THE NEGATIVE
4
NATIONAL BARFING CHAMPION
NBC PEACOCK TURKEY
MORT DRUCKER

Family Tides

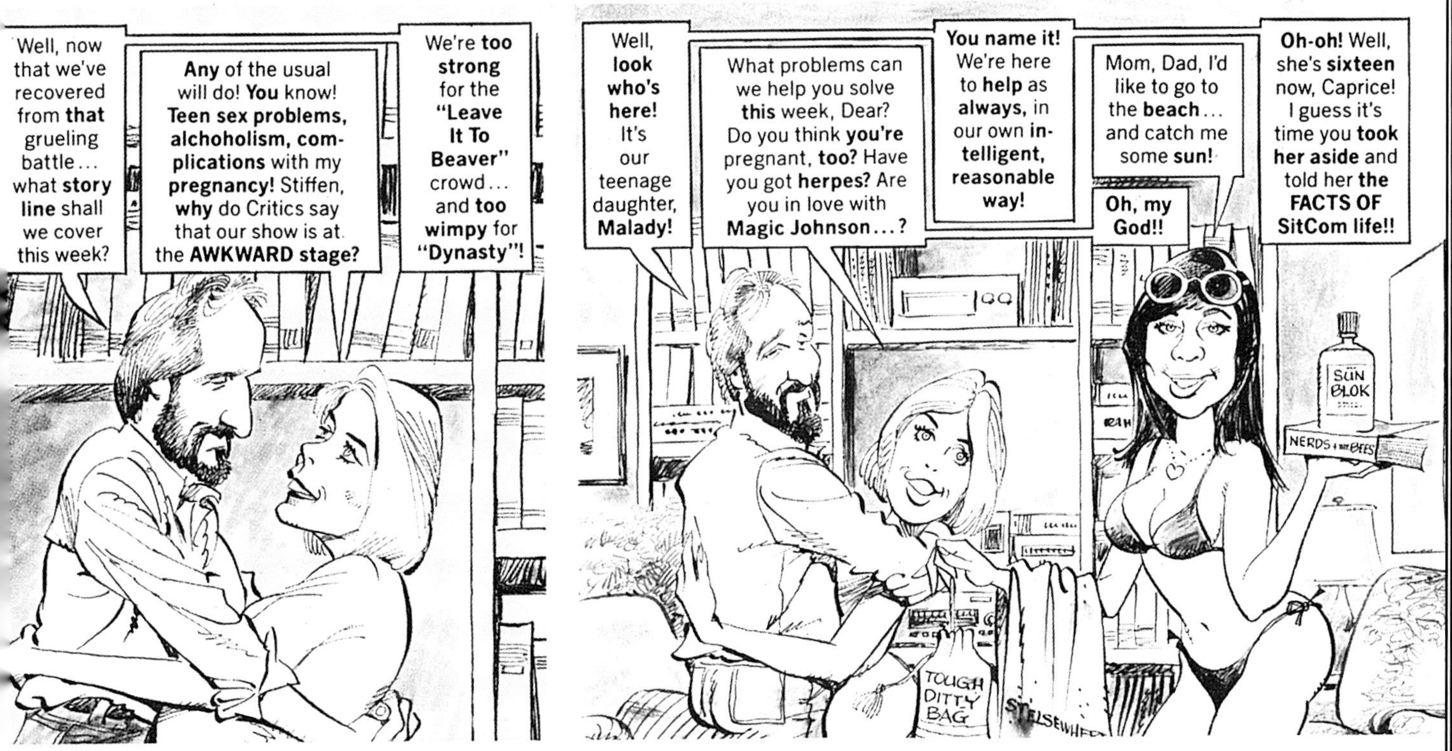
Well, now that we've recovered from that grueling battle... what story line shall we cover this week?
Any of the usual will do! You know! Teen sex problems, alchoholism, complications with my pregnancy! Stiffen, why do Critics say that our show is at the AWKWARD stage?
We're too strong for the "Leave It To Beaver" crowd... and too wimpy for "Dynasty"!
Well, look who's here! It's our teenage daughter, Malady!
What problems can we help you solve this week, Dear? Do you think you're pregnant, too? Have you got herpes? Are you in love with Magic Johnson...?
You name it! We're here to help as always, in our own intelligent, reasonable way!
Mom, Dad, I'd like to go to the beach... and catch me some sun!
Oh, my God!!
Oh-oh! Well, she's sixteen now, Caprice! I guess it's time you took her aside and told her the FACTS OF SitCom life!!
SUN BLOK
TOUGH DITTY BAG

ARTIST: MORT DRUCKER WRITER: LARRY SIEGEL

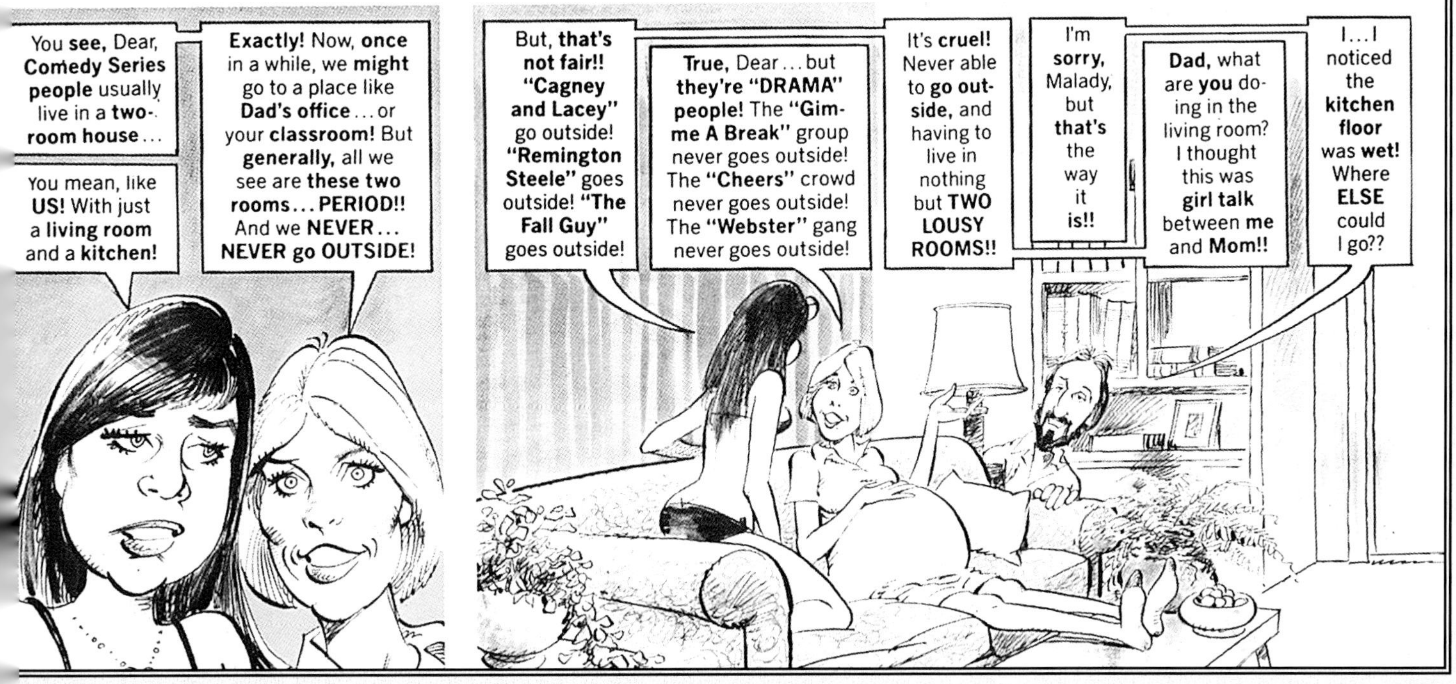
You see, Dear, Comedy Series people usually live in a two-room house...
You mean, like US! With just a living room and a kitchen!
Exactly! Now, once in a while, we might go to a place like Dad's office... or your classroom! But generally, all we see are these two rooms... PERIOD!! And we NEVER... NEVER go OUTSIDE!
But, that's not fair!! "Cagney and Lacey" go outside! "Remington Steele" goes outside! "The Fall Guy" goes outside!
True, Dear... but they're "DRAMA" people! The "Gimme A Break" group never goes outside! The "Cheers" crowd never goes outside! The "Webster" gang never goes outside!
It's cruel! Never able to go outside, and having to live in nothing but TWO LOUSY ROOMS!!
I'm sorry, Malady, but that's the way it is!!
Dad, what are you doing in the living room? I thought this was girl talk between me and Mom!!
I... I noticed the kitchen floor was wet! Where ELSE could I go??

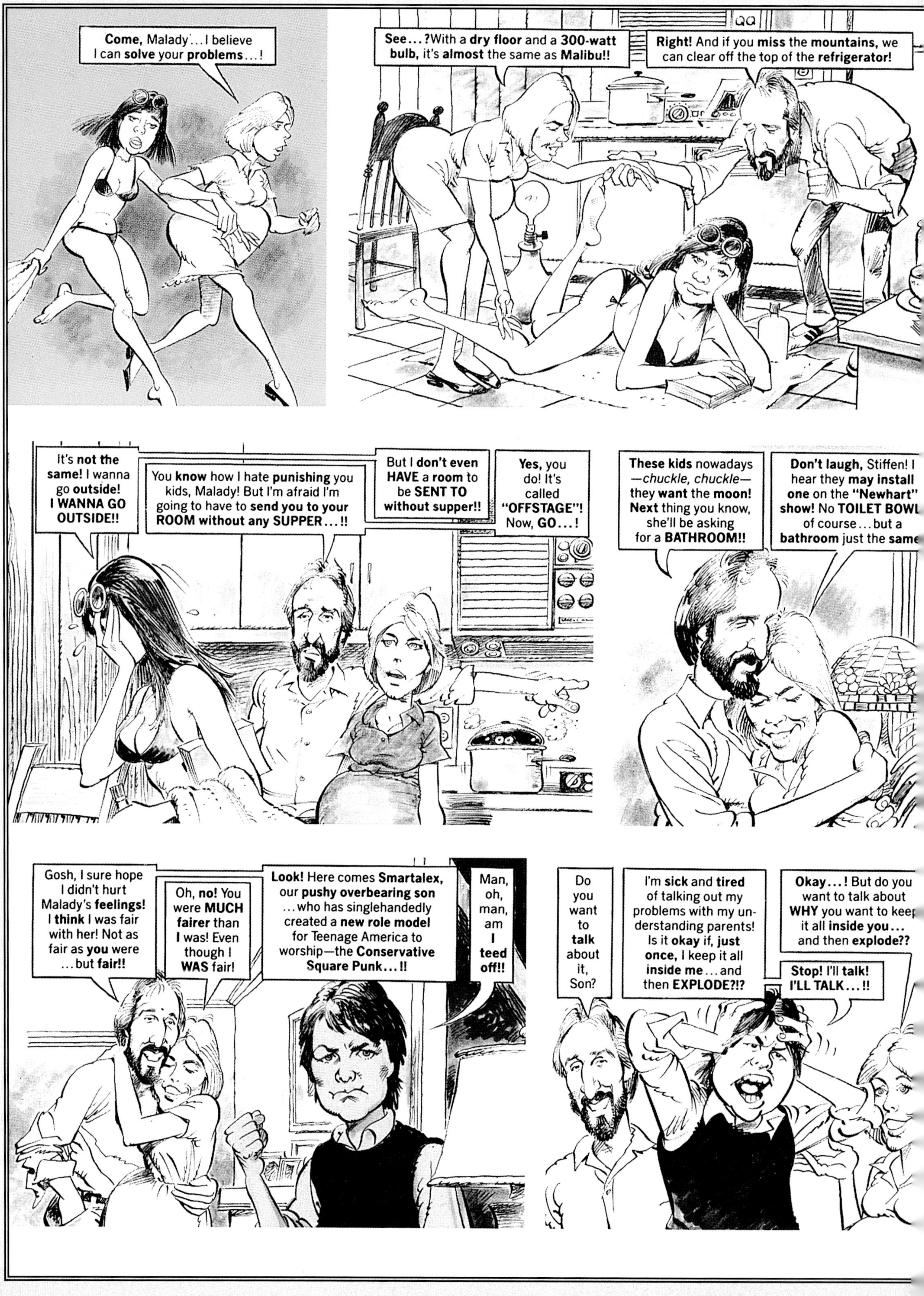
Come, Malady... I believe I can solve your problems...!
See...? With a dry floor and a 300-watt bulb, it's almost the same as Malibu!!
Right! And if you miss the mountains, we can clear off the top of the refrigerator!
It's not the same! I wanna go outside! I WANNA GO OUTSIDE!!
You know how I hate punishing you kids, Malady! But I'm afraid I'm going to have to send you to your ROOM without any SUPPER...!!
But I don't even HAVE a room to be SENT TO without supper!!
Yes, you do! It's called "OFFSTAGE"! Now, GO...!
These kids nowadays —chuckle, chuckle— they want the moon! Next thing you know, she'll be asking for a BATHROOM!!
Don't laugh, Stiffen! I hear they may install one on the "Newhart" show! No TOILET BOWL of course... but a bathroom just the same
Gosh, I sure hope I didn't hurt Malady's feelings! I think I was fair with her! Not as fair as you were ...but fair!!
Oh, no! You were MUCH fairer than I was! Even though I WAS fair!
Look! Here comes Smartalex, our pushy overbearing son ...who has singlehandedly created a new role model for Teenage America to worship—the Conservative Square Punk...!!
Man, oh, man, am I teed off!!
Do you want to talk about it, Son?
I'm sick and tired of talking out my problems with my understanding parents! Is it okay if, just once, I keep it all inside me... and then EXPLODE?!?
Okay...! But do you want to talk about WHY you want to keep it all inside you... and then explode??
Stop! I'll talk! I'LL TALK...!!

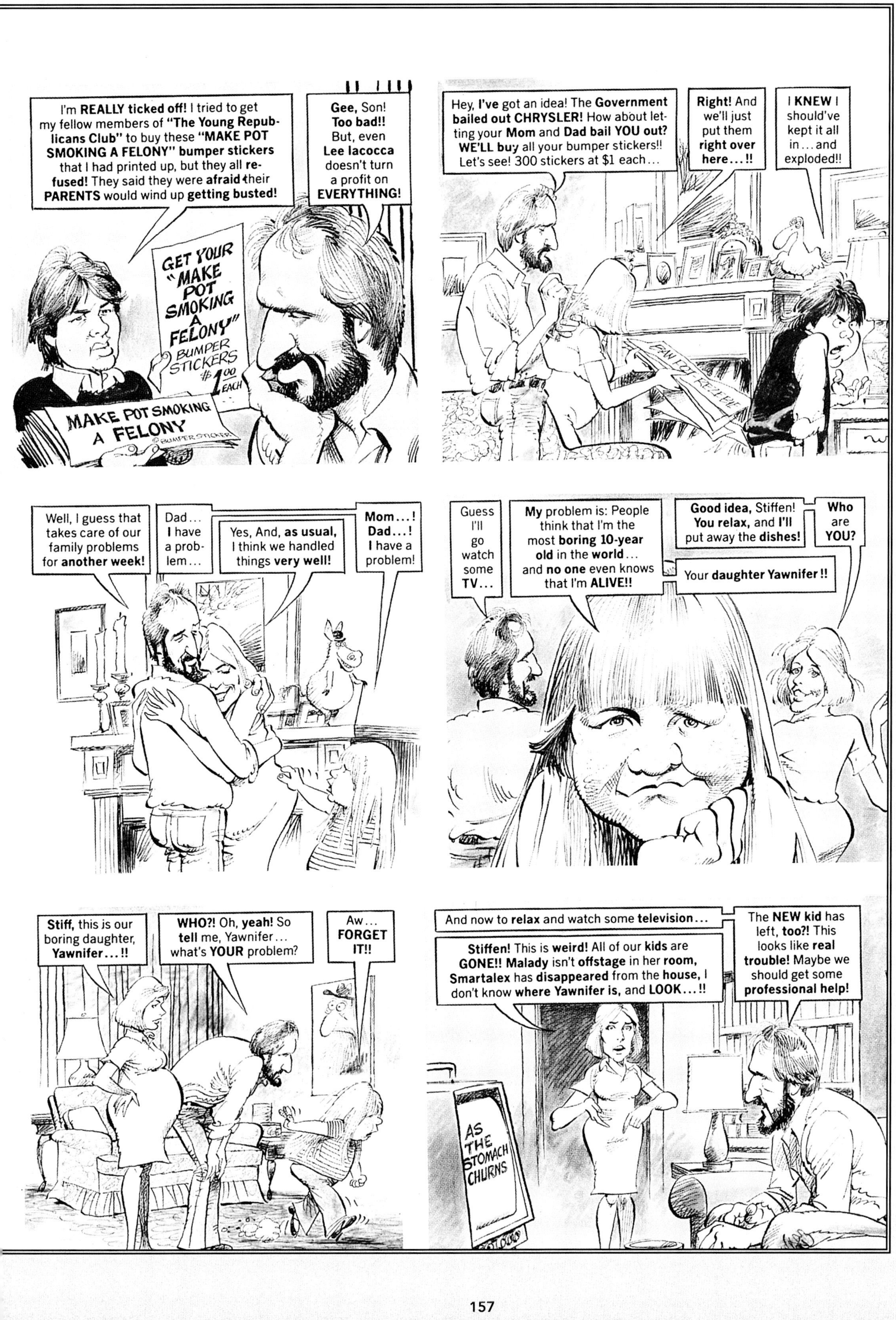
I'm REALLY ticked off! I tried to get my fellow members of "The Young Republicans Club" to buy these "MAKE POT SMOKING A FELONY" bumper stickers that I had printed up, but they all refused! They said they were afraid their PARENTS would wind up getting busted!
Gee, Son! Too bad!! But, even Lee Iacocca doesn't turn a profit on EVERYTHING!
GET YOUR "MAKE POT SMOKING A FELONY" BUMPER STICKERS $1.00 EACH
MAKE POT SMOKING A FELONY
Hey, I've got an idea! The Government bailed out CHRYSLER! How about letting your Mom and Dad bail YOU out? WE'LL buy all your bumper stickers!! Let's see! 300 stickers at $1 each...
Right! And we'll just put them right over here...!!
I KNEW I should've kept it all in... and exploded!!
Well, I guess that takes care of our family problems for another week!
Dad... I have a problem...
Yes, And, as usual, I think we handled things very well!
Mom...! Dad...! I have a problem!
Guess I'll go watch some TV...
My problem is: People think that I'm the most boring 10-year old in the world... and no one even knows that I'm ALIVE!!
Good idea, Stiffen! You relax, and I'll put away the dishes!
Who are YOU?
Your daughter Yawnifer!!
Stiff, this is our boring daughter, Yawnifer...!!
WHO?! Oh, yeah! So tell me, Yawnifer... what's YOUR problem?
Aw... FORGET IT!!
And now to relax and watch some television...
Stiffen! This is weird! All of our kids are GONE!! Malady isn't offstage in her room, Smartalex has disappeared from the house, I don't know where Yawnifer is, and LOOK...!!
The NEW kid has left, too?! This looks like real trouble! Maybe we should get some professional help!
AS THE STOMACH CHURNS

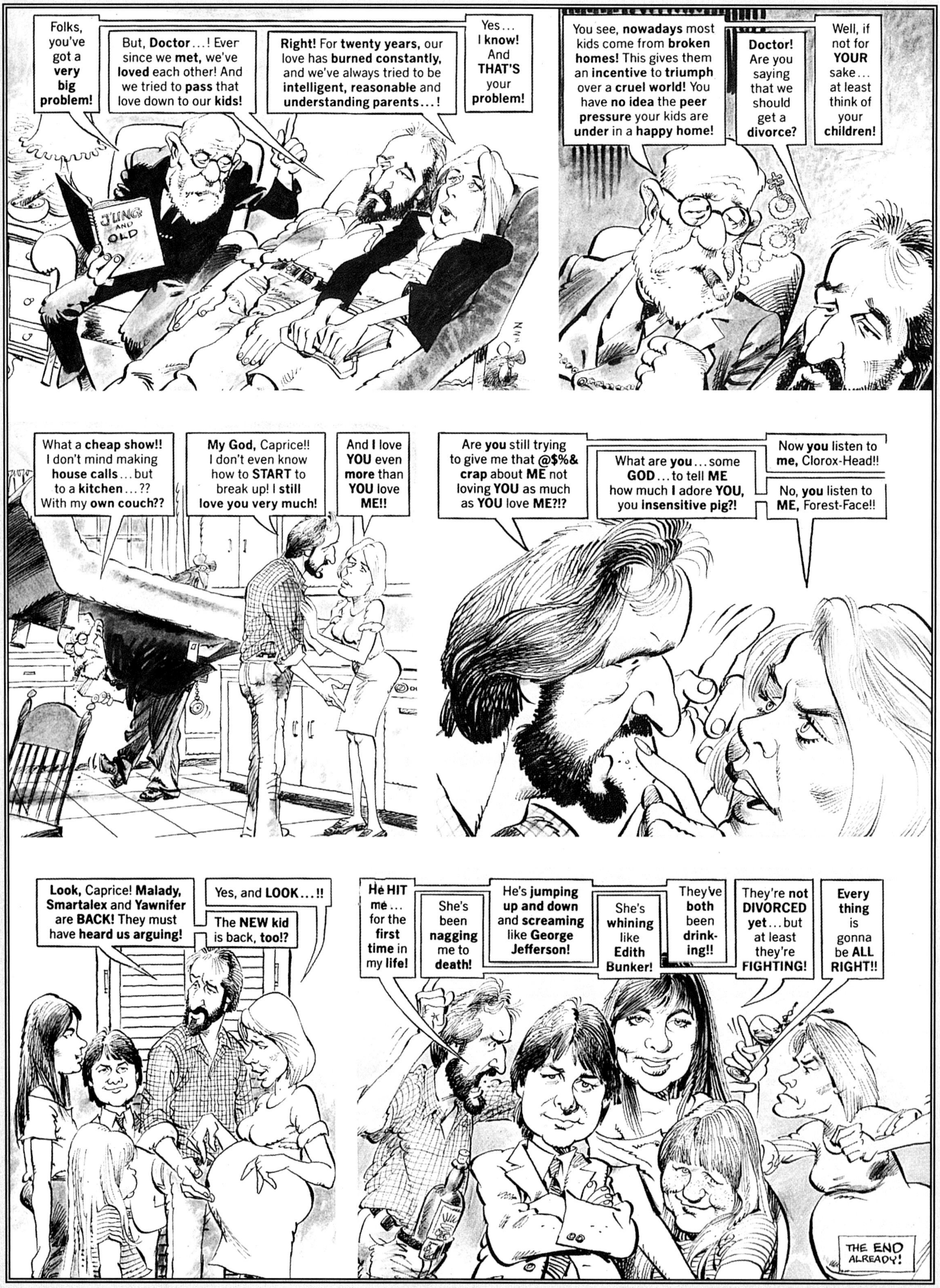
Folks, you've got a very big problem!
But, Doctor...! Ever since we met, we've loved each other! And we tried to pass that love down to our kids!
Right! For twenty years, our love has burned constantly, and we've always tried to be intelligent, reasonable and understanding parents...!
Yes... I know! And THAT'S your problem!
JUNG AND OLD
You see, nowadays most kids come from broken homes! This gives them an incentive to triumph over a cruel world! You have no idea the peer pressure your kids are under in a happy home!
Doctor! Are you saying that we should get a divorce?
Well, if not for YOUR sake... at least think of your children!
What a cheap show!! I don't mind making house calls... but to a kitchen...?? With my own couch??
My God, Caprice!! I don't even know how to START to break up! I still love you very much!
And I love YOU even more than YOU love ME!!
Are you still trying to give me that @$%& crap about ME not loving YOU as much as YOU love ME?!?
What are you... some GOD... to tell ME how much I adore YOU, you insensitive pig?!
Now you listen to me, Clorox-Head!!
No, you listen to ME, Forest-Face!!
Look, Caprice! Malady, Smartalex and Yawnifer are BACK! They must have heard us arguing!
Yes, and LOOK...!!
The NEW kid is back, too!?
He HIT me... for the first time in my life!
She's been nagging me to death!
He's jumping up and down and screaming like George Jefferson!
She's whining like Edith Bunker!
They've both been drink-ing!!
They're not DIVORCED yet... but at least they're FIGHTING!
Every thing is gonna be ALL RIGHT!!
THE END ALREADY!

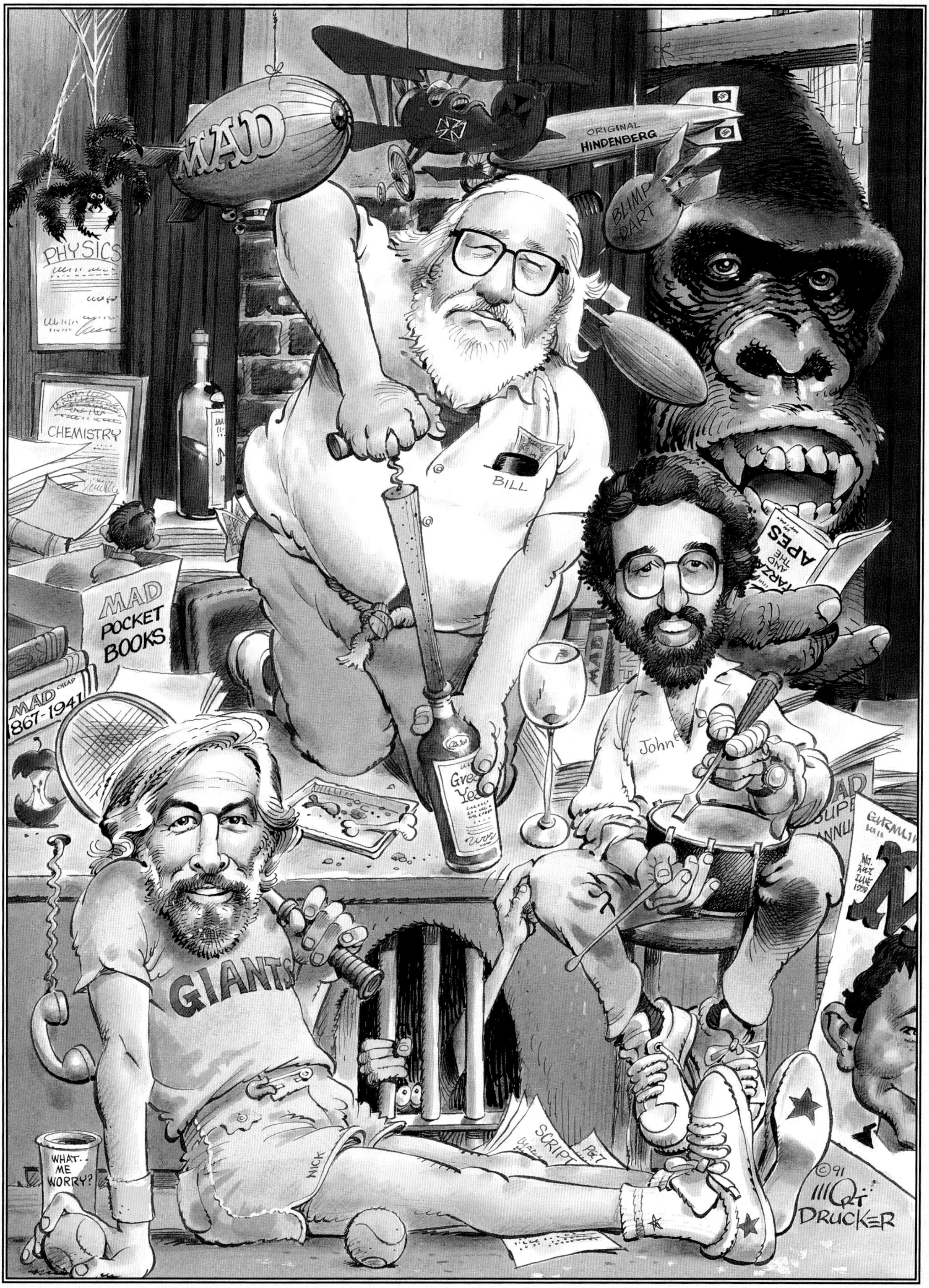
MAD
ORIGINAL HINDENBERG
BLIMP DART
PHYSICS
CHEMISTRY
BILL
MAD POCKET BOOKS
MAD
CHEAP
1867-1941
APES
John
GIANTS
WHAT- ME WORRY?
NICK
SCRIPT
©91
DRUCKER

In 1991, Mort Drucker illustrated an article about *MAD* in the trade journal *Folio's Publishing News* with a portrait of MAD Publisher William M. Gaines (pulling the cork out of a bottle of one of his collection of fine wines) and Co-editors Nick Meglin (in full tennis regalia) and John Ficarra (with his ever-present snare drum). The scene was set in Gaines's office, which indeed was decorated with model airships, as well as a full-size papier-mâché head of King Kong sculpted by Sergio Aragonés.

A ROLLING STALLONE GATHERS EVEN MORE GROSS DEPT.

It may be some comfort to realize that while life is full of surprises, Rocky films are *not!* Each one plagiarizes the one before it and adds a corny twist of its own, like in this case, patriotism! So sit back and relax with something old, little new, something borrowed and something red, white and blue...

ROC

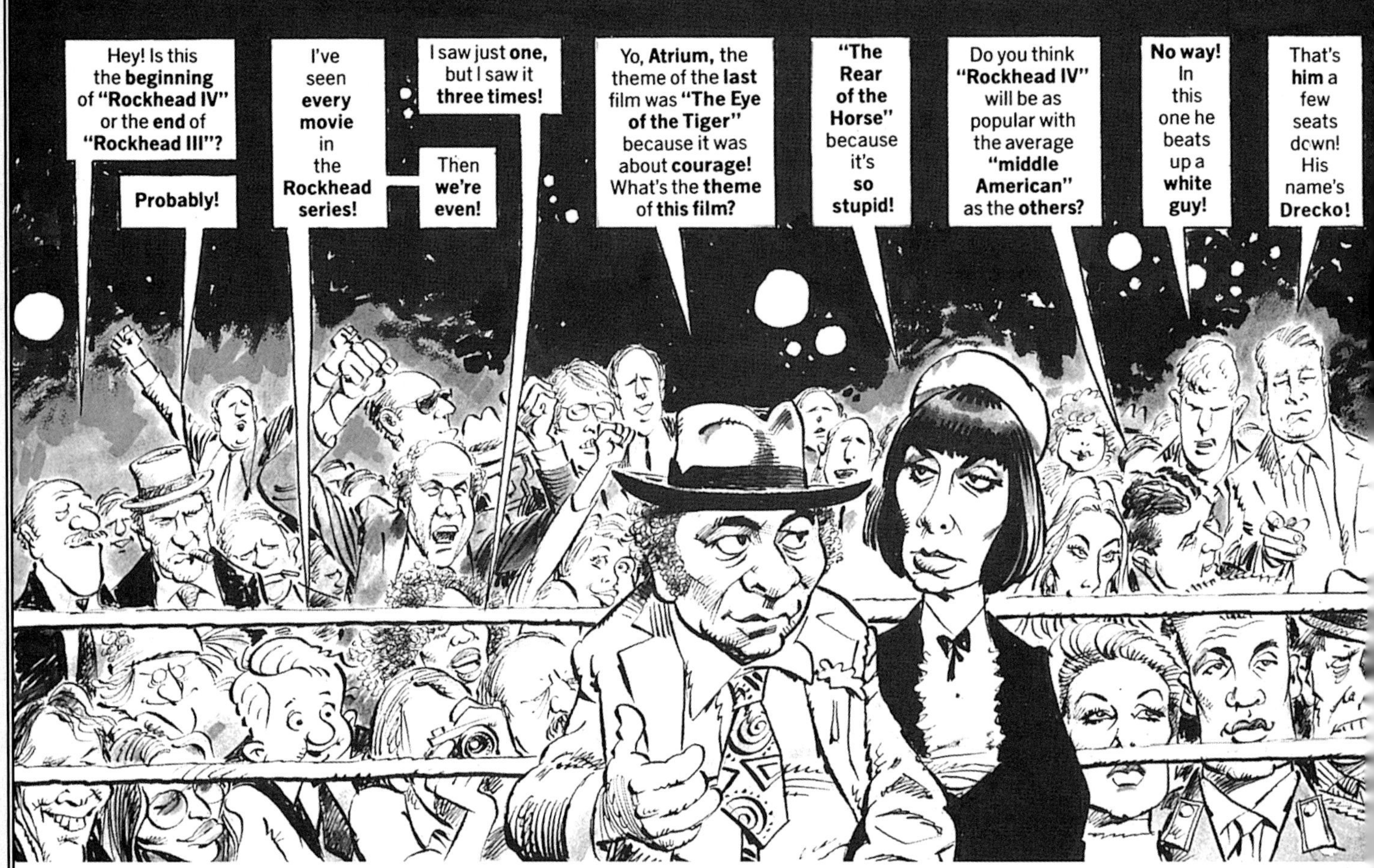
Hey! Is this the **beginning** of **"Rockhead IV"** or the **end** of **"Rockhead III"?**
Probably!
I've seen **every movie** in the **Rockhead series!**
I saw just **one,** but I saw it **three times!**
Then **we're even!**
Yo, **Atrium,** the theme of the **last** film was **"The Eye of the Tiger"** because it was about **courage!** What's the **theme** of **this film?**
"The Rear of the Horse" because it's **so stupid!**
Do you think **"Rockhead IV"** will be as popular with the average **"middle American"** as the **others?**
No way! In this one he beats up a **white guy!**
That's **him** a few seats down! His name's **Drecko!**

ARTIST: MORT DRUCK

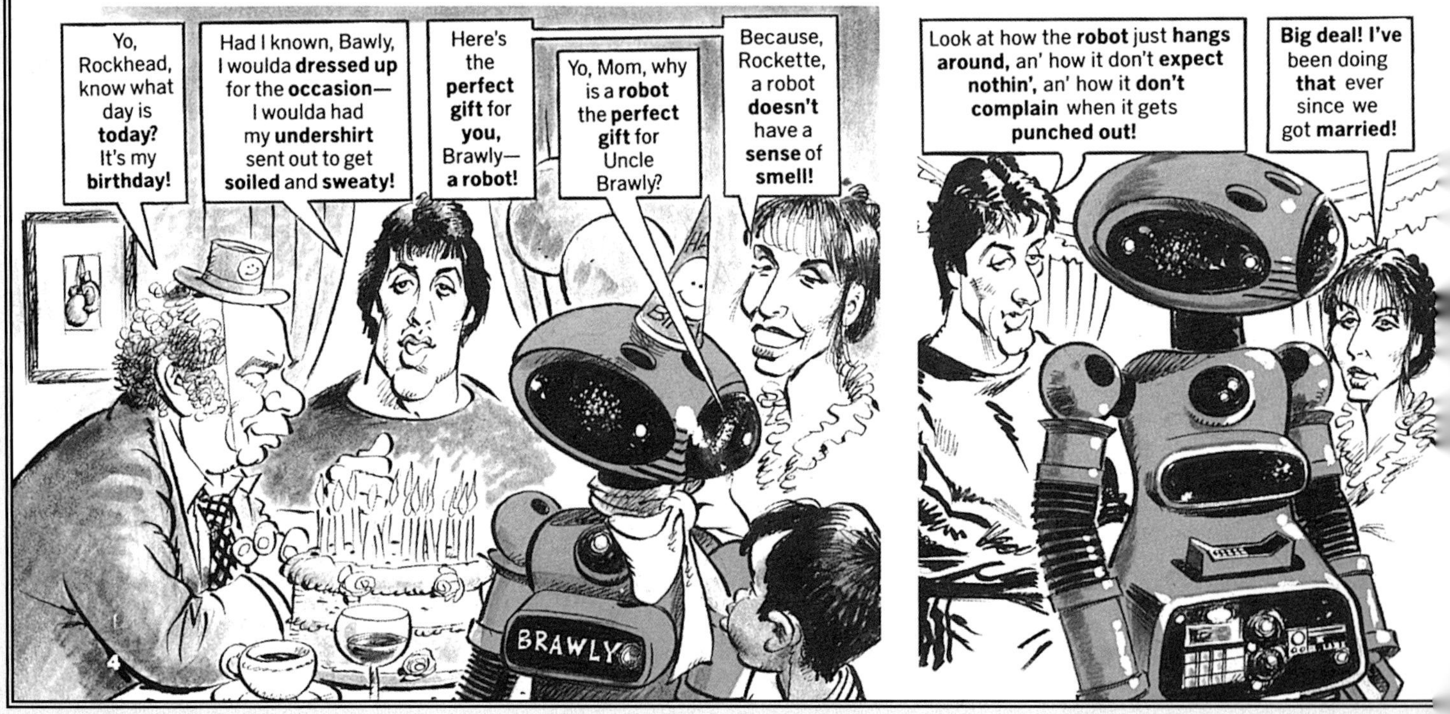
Yo, Rockhead, know what day is **today?** It's my **birthday!**
Had I known, Bawly, I woulda **dressed up** for the **occasion**— I woulda had my **undershirt** sent out to get **soiled** and **sweaty!**
Here's the **perfect gift** for **you,** Brawly— **a robot!**
Yo, Mom, why is a **robot** the **perfect gift** for Uncle Brawly?
Because, Rockette, a robot **doesn't** have a **sense** of **smell!**
BRAWLY
Look at how the **robot** just **hangs around,** an' how it don't **expect nothin',** an' how it **don't complain** when it gets **punched out!**
Big deal! I've been doing **that** ever since we got **married!**

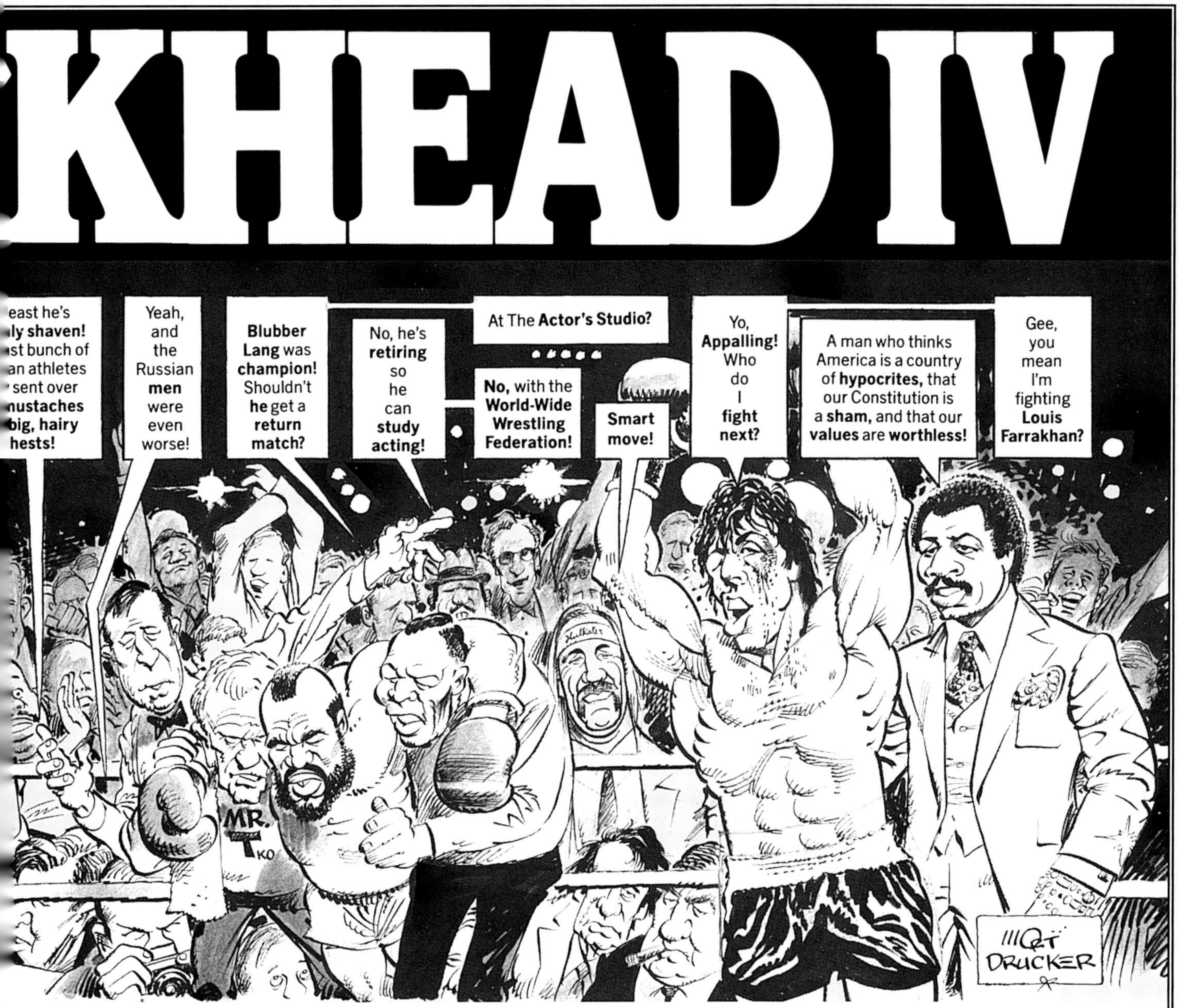
KHEAD IV
east he's ly shaven! st bunch of an athletes sent over nustaches big, hairy hests!
Yeah, and the Russian men were even worse!
Blubber Lang was champion! Shouldn't he get a return match?
No, he's retiring so he can study acting!
At The Actor's Studio?
No, with the World-Wide Wrestling Federation!
Smart move!
Yo, Appalling! Who do I fight next?
A man who thinks America is a country of hypocrites, that our Constitution is a sham, and that our values are worthless!
Gee, you mean I'm fighting Louis Farrakhan?
MR. T KO
MORT DRUCKER

TER: STAN HART

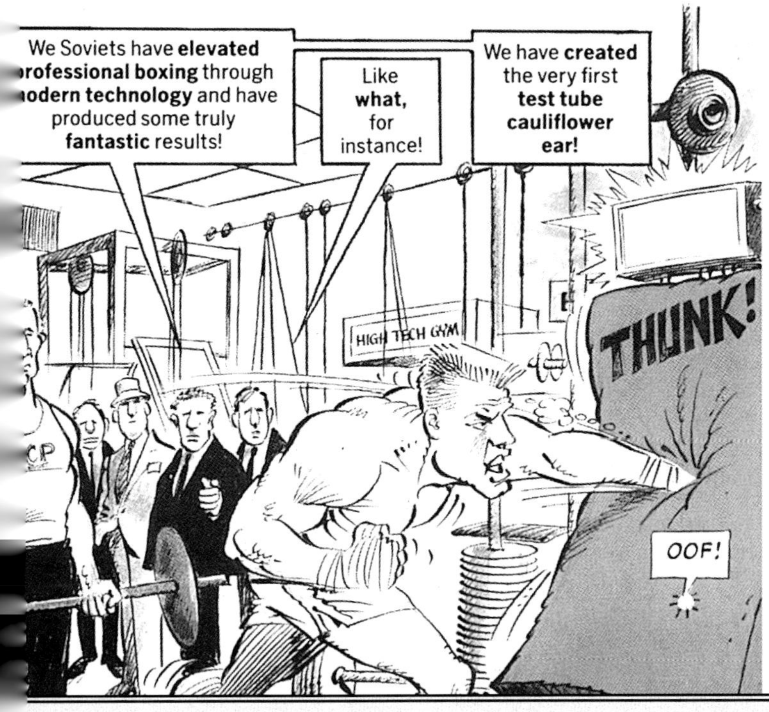
We Soviets have elevated professional boxing through modern technology and have produced some truly fantastic results!
Like what, for instance!
We have created the very first test tube cauliflower ear!
HIGH TECH GYM
THUNK!
OOF!

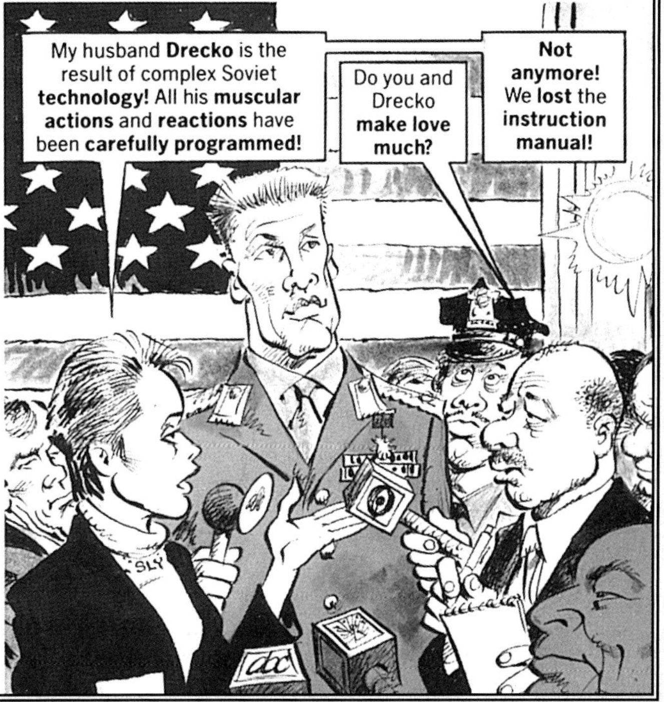
My husband Drecko is the result of complex Soviet technology! All his muscular actions and reactions have been carefully programmed!
Do you and Drecko make love much?
Not anymore! We lost the instruction manual!
SLY

I intend to come out of **retirement** and **fight** that **Russian giant!**

This is **unbelievable!** How many times do you guys go **in** and **out of retirement?**

Ahhh, you **sports writers!**

What **sports writers?** We're **film critics!**

Appalling, **why** are you doing this? What do you **want?**

The lights, the action, the glory! Without those, **what do I have?** Answer me **that,** Scallion—**what do I have?**

Let's see… 5 or 6 million bucks, time for your wife and family, a chance to work for important causes like hunger in Africa and educating ghetto kids properly…

Forget the question!

Is tough darts, **Yankee!** We will **not** fight washed-up bum like **you!**

Why not? Afraid I'll belt that blonde bag of borscht **bonkers?** You commies ain't **Red**—you're **yellow!**

Drecko will **make you pay** for saying that! He will not only **fight** you, he will **destroy** you!

Shooting off my mouth **paid off,** Scallion! I got them to accept my challenge! I'm **dying** to fight Drecko!

Yo, Appalling, **don't give away the plot!**

This fight will show **Soviet system** is **superior** to decadent **American system!**

Sez you! Only in America can a person be free to **do** what they want and **be** anything they want to be with **equal** opportunity for **all!**

I don't think those Russians will **believe** that stuff!

I'm afraid a lot of Americ- ians won't either!

Rockhead—stop the fight! Appalling's **getting killed!** I can't stand to **watch this!**

Hey, Bawly, quick! Gimme that **towel!**

You gonna **throw it in?**

No, I'm gonna put it **over my eyes**—I can't stand to **watch** this, either!

If you can **hear me,** take **two aspirins** and call me in the morning!

Yo, Doc, I think he's **dead!**

In that case, **forget** the aspirins!

I feel **awful! Last** movie, Rockhead's **trainer** died! Now Rockhead's **best pal** died!

Gee, Bawly, I didn't know you were capable of such **sentiments!**

What **sentiment!** I'm just worried about which on- of **us** gets their **ticket punched** in "Rockhead V…

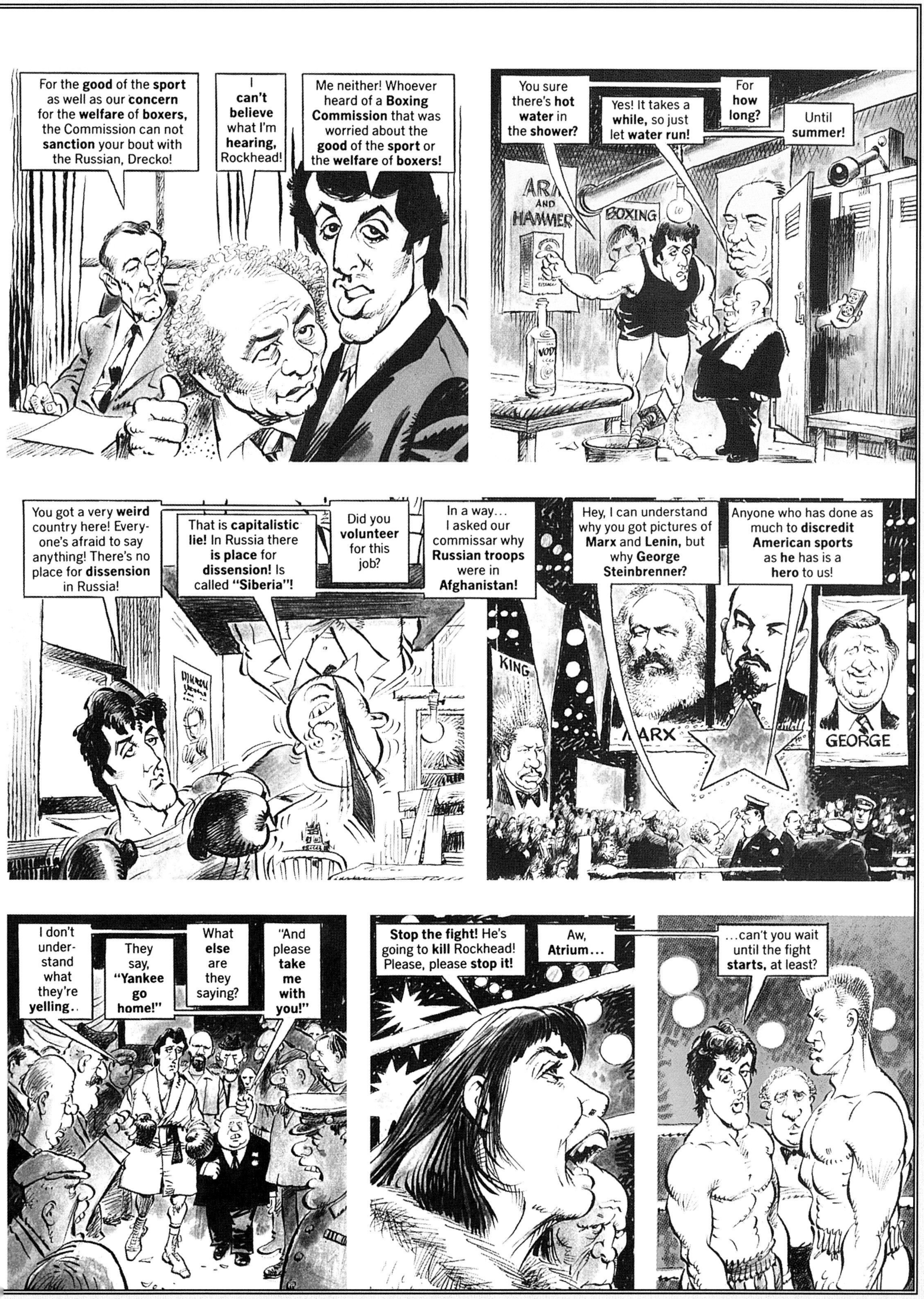
For the good of the sport as well as our concern for the welfare of boxers, the Commission can not sanction your bout with the Russian, Drecko!
I can't believe what I'm hearing, Rockhead!
Me neither! Whoever heard of a Boxing Commission that was worried about the good of the sport or the welfare of boxers!
You sure there's hot water in the shower?
Yes! It takes a while, so just let water run!
For how long?
Until summer!
ARM AND HAMMER
BOXING
You got a very weird country here! Every-one's afraid to say anything! There's no place for dissension in Russia!
That is capitalistic lie! In Russia there is place for dissension! Is called "Siberia"!
Did you volunteer for this job?
In a way... I asked our commissar why Russian troops were in Afghanistan!
Hey, I can understand why you got pictures of Marx and Lenin, but why George Steinbrenner?
Anyone who has done as much to discredit American sports as he has is a hero to us!
KING
MARX
GEORGE
I don't under-stand what they're yelling..
They say, "Yankee go home!"
What else are they saying?
"And please take me with you!"
Stop the fight! He's going to kill Rockhead! Please, please stop it!
Aw, Atrium...
...can't you wait until the fight starts, at least?

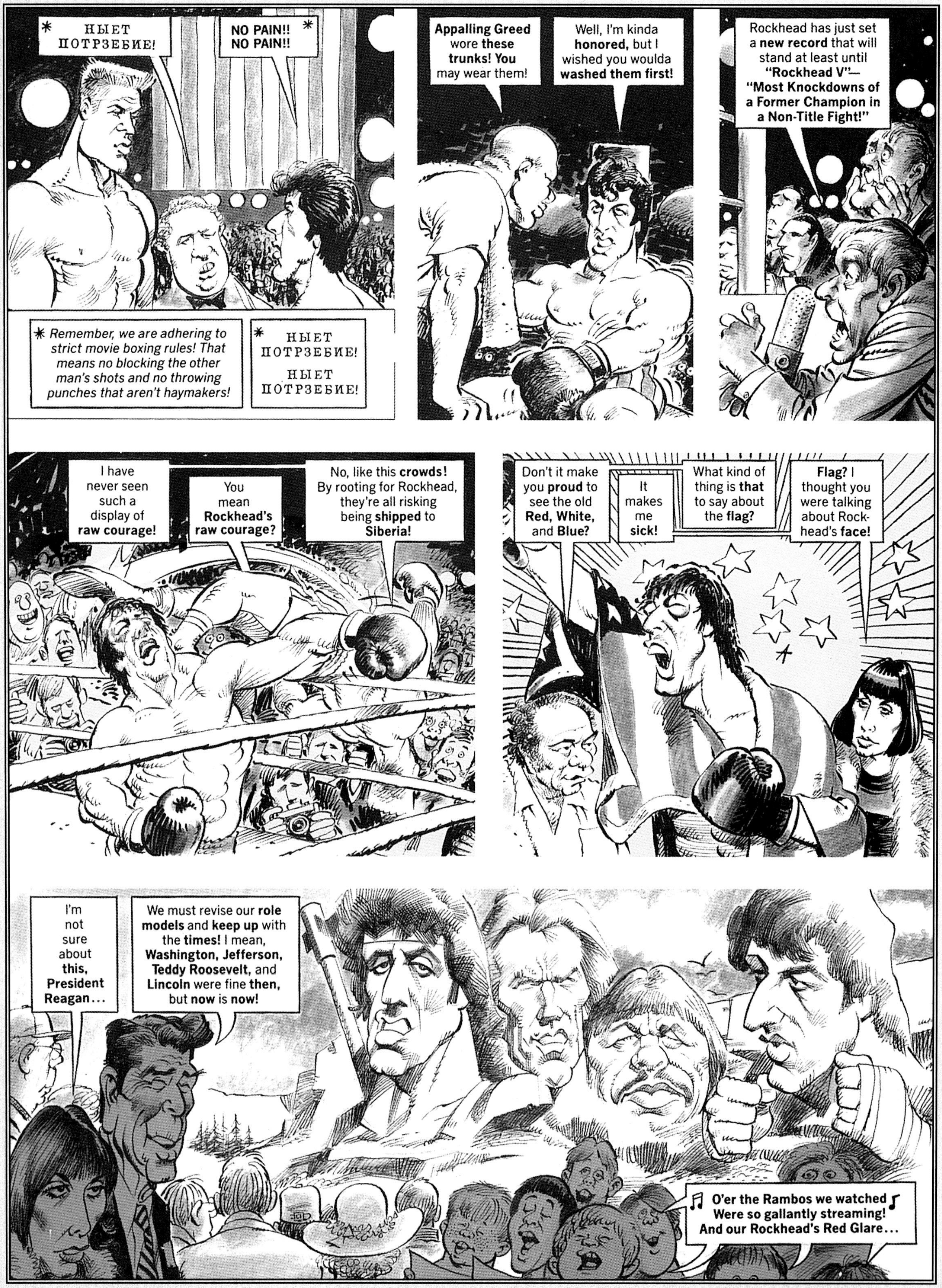
* НЫЕТ ПОТРЗЕБИЕ!
NO PAIN!! NO PAIN!! *
* Remember, we are adhering to strict movie boxing rules! That means no blocking the other man's shots and no throwing punches that aren't haymakers!
* НЫЕТ ПОТРЗЕБИЕ! НЫЕТ ПОТРЗЕБИЕ!
Appalling Greed wore these trunks! You may wear them!
Well, I'm kinda honored, but I wished you woulda washed them first!
Rockhead has just set a new record that will stand at least until "Rockhead V"—"Most Knockdowns of a Former Champion in a Non-Title Fight!"
I have never seen such a display of raw courage!
You mean Rockhead's raw courage?
No, like this crowds! By rooting for Rockhead, they're all risking being shipped to Siberia!
Don't it make you proud to see the old Red, White, and Blue?
It makes me sick!
What kind of thing is that to say about the flag?
Flag? I thought you were talking about Rockhead's face!
I'm not sure about this, President Reagan...
We must revise our role models and keep up with the times! I mean, Washington, Jefferson, Teddy Roosevelt, and Lincoln were fine then, but now is now!
O'er the Rambos we watched Were so gallantly streaming! And our Rockhead's Red Glare...

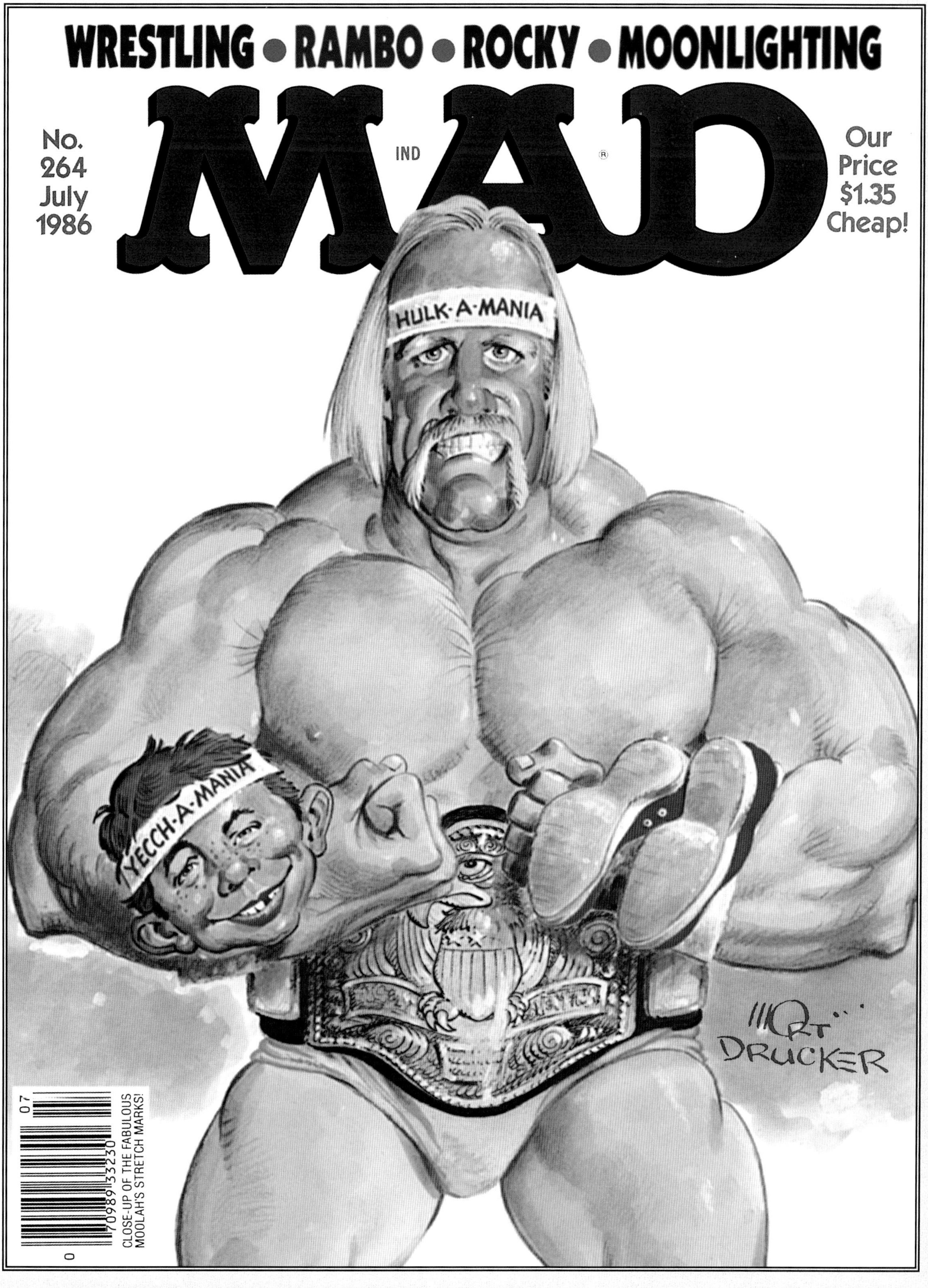
WRESTLING • RAMBO • ROCKY • MOONLIGHTING
MAD
IND
No. 264 July 1986
Our Price $1.35 Cheap!
HULK·A·MANIA
YECCH·A·MANIA
MORT DRUCKER
CLOSE-UP OF THE FABULOUS MOOLAH'S STRETCH MARKS!

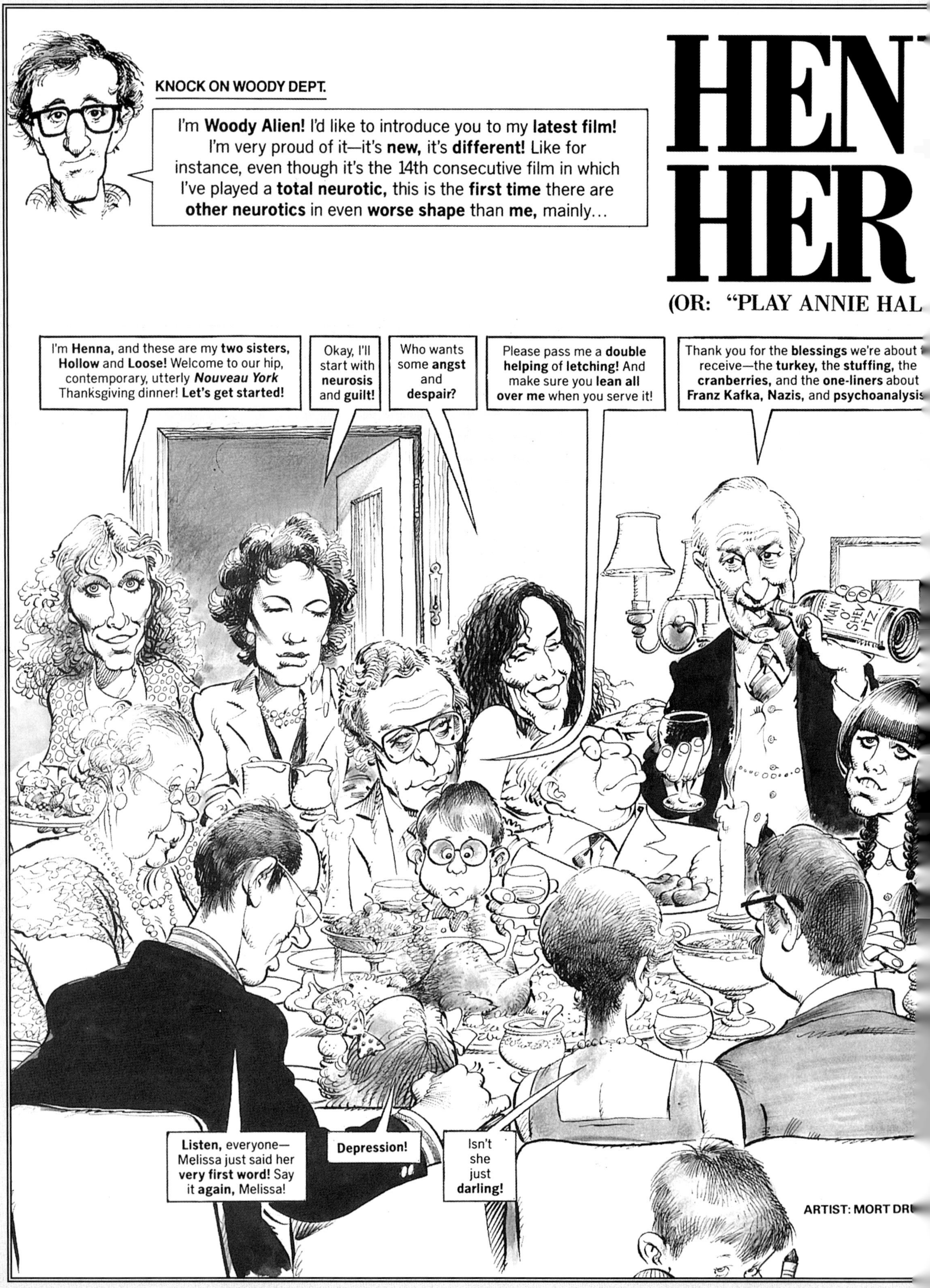
KNOCK ON WOODY DEPT.
I'm Woody Alien! I'd like to introduce you to my latest film! I'm very proud of it—it's new, it's different! Like for instance, even though it's the 14th consecutive film in which I've played a total neurotic, this is the first time there are other neurotics in even worse shape than me, mainly...
HEN
HER
(OR: "PLAY ANNIE HAL
I'm Henna, and these are my two sisters, Hollow and Loose! Welcome to our hip, contemporary, utterly Nouveau York Thanksgiving dinner! Let's get started!
Okay, I'll start with neurosis and guilt!
Who wants some angst and despair?
Please pass me a double helping of letching! And make sure you lean all over me when you serve it!
Thank you for the blessings we're about receive—the turkey, the stuffing, the cranberries, and the one-liners about Franz Kafka, Nazis, and psychoanalysis
MAN O' SHEV ITZ
Listen, everyone—Melissa just said her very first word! Say it again, Melissa!
Depression!
Isn't she just darling!
ARTIST: MORT DRU

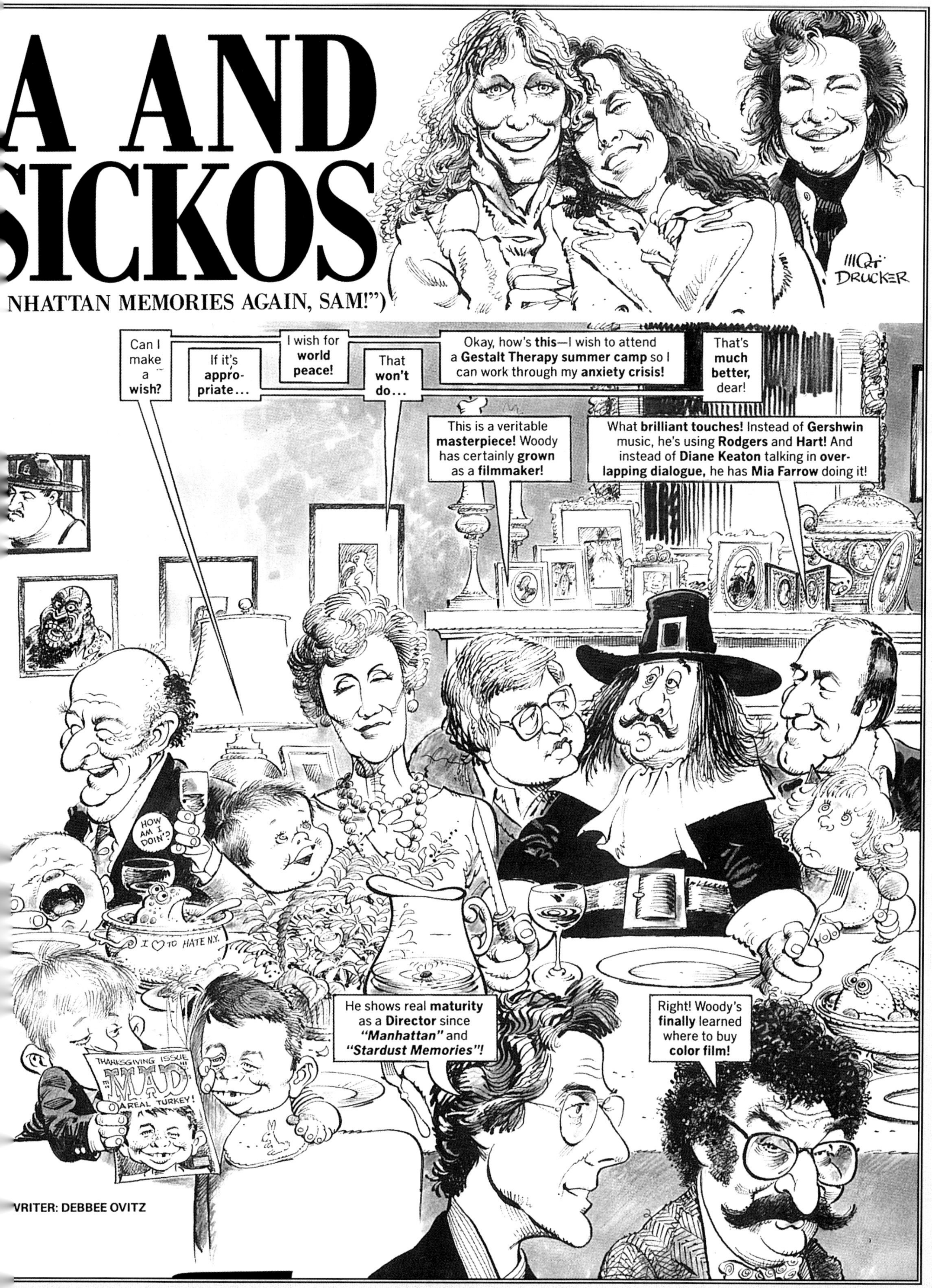
A AND
SICKOS
NHATTAN MEMORIES AGAIN, SAM!")
MORT DRUCKER
Can I make a wish?
If it's appro-priate...
I wish for world peace!
That won't do...
Okay, how's this—I wish to attend a Gestalt Therapy summer camp so I can work through my anxiety crisis!
That's much better, dear!
This is a veritable masterpiece! Woody has certainly grown as a filmmaker!
What brilliant touches! Instead of Gershwin music, he's using Rodgers and Hart! And instead of Diane Keaton talking in over-lapping dialogue, he has Mia Farrow doing it!
HOW AM I DOIN'?
I ♡ TO HATE N.Y.
He shows real maturity as a Director since "Manhattan" and "Stardust Memories"!
Right! Woody's finally learned where to buy color film!
THANKSGIVING ISSUE
MAD
A REAL TURKEY!
VRITER: DEBBEE OVITZ

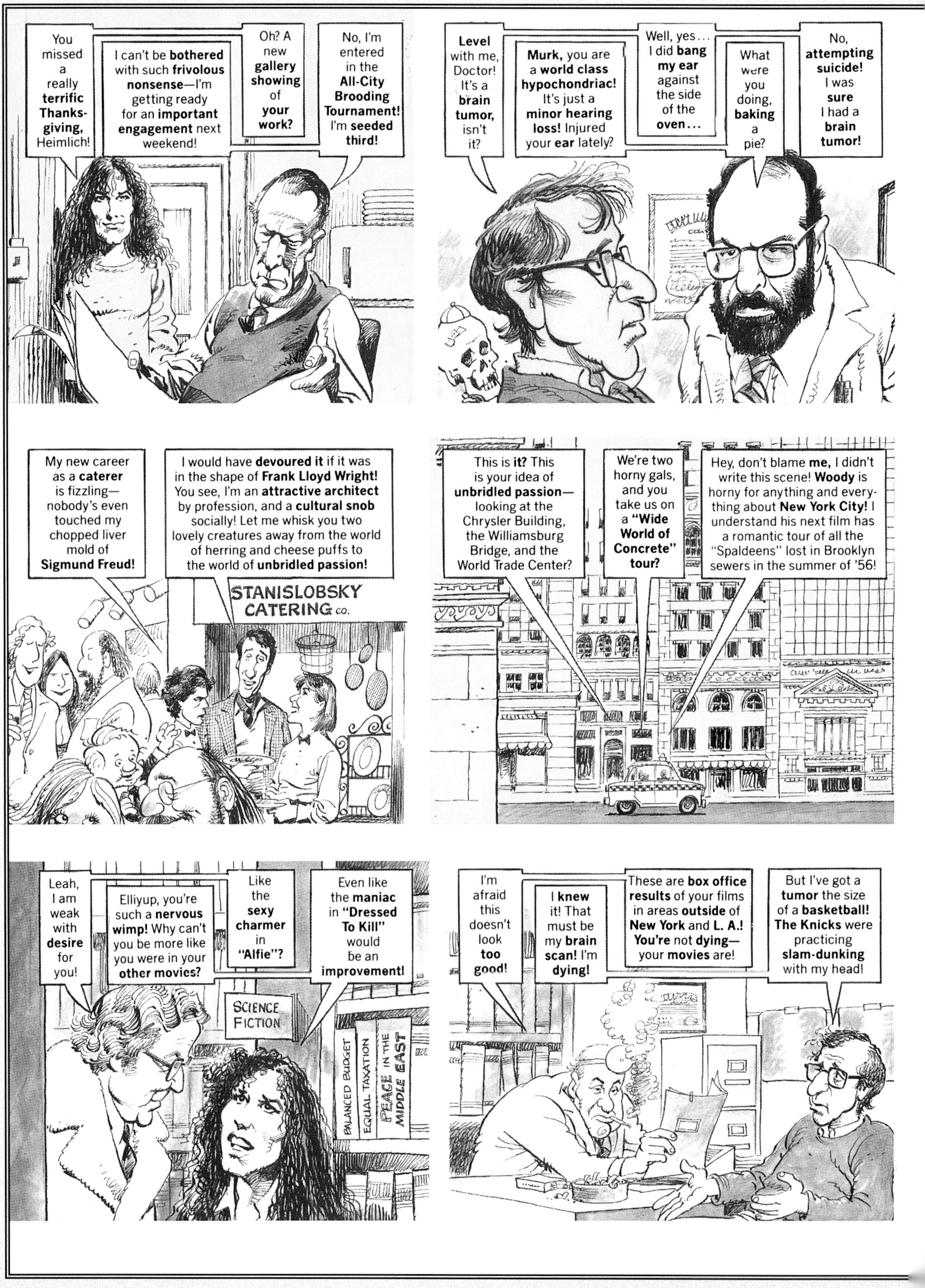
You missed a really terrific Thanks-giving, Heimlich!
I can't be bothered with such frivolous nonsense—I'm getting ready for an important engagement next weekend!
Oh? A new gallery showing of your work?
No, I'm entered in the All-City Brooding Tournament! I'm seeded third!
Level with me, Doctor! It's a brain tumor, isn't it?
Murk, you are a world class hypochondriac! It's just a minor hearing loss! Injured your ear lately?
Well, yes... I did bang my ear against the side of the oven...
What were you doing, baking a pie?
No, attempting suicide! I was sure I had a brain tumor!
My new career as a caterer is fizzling—nobody's even touched my chopped liver mold of Sigmund Freud!
I would have devoured it if it was in the shape of Frank Lloyd Wright! You see, I'm an attractive architect by profession, and a cultural snob socially! Let me whisk you two lovely creatures away from the world of herring and cheese puffs to the world of unbridled passion!
STANISLOBSKY CATERING CO.
This is it? This is your idea of unbridled passion—looking at the Chrysler Building, the Williamsburg Bridge, and the World Trade Center?
We're two horny gals, and you take us on a "Wide World of Concrete" tour?
Hey, don't blame me, I didn't write this scene! Woody is horny for anything and every-thing about New York City! I understand his next film has a romantic tour of all the "Spaldeens" lost in Brooklyn sewers in the summer of '56!
Leah, I am weak with desire for you!
Elliyup, you're such a nervous wimp! Why can't you be more like you were in your other movies?
Like the sexy charmer in "Alfie"?
Even like the maniac in "Dressed To Kill" would be an improvement!
SCIENCE FICTION
BALANCED BUDGET
EQUAL TAXATION
PEACE IN THE MIDDLE EAST
I'm afraid this doesn't look too good!
I knew it! That must be my brain scan! I'm dying!
These are box office results of your films in areas outside of New York and L. A.! You're not dying—your movies are!
But I've got a tumor the size of a basketball! The Knicks were practicing slam-dunking with my head!

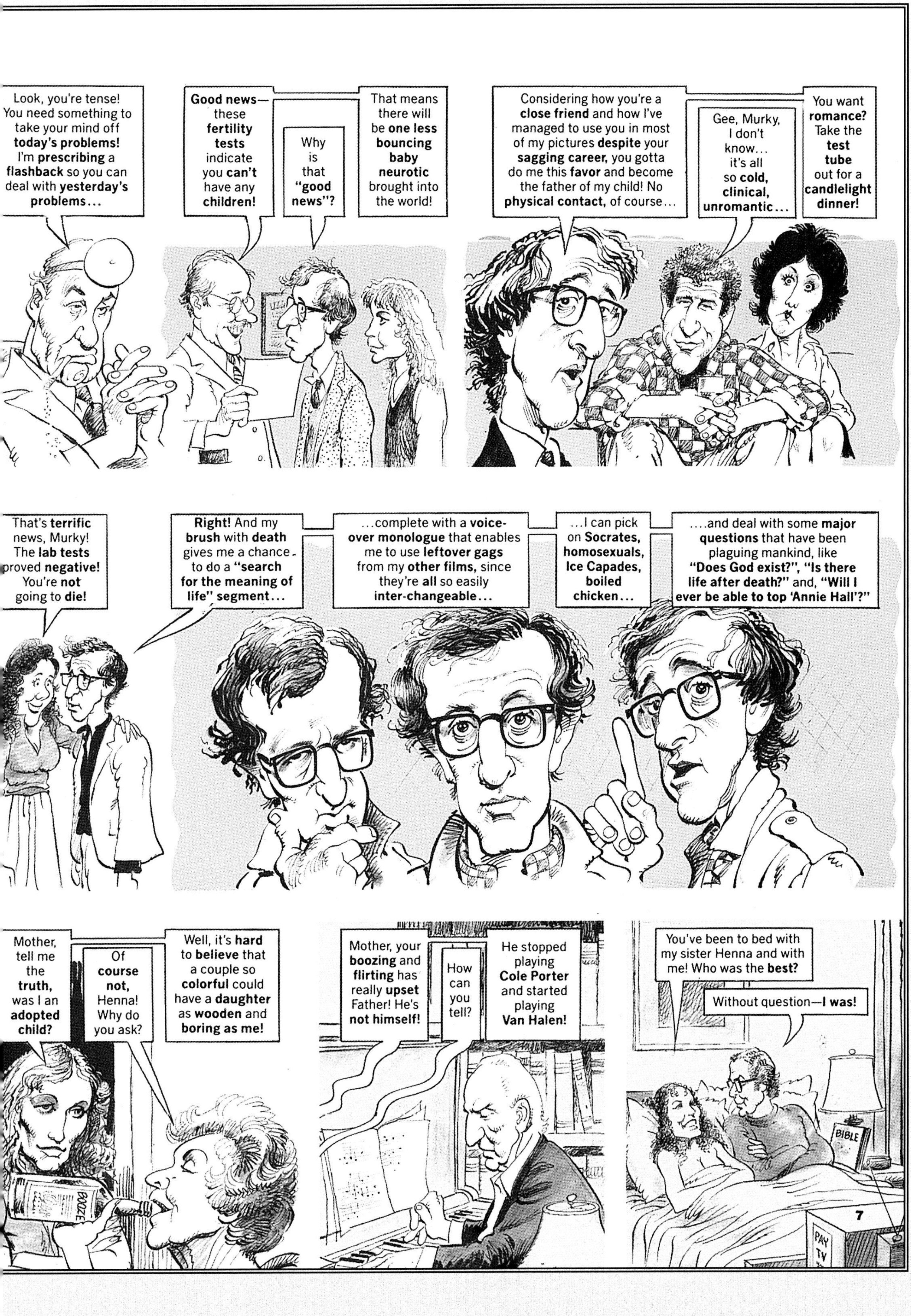
Look, you're tense! You need something to take your mind off today's problems! I'm prescribing a flashback so you can deal with yesterday's problems...
Good news—these fertility tests indicate you can't have any children!
Why is that "good news"?
That means there will be one less bouncing baby neurotic brought into the world!
Considering how you're a close friend and how I've managed to use you in most of my pictures despite your sagging career, you gotta do me this favor and become the father of my child! No physical contact, of course...
Gee, Murky, I don't know... it's all so cold, clinical, unromantic...
You want romance? Take the test tube out for a candlelight dinner!
That's terrific news, Murky! The lab tests proved negative! You're not going to die!
Right! And my brush with death gives me a chance to do a "search for the meaning of life" segment...
...complete with a voice-over monologue that enables me to use leftover gags from my other films, since they're all so easily inter-changeable...
...I can pick on Socrates, homosexuals, Ice Capades, boiled chicken...
....and deal with some major questions that have been plaguing mankind, like "Does God exist?", "Is there life after death?" and, "Will I ever be able to top 'Annie Hall'?"
Mother, tell me the truth, was I an adopted child?
Of course not, Henna! Why do you ask?
Well, it's hard to believe that a couple so colorful could have a daughter as wooden and boring as me!
BOOZE
Mother, your boozing and flirting has really upset Father! He's not himself!
How can you tell?
He stopped playing Cole Porter and started playing Van Halen!
You've been to bed with my sister Henna and with me! Who was the best?
Without question—I was!
BIBLE
PAY TV
7

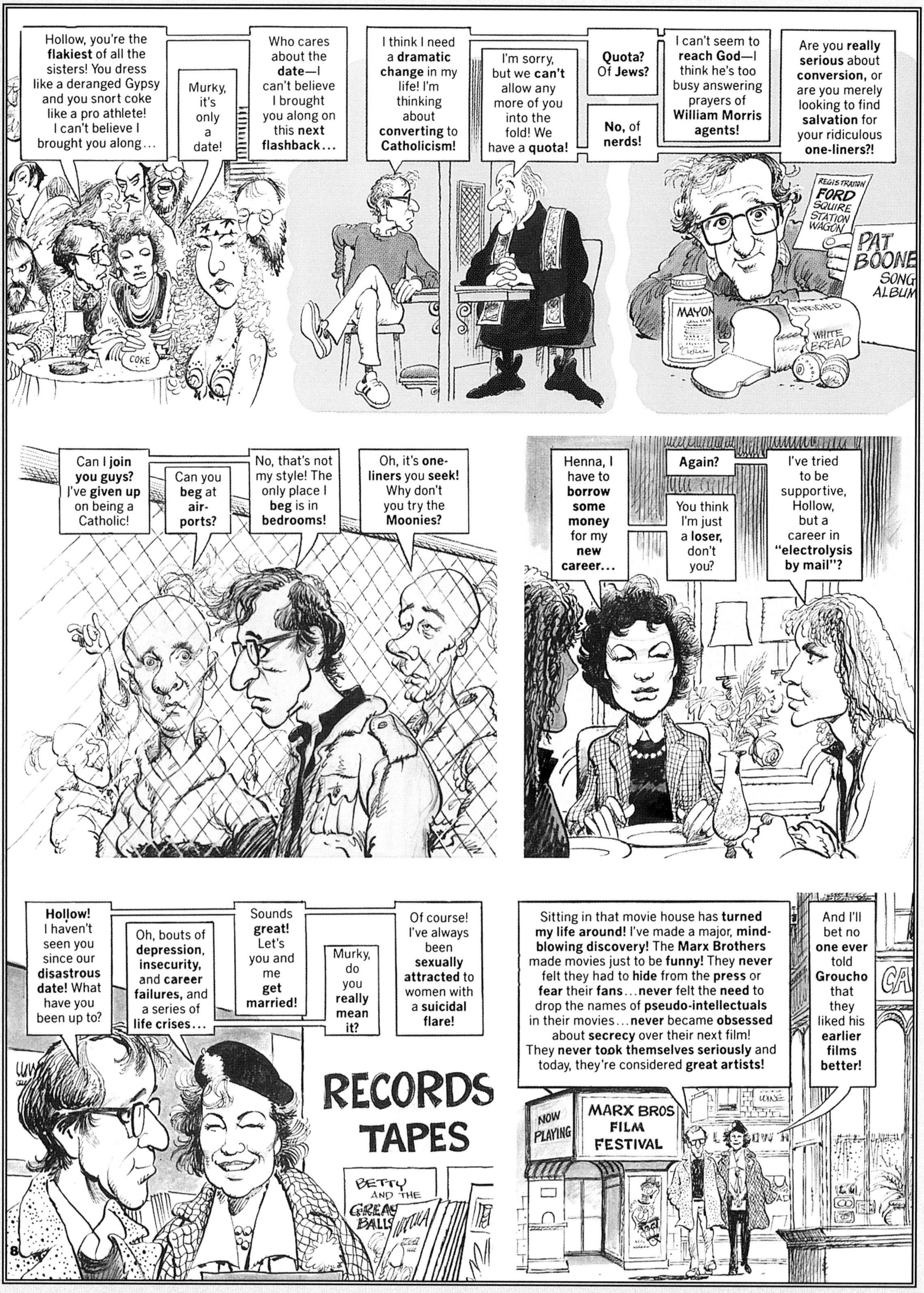
Hollow, you're the flakiest of all the sisters! You dress like a deranged Gypsy and you snort coke like a pro athlete! I can't believe I brought you along...
Murky, it's only a date!
Who cares about the date—I can't believe I brought you along on this next flashback...
COKE
I think I need a dramatic change in my life! I'm thinking about converting to Catholicism!
I'm sorry, but we can't allow any more of you into the fold! We have a quota!
Quota? Of Jews?
No, of nerds!
I can't seem to reach God—I think he's too busy answering prayers of William Morris agents!
Are you really serious about conversion, or are you merely looking to find salvation for your ridiculous one-liners?!
REGISTRATION FORD SQUIRE STATION WAGON
PAT BOONE SONG ALBUM
MAYON
WHITE BREAD
Can I join you guys? I've given up on being a Catholic!
Can you beg at air-ports?
No, that's not my style! The only place I beg is in bedrooms!
Oh, it's one-liners you seek! Why don't you try the Moonies?
Henna, I have to borrow some money for my new career...
Again?
You think I'm just a loser, don't you?
I've tried to be supportive, Hollow, but a career in "electrolysis by mail"?
Hollow! I haven't seen you since our disastrous date! What have you been up to?
Oh, bouts of depression, insecurity, and career failures, and a series of life crises...
Sounds great! Let's you and me get married!
Murky, do you really mean it?
Of course! I've always been sexually attracted to women with a suicidal flare!
RECORDS TAPES
BETTY AND THE GREAS BALLS
Sitting in that movie house has turned my life around! I've made a major, mind-blowing discovery! The Marx Brothers made movies just to be funny! They never felt they had to hide from the press or fear their fans...never felt the need to drop the names of pseudo-intellectuals in their movies...never became obsessed about secrecy over their next film! They never took themselves seriously and today, they're considered great artists!
And I'll bet no one ever told Groucho that they liked his earlier films better!
NOW PLAYING
MARX BROS FILM FESTIVAL

FRANK ON A ROLL DEPT.

SCHWARZENEGGER

WITH A TIP OF THE HAT TO HANK "HIAWATHA" LONGFELLOW

ARTIST: MORT DRUCKER WRITER: FRANK JACOBS

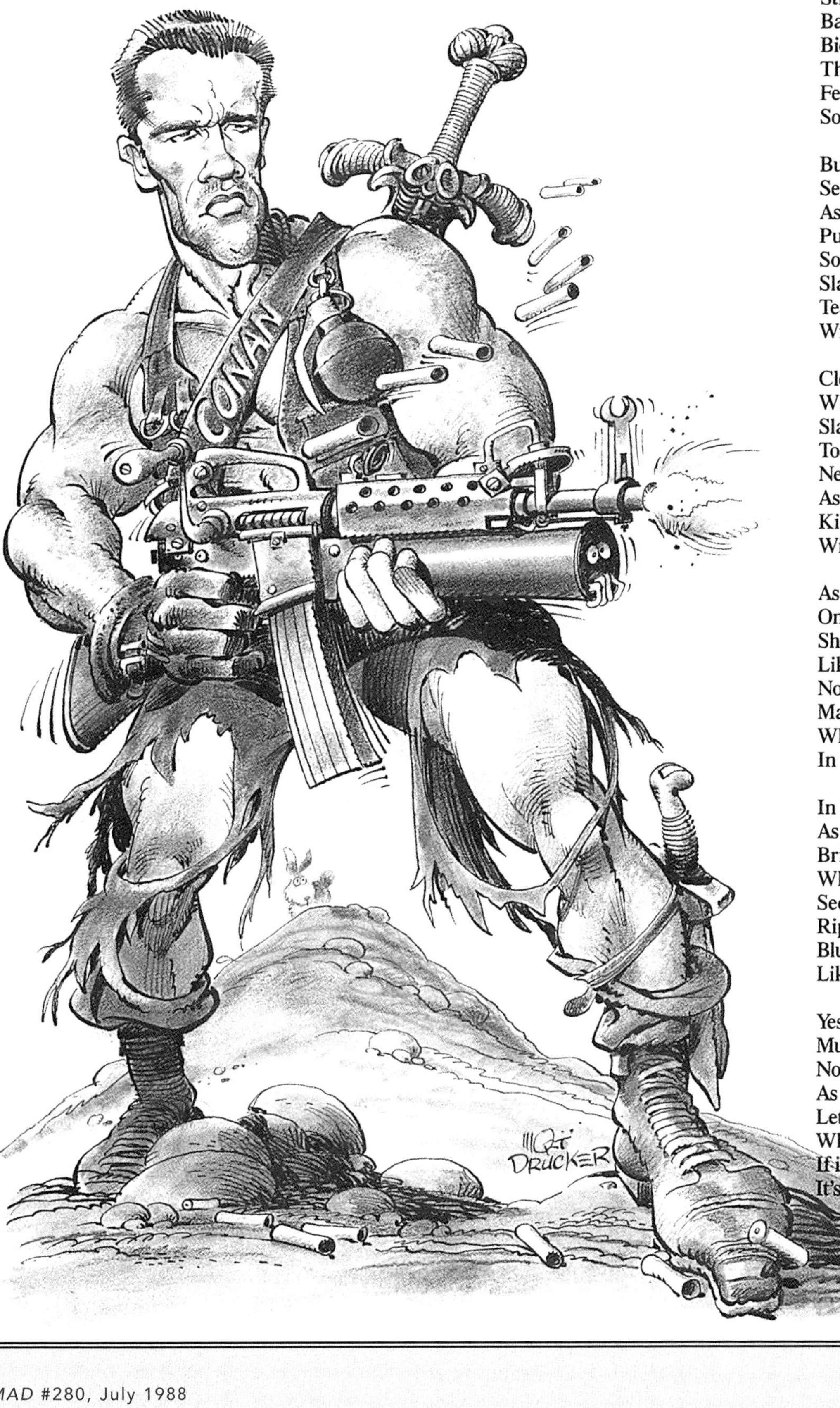
CONAN

By the shores of the Pacific,
In the town of glitz and hustle,
Strode the mighty Schwarzenegger,
Baring chest and flexing muscle;
Biceps twitched in perfect rhythm
Through his skill with isometrics, —
Feats that Letterman, on seeing,
Sought to use as Stupid Pet tricks.

But the bulging Schwarzenegger
Set his sights on goals much higher,
As the lure of movie stardom
Pumped him up with great desire;
Soon he found himself in epics,
Slaying enemies like vermin,
Tearing dialogue to pieces
With his accent, sorta German.

Clenching jaw, he raged as "Conan,"
Who, upset by double-dealing,
Slaughters half the population
To express his depth of feeling;
Next "The Terminator" starred him
As a droid bent on aggression,
Killing victims for two hours
Without changing his expression.

As a soldier in "Commando,"
On whole armies he was feasting,
Shrugging off a hail of bullets
Like a flea-bite or a bee-sting;
Not Stallone in Panavision
Matched the fury of his scowling
When in "Predator" he thrilled us
In the art of disemboweling.

In his latest quest for glory
As "The Running Man" he bears up,
Bringing down the rule of evil
While assorted foes he tears up;
See him punch out his oppressors,
Rip apart a villain's torso,
Bludgeon killers into meatloaf
Like Chuck Norris, only more so.

Yes, the massive Schwarzenegger,
Muscles rippling, tendons straining,
Now, through fame and sky-high grosses,
As a super-star is reigning;
Let the critics crucify him
When his lines he seems to louse up!
If it's brains that wins the Oscars,
It's the beef that fills the house up!

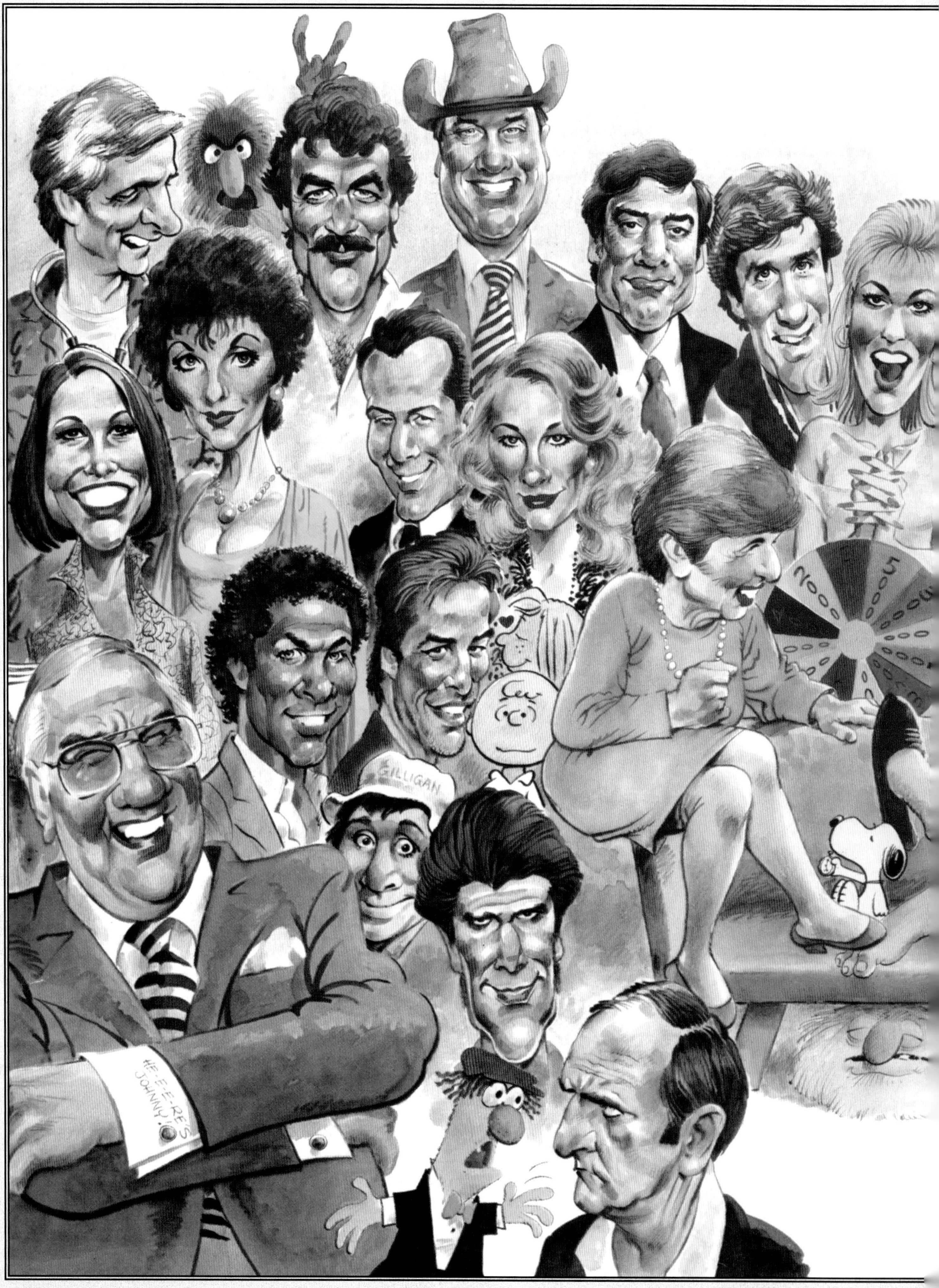
GILLIGAN
HE-E-E-RE'S JOHNNY!

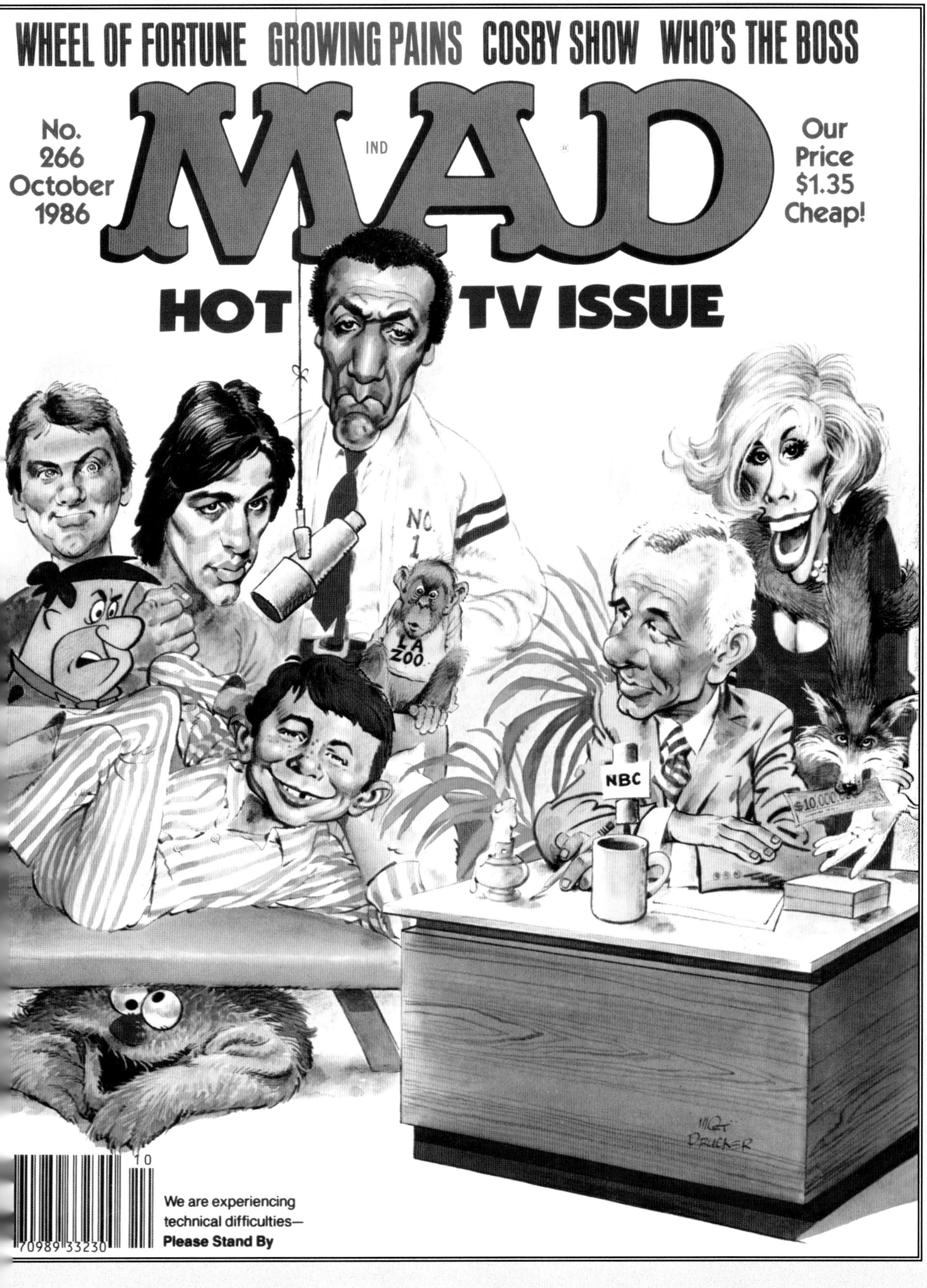
WHEEL OF FORTUNE GROWING PAINS COSBY SHOW WHO'S THE BOSS
MAD
No. 266 October 1986
Our Price $1.35 Cheap!
HOT TV ISSUE
NO. 1
LA ZOO
NBC
$10,000,000
MORT DRUCKER
We are experiencing technical difficulties—
Please Stand By

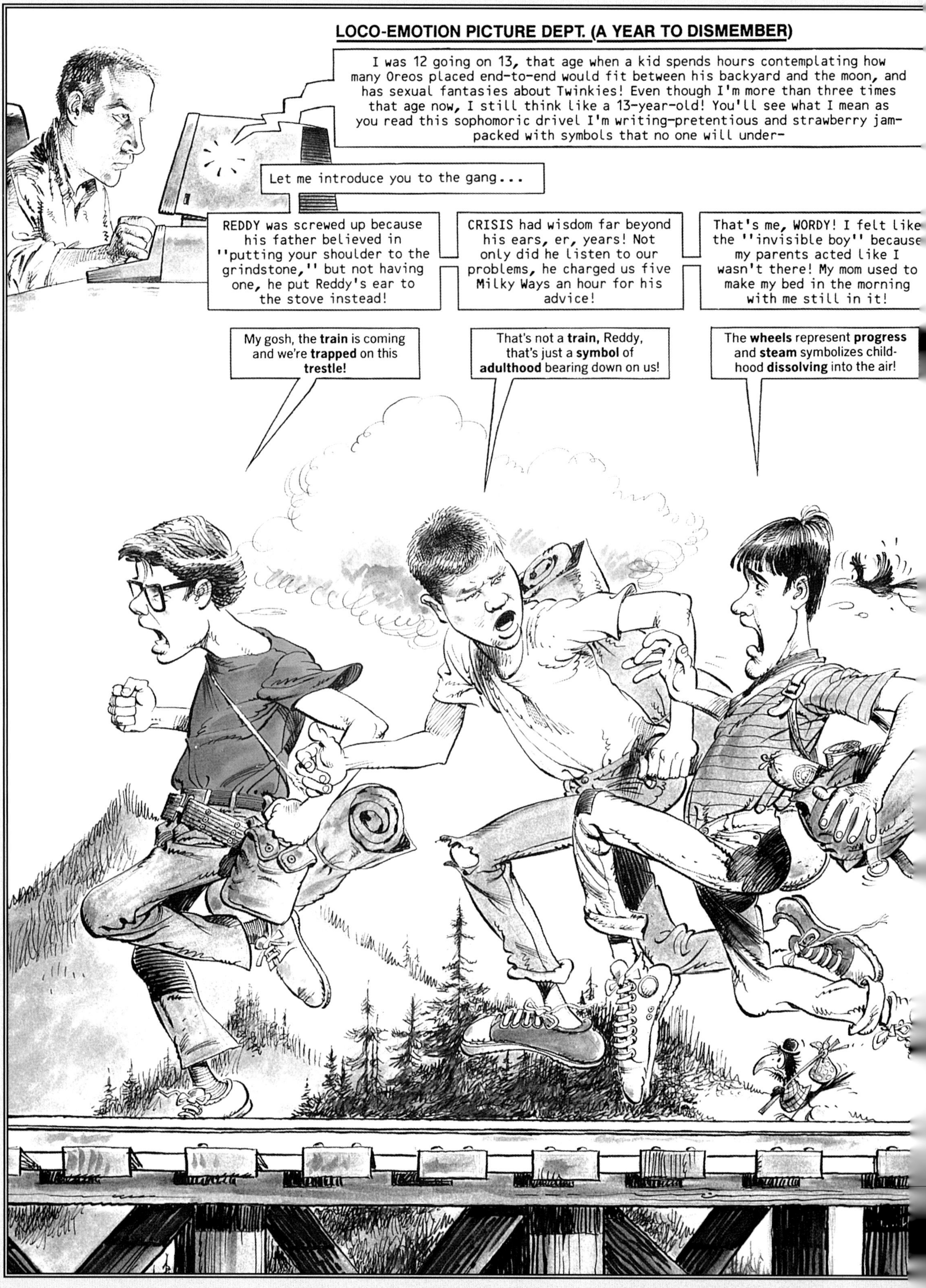
LOCO-EMOTION PICTURE DEPT. (A YEAR TO DISMEMBER)
I was 12 going on 13, that age when a kid spends hours contemplating how many Oreos placed end-to-end would fit between his backyard and the moon, and has sexual fantasies about Twinkies! Even though I'm more than three times that age now, I still think like a 13-year-old! You'll see what I mean as you read this sophomoric drivel I'm writing–pretentious and strawberry jam-packed with symbols that no one will under-
Let me introduce you to the gang...
REDDY was screwed up because his father believed in ''putting your shoulder to the grindstone,'' but not having one, he put Reddy's ear to the stove instead!
CRISIS had wisdom far beyond his ears, er, years! Not only did he listen to our problems, he charged us five Milky Ways an hour for his advice!
That's me, WORDY! I felt like the ''invisible boy'' because my parents acted like I wasn't there! My mom used to make my bed in the morning with me still in it!
My gosh, the **train** is coming and we're **trapped** on this **trestle!**
That's not a **train,** Reddy, that's just a **symbol** of **adulthood** bearing down on us!
The **wheels** represent **progress** and **steam** symbolizes childhood **dissolving** into the air!

MAD #269, March 1987

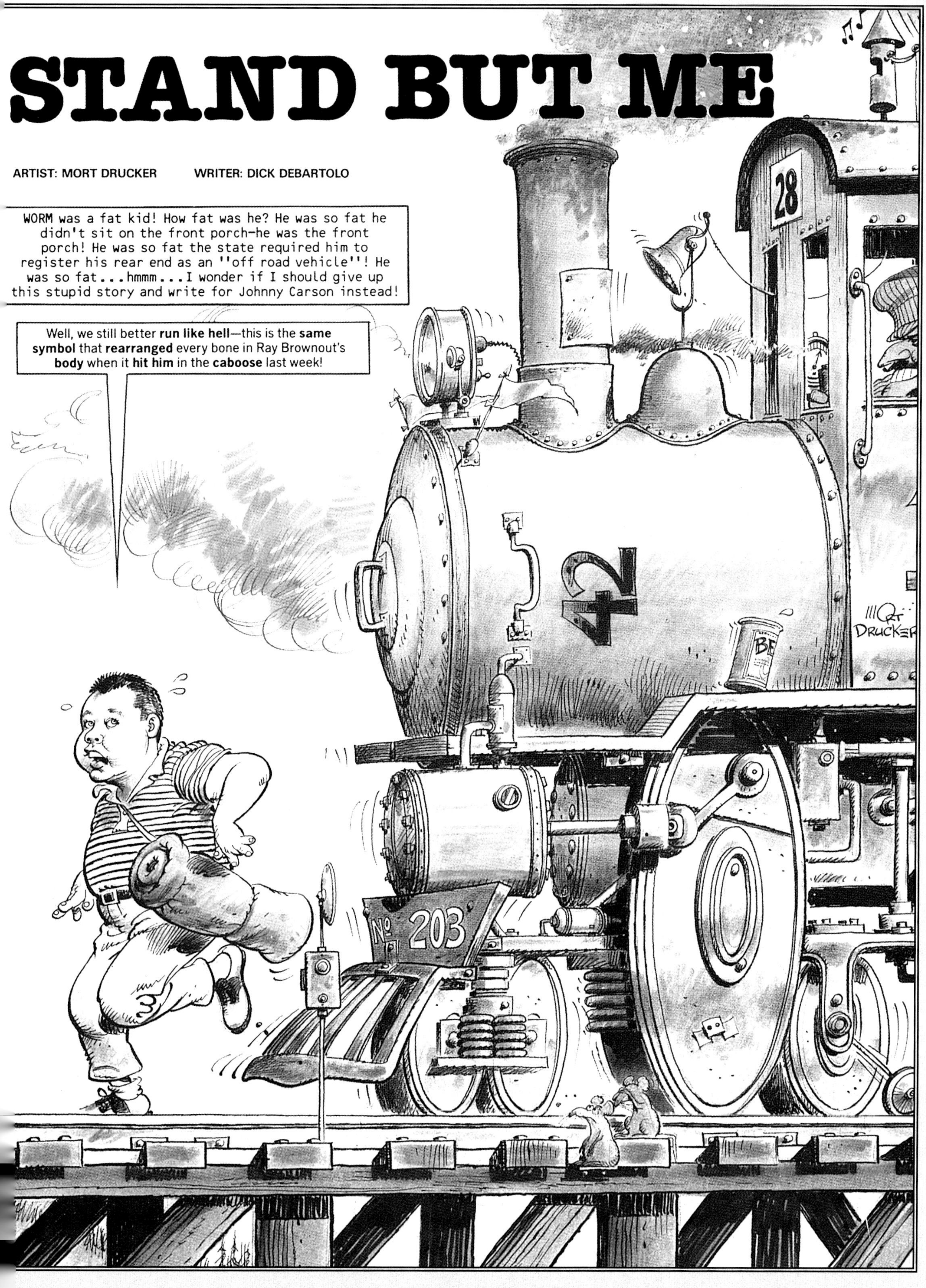
STAND BUT ME
ARTIST: MORT DRUCKER
WRITER: DICK DEBARTOLO
WORM was a fat kid! How fat was he? He was so fat he didn't sit on the front porch—he was the front porch! He was so fat the state required him to register his rear end as an ''off road vehicle''! He was so fat...hmmm...I wonder if I should give up this stupid story and write for Johnny Carson instead!
Well, we still better run like hell—this is the same symbol that rearranged every bone in Ray Brownout's body when it hit him in the caboose last week!
28
42
No 203

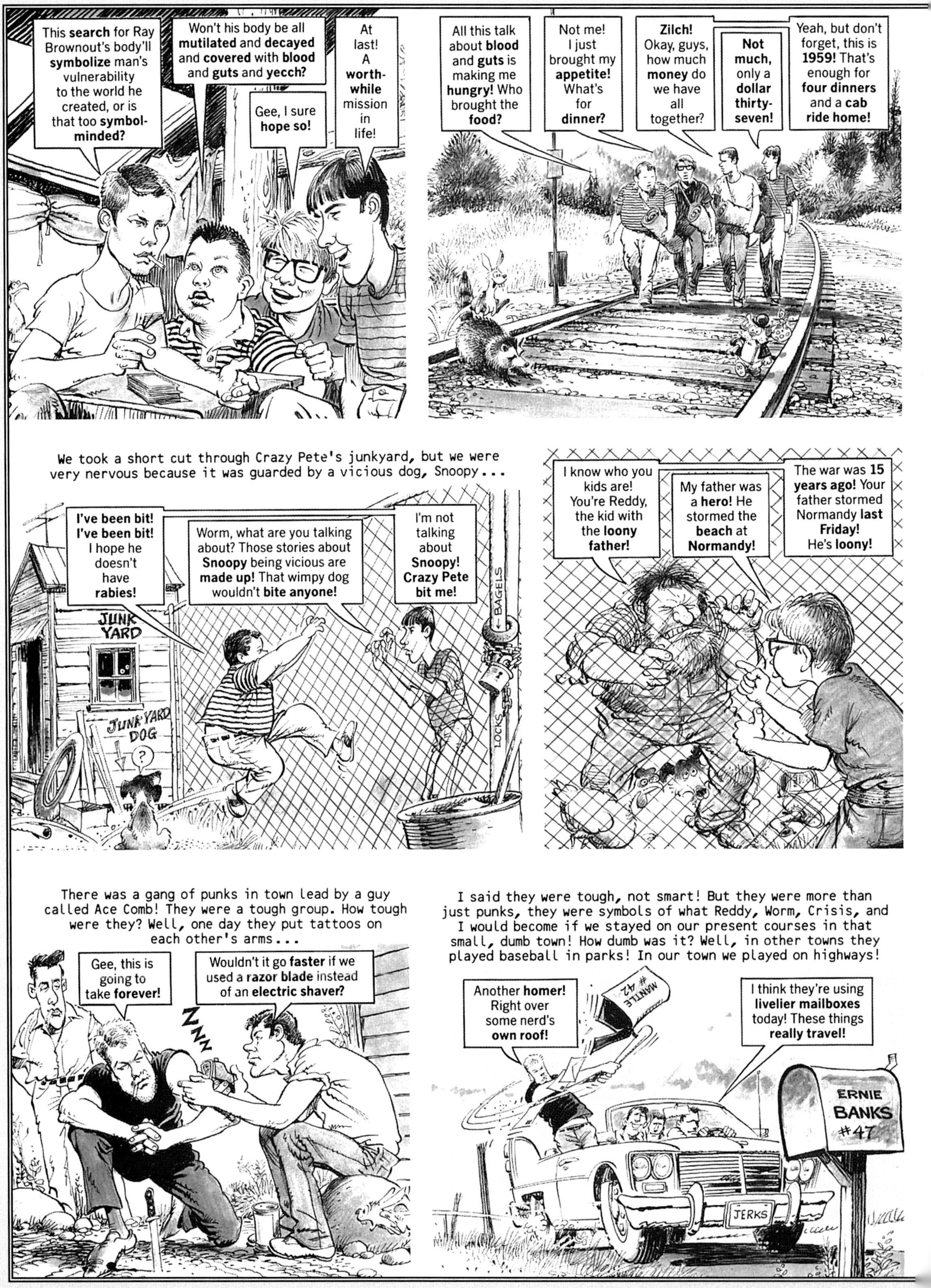
This **search** for Ray Brownout's body'll **symbolize** man's vulnerability to the world he created, or is that too **symbol-minded?**
Won't his body be all **mutilated** and **decayed** and **covered** with **blood** and **guts** and **yecch?**
Gee, I sure **hope so!**
At last! A **worth-while** mission in life!
All this talk about **blood** and **guts** is making me **hungry!** Who brought the **food?**
Not me! I just brought my **appetite!** What's for **dinner?**
Zilch! Okay, guys, how much **money** do we have all together?
Not much, only a **dollar thirty-seven!**
Yeah, but don't forget, this is **1959!** That's enough for **four dinners** and a **cab ride home!**
We took a short cut through Crazy Pete's junkyard, but we were very nervous because it was guarded by a vicious dog, Snoopy...
I've been bit! I've been bit! I hope he doesn't have **rabies!**
Worm, what are you talking about? Those stories about **Snoopy** being vicious are **made up!** That wimpy dog wouldn't **bite anyone!**
I'm not talking about **Snoopy! Crazy Pete bit me!**
JUNK YARD
JUNK-YARD DOG
BAGELS
LOCKS
I know who you kids are! You're Reddy, the kid with the **loony father!**
My father was a **hero!** He stormed the **beach** at **Normandy!**
The war was **15 years ago!** Your father stormed Normandy **last Friday!** He's **loony!**
There was a gang of punks in town lead by a guy called Ace Comb! They were a tough group. How tough were they? Well, one day they put tattoos on each other's arms...
Gee, this is going to take **forever!**
Wouldn't it go **faster** if we used a **razor blade** instead of an **electric shaver?**
ZZZ
I said they were tough, not smart! But they were more than just punks, they were symbols of what Reddy, Worm, Crisis, and I would become if we stayed on our present courses in that small, dumb town! How dumb was it? Well, in other towns they played baseball in parks! In our town we played on highways!
Another **homer!** Right over some nerd's **own roof!**
MANTLE #42
I think they're using **livelier mailboxes** today! These things **really travel!**
ERNIE BANKS #47
JERKS

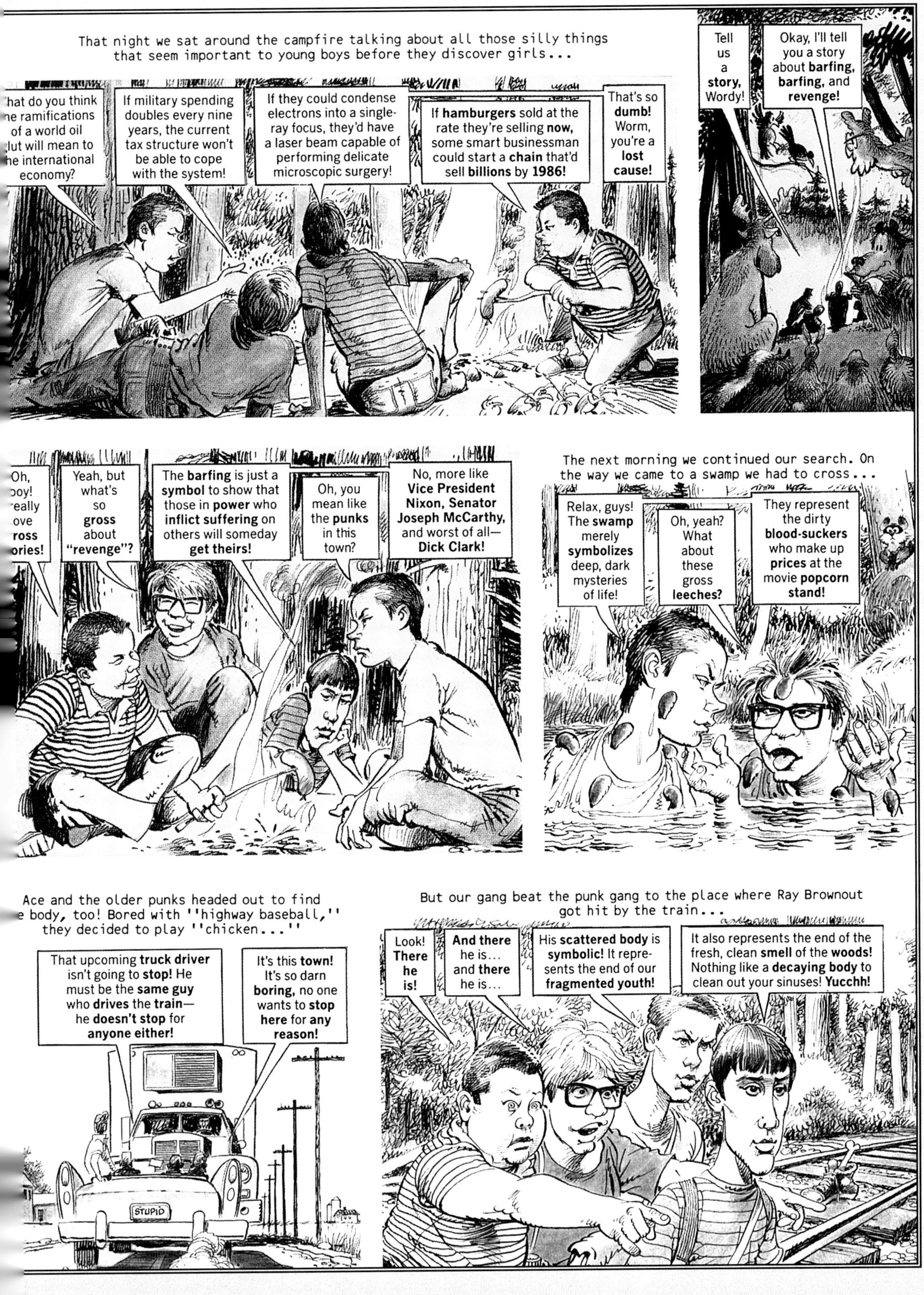
That night we sat around the campfire talking about all those silly things that seem important to young boys before they discover girls...
hat do you think ne ramifications of a world oil lut will mean to he international economy?
If military spending doubles every nine years, the current tax structure won't be able to cope with the system!
If they could condense electrons into a single-ray focus, they'd have a laser beam capable of performing delicate microscopic surgery!
If **hamburgers** sold at the rate they're selling **now,** some smart businessman could start a **chain** that'd sell **billions** by **1986!**
That's so **dumb!** Worm, you're a **lost cause!**
Tell us a **story,** Wordy!
Okay, I'll tell you a story about **barfing, barfing,** and **revenge!**
Oh, oy! eally ove ross ories!
Yeah, but what's so **gross** about **"revenge"?**
The **barfing** is just a **symbol** to show that those in **power** who **inflict suffering** on others will someday **get theirs!**
Oh, you mean like the **punks** in this town?
No, more like **Vice President Nixon, Senator Joseph McCarthy,** and worst of all— **Dick Clark!**
The next morning we continued our search. On the way we came to a swamp we had to cross...
Relax, guys! The **swamp** merely **symbolizes** deep, dark mysteries of life!
Oh, yeah? What about these gross **leeches?**
They represent the dirty **blood-suckers** who make up **prices** at the movie **popcorn stand!**
Ace and the older punks headed out to find e body, too! Bored with "highway baseball," they decided to play "chicken..."
That upcoming **truck driver** isn't going to **stop!** He must be the **same guy** who **drives the train**— he **doesn't stop** for **anyone either!**
It's this **town!** It's so darn **boring,** no one wants to **stop here** for **any reason!**
STUPID
But our gang beat the punk gang to the place where Ray Brownout got hit by the train...
Look! **There he is!**
And there he is... and **there** he is...
His **scattered body** is **symbolic!** It represents the end of our **fragmented youth!**
It also represents the end of the fresh, clean **smell** of the **woods!** Nothing like a **decaying body** to clean out your sinuses! **Yucchh!**

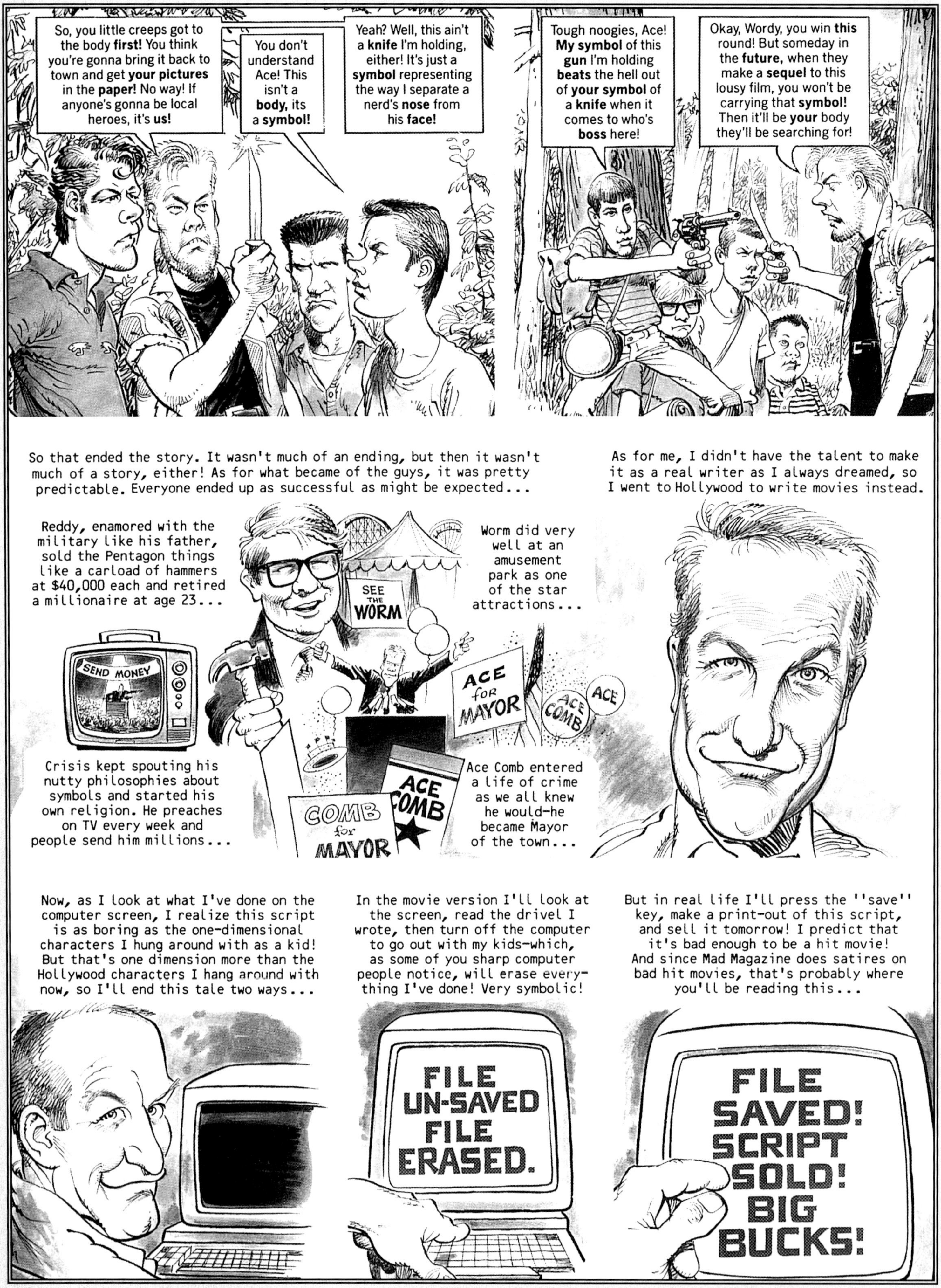
So, you little creeps got to the body first! You think you're gonna bring it back to town and get your pictures in the paper! No way! If anyone's gonna be local heroes, it's us!
You don't understand Ace! This isn't a body, its a symbol!
Yeah? Well, this ain't a knife I'm holding, either! It's just a symbol representing the way I separate a nerd's nose from his face!
Tough noogies, Ace! My symbol of this gun I'm holding beats the hell out of your symbol of a knife when it comes to who's boss here!
Okay, Wordy, you win this round! But someday in the future, when they make a sequel to this lousy film, you won't be carrying that symbol! Then it'll be your body they'll be searching for!
So that ended the story. It wasn't much of an ending, but then it wasn't much of a story, either! As for what became of the guys, it was pretty predictable. Everyone ended up as successful as might be expected...
As for me, I didn't have the talent to make it as a real writer as I always dreamed, so I went to Hollywood to write movies instead.
Reddy, enamored with the military like his father, sold the Pentagon things like a carload of hammers at $40,000 each and retired a millionaire at age 23...
SEE THE WORM
Worm did very well at an amusement park as one of the star attractions...
SEND MONEY
ACE for MAYOR
ACE COMB
ACE
Crisis kept spouting his nutty philosophies about symbols and started his own religion. He preaches on TV every week and people send him millions...
ACE COMB
COMB for MAYOR
Ace Comb entered a life of crime as we all knew he would—he became Mayor of the town...
Now, as I look at what I've done on the computer screen, I realize this script is as boring as the one-dimensional characters I hung around with as a kid! But that's one dimension more than the Hollywood characters I hang around with now, so I'll end this tale two ways...
In the movie version I'll look at the screen, read the drivel I wrote, then turn off the computer to go out with my kids—which, as some of you sharp computer people notice, will erase everything I've done! Very symbolic!
FILE UN-SAVED FILE ERASED.
But in real life I'll press the "save" key, make a print-out of this script, and sell it tomorrow! I predict that it's bad enough to be a hit movie! And since Mad Magazine does satires on bad hit movies, that's probably where you'll be reading this...
FILE SAVED! SCRIPT SOLD! BIG BUCKS!

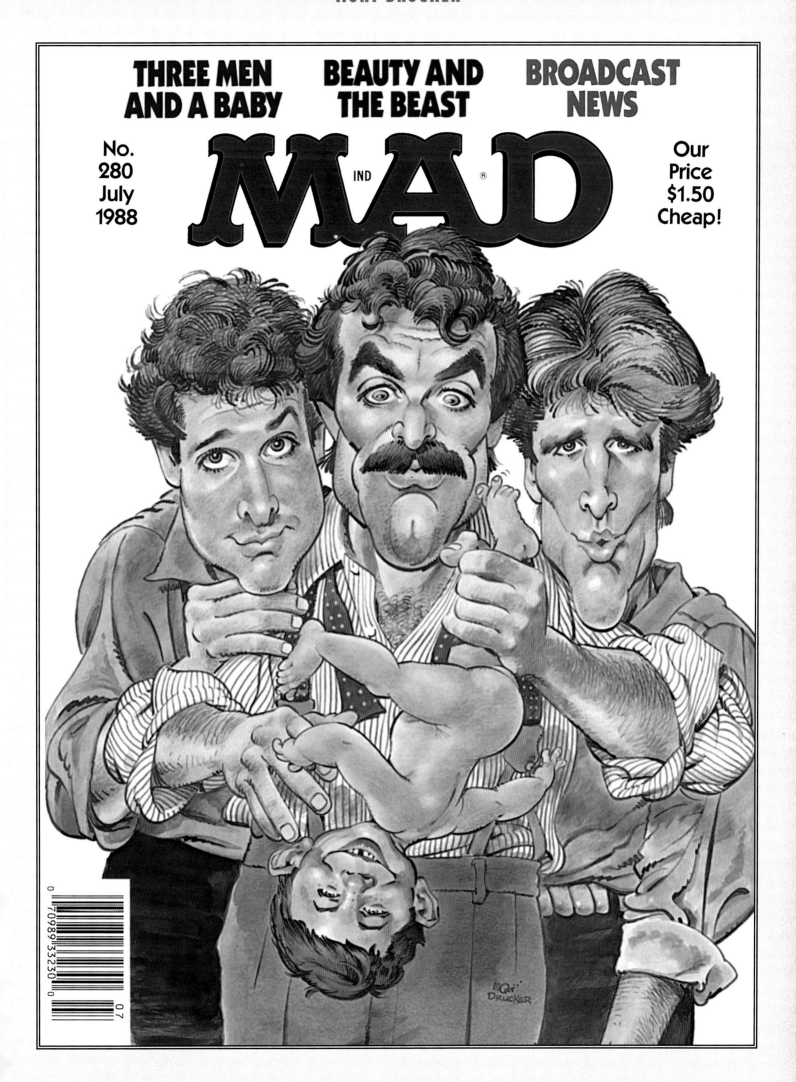

THREE MEN AND A BABY

BEAUTY AND THE BEAST

BROADCAST NEWS

No. 280 July 1988

MAD

IND

®

Our Price $1.50 Cheap!

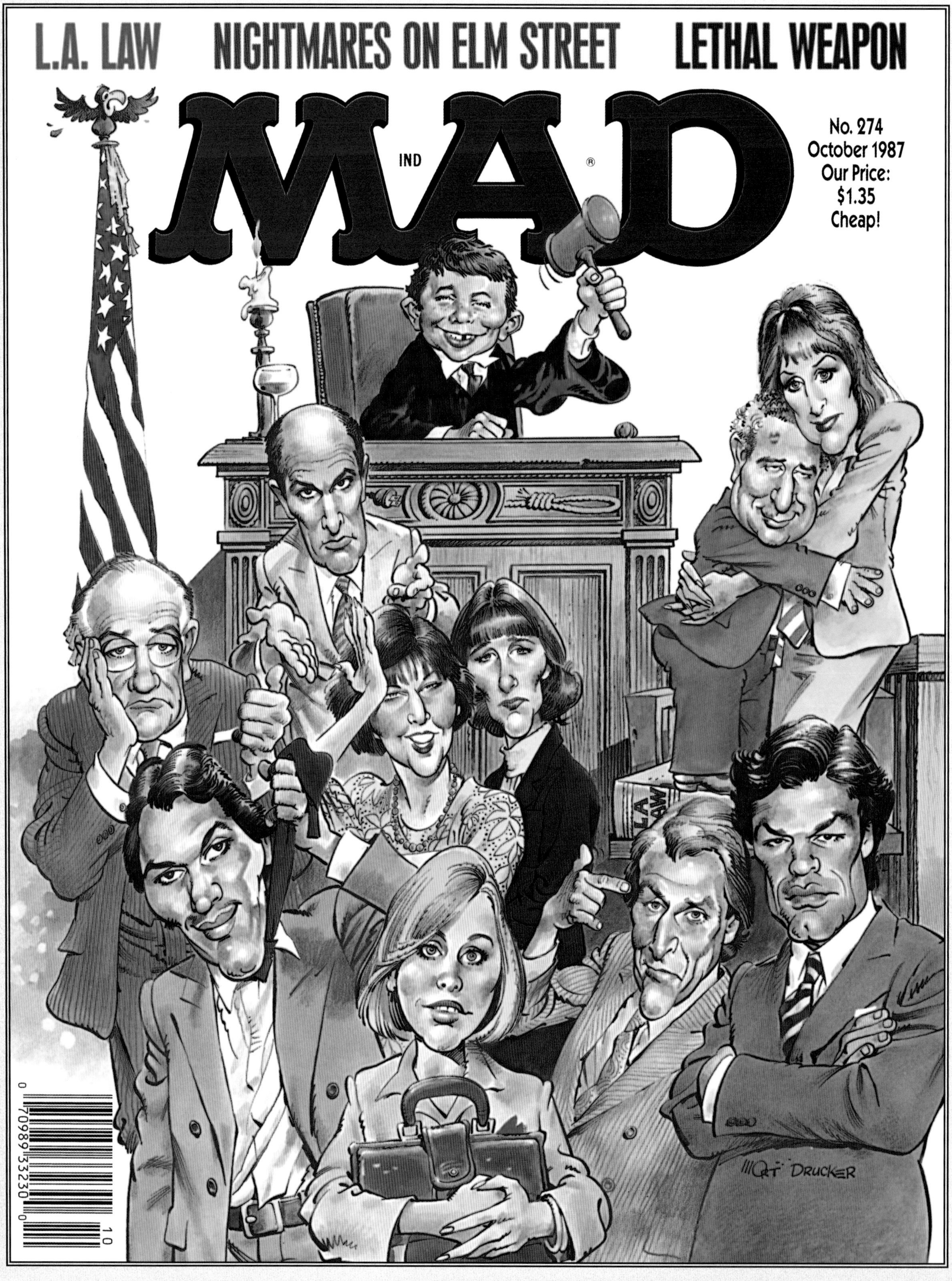
L.A. LAW
NIGHTMARES ON ELM STREET
LETHAL WEAPON
MAD
IND
No. 274
October 1987
Our Price:
$1.35
Cheap!
L.A. LAW
MORT DRUCKER

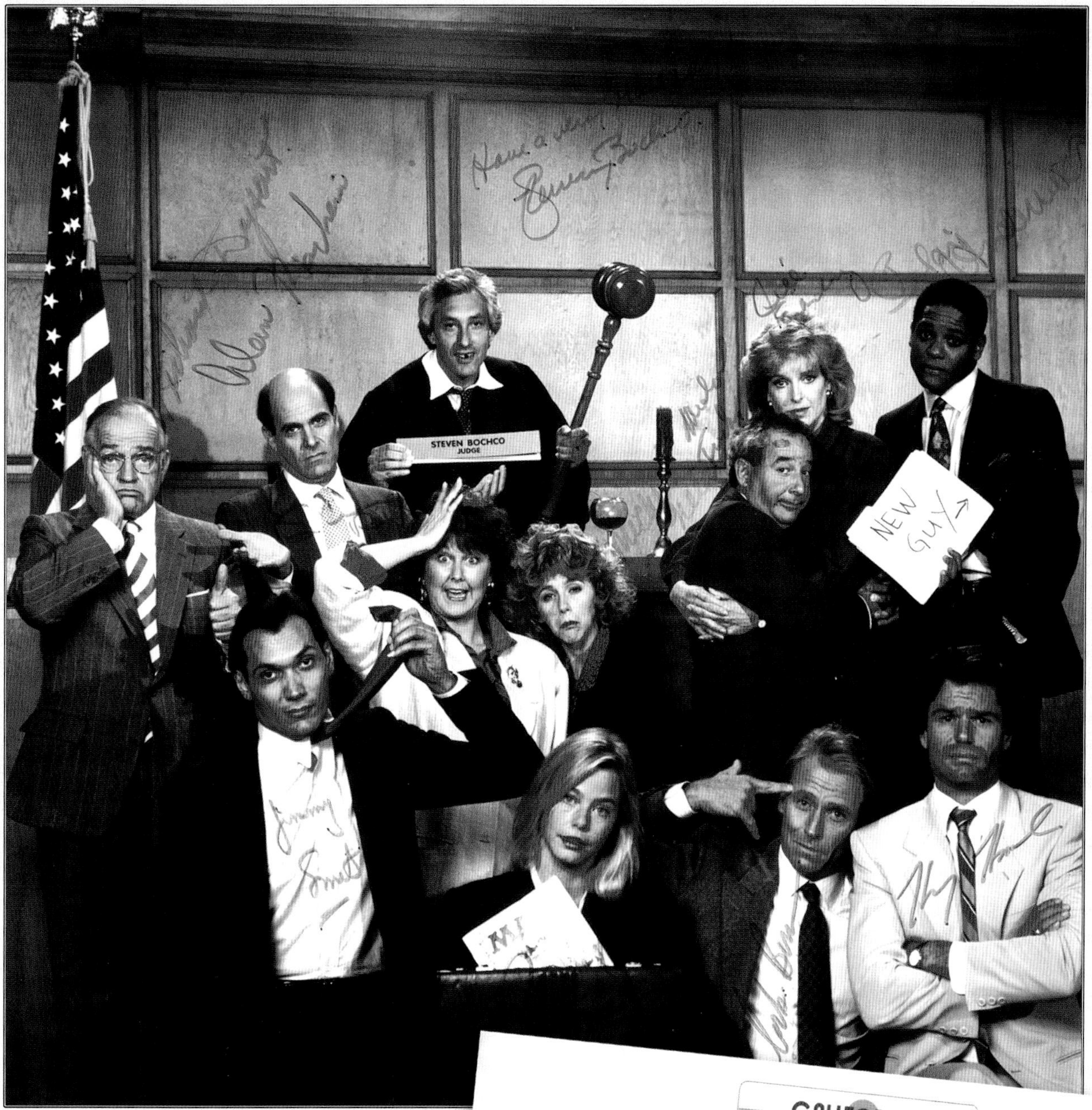
STEVEN BOCHCO
JUDGE
NEW GUY

After seeing the cover of *MAD* #274, the creator and producer of *LA Law*, Steven Bochco, sent *MAD* an unsolicited photo of the show's cast re-enacting Drucker's illustration, with Bochco replacing Alfred as judge, including a blackened-out front tooth. This photo was featured on the letters page of *MAD* #276, along with a reproduction of Bochco's letter.

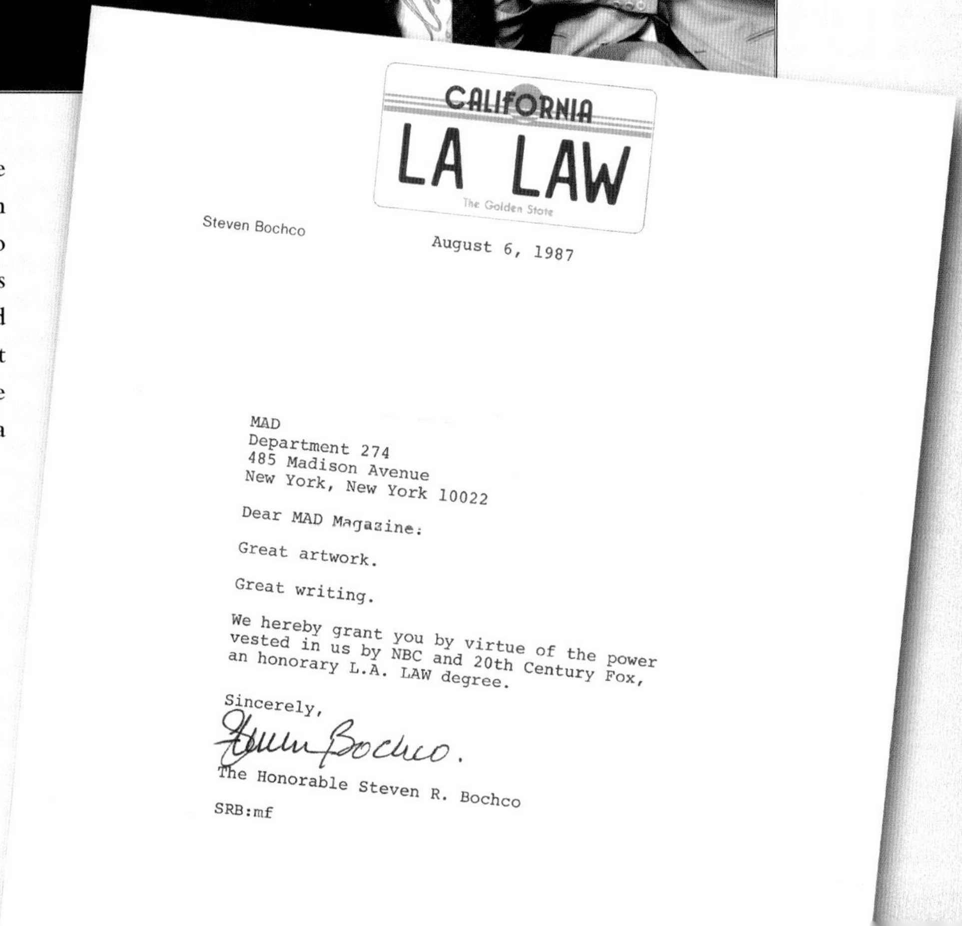

CALIFORNIA
LA LAW
The Golden State

Steven Bochco

August 6, 1987

MAD
Department 274
485 Madison Avenue
New York, New York 10022

Dear MAD Magazine:

Great artwork.

Great writing.

We hereby grant you by virtue of the power vested in us by NBC and 20th Century Fox, an honorary L.A. LAW degree.

Sincerely,

Steven Bochco.

The Honorable Steven R. Bochco

SRB:mf

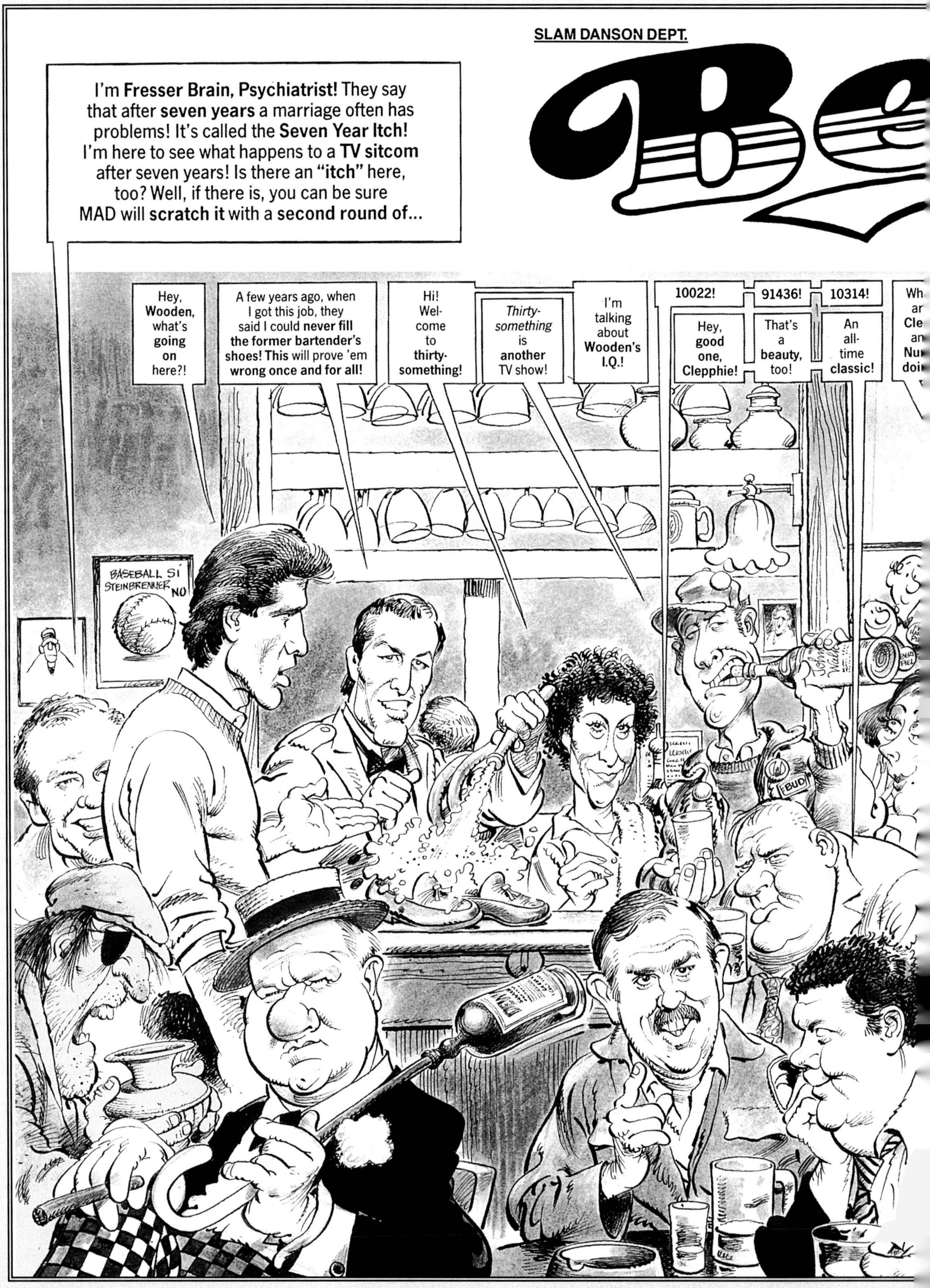
SLAM DANSON DEPT.
I'm Fresser Brain, Psychiatrist! They say that after seven years a marriage often has problems! It's called the Seven Year Itch! I'm here to see what happens to a TV sitcom after seven years! Is there an "itch" here, too? Well, if there is, you can be sure MAD will scratch it with a second round of...
Hey, Wooden, what's going on here?!
A few years ago, when I got this job, they said I could never fill the former bartender's shoes! This will prove 'em wrong once and for all!
Hi! Wel-come to thirty-something!
Thirty-something is another TV show!
I'm talking about Wooden's I.Q.!
10022!
Hey, good one, Clepphie!
91436!
That's a beauty, too!
10314!
An all-time classic!
BASEBALL SI
STEINBRENNER NO
BUD

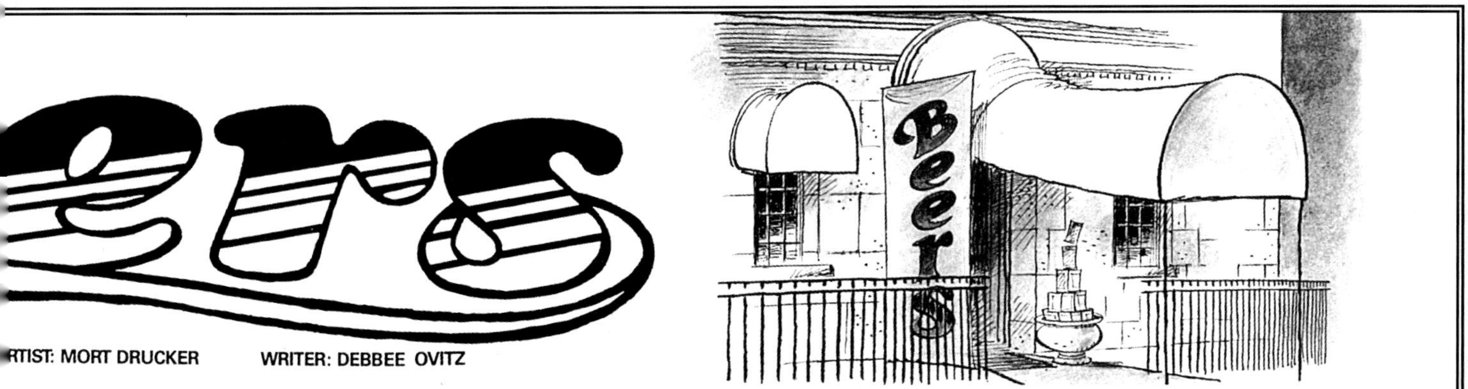
ers
Beers
RTIST: MORT DRUCKER
WRITER: DEBBEE OVITZ

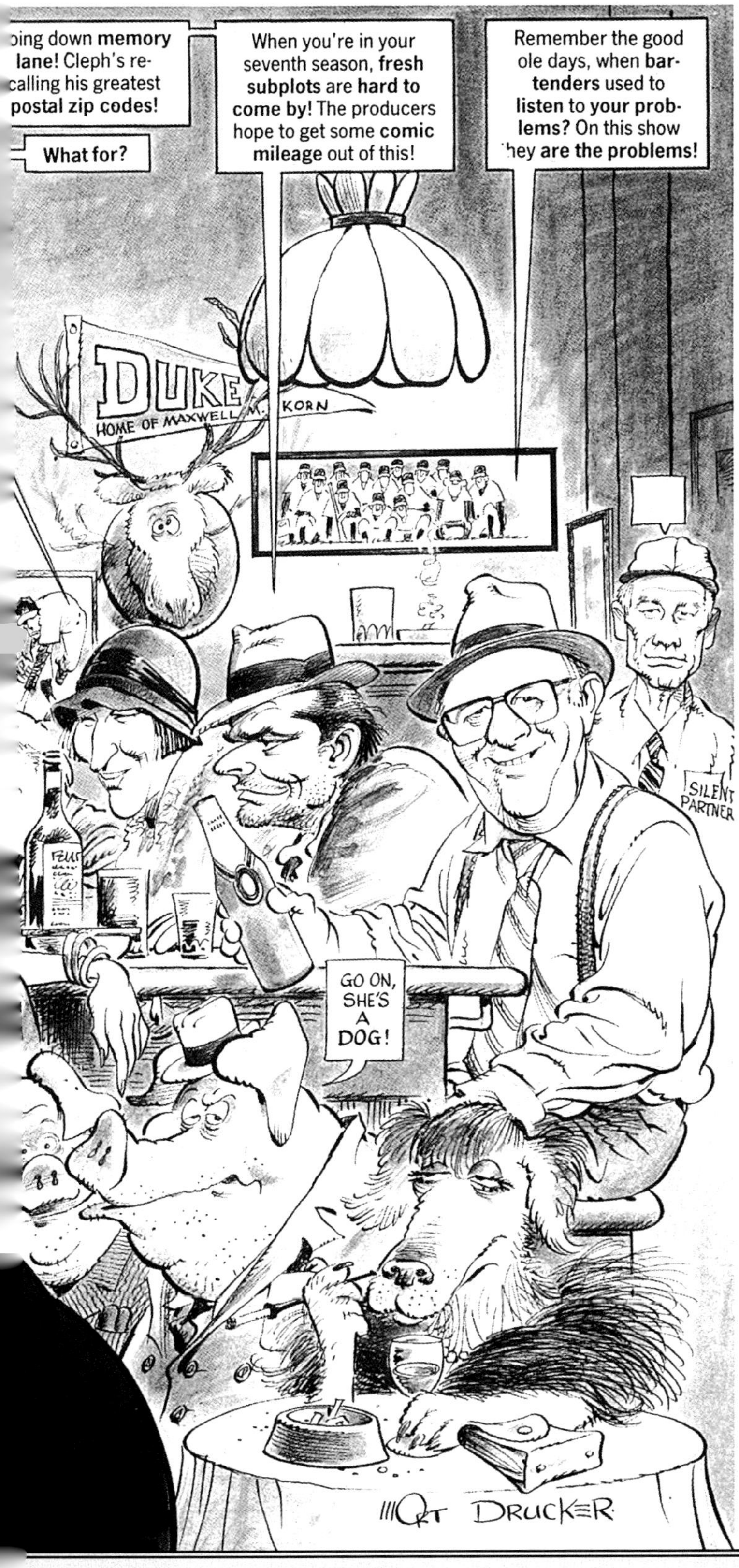
oing down memory lane! Cleph's re-calling his greatest postal zip codes!
What for?
When you're in your seventh season, fresh subplots are hard to come by! The producers hope to get some comic mileage out of this!
Remember the good ole days, when bar-tenders used to listen to your prob-lems? On this show 'hey are the problems!
DUKE
HOME OF MAXWELL M. KORN
SILENT PARTNER
GO ON, SHE'S A DOG!
MORT DRUCKER

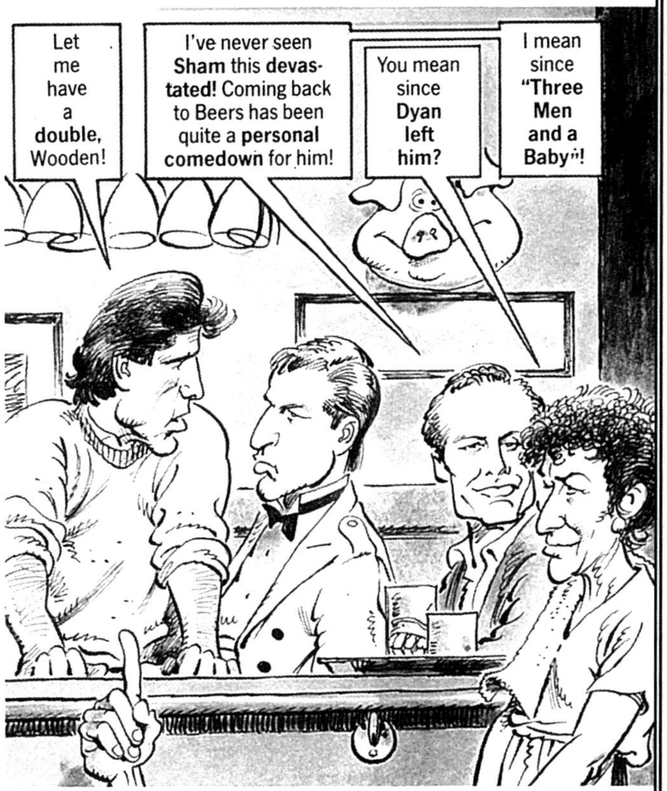
Let me have a double, Wooden!
I've never seen Sham this devas-tated! Coming back to Beers has been quite a personal comedown for him!
You mean since Dyan left him?
I mean since "Three Men and a Baby"!

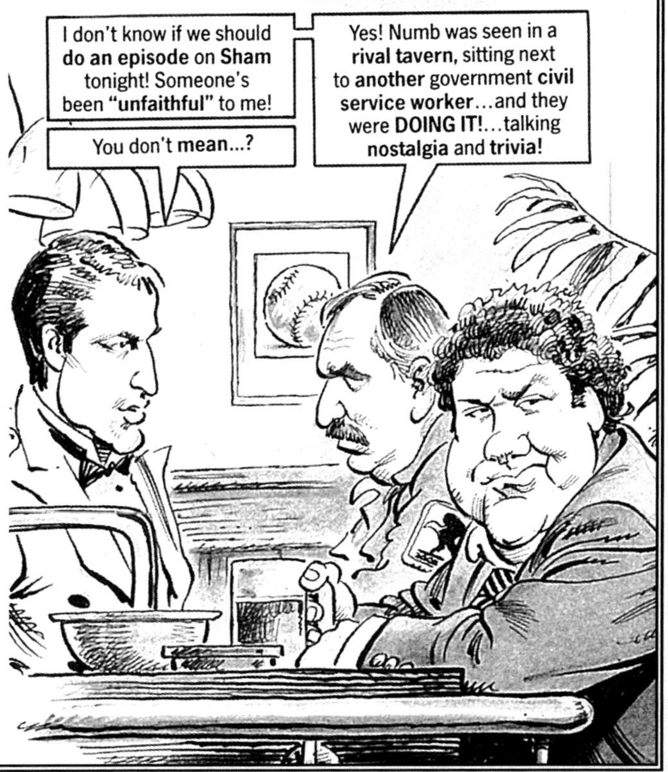
I don't know if we should do an episode on Sham tonight! Someone's been "unfaithful" to me!
You don't mean...?
Yes! Numb was seen in a rival tavern, sitting next to another government civil service worker...and they were DOING IT!...talking nostalgia and trivia!

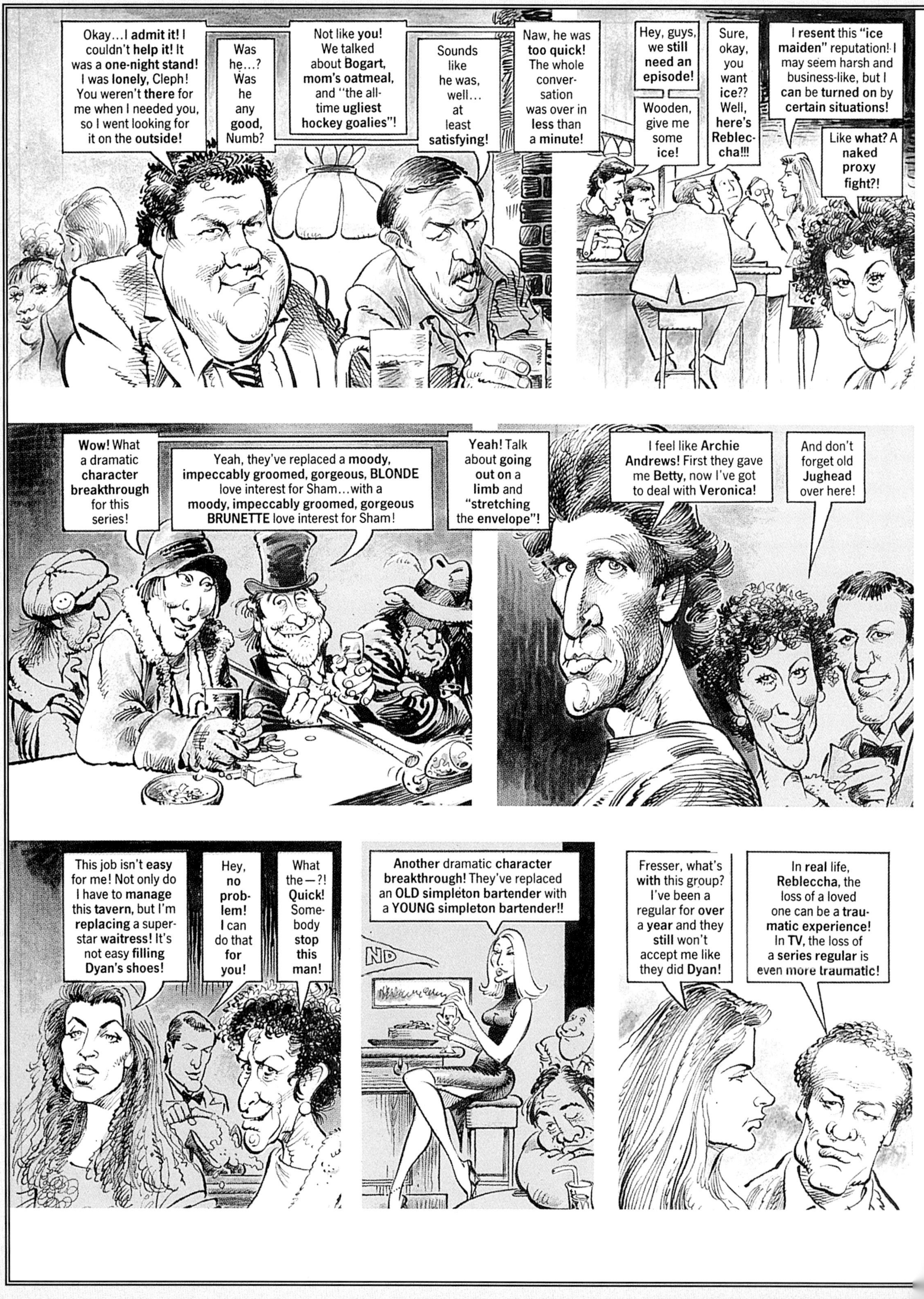
Okay…I admit it! I couldn't help it! It was a one-night stand! I was lonely, Cleph! You weren't there for me when I needed you, so I went looking for it on the outside!
Was he…? Was he any good, Numb?
Not like you! We talked about Bogart, mom's oatmeal, and "the all-time ugliest hockey goalies"!
Sounds like he was, well… at least satisfying!
Naw, he was too quick! The whole conversation was over in less than a minute!
Hey, guys, we still need an episode!
Wooden, give me some ice!
Sure, okay, you want ice?? Well, here's Reblec-cha!!!
I resent this "ice maiden" reputation! I may seem harsh and business-like, but I can be turned on by certain situations!
Like what? A naked proxy fight?!
Wow! What a dramatic character breakthrough for this series!
Yeah, they've replaced a moody, impeccably groomed, gorgeous, BLONDE love interest for Sham…with a moody, impeccably groomed, gorgeous BRUNETTE love interest for Sham!
Yeah! Talk about going out on a limb and "stretching the envelope"!
I feel like Archie Andrews! First they gave me Betty, now I've got to deal with Veronica!
And don't forget old Jughead over here!
This job isn't easy for me! Not only do I have to manage this tavern, but I'm replacing a superstar waitress! It's not easy filling Dyan's shoes!
Hey, no problem! I can do that for you!
What the—?! Quick! Somebody stop this man!
Another dramatic character breakthrough! They've replaced an OLD simpleton bartender with a YOUNG simpleton bartender!!
ND
Fresser, what's with this group? I've been a regular for over a year and they still won't accept me like they did Dyan!
In real life, Reblecca, the loss of a loved one can be a traumatic experience! In TV, the loss of a series regular is even more traumatic!

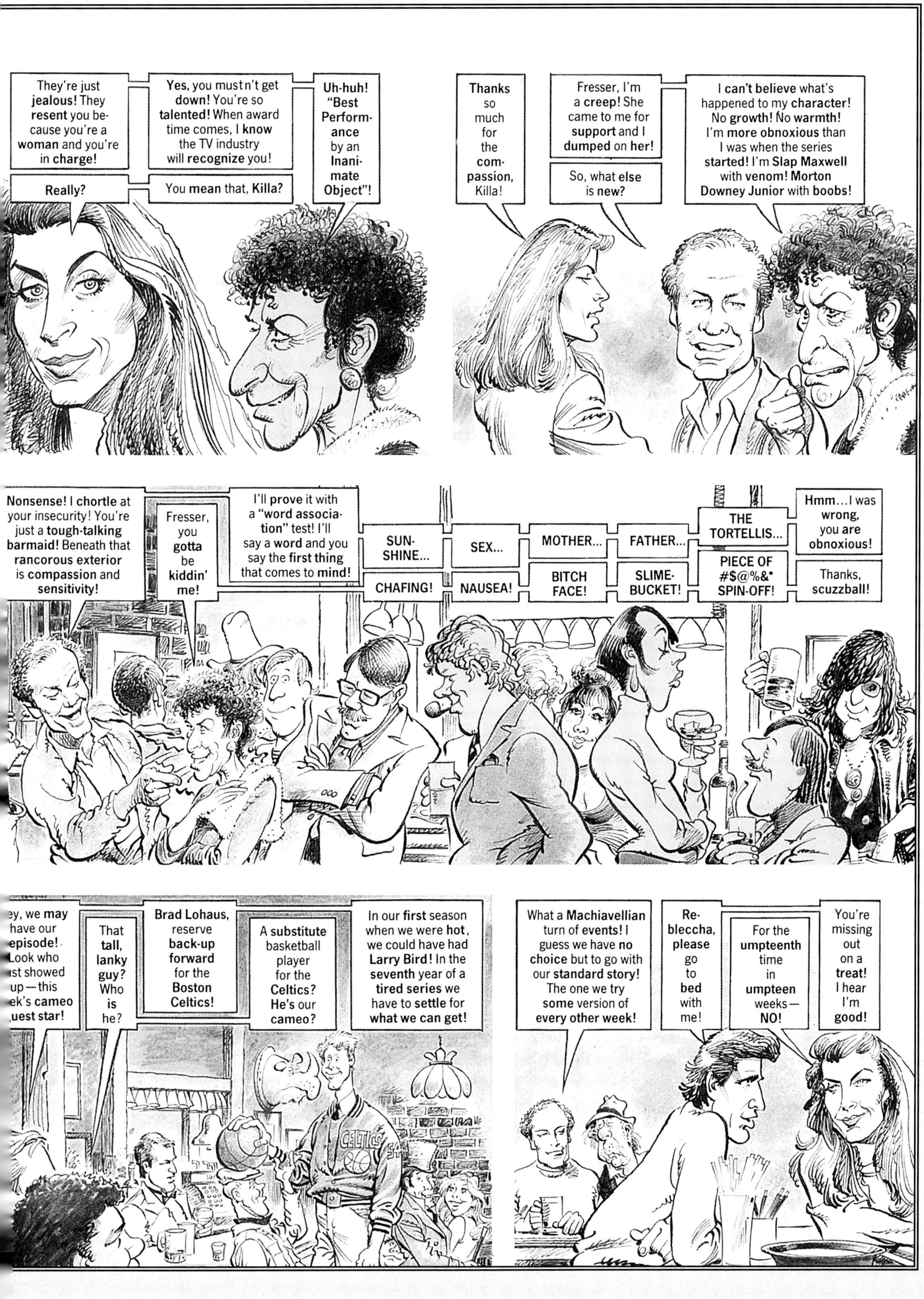
They're just jealous! They resent you because you're a woman and you're in charge!
Really?
Yes, you mustn't get down! You're so talented! When award time comes, I know the TV industry will recognize you!
You mean that, Killa?
Uh-huh! "Best Performance by an Inanimate Object"!
Thanks so much for the compassion, Killa!
Fresser, I'm a creep! She came to me for support and I dumped on her!
So, what else is new?
I can't believe what's happened to my character! No growth! No warmth! I'm more obnoxious than I was when the series started! I'm Slap Maxwell with venom! Morton Downey Junior with boobs!
Nonsense! I chortle at your insecurity! You're just a tough-talking barmaid! Beneath that rancorous exterior is compassion and sensitivity!
Fresser, you gotta be kiddin' me!
I'll prove it with a "word association" test! I'll say a word and you say the first thing that comes to mind!
SUNSHINE...
CHAFING!
SEX...
NAUSEA!
MOTHER...
BITCH FACE!
FATHER...
SLIME-BUCKET!
THE TORTELLIS...
PIECE OF #$@%&* SPIN-OFF!
Hmm...I was wrong, you are obnoxious!
Thanks, scuzzball!
ey, we may have our episode! Look who ist showed up—this ek's cameo uest star!
That tall, lanky guy? Who is he?
Brad Lohaus, reserve back-up forward for the Boston Celtics!
A substitute basketball player for the Celtics? He's our cameo?
In our first season when we were hot, we could have had Larry Bird! In the seventh year of a tired series we have to settle for what we can get!
What a Machiavellian turn of events! I guess we have no choice but to go with our standard story! The one we try some version of every other week!
Rebleccha, please go to bed with me!
For the umpteenth time in umpteen weeks—NO!
You're missing out on a treat! I hear I'm good!

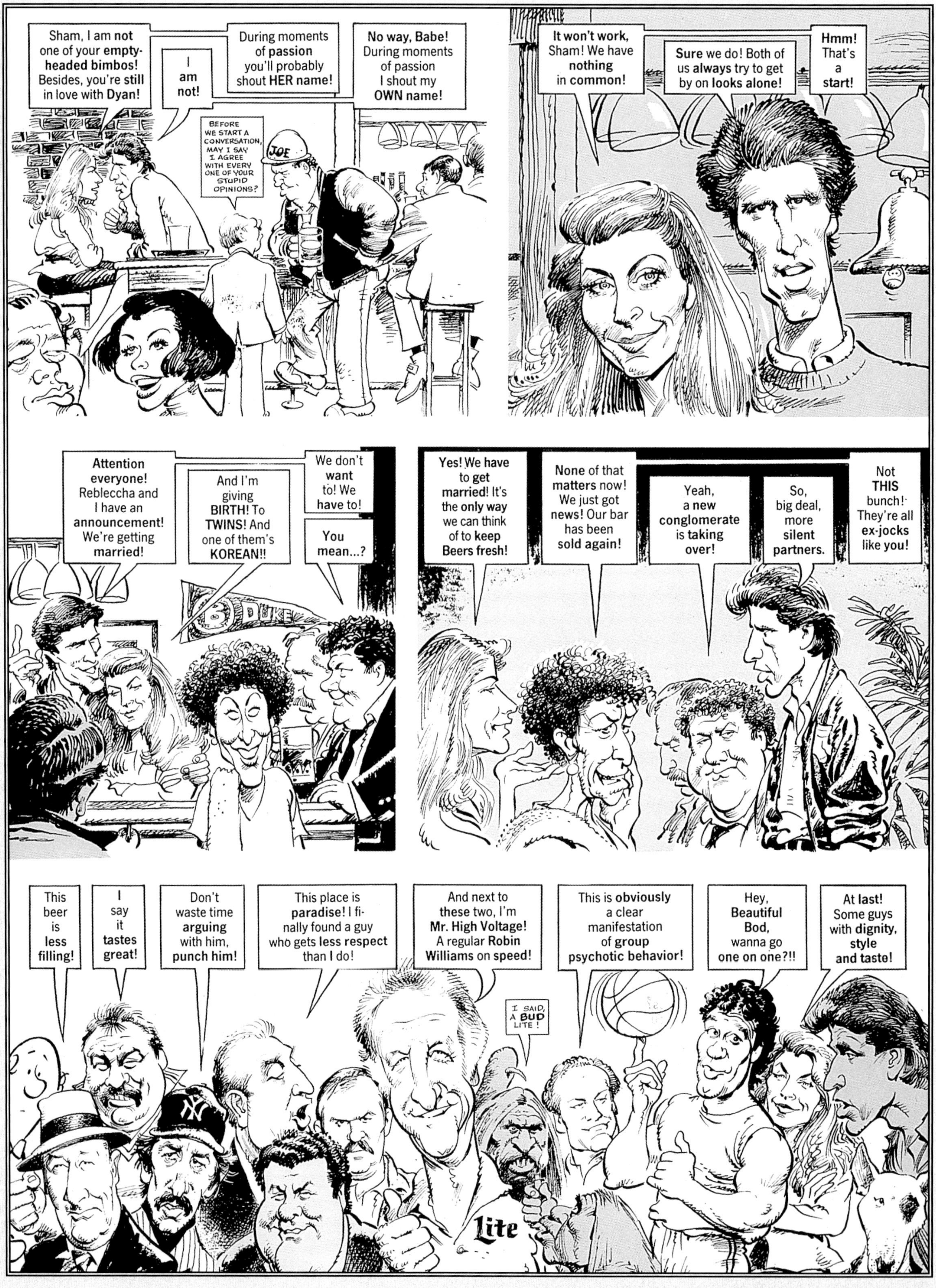
Sham, I am **not** one of your **empty-headed bimbos!** Besides, you're **still** in love with **Dyan!**
I **am not!**
During moments of **passion** you'll probably shout **HER name!**
No way, Babe! During moments of passion I shout my **OWN name!**
JOE
BEFORE WE START A CONVERSATION, MAY I SAY I AGREE WITH EVERY ONE OF YOUR STUPID OPINIONS?
It won't work, Sham! We have **nothing** in **common!**
Sure we do! Both of us **always** try to get by on **looks alone!**
Hmm! That's a **start!**
Attention everyone! Reblecchа and I have an **announcement!** We're getting **married!**
And I'm giving **BIRTH!** To **TWINS!** And one of them's **KOREAN!!**
We don't **want** to! We **have** to!
You mean...?
DUKE
Yes! We have to **get married!** It's the **only way** we can think of to **keep Beers fresh!**
None of that **matters** now! We just got **news!** Our bar has been **sold again!**
Yeah, a **new conglomerate** is **taking over!**
So, big deal, more **silent partners.**
Not **THIS** bunch! They're all **ex-jocks** like you!
This beer is **less filling!**
I say it **tastes great!**
Don't waste time **arguing** with him, **punch him!**
This place is **paradise!** I finally found a guy who gets **less respect** than I do!
And next to **these two,** I'm **Mr. High Voltage!** A regular **Robin Williams** on **speed!**
I SAID, A **BUD** LITE!
This is **obviously** a clear manifestation of **group psychotic behavior!**
Hey, **Beautiful Bod,** wanna go **one on one?!!**
At **last!** Some guys with **dignity, style** and **taste!**
Lite

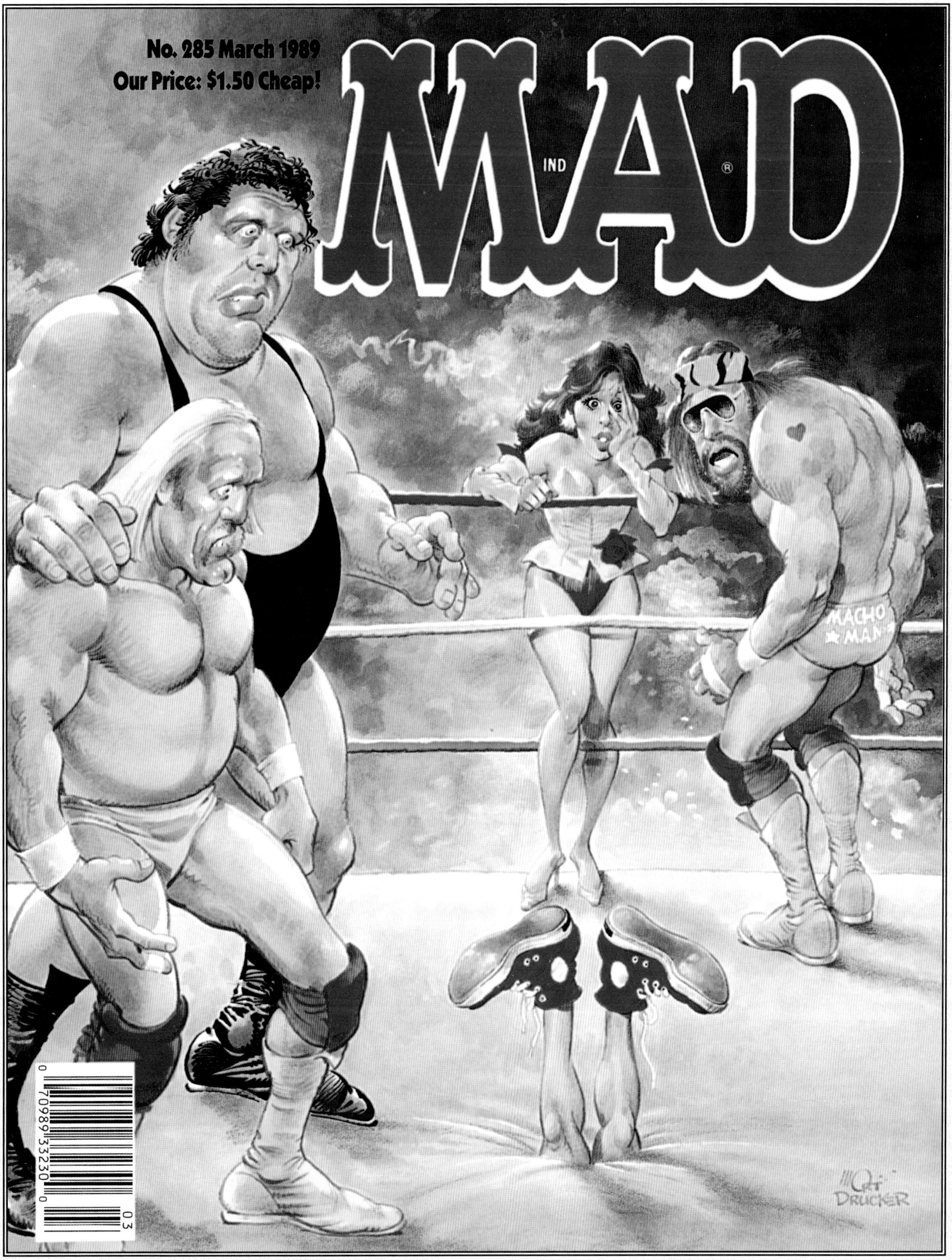
No. 285 March 1989
Our Price: $1.50 Cheap!
MAD
IND
MACHO MAN
Mort DRUCKER

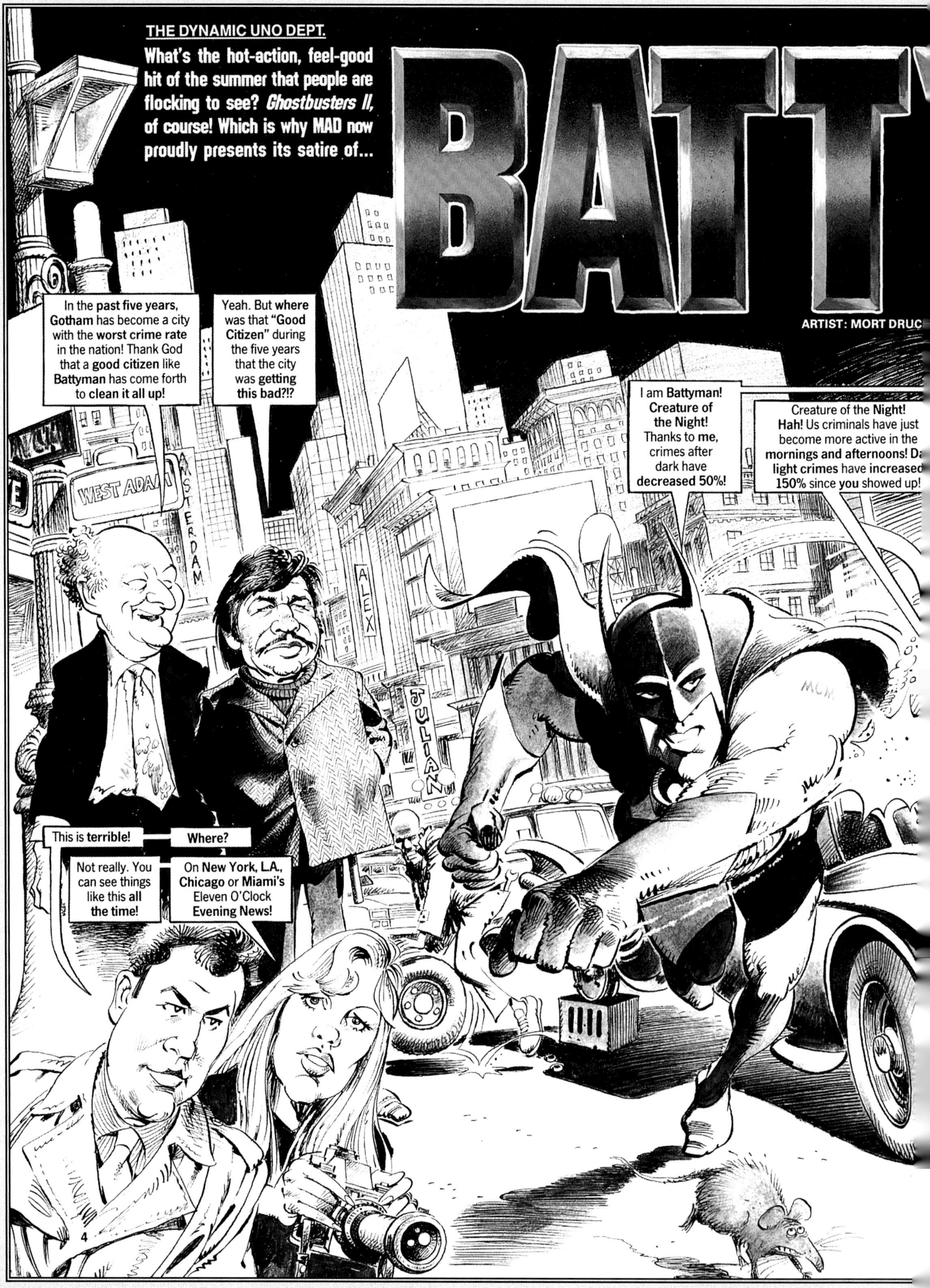
THE DYNAMIC UNO DEPT.
What's the hot-action, feel-good hit of the summer that people are flocking to see? *Ghostbusters II,* of course! Which is why MAD now proudly presents its satire of...
BATT
ARTIST: MORT DRUC
In the past five years, Gotham has become a city with the worst crime rate in the nation! Thank God that a good citizen like Battyman has come forth to clean it all up!
Yeah. But where was that "Good Citizen" during the five years that the city was getting this bad?!?
I am Battyman! Creature of the Night! Thanks to me, crimes after dark have decreased 50%!
Creature of the Night! Hah! Us criminals have just become more active in the mornings and afternoons! Da light crimes have increased 150% since you showed up!
WEST ADAM
AMSTERDAM
ALEX
JULIAN
This is terrible!
Where?
Not really. You can see things like this all the time!
On New York, L.A., Chicago or Miami's Eleven O'Clock Evening News!

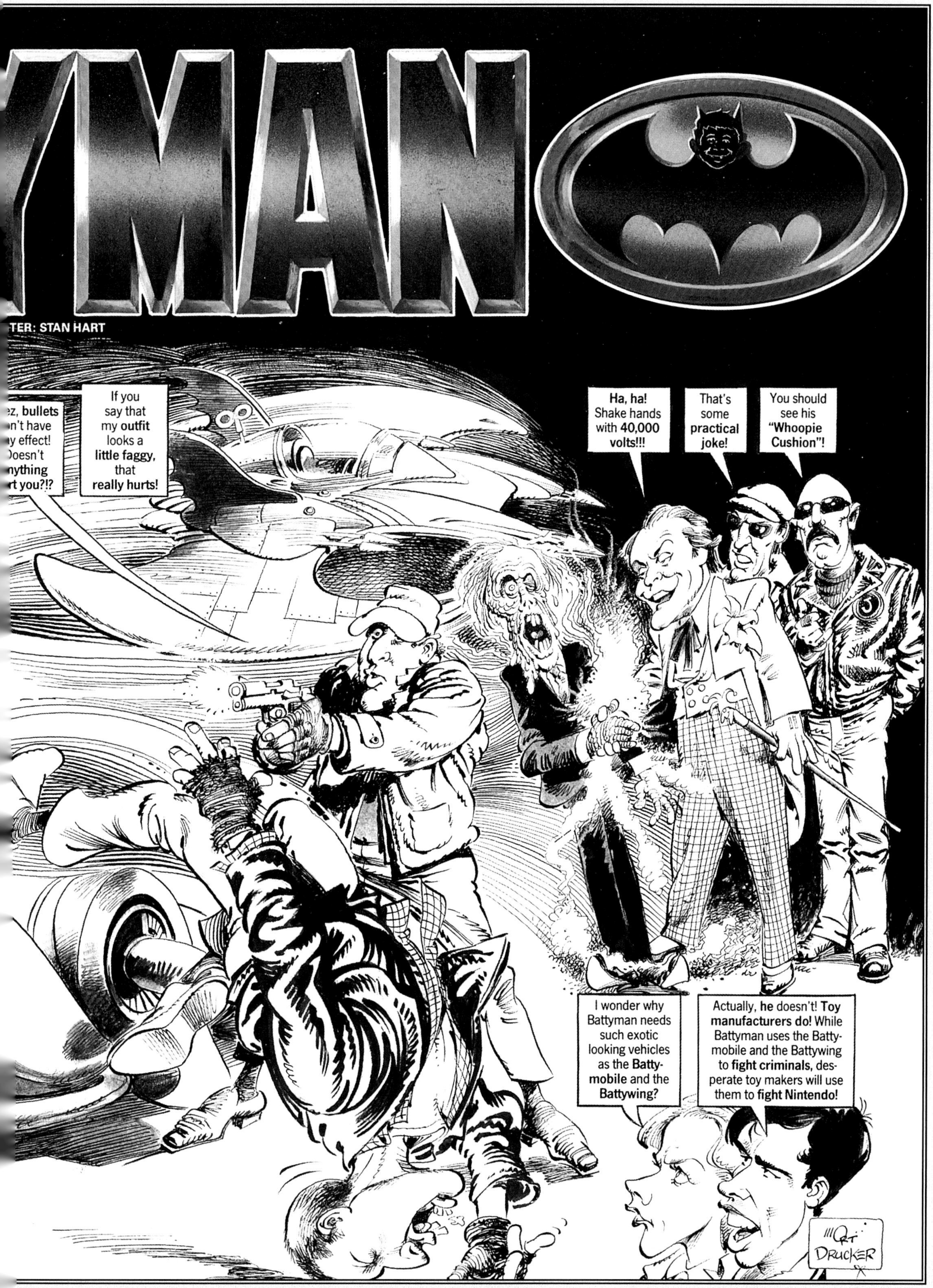
YMAN
TER: STAN HART
ez, bullets n't have y effect! Doesn't nything rt you?!?
If you say that my outfit looks a little faggy, that really hurts!
Ha, ha! Shake hands with 40,000 volts!!!
That's some practical joke!
You should see his "Whoopie Cushion"!
I wonder why Battyman needs such exotic looking vehicles as the Batty-mobile and the Battywing?
Actually, he doesn't! Toy manufacturers do! While Battyman uses the Batty-mobile and the Battywing to fight criminals, desperate toy makers will use them to fight Nintendo!
MORT DRUCKER

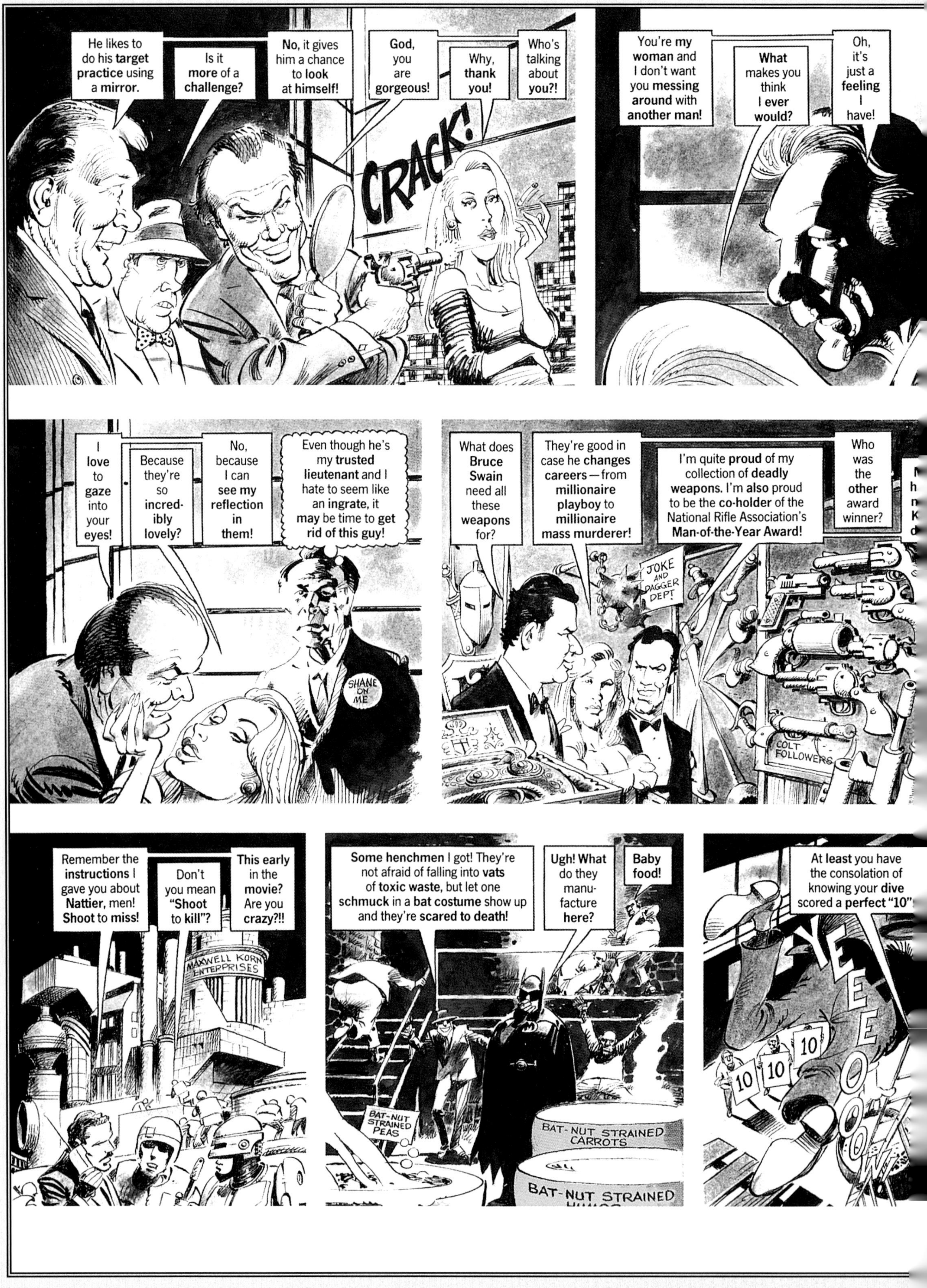
He likes to do his target practice using a mirror.
Is it more of a challenge?
No, it gives him a chance to look at himself!
God, you are gorgeous!
Why, thank you!
Who's talking about you?!
CRACK!
You're my woman and I don't want you messing around with another man!
What makes you think I ever would?
Oh, it's just a feeling I have!
I love to gaze into your eyes!
Because they're so incred-ibly lovely?
No, because I can see my reflection in them!
Even though he's my trusted lieutenant and I hate to seem like an ingrate, it may be time to get rid of this guy!
SHANE ON ME
What does Bruce Swain need all these weapons for?
They're good in case he changes careers — from millionaire playboy to millionaire mass murderer!
I'm quite proud of my collection of deadly weapons. I'm also proud to be the co-holder of the National Rifle Association's Man-of-the-Year Award!
Who was the other award winner?
JOKE AND DAGGER DEPT
COLT FOLLOWERS
Remember the instructions I gave you about Nattier, men! Shoot to miss!
Don't you mean "Shoot to kill"?
This early in the movie? Are you crazy?!!
MAXWELL KORN ENTERPRISES
Some henchmen I got! They're not afraid of falling into vats of toxic waste, but let one schmuck in a bat costume show up and they're scared to death!
Ugh! What do they manu-facture here?
Baby food!
BAT-NUT STRAINED PEAS
BAT-NUT STRAINED CARROTS
BAT-NUT STRAINED
At least you have the consolation of knowing your dive scored a perfect "10"!
10
10
10
YEEEOOOW!

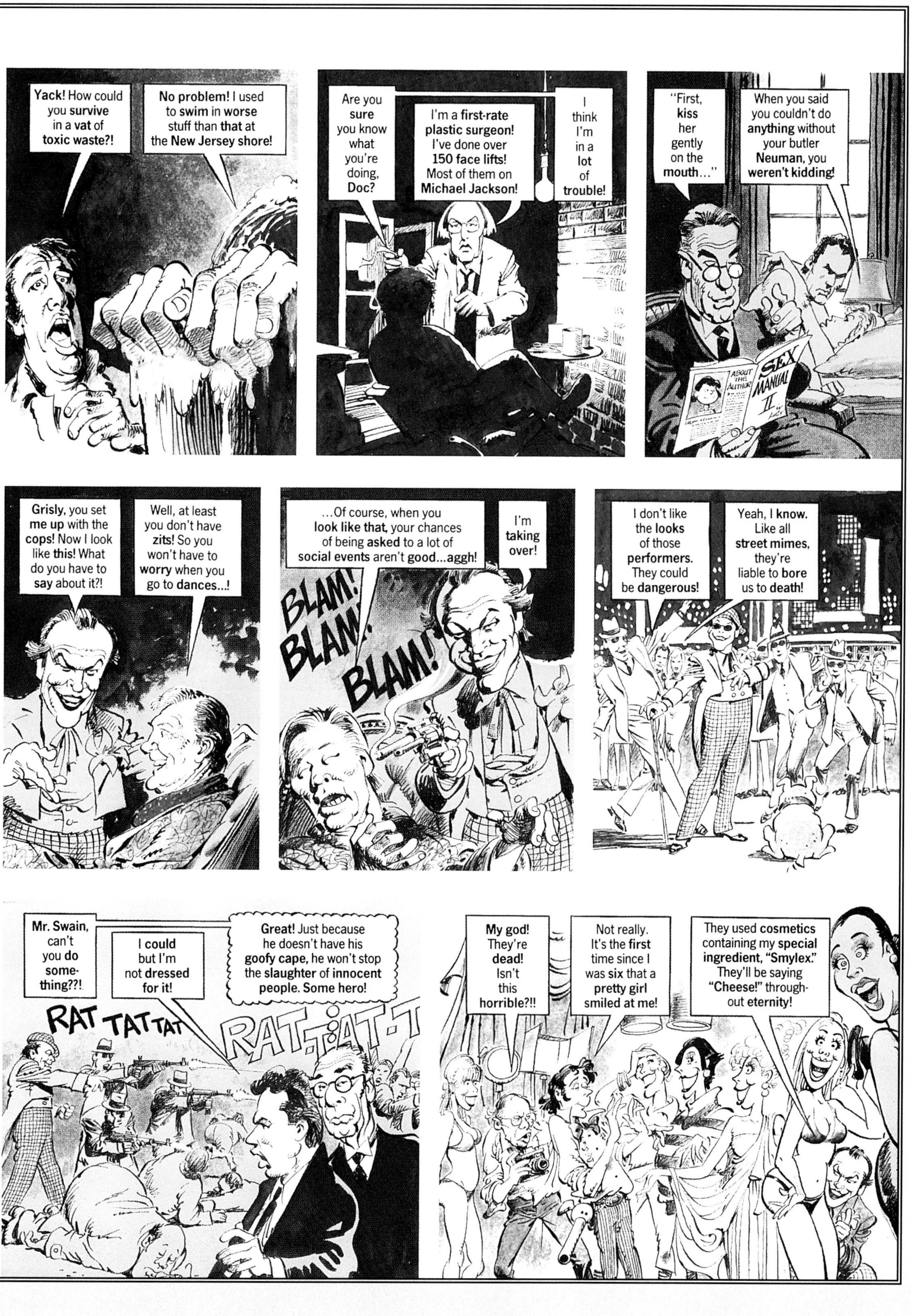
Yack! How could you survive in a vat of toxic waste?!
No problem! I used to swim in worse stuff than that at the New Jersey shore!
Are you sure you know what you're doing, Doc?
I'm a first-rate plastic surgeon! I've done over 150 face lifts! Most of them on Michael Jackson!
I think I'm in a lot of trouble!
"First, kiss her gently on the mouth..."
When you said you couldn't do anything without your butler Neuman, you weren't kidding!
SEX MANUAL II
ABOUT THE AUTHOR
Grisly, you set me up with the cops! Now I look like this! What do you have to say about it?!
Well, at least you don't have zits! So you won't have to worry when you go to dances...!
...Of course, when you look like that, your chances of being asked to a lot of social events aren't good...aggh!
I'm taking over!
BLAM! BLAM! BLAM!
I don't like the looks of those performers. They could be dangerous!
Yeah, I know. Like all street mimes, they're liable to bore us to death!
Mr. Swain, can't you do some-thing??!
I could but I'm not dressed for it!
Great! Just because he doesn't have his goofy cape, he won't stop the slaughter of innocent people. Some hero!
RAT TAT TAT
RAT-TAT-TAT-T
My god! They're dead! Isn't this horrible?!!
Not really. It's the first time since I was six that a pretty girl smiled at me!
They used cosmetics containing my special ingredient, "Smylex." They'll be saying "Cheese!" through-out eternity!

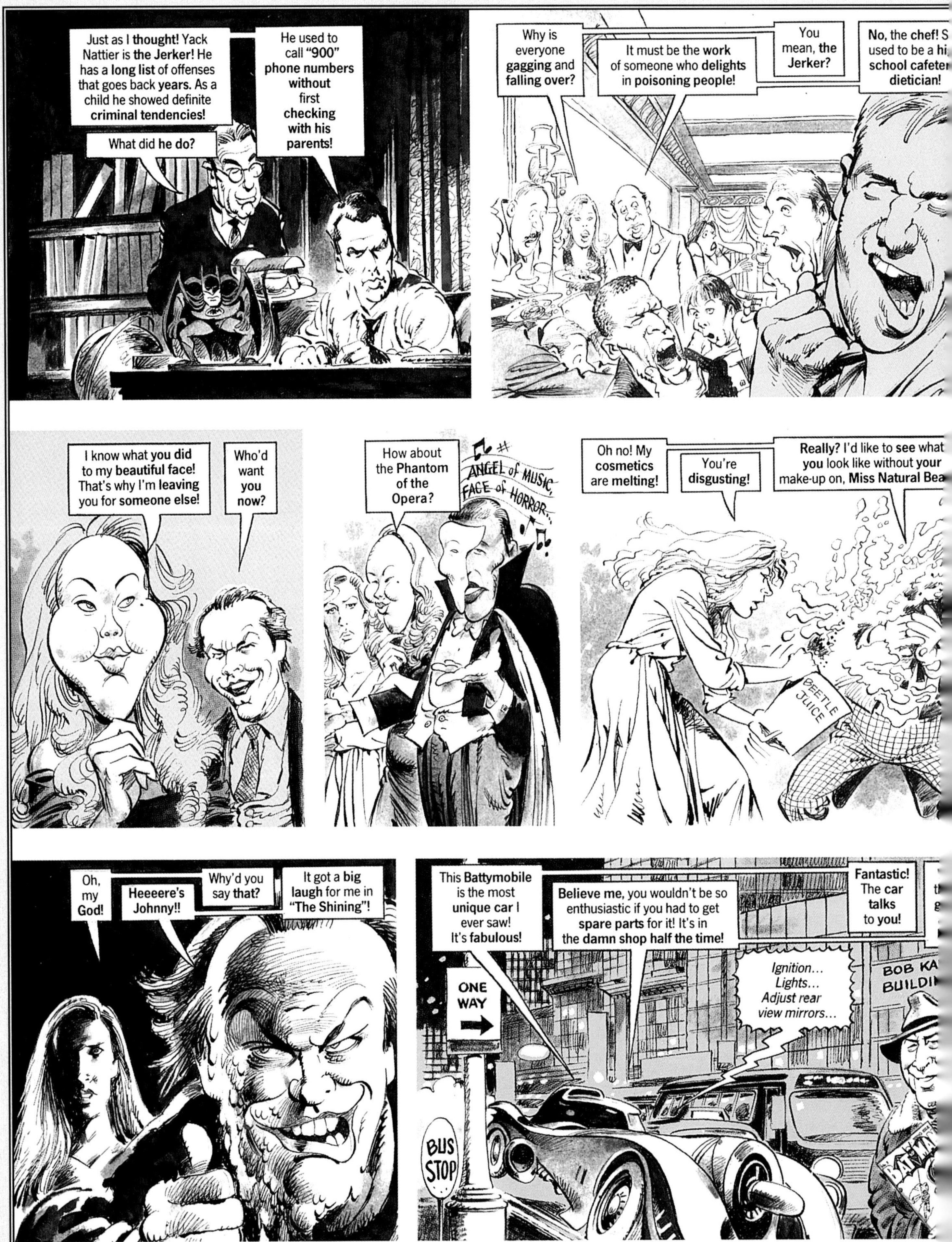
Just as I thought! Yack Nattier is the Jerker! He has a long list of offenses that goes back years. As a child he showed definite criminal tendencies!
What did he do?
He used to call "900" phone numbers without first checking with his parents!
Why is everyone gagging and falling over?
It must be the work of someone who delights in poisoning people!
You mean, the Jerker?
No, the chef! S
used to be a hi
school cafeter
dietician!
I know what you did to my beautiful face! That's why I'm leaving you for someone else!
Who'd want you now?
How about the Phantom of the Opera?
ANGEL of MUSIC, FACE of HORROR...
Oh no! My cosmetics are melting!
You're disgusting!
Really? I'd like to see what you look like without your make-up on, Miss Natural Bea
BEETLE JUICE
Oh, my God!
Heeeere's Johnny!!
Why'd you say that?
It got a big laugh for me in "The Shining"!
This Battymobile is the most unique car I ever saw! It's fabulous!
Believe me, you wouldn't be so enthusiastic if you had to get spare parts for it! It's in the damn shop half the time!
Fantastic! The car talks to you!
ONE WAY
Ignition... Lights... Adjust rear view mirrors...
BOB KA
BUILDI
BUS STOP

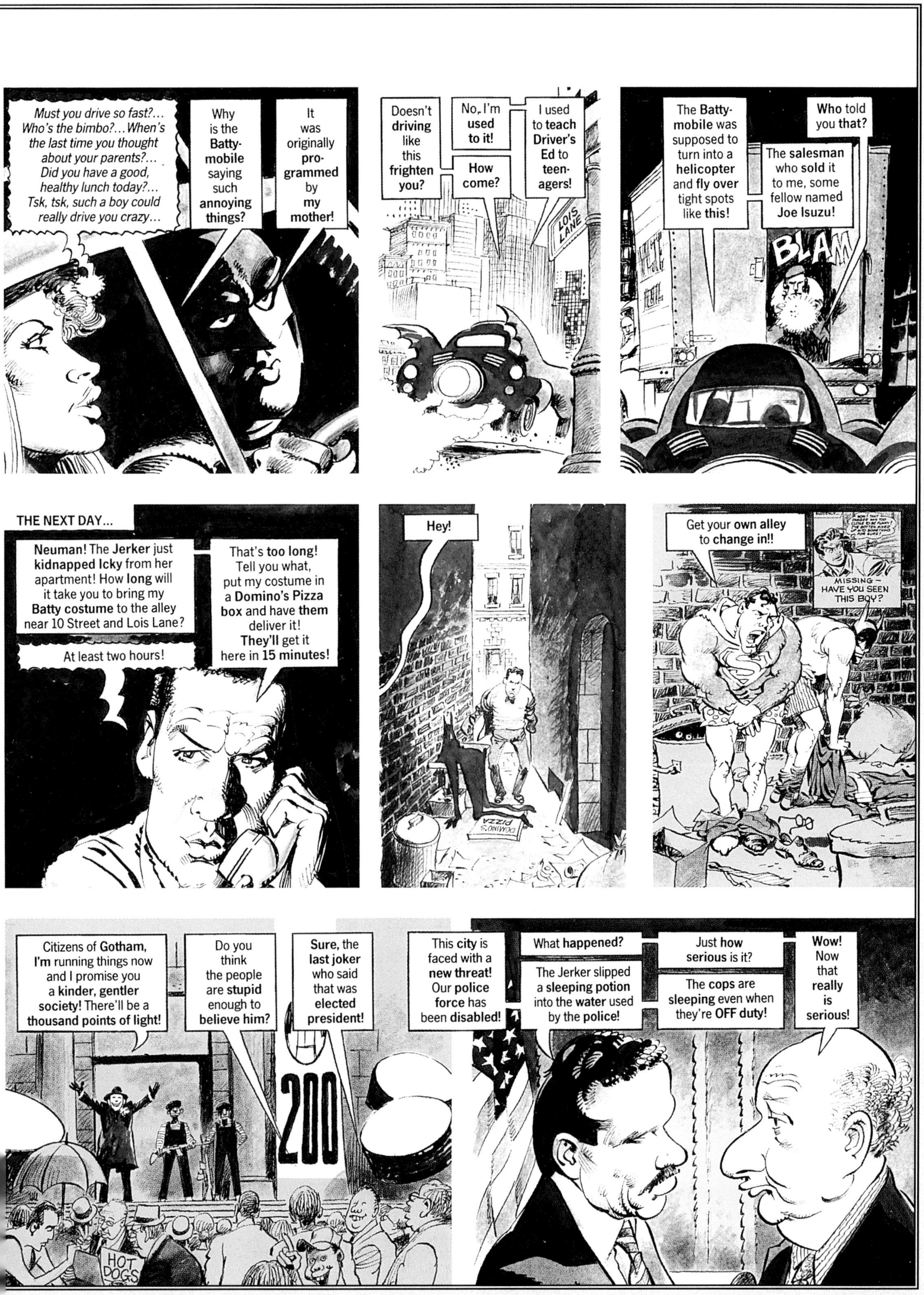
Must you drive so fast?... Who's the bimbo?... When's the last time you thought about your parents?... Did you have a good, healthy lunch today?... Tsk, tsk, such a boy could really drive you crazy...
Why is the Batty-mobile saying such annoying things?
It was originally pro-grammed by my mother!
Doesn't driving like this frighten you?
No, I'm used to it!
How come?
I used to teach Driver's Ed to teen-agers!
LOIS LANE
The Batty-mobile was supposed to turn into a helicopter and fly over tight spots like this!
Who told you that?
The salesman who sold it to me, some fellow named Joe Isuzu!
BLAM
THE NEXT DAY...
Neuman! The Jerker just kidnapped Icky from her apartment! How long will it take you to bring my Batty costume to the alley near 10 Street and Lois Lane?
At least two hours!
That's too long! Tell you what, put my costume in a Domino's Pizza box and have them deliver it! They'll get it here in 15 minutes!
Hey!
DOMINO'S PIZZA
Get your own alley to change in!!
MISSING – HAVE YOU SEEN THIS BOY?
Citizens of Gotham, I'm running things now and I promise you a kinder, gentler society! There'll be a thousand points of light!
Do you think the people are stupid enough to believe him?
Sure, the last joker who said that was elected president!
200
HOT DOGS
This city is faced with a new threat! Our police force has been disabled!
What happened?
The Jerker slipped a sleeping potion into the water used by the police!
Just how serious is it?
The cops are sleeping even when they're OFF duty!
Wow! Now that really is serious!

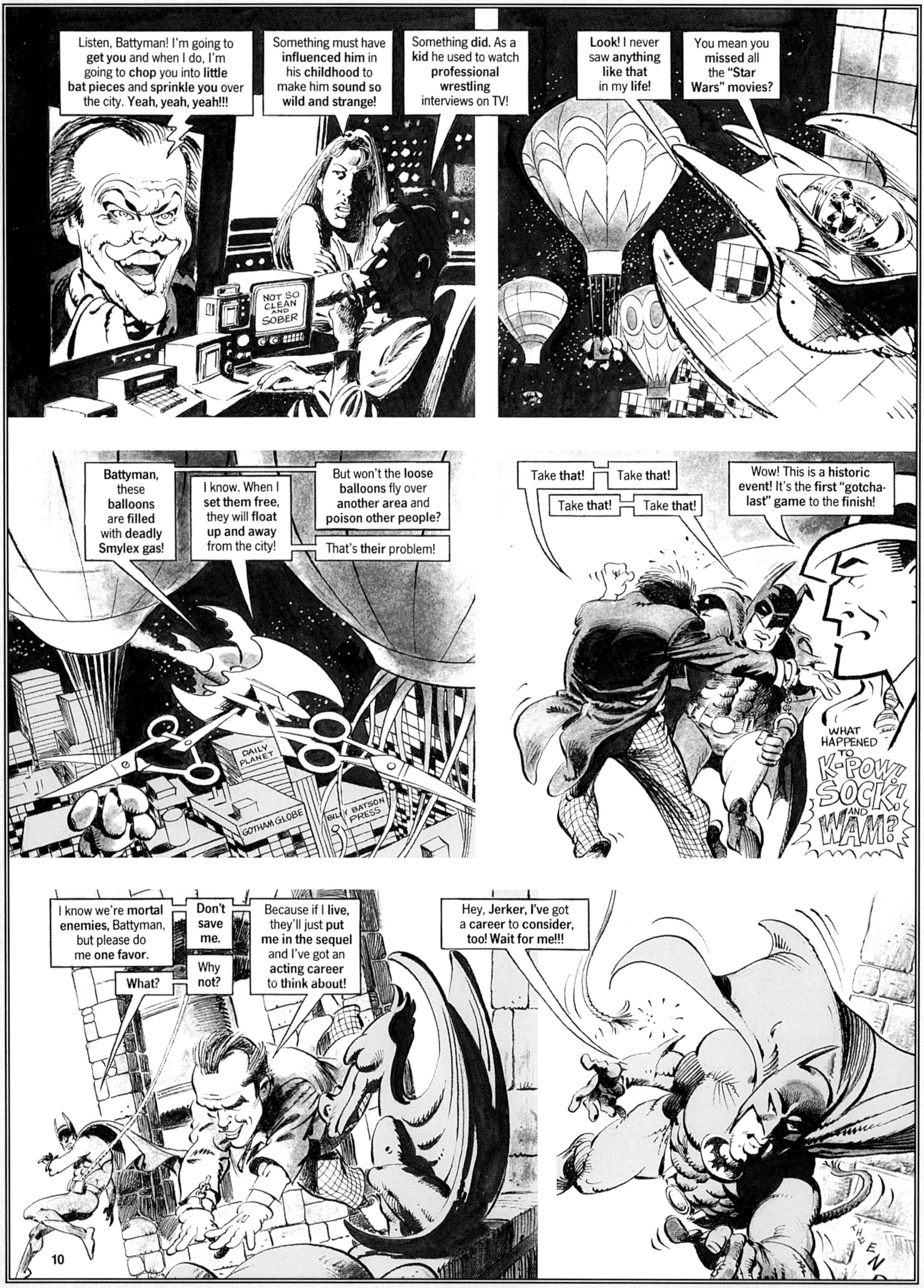

Listen, Battyman! I'm going to get you and when I do, I'm going to chop you into little bat pieces and sprinkle you over the city. Yeah, yeah, yeah!!!
NOT SO CLEAN AND SOBER
Something must have influenced him in his childhood to make him sound so wild and strange!
Something did. As a kid he used to watch professional wrestling interviews on TV!
Look! I never saw anything like that in my life!
You mean you missed all the "Star Wars" movies?
Battyman, these balloons are filled with deadly Smylex gas!
I know. When I set them free, they will float up and away from the city!
But won't the loose balloons fly over another area and poison other people?
That's their problem!
DAILY PLANET
GOTHAM GLOBE
BILLY BATSON PRESS
Take that!
Take that!
Take that!
Take that!
Wow! This is a historic event! It's the first "gotcha-last" game to the finish!
WHAT HAPPENED TO K-POW! SOCK! AND WAM?
I know we're mortal enemies, Battyman, but please do me one favor.
What?
Don't save me.
Why not?
Because if I live, they'll just put me in the sequel and I've got an acting career to think about!
10
Hey, Jerker, I've got a career to consider, too! Wait for me!!!
THE END

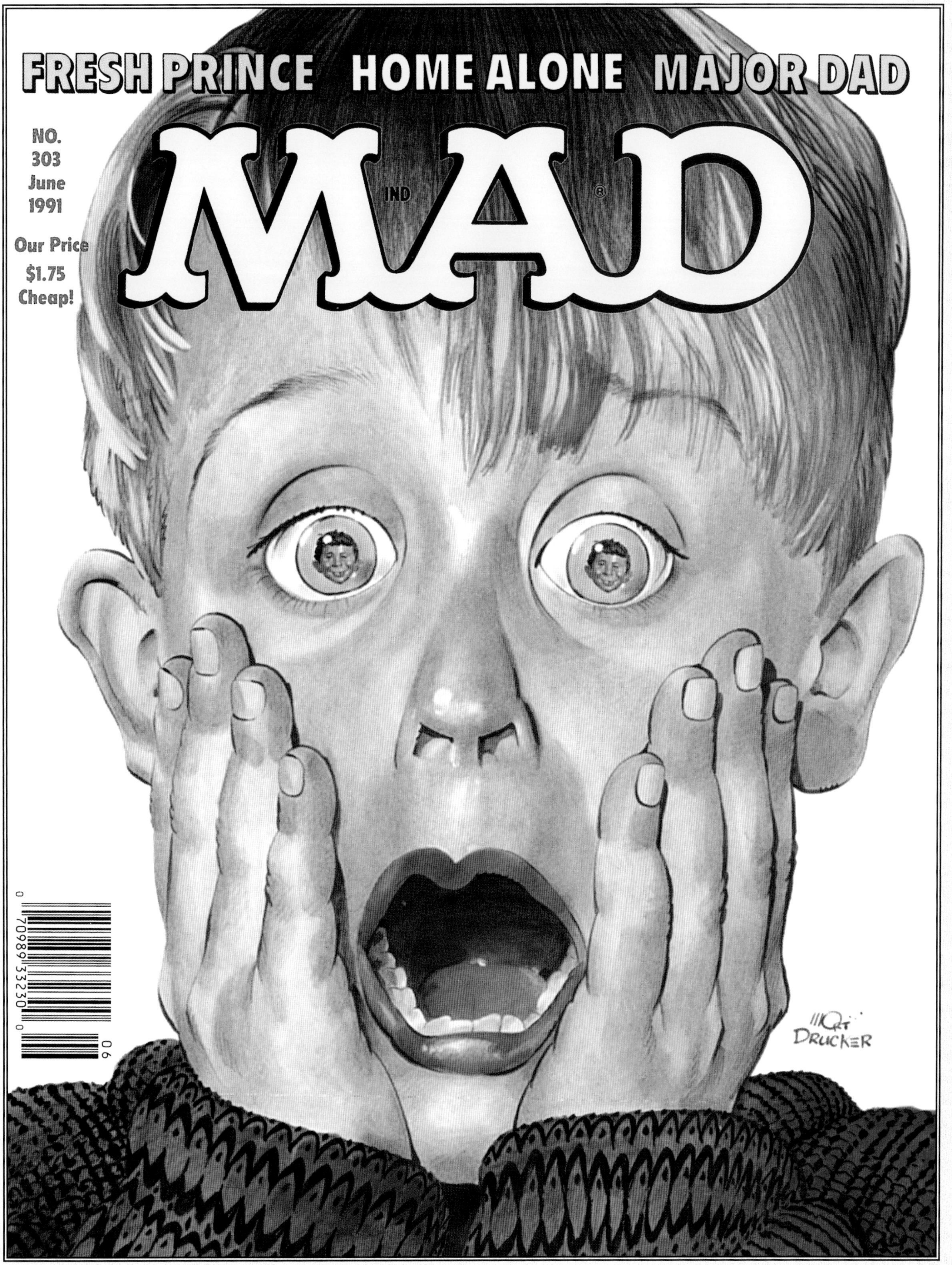
FRESH PRINCE HOME ALONE MAJOR DAD
NO. 303 June 1991
MAD
IND
Our Price $1.75 Cheap!
MORT DRUCKER

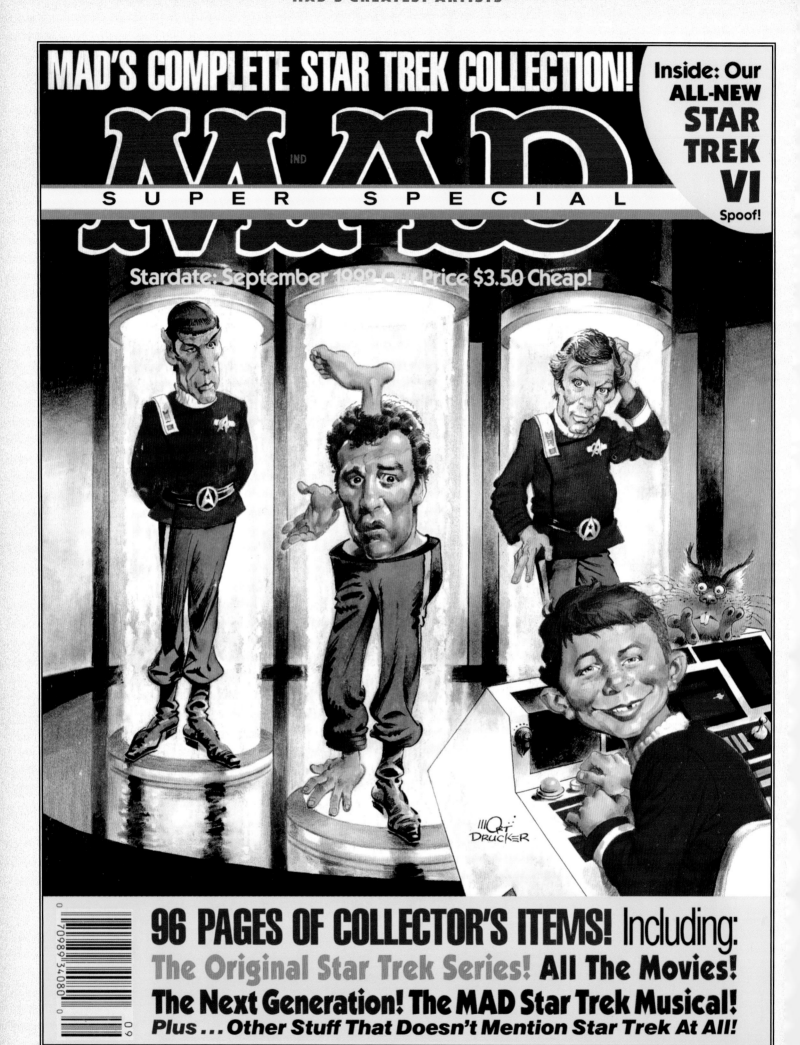

MAD'S COMPLETE STAR TREK COLLECTION!

Inside: Our ALL-NEW STAR TREK VI Spoof!

MAD

SUPER SPECIAL

Stardate: September 1992 .... Price $3.50 Cheap!

96 PAGES OF COLLECTOR'S ITEMS! Including:
The Original Star Trek Series! All The Movies!
The Next Generation! The MAD Star Trek Musical!
Plus ... Other Stuff That Doesn't Mention Star Trek At All!

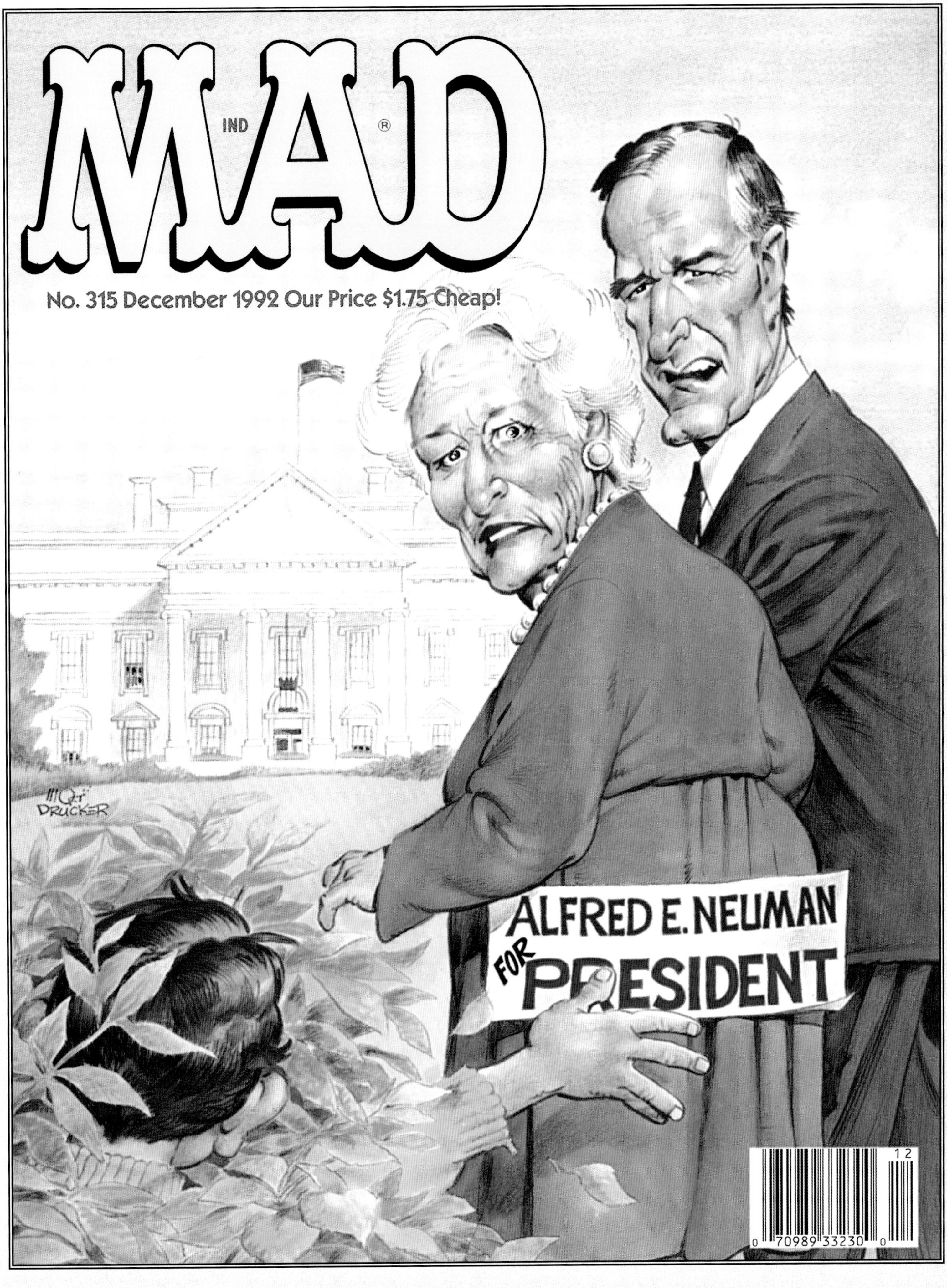
MAD
IND
No. 315 December 1992 Our Price $1.75 Cheap!
MORT DRUCKER
ALFRED E. NEUMAN
FOR PRESIDENT

SENDING UP TRIAL BUFFOONS DEPT.

In the criminal justice system, people are resented by two separate but equally offensive groups: the police who are frequently inept in their investigation of crimes, and the District Attorneys who procrastinate with the offenders! Here are their stories, told weekly in the gritty, giddy, totally shot in New York series. . .

LAW & DISORDER

ARTIST: MORT DRUCKER WRITER: DICK DEBARTOLO

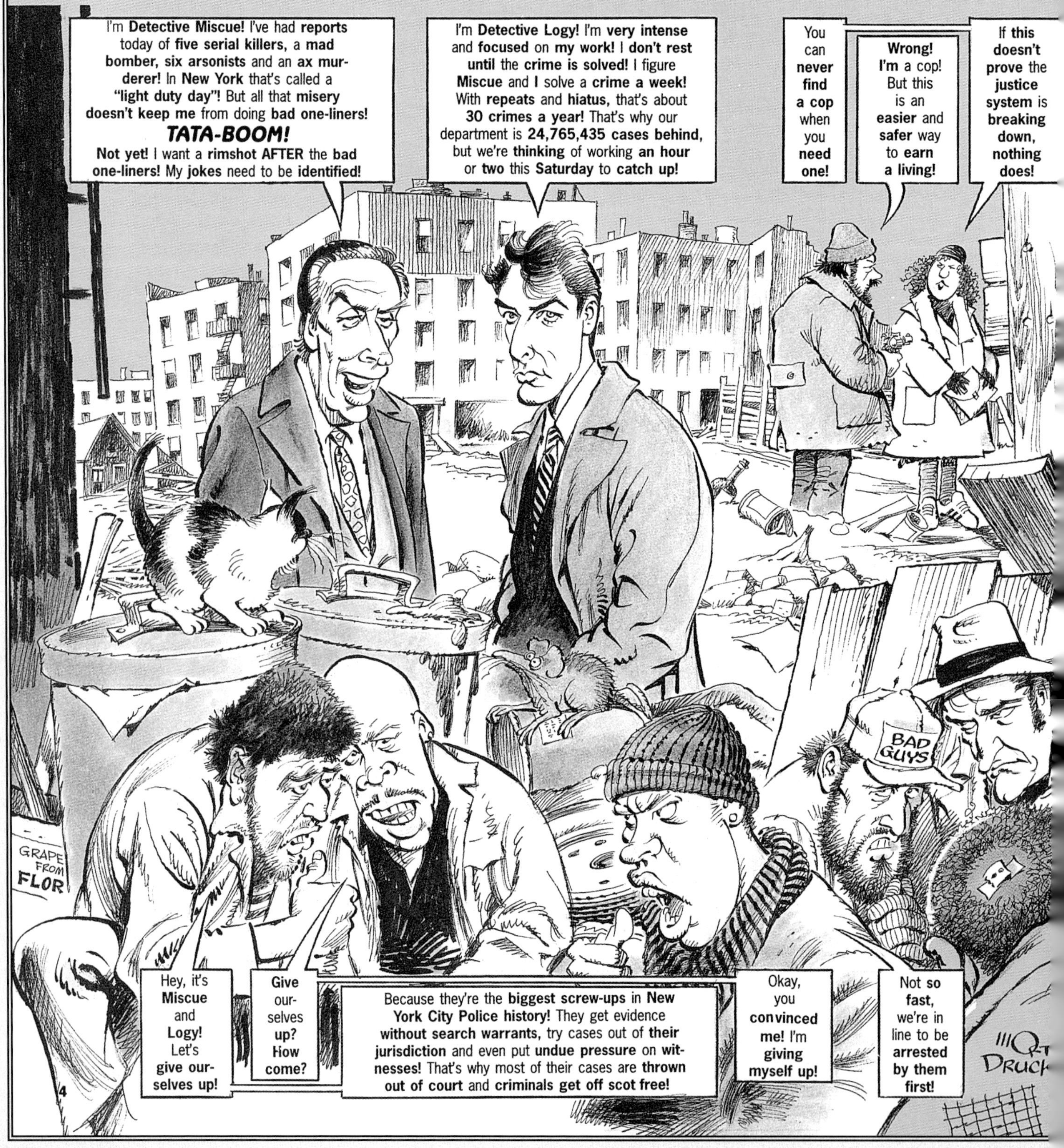
I'm Detective Miscue! I've had reports today of five serial killers, a mad bomber, six arsonists and an ax murderer! In New York that's called a "light duty day"! But all that misery doesn't keep me from doing bad one-liners!
TATA-BOOM!
Not yet! I want a rimshot AFTER the bad one-liners! My jokes need to be identified!
I'm Detective Logy! I'm very intense and focused on my work! I don't rest until the crime is solved! I figure Miscue and I solve a crime a week! With repeats and hiatus, that's about 30 crimes a year! That's why our department is 24,765,435 cases behind, but we're thinking of working an hour or two this Saturday to catch up!
You can never find a cop when you need one!
Wrong! I'm a cop! But this is an easier and safer way to earn a living!
If this doesn't prove the justice system is breaking down, nothing does!
GRAPE FROM FLOR
BAD GUYS
Hey, it's Miscue and Logy! Let's give ourselves up!
Give ourselves up? How come?
Because they're the biggest screw-ups in New York City Police history! They get evidence without search warrants, try cases out of their jurisdiction and even put undue pressure on witnesses! That's why most of their cases are thrown out of court and criminals get off scot free!
Okay, you convinced me! I'm giving myself up!
Not so fast, we're in line to be arrested by them first!

MAD #328, June 1994

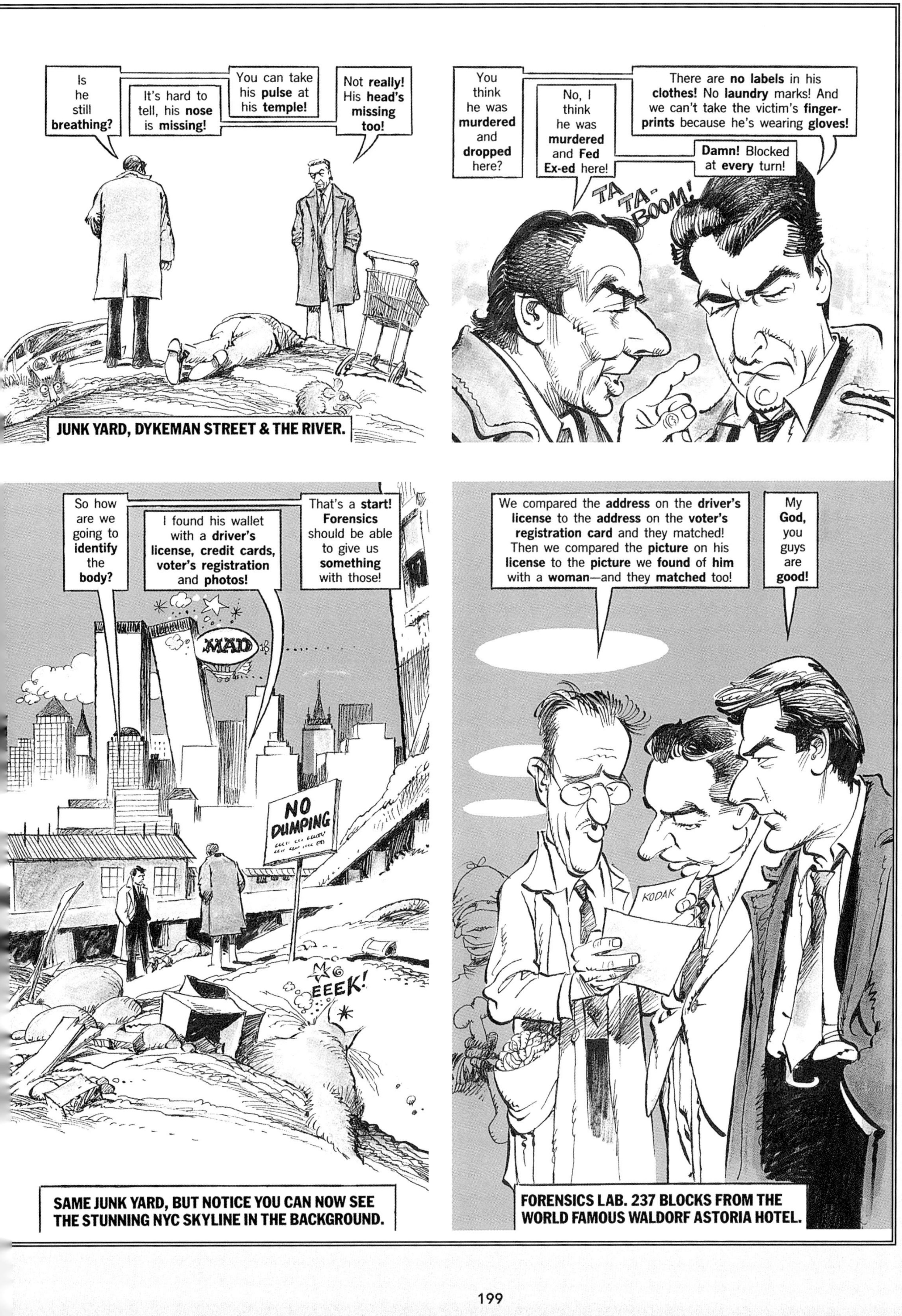

Is he still breathing?
It's hard to tell, his nose is missing!
You can take his pulse at his temple!
Not really! His head's missing too!
JUNK YARD, DYKEMAN STREET & THE RIVER.
You think he was murdered and dropped here?
No, I think he was murdered and Fed Ex-ed here!
There are no labels in his clothes! No laundry marks! And we can't take the victim's finger-prints because he's wearing gloves!
Damn! Blocked at every turn!
TA TA-BOOM!
So how are we going to identify the body?
I found his wallet with a driver's license, credit cards, voter's registration and photos!
That's a start! Forensics should be able to give us something with those!
MAD
NO DUMPING
EEEK!
SAME JUNK YARD, BUT NOTICE YOU CAN NOW SEE THE STUNNING NYC SKYLINE IN THE BACKGROUND.
We compared the address on the driver's license to the address on the voter's registration card and they matched! Then we compared the picture on his license to the picture we found of him with a woman—and they matched too!
My God, you guys are good!
KODAK
FORENSICS LAB. 237 BLOCKS FROM THE WORLD FAMOUS WALDORF ASTORIA HOTEL.

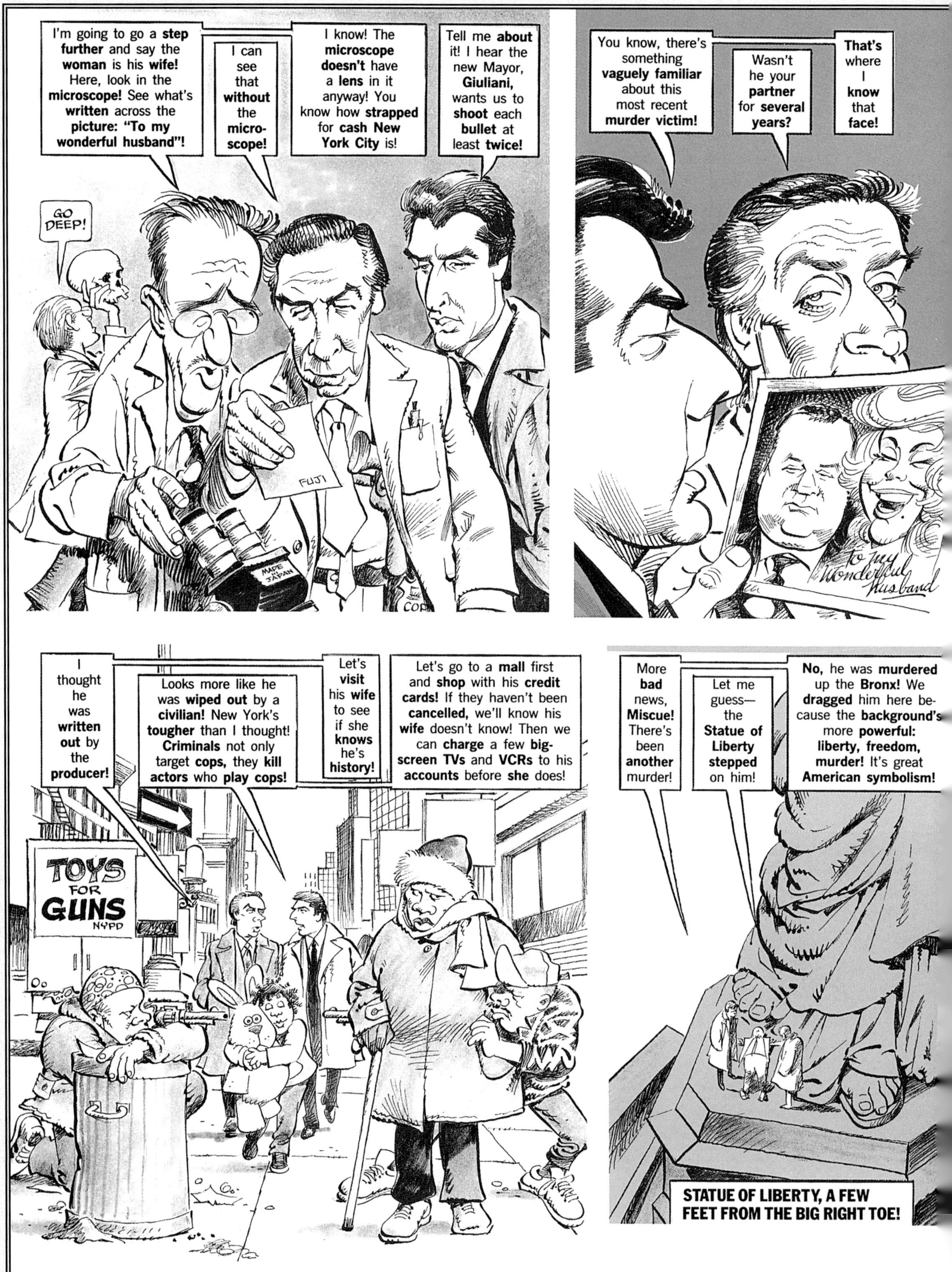
I'm going to go a step further and say the woman is his wife! Here, look in the microscope! See what's written across the picture: "To my wonderful husband"!
I can see that without the micro-scope!
I know! The microscope doesn't have a lens in it anyway! You know how strapped for cash New York City is!
Tell me about it! I hear the new Mayor, Giuliani, wants us to shoot each bullet at least twice!
GO DEEP!
FUJI
MADE IN JAPAN
You know, there's something vaguely familiar about this most recent murder victim!
Wasn't he your partner for several years?
That's where I know that face!
to my wonderful husband
I thought he was written out by the producer!
Looks more like he was wiped out by a civilian! New York's tougher than I thought! Criminals not only target cops, they kill actors who play cops!
Let's visit his wife to see if she knows he's history!
Let's go to a mall first and shop with his credit cards! If they haven't been cancelled, we'll know his wife doesn't know! Then we can charge a few big-screen TVs and VCRs to his accounts before she does!
TOYS FOR GUNS NYPD
More bad news, Miscue! There's been another murder!
Let me guess—the Statue of Liberty stepped on him!
No, he was murdered up the Bronx! We dragged him here because the background's more powerful: liberty, freedom, murder! It's great American symbolism!
STATUE OF LIBERTY, A FEW FEET FROM THE BIG RIGHT TOE!

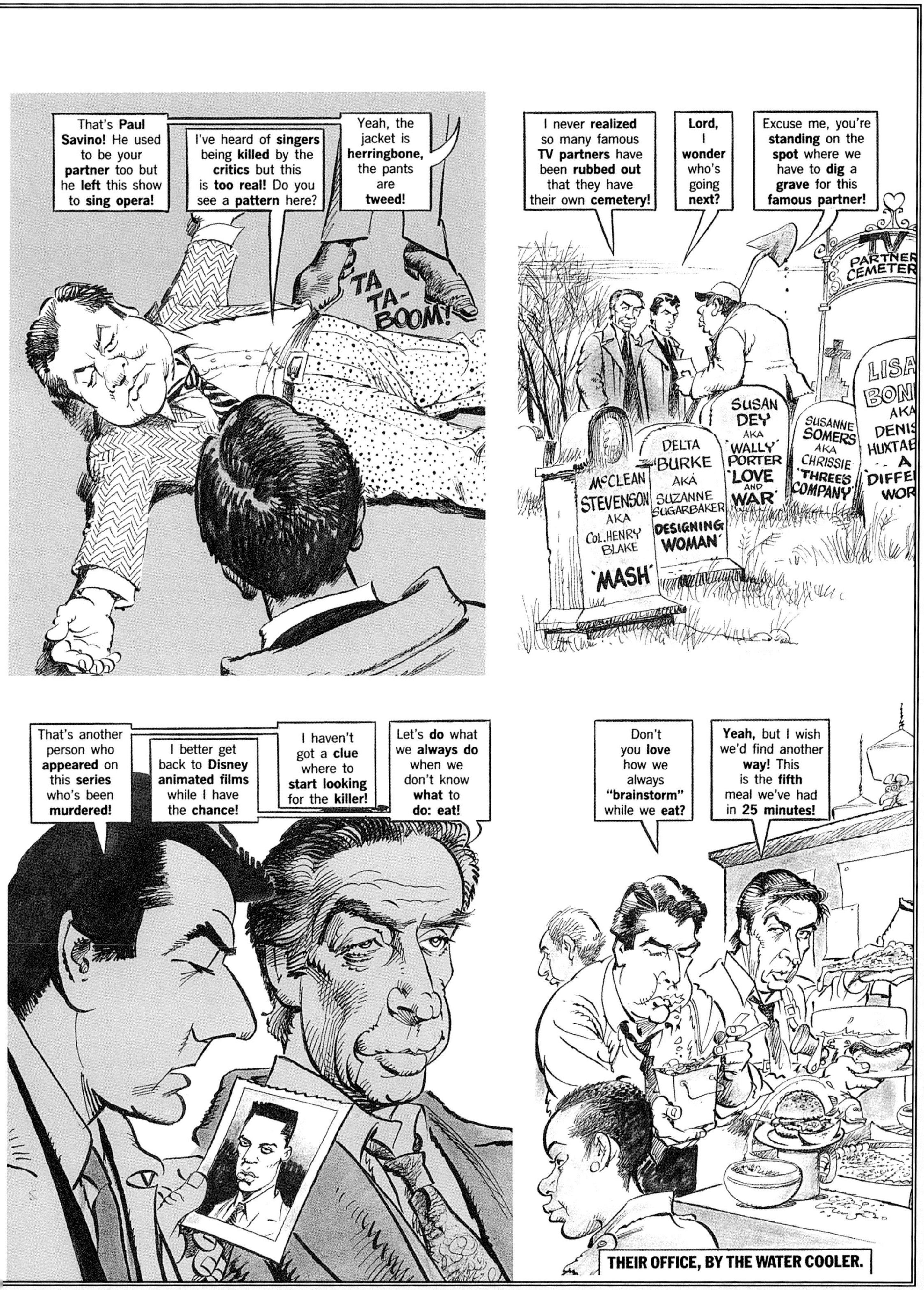
That's **Paul Savino!** He used to be your **partner** too but he **left** this show to **sing opera!**
I've heard of **singers** being **killed** by the **critics** but this is **too real!** Do you see a **pattern** here?
Yeah, the jacket is **herringbone,** the pants are **tweed!**
TA TA-BOOM!
I never **realized** so many famous **TV partners** have been **rubbed out** that they have their own **cemetery!**
Lord, I **wonder** who's going **next?**
Excuse me, you're **standing** on the **spot** where we have to **dig** a **grave** for this **famous partner!**
McCLEAN STEVENSON AKA COL. HENRY BLAKE 'MASH'
DELTA BURKE AKA SUZANNE SUGARBAKER 'DESIGNING WOMAN'
SUSAN DEY AKA 'WALLY' PORTER 'LOVE AND WAR'
SUSANNE SOMERS AKA CHRISSIE 'THREE'S COMPANY'
That's another person who **appeared** on this **series** who's been **murdered!**
I better get back to **Disney animated films** while I have the **chance!**
I haven't got a **clue** where to **start looking** for the **killer!**
Let's **do** what we **always do** when we don't know **what** to **do: eat!**
Don't you **love** how we always **"brainstorm"** while we **eat?**
Yeah, but I wish we'd find another **way!** This is the **fifth** meal we've had in **25 minutes!**
THEIR OFFICE, BY THE WATER COOLER.

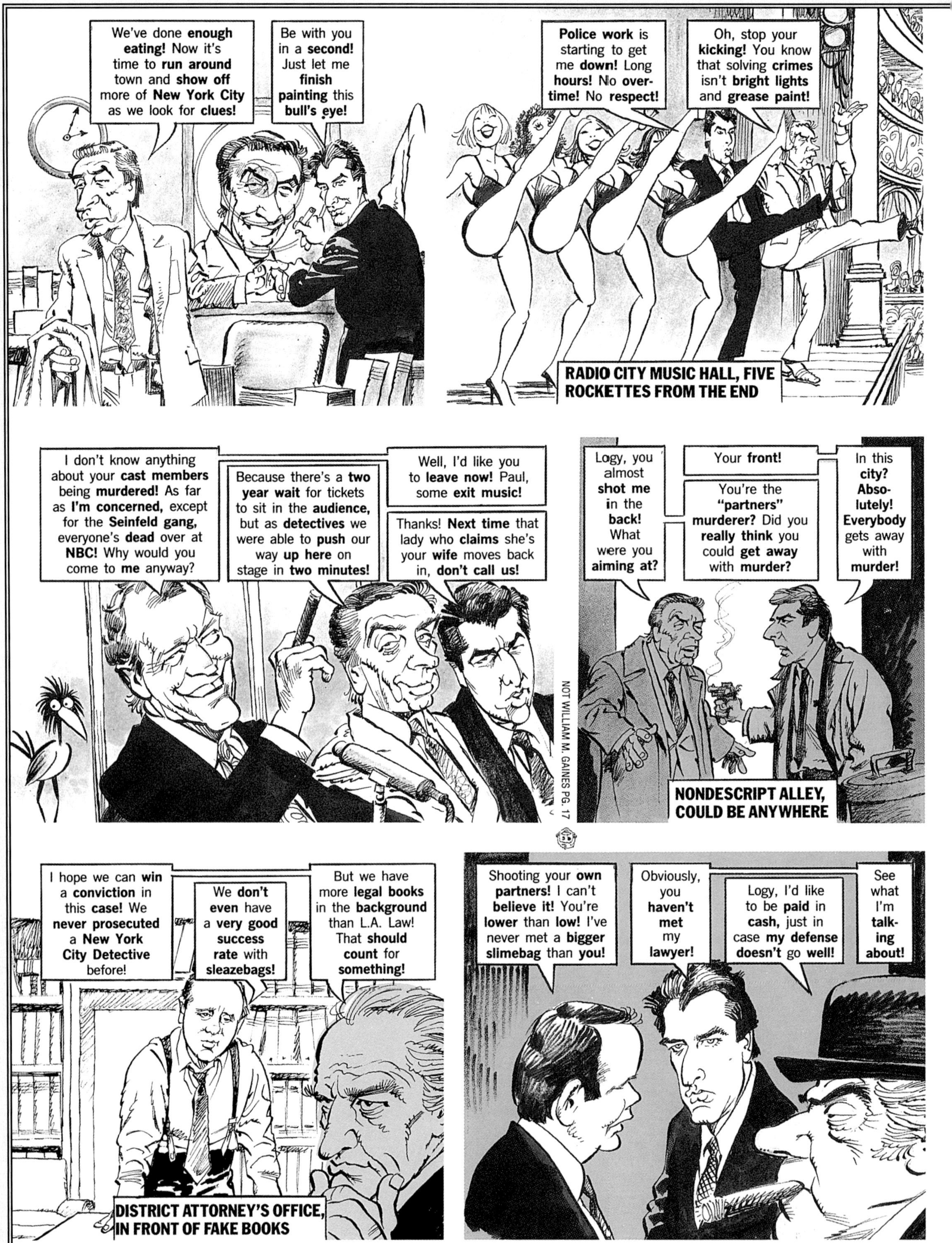
We've done enough eating! Now it's time to run around town and show off more of New York City as we look for clues!
Be with you in a second! Just let me finish painting this bull's eye!
Police work is starting to get me down! Long hours! No over-time! No respect!
Oh, stop your kicking! You know that solving crimes isn't bright lights and grease paint!
RADIO CITY MUSIC HALL, FIVE ROCKETTES FROM THE END
I don't know anything about your cast members being murdered! As far as I'm concerned, except for the Seinfeld gang, everyone's dead over at NBC! Why would you come to me anyway?
Because there's a two year wait for tickets to sit in the audience, but as detectives we were able to push our way up here on stage in two minutes!
Well, I'd like you to leave now! Paul, some exit music!
Thanks! Next time that lady who claims she's your wife moves back in, don't call us!
NOT WILLIAM M. GAINES PG. 17
Logy, you almost shot me in the back! What were you aiming at?
Your front!
You're the "partners" murderer? Did you really think you could get away with murder?
In this city? Abso-lutely! Everybody gets away with murder!
NONDESCRIPT ALLEY, COULD BE ANYWHERE
I hope we can win a conviction in this case! We never prosecuted a New York City Detective before!
We don't even have a very good success rate with sleazebags!
But we have more legal books in the background than L.A. Law! That should count for something!
DISTRICT ATTORNEY'S OFFICE, IN FRONT OF FAKE BOOKS
Shooting your own partners! I can't believe it! You're lower than low! I've never met a bigger slimebag than you!
Obviously, you haven't met my lawyer!
Logy, I'd like to be paid in cash, just in case my defense doesn't go well!
See what I'm talk-ing about!

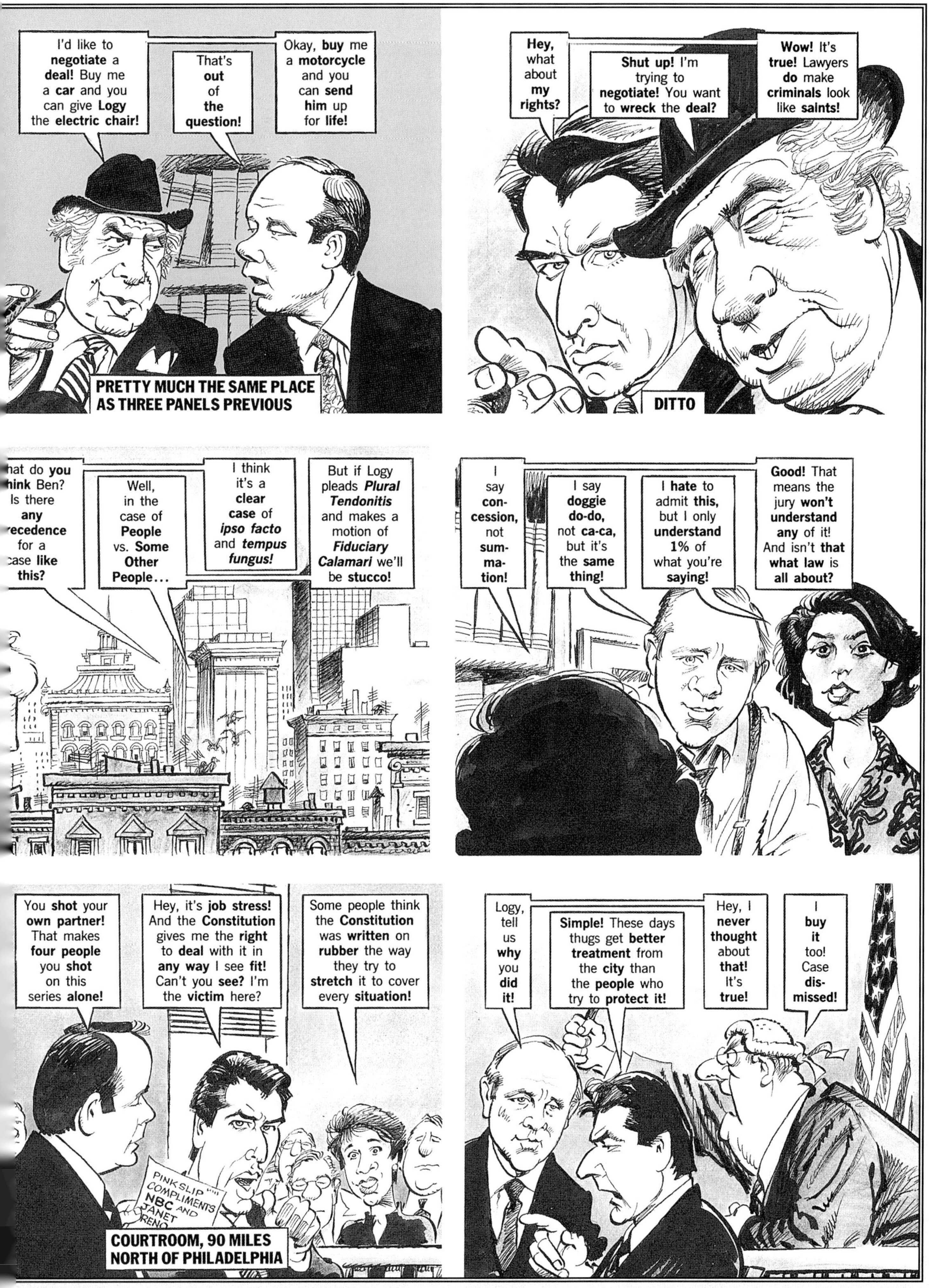
I'd like to negotiate a deal! Buy me a car and you can give Logy the electric chair!
That's out of the question!
Okay, buy me a motorcycle and you can send him up for life!
PRETTY MUCH THE SAME PLACE AS THREE PANELS PREVIOUS
Hey, what about my rights?
Shut up! I'm trying to negotiate! You want to wreck the deal?
Wow! It's true! Lawyers do make criminals look like saints!
DITTO
hat do you hink Ben? Is there any recedence for a case like this?
Well, in the case of People vs. Some Other People...
I think it's a clear case of ipso facto and tempus fungus!
But if Logy pleads Plural Tendonitis and makes a motion of Fiduciary Calamari we'll be stucco!
I say con-cession, not sum-ma-tion!
I say doggie do-do, not ca-ca, but it's the same thing!
I hate to admit this, but I only understand 1% of what you're saying!
Good! That means the jury won't understand any of it! And isn't that what law is all about?
You shot your own partner! That makes four people you shot on this series alone!
Hey, it's job stress! And the Constitution gives me the right to deal with it in any way I see fit! Can't you see? I'm the victim here?
Some people think the Constitution was written on rubber the way they try to stretch it to cover every situation!
PINK SLIP COMPLIMENTS NBC AND JANET RENO
COURTROOM, 90 MILES NORTH OF PHILADELPHIA
Logy, tell us why you did it!
Simple! These days thugs get better treatment from the city than the people who try to protect it!
Hey, I never thought about that! It's true!
I buy it too! Case dis-missed!

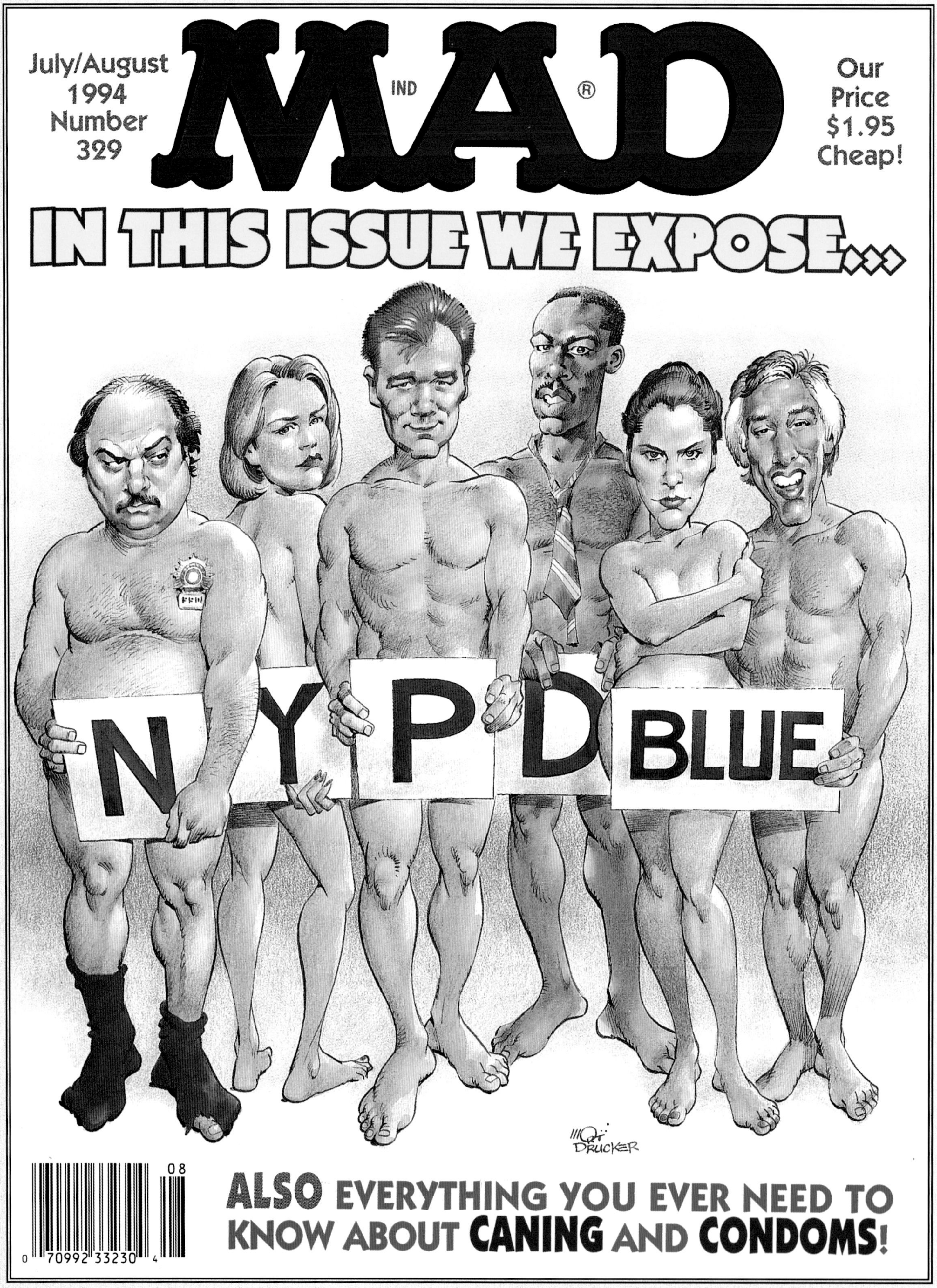
July/August
1994
Number
329
MAD
IND
®
Our
Price
$1.95
Cheap!
IN THIS ISSUE WE EXPOSE...
N Y P D BLUE
DRUCKER
ALSO EVERYTHING YOU EVER NEED TO KNOW ABOUT CANING AND CONDOMS!

A TIP OF THE CAPRA DEPT.

It's a Wonderful Life is a heartwarming film about the positive impact one man's life had on all those around him. It starred Jimmy Stewart as the troubled man who learns a valuable lesson. Over the years it's become an American classic, enjoyed by generations. *It's a Blunderful Life* is a less-than-heartwarming movie satire about the questionable impact one man's election had on all those around him. It stars Bill Clinton as the troubled politician who never seems to learn his lesson. Hopefully, this too will become an American classic enjoyed by generations. Given MAD's policy of reprinting articles over and over again in Super Specials, we think that's pretty much a done deal! Here's...

It's a Blunderful Life

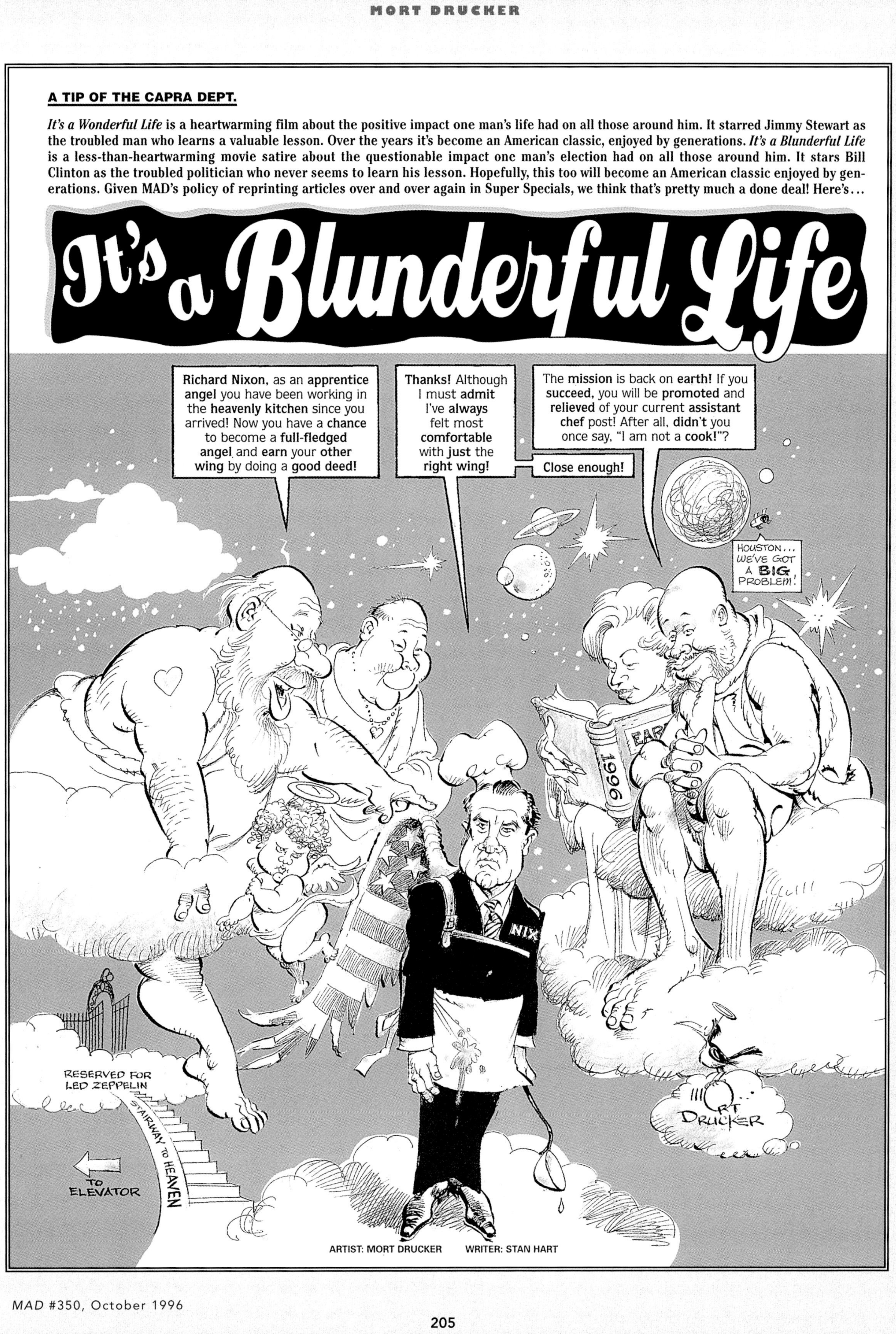
Richard Nixon, as an apprentice angel you have been working in the heavenly kitchen since you arrived! Now you have a chance to become a full-fledged angel and earn your other wing by doing a good deed!
Thanks! Although I must admit I've always felt most comfortable with just the right wing!
The mission is back on earth! If you succeed, you will be promoted and relieved of your current assistant chef post! After all, didn't you once say, "I am not a cook!"?
Close enough!
HOUSTON... WE'VE GOT A BIG PROBLEM!
1996
NIX
RESERVED FOR LED ZEPPELIN
STAIRWAY TO HEAVEN
TO ELEVATOR
MORT DRUCKER

ARTIST: MORT DRUCKER WRITER: STAN HART

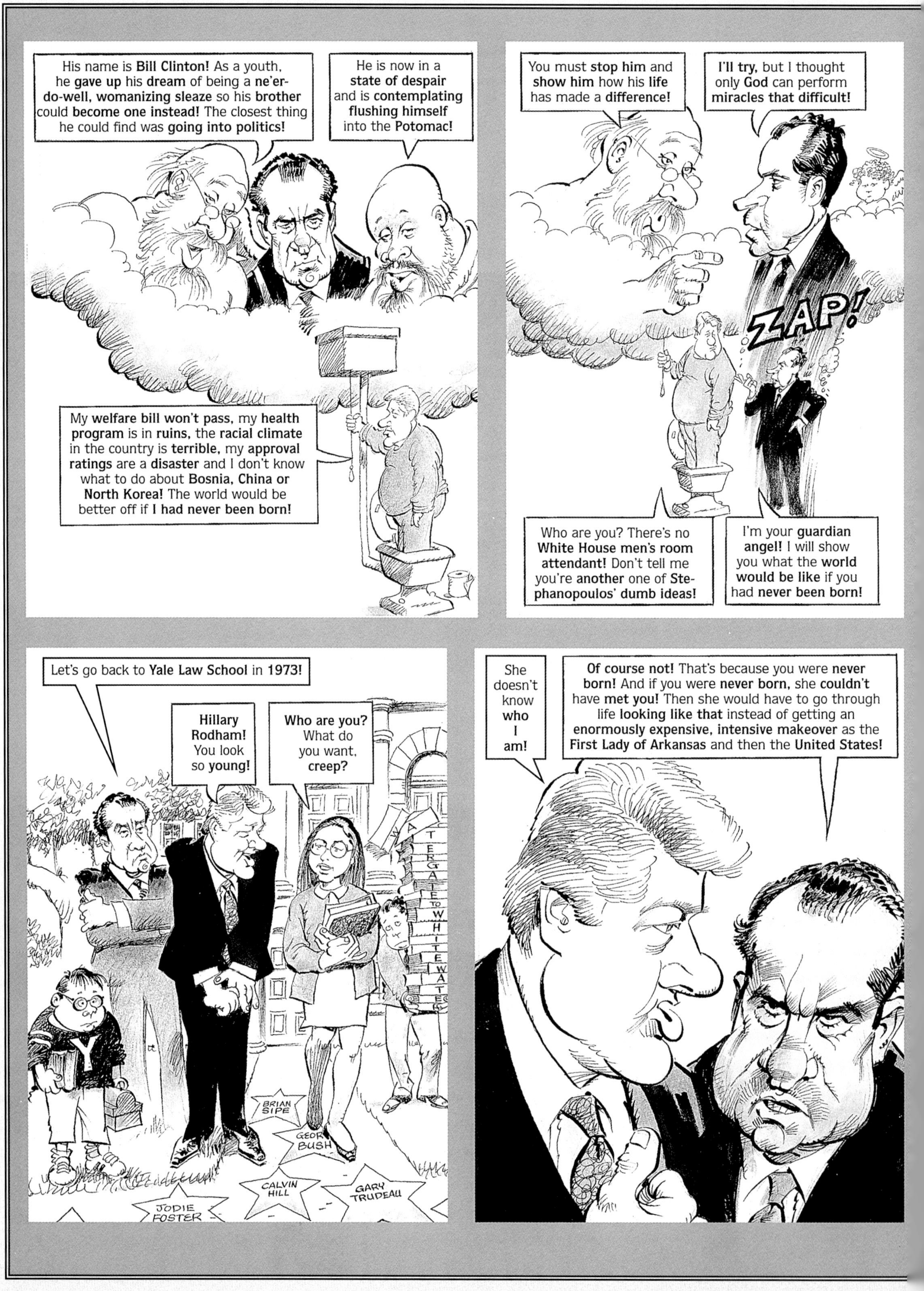
His name is Bill Clinton! As a youth, he gave up his dream of being a ne'er-do-well, womanizing sleaze so his brother could become one instead! The closest thing he could find was going into politics!
He is now in a state of despair and is contemplating flushing himself into the Potomac!
My welfare bill won't pass, my health program is in ruins, the racial climate in the country is terrible, my approval ratings are a disaster and I don't know what to do about Bosnia, China or North Korea! The world would be better off if I had never been born!
You must stop him and show him how his life has made a difference!
I'll try, but I thought only God can perform miracles that difficult!
ZAP!
Who are you? There's no White House men's room attendant! Don't tell me you're another one of Stephanopoulos' dumb ideas!
I'm your guardian angel! I will show you what the world would be like if you had never been born!
Let's go back to Yale Law School in 1973!
Hillary Rodham! You look so young!
Who are you? What do you want, creep?
WATERGATE TO WHITEWATE
Y
BRIAN SIPE
GEOR BUSH
CALVIN HILL
GARY TRUDEAU
JODIE FOSTER
She doesn't know who I am!
Of course not! That's because you were never born! And if you were never born, she couldn't have met you! Then she would have to go through life looking like that instead of getting an enormously expensive, intensive makeover as the First Lady of Arkansas and then the United States!

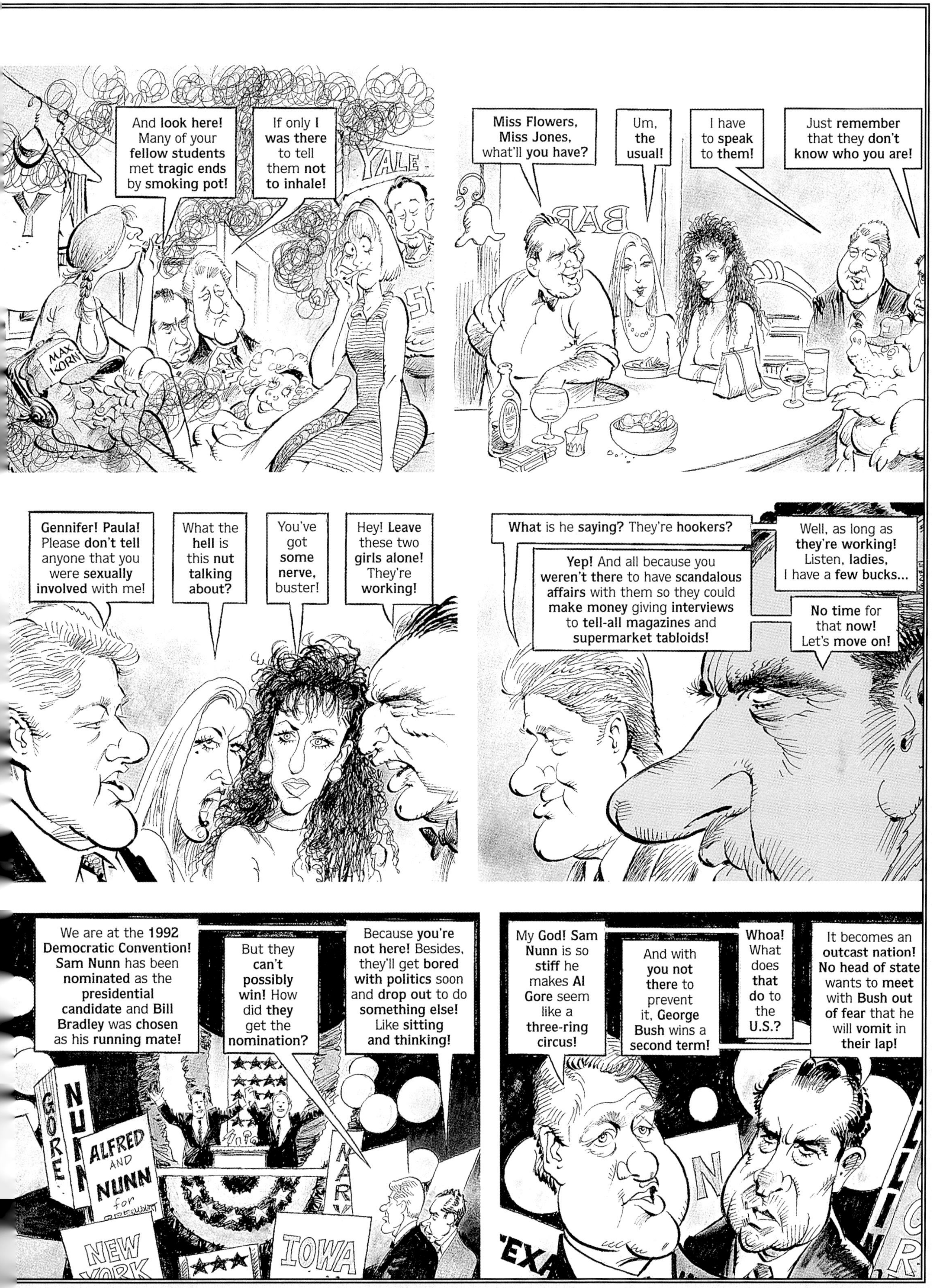
And look here! Many of your fellow students met tragic ends by smoking pot!
If only I was there to tell them not to inhale!
YALE
MAX KORN
Miss Flowers, Miss Jones, what'll you have?
Um, the usual!
I have to speak to them!
Just remember that they don't know who you are!
Gennifer! Paula! Please don't tell anyone that you were sexually involved with me!
What the hell is this nut talking about?
You've got some nerve, buster!
Hey! Leave these two girls alone! They're working!
What is he saying? They're hookers?
Yep! And all because you weren't there to have scandalous affairs with them so they could make money giving interviews to tell-all magazines and supermarket tabloids!
Well, as long as they're working! Listen, ladies, I have a few bucks...
No time for that now! Let's move on!
We are at the 1992 Democratic Convention! Sam Nunn has been nominated as the presidential candidate and Bill Bradley was chosen as his running mate!
But they can't possibly win! How did they get the nomination?
Because you're not here! Besides, they'll get bored with politics soon and drop out to do something else! Like sitting and thinking!
GORE
NUNN
ALFRED AND NUNN
IOWA
My God! Sam Nunn is so stiff he makes Al Gore seem like a three-ring circus!
And with you not there to prevent it, George Bush wins a second term!
Whoa! What does that do to the U.S.?
It becomes an outcast nation! No head of state wants to meet with Bush out of fear that he will vomit in their lap!

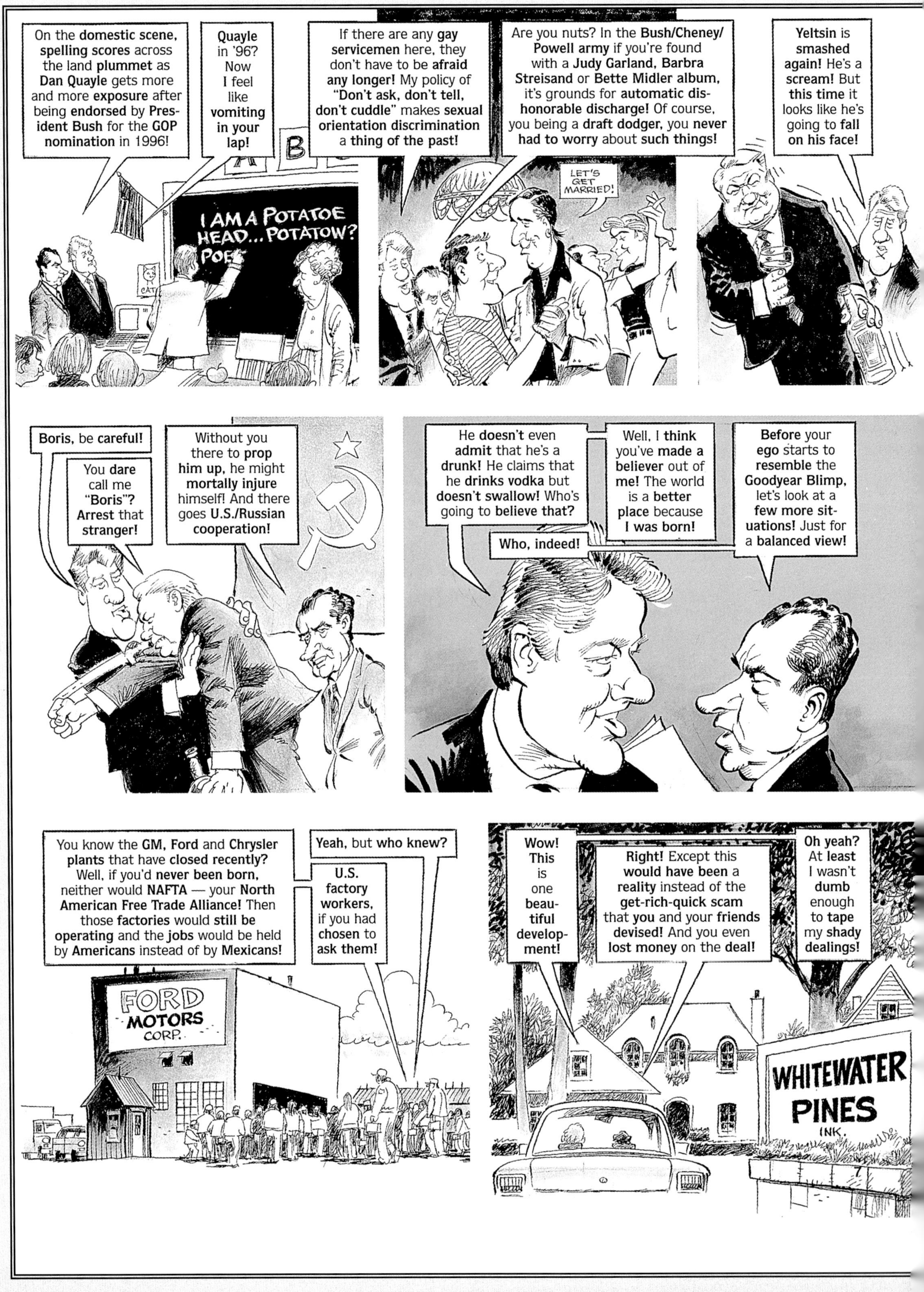
On the domestic scene, spelling scores across the land plummet as Dan Quayle gets more and more exposure after being endorsed by President Bush for the GOP nomination in 1996!
Quayle in '96? Now I feel like vomiting in your lap!
I AM A POTATOE HEAD... POTATOW? POE
CAT
If there are any gay servicemen here, they don't have to be afraid any longer! My policy of "Don't ask, don't tell, don't cuddle" makes sexual orientation discrimination a thing of the past!
Are you nuts? In the Bush/Cheney/Powell army if you're found with a Judy Garland, Barbra Streisand or Bette Midler album, it's grounds for automatic dishonorable discharge! Of course, you being a draft dodger, you never had to worry about such things!
LET'S GET MARRIED!
Yeltsin is smashed again! He's a scream! But this time it looks like he's going to fall on his face!
Boris, be careful!
You dare call me "Boris"? Arrest that stranger!
Without you there to prop him up, he might mortally injure himself! And there goes U.S./Russian cooperation!
He doesn't even admit that he's a drunk! He claims that he drinks vodka but doesn't swallow! Who's going to believe that?
Who, indeed!
Well, I think you've made a believer out of me! The world is a better place because I was born!
Before your ego starts to resemble the Goodyear Blimp, let's look at a few more situations! Just for a balanced view!
You know the GM, Ford and Chrysler plants that have closed recently? Well, if you'd never been born, neither would NAFTA — your North American Free Trade Alliance! Then those factories would still be operating and the jobs would be held by Americans instead of by Mexicans!
Yeah, but who knew?
U.S. factory workers, if you had chosen to ask them!
FORD MOTORS CORP.
Wow! This is one beautiful development!
Right! Except this would have been a reality instead of the get-rich-quick scam that you and your friends devised! And you even lost money on the deal!
Oh yeah? At least I wasn't dumb enough to tape my shady dealings!
WHITEWATER PINES INK.

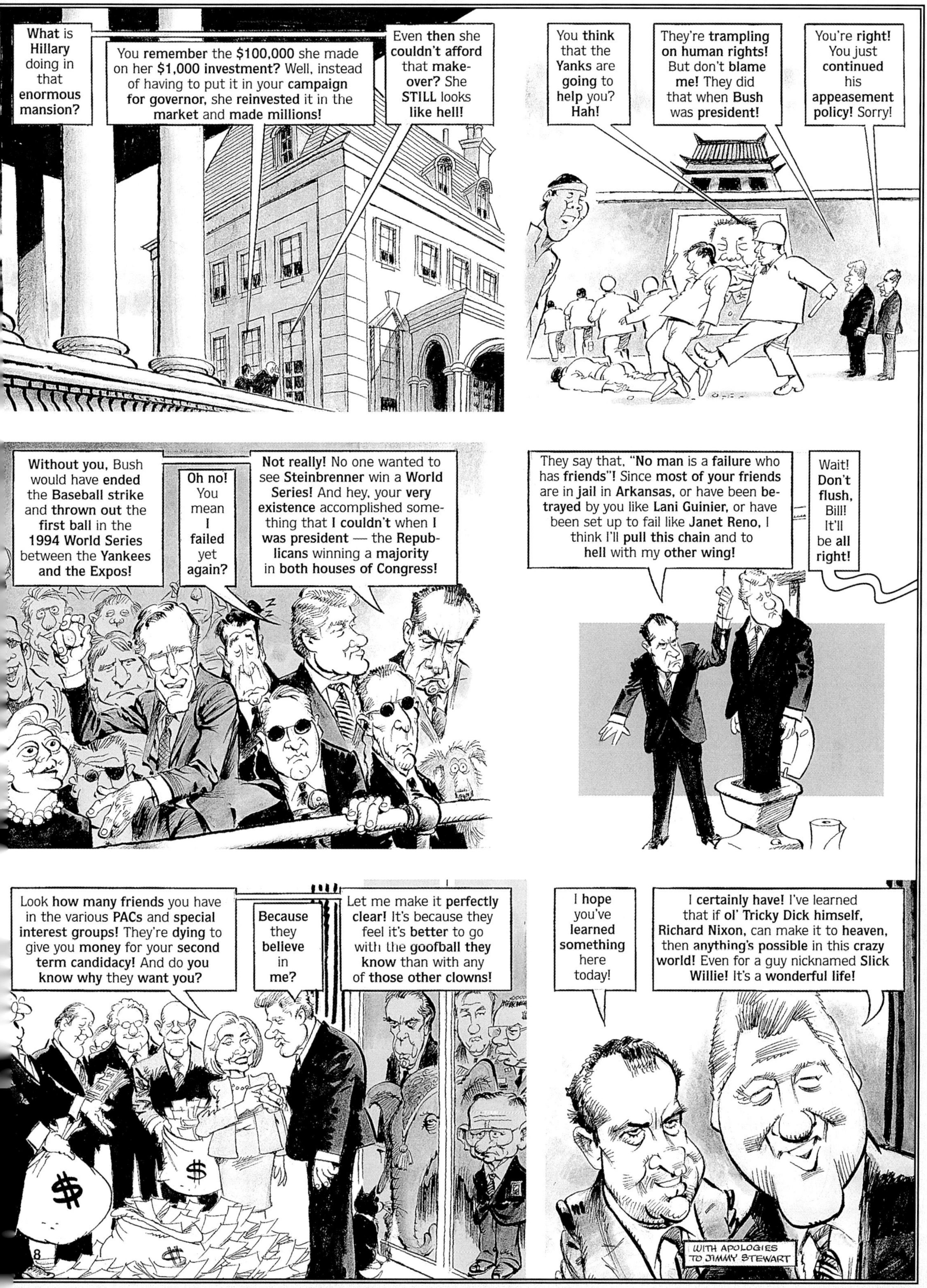
What is Hillary doing in that enormous mansion?
You remember the $100,000 she made on her $1,000 investment? Well, instead of having to put it in your campaign for governor, she reinvested it in the market and made millions!
Even then she couldn't afford that make-over? She STILL looks like hell!
You think that the Yanks are going to help you? Hah!
They're trampling on human rights! But don't blame me! They did that when Bush was president!
You're right! You just continued his appeasement policy! Sorry!
Without you, Bush would have ended the Baseball strike and thrown out the first ball in the 1994 World Series between the Yankees and the Expos!
Oh no! You mean I failed yet again?
Not really! No one wanted to see Steinbrenner win a World Series! And hey, your very existence accomplished something that I couldn't when I was president — the Republicans winning a majority in both houses of Congress!
They say that, "No man is a failure who has friends"! Since most of your friends are in jail in Arkansas, or have been betrayed by you like Lani Guinier, or have been set up to fail like Janet Reno, I think I'll pull this chain and to hell with my other wing!
Wait! Don't flush, Bill! It'll be all right!
Look how many friends you have in the various PACs and special interest groups! They're dying to give you money for your second term candidacy! And do you know why they want you?
Because they believe in me?
Let me make it perfectly clear! It's because they feel it's better to go with the goofball they know than with any of those other clowns!
I hope you've learned something here today!
I certainly have! I've learned that if ol' Tricky Dick himself, Richard Nixon, can make it to heaven, then anything's possible in this crazy world! Even for a guy nicknamed Slick Willie! It's a wonderful life!
WITH APOLOGIES TO JIMMY STEWART

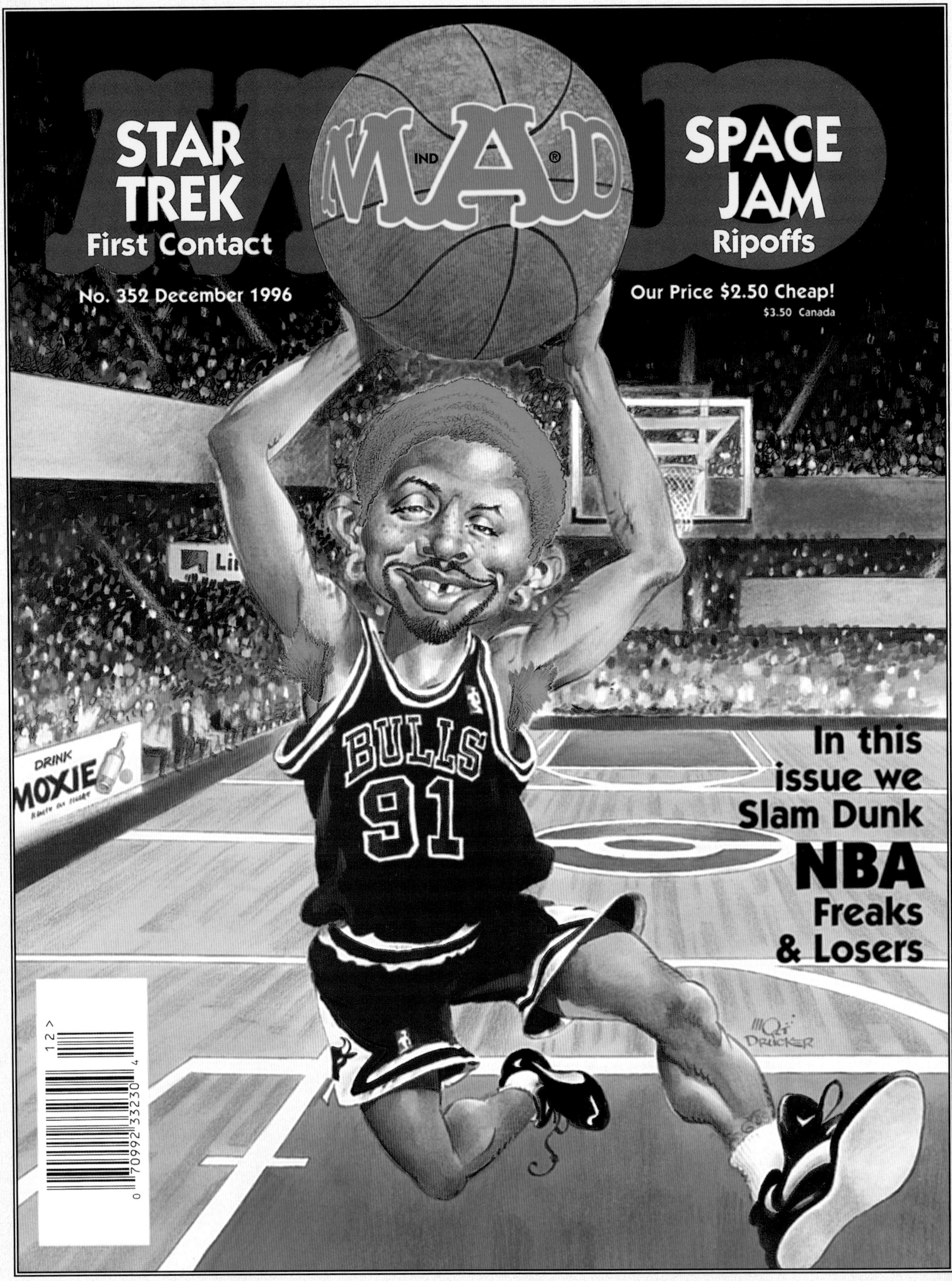
MAD
IND
®
STAR
TREK
First Contact
SPACE
JAM
Ripoffs
No. 352 December 1996
Our Price $2.50 Cheap!
$3.50 Canada
DRINK
MOXIE
BULLS
91
In this
issue we
Slam Dunk
NBA
Freaks
& Losers
DRUCKER

MAD
#1 of 4 BATMAN Covers This Month! Collect Them All For Secret Message!
YECCH!
#359 July 1997 Our Price $2.50 Cheap!
MAD
#2 of 4 BATMAN Covers This Month! Collect Them All For Secret Message!
YECCH!
#359 July 1997 Our Price $2.50 Cheap!
CHE
EAP
GiMI
MAD
#3 of 4 BATMAN Covers This Month! Collect Them All For Secret Message!
YECCH!
#359 July 1997 Our Price $2.50 Cheap!
MiCK
MAD
#4 of 4 BATMAN Covers This Month! Collect Them All For Secret Message!
YECCH!
#359 July 1997 Our Price $2.50 Cheap!
O.K., Pal, you gonna' Buy the Magazine or what?
PSYCHIATRIC HELP 5¢
THE DOCTORS ARE IN
The Clone Ranger
DRUCKER

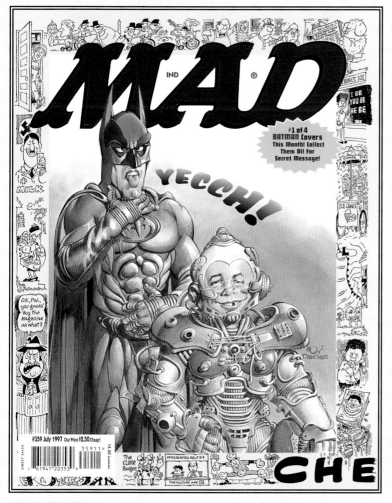

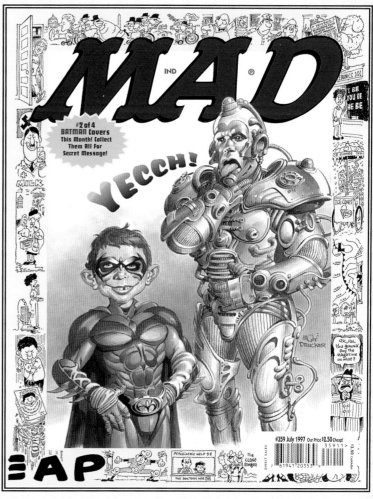

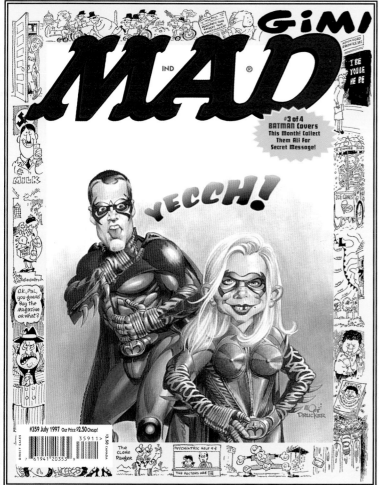

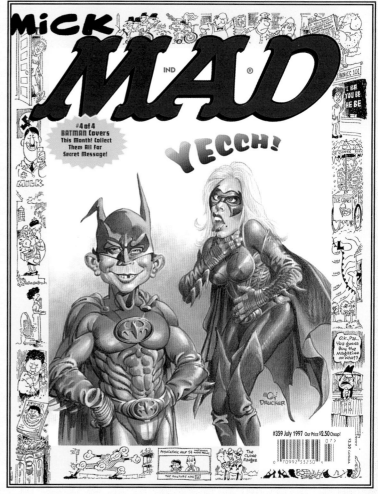

THEY GET BY WITH A LITTLE HELP FROM THEIR FRANZ DEPT.

Back in MAD #329 we told you of a gritty, New York City police drama that was atop the ratings charts. Well, here it is several years later and this police drama is still on top of the charts. Proving once again that the American viewing public knows nothing about quality television! But wait! Something's changed! There are a lot of shiny new faces (not to mention saggy new asses). It's time for a another look at this fershlugginer show. It's time for...

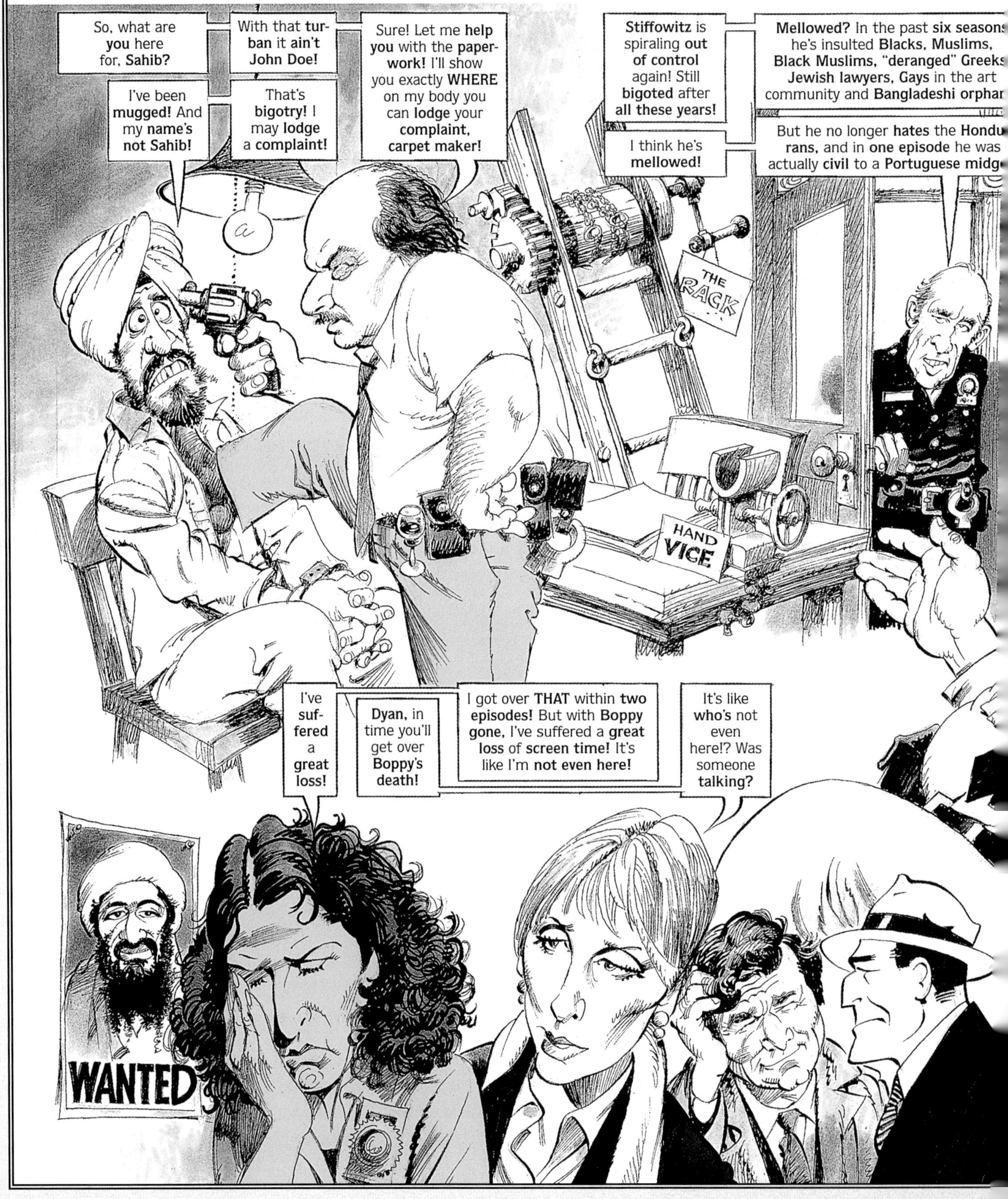
So, what are you here for, Sahib?
With that turban it ain't John Doe!
I've been mugged! And my name's not Sahib!
That's bigotry! I may lodge a complaint!
Sure! Let me help you with the paperwork! I'll show you exactly WHERE on my body you can lodge your complaint, carpet maker!
Stiffowitz is spiraling out of control again! Still bigoted after all these years!
Mellowed? In the past six seasons he's insulted Blacks, Muslims, Black Muslims, "deranged" Greeks, Jewish lawyers, Gays in the art community and Bangladeshi orphan
I think he's mellowed!
But he no longer hates the Hondurans, and in one episode he was actually civil to a Portuguese midg
THE RACK
HAND VICE
I've suffered a great loss!
Dyan, in time you'll get over Boppy's death!
I got over THAT within two episodes! But with Boppy gone, I've suffered a great loss of screen time! It's like I'm not even here!
It's like who's not even here!? Was someone talking?
WANTED

NYPD RE-DO

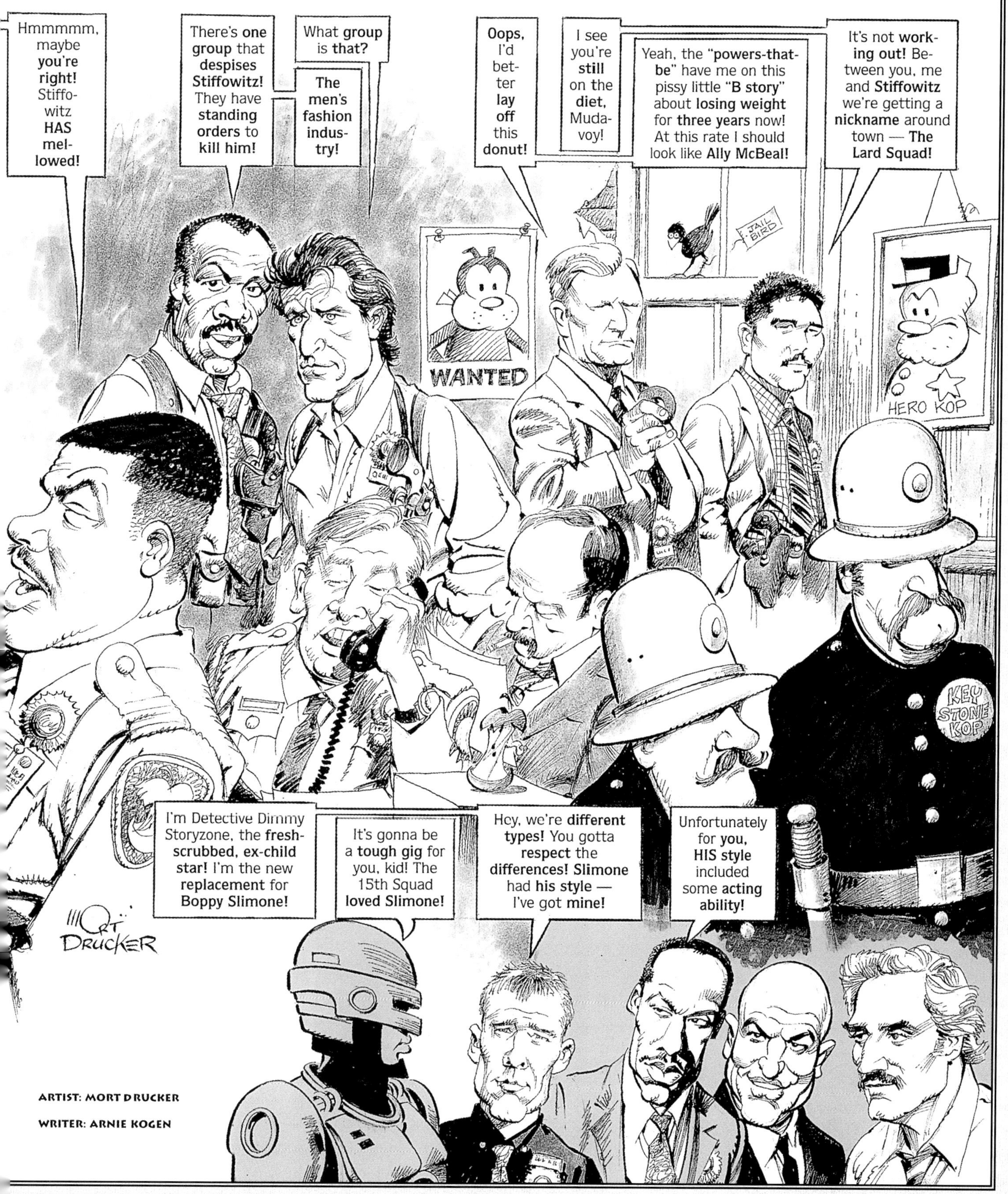
Hmmmmm, maybe you're right! Stiffowitz HAS mellowed!
There's one group that despises Stiffowitz! They have standing orders to kill him!
What group is that?
The men's fashion industry!
Oops, I'd better lay off this donut!
I see you're still on the diet, Mudavoy!
Yeah, the "powers-that-be" have me on this pissy little "B story" about losing weight for three years now! At this rate I should look like Ally McBeal!
It's not working out! Between you, me and Stiffowitz we're getting a nickname around town — The Lard Squad!
WANTED
JAIL BIRD
HERO KOP
KEY STONE KOP
I'm Detective Dimmy Storyzone, the fresh-scrubbed, ex-child star! I'm the new replacement for Boppy Slimone!
It's gonna be a tough gig for you, kid! The 15th Squad loved Slimone!
Hey, we're different types! You gotta respect the differences! Slimone had his style — I've got mine!
Unfortunately for you, HIS style included some acting ability!
MORT DRUCKER
ARTIST: MORT DRUCKER
WRITER: ARNIE KOGEN

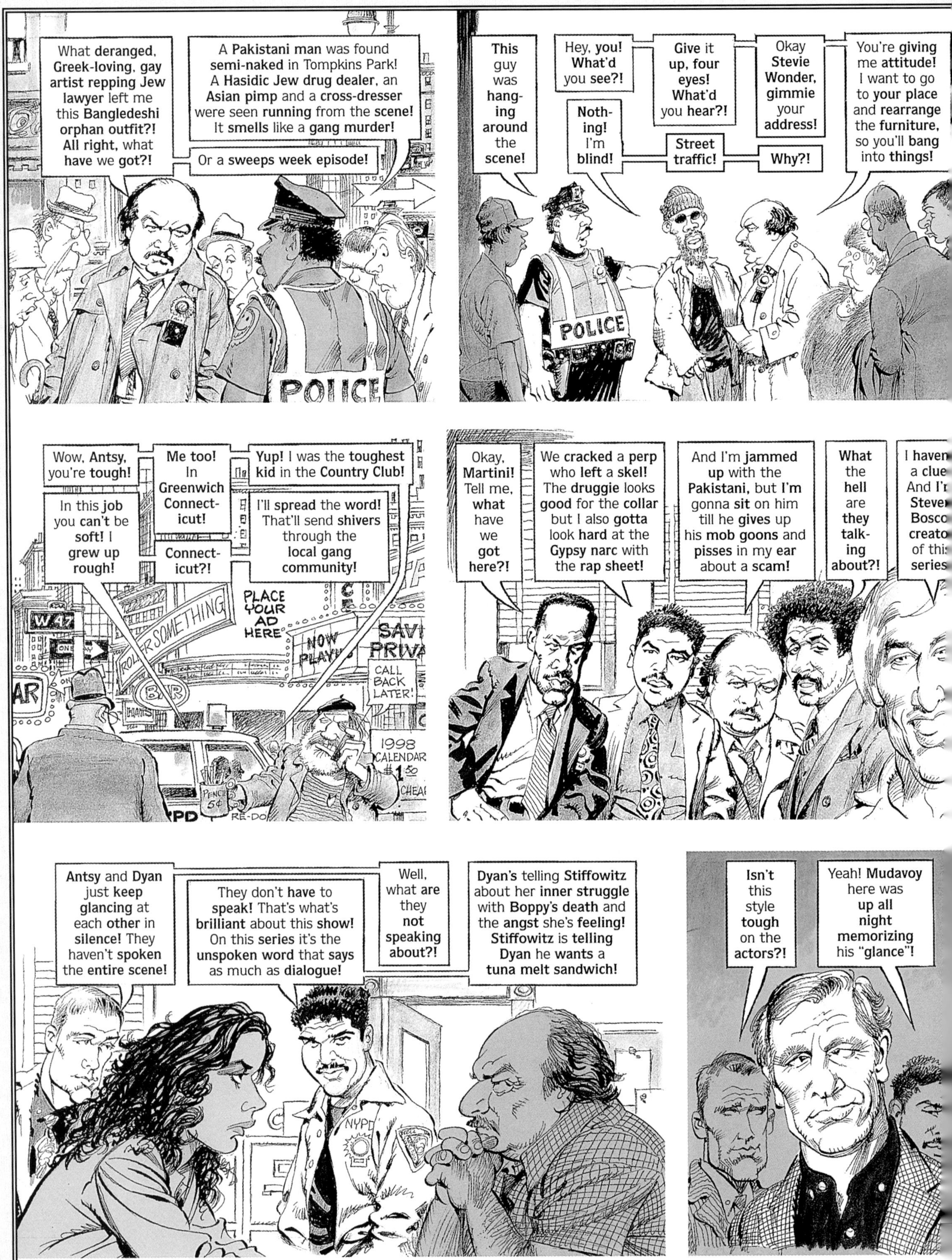
What deranged, Greek-loving, gay artist repping Jew lawyer left me this Bangledeshi orphan outfit?! All right, what have we got?!
A Pakistani man was found semi-naked in Tompkins Park! A Hasidic Jew drug dealer, an Asian pimp and a cross-dresser were seen running from the scene! It smells like a gang murder!
Or a sweeps week episode!
POLICE
This guy was hang-ing around the scene!
Hey, you! What'd you see?!
Noth-ing! I'm blind!
Give it up, four eyes! What'd you hear?!
Street traffic!
Okay Stevie Wonder, gimmie your address!
Why?!
You're giving me attitude! I want to go to your place and rearrange the furniture, so you'll bang into things!
POLICE
Wow, Antsy, you're tough!
In this job you can't be soft! I grew up rough!
Me too! In Greenwich Connect-icut!
Connect-icut?!
Yup! I was the toughest kid in the Country Club!
I'll spread the word! That'll send shivers through the local gang community!
PLACE YOUR AD HERE
ROLLER SOMETHING
CALL BACK LATER!
1998 CALENDAR $1.50
PENCILS 5¢
Okay, Martini! Tell me, what have we got here?!
We cracked a perp who left a skel! The druggie looks good for the collar but I also gotta look hard at the Gypsy narc with the rap sheet!
And I'm jammed up with the Pakistani, but I'm gonna sit on him till he gives up his mob goons and pisses in my ear about a scam!
What the hell are they talk-ing about?!
Antsy and Dyan just keep glancing at each other in silence! They haven't spoken the entire scene!
They don't have to speak! That's what's brilliant about this show! On this series it's the unspoken word that says as much as dialogue!
Well, what are they not speaking about?!
Dyan's telling Stiffowitz about her inner struggle with Boppy's death and the angst she's feeling! Stiffowitz is telling Dyan he wants a tuna melt sandwich!
NYPD
Isn't this style tough on the actors?!
Yeah! Mudavoy here was up all night memorizing his "glance"!

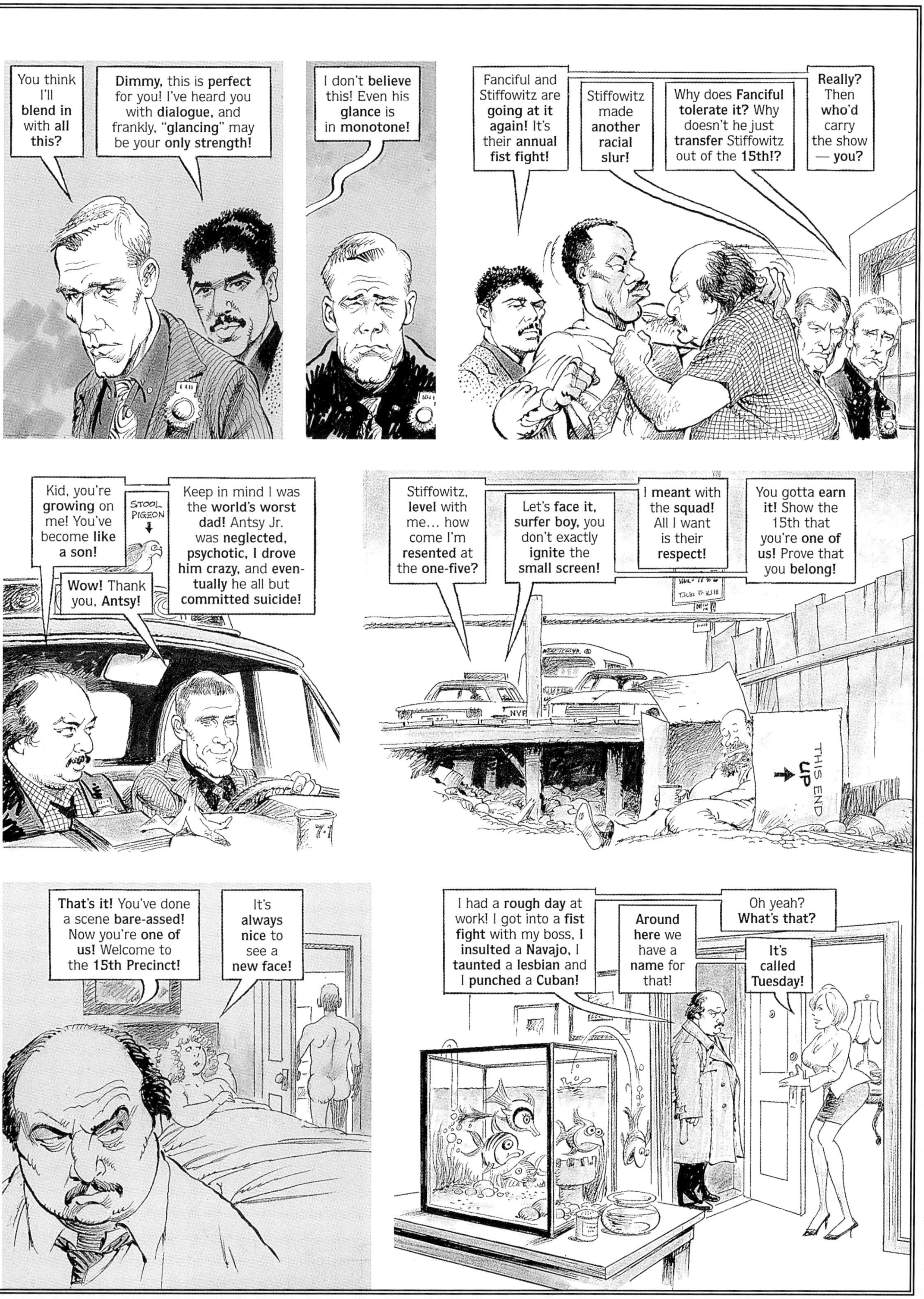
You think I'll blend in with all this?
Dimmy, this is perfect for you! I've heard you with dialogue, and frankly, "glancing" may be your only strength!
I don't believe this! Even his glance is in monotone!
Fanciful and Stiffowitz are going at it again! It's their annual fist fight!
Stiffowitz made another racial slur!
Why does Fanciful tolerate it? Why doesn't he just transfer Stiffowitz out of the 15th!?
Really? Then who'd carry the show — you?
Kid, you're growing on me! You've become like a son!
STOOL PIGEON
Wow! Thank you, Antsy!
Keep in mind I was the world's worst dad! Antsy Jr. was neglected, psychotic, I drove him crazy, and eventually he all but committed suicide!
Stiffowitz, level with me... how come I'm resented at the one-five?
Let's face it, surfer boy, you don't exactly ignite the small screen!
I meant with the squad! All I want is their respect!
You gotta earn it! Show the 15th that you're one of us! Prove that you belong!
NYP
THIS END UP
That's it! You've done a scene bare-assed! Now you're one of us! Welcome to the 15th Precinct!
It's always nice to see a new face!
I had a rough day at work! I got into a fist fight with my boss, I insulted a Navajo, I taunted a lesbian and I punched a Cuban!
Around here we have a name for that!
Oh yeah? What's that?
It's called Tuesday!

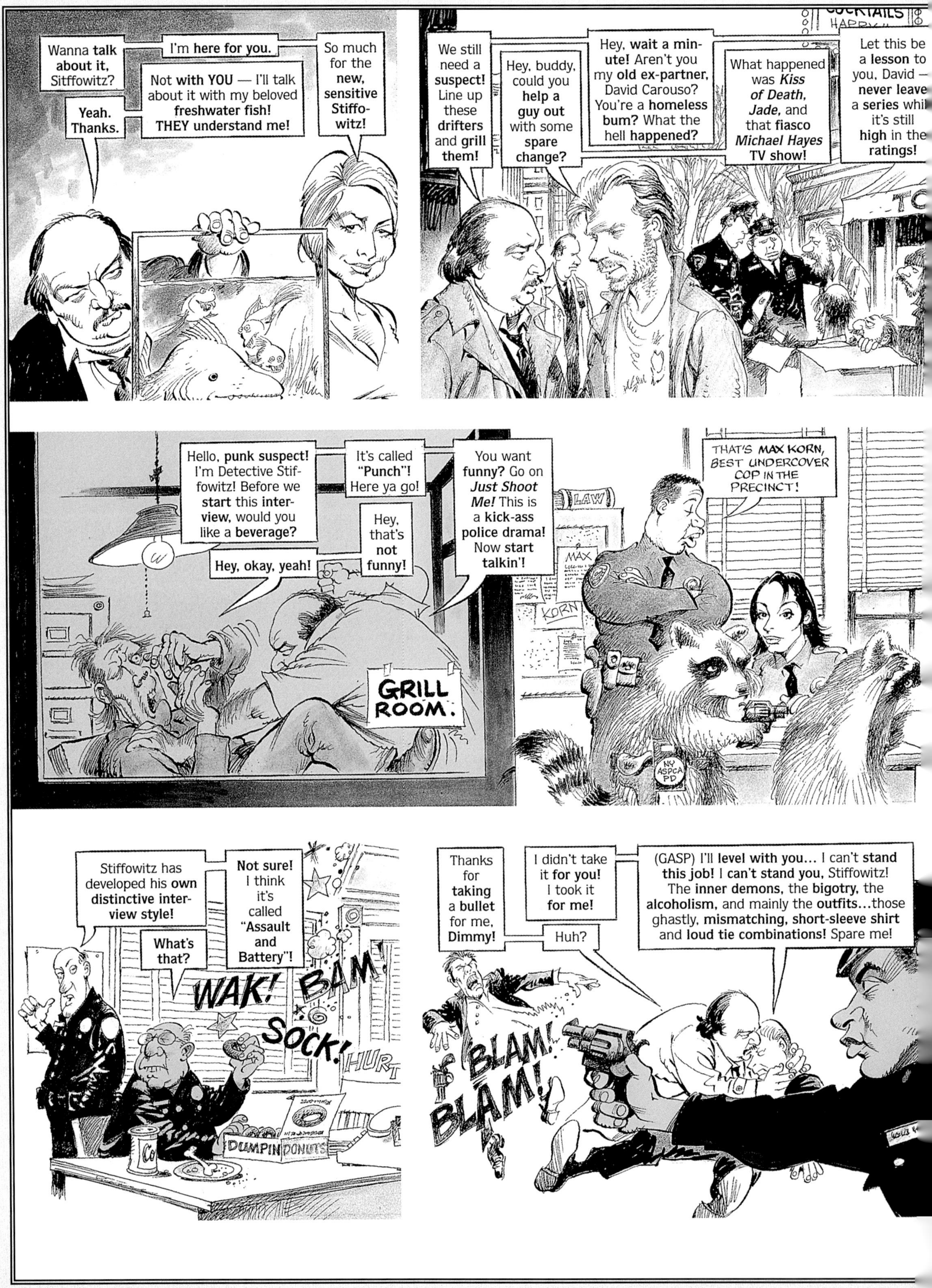
Wanna talk about it, Sitffowitz?
Yeah. Thanks.
I'm here for you.
Not with YOU — I'll talk about it with my beloved freshwater fish! THEY understand me!
So much for the new, sensitive Stiffo-witz!
We still need a suspect! Line up these drifters and grill them!
Hey, buddy, could you help a guy out with some spare change?
Hey, wait a min-ute! Aren't you my old ex-partner, David Carouso? You're a homeless bum? What the hell happened?
What happened was Kiss of Death, Jade, and that fiasco Michael Hayes TV show!
Let this be a lesson to you, David — never leave a series whil it's still high in the ratings!
Hello, punk suspect! I'm Detective Stif-fowitz! Before we start this inter-view, would you like a beverage?
Hey, okay, yeah!
It's called "Punch"! Here ya go!
Hey, that's not funny!
You want funny? Go on Just Shoot Me! This is a kick-ass police drama! Now start talkin'!
LAW
GRILL ROOM.
THAT'S MAX KORN, BEST UNDERCOVER COP IN THE PRECINCT!
MAX
KORN
NY ASPCA PD
Stiffowitz has developed his own distinctive inter-view style!
What's that?
Not sure! I think it's called "Assault and Battery"!
WAK! BAM! SOCK! HURT
DUMPIN DONUTS
Thanks for taking a bullet for me, Dimmy!
I didn't take it for you! I took it for me!
Huh?
(GASP) I'll level with you... I can't stand this job! I can't stand you, Stiffowitz! The inner demons, the bigotry, the alcoholism, and mainly the outfits...those ghastly, mismatching, short-sleeve shirt and loud tie combinations! Spare me!
BLAM! BLAM!

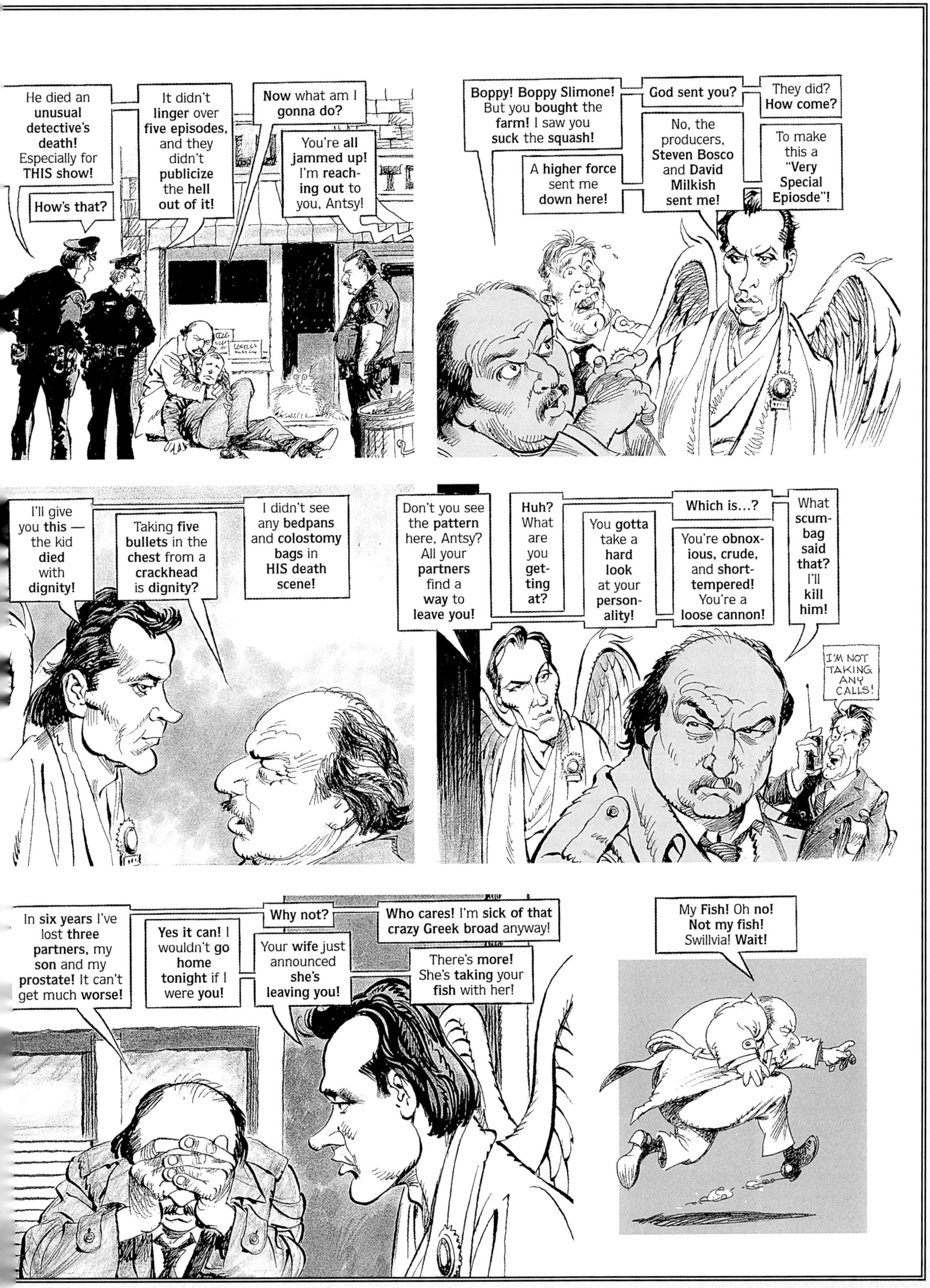
He died an unusual detective's death! Especially for THIS show!
How's that?
It didn't linger over five episodes, and they didn't publicize the hell out of it!
Now what am I gonna do?
You're all jammed up! I'm reaching out to you, Antsy!
Boppy! Boppy Slimone! But you bought the farm! I saw you suck the squash!
A higher force sent me down here!
God sent you?
No, the producers, Steven Bosco and David Milkish sent me!
They did? How come?
To make this a "Very Special Episode"!
I'll give you this — the kid died with dignity!
Taking five bullets in the chest from a crackhead is dignity?
I didn't see any bedpans and colostomy bags in HIS death scene!
Don't you see the pattern here, Antsy? All your partners find a way to leave you!
Huh? What are you getting at?
You gotta take a hard look at your personality!
Which is...?
You're obnoxious, crude, and short-tempered! You're a loose cannon!
What scumbag said that? I'll kill him!
I'M NOT TAKING ANY CALLS!
In six years I've lost three partners, my son and my prostate! It can't get much worse!
Yes it can! I wouldn't go home tonight if I were you!
Why not?
Your wife just announced she's leaving you!
Who cares! I'm sick of that crazy Greek broad anyway!
There's more! She's taking your fish with her!
My Fish! Oh no! Not my fish! Swillvia! Wait!

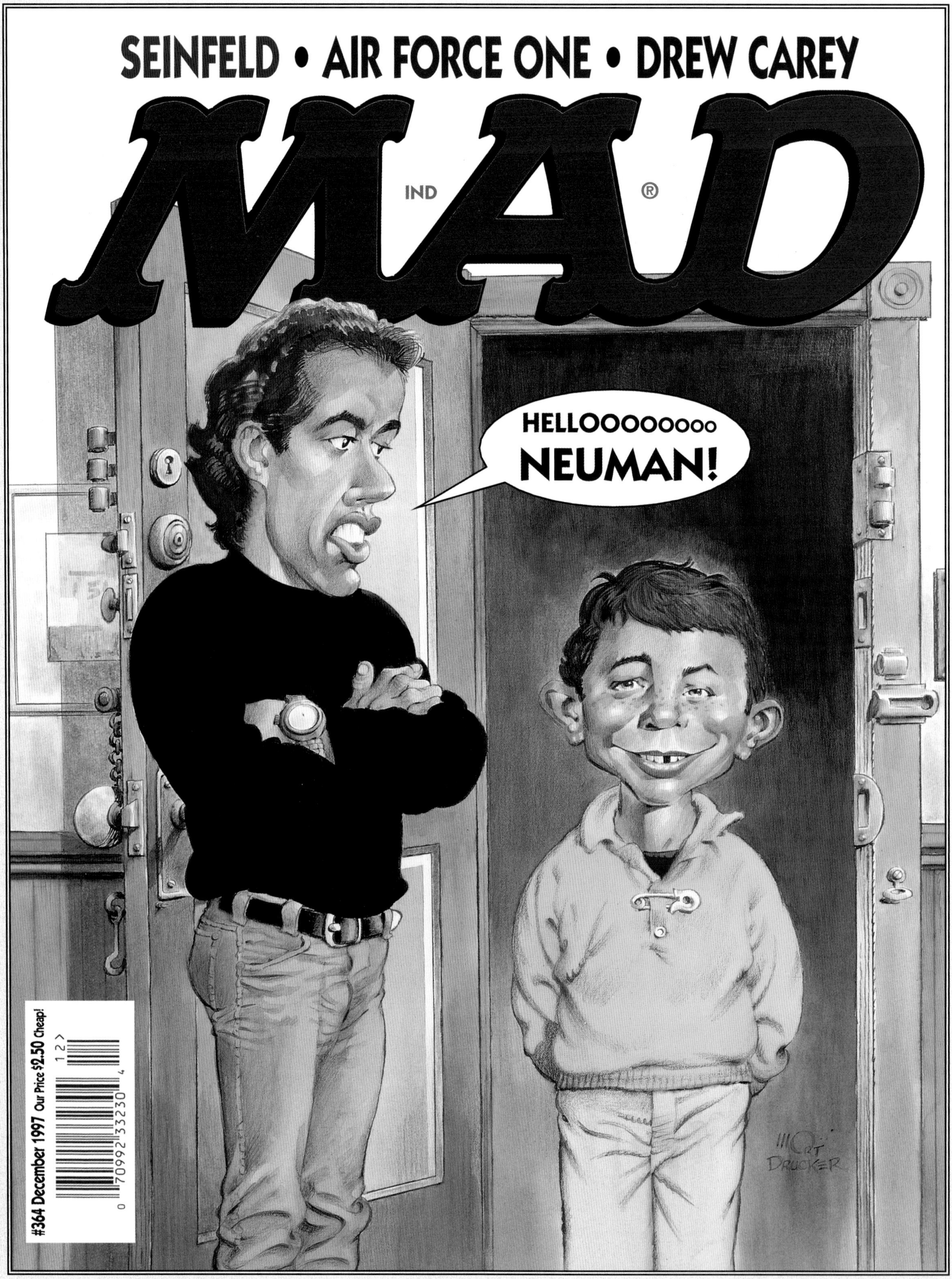
SEINFELD • AIR FORCE ONE • DREW CAREY
MAD
IND
HELLOOOOOOooo
NEUMAN!
#364 December 1997 Our Price $2.50 Cheap!
MORT DRUCKER

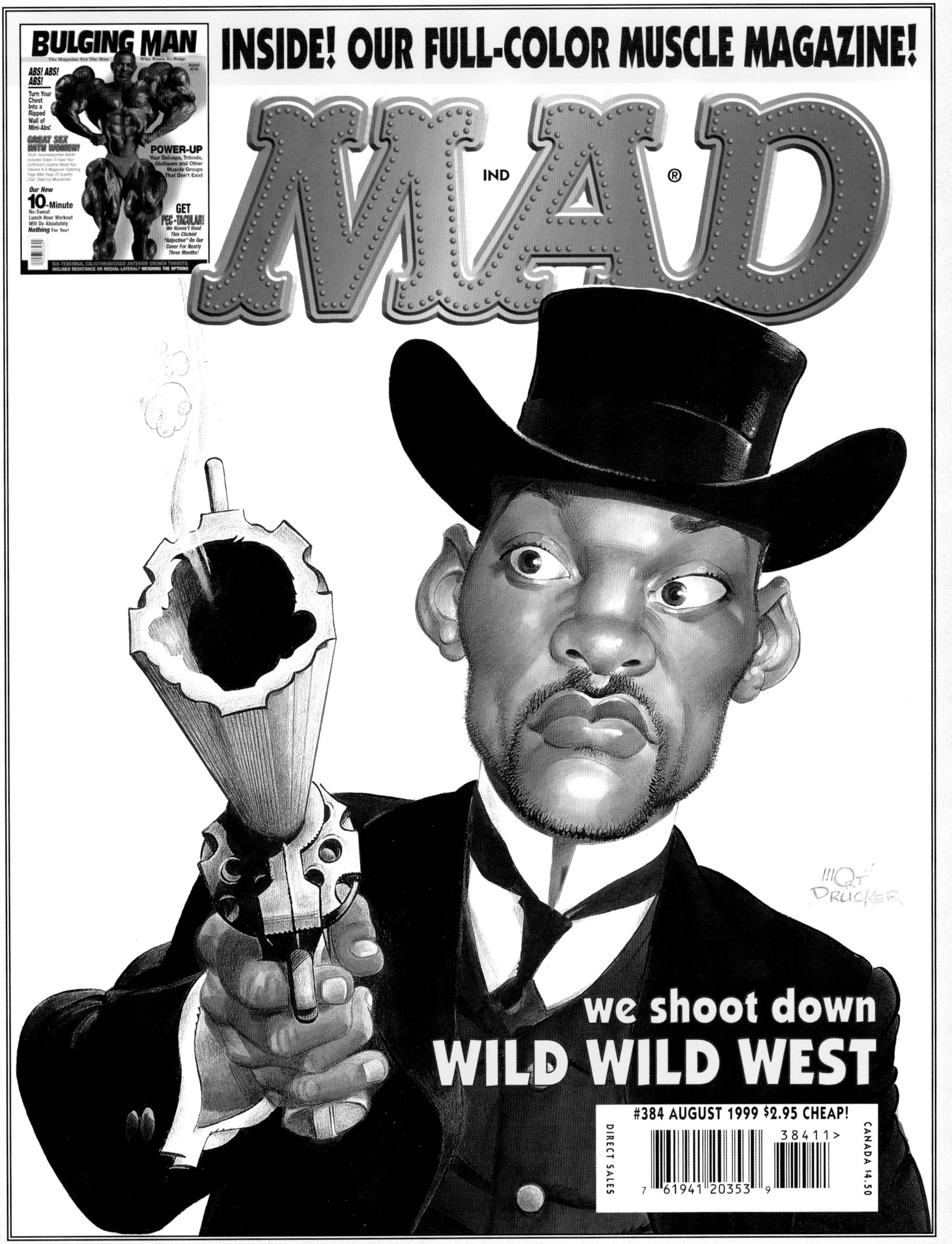
BULGING MAN
ABS! ABS! ABS!
Turn Your Chest Into a Ripped Wall of Mini-Abs!
POWER-UP
Our New 10-Minute No-Sweat Lunch Hour Workout Will Do Absolutely Nothing For You!
GET PEC-TACULAR!
INSIDE! OUR FULL-COLOR MUSCLE MAGAZINE!
MAD
IND
®
we shoot down
WILD WILD WEST
#384 AUGUST 1999 $2.95 CHEAP!
DIRECT SALES
CANADA $4.50
MORT DRUCKER

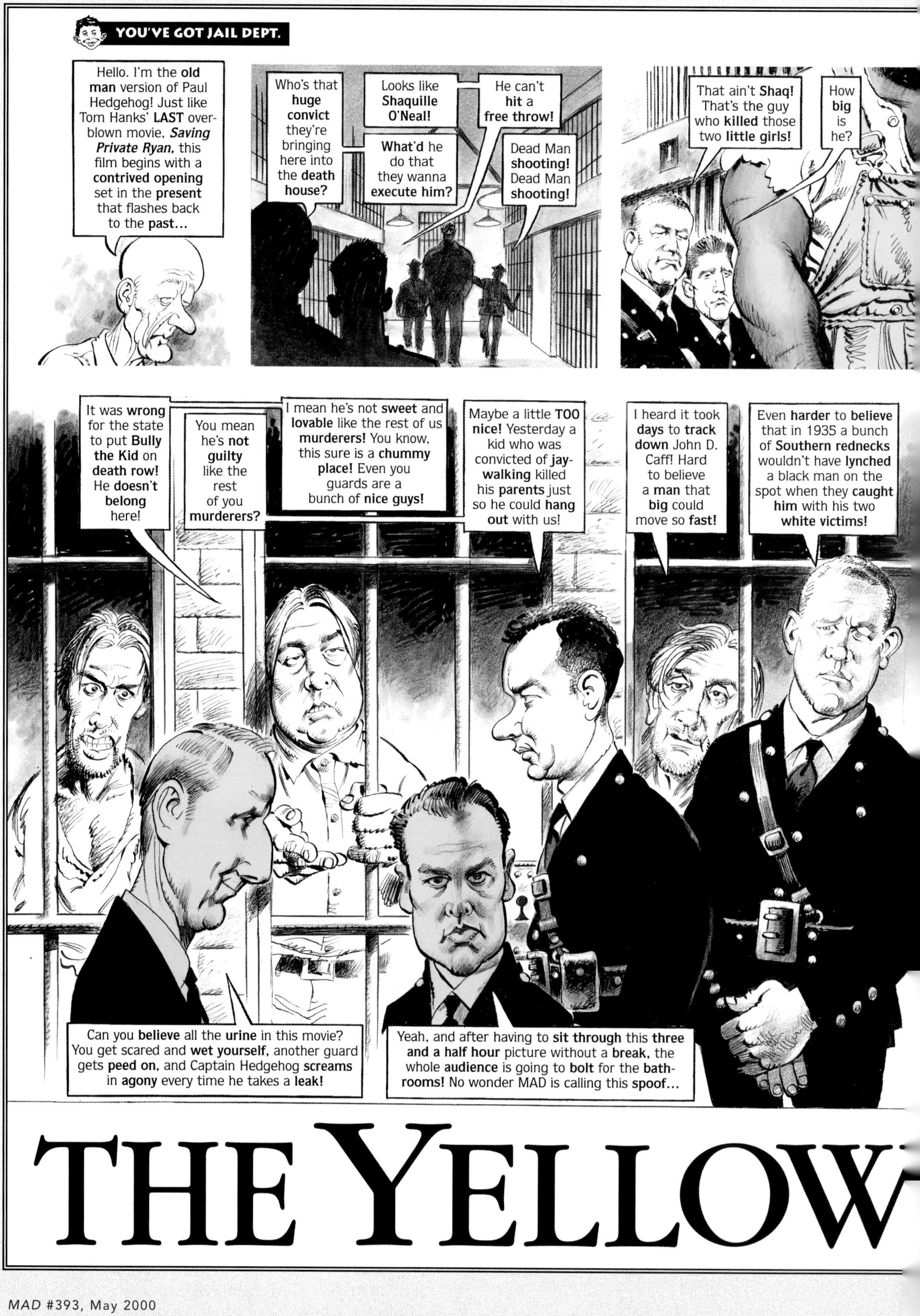
YOU'VE GOT JAIL DEPT.
Hello. I'm the old man version of Paul Hedgehog! Just like Tom Hanks' LAST over-blown movie, Saving Private Ryan, this film begins with a contrived opening set in the present that flashes back to the past...
Who's that huge convict they're bringing here into the death house?
Looks like Shaquille O'Neal!
He can't hit a free throw!
What'd he do that they wanna execute him?
Dead Man shooting! Dead Man shooting!
That ain't Shaq! That's the guy who killed those two little girls!
How big is he?
It was wrong for the state to put Bully the Kid on death row! He doesn't belong here!
You mean he's not guilty like the rest of you murderers?
I mean he's not sweet and lovable like the rest of us murderers! You know, this sure is a chummy place! Even you guards are a bunch of nice guys!
Maybe a little TOO nice! Yesterday a kid who was convicted of jay-walking killed his parents just so he could hang out with us!
I heard it took days to track down John D. Caff! Hard to believe a man that big could move so fast!
Even harder to believe that in 1935 a bunch of Southern rednecks wouldn't have lynched a black man on the spot when they caught him with his two white victims!
Can you believe all the urine in this movie? You get scared and wet yourself, another guard gets peed on, and Captain Hedgehog screams in agony every time he takes a leak!
Yeah, and after having to sit through this three and a half hour picture without a break, the whole audience is going to bolt for the bath-rooms! No wonder MAD is calling this spoof...
THE YELLOW

MAD #393, May 2000

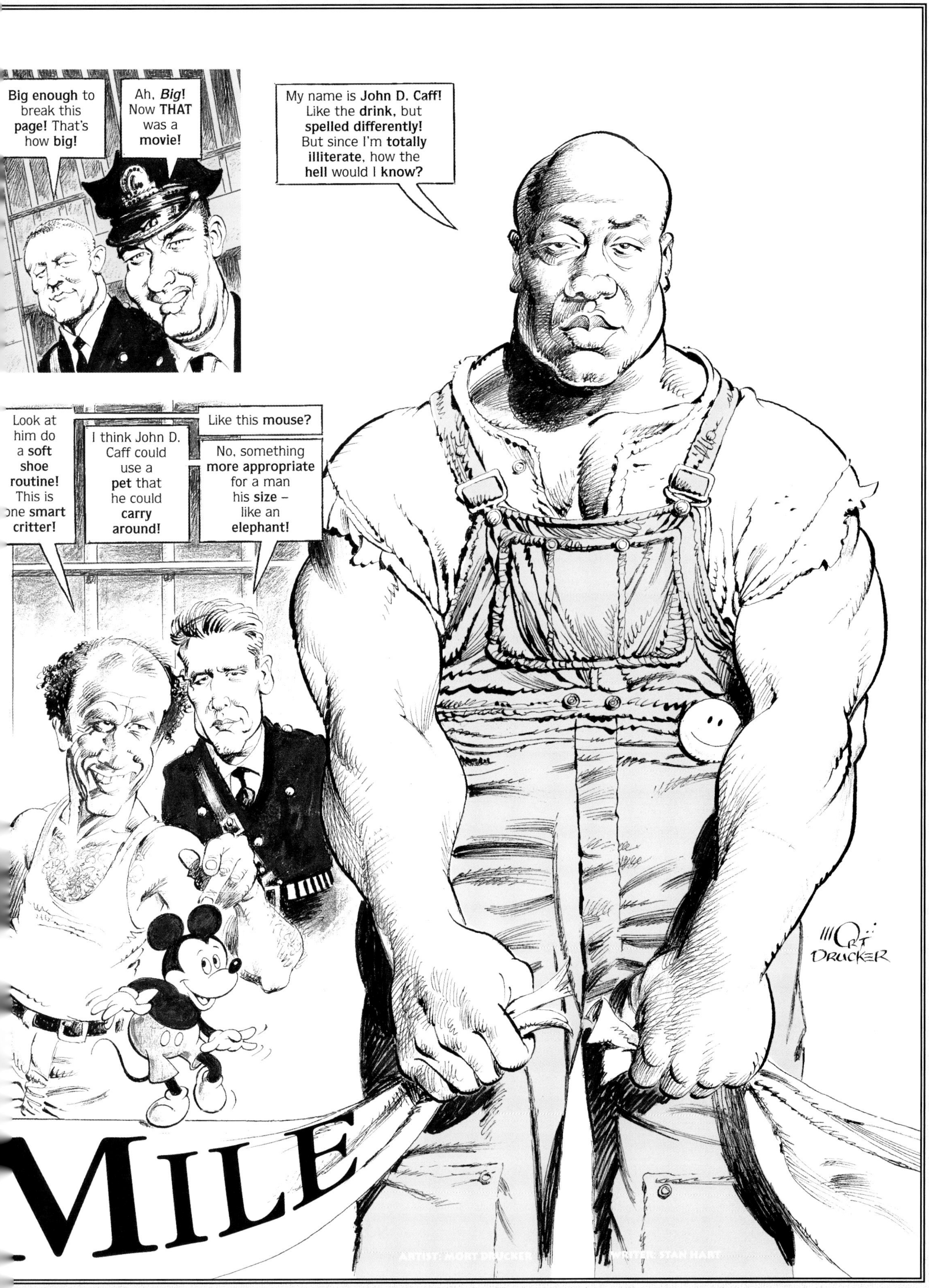
Big enough to break this page! That's how big!
Ah, Big! Now THAT was a movie!
My name is John D. Caff! Like the drink, but spelled differently! But since I'm totally illiterate, how the hell would I know?
Look at him do a soft shoe routine! This is one smart critter!
I think John D. Caff could use a pet that he could carry around!
Like this mouse?
No, something more appropriate for a man his size – like an elephant!
MORT DRUCKER
MILE
ARTIST: MORT DRUCKER
WRITER: STAN HART

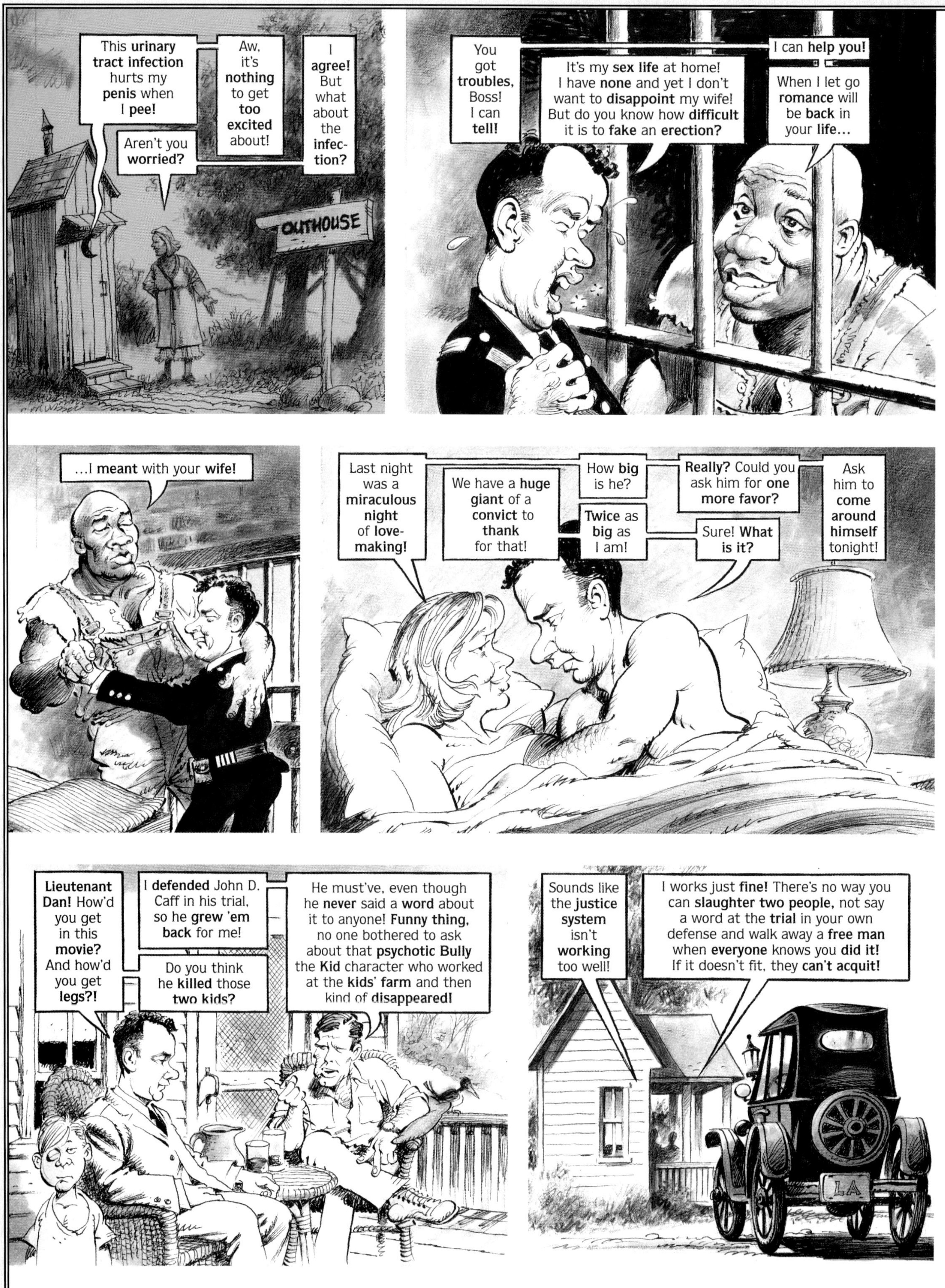
This urinary tract infection hurts my penis when I pee!
Aren't you worried?
Aw, it's nothing to get too excited about!
I agree! But what about the infection?
OUTHOUSE
You got troubles, Boss! I can tell!
It's my sex life at home! I have none and yet I don't want to disappoint my wife! But do you know how difficult it is to fake an erection?
I can help you!
When I let go romance will be back in your life...
...I meant with your wife!
Last night was a miraculous night of love-making!
We have a huge giant of a convict to thank for that!
How big is he?
Twice as big as I am!
Really? Could you ask him for one more favor?
Sure! What is it?
Ask him to come around himself tonight!
Lieutenant Dan! How'd you get in this movie? And how'd you get legs?!
I defended John D. Caff in his trial, so he grew 'em back for me!
Do you think he killed those two kids?
He must've, even though he never said a word about it to anyone! Funny thing, no one bothered to ask about that psychotic Bully the Kid character who worked at the kids' farm and then kind of disappeared!
Sounds like the justice system isn't working too well!
I works just fine! There's no way you can slaughter two people, not say a word at the trial in your own defense and walk away a free man when everyone knows you did it! If it doesn't fit, they can't acquit!
LA

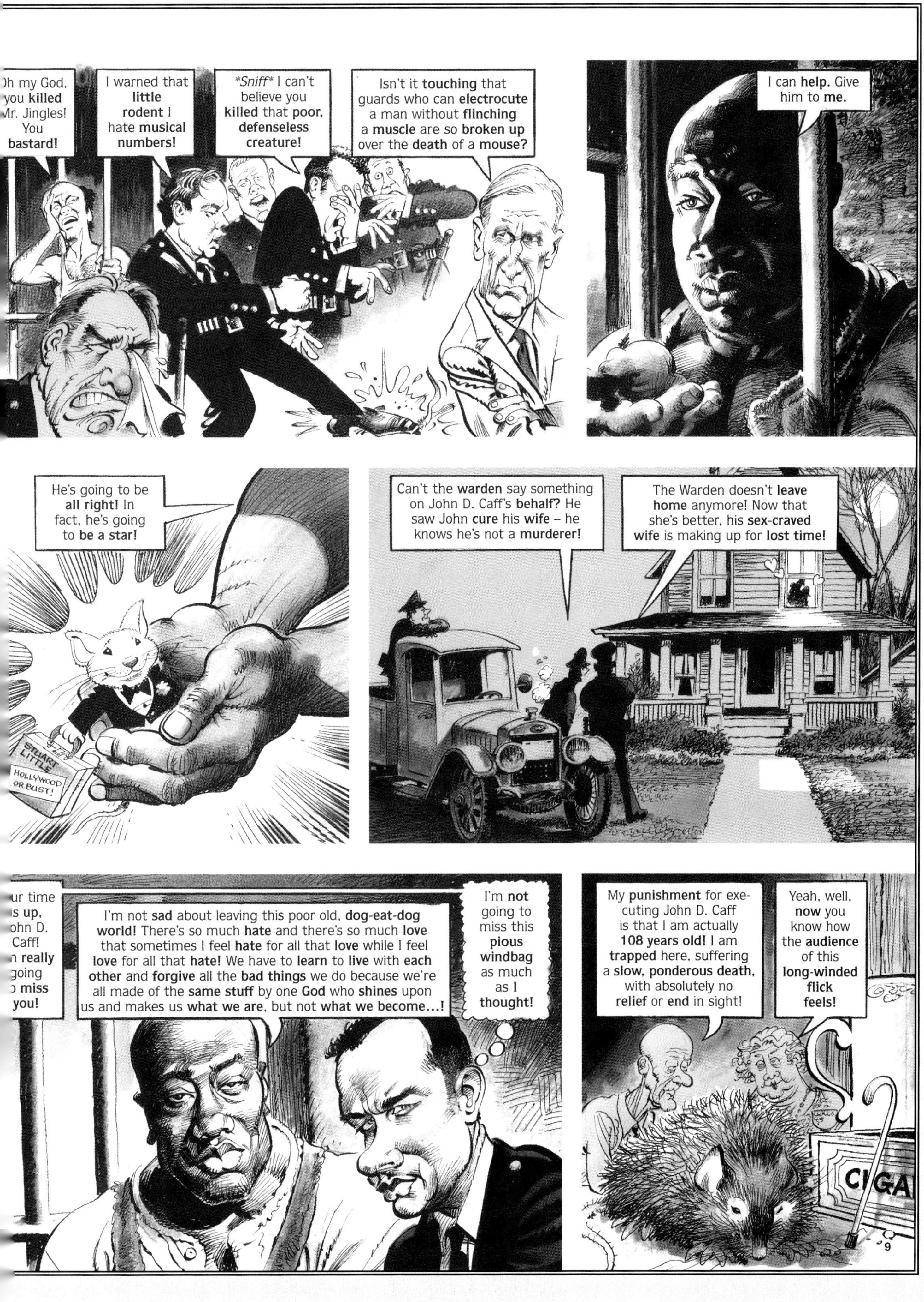

h my God, you killed r. Jingles! You bastard!
I warned that little rodent I hate musical numbers!
Sniff I can't believe you killed that poor, defenseless creature!
Isn't it touching that guards who can electrocute a man without flinching a muscle are so broken up over the death of a mouse?
I can help. Give him to me.
He's going to be all right! In fact, he's going to be a star!
STUART LITTLE
HOLLYWOOD OR BUST!
Can't the warden say something on John D. Caff's behalf? He saw John cure his wife – he knows he's not a murderer!
The Warden doesn't leave home anymore! Now that she's better, his sex-craved wife is making up for lost time!
ur time s up, ohn D. Caff! n really going o miss you!
I'm not sad about leaving this poor old, dog-eat-dog world! There's so much hate and there's so much love that sometimes I feel hate for all that love while I feel love for all that hate! We have to learn to live with each other and forgive all the bad things we do because we're all made of the same stuff by one God who shines upon us and makes us what we are, but not what we become...!
I'm not going to miss this pious windbag as much as I thought!
My punishment for executing John D. Caff is that I am actually 108 years old! I am trapped here, suffering a slow, ponderous death, with absolutely no relief or end in sight!
Yeah, well, now you know how the audience of this long-winded flick feels!
CIGA
9

spent much of my childhood poring over every panel of Mort Drucker's art in *MAD* Magazine. I'm not alone in this obsession. Many of us hoarded every issue so we could go back and revisit his art time and again, like pilgrims visiting a holy land. One of the things that always struck me about his work was his unstinting approach, regardless of the film being parodied. It wasn't just the lavish movies like *The Godfather* for which he pulled out all the stops; he did the same for *every* film. For example, I remember being blown away by his art for the 1971 low-budget "killer rats" movie, *Willard*. That Mr. Drucker conveyed so beautifully the likenesses of Ernest Borgnine and Elsa Lanchester comes as no surprise given his renowned skills, but I was just as impressed that he nailed with equal loving perfection the likenesses of actors Bruce Davison and Sondra Locke. Even as a kid reading a magazine whose only goal was to make me chortle, I recognized that this was an artist possessing professionalism and talent far beyond the norm. What sets Mort Drucker apart? What assures that his face will be the first one carved on the Mt. Rushmore of caricature artists? He never merely drew a person's likeness, he somehow gave us the *person*. The essence, the presence, even the mannerisms of those actors are ineffably captured on the page by means of some sly magic that Mr. Drucker conjures between his pen and the Bristol board. Like all the best art, it seems like purest alchemy to me. It mystifies and delights me.

Some years ago, I was rendered slack-jawed upon finding the original art of Mort Drucker's *Jaws* parody on the wall of Steven Spielberg's office, beautifully framed and reverently lit. Mind you, there are awards and honors beyond counting in that office, but it was those Mort Drucker pages that Steven was prouder of than just about anything else on display. Steven had been *Drucker-ized*, you see. For a filmmaker, it's the next best thing to getting an Oscar. In the Church of Geek, it's like being canonized.

Okay, I'll admit this now: I was so damn jealous of Steven for being Drucker-ized! Not only that, but Steven actually *owned* the pages! Oh, how I seethed with envy! Oh, how I plotted revenge!

Both envy and revenge proved petty and unnecessary, for not long after seeing those *Jaws* pages on Steven's wall, fortune smiled upon me and my film *The Green Mile* was likewise Drucker-ized in the pages of MAD. I don't know what flabbergasted me more: the fact that Mr. Drucker had chosen my film for that honor, or the stunning quality of the art he produced. (Time has not diminished the man's skills by one iota.) I use no hyperbole when I say that getting Drucker-ized was one of the thrills of my career.

I no longer have any reason to be jealous of Steven Spielberg (truly one of the world's nicest guys, and undeserving of my seething envy) because I too have been immortalized by the great Mort Drucker. Thank you, Mr. Drucker, for bestowing your blessing upon me, and for allowing me the privilege of owning those hallowed pages.

Mort Drucker didn't invent caricature art, but we should just throw the credit to him anyway, because his talent and vast influence in his highly specialized field shall never be surpassed. He is to caricature art what Frank Frazetta is to fantasy, what William Blake is to the Romantic Age, and what Michelangelo is to ceilings: an innovator, a legend, the best of the best.

—Frank Darabont
Director, *The Green Mile*

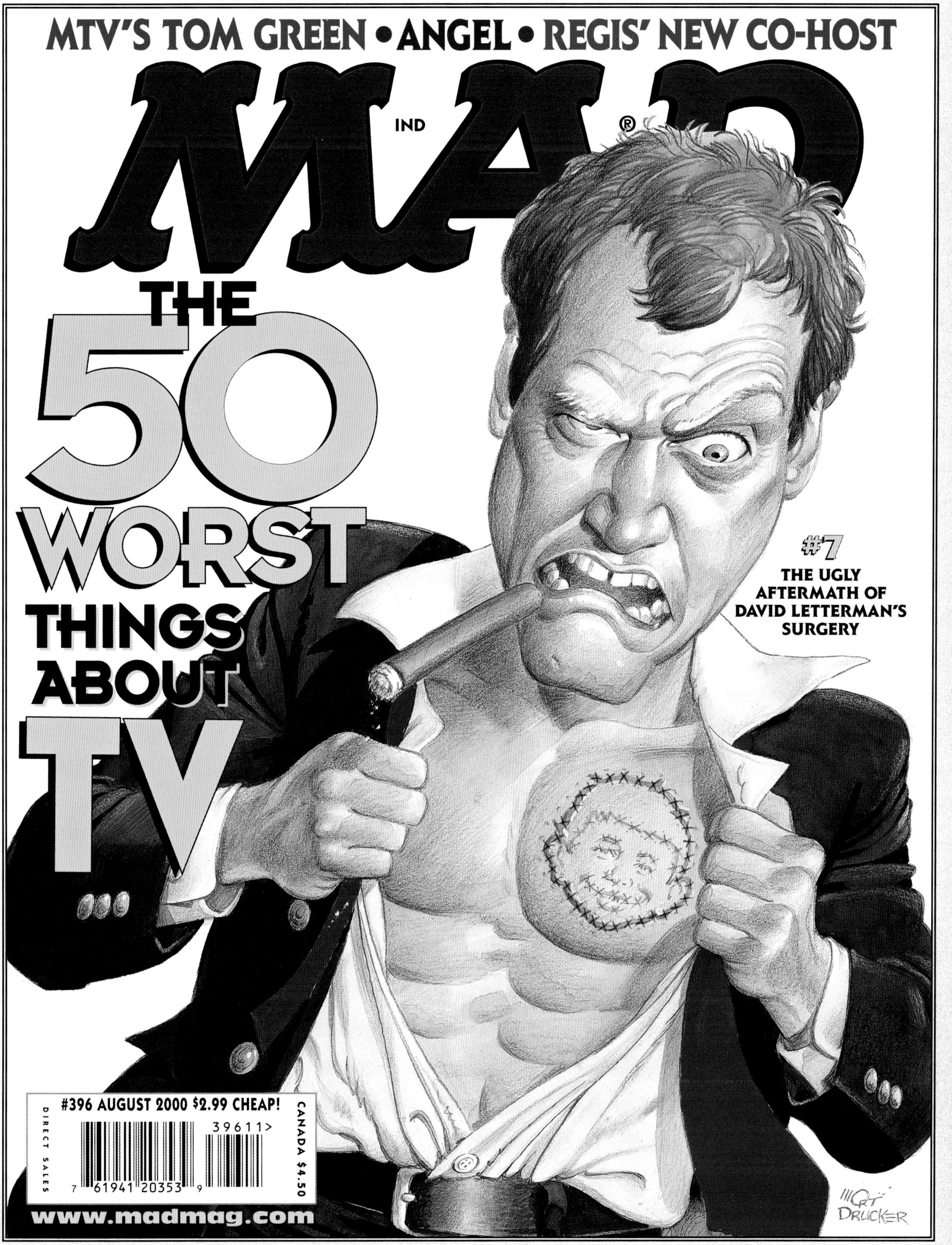
MTV'S TOM GREEN • ANGEL • REGIS' NEW CO-HOST
MAD
IND
THE 50 WORST THINGS ABOUT TV
#7
THE UGLY AFTERMATH OF DAVID LETTERMAN'S SURGERY
#396 AUGUST 2000 $2.99 CHEAP!
DIRECT SALES
CANADA $4.50
www.madmag.com
MORT DRUCKER

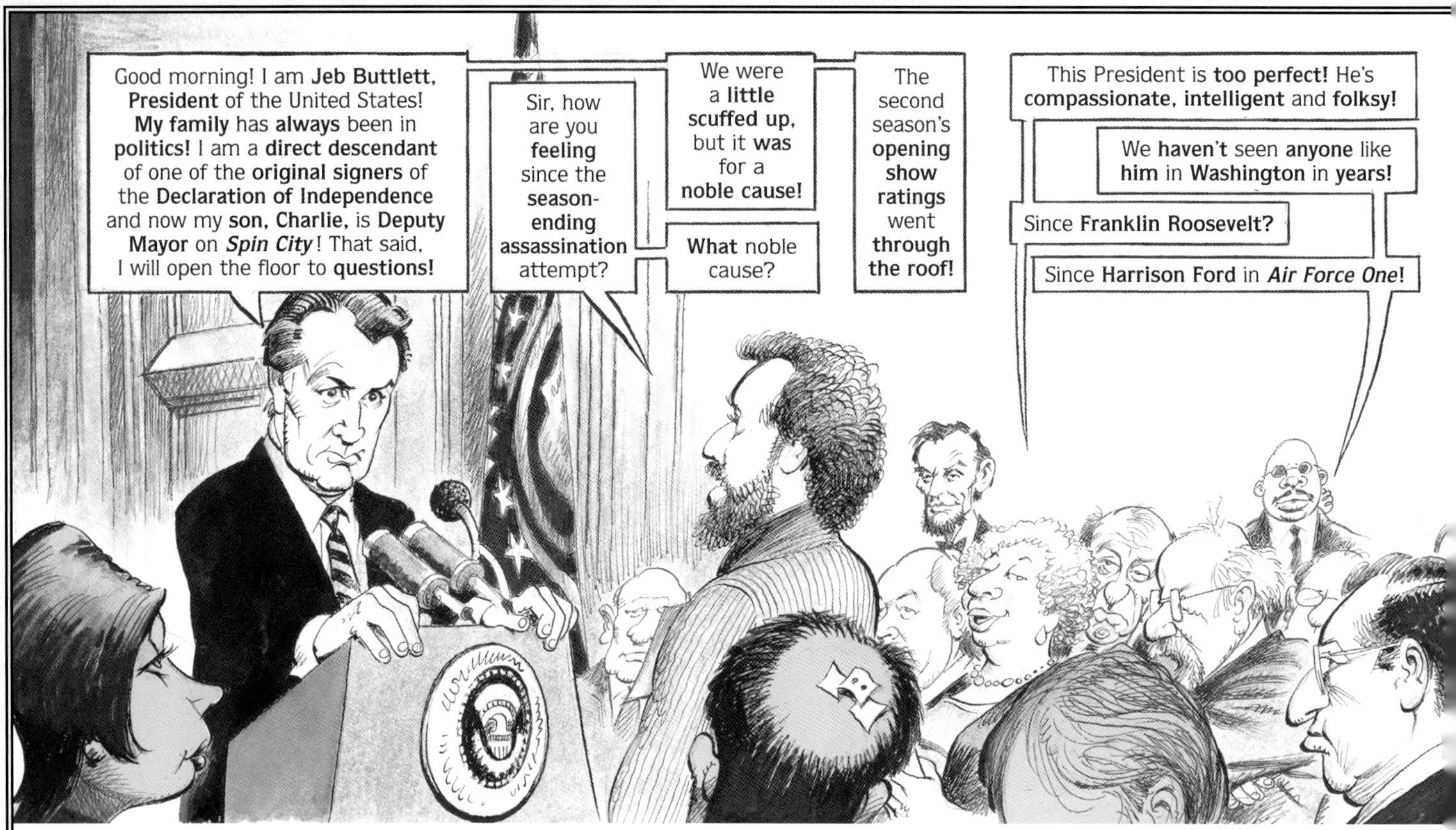
Good morning! I am **Jeb Buttlett, President** of the United States! **My family** has **always** been in **politics!** I am a **direct descendant** of one of the **original signers** of the **Declaration of Independence** and now my **son, Charlie,** is **Deputy Mayor** on ***Spin City***! That said, I will open the floor to **questions!**
Sir, how are you **feeling** since the **season-ending assassination** attempt?
We were a **little scuffed up,** but it **was** for a **noble cause!**
What noble cause?
The second season's **opening show ratings** went **through the roof!**
This President is **too perfect!** He's **compassionate, intelligent** and **folksy!**
We **haven't** seen **anyone** like **him** in **Washington** in **years!**
Since **Franklin Roosevelt?**
Since **Harrison Ford** in ***Air Force One***!

PREZ DISPENSER DEPT.

The Electoral College. Hanging chads. Voting irregularities. Frankly, we're sick of hearing about nothing but politics. We just want to sit down in front of the TV and take our minds off of the whole ridiculous process! Okay, let's see what's on...damn! It's...

THE

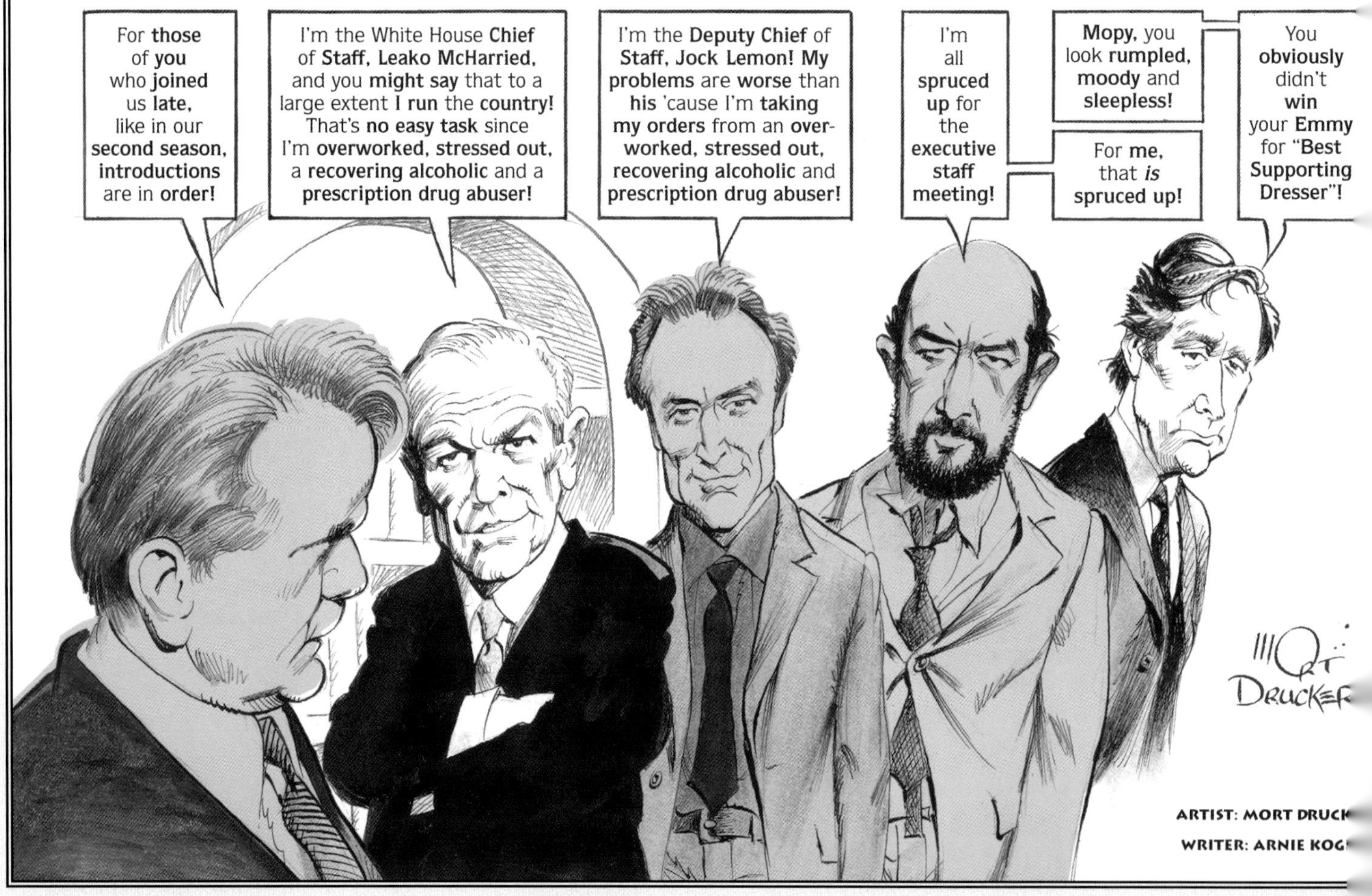
For **those** of **you** who **joined** us **late,** like in our **second season, introductions** are in **order!**
I'm the White House **Chief** of **Staff, Leako McHarried,** and you **might say** that to a large extent **I run** the **country!** That's **no easy task** since I'm **overworked, stressed out,** a **recovering alcoholic** and a **prescription drug abuser!**
I'm the **Deputy Chief** of **Staff, Jock Lemon! My problems** are **worse** than **his** 'cause I'm **taking my orders** from an **over-worked, stressed out, recovering alcoholic** and **prescription drug abuser!**
I'm all **spruced up** for the **executive staff meeting!**
Mopy, you look **rumpled, moody** and **sleepless!**
For **me,** that *is* **spruced up!**
You **obviously** didn't **win** your **Emmy** for **"Best Supporting Dresser"!**
ARTIST: MORT DRUC
WRITER: ARNIE KOG

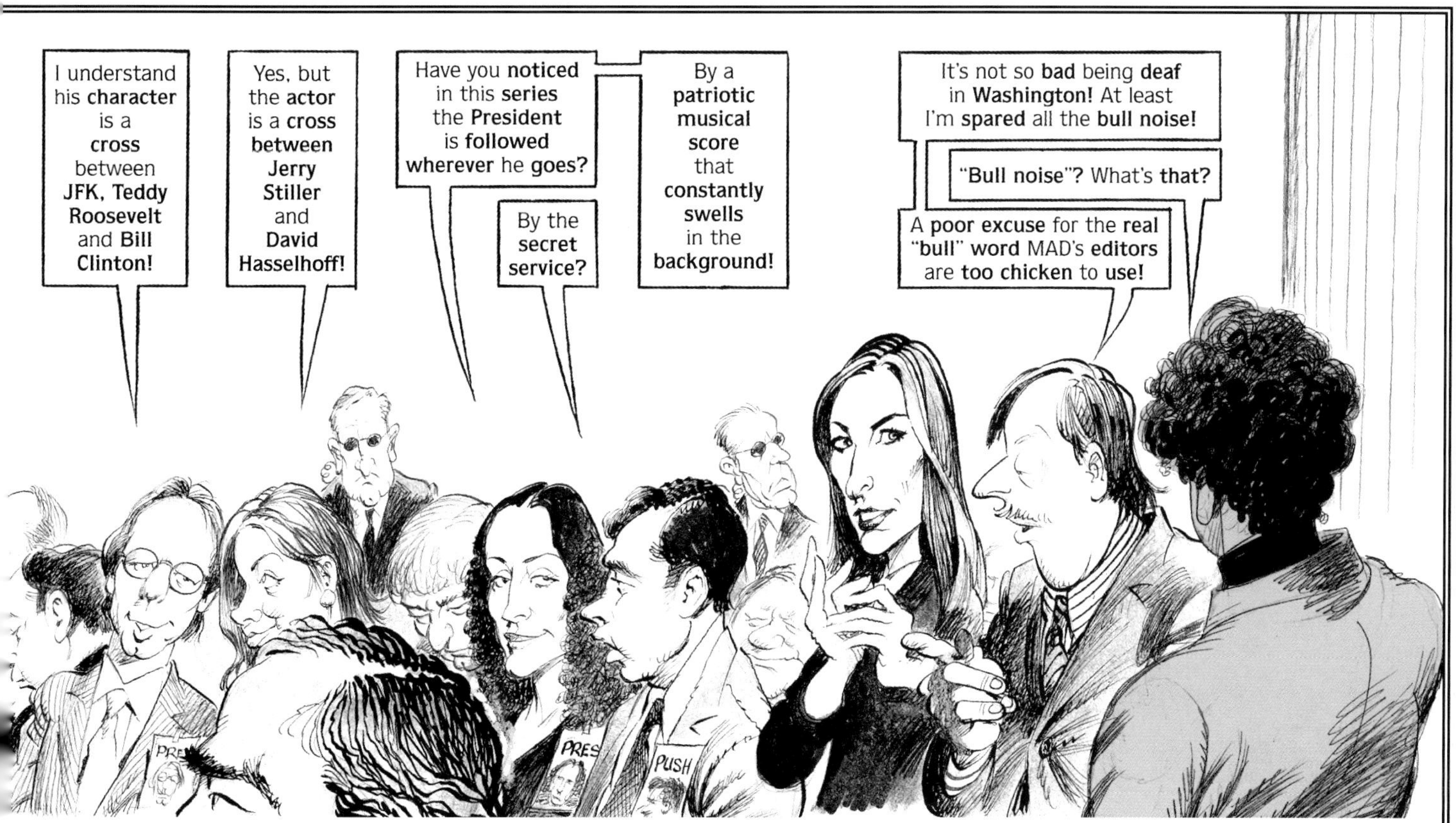
I understand his character is a cross between JFK, Teddy Roosevelt and Bill Clinton!
Yes, but the actor is a cross between Jerry Stiller and David Hasselhoff!
Have you noticed in this series the President is followed wherever he goes?
By the secret service?
By a patriotic musical score that constantly swells in the background!
It's not so bad being deaf in Washington! At least I'm spared all the bull noise!
"Bull noise"? What's that?
A poor excuse for the real "bull" word MAD's editors are too chicken to use!
PRES
PUSH

WORST WING

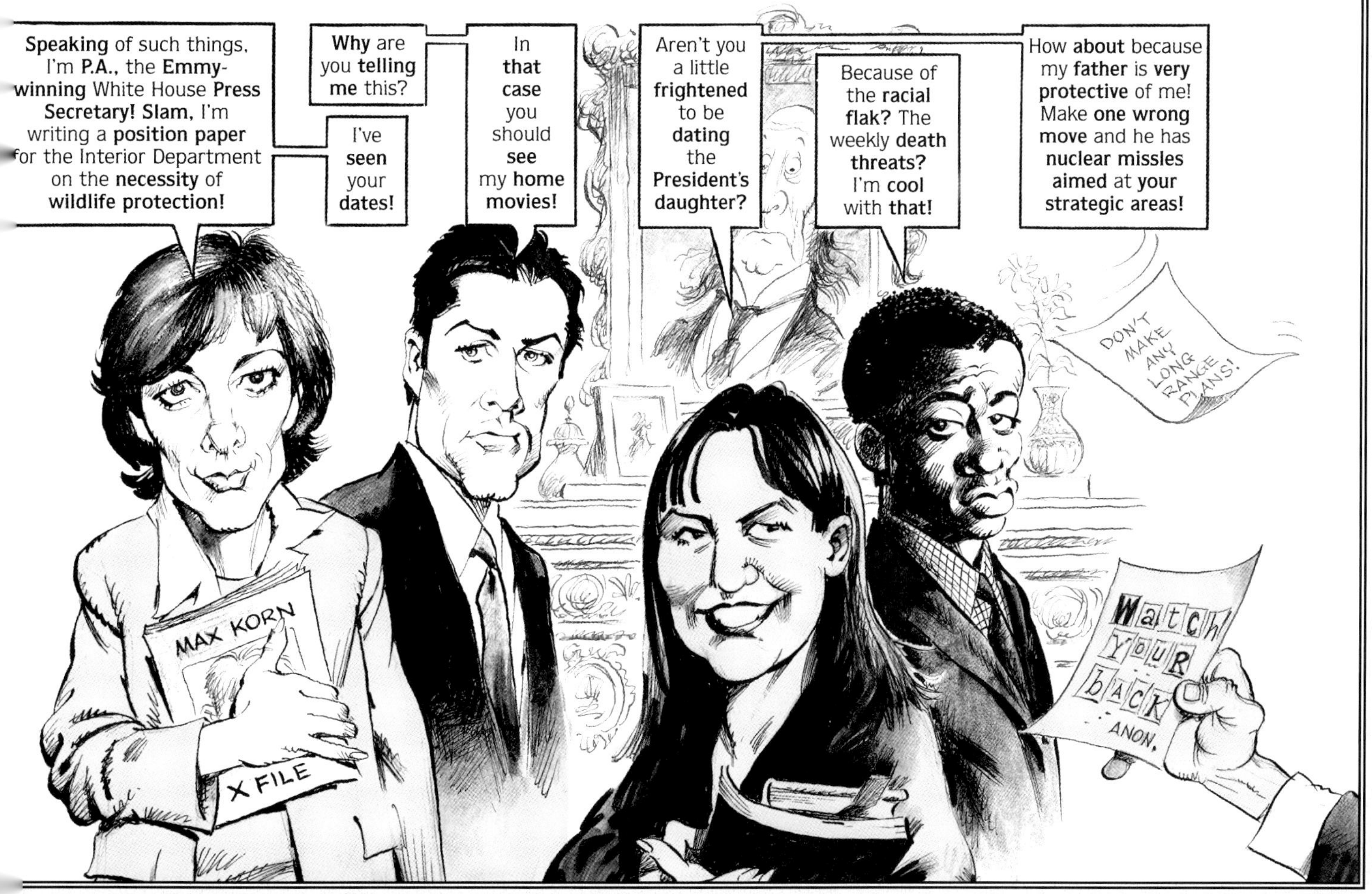
Speaking of such things, I'm P.A., the Emmy-winning White House Press Secretary! Slam, I'm writing a position paper for the Interior Department on the necessity of wildlife protection!
Why are you telling me this?
I've seen your dates!
In that case you should see my home movies!
Aren't you a little frightened to be dating the President's daughter?
Because of the racial flak? The weekly death threats? I'm cool with that!
How about because my father is very protective of me! Make one wrong move and he has nuclear missles aimed at your strategic areas!
DON'T MAKE ANY LONG RANGE PLANS!
MAX KORN
X FILE
Watch Your back
ANON.

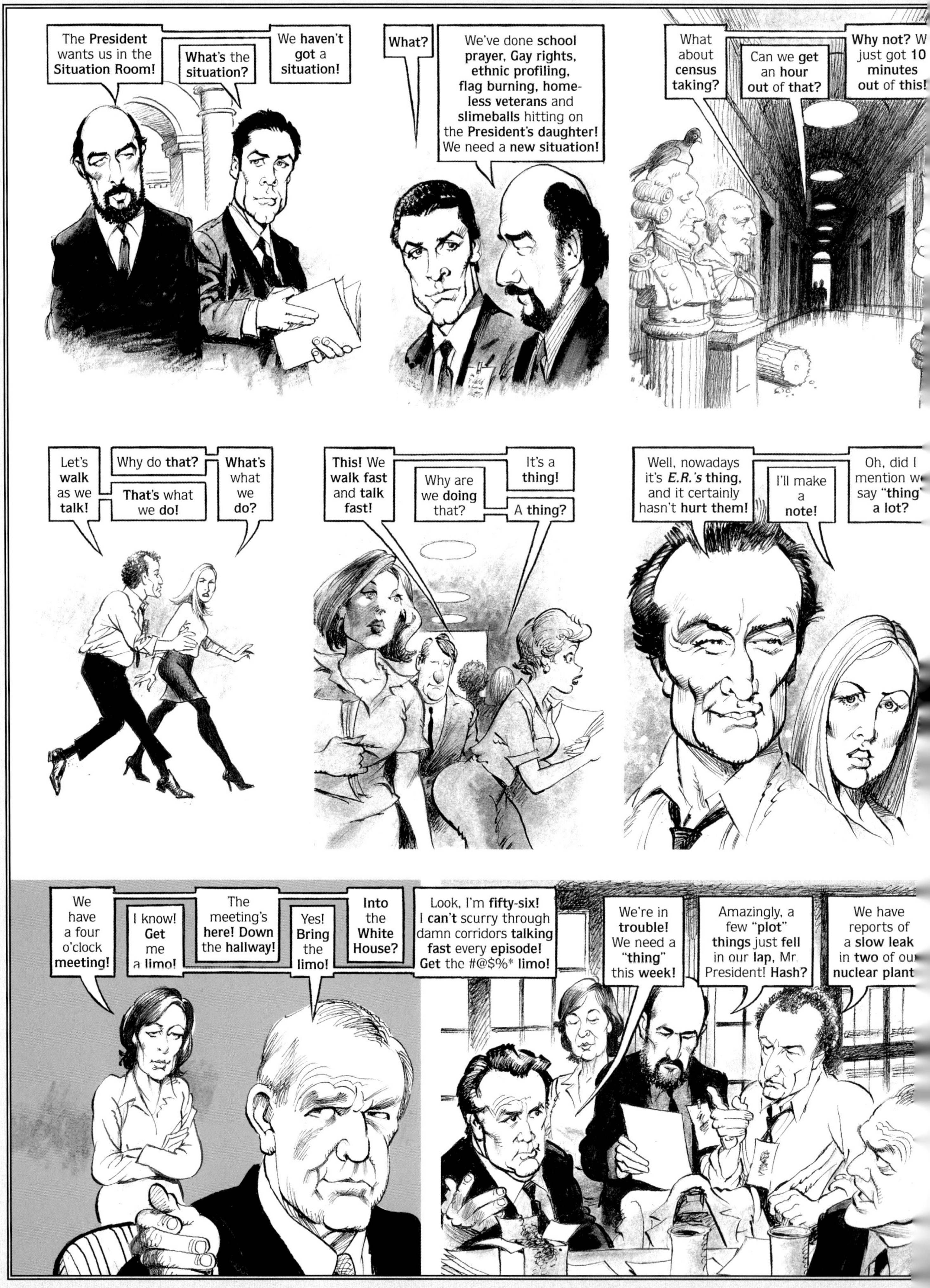
The President wants us in the Situation Room!
What's the situation?
We haven't got a situation!
What?
We've done school prayer, Gay rights, ethnic profiling, flag burning, homeless veterans and slimeballs hitting on the President's daughter! We need a new situation!
What about census taking?
Can we get an hour out of that?
Why not? W just got 10 minutes out of this!
Let's walk as we talk!
Why do that?
That's what we do!
What's what we do?
This! We walk fast and talk fast!
Why are we doing that?
It's a thing!
A thing?
Well, nowadays it's E.R.'s thing, and it certainly hasn't hurt them!
I'll make a note!
Oh, did I mention w say "thing" a lot?
We have a four o'clock meeting!
I know! Get me a limo!
The meeting's here! Down the hallway!
Yes! Bring the limo!
Into the White House?
Look, I'm fifty-six! I can't scurry through damn corridors talking fast every episode! Get the #@$%* limo!
We're in trouble! We need a "thing" this week!
Amazingly, a few "plot" things just fell in our lap, Mr. President! Hash?
We have reports of a slow leak in two of ou nuclear plant

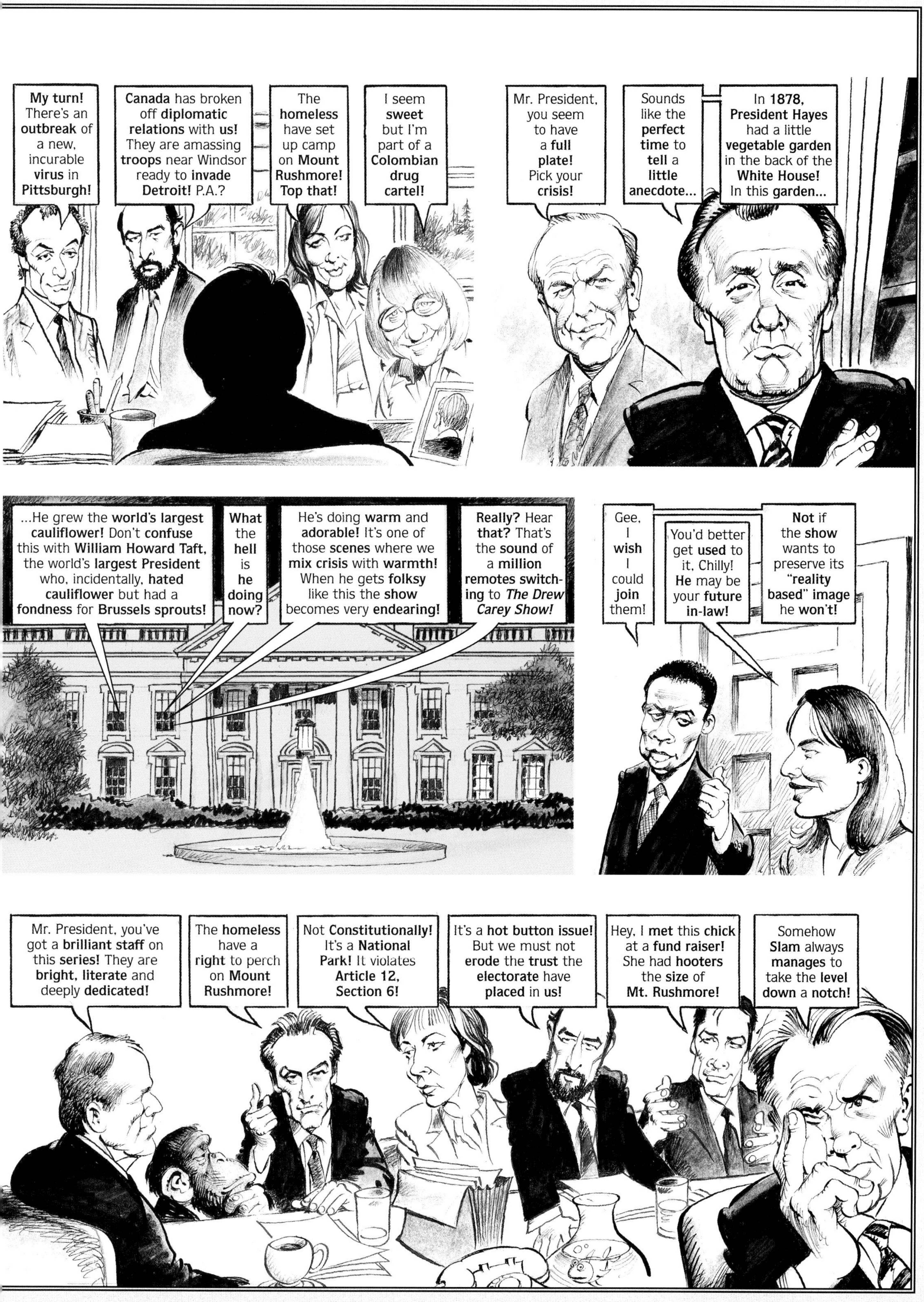

My turn! There's an outbreak of a new, incurable virus in Pittsburgh!
Canada has broken off diplomatic relations with us! They are amassing troops near Windsor ready to invade Detroit! P.A.?
The homeless have set up camp on Mount Rushmore! Top that!
I seem sweet but I'm part of a Colombian drug cartel!
Mr. President, you seem to have a full plate! Pick your crisis!
Sounds like the perfect time to tell a little anecdote...
In 1878, President Hayes had a little vegetable garden in the back of the White House! In this garden...
...He grew the world's largest cauliflower! Don't confuse this with William Howard Taft, the world's largest President who, incidentally, hated cauliflower but had a fondness for Brussels sprouts!
What the hell is he doing now?
He's doing warm and adorable! It's one of those scenes where we mix crisis with warmth! When he gets folksy like this the show becomes very endearing!
Really? Hear that? That's the sound of a million remotes switching to *The Drew Carey Show!*
Gee, I wish I could join them!
You'd better get used to it, Chilly! He may be your future in-law!
Not if the show wants to preserve its "reality based" image he won't!
Mr. President, you've got a brilliant staff on this series! They are bright, literate and deeply dedicated!
The homeless have a right to perch on Mount Rushmore!
Not Constitutionally! It's a National Park! It violates Article 12, Section 6!
It's a hot button issue! But we must not erode the trust the electorate have placed in us!
Hey, I met this chick at a fund raiser! She had hooters the size of Mt. Rushmore!
Somehow Slam always manages to take the level down a notch!

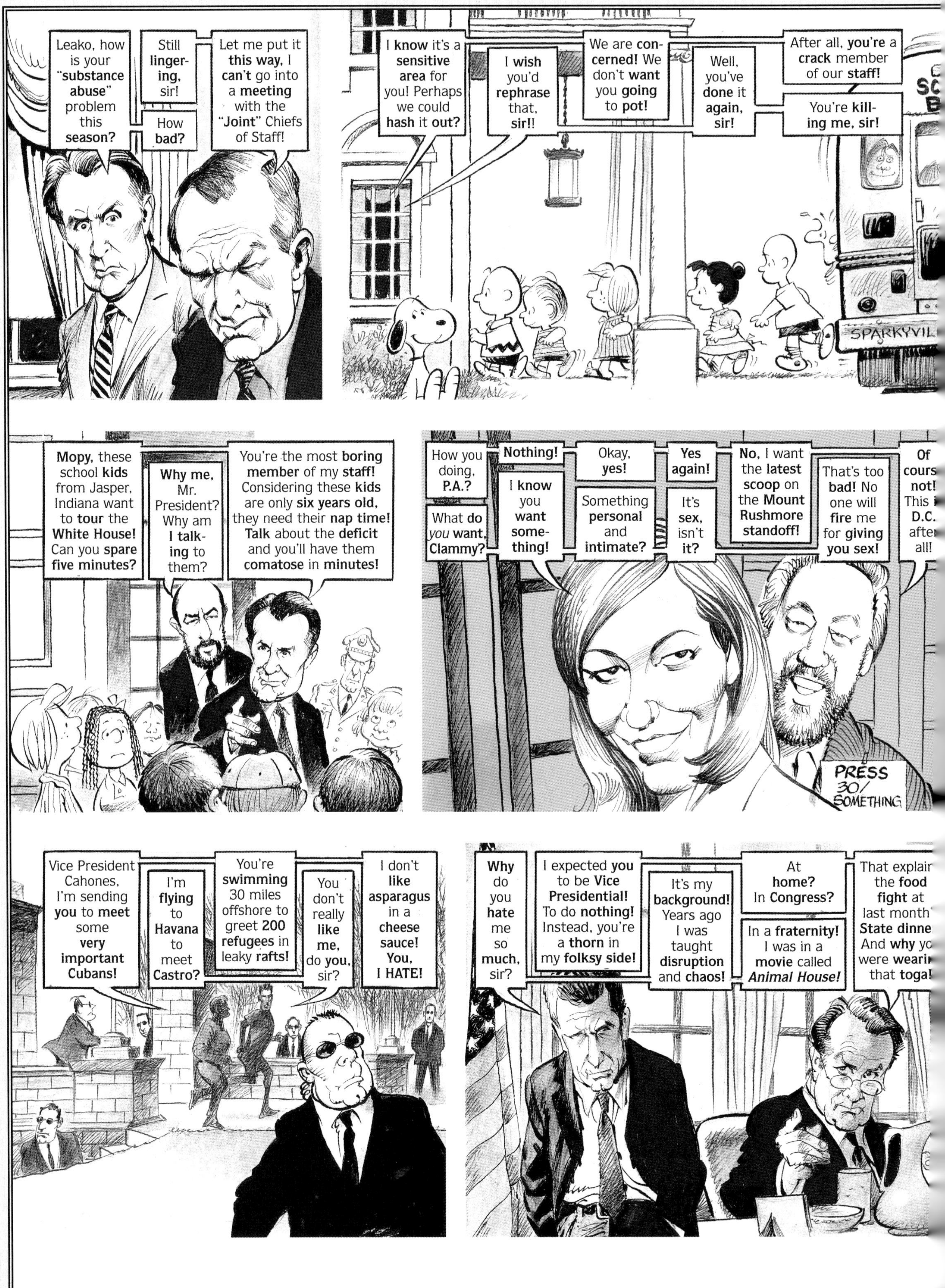

Leako, how is your "substance abuse" problem this season?
Still linger-ing, sir!
How bad?
Let me put it this way, I can't go into a meeting with the "Joint" Chiefs of Staff!
I know it's a sensitive area for you! Perhaps we could hash it out?
I wish you'd rephrase that, sir!!
We are con-cerned! We don't want you going to pot!
Well, you've done it again, sir!
After all, you're a crack member of our staff!
You're kill-ing me, sir!
SPARKYVIL
Mopy, these school kids from Jasper, Indiana want to tour the White House! Can you spare five minutes?
Why me, Mr. President? Why am I talk-ing to them?
You're the most boring member of my staff! Considering these kids are only six years old, they need their nap time! Talk about the deficit and you'll have them comatose in minutes!
How you doing, P.A.?
Nothing!
What do you want, Clammy?
I know you want some-thing!
Okay, yes!
Something personal and intimate?
Yes again!
It's sex, isn't it?
No, I want the latest scoop on the Mount Rushmore standoff!
That's too bad! No one will fire me for giving you sex!
Of cours not! This D.C. afte all!
PRESS 30/ SOMETHING
Vice President Cahones, I'm sending you to meet some very important Cubans!
I'm flying to Havana to meet Castro?
You're swimming 30 miles offshore to greet 200 refugees in leaky rafts!
You don't really like me, do you, sir?
I don't like asparagus in a cheese sauce! You, I HATE!
Why do you hate me so much, sir?
I expected you to be Vice Presidential! To do nothing! Instead, you're a thorn in my folksy side!
It's my background! Years ago I was taught disruption and chaos!
At home? In Congress?
In a fraternity! I was in a movie called Animal House!
That explai the food fight at last month State dinne And why yo were weari that toga!

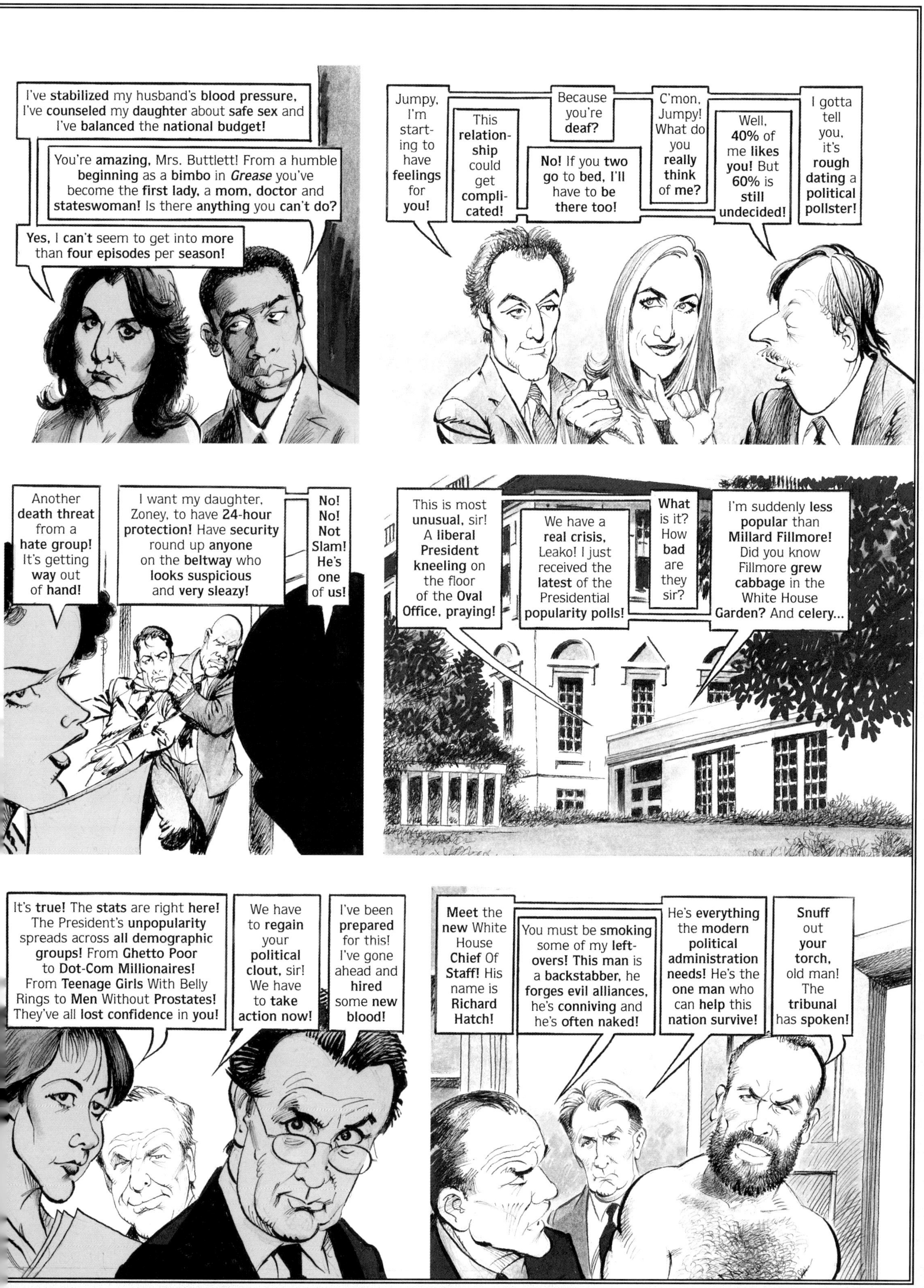
I've stabilized my husband's blood pressure, I've counseled my daughter about safe sex and I've balanced the national budget!
You're amazing, Mrs. Buttlett! From a humble beginning as a bimbo in Grease you've become the first lady, a mom, doctor and stateswoman! Is there anything you can't do?
Yes, I can't seem to get into more than four episodes per season!
Jumpy, I'm starting to have feelings for you!
This relationship could get complicated!
Because you're deaf?
No! If you two go to bed, I'll have to be there too!
C'mon, Jumpy! What do you really think of me?
Well, 40% of me likes you! But 60% is still undecided!
I gotta tell you, it's rough dating a political pollster!
Another death threat from a hate group! It's getting way out of hand!
I want my daughter, Zoney, to have 24-hour protection! Have security round up anyone on the beltway who looks suspicious and very sleazy!
No! No! Not Slam! He's one of us!
This is most unusual, sir! A liberal President kneeling on the floor of the Oval Office, praying!
We have a real crisis, Leako! I just received the latest of the Presidential popularity polls!
What is it? How bad are they sir?
I'm suddenly less popular than Millard Fillmore! Did you know Fillmore grew cabbage in the White House Garden? And celery...
It's true! The stats are right here! The President's unpopularity spreads across all demographic groups! From Ghetto Poor to Dot-Com Millionaires! From Teenage Girls With Belly Rings to Men Without Prostates! They've all lost confidence in you!
We have to regain your political clout, sir! We have to take action now!
I've been prepared for this! I've gone ahead and hired some new blood!
Meet the new White House Chief Of Staff! His name is Richard Hatch!
You must be smoking some of my left-overs! This man is a backstabber, he forges evil alliances, he's conniving and he's often naked!
He's everything the modern political administration needs! He's the one man who can help this nation survive!
Snuff out your torch, old man! The tribunal has spoken!

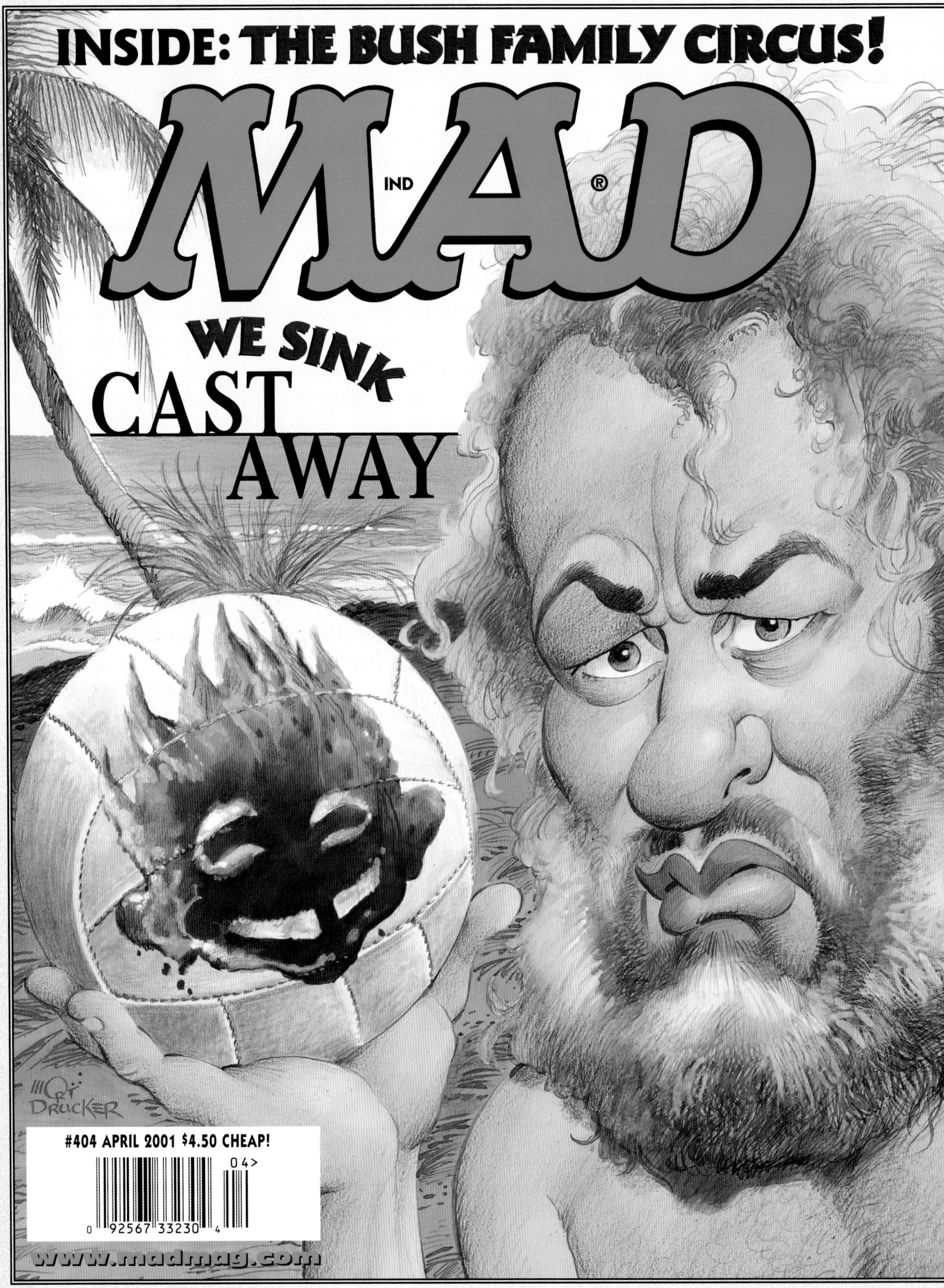
INSIDE: THE BUSH FAMILY CIRCUS!
MAD
IND
WE SINK
CAST
AWAY
MORT DRUCKER
#404 APRIL 2001 $4.50 CHEAP!
www.madmag.com

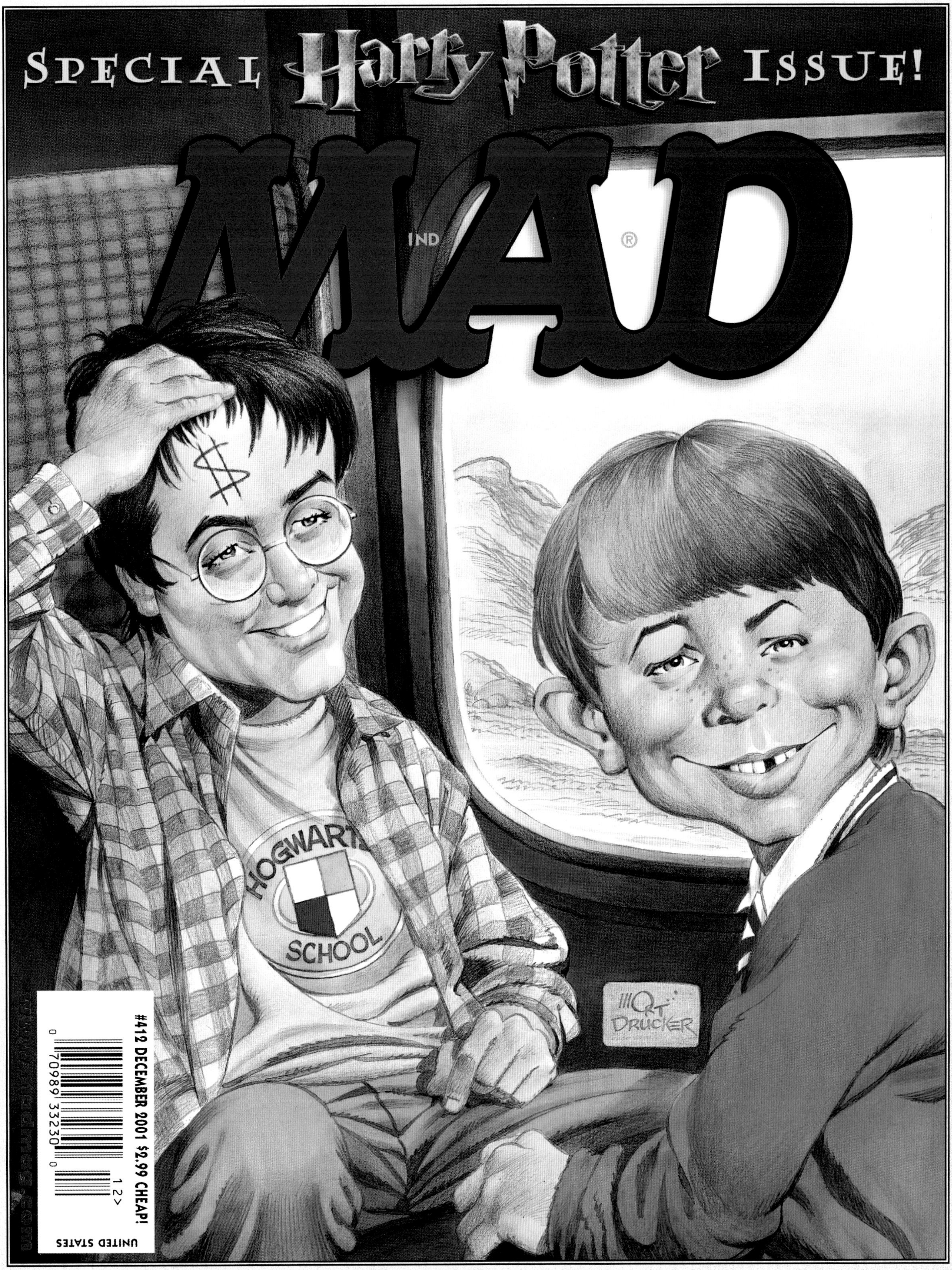
SPECIAL Harry Potter ISSUE!
MAD
$
HOGWARTS
SCHOOL
MORT DRUCKER
#412 DECEMBER 2001 $2.99 CHEAP!
UNITED STATES

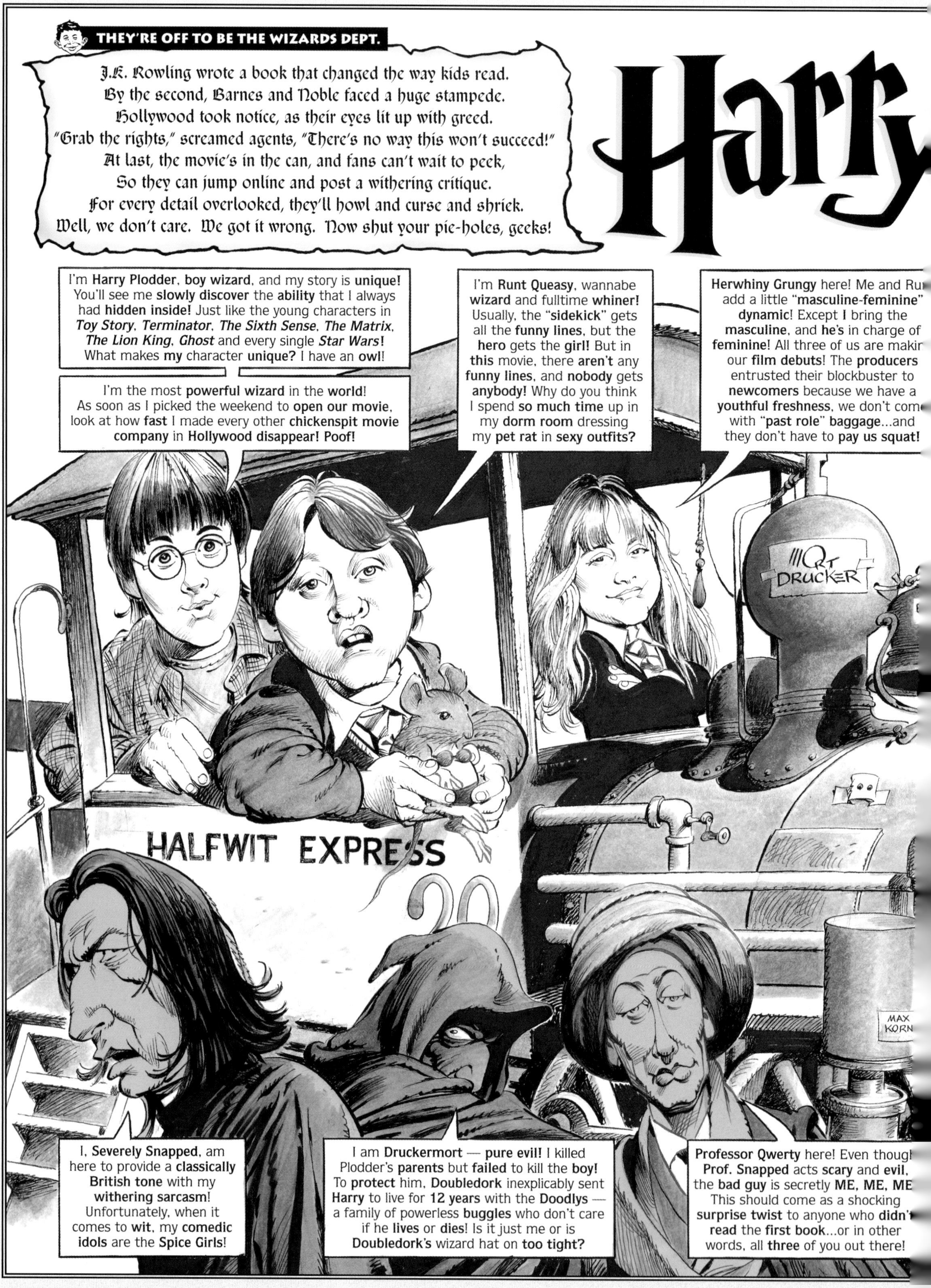
THEY'RE OFF TO BE THE WIZARDS DEPT.
J.K. Rowling wrote a book that changed the way kids read.
By the second, Barnes and Noble faced a huge stampede.
Hollywood took notice, as their eyes lit up with greed.
"Grab the rights," screamed agents, "There's no way this won't succeed!"
At last, the movie's in the can, and fans can't wait to peek,
So they can jump online and post a withering critique.
For every detail overlooked, they'll howl and curse and shriek.
Well, we don't care. We got it wrong. Now shut your pie-holes, geeks!
Harr
I'm Harry Plodder, boy wizard, and my story is unique! You'll see me slowly discover the ability that I always had hidden inside! Just like the young characters in Toy Story, Terminator, The Sixth Sense, The Matrix, The Lion King, Ghost and every single Star Wars! What makes my character unique? I have an owl!
I'm the most powerful wizard in the world! As soon as I picked the weekend to open our movie, look at how fast I made every other chickenspit movie company in Hollywood disappear! Poof!
I'm Runt Queasy, wannabe wizard and fulltime whiner! Usually, the "sidekick" gets all the funny lines, but the hero gets the girl! But in this movie, there aren't any funny lines, and nobody gets anybody! Why do you think I spend so much time up in my dorm room dressing my pet rat in sexy outfits?
Herwhiny Grungy here! Me and Ru add a little "masculine-feminine" dynamic! Except I bring the masculine, and he's in charge of feminine! All three of us are makir our film debuts! The producers entrusted their blockbuster to newcomers because we have a youthful freshness, we don't com with "past role" baggage...and they don't have to pay us squat!
HALFWIT EXPRESS
20
MORT DRUCKER
MAX KORN
I, Severely Snapped, am here to provide a classically British tone with my withering sarcasm! Unfortunately, when it comes to wit, my comedic idols are the Spice Girls!
I am Druckermort — pure evil! I killed Plodder's parents but failed to kill the boy! To protect him, Doubledork inexplicably sent Harry to live for 12 years with the Doodlys — a family of powerless buggles who don't care if he lives or dies! Is it just me or is Doubledork's wizard hat on too tight?
Professor Qwerty here! Even thoug Prof. Snapped acts scary and evil, the bad guy is secretly ME, ME, ME This should come as a shocking surprise twist to anyone who didn't read the first book...or in other words, all three of you out there!

MAD #412, December 2001

Plodder AND THE SORRY~ASS STORY

ARTIST: MORT DRUCKER WRITER: DESMOND DEVLIN

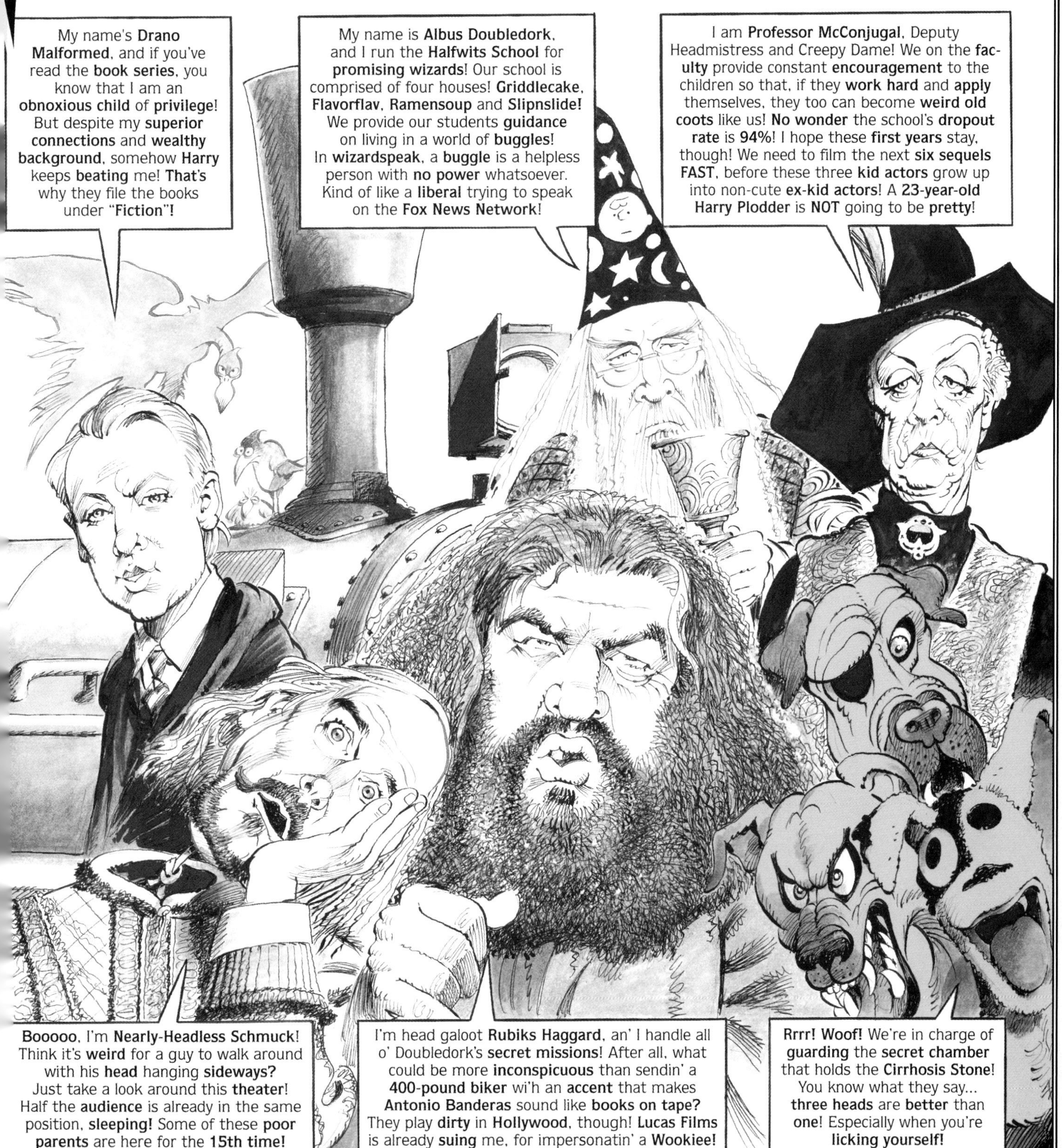
My name's **Drano Malformed**, and if you've read the **book series**, you know that I am an **obnoxious child** of **privilege**! But despite my **superior connections** and **wealthy background**, somehow **Harry** keeps **beating** me! **That's** why they file the books under "**Fiction**"!
My name is **Albus Doubledork**, and I run the **Halfwits School** for **promising wizards**! Our school is comprised of four houses! **Griddlecake, Flavorflav, Ramensoup** and **Slipnslide!** We provide our students **guidance** on living in a world of **buggles**! In **wizardspeak**, a **buggle** is a helpless person with **no power** whatsoever. Kind of like a **liberal** trying to speak on the **Fox News Network**!
I am **Professor McConjugal**, Deputy Headmistress and Creepy Dame! We on the **faculty** provide constant **encouragement** to the children so that, if they **work hard** and **apply** themselves, they too can become **weird old coots** like us! **No wonder** the school's **dropout rate** is **94%**! I hope these **first years** stay, though! We need to film the next **six sequels FAST**, before these three **kid actors** grow up into non-cute **ex-kid actors**! A **23-year-old** Harry Plodder is **NOT** going to be **pretty**!
Booooo, I'm **Nearly-Headless Schmuck**! Think it's **weird** for a guy to walk around with his **head** hanging **sideways?** Just take a look around this **theater**! Half the **audience** is already in the same position, **sleeping!** Some of these **poor parents** are here for the **15th time!**
I'm head galoot **Rubiks Haggard**, an' I handle all o' Doubledork's **secret missions**! After all, what could be more **inconspicuous** than sendin' a **400-pound biker** wi'h an **accent** that makes **Antonio Banderas** sound like **books on tape?** They play **dirty** in **Hollywood**, though! **Lucas Films** is already **suing** me, for impersonatin' a **Wookiee**!
Rrrr! Woof! We're in charge of **guarding** the **secret chamber** that holds the **Cirrhosis Stone**! You know what they say... **three heads** are **better** than **one**! Especially when you're **licking yourself!**

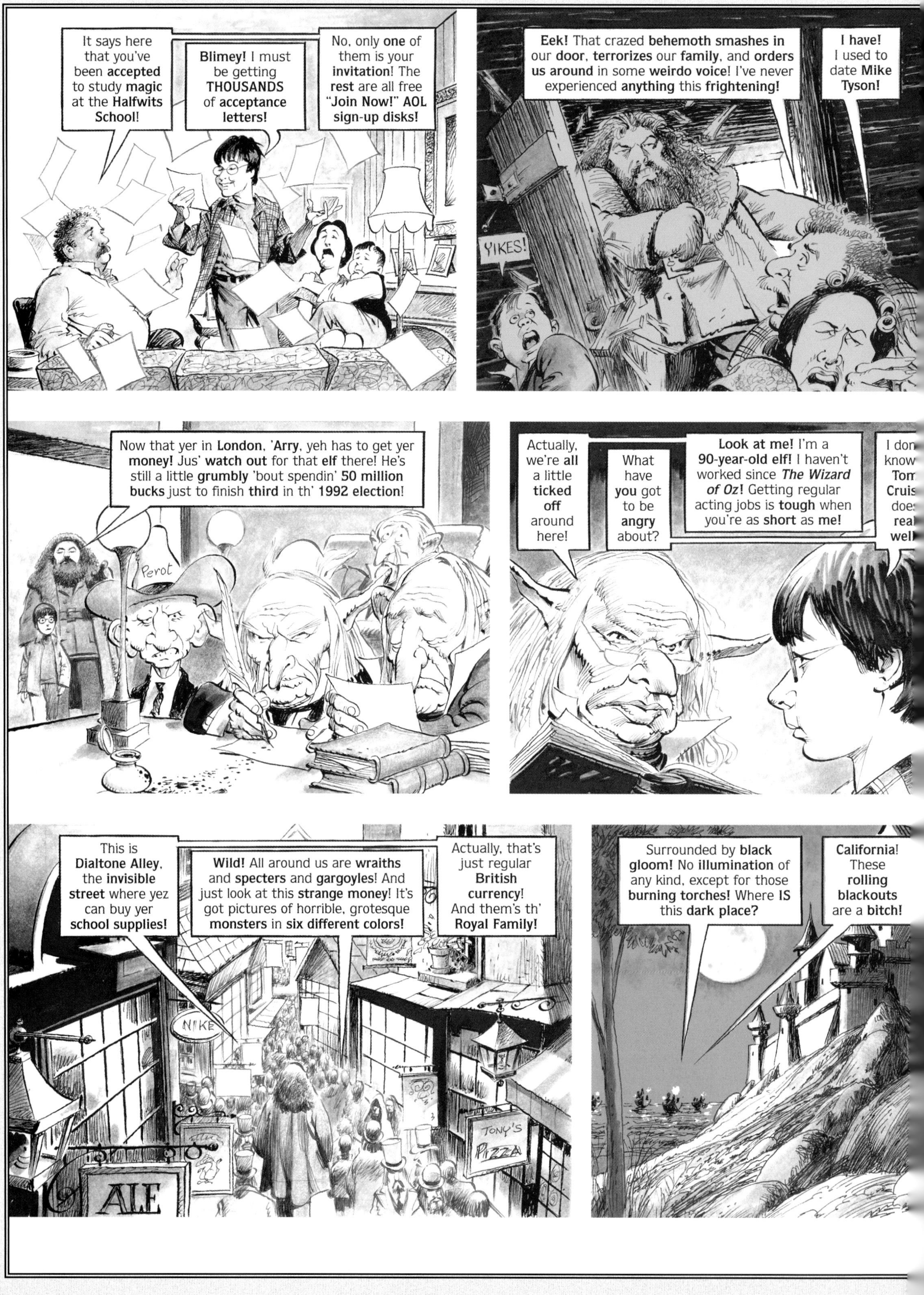
It says here that you've been accepted to study magic at the Halfwits School!
Blimey! I must be getting THOUSANDS of acceptance letters!
No, only one of them is your invitation! The rest are all free "Join Now!" AOL sign-up disks!
Eek! That crazed behemoth smashes in our door, terrorizes our family, and orders us around in some weirdo voice! I've never experienced anything this frightening!
I have! I used to date Mike Tyson!
YIKES!
Now that yer in London, 'Arry, yeh has to get yer money! Jus' watch out for that elf there! He's still a little grumbly 'bout spendin' 50 million bucks just to finish third in th' 1992 election!
Perot
Actually, we're all a little ticked off around here!
What have you got to be angry about?
Look at me! I'm a 90-year-old elf! I haven't worked since The Wizard of Oz! Getting regular acting jobs is tough when you're as short as me!
This is Dialtone Alley, the invisible street where yez can buy yer school supplies!
Wild! All around us are wraiths and specters and gargoyles! And just look at this strange money! It's got pictures of horrible, grotesque monsters in six different colors!
Actually, that's just regular British currency! And them's th' Royal Family!
NIKE
TONY'S PIZZA
ALE
Surrounded by black gloom! No illumination of any kind, except for those burning torches! Where IS this dark place?
California! These rolling blackouts are a bitch!

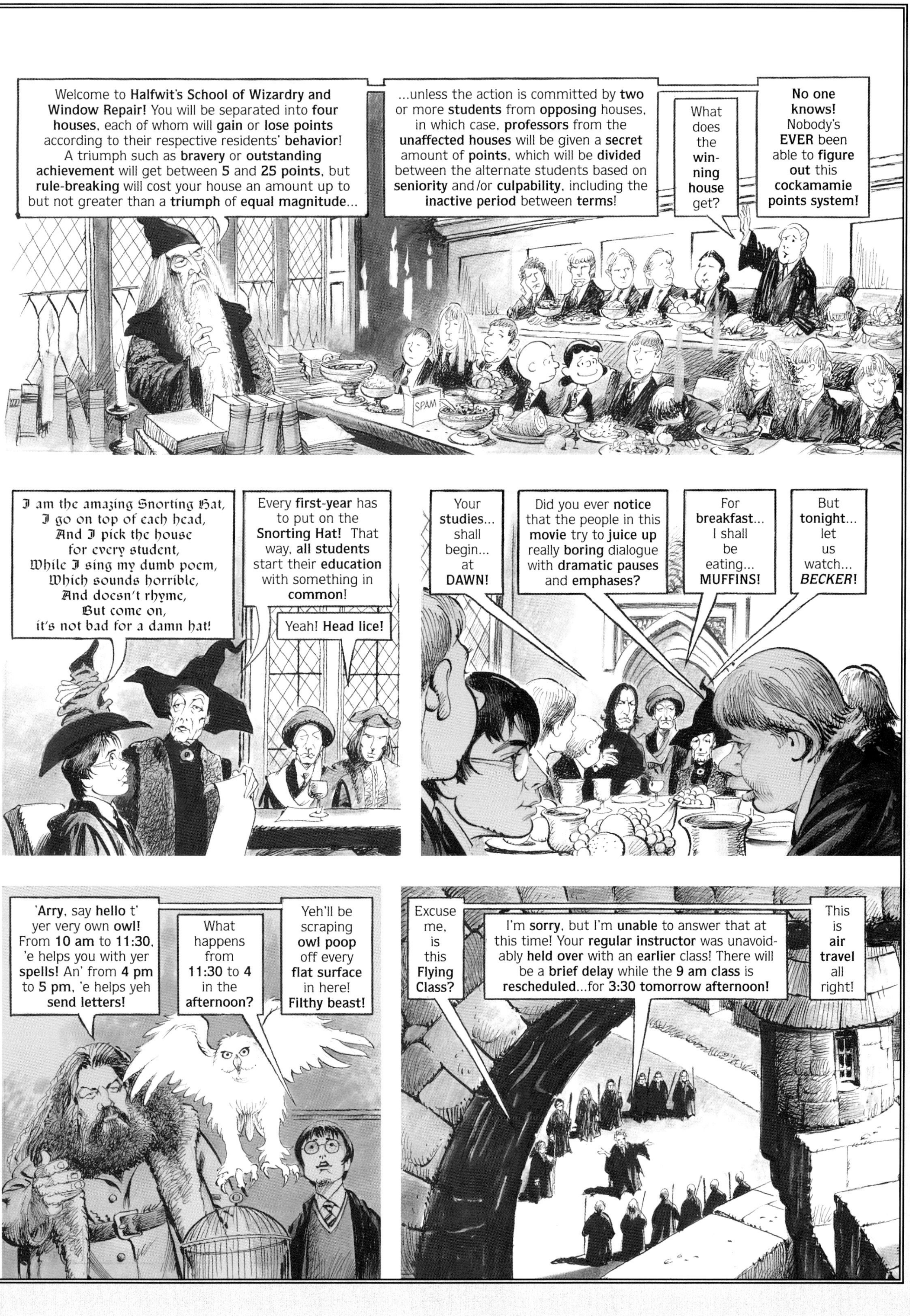
Welcome to Halfwit's School of Wizardry and Window Repair! You will be separated into four houses, each of whom will gain or lose points according to their respective residents' behavior! A triumph such as bravery or outstanding achievement will get between 5 and 25 points, but rule-breaking will cost your house an amount up to but not greater than a triumph of equal magnitude...
...unless the action is committed by two or more students from opposing houses, in which case, professors from the unaffected houses will be given a secret amount of points, which will be divided between the alternate students based on seniority and/or culpability, including the inactive period between terms!
What does the win-ning house get?
No one knows! Nobody's EVER been able to figure out this cockamamie points system!
SPAM
I am the amazing Snorting Hat, I go on top of each head, And I pick the house for every student, While I sing my dumb poem, Which sounds horrible, And doesn't rhyme, But come on, it's not bad for a damn hat!
Every first-year has to put on the Snorting Hat! That way, all students start their education with something in common!
Yeah! Head lice!
Your studies... shall begin... at DAWN!
Did you ever notice that the people in this movie try to juice up really boring dialogue with dramatic pauses and emphases?
For breakfast... I shall be eating... MUFFINS!
But tonight... let us watch... BECKER!
'Arry, say hello t' yer very own owl! From 10 am to 11:30, 'e helps you with yer spells! An' from 4 pm to 5 pm, 'e helps yeh send letters!
What happens from 11:30 to 4 in the afternoon?
Yeh'll be scraping owl poop off every flat surface in here! Filthy beast!
Excuse me, is this Flying Class?
I'm sorry, but I'm unable to answer that at this time! Your regular instructor was unavoid-ably held over with an earlier class! There will be a brief delay while the 9 am class is rescheduled...for 3:30 tomorrow afternoon!
This is air travel all right!

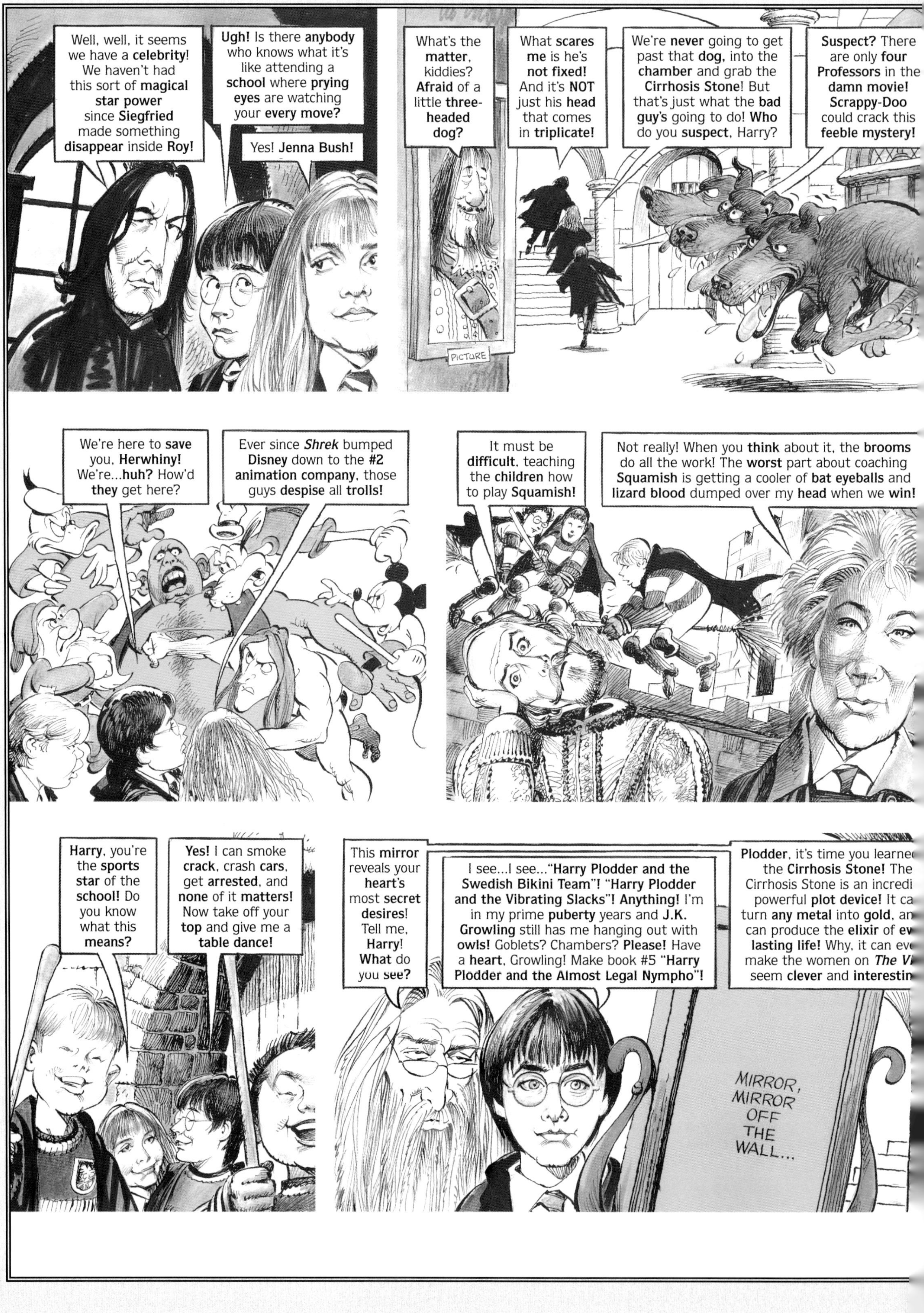
Well, well, it seems we have a celebrity! We haven't had this sort of magical star power since Siegfried made something disappear inside Roy!
Ugh! Is there anybody who knows what it's like attending a school where prying eyes are watching your every move?
Yes! Jenna Bush!
What's the matter, kiddies? Afraid of a little three-headed dog?
PICTURE
What scares me is he's not fixed! And it's NOT just his head that comes in triplicate!
We're never going to get past that dog, into the chamber and grab the Cirrhosis Stone! But that's just what the bad guy's going to do! Who do you suspect, Harry?
Suspect? There are only four Professors in the damn movie! Scrappy-Doo could crack this feeble mystery!
We're here to save you, Herwhiny! We're...huh? How'd they get here?
Ever since Shrek bumped Disney down to the #2 animation company, those guys despise all trolls!
It must be difficult, teaching the children how to play Squamish!
Not really! When you think about it, the brooms do all the work! The worst part about coaching Squamish is getting a cooler of bat eyeballs and lizard blood dumped over my head when we win!
Harry, you're the sports star of the school! Do you know what this means?
Yes! I can smoke crack, crash cars, get arrested, and none of it matters! Now take off your top and give me a table dance!
This mirror reveals your heart's most secret desires! Tell me, Harry! What do you see?
I see...I see..."Harry Plodder and the Swedish Bikini Team"! "Harry Plodder and the Vibrating Slacks"! Anything! I'm in my prime puberty years and J.K. Growling still has me hanging out with owls! Goblets? Chambers? Please! Have a heart, Growling! Make book #5 "Harry Plodder and the Almost Legal Nympho"!
Plodder, it's time you learne
the Cirrhosis Stone! The
Cirrhosis Stone is an incredi
powerful plot device! It ca
turn any metal into gold, an
can produce the elixir of ev
lasting life! Why, it can eve
make the women on The Vi
seem clever and interestin
MIRROR, MIRROR OFF THE WALL...

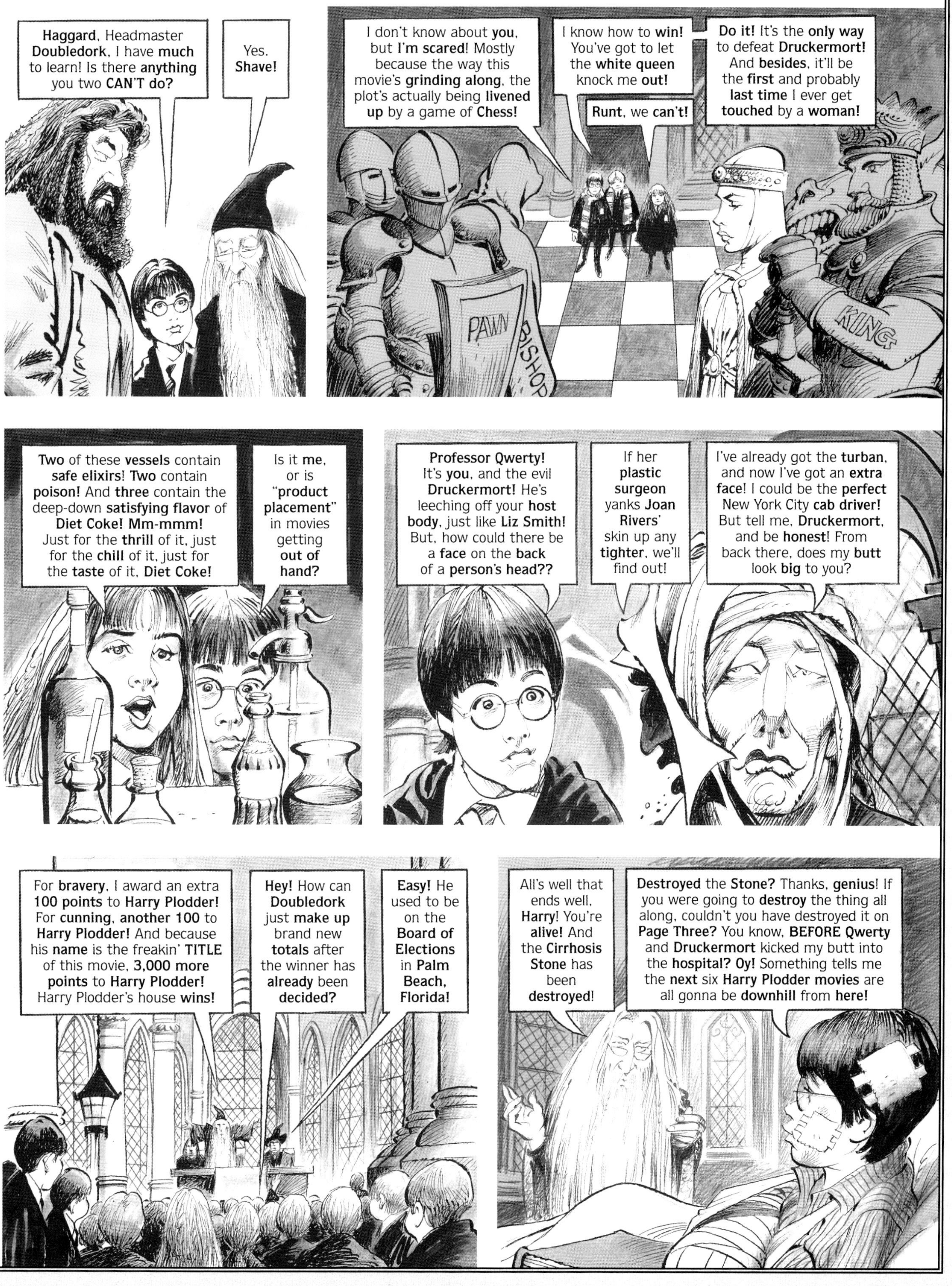
Haggard, Headmaster Doubledork, I have much to learn! Is there anything you two CAN'T do?
Yes. Shave!
I don't know about you, but I'm scared! Mostly because the way this movie's grinding along, the plot's actually being livened up by a game of Chess!
I know how to win! You've got to let the white queen knock me out!
Runt, we can't!
Do it! It's the only way to defeat Druckermort! And besides, it'll be the first and probably last time I ever get touched by a woman!
PAWN
BISHOP
KING
Two of these vessels contain safe elixirs! Two contain poison! And three contain the deep-down satisfying flavor of Diet Coke! Mm-mmm! Just for the thrill of it, just for the chill of it, just for the taste of it, Diet Coke!
Is it me, or is "product placement" in movies getting out of hand?
Professor Qwerty! It's you, and the evil Druckermort! He's leeching off your host body, just like Liz Smith! But, how could there be a face on the back of a person's head??
If her plastic surgeon yanks Joan Rivers' skin up any tighter, we'll find out!
I've already got the turban, and now I've got an extra face! I could be the perfect New York City cab driver! But tell me, Druckermort, and be honest! From back there, does my butt look big to you?
For bravery, I award an extra 100 points to Harry Plodder! For cunning, another 100 to Harry Plodder! And because his name is the freakin' TITLE of this movie, 3,000 more points to Harry Plodder! Harry Plodder's house wins!
Hey! How can Doubledork just make up brand new totals after the winner has already been decided?
Easy! He used to be on the Board of Elections in Palm Beach, Florida!
All's well that ends well, Harry! You're alive! And the Cirrhosis Stone has been destroyed!
Destroyed the Stone? Thanks, genius! If you were going to destroy the thing all along, couldn't you have destroyed it on Page Three? You know, BEFORE Qwerty and Druckermort kicked my butt into the hospital? Oy! Something tells me the next six Harry Plodder movies are all gonna be downhill from here!

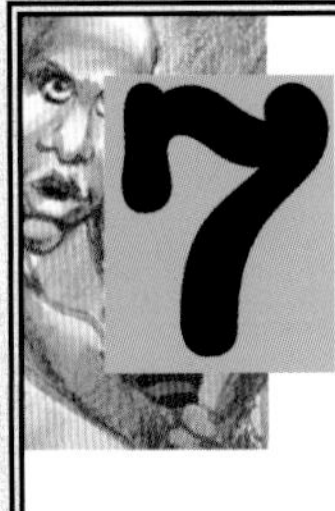

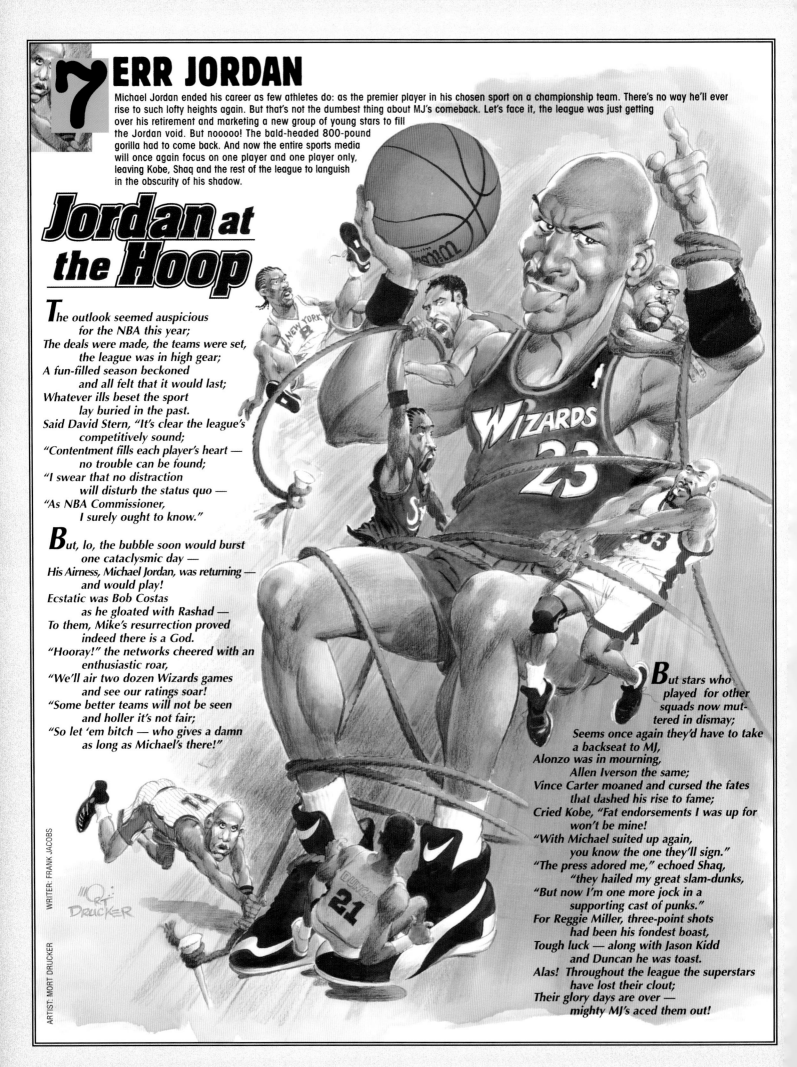

7 ERR JORDAN

Michael Jordan ended his career as few athletes do: as the premier player in his chosen sport on a championship team. There's no way he'll ever rise to such lofty heights again. But that's not the dumbest thing about MJ's comeback. Let's face it, the league was just getting over his retirement and marketing a new group of young stars to fill the Jordan void. But nooooo! The bald-headed 800-pound gorilla had to come back. And now the entire sports media will once again focus on one player and one player only, leaving Kobe, Shaq and the rest of the league to languish in the obscurity of his shadow.

Jordan at the Hoop

The outlook seemed auspicious
for the NBA this year;
The deals were made, the teams were set,
the league was in high gear;
A fun-filled season beckoned
and all felt that it would last;
Whatever ills beset the sport
lay buried in the past.
Said David Stern, "It's clear the league's
competitively sound;
"Contentment fills each player's heart —
no trouble can be found;
"I swear that no distraction
will disturb the status quo —
"As NBA Commissioner,
I surely ought to know."

But, lo, the bubble soon would burst
one cataclysmic day —
His Airness, Michael Jordan, was returning —
and would play!
Ecstatic was Bob Costas
as he gloated with Rashad —
To them, Mike's resurrection proved
indeed there is a God.
"Hooray!" the networks cheered with an
enthusiastic roar,
"We'll air two dozen Wizards games
and see our ratings soar!
"Some better teams will not be seen
and holler it's not fair;
"So let 'em bitch — who gives a damn
as long as Michael's there!"

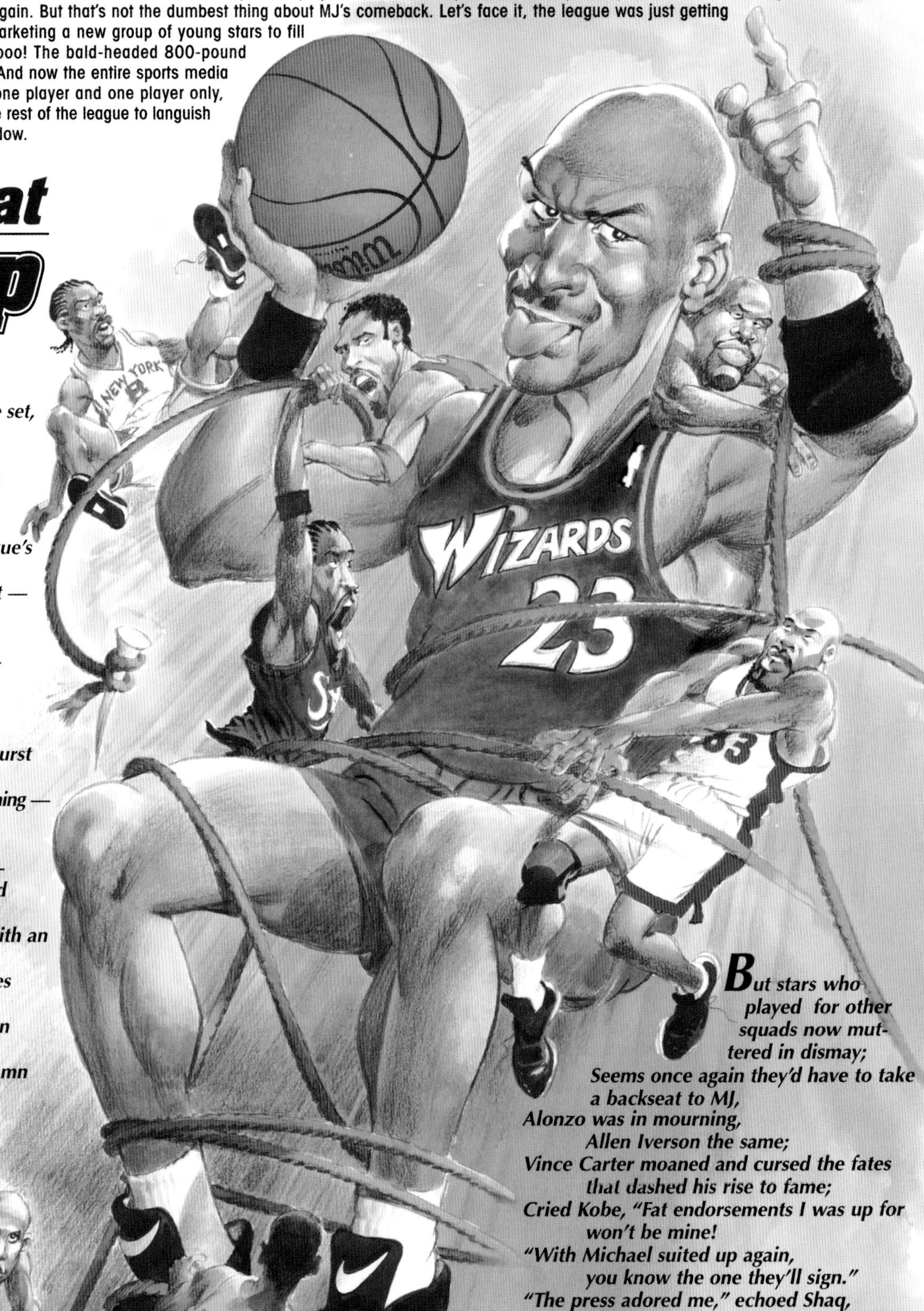

WIZARDS
23
NEW YORK
DUNCAN
21

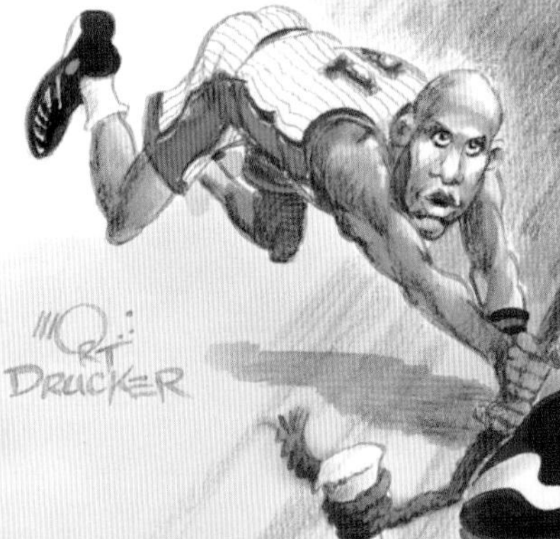

MORT DRUCKER

WRITER: FRANK JACOBS

ARTIST: MORT DRUCKER

But stars who
played for other
squads now mut-
tered in dismay;
Seems once again they'd have to take
a backseat to MJ,
Alonzo was in mourning,
Allen Iverson the same;
Vince Carter moaned and cursed the fates
that dashed his rise to fame;
Cried Kobe, "Fat endorsements I was up for
won't be mine!
"With Michael suited up again,
you know the one they'll sign."
"The press adored me," echoed Shaq,
"they hailed my great slam-dunks,
"But now I'm one more jock in a
supporting cast of punks."
For Reggie Miller, three-point shots
had been his fondest boast,
Tough luck — along with Jason Kidd
and Duncan he was toast.
Alas! Throughout the league the superstars
have lost their clout;
Their glory days are over —
mighty MJ's aced them out!

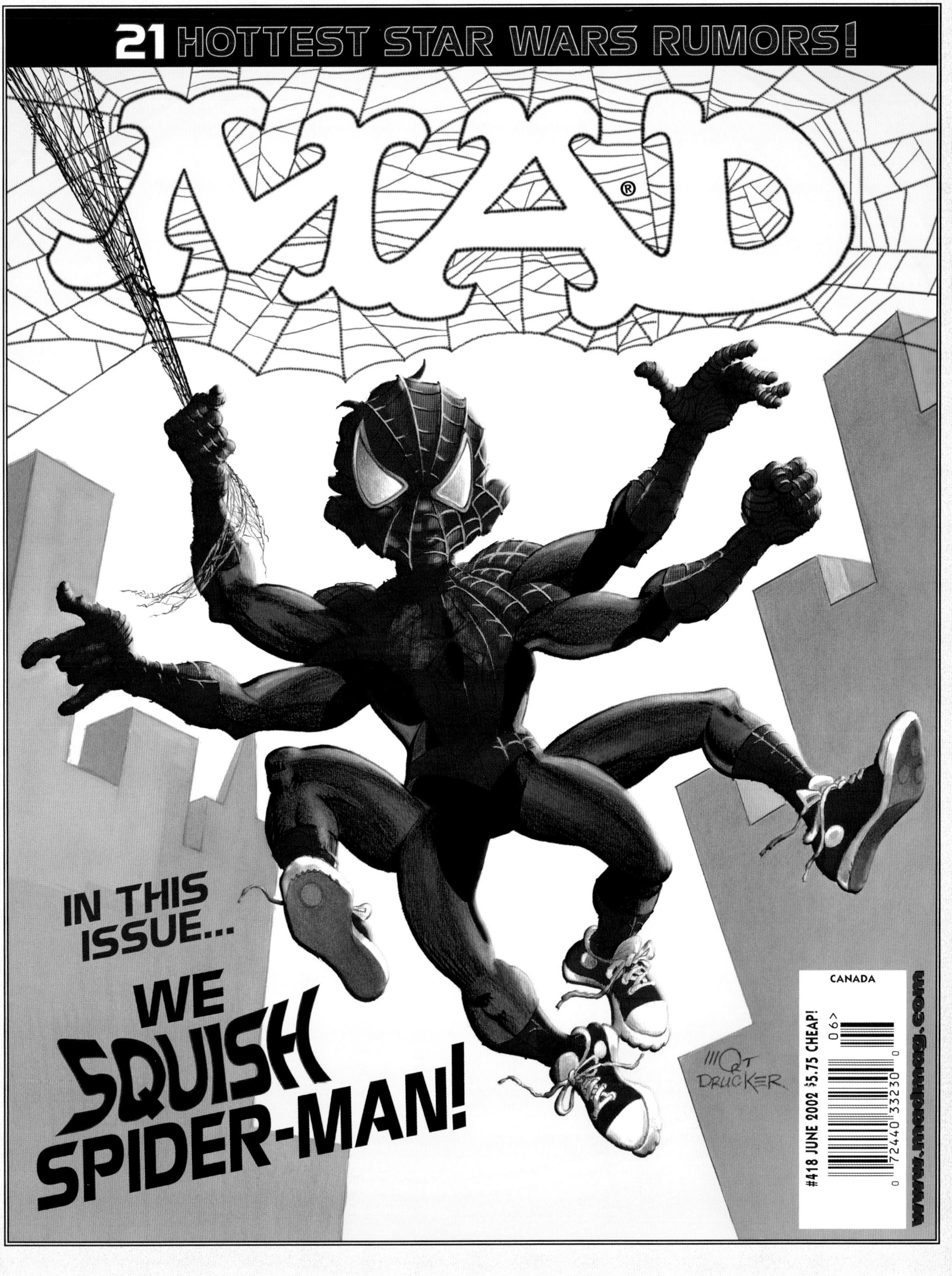
21 HOTTEST STAR WARS RUMORS!
MAD®
IN THIS ISSUE...
WE SQUISH SPIDER-MAN!
MORT DRUCKER
CANADA
#418 JUNE 2002 $5.75 CHEAP!
www.madmag.com

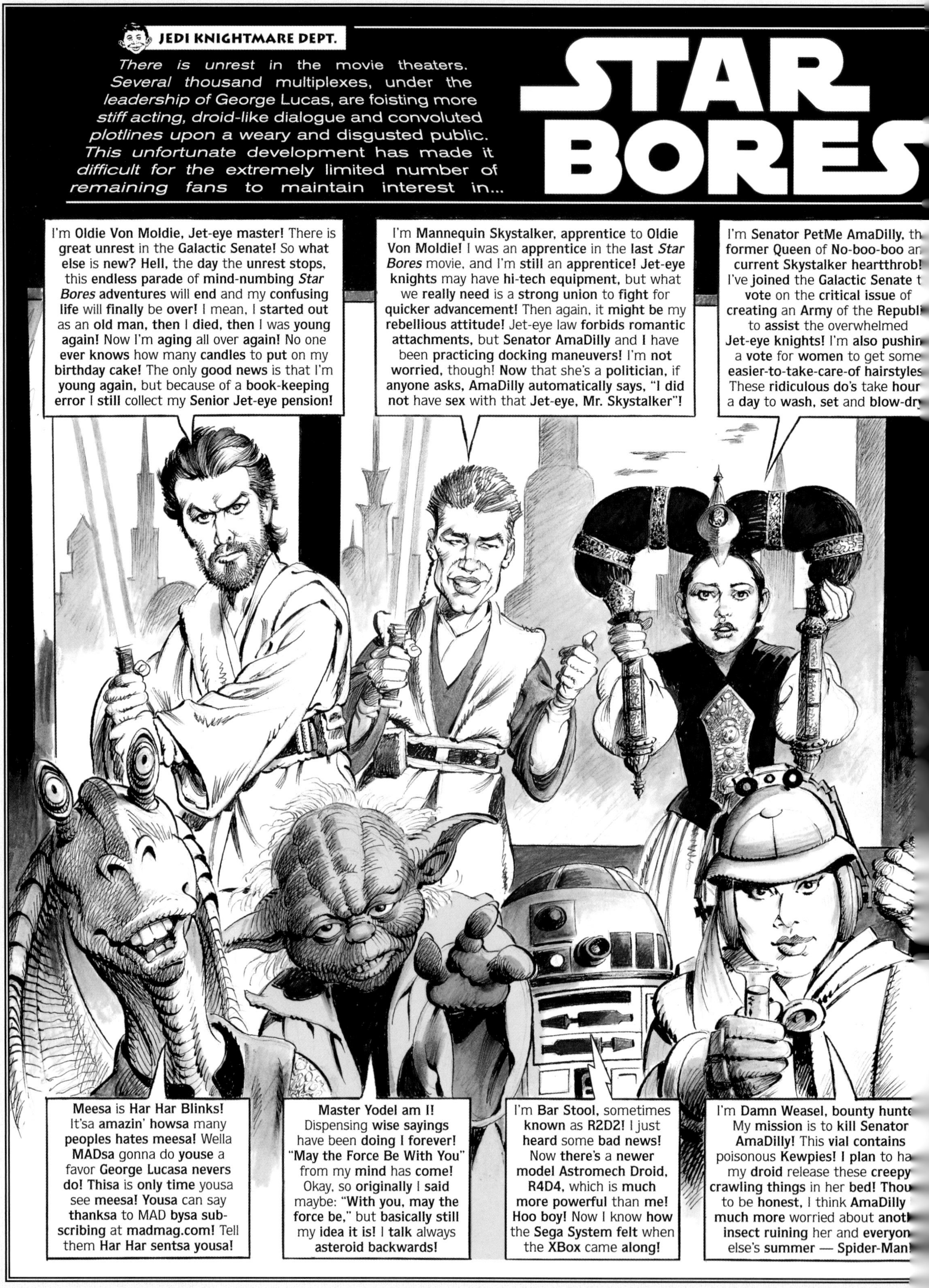
JEDI KNIGHTMARE DEPT.
There is unrest in the movie theaters. Several thousand multiplexes, under the leadership of George Lucas, are foisting more stiff acting, droid-like dialogue and convoluted plotlines upon a weary and disgusted public. This unfortunate development has made it difficult for the extremely limited number of remaining fans to maintain interest in...
STAR BORES
I'm Oldie Von Moldie, Jet-eye master! There is great unrest in the Galactic Senate! So what else is new? Hell, the day the unrest stops, this endless parade of mind-numbing Star Bores adventures will end and my confusing life will finally be over! I mean, I started out as an old man, then I died, then I was young again! Now I'm aging all over again! No one ever knows how many candles to put on my birthday cake! The only good news is that I'm young again, but because of a book-keeping error I still collect my Senior Jet-eye pension!
I'm Mannequin Skystalker, apprentice to Oldie Von Moldie! I was an apprentice in the last Star Bores movie, and I'm still an apprentice! Jet-eye knights may have hi-tech equipment, but what we really need is a strong union to fight for quicker advancement! Then again, it might be my rebellious attitude! Jet-eye law forbids romantic attachments, but Senator AmaDilly and I have been practicing docking maneuvers! I'm not worried, though! Now that she's a politician, if anyone asks, AmaDilly automatically says, "I did not have sex with that Jet-eye, Mr. Skystalker"!
I'm Senator PetMe AmaDilly, th former Queen of No-boo-boo an current Skystalker heartthrob! I've joined the Galactic Senate t vote on the critical issue of creating an Army of the Republi to assist the overwhelmed Jet-eye knights! I'm also pushin a vote for women to get some easier-to-take-care-of hairstyles These ridiculous do's take hour a day to wash, set and blow-dr
Meesa is Har Har Blinks! It'sa amazin' howsa many peoples hates meesa! Wella MADsa gonna do youse a favor George Lucasa nevers do! Thisa is only time yousa see meesa! Yousa can say thanksa to MAD bysa sub-scribing at madmag.com! Tell them Har Har sentsa yousa!
Master Yodel am I! Dispensing wise sayings have been doing I forever! "May the Force Be With You" from my mind has come! Okay, so originally I said maybe: "With you, may the force be," but basically still my idea it is! I talk always asteroid backwards!
I'm Bar Stool, sometimes known as R2D2! I just heard some bad news! Now there's a newer model Astromech Droid, R4D4, which is much more powerful than me! Hoo boy! Now I know how the Sega System felt when the XBox came along!
I'm Damn Weasel, bounty hunte My mission is to kill Senator AmaDilly! This vial contains poisonous Kewpies! I plan to ha my droid release these creepy crawling things in her bed! Thou to be honest, I think AmaDilly much more worried about anot insect ruining her and everyon else's summer — Spider-Man

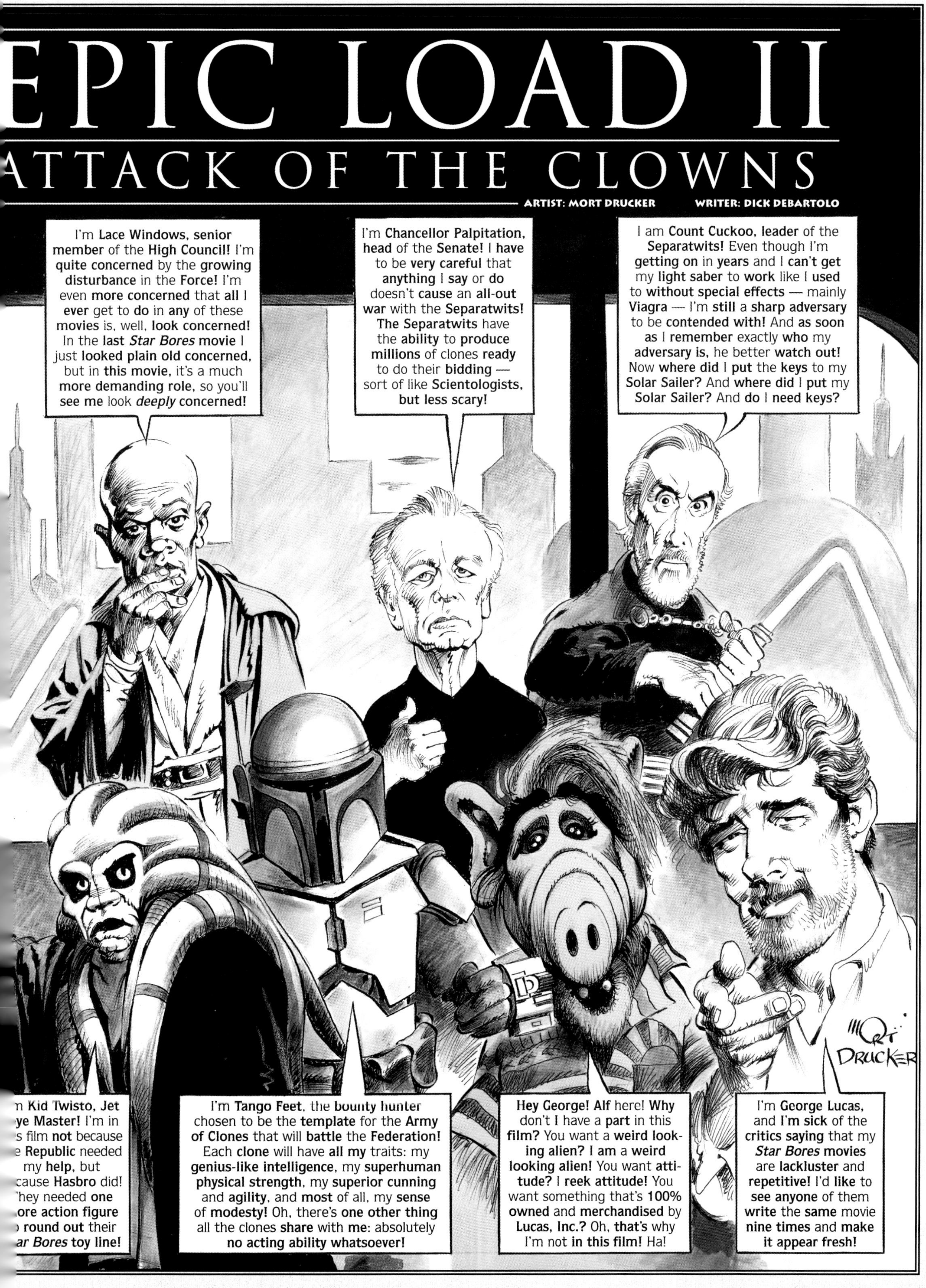
EPIC LOAD II
ATTACK OF THE CLOWNS
ARTIST: MORT DRUCKER WRITER: DICK DEBARTOLO
I'm Lace Windows, senior member of the High Council! I'm quite concerned by the growing disturbance in the Force! I'm even more concerned that all I ever get to do in any of these movies is, well, look concerned! In the last *Star Bores* movie I just looked plain old concerned, but in this movie, it's a much more demanding role, so you'll see me look *deeply* concerned!
I'm Chancellor Palpitation, head of the Senate! I have to be very careful that anything I say or do doesn't cause an all-out war with the Separatwits! The Separatwits have the ability to produce millions of clones ready to do their bidding — sort of like Scientologists, but less scary!
I am Count Cuckoo, leader of the Separatwits! Even though I'm getting on in years and I can't get my light saber to work like I used to without special effects — mainly Viagra — I'm still a sharp adversary to be contended with! And as soon as I remember exactly who my adversary is, he better watch out! Now where did I put the keys to my Solar Sailer? And where did I put my Solar Sailer? And do I need keys?
n Kid Twisto, Jet ye Master! I'm in s film not because e Republic needed my help, but cause Hasbro did! 'hey needed one ore action figure round out their ar Bores toy line!
I'm Tango Feet, the bounty hunter chosen to be the template for the Army of Clones that will battle the Federation! Each clone will have all my traits: my genius-like intelligence, my superhuman physical strength, my superior cunning and agility, and most of all, my sense of modesty! Oh, there's one other thing all the clones share with me: absolutely no acting ability whatsoever!
Hey George! Alf here! Why don't I have a part in this film? You want a weird looking alien? I am a weird looking alien! You want attitude? I reek attitude! You want something that's 100% owned and merchandised by Lucas, Inc.? Oh, that's why I'm not in this film! Ha!
I'm George Lucas, and I'm sick of the critics saying that my *Star Bores* movies are lackluster and repetitive! I'd like to see anyone of them write the same movie nine times and make it appear fresh!
MORT DRUCKER

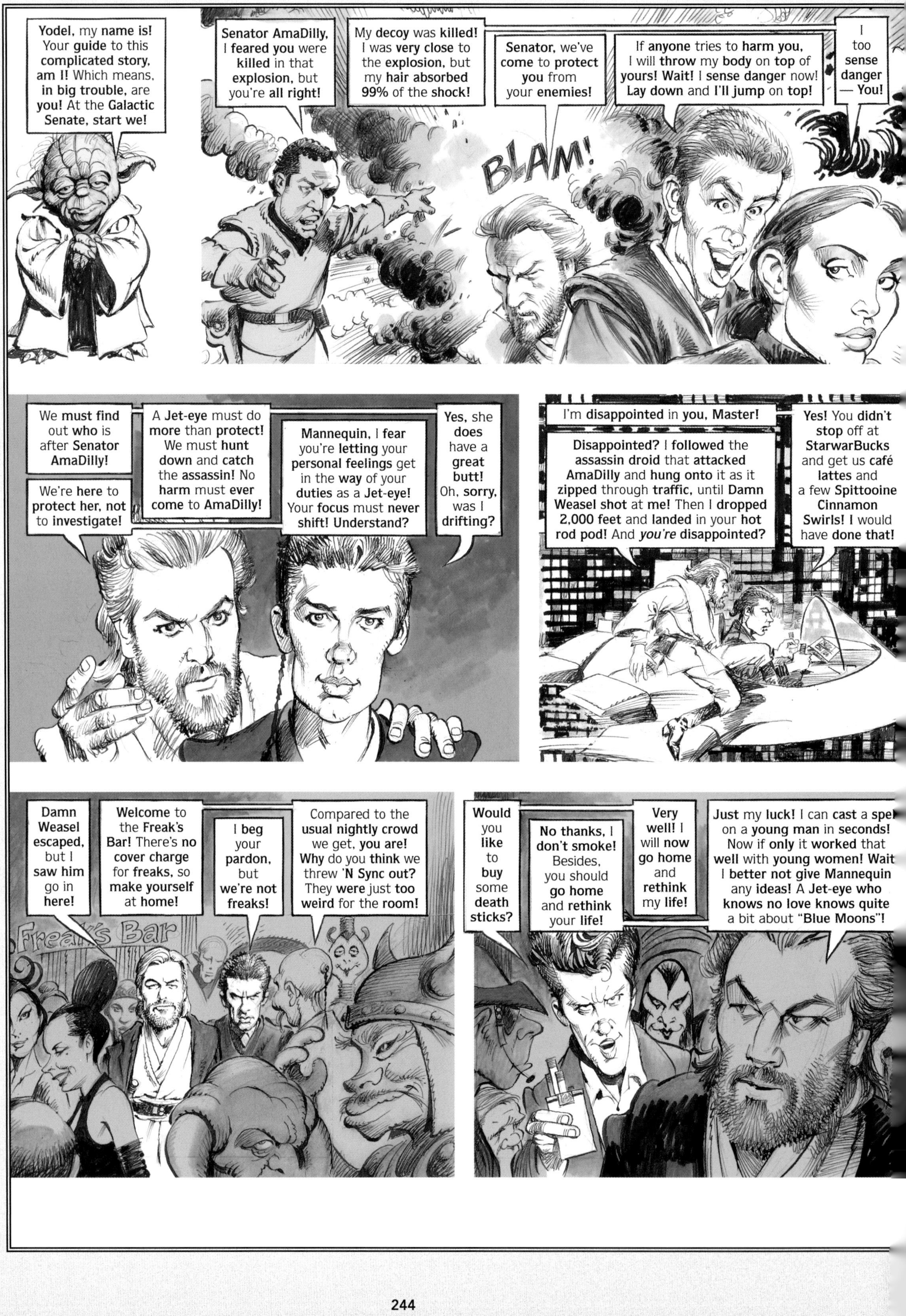
Yodel, my name is! Your guide to this complicated story, am I! Which means, in big trouble, are you! At the Galactic Senate, start we!
Senator AmaDilly, I feared you were killed in that explosion, but you're all right!
My decoy was killed! I was very close to the explosion, but my hair absorbed 99% of the shock!
Senator, we've come to protect you from your enemies!
If anyone tries to harm you, I will throw my body on top of yours! Wait! I sense danger now! Lay down and I'll jump on top!
I too sense danger — You!
BLAM!
We must find out who is after Senator AmaDilly!
We're here to protect her, not to investigate!
A Jet-eye must do more than protect! We must hunt down and catch the assassin! No harm must ever come to AmaDilly!
Mannequin, I fear you're letting your personal feelings get in the way of your duties as a Jet-eye! Your focus must never shift! Understand?
Yes, she does have a great butt! Oh, sorry, was I drifting?
I'm disappointed in you, Master!
Disappointed? I followed the assassin droid that attacked AmaDilly and hung onto it as it zipped through traffic, until Damn Weasel shot at me! Then I dropped 2,000 feet and landed in your hot rod pod! And *you're* disappointed?
Yes! You didn't stop off at StarwarBucks and get us café lattes and a few Spittooine Cinnamon Swirls! I would have done that!
Damn Weasel escaped, but I saw him go in here!
Welcome to the Freak's Bar! There's no cover charge for freaks, so make yourself at home!
I beg your pardon, but we're not freaks!
Compared to the usual nightly crowd we get, you are! Why do you think we threw 'N Sync out? They were just too weird for the room!
Freak's Bar
Would you like to buy some death sticks?
No thanks, I don't smoke! Besides, you should go home and rethink your life!
Very well! I will now go home and rethink my life!
Just my luck! I can cast a spel on a young man in seconds! Now if only it worked that well with young women! Wait I better not give Mannequin any ideas! A Jet-eye who knows no love knows quite a bit about "Blue Moons"!

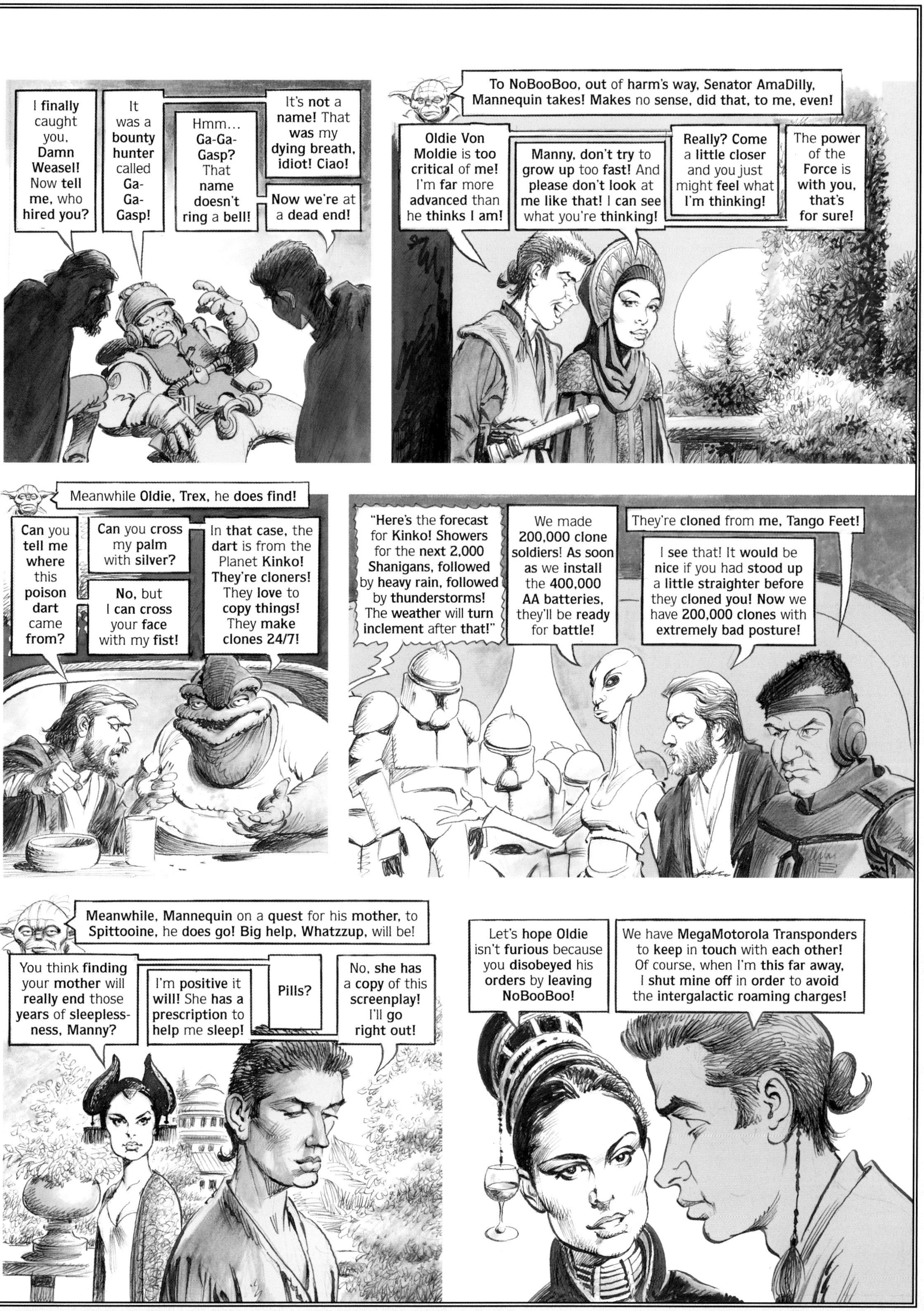
I finally caught you, Damn Weasel! Now tell me, who hired you?
It was a bounty hunter called Ga-Ga-Gasp!
Hmm... Ga-Ga-Gasp? That name doesn't ring a bell!
It's not a name! That was my dying breath, idiot! Ciao!
Now we're at a dead end!
To NoBooBoo, out of harm's way, Senator AmaDilly, Mannequin takes! Makes no sense, did that, to me, even!
Oldie Von Moldie is too critical of me! I'm far more advanced than he thinks I am!
Manny, don't try to grow up too fast! And please don't look at me like that! I can see what you're thinking!
Really? Come a little closer and you just might feel what I'm thinking!
The power of the Force is with you, that's for sure!
Meanwhile Oldie, Trex, he does find!
Can you tell me where this poison dart came from?
Can you cross my palm with silver?
No, but I can cross your face with my fist!
In that case, the dart is from the Planet Kinko! They're cloners! They love to copy things! They make clones 24/7!
"Here's the forecast for Kinko! Showers for the next 2,000 Shanigans, followed by heavy rain, followed by thunderstorms! The weather will turn inclement after that!"
We made 200,000 clone soldiers! As soon as we install the 400,000 AA batteries, they'll be ready for battle!
They're cloned from me, Tango Feet!
I see that! It would be nice if you had stood up a little straighter before they cloned you! Now we have 200,000 clones with extremely bad posture!
Meanwhile, Mannequin on a quest for his mother, to Spittooine, he does go! Big help, Whatzzup, will be!
You think finding your mother will really end those years of sleepless-ness, Manny?
I'm positive it will! She has a prescription to help me sleep!
Pills?
No, she has a copy of this screenplay! I'll go right out!
Let's hope Oldie isn't furious because you disobeyed his orders by leaving NoBooBoo!
We have MegaMotorola Transponders to keep in touch with each other! Of course, when I'm this far away, I shut mine off in order to avoid the intergalactic roaming charges!

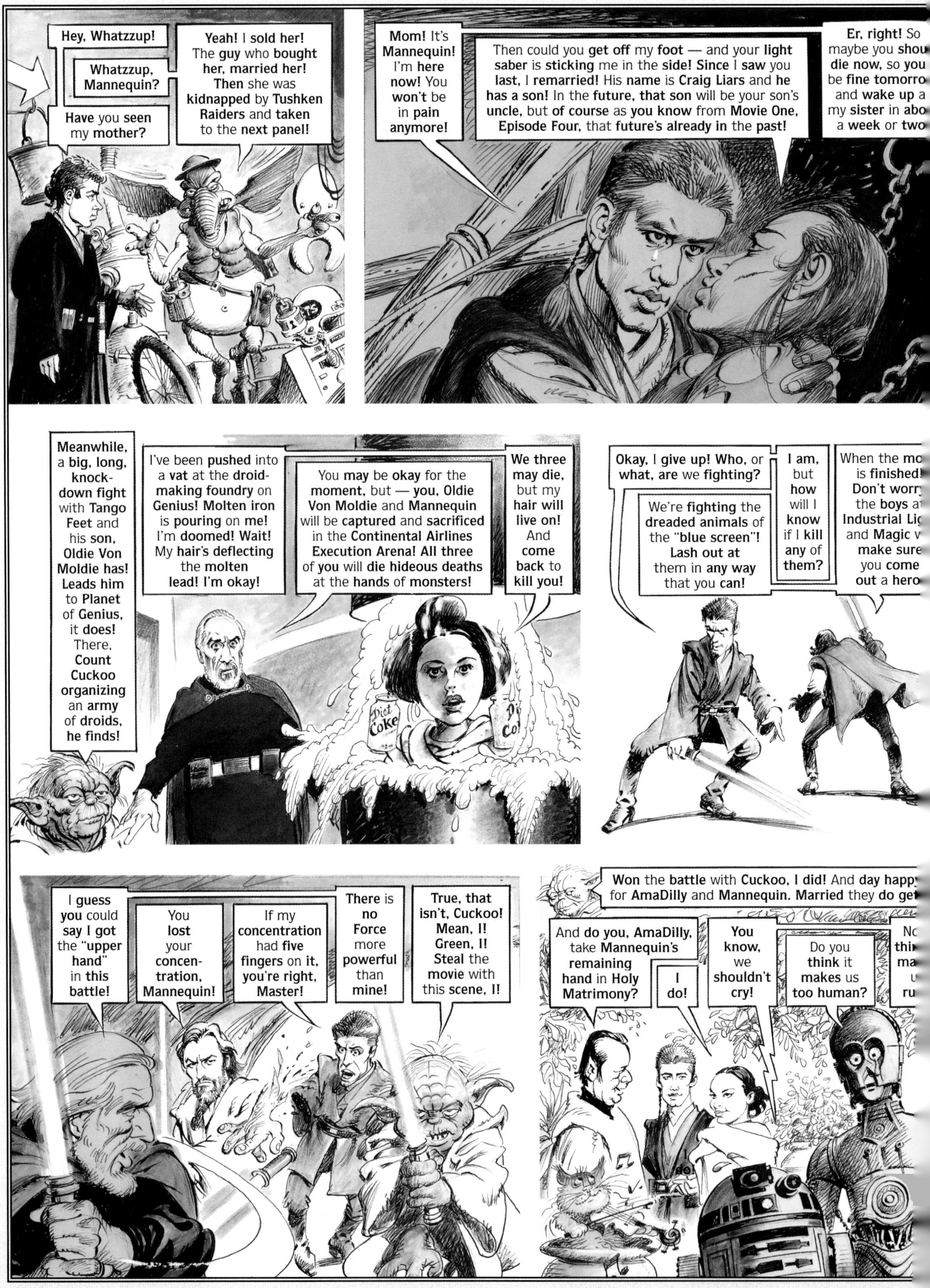
Hey, Whatzzup!
Whatzzup, Mannequin?
Have you seen my mother?
Yeah! I sold her! The guy who bought her, married her! Then she was kidnapped by Tushken Raiders and taken to the next panel!
Mom! It's Mannequin! I'm here now! You won't be in pain anymore!
Then could you get off my foot — and your light saber is sticking me in the side! Since I saw you last, I remarried! His name is Craig Liars and he has a son! In the future, that son will be your son's uncle, but of course as you know from Movie One, Episode Four, that future's already in the past!
Er, right! So maybe you shou die now, so you be fine tomorro and wake up a my sister in abo a week or two
Meanwhile, a big, long, knock-down fight with Tango Feet and his son, Oldie Von Moldie has! Leads him to Planet of Genius, it does! There, Count Cuckoo organizing an army of droids, he finds!
I've been pushed into a vat at the droid-making foundry on Genius! Molten iron is pouring on me! I'm doomed! Wait! My hair's deflecting the molten lead! I'm okay!
You may be okay for the moment, but — you, Oldie Von Moldie and Mannequin will be captured and sacrificed in the Continental Airlines Execution Arena! All three of you will die hideous deaths at the hands of monsters!
We three may die, but my hair will live on! And come back to kill you!
Diet Coke
Okay, I give up! Who, or what, are we fighting?
We're fighting the dreaded animals of the "blue screen"! Lash out at them in any way that you can!
I am, but how will I know if I kill any of them?
When the mo is finished! Don't worr the boys a Industrial Li and Magic w make sure you come out a hero
I guess you could say I got the "upper hand" in this battle!
You lost your concen-tration, Mannequin!
If my concentration had five fingers on it, you're right, Master!
There is no Force more powerful than mine!
True, that isn't, Cuckoo! Mean, I! Green, I! Steal the movie with this scene, I!
Won the battle with Cuckoo, I did! And day happy for AmaDilly and Mannequin. Married they do get
And do you, AmaDilly, take Mannequin's remaining hand in Holy Matrimony?
I do!
You know, we shouldn't cry!
Do you think it makes us too human?

Since I first read *MAD* Magazine as a kid, I've been drawn in by its mix of highbrow satire and lowbrow laughs that pokes very funny holes in the stuffiest of institutions. Mort Drucker's signature artwork captures and exaggerates the world around us and the people in it in a way that makes them more real. His caricatures are the best, and he is the artist that defines *MAD* for me.

When I had to choose an artist for the *American Graffiti* poster, Mort was the first and only person who came to mind. Since then, he's been redrawing my movies as funny parodies. You never mind being the subject of one of Mort's jokes, because he executes them so artfully.

—George Lucas
Director, *Star Wars*

IT'S NOT THE HEAT, IT'S THE STUPIDITY DEPT.

C.S.OY

Comedian Fred Allen once said, "Imitation is the sincerest form of television." So, obviously, did the creators of *CSI*. They've duplicated the exact DNA of their original Crime Scene Investigation series located in Vegas and simply moved it to the steamy tropics of Florida! Uh-huh, a copycat cadaver cop series! Same formula, new faces. And one familiar old face! Here is...

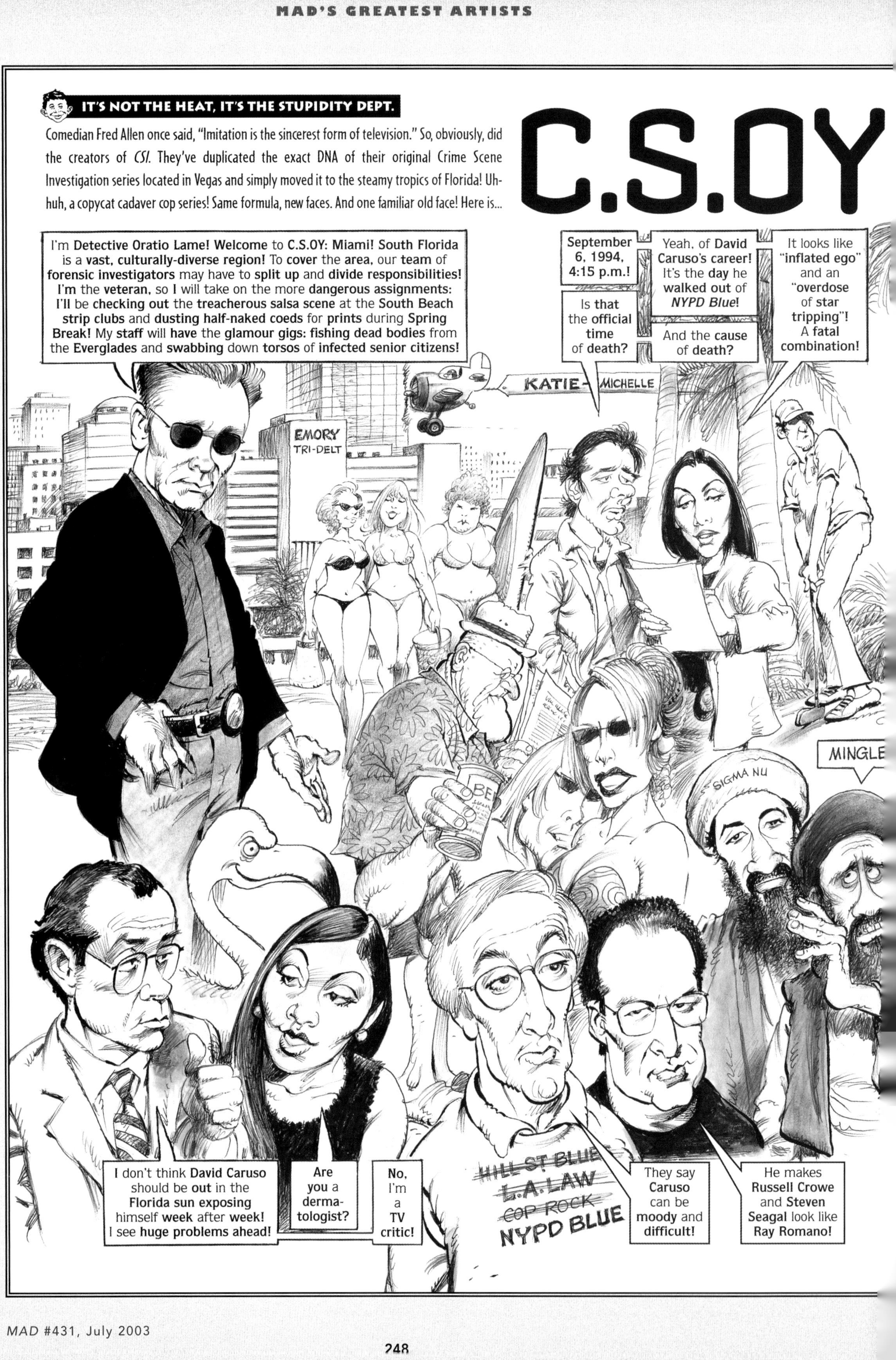

I'm Detective Oratio Lame! Welcome to C.S.OY: Miami! South Florida is a vast, culturally-diverse region! To cover the area, our team of forensic investigators may have to split up and divide responsibilities! I'm the veteran, so I will take on the more dangerous assignments: I'll be checking out the treacherous salsa scene at the South Beach strip clubs and dusting half-naked coeds for prints during Spring Break! My staff will have the glamour gigs: fishing dead bodies from the Everglades and swabbing down torsos of infected senior citizens!
September 6, 1994, 4:15 p.m.!
Is that the official time of death?
Yeah, of David Caruso's career! It's the day he walked out of *NYPD Blue*!
And the cause of death?
It looks like "inflated ego" and an "overdose of star tripping"! A fatal combination!
KATIE-MICHELLE
EMORY TRI-DELT
MINGLE
SIGMA NU
I don't think David Caruso should be out in the Florida sun exposing himself week after week! I see huge problems ahead!
Are you a derma-tologist?
No, I'm a TV critic!
HILL ST BLUE
L.A. LAW
COP ROCK
NYPD BLUE
They say Caruso can be moody and difficult!
He makes Russell Crowe and Steven Seagal look like Ray Romano!

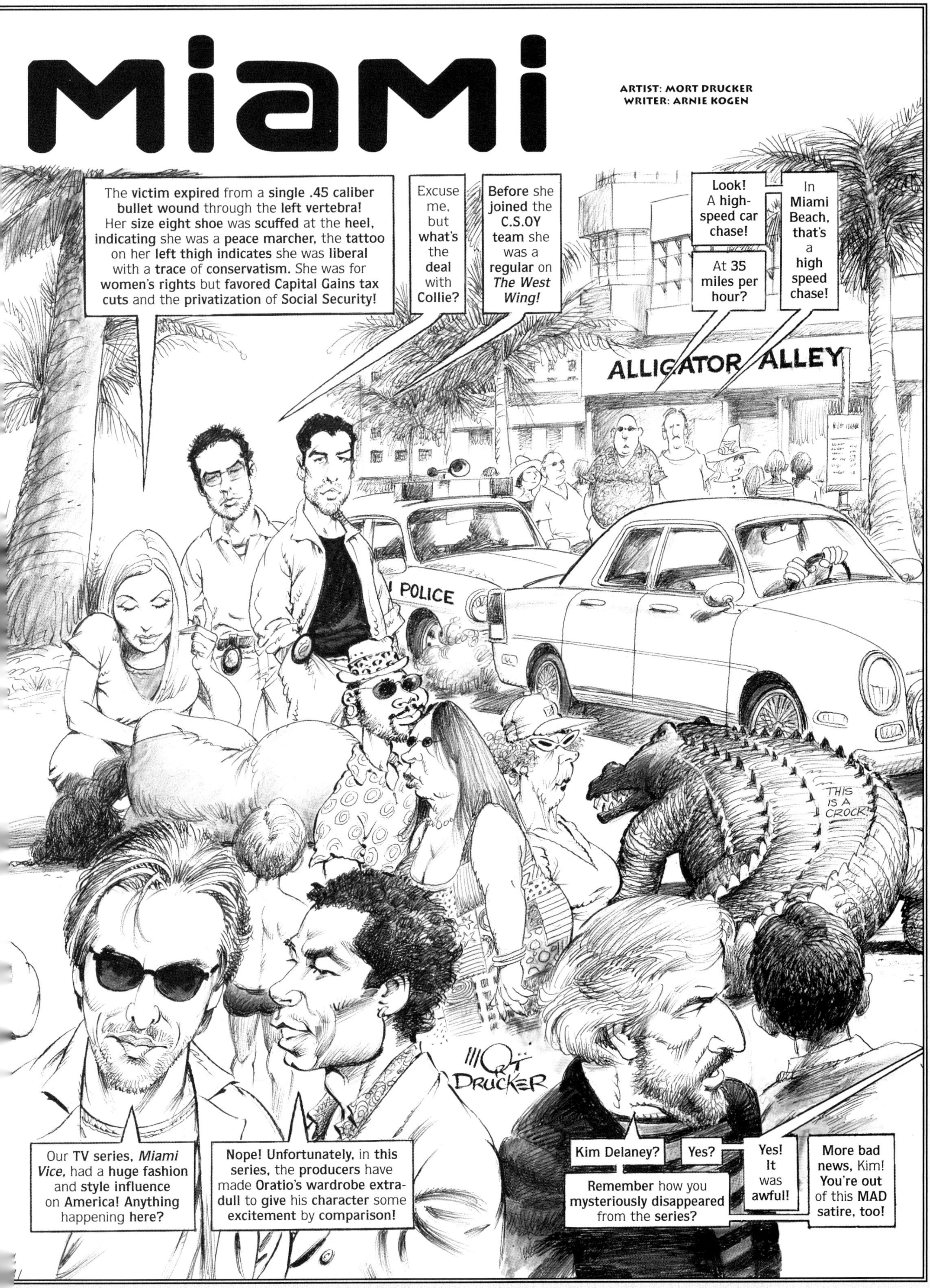

MiaMi
ARTIST: MORT DRUCKER
WRITER: ARNIE KOGEN
The victim expired from a single .45 caliber bullet wound through the left vertebra! Her size eight shoe was scuffed at the heel, indicating she was a peace marcher, the tattoo on her left thigh indicates she was liberal with a trace of conservatism. She was for women's rights but favored Capital Gains tax cuts and the privatization of Social Security!
Excuse me, but what's the deal with Collie?
Before she joined the C.S.OY team she was a regular on *The West Wing!*
Look! A high-speed car chase!
At 35 miles per hour?
In Miami Beach, that's a high speed chase!
ALLIGATOR ALLEY
POLICE
THIS IS A CROCK!
MORT DRUCKER
Our TV series, *Miami Vice*, had a huge fashion and style influence on America! Anything happening here?
Nope! Unfortunately, in this series, the producers have made Oratio's wardrobe extra-dull to give his character some excitement by comparison!
Kim Delaney?
Yes?
Remember how you mysteriously disappeared from the series?
Yes! It was awful!
More bad news, Kim! You're out of this MAD satire, too!

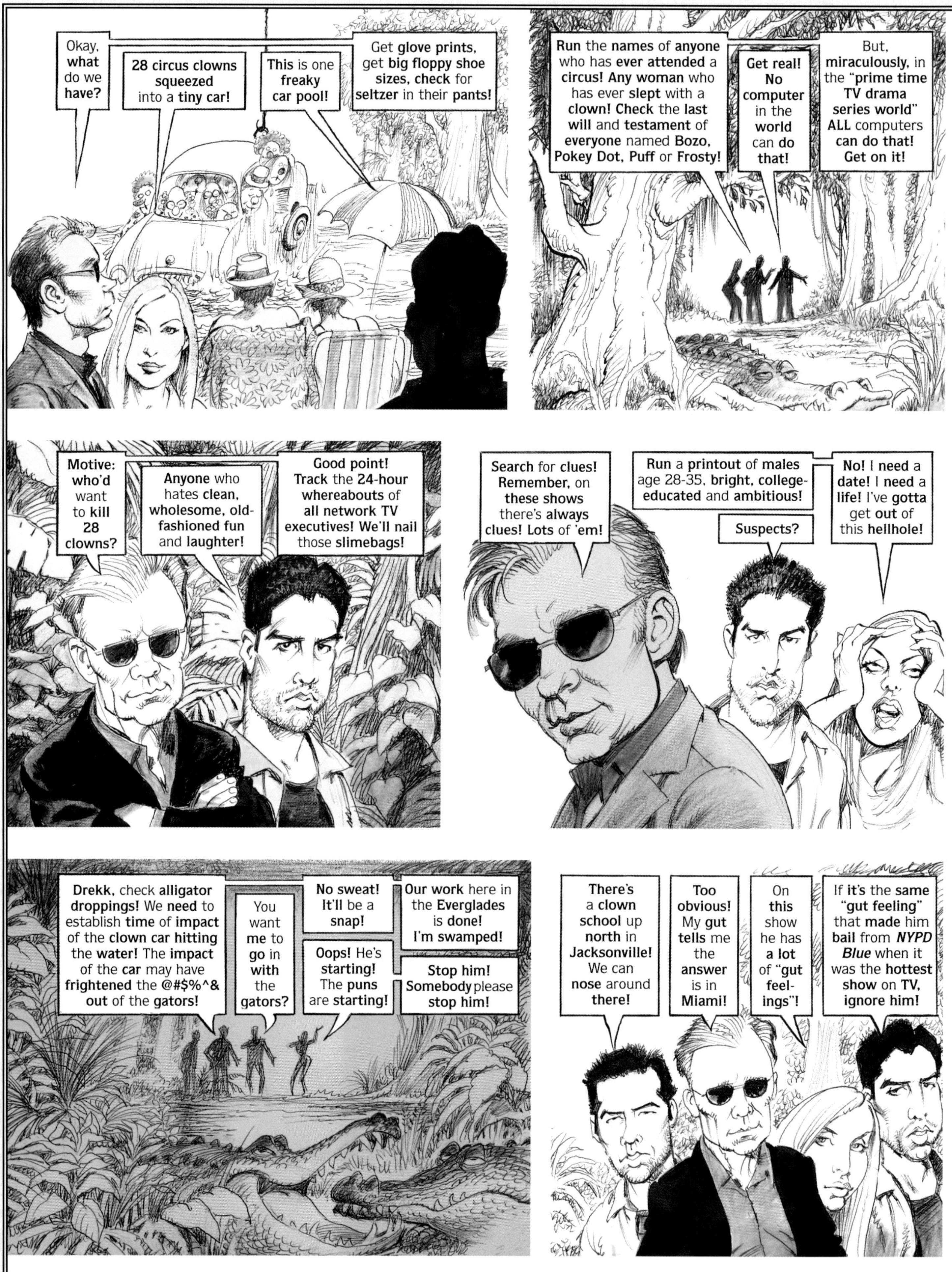
Okay, what do we have?
28 circus clowns squeezed into a tiny car!
This is one freaky car pool!
Get glove prints, get big floppy shoe sizes, check for seltzer in their pants!
Run the names of anyone who has ever attended a circus! Any woman who has ever slept with a clown! Check the last will and testament of everyone named Bozo, Pokey Dot, Puff or Frosty!
Get real! No computer in the world can do that!
But, miraculously, in the "prime time TV drama series world" ALL computers can do that! Get on it!
Motive: who'd want to kill 28 clowns?
Anyone who hates clean, wholesome, old-fashioned fun and laughter!
Good point! Track the 24-hour whereabouts of all network TV executives! We'll nail those slimebags!
Search for clues! Remember, on these shows there's always clues! Lots of 'em!
Run a printout of males age 28-35, bright, college-educated and ambitious!
Suspects?
No! I need a date! I need a life! I've gotta get out of this hellhole!
Drekk, check alligator droppings! We need to establish time of impact of the clown car hitting the water! The impact of the car may have frightened the @#$%^& out of the gators!
You want me to go in with the gators?
No sweat! It'll be a snap!
Oops! He's starting! The puns are starting!
Our work here in the Everglades is done! I'm swamped!
Stop him! Somebody please stop him!
There's a clown school up north in Jacksonville! We can nose around there!
Too obvious! My gut tells me the answer is in Miami!
On this show he has a lot of "gut feel-ings"!
If it's the same "gut feeling" that made him bail from NYPD Blue when it was the hottest show on TV, ignore him!

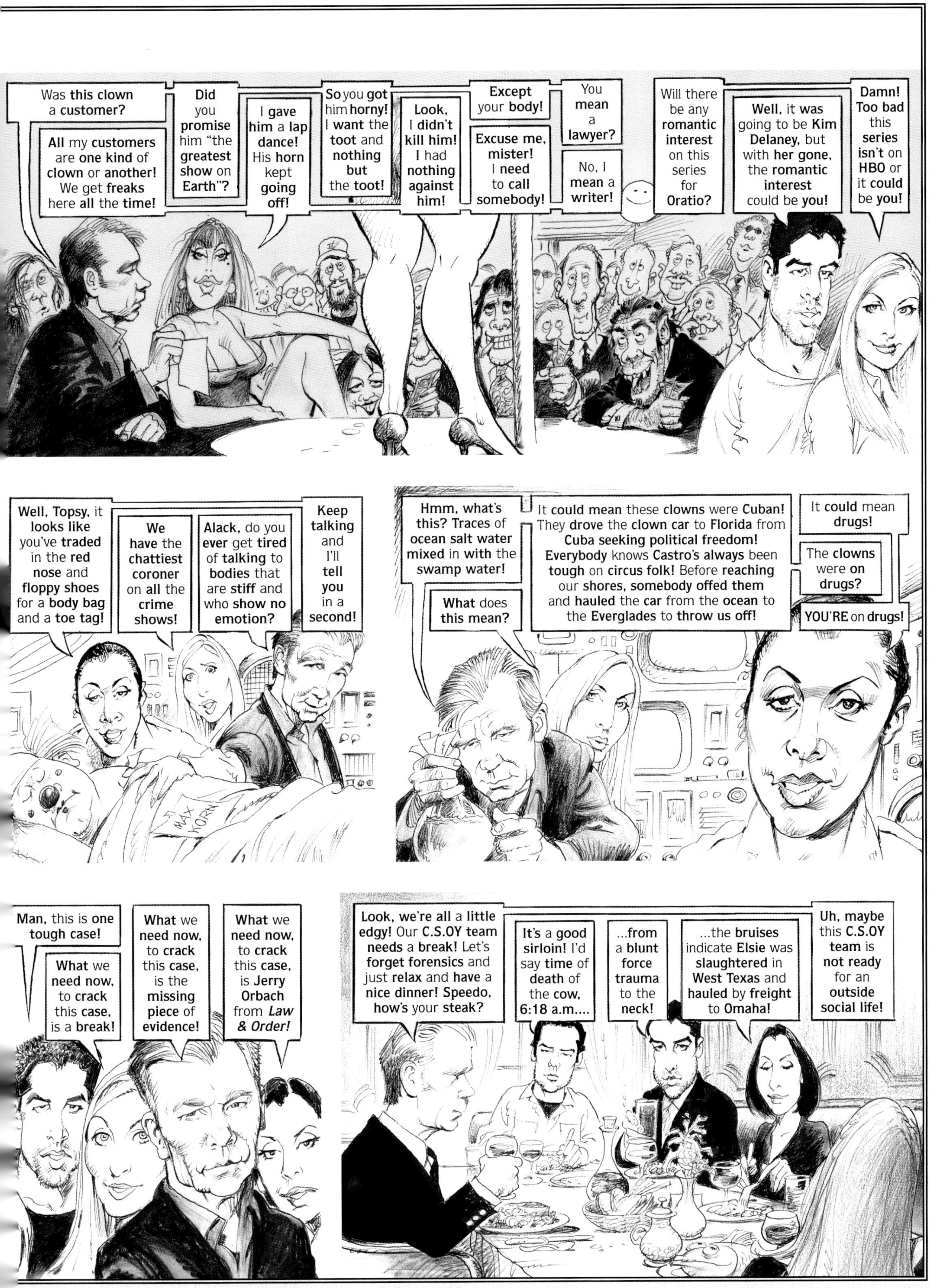

Was this clown a customer?
All my customers are one kind of clown or another! We get freaks here all the time!
Did you promise him "the greatest show on Earth"?
I gave him a lap dance! His horn kept going off!
So you got him horny! I want the toot and nothing but the toot!
Look, I didn't kill him! I had nothing against him!
Except your body!
Excuse me, mister! I need to call somebody!
You mean a lawyer?
No, I mean a writer!
Will there be any romantic interest on this series for Oratio?
Well, it was going to be Kim Delaney, but with her gone, the romantic interest could be you!
Damn! Too bad this series isn't on HBO or it could be you!
Well, Topsy, it looks like you've traded in the red nose and floppy shoes for a body bag and a toe tag!
We have the chattiest coroner on all the crime shows!
Alack, do you ever get tired of talking to bodies that are stiff and who show no emotion?
Keep talking and I'll tell you in a second!
MAX KORN
Hmm, what's this? Traces of ocean salt water mixed in with the swamp water!
What does this mean?
It could mean these clowns were Cuban! They drove the clown car to Florida from Cuba seeking political freedom! Everybody knows Castro's always been tough on circus folk! Before reaching our shores, somebody offed them and hauled the car from the ocean to the Everglades to throw us off!
It could mean drugs!
The clowns were on drugs?
YOU'RE on drugs!
Man, this is one tough case!
What we need now, to crack this case, is a break!
What we need now, to crack this case, is the missing piece of evidence!
What we need now, to crack this case, is Jerry Orbach from Law & Order!
Look, we're all a little edgy! Our C.S.OY team needs a break! Let's forget forensics and just relax and have a nice dinner! Speedo, how's your steak?
It's a good sirloin! I'd say time of death of the cow, 6:18 a.m....
...from a blunt force trauma to the neck!
...the bruises indicate Elsie was slaughtered in West Texas and hauled by freight to Omaha!
Uh, maybe this C.S.OY team is not ready for an outside social life!

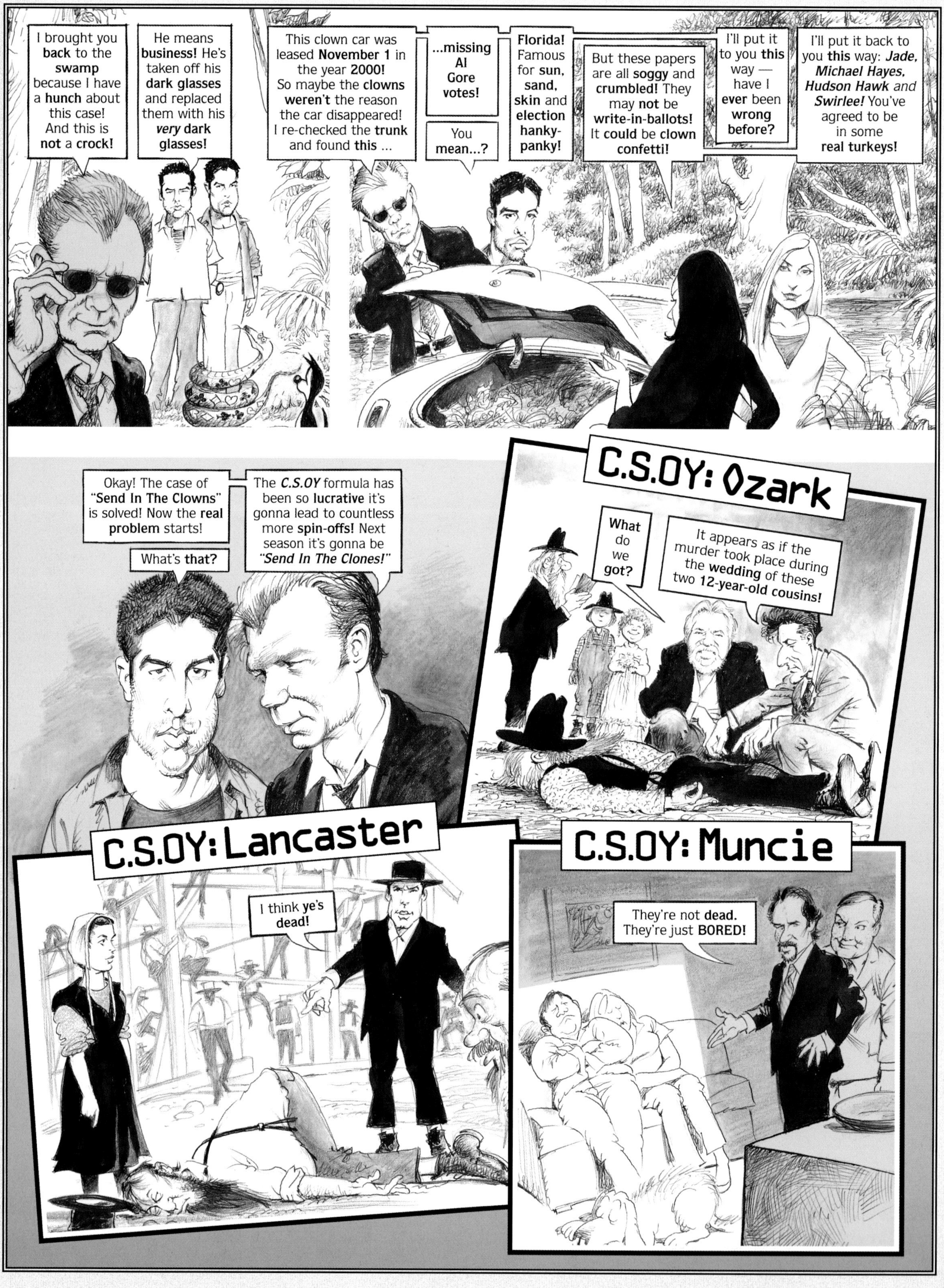
I brought you back to the swamp because I have a hunch about this case! And this is not a crock!
He means business! He's taken off his dark glasses and replaced them with his very dark glasses!
This clown car was leased November 1 in the year 2000! So maybe the clowns weren't the reason the car disappeared! I re-checked the trunk and found this ...
...missing Al Gore votes!
You mean...?
Florida! Famous for sun, sand, skin and election hanky-panky!
But these papers are all soggy and crumbled! They may not be write-in-ballots! It could be clown confetti!
I'll put it to you this way — have I ever been wrong before?
I'll put it back to you this way: Jade, Michael Hayes, Hudson Hawk and Swirlee! You've agreed to be in some real turkeys!
Okay! The case of "Send In The Clowns" is solved! Now the real problem starts!
What's that?
The C.S.OY formula has been so lucrative it's gonna lead to countless more spin-offs! Next season it's gonna be "Send In The Clones!"
C.S.OY: Ozark
What do we got?
It appears as if the murder took place during the wedding of these two 12-year-old cousins!
C.S.OY: Lancaster
I think ye's dead!
C.S.OY: Muncie
They're not dead. They're just BORED!

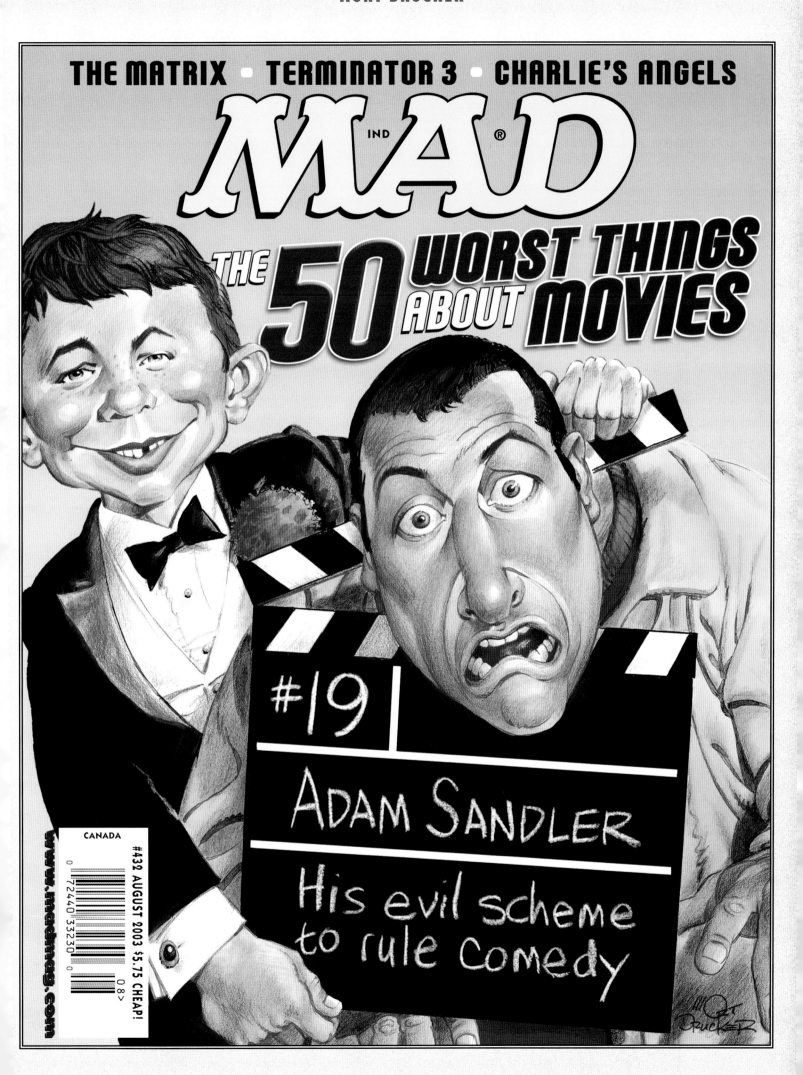

THE MATRIX • TERMINATOR 3 • CHARLIE'S ANGELS

MAD

IND

THE 50 WORST THINGS ABOUT MOVIES

#19

ADAM SANDLER

His evil scheme to rule comedy

CANADA
#432 AUGUST 2003 $5.75 CHEAP!
www.madmag.com
0 72440 33230 0
08>

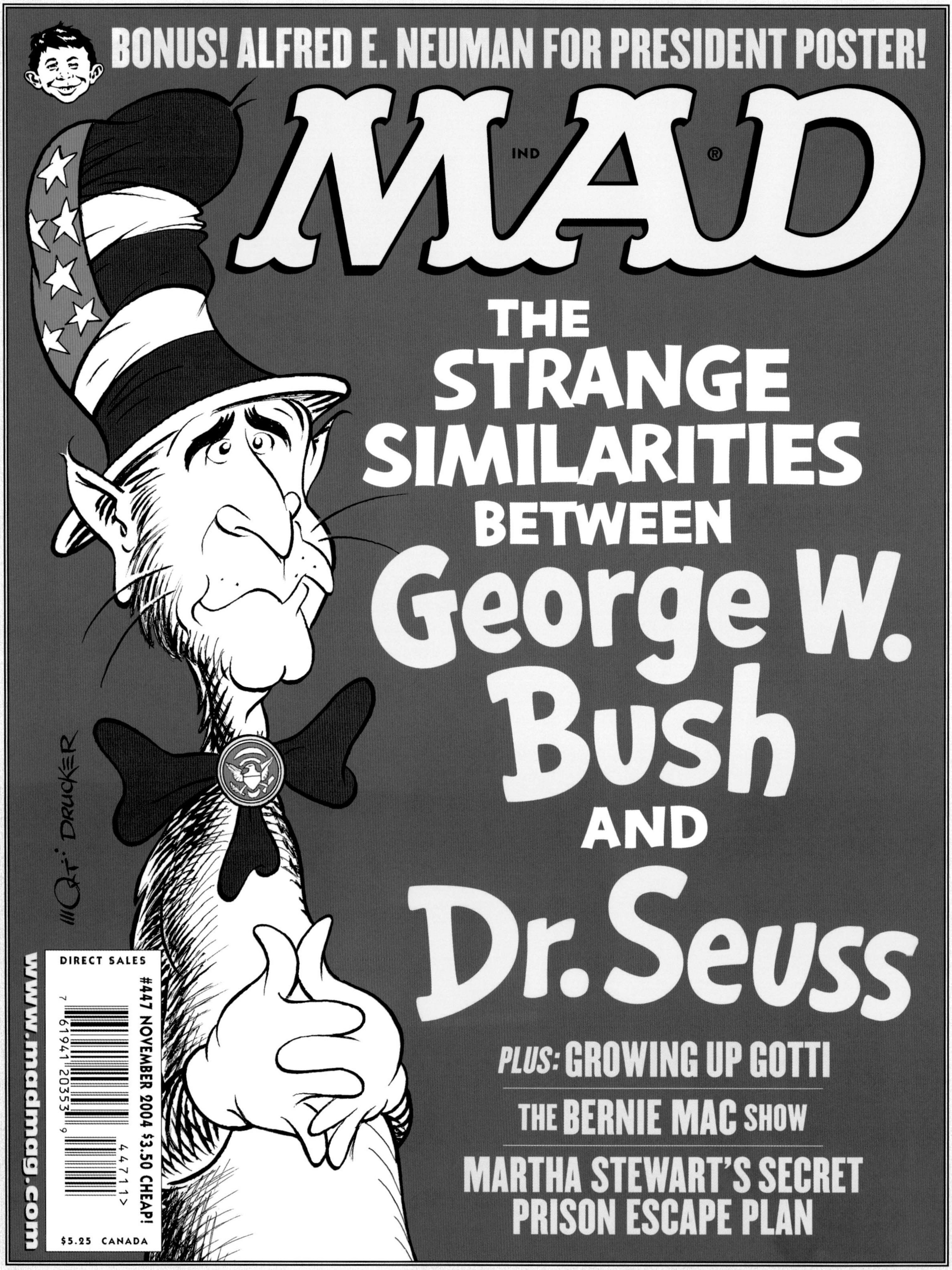
BONUS! ALFRED E. NEUMAN FOR PRESIDENT POSTER!
MAD
THE STRANGE SIMILARITIES BETWEEN George W. Bush AND Dr. Seuss
PLUS: GROWING UP GOTTI
THE BERNIE MAC SHOW
MARTHA STEWART'S SECRET PRISON ESCAPE PLAN
DIRECT SALES
#447 NOVEMBER 2004 $3.50 CHEAP!
$5.25 CANADA
www.madmag.com
DRUCKER

TOM CRUISE FROM PRETTY BOY TO "HOO BOY!"

As a Scientologist, Tom Cruise believes that all human suffering is caused by the galactic tyrant Xenu, who stacked billions of alien ghosts in volcanoes 75,000,000 years ago and then blew them up with his H-bombs. To us that sounds completely plausible, especially when compared to Tom's recent *super* crazy rants against psychotherapy and his wide-eyed, maniacal declarations of love for Katie Holmes. (Note to Katie: *Get out now!*) Damn that Xenu for making us all suffer through Cruise's weird, pathetic meltdown.

THE CHURCH OF SCIENTOLOGY PRESENTS TOM CRUISE IN...

MISSION: INSUFFERABLE

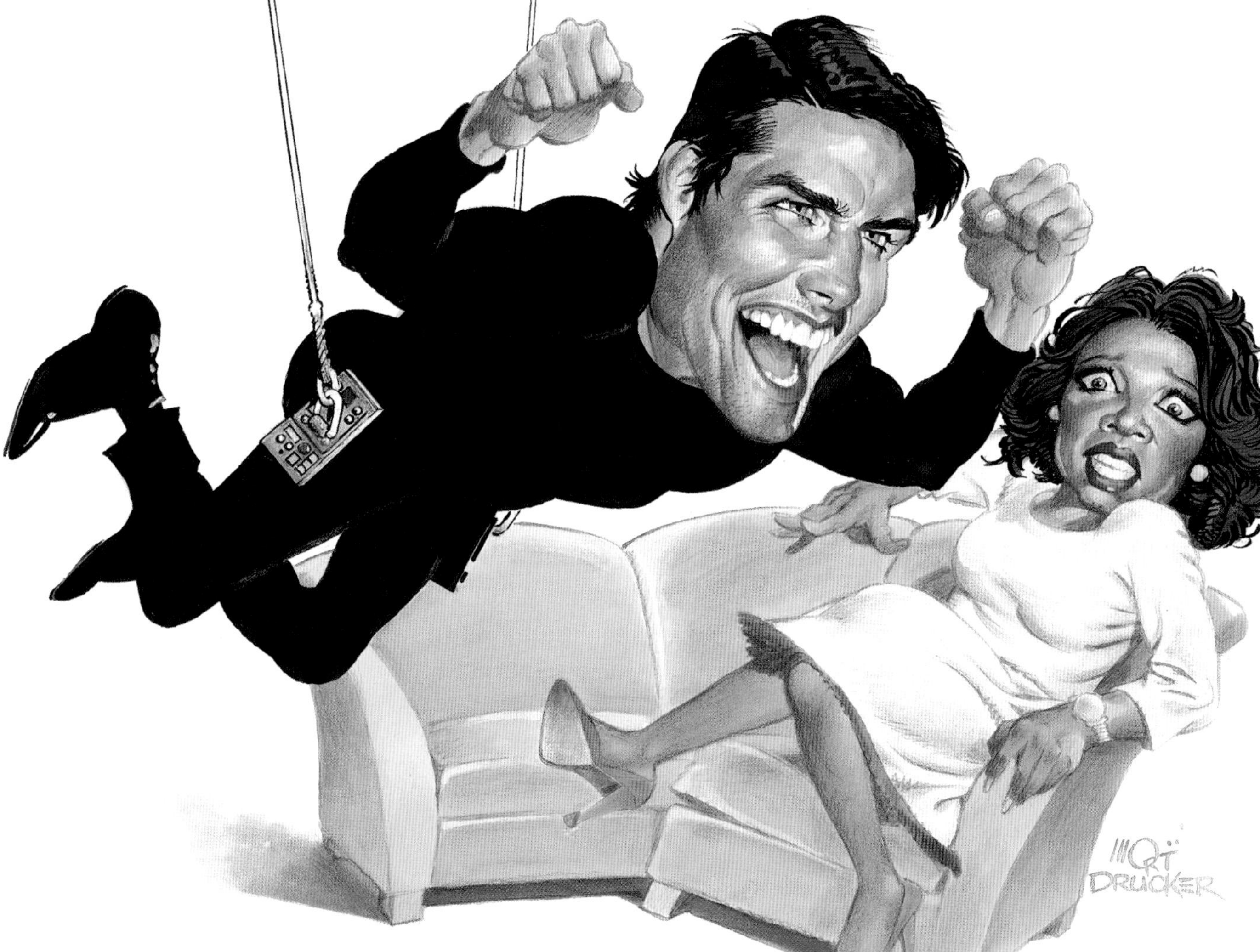
MORT DRUCKER

His mission, should he choose to accept it, is to convince the world that he really, really, really likes women, prescription drugs for mental illness are evil, and everyone must go see his new movie.

THIS MAN WILL SELF-DESTRUCT IN FIVE SECONDS.

TOM CRUISE
AS THE UNRAVELING MOVIE STAR AND AMATEUR PSYCHIATRIST

KATIE HOLMES
AS THE BRAINWASHED LOVE INTEREST WITH WEIRD SORES AROUND HER MOUTH

OPRAH WINFREY
AS THE TALK SHOW HOST WHO NEEDS TO CLEAN FOOTPRINTS OFF HER COUCH

MATT LAUER
AS THE "GLIB" MORNING ANCHOR

AND BROOKE SHIELDS AS THE LONG-SUFFERING, POSTPARTUM MOM WHO JUST NEEDS SOME EXERCISE AND A FEW VITAMINS

PRODUCED BY A GIGANTIC EGO

ARTIST: MORT DRUCKER WRITER: DESMOND DEVLIN

THE VILE, VILE WEST DEPT.

Okay, **c$%&** **s@#!%n'** MAD readers. You want an intro? Here's your **f#$%*n'** intro! There's a gritty, foul-mouthed **f%$#@n'** western series on HBO which is getting great **m%@$*r** **f&%$*n'** reviews and uses a **s&%tload** of **c&%#** **s#@%$n'** profanity even when that profanity is **f#*%$n'** unnecessary! Here is...

DREAI

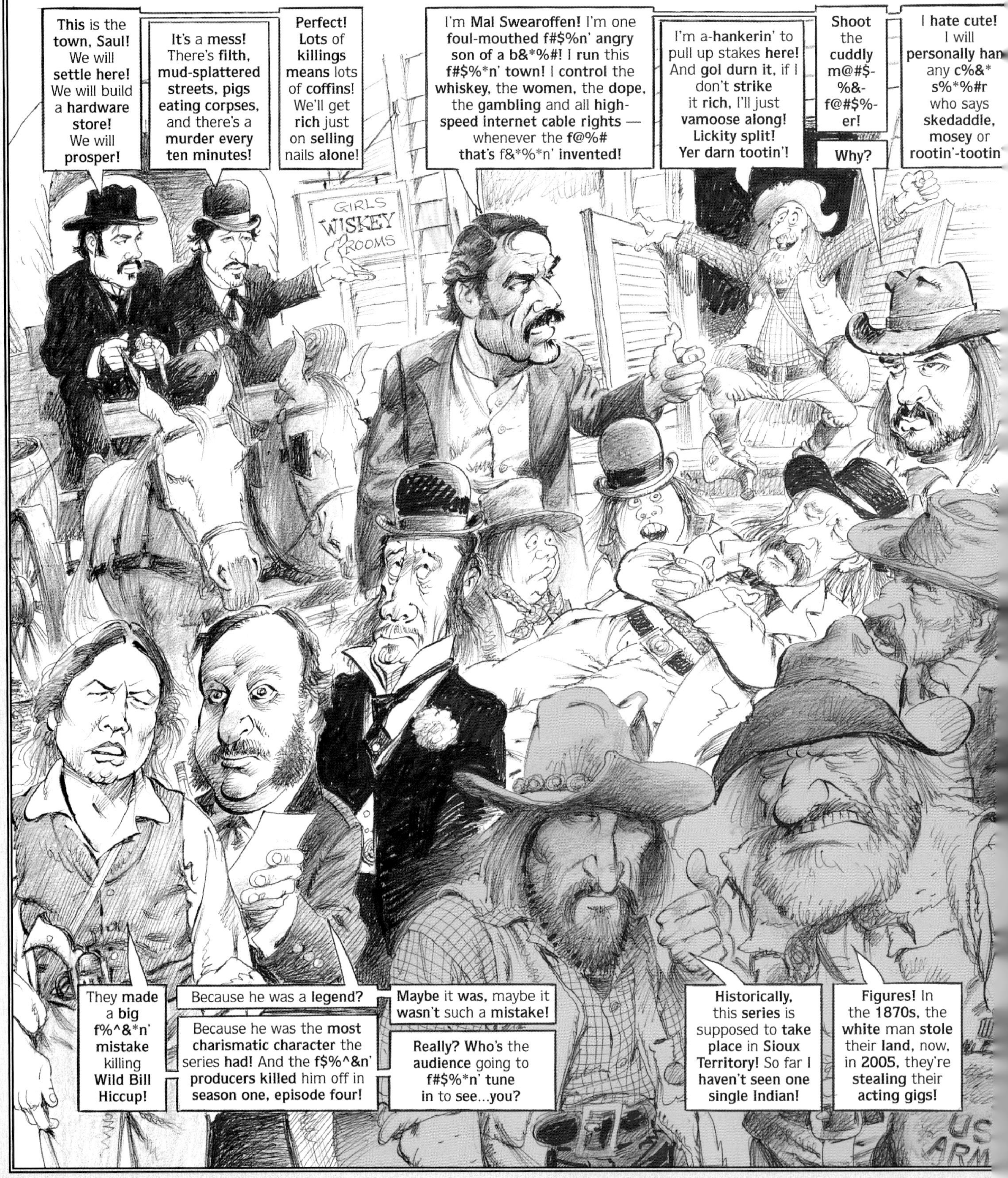
This is the town, Saul! We will settle here! We will build a hardware store! We will prosper!
It's a mess! There's filth, mud-splattered streets, pigs eating corpses, and there's a murder every ten minutes!
Perfect! Lots of killings means lots of coffins! We'll get rich just on selling nails alone!
I'm Mal Swearoffen! I'm one foul-mouthed f#$%n' angry son of a b&*%#! I run this f#$%*n' town! I control the whiskey, the women, the dope, the gambling and all high-speed internet cable rights — whenever the f@%# that's f&*%*n' invented!
GIRLS WISKEY ROOMS
I'm a-hankerin' to pull up stakes here! And gol durn it, if I don't strike it rich, I'll just vamoose along! Lickity split! Yer darn tootin'!
Shoot the cuddly m@#$-%&-f@#$%-er!
Why?
I hate cute! I will personally han any c%&* s%*%#r who says skedaddle, mosey or rootin'-tootin'
They made a big f%^&*n' mistake killing Wild Bill Hiccup!
Because he was a legend?
Because he was the most charismatic character the series had! And the f$%^&n' producers killed him off in season one, episode four!
Maybe it was, maybe it wasn't such a mistake!
Really? Who's the audience going to f#$%*n' tune in to see...you?
Historically, this series is supposed to take place in Sioux Territory! So far I haven't seen one single Indian!
Figures! In the 1870s, the white man stole their land, now, in 2005, they're stealing their acting gigs!
US ARM

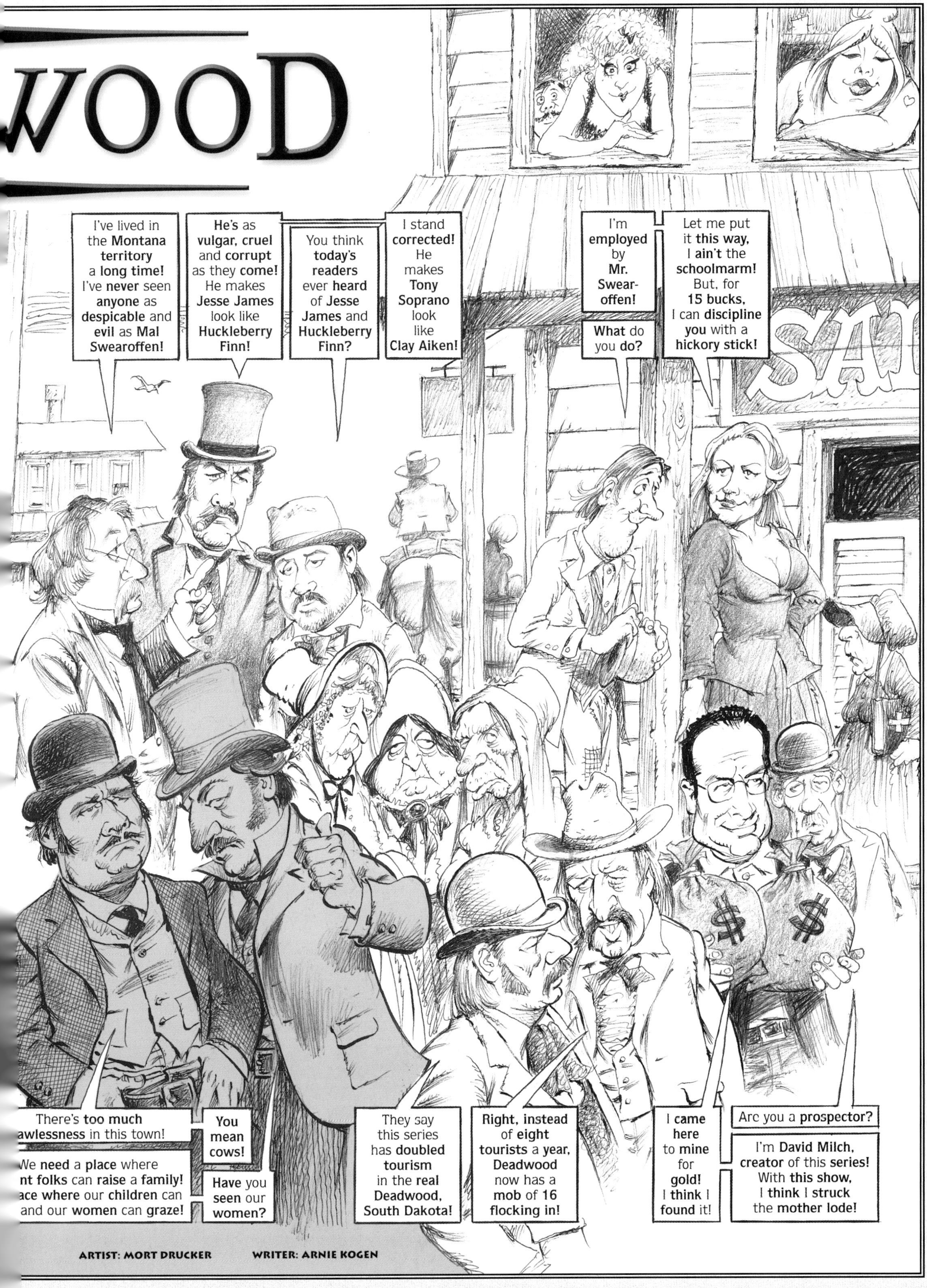
WOOD
I've lived in the Montana territory a long time! I've never seen anyone as despicable and evil as Mal Swearoffen!
He's as vulgar, cruel and corrupt as they come! He makes Jesse James look like Huckleberry Finn!
You think today's readers ever heard of Jesse James and Huckleberry Finn?
I stand corrected! He makes Tony Soprano look like Clay Aiken!
I'm employed by Mr. Swear-offen!
What do you do?
Let me put it this way, I ain't the schoolmarm! But, for 15 bucks, I can discipline you with a hickory stick!
SA
There's too much awlessness in this town!
We need a place where nt folks can raise a family! ace where our children can and our women can graze!
You mean cows!
Have you seen our women?
They say this series has doubled tourism in the real Deadwood, South Dakota!
Right, instead of eight tourists a year, Deadwood now has a mob of 16 flocking in!
I came here to mine for gold! I think I found it!
Are you a prospector?
I'm David Milch, creator of this series! With this show, I think I struck the mother lode!
ARTIST: MORT DRUCKER WRITER: ARNIE KOGEN

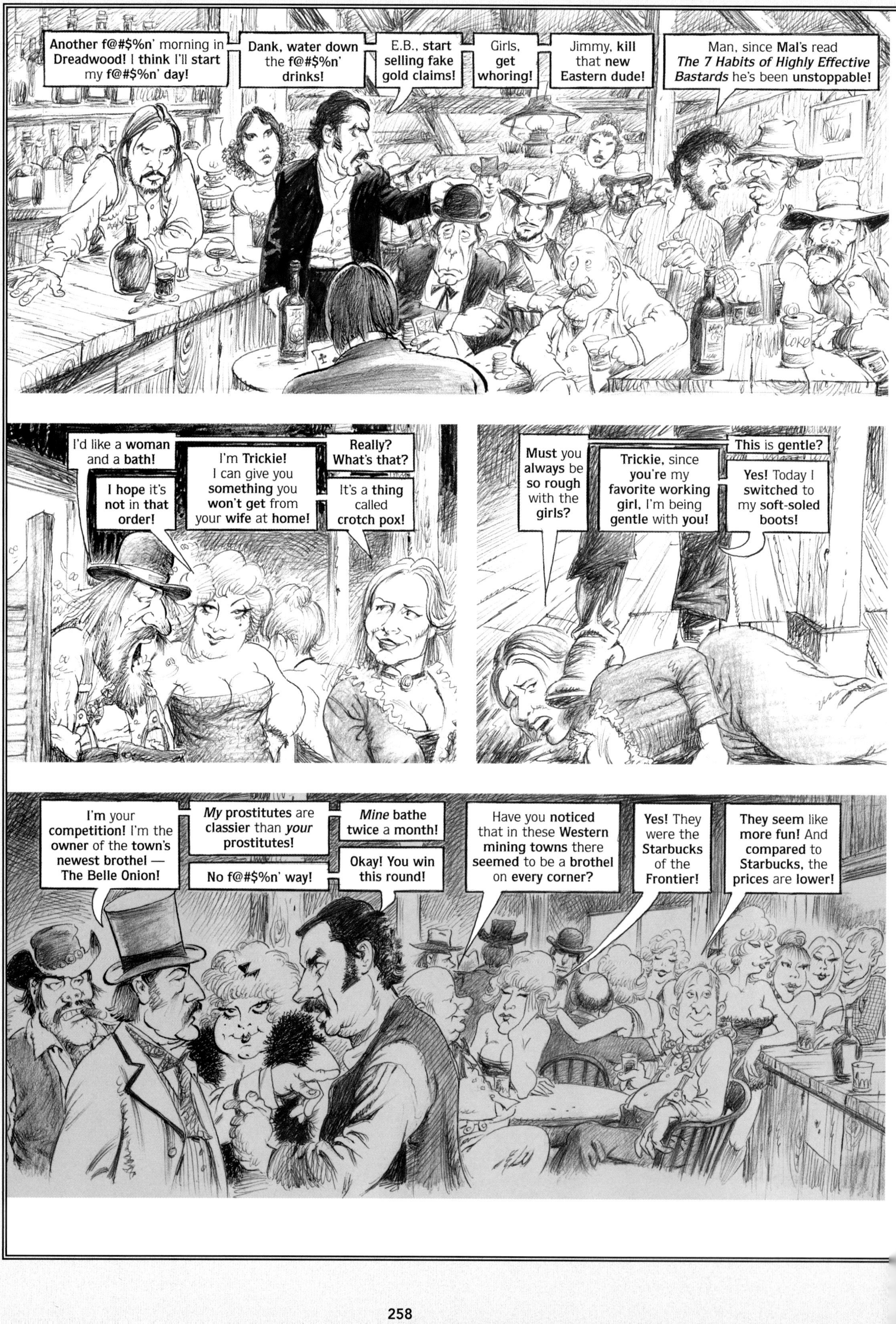
Another f@#$%n' morning in Dreadwood! I think I'll start my f@#$%n' day!
Dank, water down the f@#$%n' drinks!
E.B., start selling fake gold claims!
Girls, get whoring!
Jimmy, kill that new Eastern dude!
Man, since Mal's read The 7 Habits of Highly Effective Bastards he's been unstoppable!
I'd like a woman and a bath!
I hope it's not in that order!
I'm Trickie! I can give you something you won't get from your wife at home!
Really? What's that?
It's a thing called crotch pox!
Must you always be so rough with the girls?
Trickie, since you're my favorite working girl, I'm being gentle with you!
This is gentle?
Yes! Today I switched to my soft-soled boots!
I'm your competition! I'm the owner of the town's newest brothel — The Belle Onion!
My prostitutes are classier than your prostitutes!
Mine bathe twice a month!
No f@#$%n' way!
Okay! You win this round!
Have you noticed that in these Western mining towns there seemed to be a brothel on every corner?
Yes! They were the Starbucks of the Frontier!
They seem like more fun! And compared to Starbucks, the prices are lower!

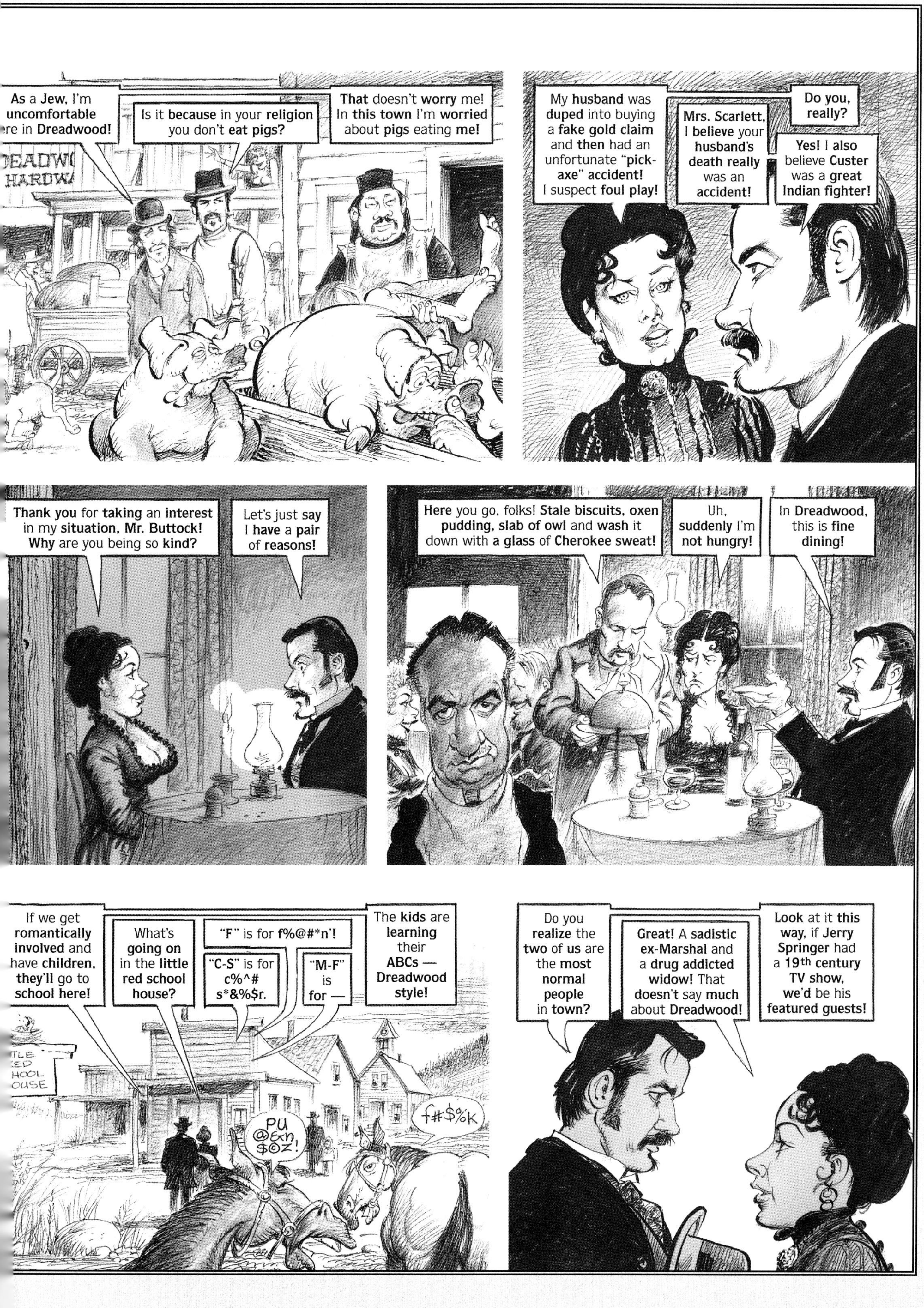
As a Jew, I'm uncomfortable ere in Dreadwood!
Is it because in your religion you don't eat pigs?
That doesn't worry me! In this town I'm worried about pigs eating me!
My husband was duped into buying a fake gold claim and then had an unfortunate "pick-axe" accident! I suspect foul play!
Mrs. Scarlett, I believe your husband's death really was an accident!
Do you, really?
Yes! I also believe Custer was a great Indian fighter!
Thank you for taking an interest in my situation, Mr. Buttock! Why are you being so kind?
Let's just say I have a pair of reasons!
Here you go, folks! Stale biscuits, oxen pudding, slab of owl and wash it down with a glass of Cherokee sweat!
Uh, suddenly I'm not hungry!
In Dreadwood, this is fine dining!
If we get romantically involved and have children, they'll go to school here!
What's going on in the little red school house?
"F" is for f%@#*n'!
"C-S" is for c%^# s*&%$r.
"M-F" is for —
The kids are learning their ABCs — Dreadwood style!
f#$%K
Do you realize the two of us are the most normal people in town?
Great! A sadistic ex-Marshal and a drug addicted widow! That doesn't say much about Dreadwood!
Look at it this way, if Jerry Springer had a 19th century TV show, we'd be his featured guests!

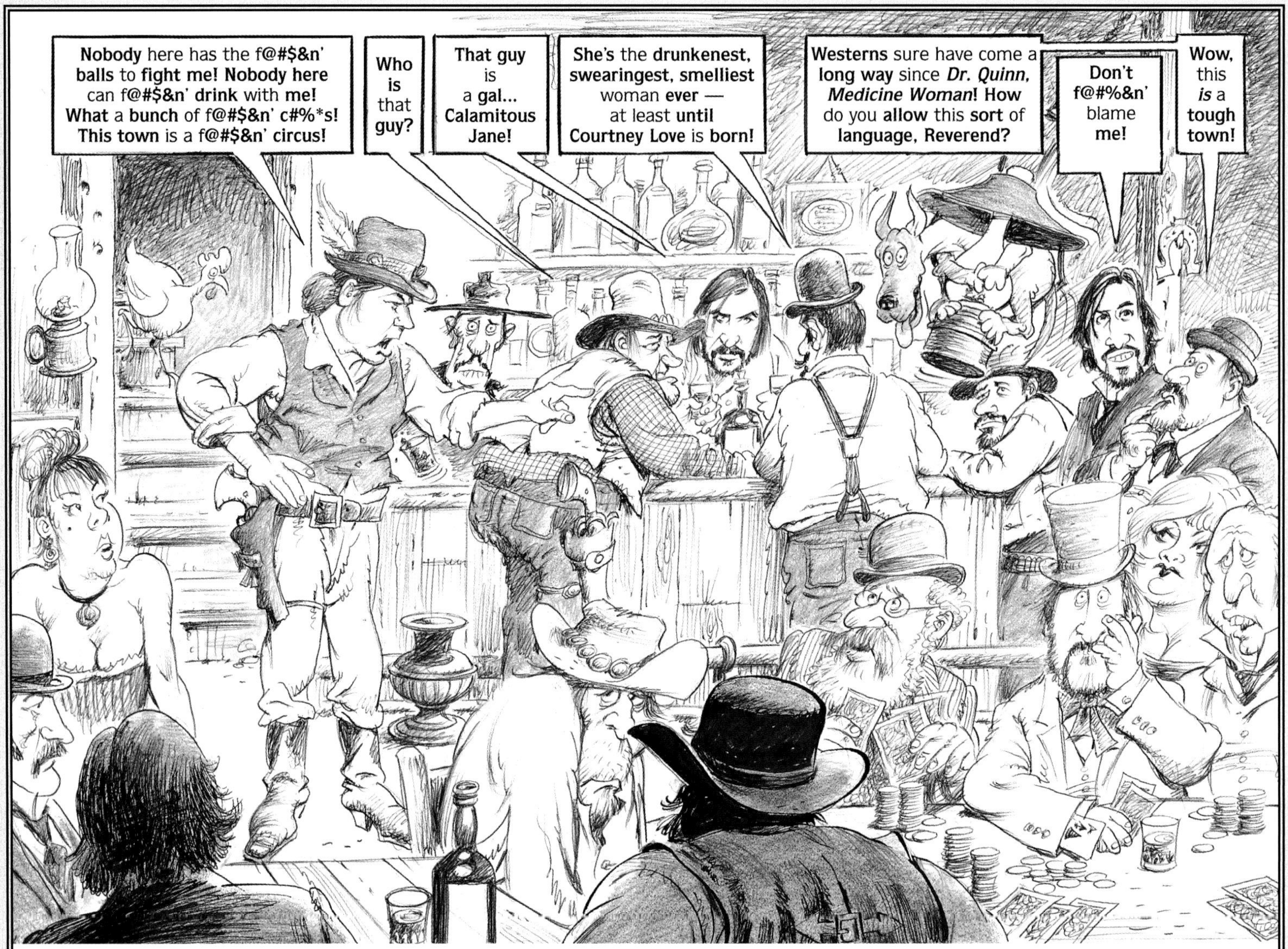
Nobody here has the f@#$&n' balls to fight me! Nobody here can f@#$&n' drink with me! What a bunch of f@#$&n' c#%*s! This town is a f@#$&n' circus!
Who is that guy?
That guy is a gal... Calamitous Jane!
She's the drunkenest, swearingest, smelliest woman ever — at least until Courtney Love is born!
Westerns sure have come a long way since Dr. Quinn, Medicine Woman! How do you allow this sort of language, Reverend?
Don't f@#%&n' blame me!
Wow, this is a tough town!

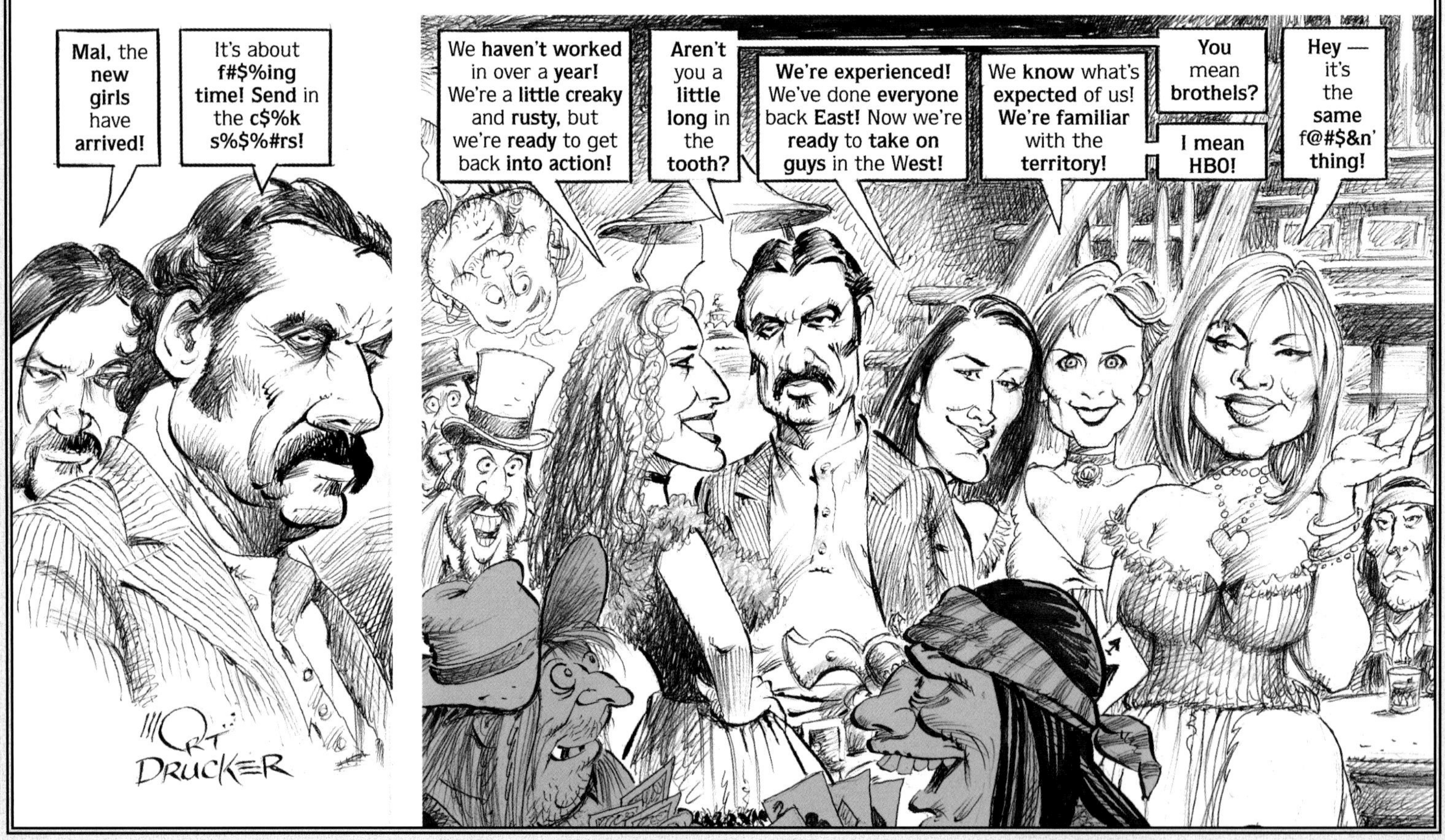
Mal, the new girls have arrived!
It's about f#$%ing time! Send in the c$%k s%$%#rs!
We haven't worked in over a year! We're a little creaky and rusty, but we're ready to get back into action!
Aren't you a little long in the tooth?
We're experienced! We've done everyone back East! Now we're ready to take on guys in the West!
We know what's expected of us! We're familiar with the territory!
You mean brothels?
I mean HBO!
Hey — it's the same f@#$&n' thing!
MORT DRUCKER

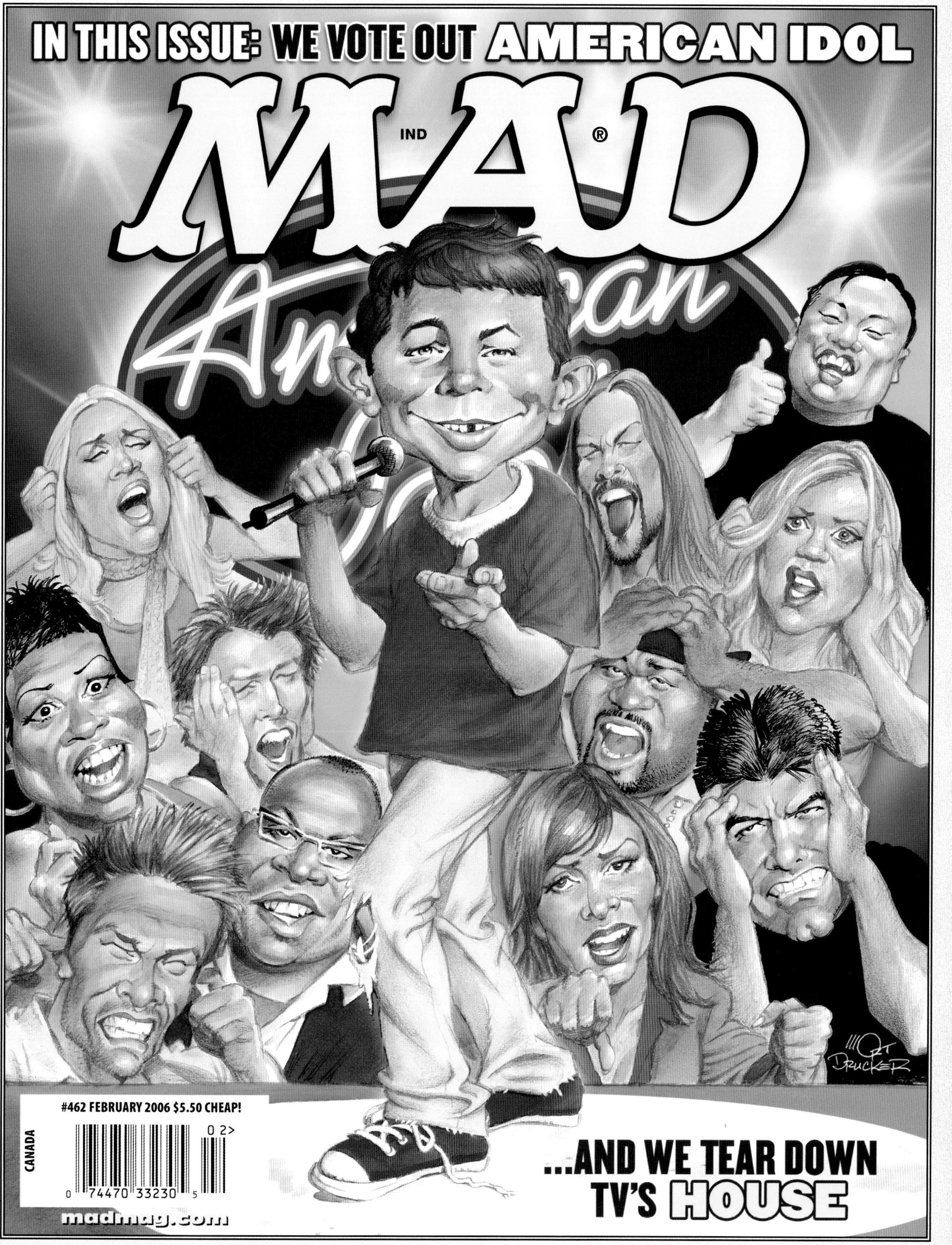
IN THIS ISSUE: WE VOTE OUT AMERICAN IDOL
MAD
IND
®
American
MORT DRUCKER
#462 FEBRUARY 2006 $5.50 CHEAP!
CANADA
...AND WE TEAR DOWN TV'S HOUSE
madmag.com

HUGH DIRTY RAT DEPT.

The Fox network seems to be successful with two types of shows. One is teen-oriented series like *The OC* and *That '70's Show*. The other is shows featuring bitter middle-aged men. Simon Cowell on *American Idol* is one of them and this guy, who makes Simon look like the Pillsbury Doughboy, is another. He stars in a new medical mystery. He's angry, he's brooding, he's unshaven, meet...

L

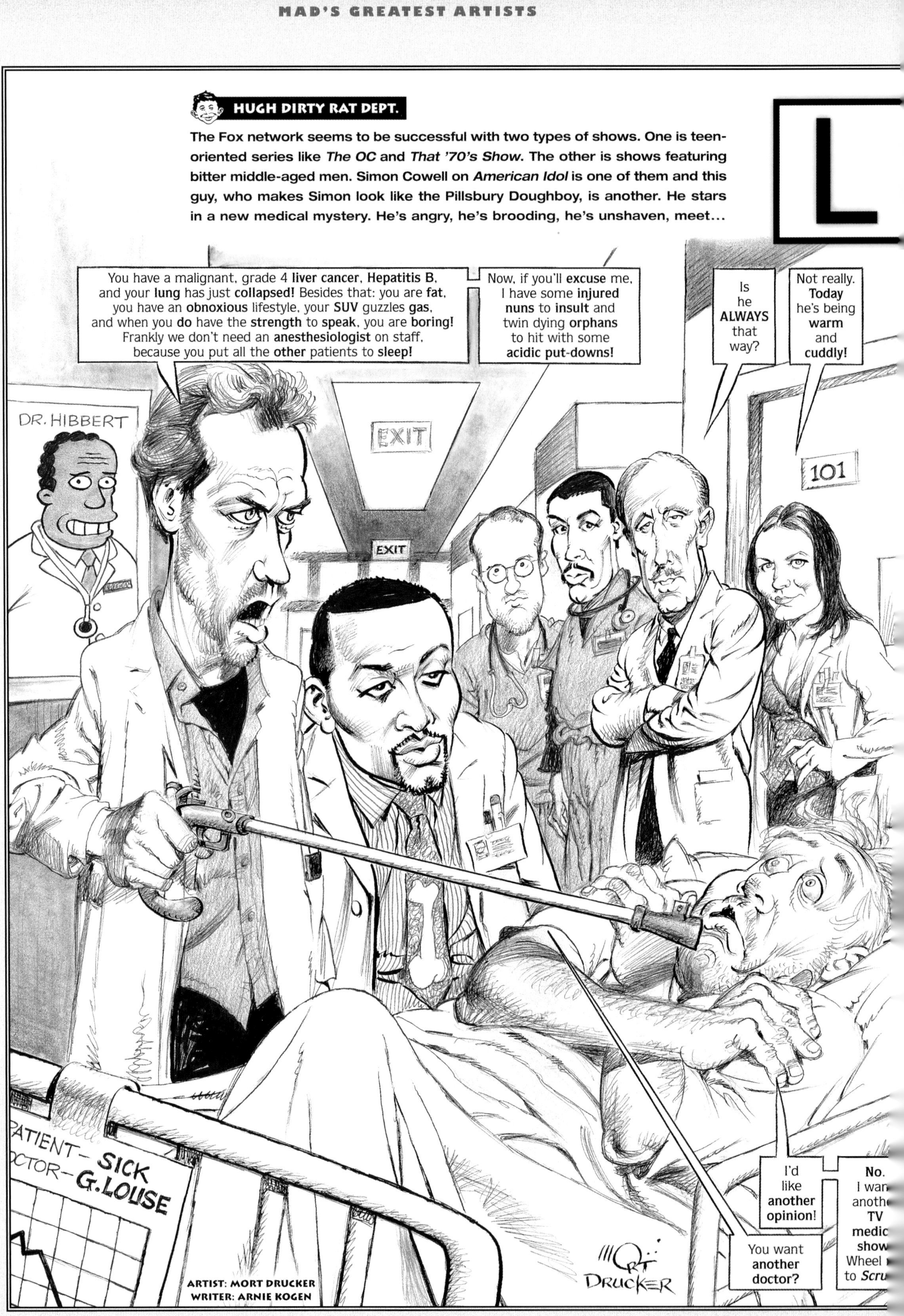
You have a malignant, grade 4 **liver cancer**, **Hepatitis B**, and your **lung** has just **collapsed!** Besides that: you are **fat**, you have an **obnoxious** lifestyle, your **SUV** guzzles **gas**, and when you **do** have the **strength** to **speak**, you are **boring!** Frankly we don't need an **anesthesiologist** on staff, because you put all the **other** patients to **sleep!**
Now, if you'll **excuse** me, I have some **injured nuns** to **insult** and twin dying **orphans** to hit with some **acidic put-downs!**
Is he **ALWAYS** that way?
Not really. **Today** he's being **warm** and **cuddly!**
DR. HIBBERT
EXIT
EXIT
101
PATIENT– SICK
DOCTOR– G. LOUSE
I'd like **another opinion!**
You want another doctor?
No. I wan anoth **TV** medic show Wheel to Scru
MORT DRUCKER
ARTIST: MORT DRUCKER
WRITER: ARNIE KOGEN

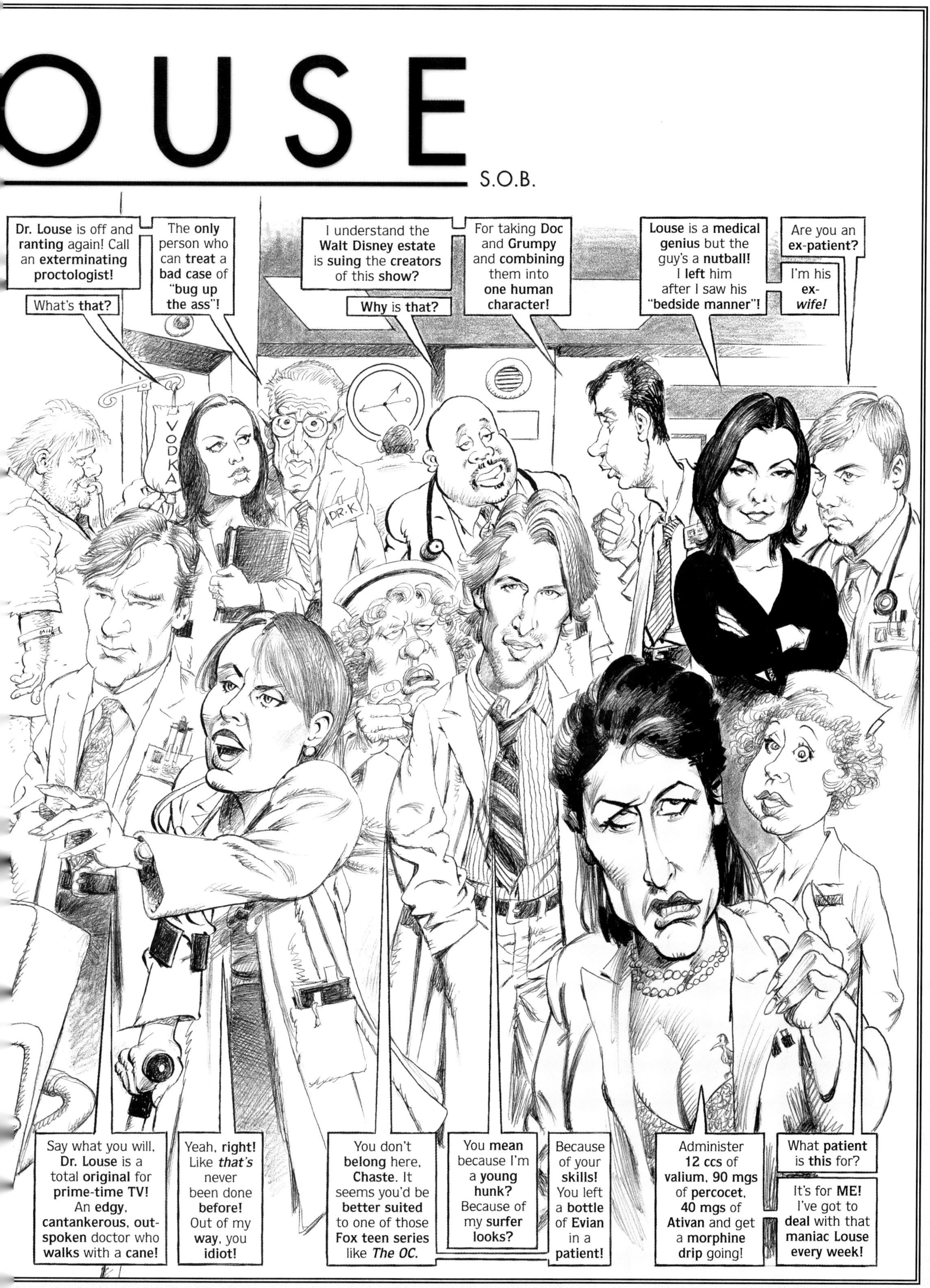
OUSE
S.O.B.
Dr. Louse is off and ranting again! Call an exterminating proctologist!
What's that?
The only person who can treat a bad case of "bug up the ass"!
I understand the Walt Disney estate is suing the creators of this show?
Why is that?
For taking Doc and Grumpy and combining them into one human character!
Louse is a medical genius but the guy's a nutball! I left him after I saw his "bedside manner"!
Are you an ex-patient?
I'm his ex-wife!
VODKA
DR. K
Say what you will, Dr. Louse is a total original for prime-time TV! An edgy, cantankerous, out-spoken doctor who walks with a cane!
Yeah, right! Like that's never been done before! Out of my way, you idiot!
You don't belong here, Chaste. It seems you'd be better suited to one of those Fox teen series like The OC.
You mean because I'm a young hunk? Because of my surfer looks?
Because of your skills! You left a bottle of Evian in a patient!
Administer 12 ccs of valium, 90 mgs of percocet, 40 mgs of Ativan and get a morphine drip going!
What patient is this for?
It's for ME! I've got to deal with that maniac Louse every week!

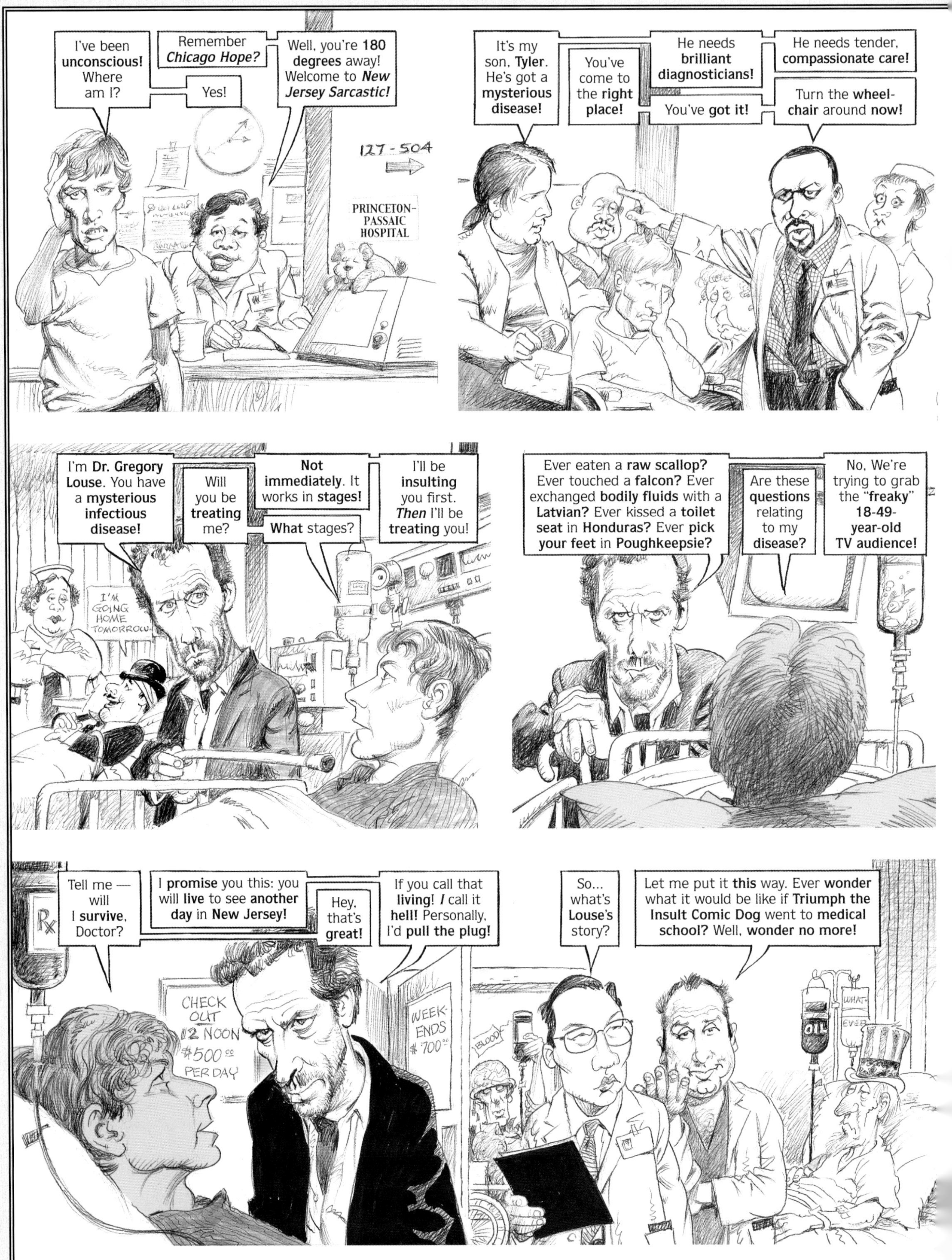
I've been unconscious! Where am I?
Remember Chicago Hope?
Yes!
Well, you're 180 degrees away! Welcome to New Jersey Sarcastic!
127 - 504
PRINCETON-PASSAIC HOSPITAL
It's my son, Tyler. He's got a mysterious disease!
You've come to the right place!
He needs brilliant diagnosticians!
You've got it!
He needs tender, compassionate care!
Turn the wheelchair around now!
I'm Dr. Gregory Louse. You have a mysterious infectious disease!
Will you be treating me?
Not immediately. It works in stages!
What stages?
I'll be insulting you first. Then I'll be treating you!
I'M GOING HOME TOMORROW
Ever eaten a raw scallop? Ever touched a falcon? Ever exchanged bodily fluids with a Latvian? Ever kissed a toilet seat in Honduras? Ever pick your feet in Poughkeepsie?
Are these questions relating to my disease?
No. We're trying to grab the "freaky" 18-49-year-old TV audience!
Tell me — will I survive, Doctor?
I promise you this: you will live to see another day in New Jersey!
Hey, that's great!
If you call that living! I call it hell! Personally, I'd pull the plug!
CHECK OUT 12 NOON $500.00 PER DAY
WEEK-ENDS $700.00
So... what's Louse's story?
Let me put it this way. Ever wonder what it would be like if Triumph the Insult Comic Dog went to medical school? Well, wonder no more!
BLOOD
OIL
WHAT-EVER

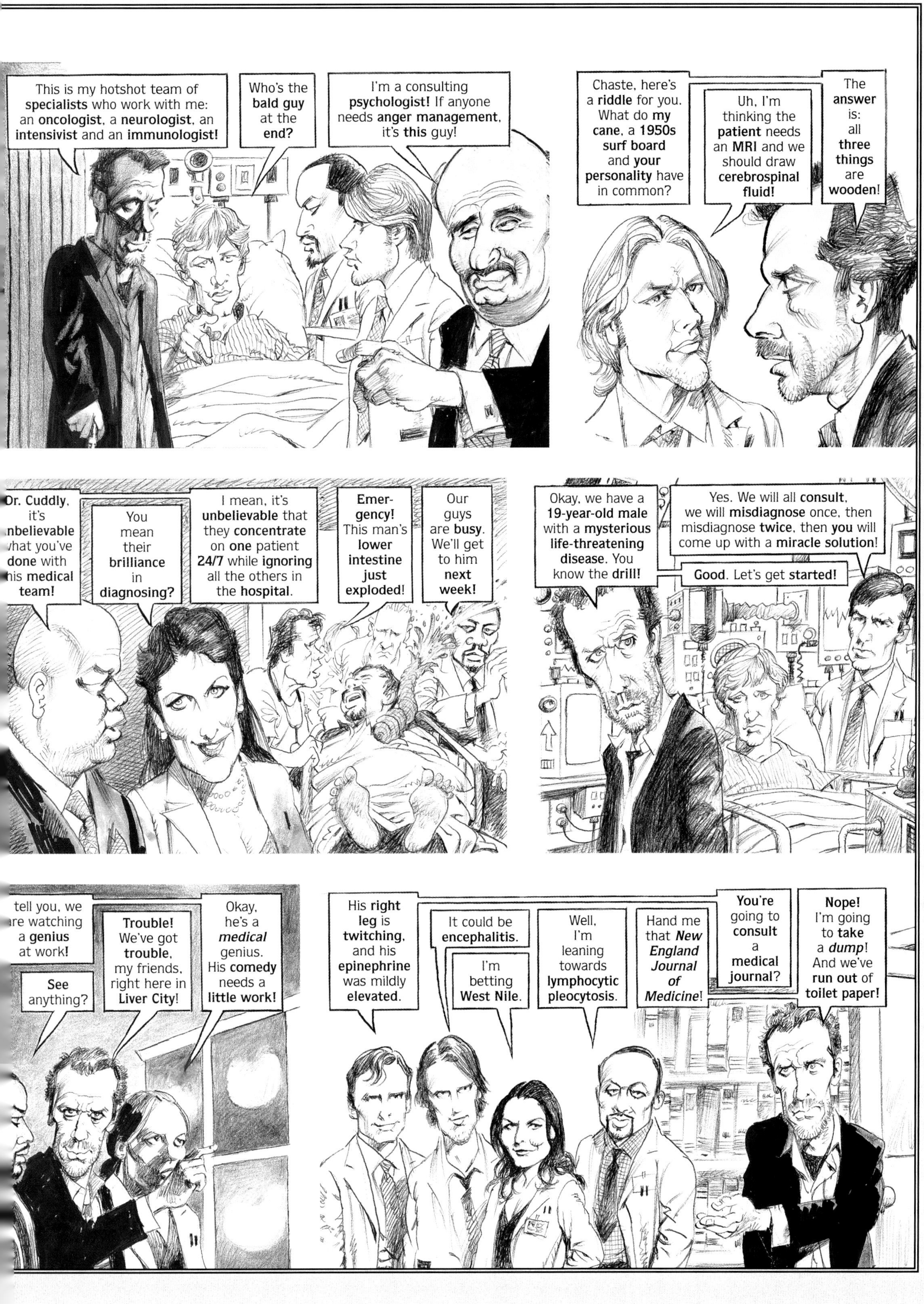
This is my hotshot team of specialists who work with me: an oncologist, a neurologist, an intensivist and an immunologist!
Who's the bald guy at the end?
I'm a consulting psychologist! If anyone needs anger management, it's this guy!
Chaste, here's a riddle for you. What do my cane, a 1950s surf board and your personality have in common?
Uh, I'm thinking the patient needs an MRI and we should draw cerebrospinal fluid!
The answer is: all three things are wooden!
Dr. Cuddly, it's nbelievable vhat you've done with his medical team!
You mean their brilliance in diagnosing?
I mean, it's unbelievable that they concentrate on one patient 24/7 while ignoring all the others in the hospital.
Emer-gency! This man's lower intestine just exploded!
Our guys are busy. We'll get to him next week!
Okay, we have a 19-year-old male with a mysterious life-threatening disease. You know the drill!
Yes. We will all consult, we will misdiagnose once, then misdiagnose twice, then you will come up with a miracle solution!
Good. Let's get started!
tell you, we re watching a genius at work!
See anything?
Trouble! We've got trouble, my friends, right here in Liver City!
Okay, he's a medical genius. His comedy needs a little work!
His right leg is twitching, and his epinephrine was mildly elevated.
It could be encephalitis.
I'm betting West Nile.
Well, I'm leaning towards lymphocytic pleocytosis.
Hand me that New England Journal of Medicine!
You're going to consult a medical journal?
Nope! I'm going to take a dump! And we've run out of toilet paper!

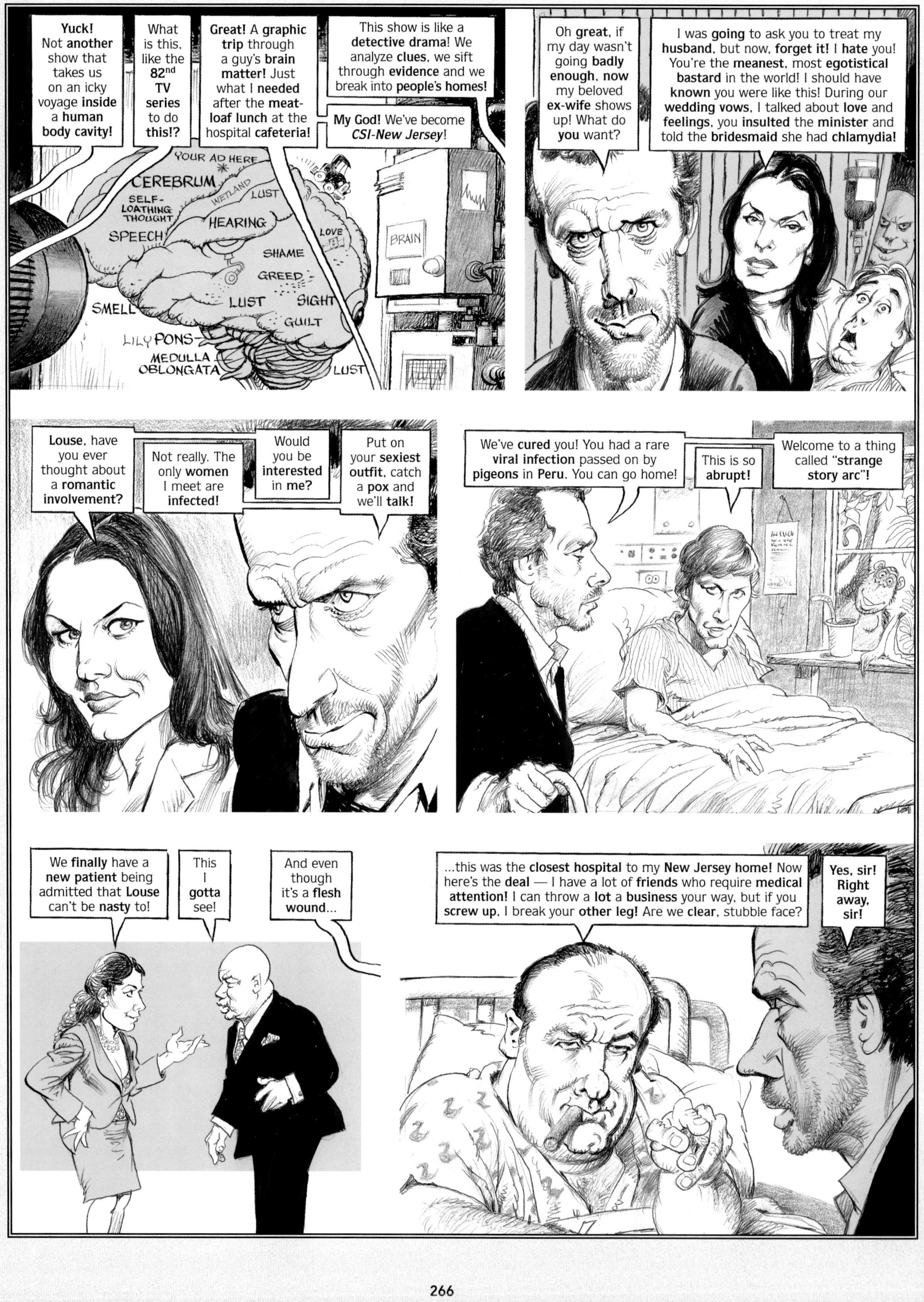
Yuck! Not another show that takes us on an icky voyage inside a human body cavity!
What is this, like the 82nd TV series to do this!?
Great! A graphic trip through a guy's brain matter! Just what I needed after the meat-loaf lunch at the hospital cafeteria!
This show is like a detective drama! We analyze clues, we sift through evidence and we break into people's homes!
My God! We've become CSI-New Jersey!
YOUR AD HERE
CEREBRUM
SELF-LOATHING THOUGHT
WETLAND
LUST
HEARING
SPEECH
LOVE
SHAME
GREED
SMELL
LUST
SIGHT
GUILT
LILY PONS
MEDULLA OBLONGATA
LUST
BRAIN
Oh great, if my day wasn't going badly enough, now my beloved ex-wife shows up! What do you want?
I was going to ask you to treat my husband, but now, forget it! I hate you! You're the meanest, most egotistical bastard in the world! I should have known you were like this! During our wedding vows, I talked about love and feelings, you insulted the minister and told the bridesmaid she had chlamydia!
Louse, have you ever thought about a romantic involvement?
Not really. The only women I meet are infected!
Would you be interested in me?
Put on your sexiest outfit, catch a pox and we'll talk!
We've cured you! You had a rare viral infection passed on by pigeons in Peru. You can go home!
This is so abrupt!
Welcome to a thing called "strange story arc"!
We finally have a new patient being admitted that Louse can't be nasty to!
This I gotta see!
And even though it's a flesh wound...
...this was the closest hospital to my New Jersey home! Now here's the deal — I have a lot of friends who require medical attention! I can throw a lot a business your way, but if you screw up, I break your other leg! Are we clear, stubble face?
Yes, sir! Right away, sir!

The influence of Mort Drucker on readers of *MAD* Magazine cannot be overstated. I remember with vivid clarity sitting in my elementary school classroom, while I was supposed to be working, desperately trying to copy his brilliant caricature style. It didn't work. Not then and not now. Drucker's eerie ability to absolutely capture the heart and soul of his subjects—and put them in hysterical tableau—is unmatched by anyone. Even the way he signed his work was something of inspiration; I remember as a kid trying to create my own signature in a style as cool as Drucker's. I wished I had an "M" and an "O" in my name so I could do the three lines and circle thing like he did. I am and always was, like so many others, a huge fan of Mort Drucker. One of the greatest comic artists of all time.

—J.J. Abrams
Filmmaker

WHOSE LION IS IT ANYWAY? DEPT.

If we're to believe the hype, this movie is more than a mere movie. It's a Christian allegory with strong messages about sacrifice and forgiveness! And we hate to say it, but they're right! You sacrifice ten hard-earned bucks to see it, and there is no forgiveness offered from the producers for wasting two and half hours of your time! Come on, this is basically a re-tread of the first *Yawnia* movie! If you don't believe it, you'll have to forgive us as we sacrifice the next four pages pointing out all the absurdies in...

THE CHRONIC
YAW

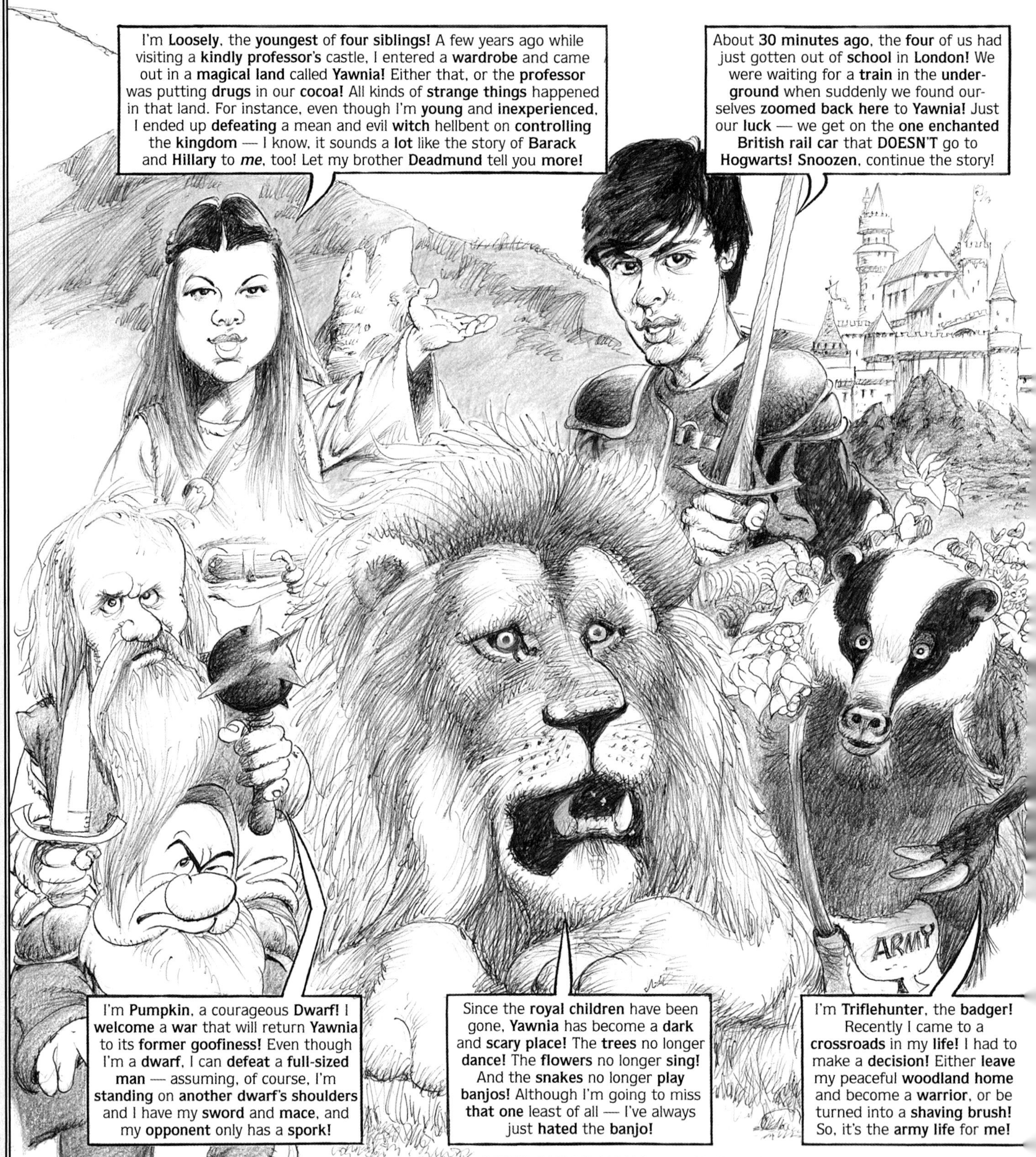

I'm Loosely, the youngest of four siblings! A few years ago while visiting a kindly professor's castle, I entered a wardrobe and came out in a magical land called Yawnia! Either that, or the professor was putting drugs in our cocoa! All kinds of strange things happened in that land. For instance, even though I'm young and inexperienced, I ended up defeating a mean and evil witch hellbent on controlling the kingdom — I know, it sounds a lot like the story of Barack and Hillary to *me*, too! Let my brother Deadmund tell you more!
About 30 minutes ago, the four of us had just gotten out of school in London! We were waiting for a train in the underground when suddenly we found ourselves zoomed back here to Yawnia! Just our luck — we get on the one enchanted British rail car that DOESN'T go to Hogwarts! Snoozen, continue the story!
I'm Pumpkin, a courageous Dwarf! I welcome a war that will return Yawnia to its former goofiness! Even though I'm a dwarf, I can defeat a full-sized man — assuming, of course, I'm standing on another dwarf's shoulders and I have my sword and mace, and my opponent only has a spork!
Since the royal children have been gone, Yawnia has become a dark and scary place! The trees no longer dance! The flowers no longer sing! And the snakes no longer play banjos! Although I'm going to miss that one least of all — I've always just hated the banjo!
ARMY
I'm Triflehunter, the badger! Recently I came to a crossroads in my life! I had to make a decision! Either leave my peaceful woodland home and become a warrior, or be turned into a shaving brush! So, it's the army life for me!

WRITER: DICK DEBARTOLO ARTIST: MORT DRUCKER

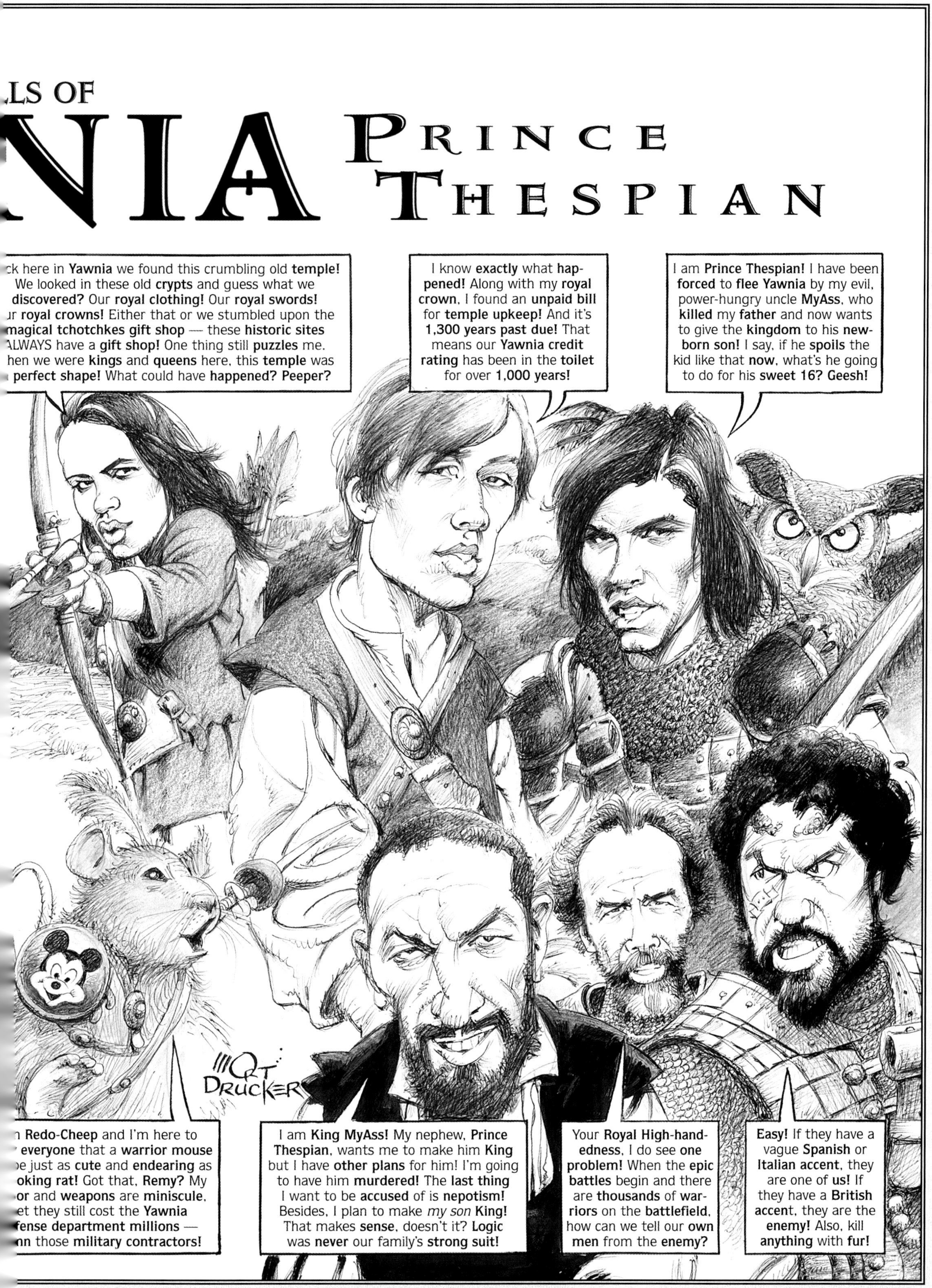

.LS OF
NIA PRINCE THESPIAN
ck here in Yawnia we found this crumbling old temple! We looked in these old crypts and guess what we discovered? Our royal clothing! Our royal swords! ur royal crowns! Either that or we stumbled upon the magical tchotchkes gift shop — these historic sites ALWAYS have a gift shop! One thing still puzzles me. hen we were kings and queens here, this temple was perfect shape! What could have happened? Peeper?
I know exactly what happened! Along with my royal crown, I found an unpaid bill for temple upkeep! And it's 1,300 years past due! That means our Yawnia credit rating has been in the toilet for over 1,000 years!
I am Prince Thespian! I have been forced to flee Yawnia by my evil, power-hungry uncle MyAss, who killed my father and now wants to give the kingdom to his newborn son! I say, if he spoils the kid like that now, what's he going to do for his sweet 16? Geesh!
MORT DRUCKER
n Redo-Cheep and I'm here to everyone that a warrior mouse be just as cute and endearing as oking rat! Got that, Remy? My or and weapons are miniscule, et they still cost the Yawnia fense department millions — nn those military contractors!
I am King MyAss! My nephew, Prince Thespian, wants me to make him King but I have other plans for him! I'm going to have him murdered! The last thing I want to be accused of is nepotism! Besides, I plan to make my son King! That makes sense, doesn't it? Logic was never our family's strong suit!
Your Royal High-handedness, I do see one problem! When the epic battles begin and there are thousands of warriors on the battlefield, how can we tell our own men from the enemy?
Easy! If they have a vague Spanish or Italian accent, they are one of us! If they have a British accent, they are the enemy! Also, kill anything with fur!

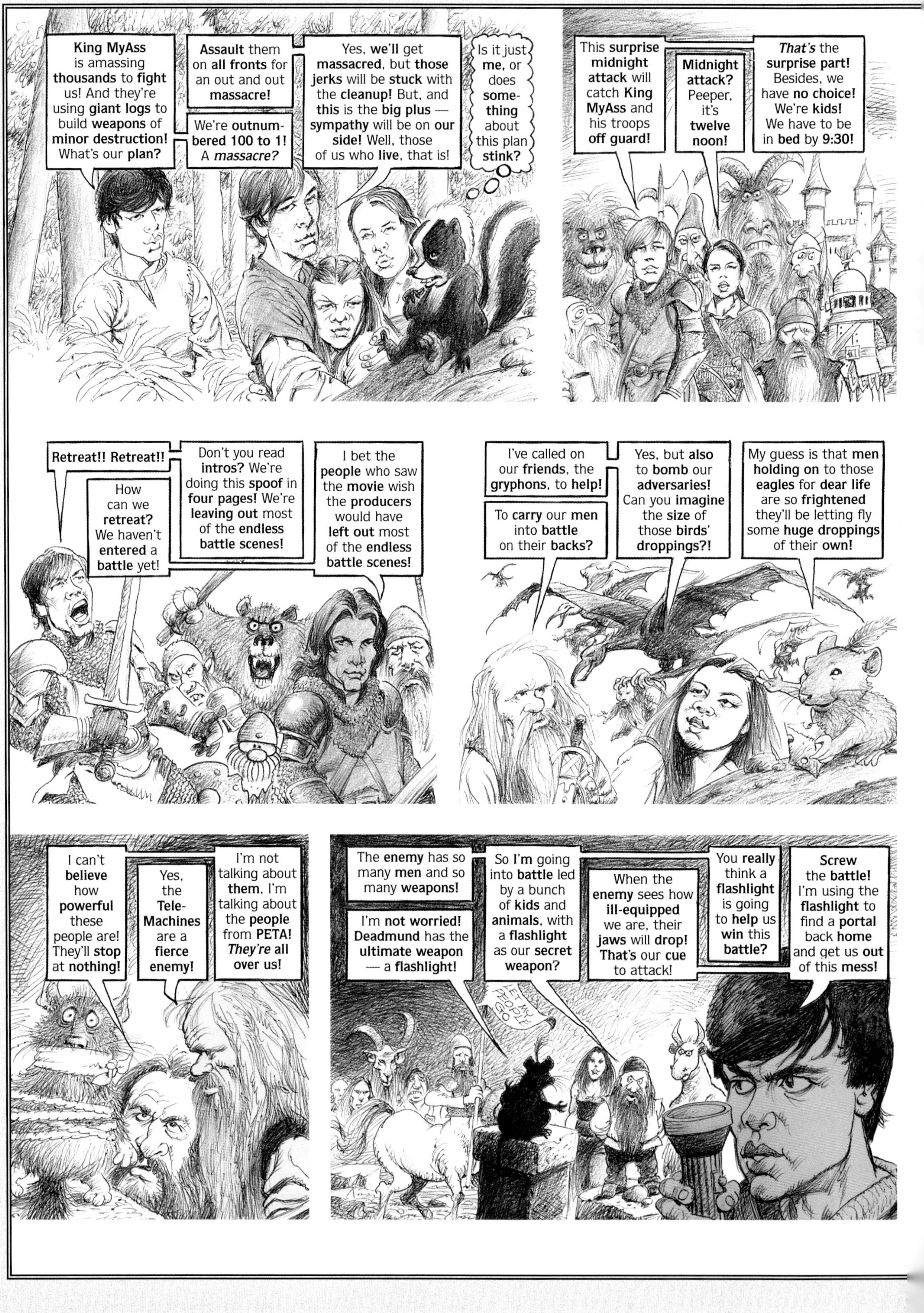
King MyAss is amassing thousands to fight us! And they're using giant logs to build weapons of minor destruction! What's our plan?
Assault them on all fronts for an out and out massacre!
We're outnumbered 100 to 1! A massacre?
Yes, we'll get massacred, but those jerks will be stuck with the cleanup! But, and this is the big plus — sympathy will be on our side! Well, those of us who live, that is!
Is it just me, or does something about this plan stink?
This surprise midnight attack will catch King MyAss and his troops off guard!
Midnight attack? Peeper, it's twelve noon!
That's the surprise part! Besides, we have no choice! We're kids! We have to be in bed by 9:30!
Retreat!! Retreat!!
How can we retreat? We haven't entered a battle yet!
Don't you read intros? We're doing this spoof in four pages! We're leaving out most of the endless battle scenes!
I bet the people who saw the movie wish the producers would have left out most of the endless battle scenes!
I've called on our friends, the gryphons, to help!
To carry our men into battle on their backs?
Yes, but also to bomb our adversaries! Can you imagine the size of those birds' droppings?!
My guess is that men holding on to those eagles for dear life are so frightened they'll be letting fly some huge droppings of their own!
I can't believe how powerful these people are! They'll stop at nothing!
Yes, the Tele-Machines are a fierce enemy!
I'm not talking about them, I'm talking about the people from PETA! They're all over us!
The enemy has so many men and so many weapons!
I'm not worried! Deadmund has the ultimate weapon — a flashlight!
So I'm going into battle led by a bunch of kids and animals, with a flashlight as our secret weapon?
When the enemy sees how ill-equipped we are, their jaws will drop! That's our cue to attack!
You really think a flashlight is going to help us win this battle?
Screw the battle! I'm using the flashlight to find a portal back home and get us out of this mess!

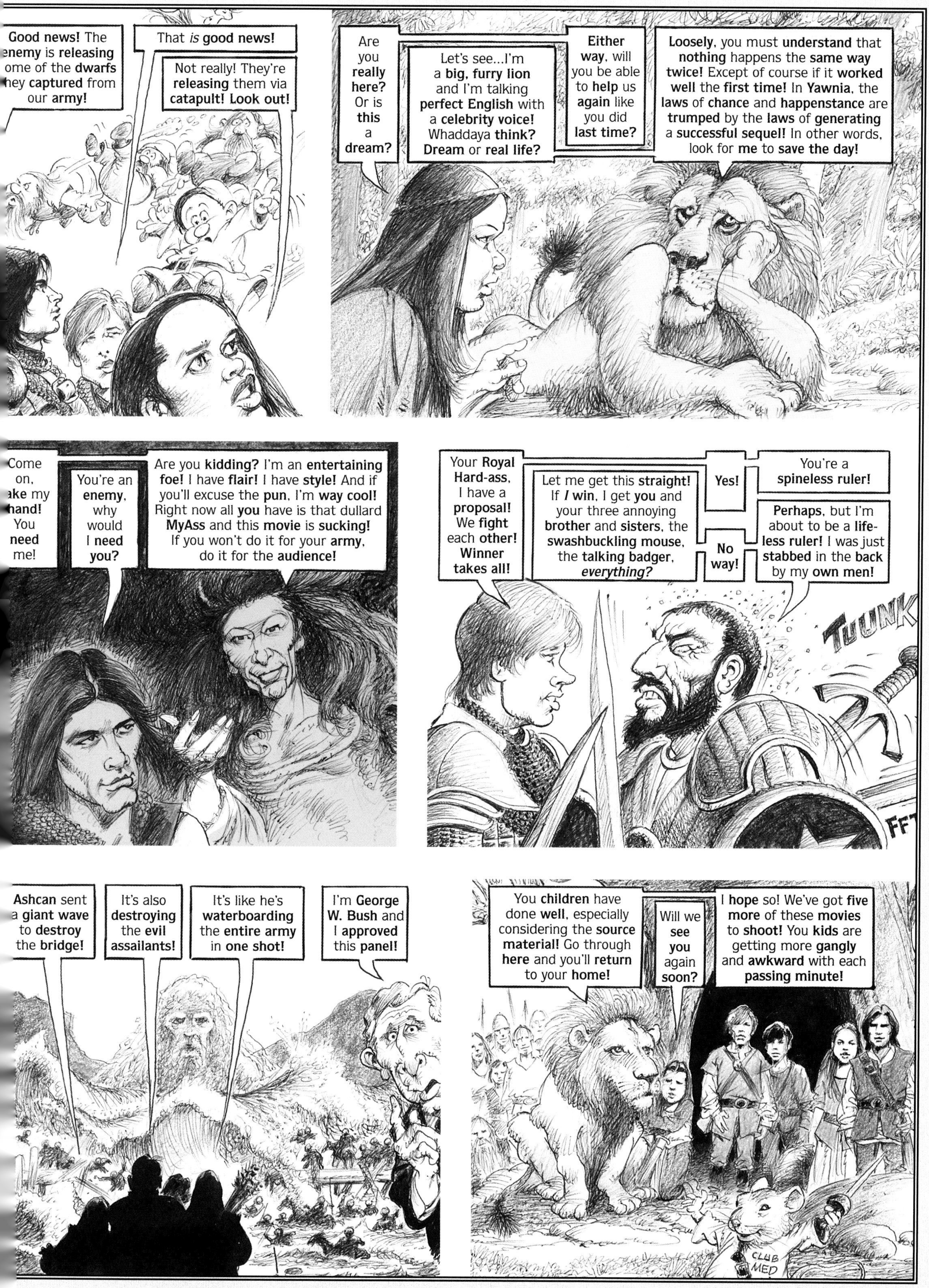
Good news! The enemy is releasing ome of the dwarfs hey captured from our army!
That *is* good news!
Not really! They're releasing them via catapult! Look out!
Are you really here? Or is this a dream?
Let's see...I'm a big, furry lion and I'm talking perfect English with a celebrity voice! Whaddaya think? Dream or real life?
Either way, will you be able to help us again like you did last time?
Loosely, you must understand that nothing happens the same way twice! Except of course if it worked well the first time! In Yawnia, the laws of chance and happenstance are trumped by the laws of generating a successful sequel! In other words, look for me to save the day!
Come on, ake my hand! You need me!
You're an enemy, why would I need you?
Are you kidding? I'm an entertaining foe! I have flair! I have style! And if you'll excuse the pun, I'm way cool! Right now all you have is that dullard MyAss and this movie is sucking! If you won't do it for your army, do it for the audience!
Your Royal Hard-ass, I have a proposal! We fight each other! Winner takes all!
Let me get this straight! If *I* win, I get you and your three annoying brother and sisters, the swashbuckling mouse, the talking badger, *everything?*
Yes!
No way!
You're a spineless ruler!
Perhaps, but I'm about to be a life-less ruler! I was just stabbed in the back by my own men!
TUUNK
FFT
Ashcan sent a giant wave to destroy the bridge!
It's also destroying the evil assailants!
It's like he's waterboarding the entire army in one shot!
I'm George W. Bush and I approved this panel!
You children have done well, especially considering the source material! Go through here and you'll return to your home!
Will we see you again soon?
I hope so! We've got five more of these movies to shoot! You kids are getting more gangly and awkward with each passing minute!
CLUB MED

FRANK ON A ROLL DEPT.

There's been a lot in the news lately about the U.S. government bailout of the nation's financial system. At least that's what we hear...the economy's so bad we had to sell our TV. And these days, who can afford to buy a newspaper? If you're in the same sinking boat as we are, now's your chance to catch up on the story with...

The Bailout Hymn of the Republic

ARTIST: MORT DRUCKER

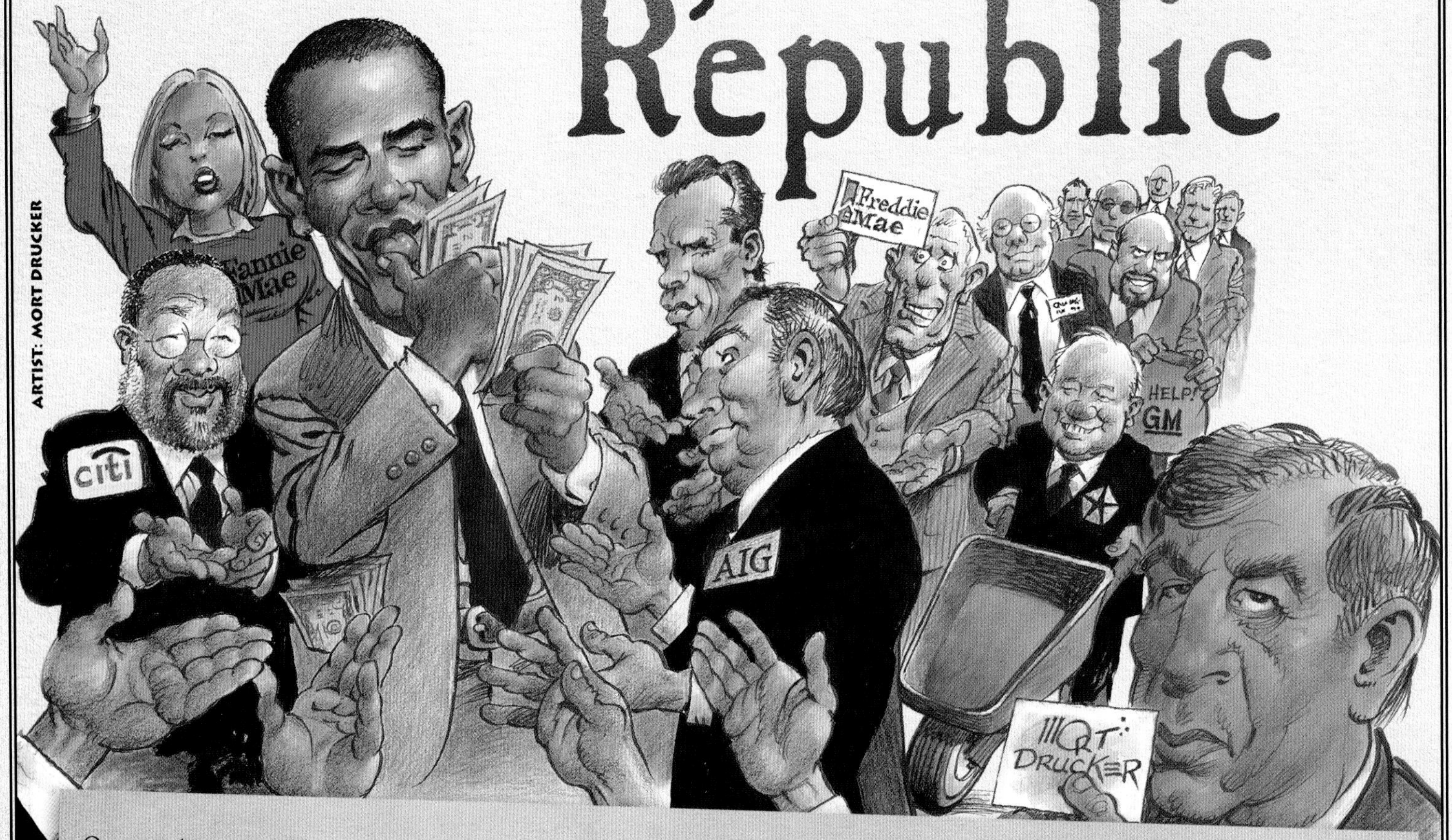
Fannie Mae
citi
Freddie Mae
AIG
HELP! GM
MORT DRUCKER

Our eyes have seen the sorrow
of a nation going bust,
Filled with bankers and politicos
that none of us can trust,
Not to mention Wall Street profiteers
who fill us with disgust —
Our hopes and dreams are gone!

Lordy, lordy,
how they blunder!
Major banks
now going under!
Years of savings
torn asunder —
Our hopes and dreams are gone!

We've beheld the massive layoffs
at Alcoa and Mattel,
At Home Depot, Nike, Target, (gulp!)
at Microsoft as well;
Will your ass soon join the masses
of discarded personnel?
The glory years are gone!

State by state,
our woes are spreadin' —
Day by day
we're surely headin'
Down the road
to Armageddon —
The glory years are gone!

With Obama in the White House
we can sit back and relax,
Though he's tried to push through nominees
who've cheated on their tax,
And his spending spree's enormous
and will stretch us to the max,
We all must cheer him on!

Glory, glory,
idolize him!
Praise his name
and lionize him!
Shame on all
who satirize him –
We all must cheer him on!

WRITER: FRANK JACOBS